A guide to teaching practice

A guide to teaching practice

Fourth edition

Louis Cohen, Lawrence Manion and Keith Morrison

London and New York

First published 1996
by Routledge
11 New Fetter Lane, London EC4P 4EE

Simultaneously published in the USA and Canada
by Routledge
29 West 35th Street, New York, NY 10001

Typeset in Times by Solidus (Bristol) Limited
Printed and bound in Great Britain by Clays Ltd, St. Ives PLC

British Library Cataloguing in Publication Data
A catalogue record for this book is available from the British Library

Library of Congress Cataloguing in Publication Data
Cohen, Louis, 1928–
    A guide to teaching practice / Louis Cohen, Lawrence Manion, and
    Keith Morrison. — 4th ed.
        p.   cm.
    Includes bibliographical references and index.
    1. Student teaching—Great Britain. 2. Teachers—Training of—
    Great Britain. I. Manion, Lawrence. II. Morrison, Keith (Keith
    R. B.) III. Title.
LB2157.G7C64   1996   96-7564
370'.7'33—dc20

ISBN 0-415-14221-0

Contents

List of boxes

Foreword to the fourth edition

It is seven years since the third edition of *A Guide to Teaching Practice* was published and we are indebted to Routledge for the opportunity of updating the text with a fourth edition. Keith Morrison joins Louis Cohen and Lawrence Manion as co-author to map the dramatic changes that have taken place since 1989 to the aims, content, pedagogy, evaluation and assessment of teaching and learning. The book has been comprehensively rewritten, with inclusion of several major new topics:

Some perspectives on teaching and learning,
Preparation and planning,
Beginning curriculum planning,
Practising teaching – primary teaching, secondary teaching,
Mixed-ability teaching,
Language in the classroom,
Equal opportunities,
Management and control in the classroom,
The classroom environment and situational factors,
Assessment, record-keeping and records of achievement.

The fourth edition also includes outlines and/or discussion of:

1 The Education Reform Act of 1988.
2 The national curriculum of England and Wales.
3 The rise of local management of schools.
4 The growth of managerialism in education.
5 The context of curriculum planning within a whole-school framework.
6 The increased emphasis on quality-assurance and quality-control mechanisms.
7 The politicisation of education and the intervention of a centralist government.
8 The growing numbers and types of educational innovations.
9 The rise of consumerism and quasi-market models of education.
10 The return of an extended version of a back-to-basics curriculum.

11 The strengthening of the relationship between education and the economy.
12 The growing concern for school effectiveness.
13 The development of diversity in educational provision and its impact on preparation for teaching.
14 The rise of competency-driven views of curriculum design, development, content and assessment.
15 The impact of information technology on flexible learning, resource-based learning and student-centred learning.
16 The extent of assessment-driven curricula and reforms in assessments and examinations.
17 The development of new initiatives in education such as: the rise of records of achievement, schools and industry links, vocational qualifications, modular curricula, subject-specialist teaching in primary schools, alterations to management structures in secondary schools, cross-curricular issues and collegial planning in secondary schools.
18 Changes to the purposes, contents, assessment and management of courses of initial teacher education.
19 The development of school-based training and partnership models of initial teacher education.
20 The shrinking role of local education authorities and the reduction of teacher autonomy and decision-making.
21 The changing nature of teacher induction and mentoring.

We should like to think that the comprehensive updating of the fourth edition will ensure that *A Guide to Teaching Practice* continues to be a major, standard text on preparing student teachers to work in contemporary classrooms.

Louis Cohen Ph.D., D.Litt. is Emeritus Professor of Education at Loughborough University. Lawrence Manion Ph.D. is former Principal Lecturer in Music at Didsbury School of Education, Manchester Metropolitan University. Keith Morrison Ph.D. is Senior Lecturer in Education in the School of Education at Durham University.

Acknowledgements

We are indebted to the following for allowing us to make use of copyright material:

Macmillan, for *Class Management and Control: a Teaching Skills Workbook*, by E. C. Wragg (DES Teacher Education Project with Focus books); Heinemann, for *Language in Culture and Class* by A. D. Edwards and V. J. Furlong; Cassell, for *Reflective Teaching in the Primary School* by A. Pollard and S. Tann, *Changing English Primary Schools? The Impact of the Education Reform Act at Key Stage One* by A. Pollard, P. Broadfoot, P. Croll, M. Osborn, D. Abbott; George Allen & Unwin, for *Learning in the Primary School* by K. Haslan and *Classroom Control: a Sociological Perspective* by M. Denscombe; Basil Blackwell, for *School Discipline: a Whole-School Approach*, by C. Watkins and P. Wagner and *Teaching Infants* by T. Kerry and J. Pollitt; McGraw Hill, for *Multicultural Teaching; A Guide for the Classroom* by M. Saunders; NFER/Nelson, for *Educating Pupils with Special Needs in the Ordinary School* by S. Hegarty, K. Pocklington and D. Lucas; Paul Chapman Publishing Ltd., for *Relationships in the Primary Classroom* by P. J. Kutnick; Longman, for *A Practical Guide to Improving your Teaching* by E. Perrott; *Educational Research*, for the article 'Curriculum Planning in Multicultural Education' by R. Jeffcoate in vol. 18 (3) pp. 192-200; the Development Education Centre [Birmingham] for *A Sense of School* by C. McFarlane and S. Sinclair; Routledge, for *Learning to Teach in the Primary School*, by A. Proctor, M. Entwistle, B. Judge and S. McKenzie-Murdoch, *Explaining* by E. C. Wragg and G. Brown, *Questioning* by G. Brown and E. C. Wragg; Routledge and Kegan Paul, for *Tractatus Logico-Philosophicus* by L. Wittgenstein; Trentham Books Ltd. and The Runnymede Trust, for *Equality Assurance in Schools*; Bodley Head, for *Zen and the Art of Motorcycle Maintenance* by R. Pirsig; School Curriculum and Assessment Authority, for *Planning the Curriculum at Key Stages 1 and 2*, SCAA (1995), *A Curriculum for All*, NCC (1989), *The National Curriculum for Pupils with Severe Learning Difficulties*, NCC (1992); Crown copyright is reproduced with the permission of the Controller of HMSO for: *Records of Achievement:*

a Statement of Policy by the Department of Education and Science (1984), *The National Curriculum from 5-16: a Consultation Document* by the Department of Education and Science (1987), *Education Observed 5: Good Behaviour and Discipline in Schools* (1989 edition) by the Department of Education and Science (1989), *National Record of Achievement* letter to accompany the publication of the National Record of Achievement by the Department of Education and Science and the Employment Department (1991), *National Record of Achievement: a Business Guide* (ref. PP3/2267/891/55) by the Employment Department, *Circular 9/92* by the Department for Education (1992), *Circular 14/93* by the Department for Education (1993), *Curriculum Organisation and Classroom Practice in Primary Schools: a Discussion Paper* by the Department for Education, written by R. Alexander, J. Rose and C. Woodhead (1992), *Mathematics in the National Curriculum* by the Department for Education (1995), *Guidance on the Inspection of Schools* by the Office for Standards in Education (1995); Taylor and Francis, for *Developing Topic Work in the Primary School*, by S. Tann; Ward Lock Educational, for *The Integrated Day – Theory and Practice*, by J. Walton (ed.).

Part I

Some perspectives on teaching and learning

Education is context-specific and context-dependent. Context refers to the settings or surroundings in which education takes place. A student teacher is faced with the exciting but challenging task of assimilating a variety of contexts very rapidly when embarking upon teaching practice, whether during a course of initial teacher pre-service education or as a newly qualified teacher entering a first appointment in a school. These contexts vary from the very broad and general macro-contexts at a societal level to the very specific micro-contexts of a particular individual in a particular school, class and lesson. The prospect can be daunting, as we see in some student teachers' concern for short-term survival in a new classroom. The thrust of this book is to support students in their initial teaching experiences – the micro-contexts of everyday life in classrooms. However, localised education is set in broader contexts of society. This part of the book sets the contemporary scene for daily teaching and learning in these broader contexts. It also describes some of the major themes of education in the last decade.

The convention used in discussions here and throughout the book will be to refer to students in initial teacher education as 'student teachers' and to children and young adults attending school as 'students'.

Chapter 1

The politicisation of education

Education has been the subject of increasing political debate for two decades. It is hard to understate the effects of a *dirigiste*, interventionist government dominated by the Thatcherite agenda of introducing market principles into education.

The economic aspect of government policy affects funding issues for education. Since the 1988 Education Act[1] there has been a clear market ideology in education that embraces: *competition, consumerism, individualism, choice, diversity,*[2] *privatisation, quality control, efficiency and information.*[3] These features include:

- A common national curriculum, coupled with formal assessment at ages 7, 11, 14 and 16 to enable schools to be compared to each other in 'league tables' of test results; schools themselves organise their 'delivery' of the national curriculum.[4]
- The abandoning of ceiling numbers for schools, together with 'open enrolment' (i.e. no catchment areas), designed to enable 'good' schools ('magnet schools') to flourish and 'poor' schools ('sink schools') to close – though, in fact, Brighouse and Tomlinson[5] indicate that 'sink' schools do not close, they are simply starved of resources for improvement because of the *per capitum* funding formula. In this respect Apple[6] argues that schools become locators of social class. Indeed Tomlinson[7] points out that it is perhaps an irony that many 'good' schools do not wish to expand simply because their existing size has contributed to their success.
- The increased number of types of schools available for 'consumers', for example 'grant maintained schools' (those schools that have opted out of local authority control); city technology colleges (whose funding was originally intended to be derived from industry); and sixth form colleges (which compete with comprehensive schools and colleges of further education for recruitment).
- The delegation of budgetary control away from local education authorities (LEAs) and into schools (i.e. local management of schools – LMS).

LEAs still maintain control over certain aspects of the upkeep of buildings; many schools raise money themselves to purchase resources and computers and to fund educational visits and music tuition.

- The increased power of schools' governing bodies, which now control, for example: budgets, staffing, resources, appointments, decisions on curricula, exclusions and behaviour policies.

- The rise of the internal market *within* and *between* schools, causing competition for funding between subject areas/departments/age phases[8] and between schools (which previously had been able to work together in partnership[9]) to attract students – each student bringing a *per capitum* sum of money into a school. The effects of the formula for funding schools which works on 'average' staff costs means that experienced teachers cost considerably more than newly qualified staff and can thereby, in some cases, take schools into financial deficit, giving rise to staff reductions, loss of resources and increasing class sizes.

- The strengthening of links with parents, industry and commercial sponsors.

- The increase in quality-assurance mechanisms: four-yearly inspections; records and policy documentation of every aspect of a school's work; the publication of examination and formal assessment results; the requirement for whole-school planning that is set out in school development plans;[10] the attention that is being given to 'school effectiveness'[11] and 'school improvement' programmes[12] (leading many schools into schemes for external recognition of excellence, e.g. Total Quality Management, Investors in People, British Standard 5750); greater accountability (e.g. governors must hold an annual meeting with parents); preparation of school prospectuses; the issuing by the government of a Parents' Charter.[13]

- The rise of a 'managerialist' mentality in schools, with line-management staffing structures, bureaucratisation, the rise of schools' 'development planning'.

In 1992 a government-commissioned report, *Curriculum Organisation and Classroom Practice in Schools*,[14] made clear its concern that the funding formula for schools, whereby primary schools received less *per capitum* money than secondary schools, could not be justified. Indeed evidence from the USA's *Head Start* project[15] suggests that extra resourcing for primary schools has longer-term beneficial effects than extra resourcing for secondary schools. The importance of nursery and early-years education was given added recognition by the National Commission on Education[16] and the belated governmental response in 1995 of vouchers to pay for approximately half of a child's nursery education.[17]

The combination of formula funding and open enrolment leads to many schools coming to regard students as 'economic units'. Funding for schools generally has been squeezed by the government at the same time as devolution of budgetary control to schools themselves has come into operation fully. One could argue that the effects of these moves are to divert responsibility for schools' effectiveness away from government and on to the shoulders of schools. Yet at the same time the government has dismantled the power and support of LEAs, thereby enabling government policy to be put directly into schools without a middle tier of power to challenge, mediate or support this policy. Indeed two organisations of the 'New Right' in education[18] – the Centre for Policy Studies[19] and the Adam Smith Institute[20] – were unequivocal in arguing that LEAs were part of the problem of, rather than part of the solution to, alleged declining standards. The former local authority advisors have been transmogrified into arms of the government's inspectorate, ceding their supportive role to a punitive and judgmental role.[21] Partnerships between schools and the advisory service have given way to suspicion and hostility.

Nor does the economic aspect of government policy for education end there. The relationship between economics and education reaches further into the heart of the school curriculum, a theme that was signalled by the former secretary of state, Keith Joseph, in his comment that the role of business and free enterprise in the modern world had to be introduced into schools.[22] For example, children from the age of 5 have to study Education for Economic and Industrial Understanding[23] and Careers Education and Guidance,[24] these being two of the five *cross-curricular themes* that are prescribed for schools (though at the moment they are non-statutory). When one looks at the documentation of these two themes it is very clear[25] that they legitimise a free-market capitalist, materialist, competitive economy and delegitimise alternatives to this (either by silence on and under-representation of them or by refusing to problematise the *status quo*).

In the secondary field the response to the perceived need to emphasise the link between education and the economy has been a renewed call for vocational qualifications to be accorded the same status as academic qualifications[26] (still given the *imprimatur* of a 'gold standard' in the debate over A-levels). The credentialising of vocational education was given impetus with the Technical and Vocational Education Initiative in the 1980s and the Certificate of Prevocational Education and the B Tec courses in the early 1990s. A process of much-needed reform and rationalisation of the post-16 sector was begun in the mid-1990s[27] that resulted in a standardisation of levels of awards for qualifications in National Vocational Qualifications (NVQs) and the rise of the General National Vocational Qualification (GNVQ). Further, the links between schools and industry, augured in James Callaghan's speech at Ruskin College in 1976 and fostered in the 1980s under the banner of 'education for enterprise', have been strengthened through 'compacts' and schemes to involve students in periods of work experience during their school careers. One should not overlook, also, the requirement that every school's governing body must include a representative from industry.

One could argue, echoing Hall *et al.* in 1978,[28] that a political debate about education has been deliberately orchestrated to give greater legitimacy to a government that is experiencing legitimation, economic and political crises.[29] The nature of this orchestration in the media has been to set up unrealistic and simplistic polarities that enable the government to make primary and secondary schools visible targets of opprobrium, caricaturing them as failing in all sorts of ways, to expose what it sees as the targets of poor practice, and thereby to set and legitimise its own political agenda for improving schools. Some of these polarities are shown in Box 1.

Box 1

Simplistic polarities in education

1   Traditional *versus* progressive education in primary schools.
2   Whole-class teaching *versus* group work in primary schools.
3   Subject teaching *versus* topics/integrated approaches in primary schools.
4   Subject specialist teachers *versus* generalist teachers in primary schools.
5   Setting/homogeneous-ability groups *versus* mixed-ability groups.
6   'Basics' *versus* 'frills'.
7   Prescribed curricula *versus* freedom to decide curricula.
8   'Cultural restoration' *versus* relativism.
9   'Standards' *versus* permissiveness and failing performance.

What we are seeing in education, then, is an attempt by government to control the organisation, contents (including time allocations),[30] purposes and outcomes of education. The government's advocacy of the left-hand side of the polarities combines with its proscription of the right-hand side to bring about a massively over-determined system of education.[31] Government policy has issued from and accords with the policies of the 'New Right' *Centre for Policy Studies*, the *Adam Smith Institute*, the *National Council for Educational Standards*, and the *Hillgate Group*, self-styled leaders of conservative reform in educational policy.[32] One of their aims was to move education out of the hands of educationists and into the hands of consumers – a shift known as *producer capture*. The Adam Smith Institute's adoption of this phrase,[33] fittingly perhaps in 1984, resonates through the 1980s and 1990s in the distrust of teachers, researchers and those with a professional interest in education.

The truth of the matter is more complex than the polarities suggest. Let us deal with each of them in turn briefly.

1. After the publication of the Black Papers in Education in the late 1960s progressive education was demonised, being blamed for the breakdown of society and creating a moral panic about education as the root cause of a lax, rebellious, work-shy youth whose presence diminished the economic performance of the UK. There was a putative dereliction of duty by teachers: instead of teaching they allowed children not to learn or to choose what to do; freedom and responsibility became license and under-achievement. This was largely a myth, as the extent of progressive education was confined to five or six LEAs; indeed Galton et al.[34] argue that: 'The kinds of practice endorsed in the Plowden Report were only partially implemented. Most of the changes which have been carried out concerned the organisational structure of the classroom and have had far less to do with the curriculum content and teaching and learning processes.' The evidence of falling standards was at best equivocal and the link between primary education and economic performance was unproven. Nevertheless sufficient noise was made to legitimise advocacy of the teacher's role as an instructor and trainer combined with authoritarian discipline.[35] The government turned its back on research evidence and academics who condemned such a crude polarisation.

2. In 1992 an influential publication on primary education in Leeds[36] led to its author being one of the 'three wise men' who reported to the government in the same year that group work had gone too far and that multiple groups undertaking different activities at the same time reduced the effectiveness of teachers and the achievements of children. This echoed some of the school-effectiveness literature that had been accumulating in the 1980s,[37] but neglected a significant piece of research in 1980 by Galton and Simon[38] which found that, though children sat in groups, overwhelmingly they worked as *individuals*; groups were a seating arrangement rather than a learning arrangement. The 'three wise men's' report, *Curriculum Organisation and Classroom Practice in Primary Schools*, and the follow-up report from OFSTED[39] were misrepresented in the press as advocating a wholesale return to whole-class teaching, whereas, in fact, the reports had argued for an *increase* in whole-class teaching, a *reduction* in the number of different types of activity and curriculum areas taking place at any one time (to a maximum of four), and the *need for a variety and balance* of teaching styles that still retained an *eclectic diversity* driven by the criterion of *fitness-for-purpose*.

3. Though there is evidence since the Primary Survey in 1978[40] that topic approaches tended to lead to undemanding work, a narrow curriculum and repetition through a child's primary school years, this was interpreted as a call to *replace* topic work rather than a call to *improve* topic work and progression.[41] The argument that topic work might accord with the holistic, integrated way in which children viewed the world cut little ice with the proponents of a national curriculum concerned to frame the curriculum in

traditionalist subject terms and to assess children in their achievements of academic, subject knowledge. One could argue that a sop was handed out to teachers when it was indicated that the *delivery* of the national curriculum was for the teachers to decide, i.e. that topic approaches could still take place. Many primary schools struggled – and still struggle – to cast a subject-framed and subject-assessed curriculum in terms of a topic approach, though clearly there has been an increase in subject teaching. A statutory national curriculum in fact might give children an 'entitlement' to a broader and more balanced curriculum than was experienced in the years preceding the Education Reform Act of 1988, a feature that was evidenced in HMI and government reports throughout the 1980s.

4. Not only was there an advocacy of subject *teaching* but this was reinforced by the government's suggestion – supported in the 1980s by the then HMI[42] – that there was a case for having subjects taught by *subject specialists* (the secondary model of teaching), particularly in the upper end of the primary school.[43] HMI had acknowledged for over a decade that this practice existed for certain subjects – music, PE, RE – but it was suggested that this should now be extended. This would putatively raise standards in the primary schools as teachers would have the opportunity to use their own academic subject knowledge more fully. The jury is still out on how far this hypothesis is correct.

5. Advocacy of subject teaching in primary schools, by specialist or generalist teachers, went hand-in-glove with advocacy of setting *across* classes in large primary schools or *within* classes in primary schools where each class had a different age group (perhaps given greater impetus since the rise in class sizes and the dip in demographic trends has led to mixed-age classes), principally in one or more of the three core subjects of the national curriculum – in terms of frequency it tended to be first mathematics, then language, then science.

The move to setting in primary (and secondary schools) was seen as a way of breaking down the tyranny of the worksheet for mixed-ability teaching – teaching by proxy – increasing the teacher's role as an instructor, and allowing the most and least able children to have work that was matched to their abilities. This built on research by Bennett *et al.*[44] which showed serious shortcomings in teachers' abilities to match work to children's abilities in mathematics and language, with junior-age teachers being less successful than infant-age teachers – in some cases over 50 per cent of tasks were incorrectly matched. (That this considerably overstates the precision that can *ever* be achieved in matching was argued convincingly by Davis,[45] though, it seems, this did not feature in the work of policy-makers.) It was suggested that many teachers taught to a notional 'average' pupil and that differentiated work had to be devised in order to improve matching. (That this runs counter to the principle of whole-class teaching advocated by the same government was apparently not seen as problematic.)

Moreover, the advocacy of homogeneous groupings could not be supported by the available research evidence, which showed that the argument that mixed-ability grouping in primary and secondary schools failed to 'stretch' children sufficiently was at best equivocal except in the case of the 'top' 1 or 2 per cent of the population (whose abilities similarly might not be matched with other organisational and pedagogic arrangements advocated by governments!).[46] Moreover, the advocacy of homogeneous ability groups failed to recognise within-group differences[47] and the well-established evidence that motivation is a key determinant of effective learning and that social processes and dynamics can exert as great an influence on effective learning as academic similarity.[48] Indeed, the 'three wise men's' report argued for four types of teacher in the primary school: the *generalist* (who teaches most of the curriculum and who probably specialises in an age-range rather than a subject); the *generalist/consultant* (who combines a generalist role with cross-school co-ordination and advice in one or more subjects); the *semi-specialist* (who teaches her/his subject but also has a generalist and/or consultancy role); the *specialist* (who teaches her/his subject full-time).

What is being suggested in the 'three wise men's' report is that effective teaching uses different types of teacher and that *pedagogic* as well as *subject* knowledge is important. This resonates with a current debate in primary education. In one camp is Bennett,[49] who argues that increasing teachers' *subject knowledge* will raise standards; in the other camp is Galton,[50] who argues that effective *pedagogy* and *pedagogical knowledge* will raise standards. Clearly there is a need to combine both, itself a feature of Alexander's[51] advocacy of the need for teaching to put aside ideology.

6, 7, 8. These three areas cluster together because their focus is on curriculum content. There is clear evidence in the national curriculum of a return to 'basics': language, mathematics and science are the three 'core' areas of the national curriculum; their contents were the first to be published by the DFE; they are the only subjects in which compulsory formal, standardised assessment takes place. They have the highest status and time in the curriculum. Indeed, John Major, speaking at a Conservative conference, said: 'People say that there is too much jargon in education. So let me give you some of my own. Knowledge, discipline, tables, sums, dates, Shakespeare, British history, Standard English, grammar, spellings, marks, tests.' This echoes the views of the 'cultural restorationists'[52] (e.g. Scruton, O'Hear, Lawlor, Marenbon, Marks – all of whom have been members of the New Right groups identified earlier) whose impact on: (a) the history curriculum has been to increase the amount of British history children study, with an emphasis on the history of white, male, imperial conquests and successes, Victorian values and the time when Britain ruled the waves; (b) religious education in state schools has been to compel schools to have a daily act of worship that is largely Christian in character; (c) the music curriculum has been to reaffirm the traditional 'great masters' of music and minimise music from other cultures (both within and outside the UK). That this return to a traditionalist curriculum was seen as a counterweight to the perceived relativism of a post-modernist society resonates with the reaction against the perceived moral permissiveness and the decline in standards of social, economic, ethical and religious behaviour that, as was suggested earlier, was the alleged result of progressivism. No longer can teachers be trusted to decide with children what is to be important knowledge. In an age marked by diversity, rapid change, differentiation and ambiguity, it is a striking irony that the government is prescribing a fixed, academic, traditionalist, uniform curriculum reinforced by a return to traditional forms of examination.

Moreover, the view of *progression* that is embedded in the national curriculum, where it is assumed that all children will learn in the same sequence, and that differentiation is largely a matter of the *speed* at which children will proceed through ten fixed stages, turns its back on the constructivist view of learning which argues that learning is recursive, eclectic, non-linear and piecemeal, progressing by means of processes of assimilation and accommodation of constructs and concepts. Indeed, there is evidence to show that some children who were able to meet the criteria for Level 3 of the national curriculum were unable to meet the criteria for Level 2![53] The simplistic view of learning and progression in the uniform national curriculum dooms a sector of the school population to failure simply because they learn in a different order or a different way. This failure is then compounded – bringing with it all the problems of motivation and lowering of self-esteem – by the publication of 'league tables' of results in the media. Again, it is ironical that a government so publicly committed to raising standards has put in place a system which may lead to falling standards in some children.

9. The denotation of 'standards' pulls together several strands of the previous eight points from Box 1. Standards can be moral, ethical, social, economic and personal, as set out above in connection with the proscription of progressivism. They can also be *academic* (though, clearly, the link to the country's economic performance is an important function of academic standards). The rise of assessment and increased attention to examinations in schools has figured largely in schools' curricula and teaching and risks having a backwash effect on the curriculum, as schools are concerned to ensure that their published results in 'league tables' show them in a favourable light. In a worst-case scenario, staff may risk dismissal if the children do not score highly in national tests. (It is now in school governors' powers to dismiss teachers, even though, as Sockett[54] pointed out years ago, this is morally indefensible as teachers cannot be called to account for aspects of students' performances over which they have little or no control.)

The proposed uses of assessment in the TGAT Report[55] – to be diagnostic, criterion-referenced, formative and linked to progression (e.g. to matching) – have been usurped by test results being used summatively, normatively, comparatively and for public accountability. Many teachers have already commented that the test results, obtained through the expenditure of vast amounts of time and millions of pounds of money, tell them little that they did not already know. Nevertheless, the tests go on; a government that has had to replace one secretary of state for education in 1994 for his unyielding attitude to flawed tests shows no signs of relaxing its commitment to this aspect of the Parents' Charter, the ascription of a simplistic grade or unreliable index of a school's achievements, in the belief that this is politically attractive to voters. In this respect the positive developments in assessment and recording (e.g. through records of achievement) do little to allay teachers' fears that an assessment-driven curriculum, where the assessments are narrow and are undertaken in large part through written tests, will suppress creativity, enjoyment, responsibility and self-esteem.

In secondary education we are witnessing a reduction in 'coursework' as a means of assessment of achievement at GCSE level, regardless of the fact that there is a gender differential[56] whereby girls achieve more highly in coursework than boys, with the differentiation reversed in respect of formal written examinations.

The first version of the national curriculum appeared some short time before the introduction of formal assessment. This and the second version overloaded the primary curriculum massively in the level of detail, the amount of detail that had to be covered, and the amount of planning that teachers would have to do in telescoped time-scales. Quite properly, teachers voiced great concern about and disagreement with this level of prescription. Indeed, in 1994 and 1995 a major review of the national curriculum and post-16 education was conducted by the chairman of the Post Office and the national lottery, Ron Dearing. His revised national curriculum appears at first sight to be much slimmer and more able to support a measure of teacher autonomy. At the same time as the Dearing version of the national curriculum was disseminated, together with a promise from government that there would be a five-year moratorium on changes to the curriculum,[57] much greater attention was given to assessment, as a new wave of assessments was beginning for 11-year-olds. One of the effects of this was to divert attention away from curriculum content. With increased attention given to assessment the danger is that the *agenda* of the curriculum – the curriculum content – is not subjected to the degree of critique that it received formerly. If one examines the content of the revised curriculum, one sees that although there is a reduction in the level of detail and the amount of material to be covered, the comments about the history, music and RE curricula mentioned earlier still apply. The nationalistic, cultural-restorationist agenda remains the same. It is as problematic as ever, under-representing the cultural backgrounds and contexts of large numbers of UK citizens.

The principal current political debates and concerns in education are summarised in Box 2.

Box 2

Principal current themes in education

1   The influence of an authoritarian, *dirigiste* government in crisis, seeking control of the educational agenda.
2   The operation of market forces, consumerism and Thatcherism in education.
3   The effects of the funding formula.
4   The reduction in resources – human and material.
5   Teacher morale and unrest.
6   The economic focus of curriculum content.
7   The polarisation of issues in order to gain legitimacy.
8   The castigation of progressive education.
9   The control of curriculum content.
10 Back to basics and cultural restoration.
11 Subject-based or topic-based teaching (control of curriculum organisation).
12 Whole-class/multiple-group teaching (control of pedagogy).
13 Mixed-ability/homogeneous-ability groups (control of pedagogy).
14 Subject specialist teaching (control of pedagogy).
15 The effects of information technology on pedagogy.
16 Increased assessment activity (control of assessment).
17 Concern for improved matching.
18 Restricted views of progression and learning.
19 Reduced teacher autonomy.
20 Moves towards school effectiveness.
21 Increasing teachers' subject and pedagogic knowledge.
22 Disrespect for research evidence.
23 The rise of vocational educational and vocational qualifications.
24 The standardisation and rationalisation of vocational qualifications.

Box 2 shows how the several pieces of a complicated jigsaw fit together in a political reading of education. Casting the discussion in a political mode reflects not only the significance of the politicisation of education but the fact that the response to this has been a growing authoritarianism in education that reveals itself in a thirst for central control concealed behind a rhetoric of increased consumerism and devolution. External pressures for change in the curriculum, pedagogy, organisation and management of schools and the staff who work in them have been defended on the grounds of the need to bring teachers and curricula into line with developments in the late twentieth century and to guarantee a broad, balanced, relevant, differentiated, sequenced and well-matched curriculum for every student. However, the costs of these policies in terms of declining teacher morale, a flight from the teaching profession and premature retirements are striking. Perhaps only a government that contributed to an economic recession in the 1980s and 1990s would have confidence in being able to staff schools from the reserve army of the unemployed.

Chapter 2

Information technology and changes in teaching and learning

Lest this analysis of current pressures on education should appear merely negative, one can point to many innovations and developments in education over the last decade that were not directly the result of external political pressure. Indeed, in the case of the introduction of information technology and records of achievement in schools the government did provide funding from the Department of Employment and the Department for Education respectively. One can identify two major sets of initiatives in education that impact very directly on schools: the first of these is the rise in information technology and the second is the changes being wrought in pedagogy – the organisation, structure and styles of teaching and learning. Indeed, the two inform each other.

The rise of information technology introduces the possibility of new, individualised, co-operative, problem-solving, student-centred learning and flexible learning approaches that were not practically possible before. This has implications for the teacher's role and 'authority', particularly when many students are currently more computer-literate than their teachers and where internet, e-mail, public-access databases, networking, interactive programs, virtual reality and powerful PC programs combine with the rapid obsolescence of knowledge to render problematic the notion of what is important, fixed and enduring knowledge. Further, it is not difficult to envisage the role of the teacher changing from a deliverer of fixed knowledge to a facilitator and supporter of student-centred learning. Learning becomes negotiated.

Being able to access and to interact with information and information systems across the globe at the touch of a button suggests firstly that the certainty of which knowledge (or medium) is important is exploded and secondly that a premium is placed on skills teaching. At their lowest level these are practical skills so that students can access and manipulate data; at their highest level these are skills of evaluation, critical thinking and the exercise of judgement in deciding what is relevant knowledge in a postmodernist, relativist world! The ability to be autonomous and to stand upright when all around is changing has much to recommend it.

The opening up of technology and knowledge gateways has major implications for schooling, not the least of which is to call into question the long-term contribution of schools to education. It was Toffler[1] who argued that many schools currently face backwards into an industrial age and that, in order to avoid 'future shock', they need to move beyond being second-wave institutions for second-wave industrial society and become third-wave institutions for the third-wave − information-rich − society. Schools will no longer be solely dispensers of knowledge but social sites[2] with flexible learning, flexible timetabling, flexible curricula and flexible teaching arrangements. That this is already becoming a reality is evidenced in 'flexible-learning' suites in secondary schools and colleges where multimedia resources combine with individualised teaching and personal tutoring systems to support student-driven learning in terms of contents and learning styles. Flexible learning is predicated on managing student/teacher partnerships, managing students' uses of resources and managing students' negotiated learning pathways.[3] Indeed, one could argue that the only brakes on this are the considerable resource implications and the straitjacketing, backwash effect of a traditionalist examination system.

One can observe, perhaps, a contradiction in current policies for teaching. On the one hand society is undergoing massive structural changes and the future contents of the curriculum are, in principle, less certain; on the other hand the national curriculum not only fixes the curricular knowledge that is deemed important but the terminology of 'curriculum delivery' implies a one-way model of teaching wherein the teacher pours new knowledge into empty or nearly empty heads, rendering good the previously educationally deficient student. This is a deficit model. It implies a passive view of learning which takes scant account of the developments in learning theory that indicate the power of constructivism and metacognition in students, i.e. where students create their own conceptual structures and assimilate and accommodate new experiences and learning into them, and where the raising of students' awareness of 'learning how to learn' figures significantly in successful memorising, retention, recall and use of concepts.

It is unavoidable that the extended use of information technology will bring a revolution in teaching and learning, just as it has brought a revolution in knowledge and its acquisition. Technology is transforming society: for example, bringing unemployment into high relief and severing the link between certification (credentialism) and opportunities for employment.[4] The rise of a disaffected underclass is already giving rise to oppositional behaviour in schools, where 'education for leisure' is becoming a euphemism for containing the unemployed[5] and where education is challenged as the principal guarantor of success. Indeed, Handy[6] writes that employment patterns will alter from 'careers for life' into a situation where an increasing number of people will be employed on a fixed-term or short-term basis, with fewer permanent members of an organisation taking on increased amounts of work.

Handy argues that individuals will offer themselves for employment and employers will look at the 'portfolio' of experiences and qualifications each person has gained on a self-directed pathway. The implications of this directly relate to, and are reflected directly in, the contents and structure of education. 'Portfolios of achievements' are already well established in the National Record of Achievement that is kept by each school leaver. This is designed to document a wide range of achievements and experiences, both in school and out of school. It makes specific reference to the need for students to plan for future education and training needs, i.e. to address *action planning*.

Chapter 3

Action planning in teaching and learning

Action planning is a central *leitmotiv* of this book; it follows from an analysis of past achievements and implications for planning of pathways of learning that still lie ahead. The rise of action planning is a response to flexible learning systems[1] which, in turn, are a response to the realisation of the potential of information technology to transform the workplace – in school or outside. Opportunities for action planning reach further still; many schools have moved to modular programmes, particularly at the secondary and post-16 phases, where students negotiate with teachers to follow combinations of compulsory and optional modules that contribute to a rounded and yet specialised programme of learning. Modular programmes have several attractions:[2]

- they are learner-centred and responsive to individual needs;
- greater autonomy and responsibility for planning learning is devolved to students, building in 'ownership' of the learning process;
- students can both specialise and follow generalist, all-round education;
- they enable learning to be focused and organised into easily manageable units;
- they enable students to develop their own 'portfolios' of achievements;
- assessment is continuous rather than summative (at the end of many years of schooling); frequent feedback is available;
- the comparatively open pathways through modules can be more individualised than longer courses;
- they enable cross-curricular, cross-department planning and collegiality to develop;
- they are outcome-focused and objectives-driven;
- they are premised on a personalised approach to teaching and a personal tutor system, i.e. they acknowledge the significance of one-to-one discussions in planning pathways, setting targets and action planning;
- they enable small amounts of learning and achievements to be recognised and qualified, enhancing student motivation;
- they are competence-driven.

Modular programmes go hand-in-glove with flexible-learning systems as, being made up of short units of study, they enable individually tailored patterns of study to be planned that follow a cycle of: (i) reflection on and analysis of learning undertaken → (ii) identifying new needs → (iii) planning new targets (objectives) → (iv) planning how to reach those targets (action planning) → (v) following appropriate courses to achieve those targets → (vi) evaluating the achievement of the targets → re-entering the cycle of reflection and planning. Action planning, like many modular programmes, is atomistic; being outcome-focused it operationalises the knowledge and skills to be learnt. It is fundamentally a *practical* exercise, setting out the *intended learning outcomes* and *competences* that will be achieved by students. It requires students (and courses) to specify objectives; objectives are cast in practical, measurable, often observable terms. This renders them eminently attractive to a government concerned with being able to 'measure' standards and improve standards by specifying specific courses of action (following a national curriculum) and casting its national curriculum in an objectives-based model. Though some would argue against the atomistic and competence-based sympathies of action planning, suggesting that it under-states the longer-term, unmeasurable yet immeasurably important aspects of education,[3] it cannot be denied that it is a powerful device for focusing the planning of curricula, teaching and learning.

It is difficult to understate the importance of action planning. For example, the High Scope project[4] with very young children uses a cycle of Plan → Do → Review; school development plans use an action-planning approach; records of achievement require action planning; and modular courses facilitate an action-planning approach. At student-teacher level (discussed below) the model of development is competence-driven, requiring students to meet named 'exit criteria' and standards of competence in order to qualify.[5] At the level of planning both the whole curriculum and individual lessons, action planning – the setting of objectives – is an efficient way of approaching teaching and learning; indeed, the objectives model is one of the main foundations of this book. The statutory national curriculum is based on an objectives model (where, for objectives, read 'attainment targets').

For student teachers facing a teaching practice with a series of classes of thirty-five students for hour-long slots of time the notion of flexible learning is, perhaps, a brave new world that is many years in the future. Nevertheless, the notion of action planning is contemporaneous; it can work here and now. Even those students who draw back from modular, flexible learning as an artefact of the future can take several lessons from the debate, for example:

- the need for target setting and action planning;
- the opportunities provided by objectives-based planning;
- the opportunities provided by competency-based planning;
- the need to involve students in planning learning;

- the need to communicate the purposes of teaching and learning situations;
- the need to specify intended learning outcomes.

The remainder of this book takes up the theme of action planning for student teachers as well as school students. Objectives-based planning for curricula and teaching accords with action planning,[6] structuring and communicating intentions for teaching and learning, target-setting and recording achievements in students' profiles, professional self-development of student teachers, appraisal of serving teachers, competency-based teaching, learning and assessment, and school development planning.[7] There are, then, many powerful reasons to take seriously the notion of action planning and its partner, objectives-based planning.

How does this impact on student teachers? Whilst the rest of the book unpacks the implications for planning curricula, teaching, learning, behaviour, assessment, evaluation and self-evaluation, this part would be incomplete without mention of significant recent changes in the preparation of newly qualified teachers. It is to this question of setting the ground for the micro-level contexts of educational analysis that we now turn.

Chapter 4

The impact of school-based initial teacher education

There have been several recent major changes in the initial preparation of newly qualified teachers in the United Kingdom:

- The establishing of the Teacher Training Agency, a government quango.
- An increase in the amount of time that student teachers spend in schools.
- Moves to reduce the role of institutions of higher education.
- A move to competence-based planning and assessment of student teachers.[1]
- An increasing role of schools in developing partnerships with institutions of higher education and taking shared responsibility for the preparation of newly qualified teachers.[2]
- The rise of 'mentoring' in schools.[3]
- An increase in the level of government prescription for the contents of, time allowances for, and assessments in, initial teacher education courses.

No longer do student teachers lead a closeted existence in schools of education and colleges of higher education, foraying infrequently into the 'real world' of primary and secondary schools. Instead student teachers spend large portions of time (over 50 per cent of course time) in schools; their courses typically are planned around school experiences and contacts. Some of the roles of college and university tutors have been ceded to mentors in school (discussed below).

THE SIGNIFICANCE OF COMPETENCE-DRIVEN COURSES AND ASSESSMENT

A major issue in teacher education has been the introduction of specified competences that student teachers should demonstrate. The DFEE requires that the development of these competences should be monitored throughout the period of initial training.[4] This enables the 'value-added' dimension of courses and student teachers' development to be assessed – in other words, how much the student has profited from the course. There is a parallel to this in early-years education in the rise of 'baseline assessment' of a child upon entry to school at 4 or 5 years in order for her or his rate and nature of *progress* to be assessed when s/he comes to the point of formal assessment at age 7.

Assessment of the nature and degree of competences of students upon entry to courses of initial training is designed to enable programmes to be developed that will be tailored to the differential needs, rates of development and areas of development in student teachers. The partner to competence-based initial training that enables differential progression in student teachers to be addressed is the increase in mentoring, where a named mentor in school has responsibility for the specific development of specific competences in specific students. For intending secondary school teachers the required competences are set out in five main areas: subject knowledge; subject application; class management; assessment and recording of pupils' progress; further professional development. The specific competences for newly qualified secondary teachers are set out below:

Subject knowledge

2.2   Newly qualified teachers should be able to demonstrate:

2.2.1   an understanding of the knowledge, concepts and skills of their specialist subjects and of the place of these subjects in the school curriculum;

2.2.2   knowledge and understanding of the national curriculum and attainment targets (NCATs) and the programmes of study (PoS) in the subjects they are preparing to teach, together with an understanding of the framework of the statutory requirements;

2.2.3   a breadth and depth of subject knowledge extending beyond PoS and examination syllabuses in school.

Subject application

2.3   Newly qualified teachers should be able to:

2.3.1   produce coherent lesson plans which take account of NCATs and of the school's curriculum policies;

2.3.2   ensure continuity and progression within and between classes and in subjects;

2.3.3   set appropriately demanding expectations for pupils;

2.3.4   employ a range of teaching strategies appropriate to the age, ability and attainment level of pupils;

2.3.5   present subject content in clear language and in a stimulating manner;

2.3.6   contribute to the development of pupils' language and communication skills;

2.3.7   demonstrate an ability to select and use appropriate resources including information technology.

Class management

2.4   Newly qualified teachers should be able to:

2.4.1 decide when teaching the whole class, groups, pairs, or individuals is appropriate for particular learning purposes;

2.4.2 create and maintain a purposeful and orderly environment for the pupils;

2.4.3 devise and use appropriate rewards and sanctions to maintain an effective learning environment;

2.4.4 maintain pupils' interest and motivation.

Assessment and recording of pupils' progress

2.5   Newly qualified teachers should be able to:

2.5.1 identify the current level of attainment of individual pupils using NCATs, statements of attainment and end of key stage statements where applicable;

2.5.2 judge how well each pupil performs against the standard expected of a pupil of that age;

2.5.3 assess and record systematically the progress of individual pupils;

2.5.4 use such assessments in their teaching;

2.5.5 demonstrate that they understand the importance of reporting to pupils on their progress and of marking their work regularly against agreed criteria.

Further professional development

2.6   Newly qualified teachers should have acquired in initial training the necessary foundation to develop:

2.6.1 an understanding of the school as an institution and its place within the community;

2.6.2 a working knowledge of their pastoral, contractual, legal and administrative responsibilities as teachers;

2.6.3 an ability to develop effective working relationships with professional colleagues and parents, and to develop their communication skills;

2.6.4 an awareness of individual differences, including social, psychological, developmental and cultural dimensions;

2.6.5 the ability to recognise diversity of talent including that of gifted pupils;

2.6.6 the ability to identify special educational needs or learning difficulties;

2.6.7 a self-critical approach to diagnosing and evaluating pupils' learning, including a recognition of the effects on that learning of teachers' expectations;

2.6.8 a readiness to promote the moral and spiritual well-being of pupils.

For intending primary school teachers the required competences are set out in six main areas: curriculum content, planning and assessment (with respect to the whole curriculum and to subject knowledge); application and assessment and recording of pupils' progress; teaching strategies (with respect to pupil learning and teaching strategies and techniques); further professional development. The specific competences for newly qualified primary teachers are set out below:

Curriculum content, planning and assessment

A. Whole curriculum

2.2   Newly qualified teachers should be able to:
2.2.1   demonstrate understanding of the purposes, scope, structure and balance of the primary curriculum as a whole;
2.2.2   ensure continuity and progression within the work of their own class and with the classes to and from which their pupils transfer;
2.2.3   exploit, in all their teaching, opportunities to develop pupils' language, reading, numeracy, information handling and other skills.

B. Subject knowledge and application

2.3   Newly qualified teachers should be able to:
2.3.1   demonstrate knowledge and understanding of the subjects of the primary curriculum which they have studied, at a level which will support effective teaching of those subjects;
2.3.2   use that knowledge and understanding to plan lessons, teach and assess pupils in the core subjects of the national curriculum and those other subjects of the primary curriculum covered in their course; newly qualified teachers may need some guidance and support in some of these subjects.

C. Assessment and recording of pupils' progress

2.4   Newly qualified teachers should be able to:
2.4.1   test, assess and record systematically the progress of individual pupils;
2.4.2   judge how well each pupil performs against appropriate criteria and standards by identifying individual pupils' attainment, with reference to relevant national curriculum requirements;
2.4.3   use such testing and assessment in their planning and teaching;
2.4.4   provide oral and written feedback to pupils on the processes and outcomes of their learning;
2.4.5   prepare and present records on pupils' progress to parents.

Teaching strategies

A. Pupil learning

2.5   Newly qualified teachers should be able to:

2.5.1 identify and respond to relevant individual differences between pupils;

2.5.2 show awareness of how pupils learn and of the various factors which affect the process;

2.5.3 set appropriate and demanding expectations of their pupils;

2.5.4 devise a variety and range of learning goals and tasks and monitor and assess them.

B. Teaching strategies and techniques

2.6   Newly qualified teachers should be able to:

2.6.1 establish clear expectations of pupil behaviour in the classroom and secure appropriate standards of discipline;

2.6.2 create and maintain a purposeful, orderly and supportive environment for their pupils' learning;

2.6.3 maintain pupils' interest and motivation;

2.6.4 present learning tasks and curriculum content in a clear and stimulating manner;

2.6.5 teach whole classes, groups and individuals, and determine the most appropriate learning goals and classroom contexts for using these and other teaching strategies;

2.6.6 use a range of teaching techniques, and judge when and how to use them;

2.6.7 employ varying forms of curriculum organisation, and monitor their effectiveness;

2.6.8 communicate clearly and effectively with pupils through questioning, instructing, explaining and feedback;

2.6.9 manage effectively and economically their own and their pupils' time;

2.6.10 make constructive use of information technology and other resources for learning;

2.6.11 train pupils in the individual and collaborative study skills necessary for effective learning.

Further professional development

2.7   Newly qualified teachers should have acquired in initial training the necessary foundation to develop:

2.7.1 a working knowledge of their contractual, legal, administrative and pastoral responsibilities as teachers;

2.7.2   effective working relationships with professional colleagues (including support staff) and parents;

2.7.3   the ability to identify and provide for special educational needs and specific learning difficulties;

2.7.4   the ability to evaluate pupils' learning and recognise the effects on that learning of teachers' expectations and actions;

2.7.5   a readiness to promote the spiritual, moral, social and cultural development of pupils;

2.7.6   their professional knowledge, understanding and skill through further professional training and development;

2.7.7   vision, imagination and critical awareness in educating their pupils.

The remainder of this book addresses the full range of the DFEE competences. Part II addresses the DFEE competences contained within the subsections 2.2, 2.3 and 2.6 for secondary student teachers, and 2.2, 2.3, 2.5 and 2.7 for primary student teachers. Part III addresses the DFEE competences contained within the subsection 2.3 and 2.4 for secondary student teachers and 2.5 and 2.6 for primary student teachers. Part IV addresses the DFEE competences contained within the subsection 2.5 for secondary student teachers, and 2.4 for primary student teachers. It can be seen, then, that this book addresses the complete range of DFEE competences for both primary and secondary student teachers.

For intending primary school teachers the achievement of these competencies is overlaid with three levels of subject competence guidelines that build on prior knowledge, new knowledge gained in the course, and the ability to combine academic with pedagogical knowledge of the subject. Level 1 reflects basic familiarity with the subject though the beginning teacher remains largely 'outside' the subject. Level 2 reflects the beginnings of enhanced subject competence, including a 'stronger sense of the concepts and methodology of the subject',[5] though these are largely in terms of received frameworks and approaches. Level 3 is 'the achievement of insight into the structures, concepts, content and principles of a subject, together with a secure understanding of how to teach it, the ability to exercise autonomy over approaches and resources, and the infectious enthusiasm which is associated with thorough subject mastery',[6] and where the person is 'inside' the subject.

One can see many similarities between the secondary and primary sets of competences. There are several points to note about the DFEE competences:

- *The competences are inert and comparatively content-free; they need to be applied, interpreted and assessed in context.*

First, this raises the difficult issue of what those appropriate contexts might be, in how many contexts and teaching situations the competences need to be demonstrated, how consistently and for how long before a student teacher is deemed to have met the competence level required. Opportunities for

development and demonstration of the competence(s) must be present; this has implications for the contents of teaching practice. Secondly, McCulloch[7] raises the problem of how to infer achievement of unobservable competences (e.g. understanding) from observed behaviour. Thirdly, there is the matter of the level of expertise required to be able to detect and recognise competence – it may exist but student teachers and observers (e.g. mentors) may not recognise it. The work of Eisner[8] is pertinent here, as he argues that teachers need a degree of *connoisseurship* to be able to judge good practice; just as a wine connoisseur develops gustatory connoisseurship through cultivation and refinement of the palette so the teacher as an 'extended professional' has to be able to develop expertise through reflective practice.

- *Each competence is undifferentiated.*

It is impossible to tell from looking at the lists of competences what the differences might be between the demonstration of a particular competence at the beginning and the end of a student teacher's course of initial training, between 'threshold' and 'exit' abilities.[9] A negative interpretation of this might be that the DFEE competences in fact are not true competences at all, for true competences, like behavioural objectives, are criterion-referenced, that is, they specify intended terminal behaviour, the conditions in which the behaviour is to occur and the criteria of acceptable performance.[10] There is a need for the competences to be 'operationalised'. A more positive interpretation recognises that there is some degree of latitude for student teachers, mentors and supervisors to interpret and plan for the development of the competences in question – a window of opportunity for the exercise of professional judgement. What is required is a clarification of what the standards and criteria will be for assessing minimum (untutored), medium (learnt) and maximum (expert) achievement of the competence in question. Of course, the problem that follows from this is the need for reliability – parity, consistency and transparency – of assessments, necessitating a moderation exercise so that all parties understand and agree the level descriptions. A further problem arises in that, in the interests of assessment, it may be difficult to avoid recasting competences in narrowly behavioural, skills-based terms.

- *Each competence is itself an amalgam of different types, numbers and orders of sub-component competences.*

For example, Whitty and Willmott[11] indicate that some competences are task-related, some person-related, some are generic, some discrete, some are low level and others are of a higher order. The operationalisation of each competence risks the same problems as behavioural objectives, *viz.* that it becomes impossible to avoid devising and endeavouring to complete lengthy lists of sub-components for each competence – an unworkable system.[12] As before, in the absence of strict guidelines and procedures from the DFEE, a degree of professional judgement can be exercised by those involved in assessing and planning for the achievement of the competences.

Since the inception of the competence-based movement in initial teacher education the achievement of competences is often recorded in a developing profile or portfolio by each student teacher; it has been suggested above that the compilation of a portfolio of achievements is an integral part of student teachers' development. Further, it has been suggested above that competences feature significantly in action planning. What is being suggested is that an action plan is the outcome of a review of present achievements of competences and a process wherein the student teacher is guided into electing which competences need to receive attention and when they are to be addressed – in schools and during a student teacher's course. If a student is to develop competences during the course then an initial appraisal of 'threshold' performance is necessary and becomes the springboard into future action planning. Though the nature of the competence-driven development of students in principle is student-driven, the reality of the situation is that students often do not have the appropriate background to assess their own performance or to plan for its development. Indeed, that is why they come on the course in the first place!

At one level it is possible to meet this by experienced and significant others – often tutors – *prescribing* a route or sequence through the lists of DFEE competences. One example of this is in a possible sequence through the clusters of competences for the intending primary school teacher, Box 3. This sequence draws on the experience of tutoring many student teachers before the first whisper of competence-based training was heard. It addresses from very early on the questions that are usually uppermost in student teachers' minds: can I keep order? Can I avoid a riot?

Box 3 An overall sequence for developing competences

> **Discipline → Teaching Techniques → Teaching and Learning Styles → Curriculum Planning → Assessment → Further Professional Development**

Moreover, this box recognises that very little teaching, attention to teaching and learning styles, and curriculum planning can be considered unless discipline has been established. It also reflects the sequence in which student teachers learn to teach during their teaching practice: initially they work alongside a teacher, taking the initiative from the teacher; they typically begin by working with small groups, trying out teaching techniques and teaching and learning styles (discussed in Parts II and III). Gradually the responsibility for curriculum planning (initially perhaps for a small group, increasing by stages as confidence grows) passes from the class or subject teacher to the student teacher. The student teacher can next begin to take stock of individual differences in the students and plan appropriately for differentiation and progression, both of which are contingent on formal and informal assessment (discussed in Part IV). Though the student teacher in fact begins her/his 'professional' development from the point of entry to the course, this label is usually reserved for the in-service professional development of recently and distantly qualified teachers – it is an issue which may not be uppermost in the mind of the novice student teacher.

Box 4 takes the elements and sequence of Box 3 and relates them to specific competences for intending primary school teachers.

Box 4 A detailed sequence of competences

Discipline and relationships
(e.g. being proactive, vigilance, transitions, routines and rules, controlling movement, setting realistic and manageable tasks, acting reasonably and fairly, use of praise and encouragement, being clear in demands and expectations, promoting a positive environment, communicating, timing, developing motivation in children, maintaining tolerance and a sense of humour)

2.4.4; 2.5.1; 2.5.3; 2.6.1; 2.6.2; 2.6.3; 2.6.4; 2.6.6; 2.6.8; 2.6.9; 2.6.11; 2.7.3; 2.7.4

↓

Teaching techniques
(e.g. introducing, explaining, questioning, summarising, use of voice, dividing attention, listening, eliciting, demonstration, giving feedback, class, group and individual teaching, timing, beginning, continuing, finishing, transitions)

2.4.4; 2.5.1; 2.5.2; 2.5.3; 2.5.4; 2.6.1–2.6.11; 2.7.3; 2.7.4; 2.7.7

↓

Teaching and learning styles
(e.g. use of whole-class, group, individual work, formal, informal, didactic, experiential, gain insights into how children are learning and what affects this)

2.5.4; 2.6.4; 2.6.5; 2.6.6; 2.6.7; 2.6.8; 2.6.9; 2.6.10; 2.6.11; 2.7.2; 2.7.3; 2.7.4

↓

Curriculum planning and organisation
(e.g. subjects, topics, cross-curricular skills, matching, differentiation, breadth, balance, continuity, progression, sequence, timing, subject knowledge, coverage of attainment targets and programmes of study, analysis of task demands and task, drawing up schemes of work and lesson plans, communicating purposes to children, providing for children with special educational needs, creativity and imagination)

2.2.1; 2.2.2; 2.2.3; 2.3.1; 2.3.2; 2.4.2; 2.4.3; 2.4.4; 2.5.1; 2.5.3; 2.5.4; 2.6.3; 2.6.7; 2.6.9; 2.6.10; 2.6.11; 2.7.2; 2.7.3; 2.7.4; 2.7.5; 2.7.6; 2.7.7

↓

Monitoring/Assessing progress
(e.g. providing valid diagnoses, diagnostic teaching, judging, recording, observing, reporting, use of level descriptions and end of key stage statements, covering core and foundation subjects and other aspects of children's development, selecting appropriate assessment criteria, providing feedback, providing for children with special educational needs)

2.3.2; 2.4.1–2.4.5; 2.5.2; 2.5.4; 2.6.3; 2.6.7; 2.7.3; 2.7.4; 2.7.7

↓

Further professional development
(e.g. subject and pedagogical knowledge, acting on advice, legal and contractual responsibilities, effective working and interpersonal relationships with other adults)

2.7.1–2.7.7

It can be seen that the competences are addressed not only during teaching practice but as part of courses offered by institutions of higher education. The criteria for assessing coursework and teaching practice need to be harmonised to complement and support each other within the context of the DFEE competences.

The operation of mentoring

The success of the use of competences for developing and assessing student teachers' achievements relies on the sensitive support given to the student in the school by the mentor and in the institution of higher education by the appropriate tutor. The development of a realistic action plan by, with and for students is often the outcome of a review with a mentor. A mentor is a named teacher in the school (often in a middle or senior management position) who has responsibility for:

- advising student teachers how to teach their particular subjects;
- developing student teachers' understandings and appreciation of how students learn and how learning can be planned;
- advising student teachers on class management and the planning of curricula and assessment;
- taking overall school responsibility for those elements of initial teacher education courses that include school-based assignments and projects;
- assessing the performance and development of student teachers' competences in teaching, subject knowledge and application, classroom performance, assessment and record-keeping and professional development.[13]

In short, the mentor has a significant role to play in the student teacher's development as a reflective practitioner.[14] The role of the mentor is multifaceted and complex, for in addition to providing content and skills-focused advice and support there is a large interpersonal and psychological dimension. The mentor acts as a support for the student teacher, motivating, raising awareness, providing feedback and advice, reviewing sessions and guiding future planning, acting as a 'critical friend' – an unthreatening source of student-teacher improvement, in some cases simply being on hand to discuss matters with the student teacher as they arise in school, and acting as a link person between the school and the college or university tutor.[15] Being a mentor requires the ability to employ several sensitive and sophisticated skills,[16] for example:

- being a model of good teaching practice;
- listening, responding and advising;
- understanding situations through the eyes of the student teacher – empathy;
- showing a willingness to work with the student teacher in a variety of situations – the development of mutual trust;
- observing the student teacher closely and identifying specific issues for discussion;
- conducting reviews and appraisals of lessons in a supportive manner;
- advising on action planning and negotiating pathways for student-teacher development in school;
- organising the contacts that student teachers have with other colleagues;
- timetabling formal review meetings;
- planning induction and teaching programmes of balanced and broad experiences for student teachers.

A student teacher has a reasonable expectation of guided support from the mentor. Reciprocally, a mentor has a reasonable expectation of co-operation in meeting negotiated targets by the student teacher. Typically a mentor will discuss the teaching file and lesson plans with the student teacher, negotiating what the mentor will be observing. The mentor then observes her/him teaching one or more of these lessons each week. Following the observation the mentor conducts a review meeting with the student teacher during which feedback is given and debriefing occurs. This meeting is timetabled and is designed to provoke reflection on the part of the student teacher – both through the setting of a predetermined agenda and in the opportunity for an open discussion about other matters. At the meeting an action plan for further development will be agreed.

Not only does the mentor have an important substantive role to play in the professional development of the student but s/he has an important facilitatory role to play. For example, the mentor is the link not only to the college or university tutor but to teacher colleagues in the school. So, for example, the mentor might arrange for a student teacher to be attached for some time to another member of staff, to meet other departmental staff (in secondary schools) or teachers of other age phases (in primary schools); the mentor may put the student teacher in touch with a colleague with a particular expertise, e.g. information technology, multimedia resources, music, contacts with outside organisations and agencies, etc. The mentor will apprise the student teacher of protocols, rules and routines in the school – in short, the 'hidden curriculum'. The hidden curriculum for students where, as Jackson[17] argued convincingly, they learn to live with crowds, praise, power, denial, public evaluation, rules and routines, applies equally to student teachers. Indeed, Holt's claim[18] that learning the hidden curriculum is more important for student success in school is equally true for student teachers; the mentor is the facilitator of that learning. The rest of this book, specifically and by implication, raises several issues that student teachers may wish to address with mentors.

The move to mentoring in schools accords significance to the part that experienced teachers can play in the initial preparation of teachers. Some schools do not wish to follow the mentoring road, arguing that it is too time-consuming, expensive (in supply-teacher cover) and onerous for teachers, whose prime responsibility is to teach children. Indeed, these sentiments often accord not only with parents but with governing bodies concerned that standards do not fall because students are taught by novice student teachers.

Chapter 5

An overview of the national curriculum of England and Wales

Perhaps the singularly most important feature of preparation and planning since the last edition of this book was issued has been the introduction and development of the national curriculum of England and Wales (hereafter called the national curriculum). Given statutory status in 1988, the national curriculum has been the subject of intense debate, and has been modified several times since its inception.

This is not the place to discuss the minutiae of that debate. Rather we consider it more appropriate to set out those aspects of the national curriculum that impinge on a student teacher's preparation and planning. Early versions were very detailed and specific on the contents (and, in many cases, the pedagogy) of what students should be taught, provoking much opposition from teachers, not only for being over-prescriptive but for being unworkable. Too much content was being prescribed; the level of detail constricted the exercise of professional autonomy of teachers too greatly; the ten-level sequence for planning progression did not fit the order or manner in which children learnt; it was difficult for teachers to incorporate the national curriculum into their existing organisation of curricula (for example, the national curriculum was framed in terms of subjects whereas many primary schools planned in terms of topics) or to harmonise it with the requirements of GCSE syllabuses and examinations; it was difficult to establish links between elements of the curriculum; the overload on teachers to have the national curriculum in place within a telescoped time-scale created inordinate stress and demoralisation, particularly when their planning for the first two versions subsequently had to be scrapped as new orders for the curriculum were prepared.

Suffice it to say here that, as a result of professional opposition and the political embarrassment caused by the fall-out from this opposition, the national curriculum was trimmed, following a report prepared by Ron Dearing in 1993–5. The government accepted Dearing's recommendations almost without reservation. Some would argue that the unseemly haste with which the government agreed to Dearing's proposals was a last-ditch attempt by the former secretary of state for education, John Patten, to save his political skin (in vain, as it turned out!). The revised national curriculum (the third main version since its inception) is less detailed, though arguably still just as prescriptive, and it still includes the frameworks set out in the first two versions.

The national curriculum applies to students of ages 5–16; it is organised into *key stages* that are age-related. Key Stage 1 is for 5–7-year-olds; Key Stage 2 is for 7–11-year-olds; Key Stage 3 is for 11–14-year-olds; Key Stage 4 is for 14–16-year-olds. It comprises *statutory elements* (core and foundation subjects and religious education) and *non-statutory elements* (cross-curricular dimensions, skills and themes) as follows: core subjects (English, mathematics, science, technology, defined as information technology (IT) and design technology (DT)); foundation subjects (history, geography, music, art, physical education (PE), a modern foreign language (MFL) for secondary students); religious education (RE); cross-curricular elements (see Box 5). The framing of the national curriculum is described variously in terms of: (i) *subjects* for each key stage (KS), (ii) *attainment targets* (ATs), (iii) *programmes of study* (PoS), (iv) *level descriptions* (LDs) and *end of key stage statements* (EOKSS). Programmes of study can be found for every statutory element of the national curriculum.

The national curriculum is set out in Box 5, with an indication, by a bullet point, of whether *level descriptions* or *end of key stage statements* are being used.

In terms of the framing of *subjects* one can see in Box 5 that the national curriculum is not uniform: physical education replaces attainment targets with areas of study; art, music and physical education have end of key stage statements rather than level descriptions (while the cross-curricular issues have neither). These differences extend further when one examines the national curriculum documents in more detail, for in many of the subjects different themes appear at different key stages. For example, in mathematics *communicating mathematically* only appears at KS3 and KS4; in science *inheritance and evolution* only appear at KS4; in technology *control with systems* only appears at KS3 and KS4; in PE *outdoor and adventurous activities* only appear at KS3 and KS4.

In terms of *pedagogy*, though the government indicated that the national curriculum would leave room for schools and teachers to decide how to deliver the contents,[1] the document in fact contains specific principles for pedagogy. For example, in mathematics students should: have experience of practical tasks and real-life problems; compare their ideas and methods with others; discuss shapes and movements; link work purposefully with other subjects; talk about and explain their mathematics; make 2D and 3D shapes; discuss common events; explore shape and space practically; solve problems by drawing, measuring and calculation. In English students should: contribute to discussion, both in talking and responding to others; remember specific points that interested them and to listen to others' reactions; be given

Box 5 An overview of the national curriculum

Subject	Attainment targets	LDs	EOKSS
English	AT1: Speaking and listening	•	
	AT2: Reading	•	
	AT3: Writing	•	
Mathematics	AT1: Using and applying mathematics	•	
	AT2: Number and algebra (for KS3 & KS4)	•	
	AT3: Shape, space and measures	•	
	AT4: Handling data (not for KS1)	•	
	Further material (for KS4)		
Science	AT1: Experimental and investigative science	•	
	AT2: Life processes and living things	•	
	AT3: Materials and their properties	•	
	AT4: Physical processes	•	
IT	AT1: Information technology capability	•	
DT	AT1: Designing	•	
	AT2: Making	•	
MFL	AT1: Listening and responding	•	
	AT2: Speaking	•	
	AT3: Reading and responding	•	
	AT4: Writing	•	
Geography	AT1: Geography	•	
History	AT1: History	•	
Art	AT1: Investigating and making		•
	AT2: Knowledge and understanding		•
Music	AT1: Performing and composing		•
	AT2: Listening and appraising		•
PE	Areas of activity		•
RE			

Cross-curricular issues:

Dimensions:	Equal opportunities; multicultural education; special educational needs.
Skills:	Communication; numeracy; problem-solving; study; personal and social; information technology.
Themes:	Education for Economic and Industrial Understanding; Health Education; Careers Education and Guidance; Environmental Education; Education for Citizenship.

opportunities to respond to drama they have watched as well as that in which they have participated; be given the opportunities to communicate to a wider range of audiences; have opportunities to listen to a range of people and media; take roles in group discussion; adjust their talk to suit the circumstances in formal and informal situations; take part in scripted and unscripted plays; draw on the various methods of teaching reading in a balanced and coherent way; read on their own, with others and to the teacher, including both independent and shared reading of play scripts and other texts by groups and the whole class; see their teacher write; read their work aloud; be taught to write for a range of readers; develop their ability to analyse and criticise their own and others' writing. In science students should: have first-hand experience; be encouraged to use a practical approach to finding out about their immediate surroundings and to develop an understanding of scientific ideas; have opportunities to test ideas; have opportunities to carry out experimental and investigative work in a wide range of contexts. In technology students should: use a variety of applications; create presentations for particular audiences. In art students should: be encouraged to develop their creative, imaginative and practical skills through a balanced programme of art, craft and design activities, working individually, in groups and as a whole class. In PE students should: begin to work with a partner and talk about what they and others have done; work alone and with others and engage in co-operative or competitive tasks which test their ability to solve problems and make decisions. In geography students should: make and use their own maps; use fieldwork where appropriate.

In terms of the *whole curriculum* the national curriculum is designed to address certain features that were signalled in 1985 by the then HMI:[2] breadth, balance, relevance; continuity; progression and differentiation. These issues will be discussed later in this book. Suffice it here to say that, even though they are problematic,[3] the level of prescription in the national curriculum attempts to ensure: *breadth, balance* and *relevance* by prescribing the contents of the curriculum; *continuity* by prescribing the curriculum from ages 5 to 16 largely in subject terms; *progression* by describing ten levels within subjects. Within the national curriculum documents one can discover several views of progression: development of enquiring attitude; growing attention, concentration and ability to sustain study; a greater range of purposes, applications, activities, audiences, resources/equipment, demands and contexts; a greater quantity of knowledge, skills, understandings, breadth and depth of study; greater complexity of ideas, concepts, sequences, stages and applications; greater independence, autonomy and ability in organising, planning, implementing, evaluating and recording work; expanding means of communication, responsive to different audiences; greater use of higher-order thinking (e.g. analysis, synthesis, enquiry, evaluation, appreciation, prediction, problem-solving, explanation); a greater degree of application, practical implementation and ways of working; movement from the immediate, familiar and present to the more distant, unfamiliar and past/future; greater confidence, responsibility and responsiveness; greater appropriacy and consistency of selection and utilisation of material and skills (fitness for purpose) and acquisition of relevant information (exercise of judgement); greater structure to their own work; drawing links and relationships between different areas of knowledge; increasing skill. *Differentiation* in the national curriculum is addressed by implying that children work through the levels at different rates.

With regard to the *cross-curricular issues* there is an expectation that each subject, where relevant, will address cross-curricular dimensions, skills[4] and themes. These all have implications for managing the planning and contents of curricula and pedagogy. Clearly a collegial model of planning is implied, so that co-ordination, coherence, sequence, avoidance of overlap, attention to progression and the nature of students' exposure to the issues are addressed. Cross-curricular matters cross subjects, departments, faculties, age phases; indeed, Morrison[5] argues that the cross-curricular themes offer some of the most exciting and innovative forms of planning and implementation in schools.

In terms of planning, the former National Curriculum Council[6] identified five main ways in which the cross-curricular themes could be organised:

- taught through national curriculum and other subjects;
- whole-curriculum planning leading to blocks of activities (e.g. a series of subject-based topics which last for varying periods of time);
- as separately timetabled themes;
- as part of a programme of personal and social education;
- through 'long-block' timetabling (e.g. 'activity weeks').

Morrison[7] takes this further, echoing the discussion in Chapter 2, arguing that modular and flexible-learning approaches can also be used to deliver the cross-curricular themes. He also identifies many strengths and weaknesses in these several forms of timetable and organisation.

In terms of *pedagogy*, the National Curriculum Council suggested some imaginative ways of learning that take the students out of school and involve considerable degrees of active involvement. In the *Curriculum Guidance*[8] documents which accompanied the non-statutory cross-curricular themes there are several suggestions for teaching and learning styles:

- a reliance on practical activities and students' decision-making;
- active learning and exploratory activities;
- learning by first-hand experience and participatory approaches;
- the use of problem-solving;
- the flexible use of a wide range of teaching methods and resources;
- the matching of content with pedagogy (so that students learn in the manner most fitting to the contents);

- the development of collaborative teamwork (teams of students and teachers);
- the development of students' self-directed, autonomous planning and learning;
- the development of small-scale projects within and outside school;
- the establishing of links and partnerships between the school and the wider community.

Not only does the national curriculum comprise matters to be taught and ways in which they can be taught and learned, but it also covers issues in *assessment*. The School Curriculum and Assessment Authority prescribes what will be assessed in students' achievements of it and how some of that assessment will operate. This is a substantial topic and will be discussed more fully in Part IV.

Our intention in presenting this introduction to the national curriculum is to indicate that when student teachers go into schools and discuss what and how they will be teaching, to whom and with whom, they will encounter very many changes from the days when student teachers were able to have a 'free hand'. Schools are required to have a yearly plan that indicates the main contents and organisation of the curriculum. Student teachers going into schools can expect to be told what they will be teaching and to have explained to them the context of their teaching in terms of the plans that have been drawn up by the school, the department and faculty, the age-phase leaders, curriculum leaders and co-ordinators, subject and age-phase teams as well as individual teachers with whom they will have contact. Though there may be latitude in planning specific activities and pedagogical matters, student teachers will have to slot into the school curriculum planning that has already preceded their arrival in school. To some extent they will have to work within the frameworks of a *received* curriculum, the parameters and contents of which teachers, in turn, have received from external sources.

In many respects the need to operate within a received curriculum can be very helpful to student teachers as it provides a considerable amount of support and guidance on what to teach and what will be matched to particular students, groups and whole classes. Within these parameters student teachers are free to consider other aspects of planning and pedagogy in more detail, with reduced stress.

This part of the book has set out a range of macro- and micro-contexts in the current educational debate. It has shown that education is an 'essentially contested concept',[9] problematic and not susceptible to simple recipes for success. This places a responsibility upon student teachers to nurture their own development as reflective practitioners, constantly aware of the shifting currents of debate and practice, and becoming increasingly able to exercise autonomy, collegiality and professional judgement in schools. Our introduction has touched the tips of several icebergs of the educational debate. Both at a macro-level and a micro-level the issues that have been selected for discussion here have not only tried to capture and represent the climate of education but have deliberately signalled that education and schooling have to change and to cope with change in the society outside schools. Change will continue to occur, and in all quarters. That said, there are some powerful constants in education which are taken up throughout the remainder of this book: the centrality of interpersonal relationships; the need to consider aims and values; the benefits of an objectives-based approach to planning; the need for careful preparation, planning and recording; the need to be sensitive to the complexity of issues in the organisation of classrooms, curricula, discipline, pastoral aspects, pedagogy, assessment and evaluation. The challenge for student teachers to absorb and keep pace with all of these issues is as exciting as it is worthwhile.

Part II

Preparation and planning

INTRODUCTION

Part II addresses the DFEE competences (see Part I) contained within subsections 2.2 and 2.3 for both primary and secondary student teachers, subsection 2.6 (secondary) and 2.5 and 2.7 (primary). One of the most crucial factors in the teaching-practice situation for the student teacher is preparation – finding out as much as possible about the school beforehand, formulating aims and objectives purposefully, selecting appropriate content, deciding the best methods of presentation and writing the actual lesson notes. It is our purpose in this section to examine in some detail the components listed above so that the reader's preparation may be more thorough and meaningful, meeting his or her needs, together with those of school and college, more satisfactorily.

Student teachers can adopt a variety of roles on teaching practice. Some of these arise from their status *qua* student teachers. One such role is that of *experimenter*. The theory and training they have received prior to their first practice and subsequently cannot possibly provide them with answers for all the problems and contingencies they are likely to encounter in the school and the classroom. There are no straightforward recipes for successful teaching that can be applied in all situations: the exercise of informed judgement is required. This moves teachers out of the realms of technicism, working in a strictly mechanistic fashion, towards roles as creative reflective practitioners. At best, they will provide general principles and guidelines as a basis for action. For this reason, they must be prepared to interpret and apply these principles and guidelines in specific situations and it is here that they can assume their experimenter role. Inevitably, some of their endeavours will not work out, but such occasions can be just as educative as the successful ones. It is in the preparation and planning stages, therefore, that we recommend student teachers to see themselves as experimenters from time to time, for it is in this capacity that they will be able to think out imaginative and innovatory approaches to traditional problems and to decide in what ways theory can inform practice. Naturally, experimenting will involve a certain amount of risk-taking. Providing risks are carefully calculated the advantages will outweigh the disadvantages.

As we intimated earlier, we shall be adopting the *objectives model* as a basis for our discussions on preparation and planning. Briefly, this involves specifying the desired outcomes of the learning situation in advance so that the means of achieving them can be ordered in a logical and systematic way. The objectives model itself is associated with the rational approach to curriculum planning and as such has it critics. Those holding progressive views on education, for example, would argue that such an approach, in which the teacher pre-specifies the learning outcomes, ignores objectives the children may have and tends to discount the value of unintended outcomes. As one writer[1] puts it: 'The teacher's task is not to prespecify outcomes, rather to place children in learning situations which stimulate them in a host of ways but whose outcomes will emerge gradually from the constant interaction and negotiation between teacher and pupil.' Other critics point to the mismatch between the cold rationality of the objectives model and the constantly changing realities of school life. Shipman,[2] for instance, writes:

> Curriculum development does not proceed through a clear cycle from a statement of objectives to an evaluation of the learning strategies used. It consists of interaction, accommodation and compromise. Horse trading and horse sense are the concrete curriculum scene, not the clinical alignment of means with ends that is the official version.

While conceding that such criticisms are perfectly valid, we for our part share the belief of the objectives school that the purpose of formal education is to bring about desired changes in children.[3] Indeed, it is a salutary exercise to ask oneself what students are able to do at the end of the lesson that they were unable to do at the beginning. The strengths and weaknesses of objectives are summarised in Box 6. It can be seen that several strengths also appear as claimed weaknesses. This indicates the ideological nature of aspects of the debate, reflecting the personal preferences of their advocates or critics. If we want students to acquire certain kinds of knowledge and skills and to develop particular attitudes, we must identify these propensities at the outset and formulate them in terms of aims and objectives. At the same time, we do not necessarily see them as fixed and unchanging; all kinds of chance factors are operating in the classroom which will affect our planning. There is, moreover, room for accommodation and modification. Indeed, we would agree with Jeffcoate[4] when he said:

> Prespecified objectives should not acquire the status of sacrosanct unalterable absolutes. Instead they should be open to constant review, adaptation and revision ... Hilda Taba[5] best conveys this notion of flexibility in the definition and use of objectives when she suggests they should be seen as 'developmental', representing 'roads to travel rather than terminal points'.

Box 6

Strengths and weaknesses of behavioural objectives

Strengths

1 They are performance-based, measurable and observable.
2 They are easily communicated to teachers and students.
3 They facilitate organisation by specifying goals and outcomes.
4 They clarify thinking and planning and resolve ambiguities.
5 They are 'teacher-proof' and clear to anxious teachers.
6 They are highly prescriptive.
7 They make clear assessment and evaluation criteria.
8 They specify behaviours.
9 They render planning logical, sequential and linear.
10 They expose trivialities and emphases.

Weaknesses

1 They are highly instrumental, regarding education as instrumentally rather than intrinsically worthwhile.
2 They render students and teachers passive recipients of curricula rather than participants in a process of negotiation.
3 They only cover the trivial, concrete and observable aspects of education, thereby neglecting longer-term, unobservable, unmeasurable, deeper-seated aims and elements.
4 Education becomes technicist, tending towards low-level training rather than high-level thinking.
5 Because they are 'teacher-proof' they build out teachers' autonomy.
6 They lead to predictability rather than open-endedness, discovery, serendipity, creativity and spontaneity.
7 The *process* of education is overtaken by *outcome dependence*.
8 They replace the significance of *understanding* with an emphasis on *behaviour*.
9 Epistemologically they mistake the nature of knowledge, seeing it as *products* and *facts*, supporting a *rationalist* rather than an *empirical* view of knowledge.
10 They mistakenly 'parcel up' and atomise knowledge.

Source Morrison and Ridley

The great attraction of objectives is that, carefully constructed, they provide criteria for evaluation and assessment. This is in direct keeping with the notion of action planning that was raised in Part I. Moreover, as was mentioned in Part I, the national curriculum is cast in an objectives model. It will be argued later that by stating objectives student teachers will have a set of criteria to use to judge the effectiveness of the lesson, i.e. the extent to which the objectives were reached.[6] The teaching–learning process is improved by (1) informing the children of the outcomes of their efforts; and (2) checking these same outcomes against the original aims and objectives to assess the extent to which they have been achieved.

It must be emphasised that the separation of the teaching–learning process into stages is necessary for the purposes of analysis and subsequent discussion. In practice, however, some stages may interact with others and occur at the same time. Objectives, for example, cannot really be separated from the means of achieving them, nor the content of a lesson from the methods of teaching and learning being used.

An objectives model can apply at several levels and to several areas. For example, one can have whole-school curriculum objectives, objectives for a year group or a curriculum subject, for schemes of work, for individual lessons, for groups of students, for individual students. One can have objectives for curricula, for physical, emotional and social environments, for behaviour and discipline, for teaching and learning styles, for addressing special needs, for equal opportunities, for school improvement.

Chapter 6

The preliminary visit

Student teachers are normally given the opportunity to visit their schools before the period of teaching practice formally begins. This may take the form of an observation week or a system of school attachments in the period leading up to the block practice. The following points will be of interest to student teachers offered such facilities.

THE PURPOSE OF THE PRELIMINARY VISIT

The preliminary visit enables the student teacher to meet the headteacher, the mentor or teacher in charge of students (where such an office exists), and the rest of the staff; to become acquainted with his or her class or subject teacher; to see the students he or she will be teaching; to get to know the nature, layout and resources of the school; and to gather specific information relevant to the work he or she will undertake during the practice.

WHAT TO LOOK FOR AND WHAT INFORMATION TO COLLECT

It follows from what we said in the preceding paragraph that to make the most of the preliminary visit, the student teacher must systematically take note of and, where he or she feels it helpful, record those aspects of the school's organisation, policy and methods in so far as they will relate to his or her own work in the school.[1] To help in these respects, we offer the following guidelines which arise from: the physical features; the school in general, its philosophy; grouping of students; the school's expectations of student teachers; policies and other relevant documentation (e.g. the school prospectus); significant people and organisational matters; the classroom, control and discipline, rules, routines and protocols (e.g. for involving others); resources; record-keeping; timetabling, curriculum organisation and planning; teaching and learning styles used; other adults involved (e.g. support assistants) and particular information to record (e.g. resources, schemes of work, details of students, timetable, curriculum planning, use of the photocopier, accessing resources – including computers, television and video). We stress that some of the points raised, e.g. in the physical features, may be more pertinent to the work of the primary teacher than the secondary specialist.

The physical features

We suggest you begin by investigating features and resources of the neighbourhood in which the school is situated. Some of these may prove to be relevant to the lessons you will be teaching and organising, e.g. the social nature of the area – is it urban, suburban or rural, for instance? You could then build up a basic topography of the locality to include the pattern of the main roads; churches and other buildings of significance; places of historical, geographical or social interest; recent developments; means of transport; details of houses, shops, businesses and industries; parks and beauty spots; museums; canals, rivers and bridges; docks; reservoirs; and markets. If there is a library near by, the librarian may be able to supply information on local history, or even arrange a special display for your class.

The *layout of the school* should next engage your attention. Observe the general architectural style. Is the school's design conventional, or open plan, for example? Approximately how old is the building? When might it have been built – in the late Victorian period or between the wars, for instance? Has the school an annex or other buildings on another site? The latter is quite common where previously separate schools have merged as a result of reorganisation. Find out where the head's room, the staffroom, the general office and assembly hall are to be found (if these are not immediately apparent). Are any rooms used for specialisation? Where are these located? How is their use timetabled? Is there an audio-visual centre? Or a resources centre? How are the rooms numbered? If the school is a single-storey construction and extensive in its layout, you may find it useful initially to draw a rough plan of the building.

The school in general

Find out how many pupils there are in the school, the size of its annual intake and the approximate location of its catchment area or areas. The school's recent history may prove interesting, especially if it includes reorganisation.

The school's ethos has an important bearing on the work of both teachers and students. Check nerve-points in the school's life to ascertain what the prevailing atmosphere is like, e.g. the staffroom or morning assembly. Make provisional assessments of the quality of the relationships between the head and the staff, between staff and students, and among the staff themselves. If the school has a healthy atmosphere, you should have little difficulty fitting in and helping to maintain it. Where the atmosphere is less than wholesome, however, then you must decide what personal and professional qualities you can display that will improve it.

The prevailing system of *control and discipline* operating in the school is of very great importance and you should find out how it works. What are the school rules, for example? Are they do's or don'ts? Who decides the rules? How explicit are they? Do all members of staff enforce them? What rewards and punishments are used? Who determines them? How effective are they? Which rules are broken? And how often? How are the more extreme forms of misbehaviour like classroom violence handled? (See Box 7 for the kinds of behaviour governed by rules.)

Box 7

Classroom rules

In their study of classroom rules, Hargreaves, Hestor and Mellor began by grouping rules into five themes, as set out below with brief explanatory comment. We suggest you use these themes as a starting point to determine the rules operating in the class, or classes, you will eventually be teaching. Begin by asking the teacher what rules are embraced by a particular theme, then use your powers of observation to see whether these actually conform to what is practised.

1   *The talk theme* Many of the rules related to areas of pupil talk. One of the most frequent teacher statements was 'stop talking'. We included in this theme all talk-related conduct, such as noise and laughter.
2   *The movement theme* The many rules about standing and sitting, entering and leaving the room, moving around the classroom, belonged to a common movement theme.
3   *The time theme* This included the rules about arriving late, about 'wasting time' and about the time taken by pupils to complete tasks assigned to them.
4   *The teacher–pupil relationship theme* The ways in which pupils were expected to treat the teachers were a common focus for a variety of rules. The most obvious rules covered obedience, manners and insolence.
5   *The pupil–pupil relationship theme* This included all the rules about how the pupils were expected to treat one another. Examples would be rules about fighting, name-calling and the various forms of interfering with another pupil and his work.

Source Hargreaves, Hestor and Mellor[2]

Alternatively, how do individual teachers cope where there is no such clearly defined framework of rules? Or where an ineffectual one exists? Or where chaos reigns? Which teachers appear to be most effective in such circumstances? And why? How will *you* relate to one or other of these situations when you have to work in the school?

It can also be of value to find out what the school's *philosophy of education* is. Naturally, it will not be voiced explicitly, and there may even be a clash of philosophies in some schools. However, one can get some idea of the way in which teachers think by studying the organisation of the school and the lessons. Some schools, for example, foster and encourage competition; others, co-operative behaviour. Some enforce a school uniform, others do not. Some are restrictive and authoritarian; others, by contrast, encourage autonomy and freedom of expression. Teaching methods are another obvious indication of a school's philosophy or philosophies. An important question arises for the student teacher in this connection: given an established system of teaching in the school, how does he or she fit in? The answer is that whereas the student teacher will generally adopt whatever method or methods are already in use, especially if they are well-tried and effective, there is no reason why he or she should not introduce alternative ones. One could, for instance, employ group methods with a class that had only experienced the traditional or teacher-

Box 8

Contrasting value-systems behind classical, romantic and modern perspectives on the curriculum

Davis distinguishes three perspectives that reflect developing educational thought in this century. Each perspective rests upon different assumptions and reflects different value structures. Using the characteristics identified below, decide what kind of perspective your school adopts towards the curriculum.

Classical perspective	*Romantic perspective*	*Modern perspective*
class teaching	individualised learning	flexible grouping
autocratic	*laissez-faire*	participative
conservative	abdication	liberal
subject emphasis	method emphasis	process emphasis
teacher-dominated	child-centred	inquiry-centred
teaching aids	audio-visual	learning resources
discipline	freedom	experience
skills	discovery	creativity
active	reactive	transactive
certainty	confusion	probability
competitive	co-operative	growth
other-directed	inner-directed	self-fulfilling
discipline	freedom	responsibility
doing things to	doing things for	doing things with

Source Davis[3]

centred approach. As a matter of courtesy, however, the class teacher should be consulted before introducing such a change, not the least reason being that rearrangements of the room may be required. Box 8 summarises three contrasting perspectives on educational thought in the twentieth century that may help the reader identify the school's philosophy.

It is particularly important to discover what forms of grouping are employed in the school: horizontal, vertical or transitional, for instance. Likewise, where integrated days and integrated curricula operate, how are they organised? Where other features such as mixed-ability grouping and team-teaching obtain they too should be investigated. A student teacher placed in a school where one or more of these approaches are used should make a special effort to find out how work and routines are organised.

It can also be helpful to get to know something of the school's expectations of you with respect to time of arrival, attendance at morning assembly, involvement with extra-curricular activities, free periods, leaving the school premises, dress, general appearance, preparation of lessons and behaviour *vis-à-vis* the rest of the staff. Box 9 provides a list of basic points one should try to keep in mind on teaching practice.

Box 9

Professional courtesy on teaching practice

1   If you are absent, let the school know promptly.
2   On return from an absence, let the headteacher know you're back. Do not let him/her find out from hearsay.
3   Lateness calls at least for an apology and possibly an explanation.
4   Be respectful to senior colleagues, e.g. concerning chairs in the staffroom.
5   Be prompt, tidy and accurate in whatever administrative work you have to do, e.g. registers.
6   Maintain adequate standards of dress and appearance.
7   Leave a classroom tidy and the blackboard clean at the end of a lesson.

There will be a number of *significant people* in the school whom you should at least meet and, better still, become acquainted with. These will include the head (or heads, if there is an upper and lower school), his or her deputy, the teacher in charge of students and the class teacher(s) with whom you will be working. It can also be useful to introduce yourself to the school secretary, technicians or laboratory assistants (where relevant), and the caretaker.

Finally, if the school has its own librarian, find out what the procedures are (1) for borrowing books for yourself, and (2) for utilising the library's resources with the children you will be teaching, in topic or project work, for example. You can save yourself a lot of time and trouble by preliminary enquiries of this kind before your block practice begins.

The classroom

We have already stressed the importance of finding out what system of *control and discipline* operates in the school. It is even more important to ascertain what management and control systems are used in the class(es) you yourself will be teaching. Where the class is taught chiefly by one teacher, make a note of established rules and routines, especially those relating to day-to-day matters such as speaking to the teacher, moving about the room, asking

Box 10

Classroom routines

The following checklist was designed by Haysom and Sutton for use in science lessons. Selecting whatever items you feel relevant, use them in one of your observation lessons to discover the rules and routines governing the classroom behaviour of the pupils.

Is it the standard practice for pupils to:

> stand up at the beginning of a lesson?
> choose where they sit?
> go to allotted spaces?
> work in self-selected groups?
> help each other in their work?
> expect not to consult each other?
> put hands up before speaking to the teacher?
> speak directly to the teacher, butting in at any time?
> be silent when the teacher begins to speak?
> carry on with what they're doing when the teacher speaks?
> leave the room on own initiative?
> move about freely during lessons?
> compose their own notes?
> copy notes from the board?
> be expected to have with them pencils, rulers, rubbers, etc.?
> be allowed to borrow these items?
> be allowed, if they finish early, to get on with homework?

You may feel it necessary to extend this list to accommodate rules and routines making up the standard practice in the particular situation you find yourself in.

Source Haysom and Sutton[4]

and answering questions, talking, finishing early and so on. (To help you make a start in these respects, we have listed guidelines in Boxes 7 and 10.)

UNDERSTANDING RULES AND ROUTINES

We cannot overstate the importance of the student teacher understanding the 'hidden curriculum'. The hidden curriculum 'oils the wheels' for the smooth running of the school and of the classes of students within it. In coining this term Jackson[5] suggested that a key factor of students' success in school was their ability not only to learn, but to work within, the hidden curriculum of the school.[6] Indeed, he argued that survival and success in school was a function of students' achievements in the hidden rather than the formal curriculum. Exactly the same is true for the student teacher. Jackson argues that *students* in school have to learn very quickly to live with rules, routines, crowds, praise, power, denial and delay. So, too, do *student teachers*. The student teacher's success depends in part on his or her ability to understand and work within the hidden curriculum of the school.

Some of the elements of the hidden curriculum are enshrined in the formal administrative and managerial aspects of the school at a whole-school level. For example, schools will have protocols for handling students who arrive late for lessons, students who seek permission to be out of school, movement around the school, arrangements for break times and lunch times, use of the school library, access to computers, incidence of illness during school time, disciplinary matters, wearing uniform and jewellery, completing homework, failure to bring the correct equipment for lessons, matters of confidentiality, pastoral and tutorial responsibilities, meeting parents, handling complaints, ordering and collecting stock from central resource areas, use of the telephones, dealing with and reporting accidents (i.e. health and safety matters). The student teacher will need to find out about the formal arrangements for all of these matters so that he or she knows exactly what to do and whom to contact in particular circumstances. Some of these matters are contained in school prospectuses, others are contained in 'information for staff' booklets, others might be found out in conversation with the mentor, link tutor and other teachers.

Not only are there rules and routines at a whole-school level; at a classroom level the student teacher will need to ascertain very quickly – from observation and discussion with relevant parties (e.g. the teachers with whom he or she will be working) – the rules and routines that individual teachers adopt with different classes. Knowledge and practice of these provides security for students and for student teachers alike. Within each class there will be several strategies that teachers routinely use to ensure that learning is productive, efficient and effective and that behaviour is acceptable. These routines and rules operate at every stage of the lesson. Examples of the practical matters that the student teacher will need to find out about are as follows:

Rules and routines at different points during the lesson

At the beginning of the lesson

- how the students enter the classroom and where they sit;
- how the teacher gains and maintains the students' attention;
- what the teacher does when students arrive without appropriate materials (e.g. books, pens, paper, sports equipment).

During the transition from the introduction to the lesson

- how the teacher manages the transition from the introduction to the subsequent activities of the students;
- what the teacher does, says, where he or she stands, where he or she goes, how he or she uses his or her voice and non-verbal behaviour immediately prior to the transition, during the transition, immediately after the transition.

During the lesson

- whether, how and in what numbers the students are able to move around the classroom;
- how the students access, use and replace resources;
- how students may ask for the teacher's attention;
- in what kinds of activity collaborative work is acceptable;
- when, where and how much talk is acceptable to the teacher;
- how the teacher gains and maintains silence and 'on-task' behaviour;
- what verbal and non-verbal means the teacher uses to gain and maintain the smooth running of the lesson;
- how the teacher handles difficult situations and students;
- how the teacher gives praise/rewards/sanctions/punishments – and for what;
- how the teacher handles difficult questions;
- how the teacher deals with unacceptable behaviour (to him or her and to other students);
- how the teacher copes with students who work more slowly/more quickly than others (i.e. what the teacher does with students who do not complete work in the lesson and with students who complete work before the lesson time has elapsed);
- how the teacher balances his or her *instructional, procedural* and *managerial* talk;
- how the teacher circulates round the class and monitors everything that is happening;
- how the teacher keeps up with marking during the lesson;

- how the teacher responds to different requests and to different students (verbally and non-verbally).

Towards the end of the lesson

- how the teacher draws the lesson to a conclusion in practical management terms – what he or she does and says;
- how students clear away and return apparatus and materials;
- how the work is gathered together for the teacher – who does it, where it is put;
- how students are to be seated at the end of the lesson;
- how the teacher draws together – summarises – the cognitive aspects of the lesson;
- how the teacher dismisses the class.

More specifically, the student teacher may find it useful to focus on a specific feature of a lesson. In this case he or she will need to plan in advance what he or she will be looking for – perhaps by posing a series of questions. For example, let us imagine that he or she wishes to see what strategies the class teacher uses to motivate students during a lesson. The questions that the student teacher might wish to ask are contained in Box 11.

Student teachers are not normally in the school or with a group of students long enough to enable them to introduce their own way of working. They inherit a set of rules and routines, and would be ill advised to try to overturn an established way of working with a class for the comparatively short duration of a teaching practice. This is not to deny the need for student teachers to try new ways of teaching and to experiment to some extent; it is to suggest that if the student teacher wishes to try something different he or she discusses it first with the class teacher.

Observe what sanctions the teacher employs with her class in order to enforce the rules. Are individuals kept in after school, for instance, or are they asked to stay behind at the end of a lesson, or reprimanded in front of the other children? Does isolation of deviant students figure in a teacher's tactics? On a more positive note, find out what kinds of rewards the teacher uses. If the class is taught by other teachers, you can subsequently compare the different methods of control used and check how the class responds to them. The advantages of ascertaining prior knowledge on these matters is that you will then be able to relate your own control systems to the existing framework where this proves to be effective.

The reality of classroom life, unfortunately, is often very different from what one would like to see. Control systems may be either ineffective or non-existent. Where this is the case, you will have to decide what you can do to achieve some measure of control over the class when you eventually take over. In this connection, we recommend you read the chapter dealing with

Box 11

Motivation: Questions for use in an observation lesson

1   What techniques and approaches, if any, did the teacher use at the outset of the lesson to engage the class's interest?
2   How did he or she sustain the interest, once aroused?
3   How did he or she deal with the problem of flagging motivation?
4   In what ways did the teacher capitalise on the children's own interests?
5   Could any parts of the lesson be explained in terms of the concepts of intrinsic and extrinsic motivation? Did the teacher, for example, arouse the students' curiosity, challenge them or offer them some form of reward?
6   What part did *feedback* play in the lesson? How was it conveyed? And what was its effect on the class?
7   Could you establish any relationship between motivation and (a) social class; (b) ability; (c) age; (d) sex; or (e) aspects of the subject being taught or investigated?
8   What effect did the *personality* of the teacher appear to have on the overall success (or failure) of the lesson?
9   Were threats used as a means of motivating the students?
10   Examine the relationship between motivation and the instructional approach or approaches used by the teacher, e.g. formal class teaching; discussion; group work; guided instruction; etc.
11   How would you describe (a) the teacher's attitudes towards his or her class, and (b) his or her expectations of their performance? Could either of these be seen to affect his or her class's motivation?
12   Which forms of motivation did the class appear to respond to best?

---

management and control in the classroom (p. 281).

Successful class teachers' methods of organisation will have evolved in the light of their experience and knowledge of the particular students they teach. The student teacher does not have this experience or knowledge nor, obviously, the time to acquire them, so it is advisable to perpetuate effective routines established by the class teacher throughout the period of teaching practice (e.g. What is the established procedure for tidying up at the end of an art lesson? Or what is a child expected to do if he or she finishes an allotted task five minutes before the rest of the class?). Studying the classroom routines of an experienced and successful teacher requires close observation because the most effective methods are often the least obvious.

What should student teachers do, however, when they find themselves working with a disorganised teacher who has no routines? Having made a quick assessment of the position, they must then decide what they can do to improve the situation, even though the extent of their influence is limited (they are, after all, in a position of dependence in a host school, and perhaps only teaching two or three lessons each day). Between the preliminary visit and the block practice, they should decide on a few basic classroom rules and routines to discuss with the class. They can thus improve the original situation at worst marginally and at best significantly.

PARTICULAR INFORMATION TO RECORD

You will need to bring back a certain amount of information from your preliminary visit, chiefly for your own use. It is important to find out details of the *resources and equipment* available in the school – the size and range of the library, the audio-visual equipment you may use, apparatus you may require, facilities for typing and duplicating, resources for individual and group work (topics and projects, for example). Teachers of practical subjects like PE or specialist subjects like art or music need to be particularly alert in this respect. A games teacher, for instance, may want to know how many badminton rackets are available; an art specialist, whether there is a sink in the room he or she will be using; and a music teacher, the extent of facilities for creative music-making. Teachers of science subjects, too, will need to anticipate equipment they will need for practical work, particularly whether there is sufficient equipment for class practicals. Find out about health and safety matters, too.

You will need to gather details of the *schemes of work* you will be required to teach, together with any explanatory or ancillary information your class teacher may provide. These aspects are examined in more detail later in this section.

Coupled with details of schemes of work is the need for *information on the students you will be working with*, together with some indication of their previous experience and learning in the subject areas you will be teaching. This kind of information is crucial, as you need to know where to begin your work. Unwittingly going over ground already covered or beginning at a point or level beyond the class's understanding can be a disastrous start. The obvious source of information of this nature is the class teacher. If he or she keeps records on each student, ask if you may have a look at them.

Difficulties sometimes arise when a class teacher does not remember what his or her class has done previously, or is not clear, or is even reluctant to disclose such information. Where this occurs, you must consult either the teacher in charge of students in the school, or the head of department, or your supervising tutor. One or other of these will advise you.

You may find that you are involved in teaching courses leading to state or external examinations such as GCSE, GCE Advanced Level, the Scottish Certificate of Education, or additional arrangements. If you are, and are unfamiliar with the nature of these systems, get hold of an introductory guidebook relevant to your needs. One important innovation in the GCSE is the inclusion of compulsory coursework for examination, something you may very well be involved with if you are a secondary specialist.

The preliminary visit also gives you the opportunity to ascertain details of text books, workcards/worksheets and other material used by the class. Where you feel it necessary, borrow copies or examples of the ones you will be using as they will help you when planning your lessons.

Details of *topic work* and related approaches, where relevant, should also be noted. These could include organisational procedures: individual or group work, for example; topics recently covered; the stage of development of the class or individuals in this kind of learning; and ways in which topics have been presented and evaluated in the past.

Specific information on the class(es) you will be teaching should include:

- The name of the class and, if relevant, the significance of the name.
- The size of the class (the number of students makes a difference to the organisation and presentation of the various subject areas and curricular activities).
- The average age of the class, or its range if it is inter-age.
- The band/stream of the class, or range of ability.
- The names of the students and a seating plan (the latter can be particularly useful in the early stages of the practice as an aid to getting to know a class).
- Details of groups (if appropriate) – their organisational basis.
- Details of students with special needs (again where relevant) – ones with emotional problems, communication difficulties, physical disabilities or home-background problems, for instance.
- Details of problematic students, in terms of control and discipline, together with suggestions from the class teacher as to possible ways of handling them.

In addition to points already discussed, the student teacher may find it useful to record information about:

- timetabling of fixed times (e.g. use of the hall);
- handling dinner money;
- use of support assistants;
- when parent helpers come in and what they do;
- which teachers have responsibilities and what they are responsible for;
- arrangements for planning times with other teachers (i.e. team meetings);
- whether students can take school property home (e.g. reading books);
- whether the students go to another teacher, and if so, when, where, what for;
- whether students join other classes, if so, when, where, what for;
- which work is done in books, jotters, loose-leaf sheets;
- permission for going to the toilet;

- how the day starts;
- how the children change their reading books (for primary schools);
- the school handwriting style(s);
- which children print and which children do 'joined-up' writing (largely for primary schools);
- which students it is advisable to keep apart;
- seating arrangements and layout of the classroom.

The *nature of organisation of the timetable operating in the school* should be noted – whether it is fully structured, partially structured or completely unstructured, for example; or whether it is organised over a five- or six-day week.

Finally, details of *your own timetable* should be recorded. These will include:

- lesson details – their times and duration;
- class(es) and subjects or activities to be taught or organised;
- indications of rooms and locations to be used (Room 3, Main Building; Room 23, Lower School: Room 7, Annexe, for instance);
- details of other teachers' lessons you will be observing (where appropriate);
- non-contact periods;
- extra-curricular activities (if relevant: science society after school on Mondays, choir practice Thursday lunchtimes, for example);
- indications of when the school will be closed in the course of the practice period (local elections, half-term, special holidays);
- indications of when you will be prevented from teaching your normal timetable (because of school examinations, for example, or rehearsals for a school play);
- the name of the school, its address and its telephone number; the names of the headteacher, the teacher in charge of student teachers (if appropriate) and of the class teacher(s).

The range of suggestions given above on what information to collect includes little reference to the kinds of problems and pitfalls you may encounter in seeking this information. We conclude this section, therefore, by highlighting some of them and indicating possible ways of dealing with them.

First, there is the problem of time. Some students spend as much as a whole week on their preliminary visit, but others are not so fortunate. If you are only in for one day and time does therefore present a problem, decide on an order of priorities and begin by noting the most immediately important information that you need. The remainder can then be collected visit by visit, or during the first week of the practice itself. Even in the most favourable circumstances, it is going to take time to build up a total picture of the school, so do not expect to do it in half a day.

A second kind of problem may arise when you are confined to one or two rooms during your initial visit (if this only lasts one day) and cannot therefore move about the building. It has been known for a student on returning to college to say, 'But I hardly moved out of the head's room all day.' What you must do if you are in this position is to ask politely and tactfully if you may see other features of the school as you will be required to make fruitful contributions to discussions with your college tutor and perhaps other students on returning to college.

A third point concerns the more intangible and elusive aspects of school life. We mentioned above, for instance, the value of finding out something of the school's philosophy of education so that one can relate to it more effectively. This, however, can sometimes be a frustrating quest, as rarely is it voiced; nor is it likely to be the subject of staffroom conversation. We suggest you study Box 8 and use the checklists provided as a starting point. What is not immediately apparent can be discovered by asking questions.

One final point: what do you do when essential information is just not forthcoming? Or when the source of it is unreliable? Or when it is misleading? You cannot complain to the head, or ask the students! The best course is to ask the teacher in charge of students to help you, or possibly the tutor from the HE institution who will be supervising you during the practice.

Chapter 7

Aims and objectives

TERMINOLOGY

A student teacher hopefully seeking guidance from the literature on *education intention* must feel like turning away in dismay. The whole area abounds in terminological confusion, being replete with words like aims, goals, tasks, objectives, learning outcomes, used freely and apparently indiscriminately. The word *aim*, for instance, formerly possessed a degree of specificity in the context of teacher education which it now appears to have lost; the words *aim* and *objective* are often used with an implied synonymity; and even the word *objective* connotes different things to different people. This confusion may result in part from national differences for, as Davis[1] has pointed out, British educators have been more interested in defining aims than in stating objectives, while American teachers have tended to think in terms of more concrete objectives.

Our purpose at this point, then, is to attempt to remove some of the confusion befogging these matters by defining terms as we shall use them in this book so that readers will at least have a reasonably systematic and consistent interpretation in the pages that follow.

Two key words will be used – *aim* and *objective*. Both refer to expressions of educational intention and purpose, but each will express varying degrees of generality and specificity respectively. In this latter respect, both meet the need to discuss educational ends at different levels depending on the issues at stake. An *aim* we will define as a general expression of intent, and the degree of generality contained in the statement may vary from the very general in the case of long-term aims to the much less general in the case of short-term aims. An *objective*, by contrast, is characterised by greater *precision* and *specificity*. Again, at one extreme will be objectives that are fairly specific, and at the other, objectives that are extremely so.

Long-term aims form the basis of a school's *raison d'être*, thus defining the nature and character of its overall educational programme in relation to societal and individual needs. Short-term aims will constitute the logical starting point for curricula construction and devising schemes of work.

Objectives expressing varying degrees of specificity will be derived from such aims, especially the short-term ones, and will represent their translation into specific and tangible terms necessary for planning a course of lessons, individual lessons or units of learning on which the ultimate realisation of the aims depends.

The following examples of aims and objectives will help the reader to see the distinction between them more clearly. Try to locate the particular examples in each category along hypothetical continua of generality and specificity respectively.

Aims

1   To provide children with the opportunity to acquire a knowledge and understanding of the society in which they live.
2   To develop an understanding and tolerance of the world's major religions.
3   To enable pupils to develop an appreciation of art in the twentieth century.
4   To introduce the class to the concept of heat.
5   To educate the whole child.

Objectives

1   To introduce the class to the principal characteristics of the violin.
2   A review of the events leading up to the First World War.
3   To further the students' appreciation of Hardy's 'The Darkling Thrush'.
4   The children will circle ten sentences in a given passage of propaganda which are indicative of the author's bias.
5   The pupils will list and identify six different figures of speech in a set prose passage.

One final point: designers of educational programmes cannot always be too legislative on the question of what constitutes an aim and what constitutes an objective. What a teacher plans to do with a given statement of intent is the ultimate determinant of its nature. Aim (4) above, for instance, *to introduce the class to the concept of heat*, could conceivably form the basis of a lesson of one hour, in which case it would be seen as an objective. Alternatively, objective (1) listed above, *to introduce the class to the principal characteristics of the violin*, could equally form the basis of four weekly lessons, in which case it would be more appropriately labelled an aim.

SOME CHARACTERISTICS OF AIMS

Aims constitute the basic elements in educational planning. Although existing at different levels of generality, collectively they make up the building blocks of the total programme. The most general aims (referred to as 'ultimate goals' by Wheeler[2]), being broad and often abstract in their expression, will simply offer guidance as to the general direction of educational intention and will in no way indicate particular achievements within specified time-limits (e.g. *to prepare children to meet the challenges of a technological age*). Aims of this nature, frequently social in character, express basic concepts of the purpose of the school and 'the expected end-products of an education carried out over time' (Wheeler). In this sense aims are perhaps synonymous with values.

At other levels, aims will express less generality (referred to as 'mediate goals' by Wheeler). Such will form the basis of curricula (e.g. *to achieve certain specified standards in the skills of reading and writing*). Unlike the more general aims noted above, they will suggest tangible achievements and imply rather more specified time-limits. They are often statements of what can be expected to have been achieved at given stages over the formal educational period. Box 12 gives further examples of such aims from the primary sector.

Box 12

General aims in primary education

1   The child should know how to convey his meaning clearly and accurately through speech for a variety of purposes.
2   The child should be able to listen with concentration and understanding.
3   The child should be able to read fluently and accurately at a minimum reading age of 11.
4   The child should be able to read with understanding material appropriate to his or her age-group and interests.
5   The child should know how to write English appropriate to different formal purposes.
6   The child should know how to observe carefully, accurately and with sensitivity.

Source Ashton, Kneen and Davies[3]

By now you will have realised that there is a relationship between the degree of generality expressed in an aim and the time-limit within which it can be expected to have been achieved. It may be expressed thus: the more general the aim, the more difficult to specify when it will be achieved, or, conversely, the less general the aim, the greater the likelihood of its being achieved within definable and predictable time-limits. Thus, *to prepare children to meet the challenges of a technological age* could only be achieved at some time in the relatively distant future; one could not be any more specific than that. The aim *to achieve certain specified standards in the skills of reading and writing*, however, could conceivably be achieved by, at the latest, the age of 16.

This relationship has very real and practical implications for the student teacher on teaching practice. Since he or she is only in school for a comparatively short time (four, six, eight or ten weeks, depending on the college or university and the particular block practice), the aims that will form the basis of his or her schemes of work may be even *less* general than the 'mediate' ones referred to above.

Now the relevance of aims for the student teacher is that they make up one of the major sources from which lesson objectives are derived; and it is essential to understand the relationship between aims and objectives, and between schemes of work and the individual lessons to be taught. This set of interrelationships can be expressed in a simple diagram:

In conclusion, you may find the following checklist useful when formulating aims for schemes of work:

1   Does the aim express the appropriate level of generality?
2   Is it expressed simply, clearly and economically?
3   Does its content relate to the ability and previous experience of the class?
4   Can an appropriate number of lesson objectives be derived naturally from it?
5   Is it attainable in relation to the facilities and time available?

TWO KINDS OF OBJECTIVES: (1) BEHAVIOURAL AND (2) NON-BEHAVIOURAL

It has been established that *objectives* are formulations of educational intent much more specific and precise than aims. While the latter serve to indicate the overall direction and purpose of educational activities they are, by comparison with objectives, lacking in specificity. They are thus of little immediate value to the teacher in planning a particular lesson or unit of learning in that they cannot inform his or her decisions on precise content, teaching strategy and evaluation. To meet these needs, the teacher must utilise *objectives* for individual lessons (Wheeler[4] refers to them as 'proximate goals'). An example of objectives is given in Box 13, together with their referent – Hardy's poem (Box 14).

Box 13

An example of a non-behavioural and a behavioural lesson objective in poetry

Non-behavioural
To further the class's understanding of Hardy's 'The Darkling Thrush'.

Behavioural
At the end of a forty-five-minute lesson on Hardy's 'The Darkling Thrush' the class will be able:

1   To detail the images which conjure up a landscape of winter and death.
2   To compare the rhythms of the winter mood with those associated with the thrush.
3   To explain the meanings in context of, or give synonyms for: coppice, spectre, bine-stems, crypt, canopy, germ, fervourless, illimited, gaunt, carollings, terrestrial, air.
4   To account briefly for the poem's date (31 December 1900).
5   To assess whether the poem is mainly pessimistic or optimistic in meaning.
6   To describe their own emotional responses to the poem.

If you scrutinise the five examples of objectives given in our discussion on the terminology of aims and objectives, you will notice that numbers (4) and (5) differ from numbers (1), (2) and (3) in that they refer to overt, visible and therefore potentially quantifiable student behaviours which the teacher hopes to bring about (the students *will circle* ten sentences ..., the students *will list and identify* six figures of speech ...). These are examples of *behavioural objectives* and as such identify the learner's overt achievements. Examples (1), (2) and (3), however, refer to more intangible qualities and being open-ended do not explicitly state the behavioural outcomes (*To introduce the class to ..., A review of ..., To further the students' appreciation of...*). These may be referred to as *non-behavioural objectives* since they do not specify the precise terminal behaviour by means of which a teacher can assess whether his objectives have been achieved. They may indicate what the teacher plans to do (To introduce the class to ...), or list the elements of content in some way or other (A review of ...), or invoke patterns of behaviour in abstract terms (appreciation of ...). None of these manifestations can be perceived directly or measured, however.

Box 14

The Darkling Thrush
by
Thomas Hardy

I leant upon a coppice gate
    When frost was spectre-gray,
And Winter's dregs made desolate
    The weakening eye of day.
The tangled bine-stems scored the sky
    Like strings of broken lyres,
And all mankind that haunted nigh
    Has sought their household fires.

The land's sharp features seemed to be
    The Century's corpse outleant,
His crypt the cloudy canopy,
    The wind his death-lament.
The ancient pulse of germ and birth
    Was shrunken hard and dry,
And every spirit upon earth
    Seemed fervourless as I.

At once a voice arose among
    The bleak twigs overhead
In a full-hearted evensong
    Of joy illimited;
An aged thrush, frail, gaunt, and small,
    In blast-beruffled plume,
Had chosen thus to fling his soul
    Upon the growing gloom.

So little cause for carollings
    Of such ecstatic sound
Was written on terrestrial things
    Afar or nigh around,
That I could think there trembled through
    His happy good-night air
Some blessed Hope, whereof he knew
    And I was unaware.
                                    December 1900

Behavioural objectives, if used competently, are tools which can do much to improve teaching and learning. It is important to remember, however, that they are not in and of themselves better than non-behavioural ones. Each type has its place and contributes in its own way to the enhancement of learning. It would therefore be naive and doctrinaire to claim that all objectives could be specified in precise behavioural terms. Some subject areas and certain kinds of learning – especially in the realms of attitudes, feelings and values – are not amenable to such specification and quantification; and 'open-endedness' is the *sine qua non* of teaching methods emphasising creativity and discovery. We recommend therefore that you give careful thought to which of your lessons should lead towards behavioural objectives and which to non-behavioural ones. In order to help you with such decisions, a little more will now be said about behavioural and then non-behavioural objectives.

SOME CHARACTERISTICS OF BEHAVIOURAL OBJECTIVES

A behavioural objective indicates a desired state in the learner, what a student will be able to do after a prescribed lesson, a behaviour that can be perceived by the teacher's unaided senses. When the learner can *demonstrate* that he has arrived at this state, he will then be deemed to have achieved the objective (e.g. the student teacher *will select* five behavioural objectives from a list of fifteen miscellaneous aims and objectives). Thus the behavioural objective describes the desired outcome of a lesson in such a way that most people can agree that the lesson has been a success or a failure.

Other terms used to describe behavioural objectives include *measurable objectives, learner objectives, instructional objectives, performance goals* and *terminal objectives.* All these terms emphasise the importance of (1) writing objectives that describe what a student should be able to do after he completes a learning experience; and (2) describing the behaviour in such a way that it can be observed and measured.

So far, so good. But what are the characteristics of meaningful behavioural objectives? And how does one write them so as to maximise the probability of achieving them?

The most important characteristic concerns the need to identify the terminal behaviour of the learner that the teacher desires. Thus a behavioural objective is useful to the extent that it indicates what the learner must be able to *do*, or *say*, or *perform* when he is demonstrating his mastery of the objective. It must describe *observable* behaviour from which the teacher can infer particular mental skills. This observable behaviour or performance may be *verbal* or *non-verbal.* Thus the learner may be asked to respond to questions orally or in writing, to demonstrate his ability to perform a certain skill or to solve a practical problem.

A second characteristic follows from the first and arises from the need for specificity and precision in phrasing the behavioural objective. There are many words which we use in everyday life that meet our need to communicate with others well enough. But for behavioural objectives they are often too general and vague. Consider the following two columns of words:

to know	to write
to understand	to explain
to be aware of	to demonstrate
to appreciate	to evaluate
to be familiar with	to list
to grasp	to construct

The words and phrases in the left-hand column are too vague and imprecise to be of use in the formulation of behavioural objectives. They are ambiguous and open to various interpretations (they are, of course, perfectly legitimate as aims and non-behavioural objectives, where their very ambiguity can be an advantage). The terms in the right-hand column, however, are more precise, open to fewer interpretations *and indicate what the learner will be doing when demonstrating that he has acquired information or skills that will contribute to, or lead to, knowing, understanding, appreciating or grasping.* Objectives using such words, then, will have been given behavioural specification. Thus if a student can *list* events in Europe leading up to the First World War and can *evaluate* their significance, his teacher can *infer* that he has some *understanding* of the subject.

A note of caution needs to be sounded here. It must not be assumed that *understand* and *list* are one and the same simply because one substitutes for the other. As Hirst[5] has pointed out, states of mind should never be confused with the evidence for them. That a child can list events in Europe leading up to the First World War merely indicates minimal student mastery of the facts which, together with the achievement of related objectives on other occasions, may lead to fuller understanding subsequently. The same caution applies to similar pairings.

As suggested in parentheses above, the kinds of words listed in the left-hand column are perfectly acceptable in the wording of aims and *non-behavioural objectives*. The problem for the student teacher is knowing how to translate words and phrases of this kind into observable behaviours. Perhaps the best way is to take a simple example. It begins by stating an aim of moderate generality. From this is derived a *non-behavioural* objective in which the crucial phrase is *to develop ... awareness of.* This is then translated into a *behavioural* objective, the phrase now being replaced by the word *list*.

Aim

To further the class's
understanding of the
significance of propaganda
in the twentieth century

↓

↓

Non-behavioural objective		Behavioural objective
To develop the child's awareness of an author's bias in selected extracts	→	The child will *list* six sentences from a passage of propaganda that reveal bias and indicate which viewpoint the author holds

The problem is thus one of replacing open-ended infinitives such as *to appreciate, to understand, to develop an awareness of* and so on, with appropriate 'hard and clear' action verbs such as *to state, to write, to demonstrate, to identify, to distinguish, to construct, to select, to order, to make* and *to describe*. Rowntree's[6] example illustrates the point: a student would be able *to design* an experiment, *list* the precautions to be taken, *describe* his results, *evaluate* conflicting interpretations, *participate* in out-of-class discussions, etc. Gerlach and Ely[7] consider that all 'action' infinitives of this kind have their roots in five basic types of behaviour, namely, *identifying, naming, describing, ordering* and *constructing*.

Two further characteristics of behavioural objectives may be mentioned in order to sharpen the focus even further. The first concerns the conditions under which mastery of behavioural objectives will be tested. These could include such factors as time limitations, evaluative procedures or situational factors (see below for examples). The second characteristic relates to the standards by which the objective is to be judged. These may include such conditions as the percentage of problems a child must answer correctly; the number of correct answers he or she must obtain; or the tolerance within which he or she must learn.

In summary, behavioural objectives should ideally contain the following four elements:

1 An indication of *who* is to perform the desired behaviour (the student, the learner, the class).
2 A precise and succinct statement of the *specific terminal behaviour* that the learner is to perform. This will indicate what he will actually *do* and will comprise an 'action' verb and its object (list the events, identify the causes, write an essay).
3 Specifications of the *relevant conditions* under which the behaviour is to be performed. These will indicate the givens, the limitations, the restrictions imposed on the student when demonstrating the terminal behaviour (time factors, details of materials, equipment, information, sources to be used or not used).
4 Reference to the *standard* that will be used to evaluate the success of the product or performance (80 per cent correct; 7 out of 10 correct; will give 6 reasons for).

Wiles and Bondi[8] indicate that behavioural objectives are helpful because they address the ABCD rule, specifying the *Audience* of the objective (who will be displaying the behaviour), the intended *Behaviour* to be demonstrated, the *Context* of the behaviour – the tasks, activities and resources, and the *Degree* of completion – the criteria for assessing successful demonstration of the behaviour.

Example: given one hour and no reference materials, the pupil will write an essay synthesising the causes and consequences of the Second World War. The essay must contain at least three of the causes and three of the consequences that were discussed in the lesson.

For further information on behavioural objectives, see the references at the end of the book.

THE STUDENT TEACHER AND BEHAVIOURAL OBJECTIVES

The example of a behavioural objective given in the preceding section, *the child will list six sentences from a passage of propaganda that reveal bias and indicate which viewpoint the author holds*, is a relatively simple one and merely illustrates the principle. It is capable of extension and may even take the form of a number of itemised sub-objectives (see Boxes 13, 15, 16 and 17 for examples). The extent of its further elaboration in this way would depend on a number of situational factors – the ability of the class or group, its previous experience in the subject area, the direction of the lesson, the teacher's knowledge of the class, his or her skill as a teacher, the methods he or she uses, and so on. Simply to frame a behavioural objective *in vacuo* without reference to the kinds of factors just noted and expect it to result in favourable outcomes is seriously to violate the principle of behavioural objectives.

The practical implications of this point for the student teacher are considerable. The use of behavioural objectives in contrast to non-behavioural ones places a much greater responsibility on the user. A behavioural objective has to be tailor-made to be effective; it will therefore require more thought and preparation in relation to the situational factors than would be the case with a non-behavioural objective. The latter, being open-ended, covert and less specific, places the onus on the learner to make of it what he will, to match it up in so far as he is able with his own cognitive structures.

It follows from this that the student teacher who is only prepared to pay lip-service to behavioural objectives and go through the motions by using superficially conceived, off-the-peg ones would be better advised to eschew them altogether. For those prepared to take them seriously, the following checklist will serve as a framework, at least initially, for setting them up:

1   Decide whether a behavioural objective is appropriate to the particular learning situation you are preparing. If it is, then proceed as follows:

Box 15

An example of a non-behavioural and a behavioural lesson objective in the visual arts

Non-behavioural
To increase the class's appreciation of Roy Lichtenstein's painting 'WHAAM!'[9]

Behavioural
At the end of a forty-five-minute lesson on Roy Lichtenstein's painting 'WHAAM!' the class will be able:

1   To identify the essential visual qualities of the composition.
2   To compare the imagery with the comic strip sources and recognise the changes it has undergone.
3   To analyse the unity of the structure within the composition.
4   To explain the significance of the composition as part of the imagery of the 1960s.
5   To separate the idea of 'depiction' in the comic strip from the idea of 'unification' in the painting.
6   To describe their personal responses to the painting.

Box 16

An example of a non-behavioural and a behavioural lesson objective in music

Non-behavioural
To develop the class's appreciation of Mendelssohn's 'Hebrides' overture.

Behavioural
At the end of a forty-five-minute appreciation lesson on Mendelssohn's 'Hebrides' overture, the class will be able:

1   To summarise in one paragraph the circumstances surrounding its composition.
2   To compare the two main themes with respect to mood, shape and instruments used.
3   To describe how Mendelssohn deals with the middle section.
4   To account for the overture's description as programme music.
5   To say whether the work is 'realistic' or 'impressionistic'.
6   To comment briefly on the performance.

Box 17

An example of a non-behavioural and a behavioural lesson objective in the visual appreciation of architecture

Non-behavioural
To increase the class's appreciation of F. L. Wright's building, Kaufmann House, 'Falling Water', Connellsville, Pennsylvania, USA.[10]

Behavioural
At the end of a forty-five-minute lesson on F. L. Wright's building, Kaufmann House, 'Falling Water', Connellsville, Pennsylvania, USA, the class will be able:

1   To recognise the essential visual and spatial qualities of the building.
2   To recognise Wright's belief in architecture's relationship to landscape and the unique suitability of a building to a site.
3   To explain what Wright meant by 'organic' architecture and 'spatial continuity' and how these relate to Kaufmann House.
4   To analyse the spatial structure of the house and recognise the unity between its parts.
5   To list the materials Wright uses and explain their integral relationship with structure, void and solid.
6   To give a brief account of their own responses to the building.

---

2   Consider the relevant situational factors the objective must relate to. These may include: the ability of the class, group or individual; the duration of the lesson; the class's previous experience of the subject; your knowledge of the class; your skill as a teacher; and the teaching methods you intend to employ.

3   Specify who is to perform the behaviour (e.g. the student, the individual, the learner, the class, the group).

4   Specify the actual behaviour in terms of 'action' infinitives (e.g. to write, to list, to enumerate, to name, to specify, to demonstrate, to distinguish, to order, to identify, to construct, to describe, to state, to mark, to compute, to supply).

5   State the result or outcomes (the product or performance) of the behaviour which will be evaluated to determine whether the objective has been achieved (an essay, six sentences..., the first four problems on page 5 ..., or whatever). This is invariably the object or object-clause of the infinitive stated in (4).

6   Specify the relevant conditions under which the behaviour is to be performed (the information, equipment, source material, etc. that the student or class can or cannot use; time limitations).

7   Indicate the standard that will be used to assess the success of the product

or performance. This will often take the form of an expression of the minimal level of performance (the percentage to be correct; so many out of ten correct; ... must list all the reasons; ... must distinguish at least *four* characteristics, etc.)

NON-BEHAVIOURAL OBJECTIVES

Tyler[11] has noted that since non-behavioural objectives are obtained from a variety of sources, they are likely to be stated in a variety of ways. A desirable common characteristic, whatever their source and whatever form they take, is that they should be expressed simply and clearly so that appropriate learning experiences may follow naturally. Tyler considers that such objectives can be conveniently placed in one or other of three groups.

First, they are sometimes expressed in a manner which indicates *what the teacher does*, e.g.

To outline the theory of relativity.
To explain the principles of operant conditions.
To introduce the work of the war poets.
To show some functions of the human ear.
To consolidate earlier work on addition and subtraction.

This is a common way of phrasing non-behavioural objectives though, as Tyler notes, because such statements tend to indicate what the teacher plans to do they are not, strictly speaking, statements of educational ends. The particular weakness of this kind of objective from the teacher's point of view is that they do not provide a satisfactory guide 'to the further steps of selecting materials and devising teaching procedures for the curriculum'.[12]

The second form often taken by non-behavioural objectives is in *stating topics, concepts, generalisations or other elements of content* to be covered in a lesson or course, e.g.

Transport problems in urban areas.
The concept of space.
The air we breathe.
Trees of the neighbourhood.
Castlereagh's foreign policy.

Here, the emphasis is on the content to be dealt with by the teacher and, like the preceding form, they are unsatisfactory in that they do not specify what the students are expected to do with the elements of content.

The third form of non-behavioural objectives identified by Tyler are those expressed in the form of *generalised patterns of behaviour* which usually relate to particular content areas, e.g.

To *develop a fuller understanding* of Picasso's paintings.

To *develop an appreciation of* the variety of architectural styles within a five-mile radius of the school.

To *increase the students' sensitivity* to manifestations of beauty in art and nature.

Behaviour patterns in this context are often expressed through infinitives like *to know, to appreciate, to be aware of, to understand,* etc. Objectives of this kind can sometimes be so generalised as to be of questionable educational value. Providing, however, they possess a *behavioural aspect* and a *content aspect,* then they are the most useful of the three forms from the student teacher's point of view. As they achieve a suitable balance between the two they will find that this will assist the structuring of their lessons and aid their decisions about teaching method, e.g. 'To further the student's knowledge of the local social services.'

Curriculum planners opposed to the use of behavioural objectives advocate the more general, flexible and open-ended approach of non-behavioural objectives. Class teachers, too, tend to prefer this broader interpretation and no doubt it is the one that student teachers are most familiar with. Arguments which have been advanced in favour of non-behavioural objectives include the following:

1   They permit the 'opening-up' process by means of which a student is able to match his own cognitive structures with the perceived content of the objectives. He must negotiate this match-making between his internal structures and the external world for himself.[13]
2   Human behaviour is broader in scope and purpose than the sum of specific bits of behaviour learned in isolation. Behavioural objectives fail to take account of the higher or more complex levels of functioning whereas non-behavioural objectives do not.[14]
3   Non-behavioural objectives also take account of the broad, interrelated categories of human activity and are often more in line with the long-term aims of the school.
4   They give both teacher and class greater room to manoeuvre, having an added flexibility and freedom.
5   Both teacher and class may engage in choice and decision-making and may try out alternative courses of action.
6   Non-behavioural objectives allow for the possibility of concomitant learning.

THE DEBATE SURROUNDING THE USE OF BEHAVIOURAL OBJECTIVES

You will have deduced from what you have just read that the issue of behavioural objectives has incurred a degree of *odium scholasticum* in some quarters. The reasons for opposition to their use are numerous. Principally, they arise from a rooted hostility to *behaviourism*, a view of psychology which in its radical form rejects concepts like 'mind' and 'consciousness' and emphasises the importance of the environment in influencing behaviour at the expense of hereditary potential. Accordingly, learning theorists adopting this extreme position, and who perceive education with similar orientations, see behavioural objectives as tools for achieving their ends. It is thus the fear that the organism will be subjected to the 'shaping' processes of this particular instructional approach without taking mental experiences into account or acknowledging the complexity of human beings that provokes reaction from its opponents. Peters,[15] for example, writes:

If the inner life of man is banned from investigation, actions which necessarily involve intentions, emotions which necessarily involve appraisals of a situation, together with imagination, memory, perception, dreaming and pain must all be ruled out as scientifically proper objects of investigation; for none of these phenomena can be described or identified without reference to consciousness. There is precious little left of human behaviour to investigate. So the sterility of this approach to human learning is not surprising.

Advocates of behavioural objectives, on the other hand, view them from the context of a systematic approach to education. For them, behavioural objectives have been a central concept in programmed learning and educational technology, their significance having been further enhanced since they were incorporated into the theory of curriculum design. While readily conceding the weaknesses of such objectives, those promoting their cause have cogently argued a case for their limited use in some contexts. MacDonald-Ross,[16] for instance, says:

For the present, behavioural objectives provide a well-worked-out tool for rational planning in education. They have made possible certain improvements in the technique of curriculum design and should not be discarded in disgust just because they fail to meet more exacting standards. But the application of these objectives should be tempered by a deep understanding of their limitations.

Further accounts and summaries of the arguments for and against the use of behavioural objectives can be found in the references.[17] By now, you must be feeling somewhat dizzy, having been confronted with the various characteristics of the two kinds of objectives. You may even feel you have been put into a position where you have to choose between one or the other. In no circumstances must you do this. You must see the relationship between them not as an *either ... or* one, but as complementary.

There will be occasions when behavioural objectives will be useful to you, once you have acquired the skills to formulate them and have had some practice in using them. Equally, there will be frequent opportunities to utilise the more familiar non-behavioural objectives.

IDENTIFYING AND WRITING OBJECTIVES

You may wish at this stage to attempt to consolidate what you have read so far by trying the following examples.

(a) Distinguishing aims and objectives

In the light of what was said earlier, which of these expressions of educational intention are objectives, and which are aims? In what circumstances could some be either?

1   To encourage young people to understand the significance of maintaining good health and physical fitness.
2   To further the children's understanding of the concept of weight by giving them practice in weighing.
3   To provide opportunities to develop an appreciation of beauty in literature, art and music.
4   To introduce the world's major religions to the class.
5   To translate ten infinitives indicating various mental states into appropriate behavioural terms.
6   To demonstrate the differences between behavioural and non-behavioural objectives.
7   To give the group practice in the use of the twenty-four-hour clock.
8   To develop interests and skills so that leisure time may be used purposefully.
9   To analyse the various parts of a popular daily newspaper.
10   To enable the student to distinguish between aims and objectives.

(b) Identifying behavioural objectives

Which of the following objectives are behavioural, and which are non-behavioural?

1   The student teacher will write down four areas within the school curriculum in which there may be difficulties in expressing the outcomes of learning in behavioural terms; and he will list one reason in each case why difficulties may arise.
2   To extend the class's knowledge of the range and variety of seashore life.
3   To identify at random four activities in the school curriculum in which learning outcomes are behavioural.
4   To develop the group's skills in the use of noun clauses.
5   To explain in one paragraph of reasonable length why it would be

inappropriate to express an aesthetic response to a work of art in behavioural terms.

6 To acquire skills in writing lesson notes to meet the needs of different teaching situations.
7 To introduce the class to Elgar's 'Enigma Variations'.
8 To write a paragraph entitled 'Traffic at rush hour' which shows the difference between similes and metaphors.
9 To give the group practice in formulating behavioural objectives.
10 State four reasons for specifying learning unit objectives in behavioural terms.

(c) Using 'action' verbs

With particular reference to the age range you intend to teach (primary, junior, middle school, secondary, etc.), frame ten behavioural objectives using these 'action' verbs:

identify	distinguish
interpret	order
describe	name
evaluate	locate
apply	construct

(d) Translating non-behavioural objectives into behavioural objectives

Translate the following six non-behavioural objectives into behavioural ones. Make sure that the latter point to observable behaviours on the part of the child or student – that is, acts that can be seen or heard.

1 To develop the group's understanding of the concept of weight.
2 To further the class's knowledge of the local environment within a three-mile radius of the school.
3 To understand something of the persuasive techniques used in TV advertising.
4 To further students' appreciation of the efficacy of behavioural objectives.
5 To give practice in creative writing.
6 To stimulate an interest in the technological developments of the past thirty years.

(e) Criteria for the evaluation of behavioural objectives

Read the following behavioural objectives and assess the extent to which they meet the criteria for behavioural objectives stipulated earlier.

1 Given a list of twenty French irregular verbs and one hour, the student will conjugate at least fifteen verbs correctly (i.e. as shown in the textbook) and translate them into their correct English equivalents.

2 Ten short melodies in the major and minor will be played to the class. Each child will identify a melody in the major by holding up a white card immediately after the tune is played, and a melody in the minor by holding up a black card immediately the tune has been played. The melodies will be played again in scrambled order and each student will be expected to respond correctly to at least seven out of the ten.

3 Given a forty-five-minute period and no reference books, the student will solve the first ten problems at the end of the chapter studied for homework. He will be required to get at least seven of these right before moving on to the next chapter next week.

(f) Aims in the primary school

Take the seven broad aims for primary education listed in Box 18 and break each one down into four or five sub-aims, in other words, aims less general than those suggested. For example, for the second aim, *ability to live and work with others*, Dean suggests the following:

(a) Developing social competence.
(b) Working with others to achieve an agreed end.
(c) Sensitivity to others.
(d) Ability to think through moral questions and make decisions about moral choice.
(e) Knowledge of our society and culture.

Box 18

Aims in the primary school

1 Self-knowledge.
2 Ability to live and work with others.
3 Skill in communication.
4 Learning skills, including the ability to reason and analyse, generate ideas and carry them through, solve problems, set goals and work towards them, evaluate, deal with evidence, make and test hypotheses.
5 A framework of understanding in the major areas of human knowledge.
6 Ability to cope with adult life as parents, workers and citizens.
7 A framework of meaning for life and a value-system.

Source Dean[18]

OBJECTIVES IN INDIVIDUALISED LEARNING

So far, we have chiefly considered aims and objectives in relation to communities, groups and classes. But they can also be used to guide and structure the learning intentions of the *individual* student, often in an independent learning situation. In addition to the intellectual, emotional and personal achievements possible with individualised objectives, there are longer-term gains to be had. The student, for example, can take greater responsibility for his or her own learning and his or her ability to learn other things is enhanced. We look briefly at three possible areas where individualised objectives are relevant; the primary school, with particular reference to students with learning difficulties, mixed-ability teaching, and projects and special studies.

In the area of primary education when a teacher is dealing with children with learning difficulties (in particular, reading), short-term individualised objectives can be specified, preferably in behavioural or performance terms, which greatly aid the teacher (and/or the parent, if he or she is involved) to keep a check on systematic and cumulative improvement. For success at this stage, objectives need to be considered in relation to frequency of instruction, the amount of practice and the kinds of rewards used. In addition, there needs to be a carefully thought-out system of recording to keep a check on progress over time. Box 19 lists these and additional features to be borne in mind when individualised objectives are used in this context. Of course, as students become older, they may also be involved in the specifying of objectives.

Box 19

Individualised objectives in programmes for children with learning difficulties

1   Specify objectives for individual child in behavioural terms.
2   Sequence them.
3   Teaching procedures.
4   Frequency of teaching.
5   Amount of practice.
6   Generalisation of learning to other contexts.
7   Rewards to be used.
8   Suitable recording system.

Where individualised objectives are used in mixed-ability teaching, possibly in conjunction with workcards, a thorough understanding of individual differences is required on the part of the teacher. As we say later in the book, it will require not only knowledge of intellectual skills but awareness of those who require more time, who lack self-confidence, or who are impulsive. Student involvement in formulating objectives is a possibility at this stage.

Individual objectives play a central role in projects and special studies. This will be particularly the case where these make up the coursework in the GCSE. We examine projects in a little more detail later in the book but student involvement is critical at the stage of formulating and negotiating aims and objectives.

CONCLUSION – SOME SUGGESTIONS

We have been concerned here with the problems surrounding the expression of educational intention. Aims were seen as general goals formulated in clear and simple language which define the nature and direction of a school's programme or an area of work within that programme. Objectives, by contrast, were seen as more precise expressions of purpose, of particular value in planning lessons and other units of learning. We then attempted to trace a path between the behavioural view, advocates of which recommend the use of behavioural objectives as their principal tool of learning, and the more traditional practices in English education which employ non-behavioural objectives.

We conclude with suggestions that will guide the reader in deciding whether to use behavioural or non-behavioural objectives. A behavioural objective may be used when the desired outcome is a skill that can be performed, or when the results of instruction can be expressed or demonstrated overtly in writing or speech (language learning, native or foreign, would apply here). The acquisition of factual knowledge may likewise be formulated in behavioural terms. Where students are experiencing some difficulty in learning, the particular problem might be broken down into simpler steps or stages, each of which could then be expressed behaviourally. Individualised learning is another area where behavioural objectives would seem appropriate; and if one is producing material for programmed learning, behavioural objectives will be required.

However, when the desired outcomes of learning are more general, developmental or complex in nature and need not, or cannot, be demonstrated by acts of fragmented behaviour, then behavioural objectives are inappropriate. For example, the aesthetic and appreciative aspects of subjects like literature, art and music are better expressed in less prescriptive ways, since they involve the building up of complex, interrelated and subjective responses and the establishing of favourable attitudes. Broad, open-ended statements of intent serve teacher and student alike better in such contexts, though it must be remembered that some of the adjuncts to appreciation (historical, biographical or social, for instance; or technical, linguistic or stylistic) are often capable of being expressed behaviourally (see, for example, Boxes 13, 15, 16 and 17).

Chapter 8

Beginning curriculum planning

The issue of planning the curriculum is central to a student teacher's school practice. It was mentioned in Part I that the days when students could elect what to teach have gone with the passing of the Education Reform Act of 1988. Student teachers can expect to go into school and, with different degrees of specificity, be told what they will be required to teach.

There are three main areas of curriculum planning that we wish to address: (a) the context and levels of planning; (b) elements of planning; (c) focuses of planning.

THE CONTEXT AND LEVELS OF PLANNING

There are several stakeholders with an interest in curriculum planning and implementation, for example those in schools and on governing bodies, the local education authority, representatives of the Office for Standards in Education (OFSTED), researchers and educationists with an interest in school effectiveness and improvement. They each have similar and complementary concerns which feed into effective curriculum planning and delivery. *The Handbook for the Inspection of Schools* sets out some useful points for curriculum planning, as shown in Box 20. These several elements from OFSTED provide student teachers (and teachers) with important criteria for evaluating their planning, implementation and assessment of curricula and students. The OFSTED framework recognises that for curriculum planning to be effective it needs to take account of external and internal factors, in short it rehearses the 'situational analysis' that was a feature of Skilbeck's model of the curriculum in Part I.

Another important context for planning draws on the literature of school effectiveness. This movement gathered impetus through research throughout the 1980s and 1990s and was concerned to identify and document the factors that made for effective schools. Several pieces of research found common factors:[1]

- effective leadership by the headteacher and senior staff, including their

Box 20

OFSTED's aspects of the curriculum

1   *Standards of Achievement* compared to national norms; application to new situations; to be as high as possible.
2   *Quality of Learning* pace; motivation; ability to use skills and understandings; progress; learning skills; attitudes to learning; variety of learning contexts.
3   *Quality of Teaching* rigour; teacher expectation; strategies; development of skills and understandings; clarity of objectives (of which children are fully aware); subject knowledge; suitable content of lessons; activities chosen to promote learning of content; engaging, interesting, motivating and challenging activities; pace; range and fitness for purpose of teaching techniques; positive relationships with children; effectiveness of lesson planning, classroom organisation and use of resources; clarity of explanations; quality of questioning; imaginativeness; links between ATs; progression, continuity, relevance, matching, differentiation, balance, richness of provision; regular and positive feedback to children.
4   *Assessment, Recording and Reporting* accurate and comprehensive records; appropriacy of arrangements for assessment; outcomes of assessment useful to pupils, teachers, parents, employers; formative assessments; frequency and regularity of reports; consistency of reporting practice; frequency of reports to parents and for transfer; regularity of review of assessment procedures; staff discussion of records received.
5   *The Curriculum* quality and range; equality of opportunity to an entitlement curriculum.
6   *Management and Administration* ethos and sense of purpose; effective leadership which is positive, which provides direction, which enables staff to understand their roles in the development of the school and which makes the best of people and resources available and which promotes positive attitudes to teaching and learning; planning (including school development plans and their usefulness as an instrument for improvement); audit of existing work and planning beyond the next school or financial year; implementation and monitoring of plans; working relationships; communication – with and among staff, parents, pupils, community; school self-evaluation and analysis of its own performance.
7   *Resources and their Management* teaching and non-teaching staff – expertise, deployment of specialist and non-specialist teachers, development (INSET and updating which are built into the school development plan), fairness of teaching loads; resources for learning – availability, accessibility and equality of access, quantity and quality, efficiency of use; in-school and out-of-school; relationship of resource provision to school development plan; accommodation – availability, condition, efficiency of use, specialist facilities, accessibility, quantity, quality, conduciveness to learning.
8   *Pupils' Welfare and Guidance* identification and meeting of pupils' academic, personal and career needs.
9   *Links with Parents and Other Institutions* informing parents and using their contributions; links to commerce and industry; quality of liaison; using others to promote learning; use of community resources; transfer documents.

Source adapted from OFSTED[2]

interest and involvement in the quality of the teaching and learning in the school and a sense of 'mission';

- a balance of collegiality and clear decision-making by senior managers;
- the establishment of clear academic goals and a widely understood set of principles for teaching – a clear thrust towards achievement and academic excellence;
- consistency of practices with regard to discipline and instruction, together with increased instructional talk;
- developed relations with parents;
- the involvement of students (in academic planning and extra-curricular activities), the development of the social basis of learning;
- an orderly atmosphere throughout the school where the promotion of positive discipline pervades all aspects of the life of the school;
- the application of careful grouping criteria within classes;
- raised teacher expectations of students, together with intellectually challenging teaching and carefully matched work;
- greater use of whole-class teaching in the primary school;
- flexible use of staff in primary schools;
- having a limited focus within lessons, together with limited organisational complexity.

It can be seen from this that effective learning has to be planned, that curriculum planning for effective learning entails attention to overall (long-term) planning, medium- and short-term planning, and planning very specifically for the contents, organisation, pedagogy and feedback of every aspect of every lesson.[3]

In addition to the *contexts* of planning, the School Curriculum and Assessment Authority[4] identifies three *levels* of planning: *long-term, medium-term* and *short-term*. This ties into the objectives model supported in this book. Long-term planning resonates with the notion of *aims*, discussed in the previous section. Medium-term planning sets *objectives* and *goals*, perhaps of a non-behavioural nature. Short-term planning – focused on *intended learning outcomes* – may be performance-based, possibly including behavioural objectives.

Long-term planning, in which the whole school, departments, subjects and faculties set out the overall curriculum framework that fits with the school's declared aims and policies, the subject orders from the School Curriculum and Assessment Authority, the time available for teaching, resources (both within and outside the schools), reference to individual students' needs, abilities and interests, the balance of subjects on the overall curriculum diet for students, the need to establish continuity and progression within and across units of work. Long-term planning will have taken place before the student teacher enters the school.

Medium-term planning, in which the programmes of work for each group

(however defined, e.g. class, year group) are set out, together with an outline of how the programmes will enable assessment to be undertaken. Medium-term planning is that which identifies units of work over a half-term or full term. The student teacher can reasonably be expected to be part of this planning when involved in a long block practice (e.g. a term or most of a term).

Short-term planning is that in which individual teachers set out what they will be teaching on a day-to-day, lesson-by-lesson basis. Clearly this is the stuff of teaching practice.

The student teacher can expect to have sight of the long-term planning that has preceded his or her teaching practice as he or she will have to fit his or her proposals into that framework. The student teacher will probably be actively concerned only with medium-term and short-term planning. With regard to medium-term planning it could well be the case that he or she becomes part of a team that plans the content and 'delivery' of the curriculum for, say, a half-term or full term. This planning would probably take place during the initial visits to the school, providing the student with sufficient guidelines to go ahead with short-term planning – the specific lessons that he or she will teach for each week and each day.

For the purposes of medium- and short-term planning the School Curriculum and Assessment Authority suggests that each unit of work comprises *continuing* and *blocked* elements. *Continuing work*[5] is that which is 'drawn from a single subject or aspect of the curriculum which:

- requires regular and frequent teaching and assessment to be planned across a year or key stage to ensure progression;
- contains a progressive sequence of learning objectives;
- requires time for the systematic and gradual acquisition, practice and consolidation of skills, knowledge and understanding'.

Hence teachers and student teachers will need to consider which aspects of the curriculum fall into the category of continuing work and how much continuing work in different curriculum areas can be managed.

Blocked work[6] is drawn 'from a single subject or aspect of the curriculum which:

- can be taught within a specific amount of time, not exceeding a term;
- focuses on a distinct and cohesive body of knowledge, understanding and skills;
- can be taught alone or have the potential for linking with units of work in other subjects or aspects of the curriculum.'

To plan for blocked work is to rehearse the discussion of modular curricula in Part I, ensuring that each block is 'distinct and cohesive'.[7]

The School Curriculum and Assessment Authority suggests that *curriculum coherence* 'can be strengthened by linking together, where appropriate, units of work from different subjects or aspects of the curriculum'.[8] This can take place when:

- 'they contain common or complementary knowledge, understanding and skills;
- the skills acquired in one subject or aspect of the curriculum can be consolidated in the context of another (e.g. the notion of generic and "transferable skills");
- the work in one subject or aspect of the curriculum provides a useful stimulus for work in another.'[9]

It is very clear, from the outline of continuing and blocked work and the need for curriculum coherence to be addressed, that a team approach is required. Gone are the days when an individual teacher could plan what she would do with her class(es); teams can be within and across subjects, departments, faculties and age phases. The student teacher will need to find out what the teams are in a school, how they operate together and of which teams he or she is to be a member or which he or she is to consult.

THE ELEMENTS OF PLANNING

Morrison[10] suggests that a full curriculum strategy addresses several features:

- a situational analysis (the contexts of curriculum planning, with reference to the wider society, the local community, and 'within-school' factors – e.g. students, teachers, resources);
- a rationale for the curriculum that is being planned for the teaching practice – its purposes, priorities and principles;
- a statement of curriculum aims and objectives for the teaching practice;
- a statement of how breadth, balance, coherence, continuity, progression, differentiation and relevance are addressed. The former DES[11] stated that all students should have a broad and balanced curriculum that was relevant to their particular needs.
- an indication of how the cross-curricular dimensions, themes and skills will be addressed;
- a plan of how the curriculum content will be addressed – its sequence (logically and chronologically), organisation (e.g. by topics and/or subjects) and resourcing (time, space, materials, staff, administrative support, money);
- an indication of teaching and learning styles to be employed;
- an indication of how assessment, evaluation and record-keeping operate.

CHARACTERISTICS OF THE CURRICULUM

It is necessary to comment upon the 'characteristics of the curriculum'[12] that have been alluded to above: breadth, balance, relevance, coherence, continuity, progression and differentiation. A series of HMI reports which predated the 1988 Education Reform Act made it clear that primary and secondary school children were receiving a partial and often narrow curriculum. In the primary school it tended to be the 'basics' with some occasional leavening from other curriculum areas, often at the whim of teachers' particular interests and abilities; in the secondary school student choice was either exercised too narrowly or insufficient options were available to students to guarantee breadth. Further, secondary education was seen to be out of touch in a changing world and with reference to preparing students for the world of work both in terms of curriculum contents and standards of achievement (a factor signalled in Callaghan's much-cited speech at Ruskin College in 1976). Hence from the late 1970s the term 'entitlement' curriculum, coined by HMI,[13] came into common parlance, arguing that every student had an entitlement to a broad, balanced and relevant curriculum, broad in the sense of addressing a wide range of curriculum areas and a wide range of contents within each curriculum area. These were termed 'areas of experience' by HMI[14] and comprised:

aesthetic and creative
human and social
linguistic and literary
mathematical
moral
physical
scientific
spiritual
technological.

They represent an augmented version of a liberal curriculum. Many found the notion of 'areas of experience' attractive as it emphasised experiential learning and permeable subject boundaries (HMI themselves indicated that children could gain mathematical experiences from art and *vice versa*[15]). However, these were overtaken by the subject-framed version of the national curriculum in 1988. Morrison and Ridley, echoing the Core Curriculum for Australian Schools,[16] argue that breadth should extend beyond curriculum content to include a student's entitlement to breadth of pedagogic styles, learning processes and experience of types of classroom organisation. In the United Kingdom a prescriptive notion of breadth has now prevailed, interpreted as the national curriculum in its several elements.

The same happened to the HMI notion of 'balance'. The open-endedness of the term was reflected in the looseness of the phraseology that HMI[17] used in defining this as 'appropriate attention' being given to the areas of experience and the 'elements of learning' – knowledge, concepts, skills and attitudes. Balance was able to be exerted not simply over the course of a week's work but in a longer time-frame; so, for example, scant attention to science in term one could be rectified by greater attention to science in term two. For secondary schools the notion of balance was accompanied in the HMI report by a castigation of too narrow an emphasis on examination syllabuses in the years immediately preceding public examinations.[18]

However, with the passing of the 1988 Education Reform Act balance was taken to mean offering all students an entitlement to the national curriculum. It is perhaps ironical now to reconsider the notion of balance in the light of the increase in formal assessments in schools and the backwash effect they have on the curriculum, and in the light of a government that was forced to back down on its prescriptions for specific time allocations for different subjects in the curriculum.

To some extent the national curriculum has silenced the debate on exactly what is meant by balance. For example, Morrison and Ridley,[19] using the analogy of a balanced diet, comment that one person's balanced diet is another's unbalanced diet because people have individual dietary needs and preferences. The analogy holds true in relation to the curriculum: to prescribe a common curriculum diet is to misrepresent the individualistic notion of balance. We know from our experience that some students need more social education than others simply to prepare them for adult life; others need more reading practice in order to be able to access the entitlement curriculum; others have a particular enthusiasm for, say, mathematics, such that to deny them an increase in this area is to demotivate them. The implication here is that the simplistic prescriptions of the national curriculum misrepresent the complexity of the issue, though the report by Alexander, Rose and Woodhead[20] argues that curriculum balance is less about time than about quality – every curriculum subject must be taught equally well. One could argue that an attenuation of the simplistic view of balance in the national curriculum can be seen in the notion of 'differentiation', wherein individual needs and differences are intended to be addressed. However, as will be discussed below, this turns out not to be the case.

In addition to curriculum breadth and balance, the notion of 'relevance' implied for HMI[21] students' entitlement to a curriculum that would serve their present and future needs as adults and workers. HMI bracketed together relevance and practicality; for students HMI advocated experiential, practical learning and problem-solving, the need to relate experiences in school to the wider society. As with the notion of breadth, so HMI's suggestion for relevance was pre-empted by the national curriculum programmes of study and cross-curricular issues, salted with reference to periods of work experience in secondary schools. It was the national curriculum that was to be relevant.

Though HMI did not specifically address curriculum 'coherence' in its 1985 report, nevertheless one can detect this as an emerging issue in the documents from the School Curriculum and Assessment Authority,[22] where, for example, planners are exhorted to try to ensure that different subjects in the overall curriculum and different areas within each subject relate to each other. So, for example, a student studying weather and climate in geography might use statistics and data about weather in mathematics, or study some important historical or religious events that turned on the weather, or undertake some poetry writing about the weather, or study (or compose) stormy and calm music. Clearly this is a matter that requires the careful co-ordination of subject teams in secondary schools and phase teams in primary schools so that the programmes of study of the national curriculum are accessed without duplication or repetition.

It is perhaps an irony that the calls for coherence, wherein logical connections are to be made across subjects, are made by the same government that has created difficulties for this very characteristic by framing the national curriculum in subject terms. The notion of coherence argues very powerfully for integrated topic work; this seems to fly in the face of the arguments against topic work that have been voiced by government representatives (discussed later).

However, there is another different but no less compelling view of coherence that interprets it as intelligibility. In this sense we move away from a prescriptive view of coherence, *viz.* the coherence that curriculum planners plan, to a constructivist view. In this latter interpretation it is the student who causes subject matter and knowledge to cohere in the sense of being able to assimilate it and accommodate it to existing conceptual structures in his or her own mind, a view that resonates with Gestalt psychology. Though we can plan for coherence to our heart's content it might not in fact occur if we do not endeavour to communicate and facilitate it in students' conceptual frameworks – their 'zone of proximal development'.[23] This argues for a view of learning through the student's eyes rather than the curriculum developer's, and echoes the salutary definition from the Schools Council[24] that the curriculum is what each child takes away. It is perhaps utopian, then, to think that student teachers can plan for coherence in a teaching practice, for coherence-as-intelligibility requires an intimate knowledge of how each individual student learns. Though the teachers in school may have some of this knowledge it is perhaps unreasonable to expect a student teacher to be able to find out very much about this in the short period of a teaching practice. The safer, if less relevant, way is to plan for curriculum coherence rather than coherence-as-intelligibility!

The notion of 'continuity' is an important educational principle, arguing that the curriculum that is planned for a teaching practice must build on students' prior curricular experiences. As we have seen earlier, the School Curriculum and Assessment Authority[25] identifies 'continuing work' as an important issue. However, Morrison and Ridley[26] argue that the notion of continuity is more extensive than this, applying to continuity of:

experiences
skills
concepts
knowledge
attitudes
in-school and out-of-school experiences
pedagogy
organisation
aims and objectives
management styles
social experiences
record-keeping

They suggest that continuity applies *vertically* as students progress through school, and *laterally* across different teachers and subjects. The latter has increased significance in primary schools with the rise in subject specialist teaching. The student teacher can plan for continuity (a) by discussing with relevant teachers what the students have done before and what they are doing in other curriculum areas, and (b) by looking at records of work undertaken.

The list above refers not only to curriculum matters but also to management matters, interpreting continuity as consistency. Since the late 1980s attention has been given to generating whole school policies on every aspect of a school's work in an attempt to bring about greater consistency of practice. For example, many policies on behaviour in school lay great stress on consistency of rewards, sanctions, referral systems, handling difficult students, being fair, and promoting positive behaviour. Moreover, the literatures both on behaviour management and on school effectiveness combine to indicate that consistency in behaviour policies has positive spin-offs in curriculum matters in terms of improved standards of student performance.[27] What we are arguing here is that a curriculum plan will make reference (if tacitly) to other aspects of school life – discipline, pedagogy, organisational arrangements.

As with the notion of coherence, the notion of continuity has two very different interpretations whose impact on practice is significant. We saw that an alternative to a prescriptive view of coherence was a view of coherence as residing in the student's mind – a constructivist interpretation. The same applies to continuity. It is the student ultimately who establishes the continuity between existing knowledge, concepts, skills, ways of working, teaching and learning styles in his or her own mind, even though we might be able to facilitate that process of building links.

This draws on the work of Vygotsky,[28] who argues that teachers ought to be able to identify the 'zone of proximal development' in students – the distance between the *actual* and *potential* intellectual, social, cognitive, emotional development in the student. This argues for careful assessment of where a student is in intellectual development, etc., in order that his or her subsequent learning can be planned without it being so close to his or her existing knowledge and abilities as to render learning boring or so distant from his or her existing knowledge and abilities as to render learning impossible. The aim is to stretch rather than to dislocate. As with the student-centred version of coherence above, it is perhaps unrealistic to imagine that a student teacher can go very far in seeing a situation through a student's cognitive lenses in the short period of a teaching practice. This is not to say that it should not be attempted; it is to argue for realistic expectations about what is possible.

The partner to continuity is 'progression'. In attending to this characteristic one is responding to HMI[29] criticisms of curriculum content in schools throughout the 1970s and 1980s, *viz.* that work was inconsequential, piecemeal, superficial, undeveloped and undemanding. The national curriculum is overtly and massively prescriptive in its interpretation of progression. Whether one agrees or disagrees with the interpretation offered at least there is a clear view of what the School Curriculum and Assessment Authority[30] considers progression to be: the cumulative, systematic and incremental acquisition of the knowledge, understandings and matters of the national curriculum through its ten-level sequence for planning and assessment purposes and its programmes of study.

It is possible, in some cases, to detect a logical sequence through the levels and programmes of study (addressing the notion of logical connections that was raised in the discussion of curriculum coherence). However, a *logical* sequence, even if it were total, which, in the national curriculum, it is not, does not necessarily imply a *psychological* sequence of learning.[31] Students' learning is eclectic, lateral and recursive rather than following the clean lines of the national curriculum. For example, what one student finds difficult another will find straightforward; what one student finds easy another finds difficult, a factor that was confirmed, as mentioned in Part I, when the formal assessments showed that some young children who could do the tasks at Level 3 were unable to do the tasks set for Level 2. There are no unequivocally objective criteria for ascribing levels of difficulty to tasks, a feature which led to the criticisms of the Rasch model for testing students undertaken by the Assessment of Performance Unit in the 1970s.[32] Indeed, there are several ways in which progression[33] can be defined that may stand as polar opposites to each other:

simple to complex / complex to simple
general to specific / specific to general
singular factors to multiple factors / multiple factors to singular factors
low order to high order / high order to low order

unique instance to overarching principle / overarching principle to unique
instance
concrete to abstract / abstract to concrete
familiar to unfamiliar / unfamiliar to familiar
present to past / past to present
present to future / future to present
near to distant / distant to near

In fact when one turns to the documentation of the national curriculum one
can see a range of different views of what constitutes progression:

1 The development of an enquiring attitude.
2 Increasing attention, concentration and ability to sustain study.
3 Greater range of purposes, applications, activities, audiences, resources,
   equipment, demands and contexts.
4 Greater quantity of knowledge, skills, understandings, breadth and depth
   of study.
5 Greater complexity of ideas, concepts, sequences, stages and applications.
6 Greater independence, autonomy and ability in organising, planning,
   implementing, evaluating and recording work.
7 Expanding means of communication, responsive to different audiences.
8 Greater use of higher-order thinking (e.g. analysis, synthesis, enquiry,
   evaluation, appreciation, prediction, problem-solving).
9 Greater degree of application, practical implementation and ways of
   working.
10 Movement from the immediate, familiar and present to the more distant,
   unfamiliar and past/future.
11 Greater confidence, responsibility and responsiveness.
12 Greater appropriacy and consistency of selection and utilisation of
   material and skills (fitness for purpose) and acquisition of relevant
   information (exercise of judgement).
13 Greater structure to students' own work.
14 Drawing links and relationships between different areas of knowledge.
15 Increasing skill.

In terms of the national curriculum, *continuing* tasks will have to
demonstrate progression within each task and *blocked* tasks will have to
demonstrate progression within and between the tasks. In planning for
progression, therefore, the student teacher has to temper the view of
progression that is sometimes implicit in the national curriculum with student-
centred and alternative views of progression. As with the notions of coherence
and continuity mentioned above, the expectation that student teachers will be
able to understand the learner in sufficient detail to be able to plan for a

learner-centred view of progression in the period of a teaching practice is almost certainly unrealistic.[34]

With regard to the final characteristic of the curriculum – 'differentiation' – this too is a response to the criticisms by HMI[35] in the 1970s, 1980s and 1990s that work is poorly matched to children's abilities. Further, a major study in 1984[36] reported not only that work was poorly matched but that teachers were blind to their underestimation of children's abilities and hence held unnecessarily low expectations of their students. In mathematics only 43 per cent of work was well matched, with 28 per cent being too difficult and 26 per cent being too easy. In language only 40 per cent of the work was well matched, with 29 per cent being too difficult and 26 per cent being too easy. Low attainers were overestimated on 44 per cent of tasks and high attainers were underestimated on 41 per cent of tasks. These figures cast serious doubt on the extent to which students were working 'at their own rate'. These are crude statistics; the full data-set is more sophisticated. The research analysed matching in terms of five types of task:

- *Incremental tasks*, involving the learning of new knowledge;
- *Restructuring tasks*, where students use familiar materials but are required to discover, invent or construct new ways of looking at a problem for themselves;
- *Enrichment tasks*, where students use familiar materials in unfamiliar contexts, i.e. applying knowledge;
- *Practice tasks*, where familiar knowledge is rehearsed to speed up thinking processes;
- *Revision tasks*, where students restore to their working consciousness knowledge that had been learnt some time previously.

The study found that underestimation included teachers setting what they thought would be incremental tasks but which, in fact, turned out to be practice tasks. Others overestimated students by setting what they thought would be practice tasks but which were, it turned out, incremental tasks.

The implications of this research are clear for student teachers: that they should conduct an analysis of the demands of the task for each individual, or more realistically, for each group of students, and adjust the demands accordingly to avoid boredom, demotivation, upset or frustration. That is not easy, for several reasons. In *practice* students, particularly perhaps inarticulate students, do not always want to reveal their weaknesses, whilst more able students do not wish to reveal their strengths as this will only attract more work![37] In *theory*, as was mentioned in Part I, the notion that one can diagnose a student's abilities with a sufficient degree of precision to be able to make more than a crude estimate of how well the work can be matched, is flawed; ability, Davis[38] argues, is not a question of operating a particular mathematics muscle or science muscle inside a student's head; it is infinitely more complex. Nevertheless, the implications are clear for planning: a careful diagnostic assessment of the students' abilities is needed in order to be able to approach anything close to a good match of work. It is unfortunate, perhaps, that this element of the formal assessment of students was originally designed to be a cornerstone of the government's assessment policies but it was dropped in favour of comparatively summative assessment which had very little formative potential.

The discussion of differentiation so far has been at a cognitive level, matching the child's abilities to the demands of different types of task – the 'zone of proximal development' mentioned earlier. However, Morrison and Ridley[39] argue for a more extended and complex view of matching. They argue for the need not only to analyse task requisites but to take account of characteristics of the learners in question: their preferred modes and ways of working and learning (e.g. on their own, in small groups, in large groups, with the teacher, without the teacher, with a lot of apparatus, with little apparatus, writing, reading, drawing, listening, talking, doing, problem-solving). The characteristics of children go beyond these preferences to include, for example, their interests, self-concept, motivation, degree of autonomy. Indeed, Withers and Eke[40] argue for a social constructivist view of matching that embraces social context and teachers' and students' discourses, i.e. 'matching' embraces more than a narrowly intellectual field. Differentiating learning will need to take account of personality characteristics, social interaction, emotional development, interest, involvement, potential for and willingness to study.

Nor does the discussion of differentiation end there, for just as there are factors that reside in students so there are important factors that reside in student teachers: their personalities, abilities, interests, preferred teaching styles, levels of subject knowledge, preferred organisational arrangements (of students, curricula, classrooms, resources), previous experiences, willingness to take risks, uses of resources, interaction with students, values, potentials. All these influence matching and differentiation.

Further, the organisational arrangements of lessons, rooms and activities can support or frustrate effectively differentiated work. Alexander, Rose and Woodhead[41] argue that over-complex patterns of classroom organisation (e.g. several groups doing several unrelated activities) can submerge the teacher with routine management issues which undermine his or her teaching role.

What we are arguing for is a notion of differentiation that moves beyond the simplistic and facile views of *differentiation by outcome* (where the same relatively open-ended task is set with the expectation that children of differing abilities will produce differentially successful outcomes) and *differentiation of input* (where different tasks are set to different children, depending on their abilities). What we are suggesting is that the student teacher will need to consider, for example, differentiation of:

- time allowances and pacing;

- the amount, type and quality of teacher attention, prompting, support, demand and challenge;
- the type of language that the teacher uses and the level and order of questioning;
- the style of teaching;
- the social arrangements, groupings and working arrangements in the class;
- the activity, task type (e.g. extension, application, practice), demands, cognitive challenge and expected outcomes;
- responsiveness to students' optimum and preferred styles of learning;
- interests and motivations of the students;
- resources and resource organisation, access and use;
- classroom organisation, layout and uses of display;
- objectives for and expectations of each student's behaviour;
- activities, e.g. problem-solving, investigational work, desk-based work, use of IT, workshop activities;
- anticipated students' responsiveness to different teaching styles and teacher behaviour – didactic, informal, authoritarian, laissez-faire;
- assessment and assessment requirements;
- differential introductions;
- student teachers' and students' responsiveness to different ways of organising the curriculum, e.g. through topics, through continuing work and blocked work, through modules, through short projects, through flexible-learning arrangements;
- expectations (social, emotional, cognitive, intellectual, physical) of students.

This is merely an introductory list,[42] the intention of which is to suggest that differentiation is not simply a matter of the speed and order in which individuals progress through the national curriculum – a naive view of the School Curriculum and Assessment Authority – but that the concept of differentiation is itself differentiated and refracted through a host of different lenses – intrapersonal, interpersonal, cognitive, affective, behavioural, cultural, and so on. In planning the curriculum, then, the student teacher is faced with a complex set of variables that, together, contribute to successful teaching. How can this complexity be addressed?

STAGING CURRICULUM PLANNING

There is a saying that the best way to eat an elephant is by eating little pieces at a time! The same applies here: although the list of factors that require planning may seem overwhelming it can be made manageable by careful staging. The following pages provide an indication of how this can be done. Essentially the process of planning involves the funnelling of issues and contents from the general to the specific, from outline areas of study to particular lessons. In essence this can follow a staged sequence, set out in Box 21. Box 21 moves from the medium term to the short term. It provides a

Box 21

A planning sequence   **General**

1 Select the area of study (e.g. a topic or curriculum subject) with reference to the programmes of study, non-statutory guidelines and attainment targets of the national curriculum.
2 Brainstorm – read around the area, collect relevant resources, investigate the possibilities in the area for study.
3 Organise the topic by curriculum areas (for primary schools) – the core and foundation subjects and the cross-curricular areas.
4 Note the knowledge, concepts, skills and attitudes that are to be developed overall and in specific lessons.
5 Identify the specific attainment targets and levels that the programme addresses.
6 Plan the sequence (logical and chronological) through the work.
7 Indicate how continuity and progression will be addressed.
8 Indicate how work will be differentiated in terms of tasks, knowledge, skills, abilities, needs and interests. Plan for differentiation of input, process and outcome.
9 Plan for good matching – looking at the type of task and the level of demand.
10 Plan appropriate resources – first-hand, second-hand, materials, time, space, display, people, e.g. whole-class, group, individual work, problem-solving, investigational work, didactic and instructional, informal, experiential, practical. Anticipate problems and how they might be addressed.
11 Plan how to introduce, develop and conclude activities and sessions.
12 Plan your evaluations and assessments.

                                                                        Specific

conceptual planning map that can be operationalised straightforwardly, comprising a divergent, all-accepting phase of planning (stages 1 and 2) and a convergent, organisational phase (stages 3–12). It addresses the features of a situational analysis and, from such an analysis, identifies priorities and practices. This concerns the third major area of planning mentioned above – the *focus* of planning, which we divide into four stages:

Stage One: a situational analysis.
Stage Two: the construction of schemes of work.
Stage Three: weekly and daily plans.
Stage Four: individual lesson plans.

These stages are addressed in order below.

Stage One: situational analysis

This draws together the material gained during the preliminary visit(s), identifying:

- the physical features of the school;
- features of the school in general;
- features of the classroom;
- particular information to record.

Out of this spring priorities to be addressed in the planning of curricula, teaching and learning. The contents of a school experience file might be presented thus:

- *Title page*: this could provide the following information:

  date of the practice;
  name of the student teacher;
  name of the school, its address and telephone number;
  name of the headteacher;
  name of the class teacher (if appropriate);
  name of the supervising tutor and mentor.

- *Page 2* and following: details of the class(es) to be taught:

  number in the class;
  its composition (i.e. boys, girls, mixed);
  age range and abilities;
  names of the students;
  a seating plan.

- A plan of the school.
- The timetable, indicating fixed slots, e.g. use of the hall, television rooms, computer suites, swimming (in primary schools), assemblies, lessons taken by other teachers (for primary schools), work experience (for secondary schools).
- Further information (e.g. notes and information on the students; details of specialist and other resources; the predominant catchment area of the students).
- Overall aims and purposes of the school, teaching practice, curriculum content (with reference to how some 'characteristics' of the curriculum

will be addressed – breadth, balance, coherence) and students' learning.
- Schemes of work.
- Charts, diagrams and words which indicate the sequence of the work, i.e. so that it is possible to see at a glance the development within each subject and activity and the relationship (where applicable) between the subject and other curriculum areas.
- Weekly plans.
- Daily plans.
- Lesson plans (with evaluations).
- Records.
- Additional materials.

It can be seen that the focus here is on medium-term and short-term planning.

Stage Two: the construction of schemes of work (i.e. planned possibilities)

Having reviewed aims and objectives in the preceding chapter, we now consider two important tools in the preparation for teaching practice: schemes of work and lesson notes. The broader aims provide a focus for a student's schemes of work and the more specific objectives provide the starting point for individual lesson notes.

A scheme of work in the context of school practice may be defined as that part of a school/class syllabus that the student teacher will be required to teach during his teaching practice. In addition to its primary function in providing an outline of the subject matter and content, it may also include information on the children (age, sex, ability, number, class, groups, etc.) as well as on organisational matters, evaluative procedures and ancillary aids. As already indicated, it is also advisable for the student teacher to find out what has gone before in the particular area he or she will be responsible for and include some reference to this in the scheme.

The scheme will therefore indicate the amount of ground a student is likely to cover in his or her stay in the host school. It will be a survey of the work he or she will undertake and will enable him or her to clarify his or her own thinking and to plan and develop those particular curriculum experiences which he or she may feel will require more time and attention in preparation. Although part of a school or class syllabus, a scheme should not be seen as fixed and rigid; modifications may be made to it in the light of new ideas or further experience of the children. One knows what the broad aim is, and there is nothing to stop one taking a detour along the route – like devoting a lesson to a topic that has arisen incidentally from the students' own interests.

In situations where the student teacher is given no clear lead from the teacher concerning schemes of work (as sometimes happens), he or she will then have to devise ones of his or her own. What he or she must avoid in such a contingency is duplicating work already done by the class. He or she must therefore tactfully ascertain from the class teacher what the position is in this respect and, where possible, discuss the schemes he or she proposes to use. When the teacher proves to be unhelpful or evasive, then the student teacher should take the matter up with the supervising tutor.

A comparable situation may arise when a student teacher is placed in a primary school. Some schools in the primary sector may have abandoned fixed timetables in which subjects are organised in isolated compartments. There may not therefore be the same need to structure the work to be covered quite so systematically. Where this is the position, the student teacher may find that he or she is responsible for his or her own schemes and for planning the timing of activities he or she will be organising. This should be done in consultation with the class teacher. The criteria to bear in mind when planning one's schemes in this context are *continuity in learning* and *progression of experience*.

WHAT TO INCLUDE IN A SCHEME OF WORK

The following information should generally be included in a scheme of work:

1 Particulars of the children in the class or group; these will cover number, age, sex, ability and stream (if appropriate).
2 Previous knowledge and experience of the class in respect of the subject matter.
3 The number and duration of the lessons, i.e. the amount of time available overall and for each lesson.
4 The aim of the scheme: an outline of the subject matter and content, possibly with objectives for each lesson or unit of learning.
5 The main content to be covered, in terms of knowledge, concepts, skills and attitudes.
6 An indication of how the scheme will demonstrate relevance, differentiation, continuity and progression.
7 An indication of how the scheme demonstrates coherence (including relatedness to other curriculum areas).
8 Some indication of organisational factors, such as: how are the pupils to learn? What kind of work units are planned – class, group or individual? Methods of teaching and learning to be employed – formal class teaching, self-direction under guidance, etc.
9 Sources of information – books, workcards, pictures, videos, speakers, visits, etc. The manner in which the children's work will be presented, for example oral, written, dramatic, folders, booklets, murals, display, exhibition, etc.
10 Means of evaluation: how are the pupils' achievements to be assessed against the lesson objectives? What criteria will be used?

11 Equipment available – books, materials, apparatus, computers, chalk-board, learning aids, audio-visual equipment, etc.
12 What the work will lead on to after the student teacher has completed the practice (i.e. when the class is returned to the class teacher).

It is usually recommended that schemes of work should be acquired or prepared before teaching practice begins. A sample is as follows:

SUBJECT . . . .   CLASS . . . .

PARTICULARS OF CHILDREN: age, sex, ability, number, groups, etc.

1 Lessons – number and duration (where appropriate).
2 Aims, objectives and priorities for each scheme (general and very specific).
3 Previous knowledge and experience of the area(s).
4 Outline of content and key concepts to be covered (possibly with lesson objectives):
   Week 1 Lesson 1, 2, etc.
   Week 2 Lesson 4, 5, etc.
5 Organisational factors, teaching styles, learning styles to be adopted.
6 Evaluative procedures and assessment evidence.
7 Equipment.

Schemes of work must demonstrate sequencing. A sequential scheme is one in which the components are logically related to one another and in which achievement of the later components will depend in large measure on having mastered the earlier ones, i.e. the notion of progression. Much successful learning in 'linear' subjects (like mathematics) depends on such organisation and continuity. Presented below are examples of two very different schemes, one from a Year 6 primary school and one from a Year 9 secondary school. But first, let us pause a moment to reflect on a continuing debate in the planning of primary-school curricula which features in the scheme of work here.

SUBJECT-BASED AND TOPIC-BASED APPROACHES TO THE PRIMARY CURRICULUM

A key feature in the planning of primary-school curricula is their framing. In particular, the debate about topics and subjects refuses to go away. The Plowden Report[43] gave legitimacy to a child-centred approach to primary curricula in which topic work featured large. This was taken up by other academics,[44] who suggested that:

• primary children naturally view the world holistically and that integrated curricula would therefore be more meaningful to them;

- children unify rather than atomise and fragment knowledge in their minds by assimilating new knowledge to existing knowledge;
- a child's 'whole personality' is best served by a holistic approach to the curriculum;
- to bind learning into subject compartments is to prevent important links between subjects from being explored and to close up channels of investigation;
- a rhythm of learning is better served by not requiring young children to switch from subject to subject, and that this should lead to the planning of topics that integrated subjects and areas of knowledge;
- parcelling up knowledge into discrete subject areas misrepresented the nature of knowledge or knowing;
- many key concepts straddle subject boundaries;
- new knowledge is not always subject-bound;
- subject-based curricula reflect traditional academic and 'preparatory school' values that are out of place in a complex, information-rich world;
- subject-based curricula, marked by strong classification and framing, i.e. with clear boundaries over which neither students nor teachers have the power to control or remove, are indicative of a conservative and elitist curriculum which reproduces inequality in society;
- transferable skills will become increasingly necessary in a changing world and that these are best served in integrated approaches.[45]

Many of these arguments in favour of a topic-based approach operated at the level of ideology and values. Hence it is not surprising to see in the literature a range of counter-arguments operating at the same level. Alexander,[46] for example, suggests that the world is only integrated if we wish to view it that way, a view that echoes Walkerdine's[47] powerful argument that what is perceived to be a 'natural and given' ability to view the world in an integrated way is in fact no more than a social construction, a production rather than an uncovering of those characteristics deemed natural in children. Entwistle[48] suggests that integrated studies provide a poor basis for acquiring knowledge in a manageable or disciplined form; Eggleston and Kerry[49] argue that to talk in terms of integration is, contrafactually, to suggest that the basic building-blocks of the curriculum are in fact the disciplines of knowledge and that it is unhelpful to students to neglect the disciplines of knowledge and their methods of enquiry. A strongly worded attack on topic work was mounted by Alexander, Rose and Woodhead,[50] who argued that to deny children access to subjects was to deny them access to some powerful ways of regarding the world. They advocated stripping out the ideological argument in favour of or against subject teaching and recognising the empirical limitations of topic work and the empirical possibilities in the promotion of subject teaching for effective learning.

Their views echo Morrison,[51] who argued that subject knowledge in teachers and subject-specialist teaching could help to raise standards because teachers with expert subject knowledge could better diagnose a student's needs and plan more carefully and knowledgeably for a differentiated and well-matched curriculum that would build in progression. He argues that a subject-specialist teacher might thereby, in fact, be more child-centred than the progressivist teachers. Indeed Alexander, Rose and Woodhead were unequivocal in their view that a teacher's subject knowledge is a critical factor in successful teaching. A series of HMI[52] reports argued that, for children in the upper end of the primary school, subject and subject-specialist teaching might bring a depth and richness to their studies that they had previously been denied. Further, Alexander, Rose and Woodhead echo the HMI reports in suggesting that much of what had passed for topic work in primary schools had been unchallenging, superficial, undemanding copying out from texts and that progression was marked by its absence over the years of a primary school child's exposure to topics.

In two follow-up reports to that of Alexander, Rose and Woodhead, OFSTED[53] argues that topics might be successful if they are carefully and co-operatively co-ordinated, if coherence and progression are planned consistently, if they address the subjects and programmes of study of the national curriculum, if they specify intended learning outcomes, objectives and assessment, and if they have a single subject bias or emphasise particular subjects. One can detect an empirical change in primary practice in respect of topic work that ensued since the Education Reform Act of 1988. In 1992 the influential report by Alexander, Rose and Woodhead[54] considered that, in practice, it would be impossible for cross-curricular topics to be pursued within a subject-framed national curriculum. In the 1993 follow-up report OFSTED noted that many primary schools had reduced the amount of cross-curricular topics and had moved to within-subject topics, for example within the field of history or science. In 1994 Pollard et al.[55] reported that since 1990 primary children in their early years were experiencing an increasing amount of single-subject teaching and that the integrated curriculum had given way decisively to a subject-based curriculum.

None the less, OFSTED reported in 1993 that only one of the seventy-four primary schools that they had visited organised their curricula entirely around subjects. It seems, therefore, that, topic work can still find a place in the delivery of the national curriculum but that the canons of coherence, coverage of the national curriculum, progression and co-ordination in topic work have to be addressed with greater rigour. It is in this respect that the remarks on the scheme of work for the Year 6 primary class have to be viewed.

AN APPROACH TO PLANNING A SCHEME OF WORK

In the case of the primary school Year 6 class, Box 22 represents the results of an initial 'brainstorming' of ideas about an integrated topic that have now

Box 22 A topic plan for a Year 6 group

Topic: Food Duration: January and February	Year Group: 6
English: AT1. Debating the location of a supermarket; should we use pesticides? drama on angry customers returning purchases; writing advertisements; should we all be vegetarians? AT2 evaluating evidence – the Kava story; language modelling – making a fish and potato pie; topic books on food; reading worksheets and information sheets; reading indexes to fruit and vegetables (non-fiction); AT3 writing recipes, letters of support/ opposition to supermarket proposal; narratives, diaries; devising a questionnaire to gather local opinion on supermarket; narrative/poetry – when I was left to make the dinner; writing a report on the survey made.	**Mathematics:** AT1, AT2. Comparing prices for different amounts of food; giving change; calculating averages; percentages and fractions (link to pie charts); comparing prices; AT4 pictograms, histograms, line graphs of likes and dislikes in food; actual food eaten (by type); venn diagrams of food types in bought products; estimation of seed density in fruits; handling data – gathering, processing and presenting data about supermarket; considering national trends in growth of fast-food outlets; problem-solving – the milk bottle and crates problem; time lines of when food is eaten.

| **Science:**
AT1, AT2 Purposes of different food types – growth, repair, protection, energy, digestion, chemical balance; ways of preserving food; healthy and unhealthy foods; nutritional and energy values; dissecting and labelling fruits;
AT3 heating and cooking food – changes (sugar, eggs, margarine, custard, milk, potatoes) – permanent and impermanent changes; making butter; decaying food; yeast and bread-making. | **Technology:**
DT. Making and calibrating a weighing machine; design and test a crispometer; making model shops and market stalls; making a 'good food' board game; making a food dominoes game;
IT computer programs – balance your diet; the fishing game; what do you eat; generate and interrogate databases on food eaten, simple statistical packages; preferences and dislikes; word processing of recipes, questionnaires; letters; accounts of how the survey was done. | **History:**
Voyages to the Spice Islands and food on board ship; typical foods in Tudor times (using facsimile first-hand documentary resources); preserving food in history. |

Box 22 continued

Geography: Locating original sources of imported food; locating fishing grounds; primary and secondary food-related industries; siting a supermarket.	Music: The prodigal son jazz; food songs with accompaniments – ostinati and pitched percussion.	PE: Emphasis on keeping healthy through exercise and diet (ref. the Happy Hearts project).
Art: Posters to indicate healthy and unhealthy foods; vegetable and fruit prints; observational drawing of still-life fruits; market scenes.	RE: Foods and festivals – Chinese new year, Divali, Easter and Christmas, Hannukah, wedding ceremonies.	EIU: arranging a tea party for a group of elderly residents – who to invite; source of finance for project; expenses and costing; supermarket packing problem from NCC EIU guideline document, p. 27.
Health ed.: Uses and abuses of alcohol; healthy and unhealthy diets; the need for exercise; nutritional value of foods; obesity and diet; safety in handling foods; dangerous effects of some foods – e.g. additives, sugar.	Careers ed.: Arranging two talks from local shopkeeper – a small shop and a large supermarket.	Environmental ed.: Effects of climate on vegetation and crops; a survey of types of shops in the locality and why out-of-town shopping is growing.
Citizenship: Legal protections for products bought; how to complain; protecting shop workers' rights and work routines; should shops open on Sundays?	Equal opportunities: Types of jobs done by women and men in shops – managers, supervisors, senior executives, cleaners, shop assistants, checkout operators; pay differentials; employment and unemployment for ethnic minorities in the food trade; making shops accessible to those unable to walk.	Cross-curricular skills: IT, problem-solving, numeracy, personal and social (through collaborative work and cross-curricular themes), communication and literary (all as indicated above).

been refined into the subject framework of the national curriculum. The student teacher has made certain that his or her proposals for the curriculum content fit with the other programmes of study from the School Curriculum and Assessment Authority for each of the subjects indicated. The programmes of study have statutory status but the cross-curricular skills, dimensions and themes do not. The student teacher has gone one stage further, which is to check that the scheme of work is correctly matched in terms of the attainment targets for each subject where applicable.

The next task, where applicable, is to address the level descriptions of the national curriculum for each attainment target so that the work is appropriately matched in difficulty to the abilities of the students (though, in fact, the level descriptions are to be used more as guides for assessment than as guides for planning). At this stage the student teacher will have to clarify how the scheme of work builds on previous knowledge, concepts, skills and attitudes, how it addresses *continuing* and *blocked* work and how it addresses progression and differentiation. What the student teacher has done so far is to create the framework for a scheme of work in each of the curriculum areas.

The final task is to devise a programme of work for each curriculum area that has a clear sequence and structure. This means moving on from outlining an overall statement of content to subject-specific, detailed descriptions of the curriculum content to be covered. The schemes of work, then, have to be subject-specific, with each one setting its aims and objectives, priorities, content, key concepts to be taught, teaching and learning styles to be employed, resources, and a delineation of what the expected assessment evidence will be during and at the end of the programme. This means that the student teacher of a primary class will have ten schemes of work – one for each of the core and foundation subjects and one for RE. To ensure genuine cross-curricularity it is envisaged that the cross-curricular dimensions, skills and themes are attached to the core and foundation subjects (where appropriate) rather than remaining as discrete curriculum areas in themselves.[56] Once the schemes of work for each subject have been planned they can be transferred rapidly (particularly if the process is computer-assisted) on to a matrix, as outlined in Box 23. Using the matrix plan in Box 23 the student teacher will be able to see how each subject will develop over the four weeks by looking across the rows. Looking vertically down the columns enables him or her to see how each subject area relates to the others in any given week. Further, looking along the rows indicates how *progression* will be addressed in each subject, whilst looking down the columns indicates how *continuity* will be addressed by identifying the relationships between activities and subject areas in a single week. This is particularly valuable if topic work is to be introduced that integrates several curriculum areas.

The second example is of a scheme of work for geography for Year 9 students, again over a four-week period, and places a strong emphasis on planning by key concepts, e.g. the concepts of (a) desertification, (b) the

Box 23 A matrix plan for a primary teaching practice

	Week 1	Week 2	Week 3	Week 4
Maths				
English				
Science				
IT				
DT				
Music				
History				
Geography				
Art				
PE				
RE				
Cross-curricular skills				
Cross-curricular dimensions				
Cross-curricular theme: EIU				
Cross-curricular theme: health				
Cross-curricular theme: careers				
Cross-curricular theme: envt. ed.				
Cross-curricular theme: citizen				

Box 24

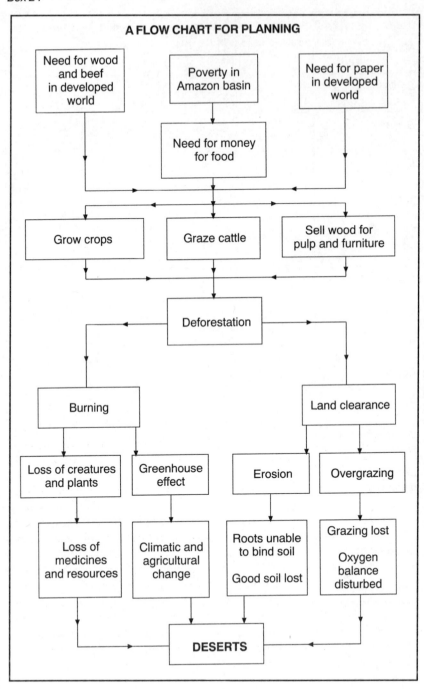

A FLOW CHART FOR PLANNING

Need for wood and beef in developed world

Poverty in Amazon basin

Need for paper in developed world

Need for money for food

Grow crops

Graze cattle

Sell wood for pulp and furniture

Deforestation

Burning

Land clearance

Loss of creatures and plants

Greenhouse effect

Erosion

Overgrazing

Loss of medicines and resources

Climatic and agricultural change

Roots unable to bind soil

Good soil lost

Grazing lost

Oxygen balance disturbed

DESERTS

economic imperatives of the developed world that lead to economic exploitation of the third world, and (c) the concept of deforestation. In conceptual terms the plan is represented in Box 24 and, in essence, falls into a four-week teaching practice thus:

Week One   The poverty of the rainforest dwellers, coupled with the need for the developed countries to have wood for pulp and furniture and beef for food, create a situation where income can be gained by deforesting the rainforests in order to sell the wood and to clear land for grazing cattle and growing crops.

Week Two   As deforestation increases (because of the need for new grazing and for more wood) the 'slash and burn' method of clearing the forest is difficult to halt because of the income it generates.

Week Three   The burning of the forest permanently upsets the climate and contributes to the greenhouse effect whilst the soil, now lacking any tree roots to hold it together, is eroded by the rain. This problem is compounded by overgrazing.

Week Four   A dust-bowl effect is caused, resulting in loss of medicines from plants, the diminution of bio-diversity, permanent climatic change, yet deforestation still continues because of the exploitation of the underdeveloped world by the developed world. Considerations of how to remedy this complete the four-week practice.

As it stands this scheme of work is incomplete, being *conceptual* only. It requires amplification by detailing aims and objectives, how it builds on previous work (i.e. progression), an indication of which parts of the scheme are *continuing* and which parts are *blocked* work, how it relates to the relevant areas of the programmes of study and the levels within the national curriculum, resources, specific content that will be approached to address the concepts listed here, teaching and learning styles, progression and differentiation, and assessment criteria and methods. Though the scheme sets out its priorities at present – the key concepts to be addressed – it needs much greater detail.

This second example is of one scheme of work for one secondary class. Typically the student teacher will be teaching several classes, so several schemes of work will be required, one for each class/set/group (falling in with the organisation of students in the school). Again, a matrix approach to planning can be useful for the student teacher, to chart the commitments and preparations that will be needed over the teaching practice. The matrix is set out in Box 25.

Box 25 A matrix plan for a secondary school practice

	Week 1 including cross-curricular themes, dimensions, skills	Week 2 including cross-curricular themes, dimensions, skills	Week 3 including cross-curricular themes, dimensions, skills	Week 4 including cross-curricular themes, dimensions, skills
Class 1:				
Class 2:				
Class 3:				
Class 4:				
Class 5:				
Class 6:				

Stage Three: making weekly and daily plans

Stages three and four of the four-stage model concern short-term planning – the tactical level of planning rather than the strategic levels of medium-term planning, clarifying specific learning objectives and intended outcomes. It was stated earlier that schemes of work are to be considered as *planned possibilities*. In several ways classrooms adhere to chaos theory![57] There is potential for disorder not only in terms of discipline but, significantly, in terms of lessons not going as originally planned; classroom processes are non-linear. Whilst the devising of schemes of work is a necessary feature of planning it is also necessary to review what takes place over a day or week, and from that review springs refinement of the scheme or lesson. There is otherwise a danger of student teachers being so over-prepared that their plans are cast in tablets of stone, unable to be altered as a result of what happens in the day-to-day activities in class. For example, it is inadvisable to draw up specific lesson plans for more than two or three days in advance in primary schools or for more than two or three lessons in a subject in secondary schools.

At the end of each lesson, day and week careful stock has to be taken of what happened in the classroom. For example, was too much or too little planned? Did the students grasp the teaching points clearly or do they need further work in the area? Did some children fail to grasp the points whilst others found them very simple, i.e. is there a need for better matching and differentiation? Had the students in fact covered some of the work prior to your teaching, and if so, what are the implications for motivation, curriculum content, teaching and learning styles, extension activities, progression and continuity? What needs to be reinforced and with whom? Did it turn out that what was planned to be straightforward proved to be very complex and confusing? How did relationships and groupings facilitate or impede learning?

What we are arguing, of course, is for evaluation to take place at the end of each lesson, day and week, and for the implications of the evaluations to be fed into subsequent modifications and coverage of the scheme of work. This is not to relegate the importance of a scheme of work. On the contrary, it is to reaffirm its central role in planning. Without it teaching and learning are literally aimless. What is being advocated here is that the students themselves have a part to play in the teaching and learning; they can cause student teachers to modify their original plans. Whilst that is to be desired, enabling students to enter the planning process, it means that a scheme of work is mutable, its timing is mutable, its sequence is mutable, its contents are mutable, its planned processes are mutable. It provides a framework rather than a blueprint. This echoes the early work of Stenhouse[58] when he describes the curriculum as a *proposal* and a *basis* for planning that is refined by, and grounded in, practice and the everyday realities of classrooms.

The implications of this view of a scheme of work render it essential that shorter-term action planning for teaching takes place as a result of reviewing events and lessons. This is the stuff of weekly, daily and lesson-by-lesson planning. For primary student teachers a weekly plan will be useful because of the extended contacts that they have with a single class of students. For some secondary student teachers a weekly plan may be useful provided that they see the students for more than one or two occasions per week (as is the case for core subjects – mathematics, English and science). For other secondary student teachers a weekly plan may not be so useful because of the limited contact that they have with students. For example, many secondary school students will only have maybe one lesson of each of the foundation subjects per week – geography, history, art, music, technology, PE, a modern foreign language, RE.

For primary student teachers a weekly planner is set out in Box 26, whilst a weekly planner for secondary school core-subject teachers is set out in Box 27. The weekly planning sheets provide a useful summary of what will be attempted. They enable student teachers to see at a glance what is happening, when it is happening, with whom, what precedes it and what proceeds from it. Because of the limited space in a weekly matrix plan student teachers, in a sense, are compelled to identify priorities. A daily plan can adopt the same format as a weekly plan, identifying priorities and the sequence of events, be it for specific students, groups or classes, depending on whether it refers to a primary school or a secondary school. A framework for a daily plan is set out in Box 28. It must be noted here that increasingly in primary schools teachers teach classes other than their 'own'; the daily plan should indicate the class that the student teacher will be teaching – i.e. it is a plan of the student teacher's programme rather than a single class's programme. This small planning matrix can act as an *aide-memoire*, reminding the student teacher of specific points, for example in connection with preparing resources, meeting others, or major teaching or organisational matters.

The example of the daily planner in Box 28 divides the day into four teaching sessions with morning, lunchtime and afternoon break. Many schools do not adhere to this plan, reducing the time of lunch breaks (often in an attempt to avert troublesome behaviour) and not having an afternoon break. In some regions of the UK this decision is also based on finances, as school heating costs can be reduced in the colder months of the year if schools finish in the mid-afternoon each day. It may be also that in any single 'session' there is more than one lesson, or there is a school assembly followed by one or more lessons before the first break. Clearly this may mean that the format of the daily planner has to be altered.

Box 26 A weekly planner for a primary school practice

Dates: Curriculum area	General and specific aims, objectives, teaching points, organisation, differentiation and progression, continuing/blocked work, grouping
Mathematics	
English	
Science	
Technology	
History	
Geography	
Art	
Music	
PE	
RE	
Cross-curric. work	

Box 27 A weekly planner for a secondary school practice

Date: Subject:	General and specific aims, objectives, teaching points, organisation, differentiation and progression, continuing/blocked work, grouping				
Classes	Lesson 1	Lesson 2	Lesson 3	Lesson 4	Lesson 5
Class 1:					
Class 2:					
Class 3:					
Class 4:					
Class 5:					
Class 6:					

Box 28 A daily plan for a primary school practice

Date:
Session 1: (Time, place, subject, group, resources, main teaching points, particular points to remember)
BREAK
Session 2: (Time, place, subject, group, resources, main teaching points, particular points to remember)
LUNCH
Session 3: (Time, place, subject, group, resources, main teaching points, particular points to remember)
BREAK
Session 4: (Time, place, subject, group, resources, main teaching points, particular points to remember)

Stage Four: individual lesson plans

The lesson plan is the clearest example of short-term planning. There is no single format for a lesson plan; it is contingent upon a number of factors, such as the school's pro-formas for lesson planning, the students, the curriculum area, the type of lesson, the individual preferences of each student teacher, the level of detail required, the level of detail that is useful. Some lessons are *introductory*, some *continue* work from a previous lesson, some *build on* and develop the work from a previous lesson, some practise skills learnt in previous lessons, some are designed to enrich and extend – laterally – points made and concepts studied in previous lessons, some *complete* a blocked unit or module of work, some lessons are overtly diagnostic (see the discussion of assessment in Part IV), some are directly concerned with 'input'. Some student teachers keep minimal lesson plans, releasing them to think creatively; others find that having to include much detail in a lesson plan helps them to think creatively, focusing their mind.

Despite these variations there are some elements that all student teachers are advised to include in their lesson plans. These include:

- *a statement of objectives* (a statement of aims may not be appropriate here because, as the earlier discussion indicated, aims are long-term, generalised and infinite, whereas objectives are short-term, specific, concrete and finite); objectives might refer to the knowledge, concepts, skills and attitudes that will feature in the lesson;
- *an indication of the subject/curriculum area* (in the terms of the national curriculum, or a topic that straddles the national curriculum subjects or works within one national curriculum subject);
- *an indication of the attainment targets, programmes of study and level descriptions* (where appropriate, defined as where they are mentioned in the national curriculum itself and whether the lesson seeks to address the national curriculum subject matter or whether it moves outside it);
- *an indication of resources to be used* (which need to be assembled and tried out by student teachers before the lesson!);
- *an indication of the time available and timing of the different stages of the lesson*, e.g. introduction, development, conclusion (to address the items from the OFSTED criteria (Box 20) mentioned earlier, in particular the items included in the *quality of learning, the quality of teaching* and *resources and their management*);
- *an indication of the intended learning outcomes* (for the students and the student teachers – student teachers experience a teaching practice in order to learn how to teach!);
- *an indication of the organisation* of the lesson – its sequence, use of resources, pedagogical intentions, groupings of students (where relevant);
- *an indication of the specific teaching points* in the lesson, perhaps framed

in terms of *key concepts, knowledge, skills and attitudes*;
- *an indication of the precise activities that will be taking place in the lesson and the times at which they will be taking place*;
- *an indication of how continuity/progression/differentiation are addressed*;
- *an indication of what the student teacher will be doing* at the various stages of the lesson, with particular groups and individuals, and what his or her priorities are for the lesson;
- *an indication* (if not already covered in the preceding points) *of criteria for evaluation of the lesson and self-evaluation of the student teacher*;
- *anticipated difficulties* (e.g. in behaviour, cognitive content, teaching points) *and how they will be addressed*;
- *an indication of assessment evidence* that the lesson will provide (so that the student teacher can complete formal assessment requirements and informal – often diagnostic – assessments).

We are suggesting here that if student teachers provide clear details of intentions for the lesson, for learning, organisation and outcomes, this facilitates evaluation and self-evaluation because the criteria for evaluation and self-evaluation have been clarified. The student teacher can then evaluate the extent to which the objectives for all aspects of the lesson have been achieved and why that was the case. This brings us back to the notion of action planning in order to facilitate review and subsequent action planning that was introduced in Part I.

In most cases student teachers are well advised to include more detail than experienced teachers in their planning. Experienced teachers have an understanding of planning, organisational and pedagogical issues which does not necessarily need to be committed to paper. Inexperienced student teachers do not possess this understanding, or possess it only in embryonic form, so it is a useful principle to over-plan rather than to under-plan.

For example, many student teachers phrase a lesson plan in terms such as 'the class will discuss such-and-such'; when they come to take the lesson they find that the students are not motivated or engaged on the task, that it seems to go nowhere and that nothing useful appears to have come out of it. It could well be that this is because the lesson plan was not clear about objectives, about what was required to come out of the discussion, what the main features of the discussion were to be, how the student teacher could prompt and lead the discussion, or about the specific questions that the student teacher was going to ask and why these questions were chosen. The lack of purpose in the plan was reflected in the implementation – anything could become relevant, any direction became acceptable. The free-floating nature of the discussion meant that it was at the whim of the students; it encouraged caprice rather than logic.

Many student teachers come to teaching practice as comparative novices in working with large numbers of students, so they are unused to phrasing questions (see the discussion of *questioning* in Part III). There is a powerful case for student teachers writing down the actual words that they will use to ask questions, to prompt discussion, to lead the discussion to a conclusion, to link the discussion to the contents of the lesson which precedes it and the activities that follow after it. What we are advocating here is that the lesson plans should be absolutely specific in their objectives and that these objectives should be made clear to students. This reinforces our argument that an objectives model of planning is a very positive organising principle.

We are not necessarily advocating that student teachers spend hour upon hour writing down every fine detail of the lesson, often as a cosmetic exercise to please a tutor or class teacher. On the contrary, we are suggesting that the student teacher will need to be explicitly clear on every aspect of the lesson and that this should be committed to paper at a level of detail and prioritisation that is useful for the professional preparation of the student teacher and helpful to colleagues – for example, class teachers, mentors, tutors from the institution of higher education, visiting examiners – so that they can both trace back through the teaching-practice file to find out how the lesson relates to previous work and understand *at speed* what is supposed to be taking place in the lesson. Further, the delineation of detail enables self-evaluation and review to have clear focuses (see the discussions of evaluations, self-evaluations, self-assessments and review later in the book).

We have argued that there are several constants that should appear in a lesson plan if it is to be useful. How these are set out in a lesson format is a matter of judgement. Some formats will provide much space for organisational matters and for details of how each group in a class will be working; other formats might emphasise the curriculum contents; others will emphasise particular teaching points or particular roles for the student teacher, and so on. The formats we provide here are examples only; clearly individual formats will depend on their appropriateness to the task in hand and on the student teacher.

Box 29 (reduced from the original A4 size) provides an example of a lesson note that attempts to address many of the contents outlined above but to avoid being too detailed – the shortage of space is deliberate in order to compel the student teacher to be selective!

Box 30 provides another format for a lesson plan which addresses the same features but is less specific, enabling the student teacher to have more room to tailor the contents to his or her own needs and priorities.

Another example of a lesson plan can be seen in Box 31. This plan, too, includes some important highlights (intended learning outcomes, activities, key teaching points, attention to differentiation, assessment data). However, it does not differentiate student teachers' and students' activities, it does not clarify the beginnings, middles, and ends of lessons (i.e. the transition points in lessons). This latter is an important omission, for it is often at the transition

Box 29 A structured lesson planner

Session/Subject	Time	Date
Objectives		ATs/LDs
Resources		
Student teacher's activities/ Intended learning outcomes	Students'/children's activities Intended learning outcomes	Assessment data
Introduction	Introduction	
Development	Development	
Conclusion	Conclusion	
Evaluation		

Box 30 A less structured lesson planner

Date: Time: Groups:

Curriculum area:

• Resources:

• Key teaching points:

• Intended learning outcomes:

• Activities/content:

• Assessment data:

• Follow up:

• Evaluation:

Box 31 An alternative loosely structured lesson plan

Curriculum area/Subject			Date
Resources			
Intended learning outcomes for student teacher	Intended learning outcomes for students/children	Main teaching points	Types of differentiation and assessment data
Evaluation			

points in the lesson, for example when a class moves from listening to the teacher or taking part in a class discussion into individual, group or practical work, that discipline problems can occur (see the discussion of *discipline* in Part III).

A fourth example of a lesson plan is less specific still (Box 32), simply highlighting key elements and leaving considerable space for the student teacher to tailor the content to his or her own needs and priorities. Whilst this has the attraction of open-endedness, this very open-endedness may leave the student teacher's thoughts and plans insufficiently structured. For example, this plan is relatively silent on the sequencing of the lesson, is totally silent on the objectives and hopes for outcomes of the lesson, and does not provide pointers to organisational features. It is a statement of content and a little of process, neglecting intentions and structure; it is neglectful of pedagogical issues.

A fifth type of lesson plan (Box 33) is particularly designed for groups within a single class or set of students.

When planning for group work it is essential to make certain that you will be able to 'be in the right place at the right time'; you cannot see to all groups at once and you need to be able to start one group working in the knowledge that they will not need your attention for, say, ten minutes, so that you are free to see to other groups. After that ten minutes you need to have planned to be free to return to the first group. Further, the tasks set must be such that you can be reasonably certain (whilst still taking account of the reference to chaos theory earlier!) that:

- the students will finish together (if that is desired), or
- that students who have completed the task before the end of the lesson are able to be gainfully employed in another activity – maybe an extension activity, or completing a previous piece of work from another occasion, or undertaking a 'holding' activity that does not require your attention but is educationally worthwhile, or
- that the stage of completion of an incomplete task is such that it is able to be picked up easily (with cognitive as well as practical ease) at a future occasion, i.e. that the main features of the task have been completed.

The significance of these points is marked. They direct attention to the need to consider carefully in planning for group work: (a) the *type* and *size* of the tasks; (b) the timing and *time-scales* of the tasks; (c) the *sequence* of the lesson so that you can use your own time most efficiently and effectively. This is a tall order. It was Bernstein[59] and Sharp and Green[60] in the 1970s who alluded to the fact that the most apparently 'free' classrooms were in fact the most planned and carefully structured; it was simply that the pedagogy was 'invisible'. This is a message familiar to teachers of very young school children – sometimes to their cost! For lesson planning, then, a device in the format must be used that will give special attention to task type, timing and

Box 32 An open-ended lesson plan

Date: Time:	Subject:	
Resources:		ATs/LDs
Student teacher's tasks and activities	Children's/students' tasks and activities	
Evaluation		

Box 33 A lesson plan for group work

Date:	Group 1	Group 2	Group 3	Group 4
09.00–09.20	Registration, news, assembly	Registration, news, assembly	Registration, news, assembly	Registration, news, assembly
09.25	*Mathematics:* Children's activities Teacher's tasks/teaching points	*Reading and writing:* Children's activities Teacher's tasks/teaching points	*Painting, shop, playdough* Children's activities Teacher's tasks/teaching points	*Sand tray, water tray, home corner* Children's activities Teacher's tasks/teaching points
09.45	→	→	*Mathematics* Children's activities Teacher's tasks/teaching points	*Reading and writing* Children's activities Teacher's tasks/teaching points
10.00–10.30	*Painting, shop, playdough* Children's activities Teacher's tasks/teaching points	*Sand tray, water tray, home corner* Children's activities Teacher's tasks/teaching points	→	→
10.45	*Measuring and recording* Children's activities Teacher's tasks/teaching points	*Mathematics* Children's activities Teacher's tasks/teaching points	*Reading and writing* Children's activities Teacher's tasks/teaching points	*Painting, shop, playdough* Children's activities Teacher's tasks/teaching points
11.15–11.55	*Sand tray, water tray, home corner* Children's activities Teacher's tasks/teaching points	*Painting, shop, playdough* Children's activities Teacher's tasks/teaching points	*Model making* Children's activities Teacher's tasks/teaching points	*Mathematics* Children's activities Teacher's tasks/teaching points
13.00	*Music corner/cassette work* Children's activities Teacher's tasks/teaching points	*Library corner* Children's activities Teacher's tasks/teaching points	*Model making (from morning)* Children's activities Teacher's tasks/teaching points	*Measuring and recording* Children's activities Teacher's tasks/teaching points
13.50–14.30	Physical Education			
14.45	*Complete audio cassette work* Children's activities Teacher's tasks/teaching points	*Complete Lego models from previous day, jigsaws* Children's activities Teacher's tasks/teaching points	*Continue model making, tidy up* Children's activities Teacher's tasks/teaching points	*Finishing the measuring and recording, tidy up* Children's activities Teacher's tasks/teaching points
15.05–15.30	Story			

sequence. An example of this is given in Box 33 – a format that is used by many teachers of young children.

In this example the time line in the left-hand column provides the student teacher with a very clear outline of what should be taking place and when; it indicates group work and whole-class work, it indicates the sequence of activities for each group and shows that each group is receiving a spread of activities over a single day. One can see, for example, that Group 1, for whatever reason, is being given longer than Group 2 for mathematics; Group 2, in turn, is being given longer for reading and writing than Group 3; it has been recognised that model-making for Group 3 requires a considerable amount of time – longer than the completion of the Lego models for Group 2; Group 4 is experiencing two types of mathematics activity – one in the morning and another in the afternoon. Group 2 finishes a Lego model from the previous day, ensuring that a comparatively large task is completed over a two-day span, so that children do not become bored because it has lasted too long.

By looking across the rows the student teacher is able to see what activities should be taking place at any one time, so that he or she can make the most use of himself or herself. For example, at 11.15 he or she may wish to concentrate on working with Group 4 because the other three groups do not necessarily require his immediate presence: the model makers (Group 3) will be getting their resources ready and putting on their protective clothing whilst Groups 1 and 2 have been able to observe the activities in the sand, water, home corner, painting, shop and playdough during the first session of the morning. When Group 4 has been started the teacher can go to Groups 3, 2 and 1, probably in that order. Once he or she has completed the round of these three groups, Group 4 will be ready for his or her attention again. At a pedagogical level this plan has to be set in the context of the debate on school and teacher effectiveness (see note 2) which questions the efficiency of learning when multiple groups of children are working on multiple curriculum areas simultaneously; that message strikes at the very heart of learning in the early years.

Though the matrix, for the sake of clarity here, has indicated that there will be children's activities and teacher's tasks, it has not indicated what these will be. A full plan for the day will probably spread over two or more sides of paper so that space is provided for a delineation of the student teacher's and children's tasks. One can speculate in this plan that the mathematics, reading and writing are *continuing* activities whilst the model-making is more of a *blocked* activity.

This type of planning could well be 'front loaded', that is, it will take a considerable amount of time to prepare for four groups but it could well last the student teacher more than one day, as children will rotate round the activities over the course of two or more days. This is an important feature of lesson planning, for it indicates that:

- each lesson draws on and relates to one or more schemes of work;
- a single *lesson* plan might last the student teacher for more than one *session*.

The folly of 'cosmetic' lesson planning is where a student teacher virtually duplicates a lesson plan from a previous day simply because the students did not complete the previous day's work. That is a sheer waste of time. Sense tells us that if a coherent lesson is planned to take two or more sessions it is unnecessary to duplicate the lesson plan for each session. In our experience this is particularly true for mathematics lessons, as (a) the concepts, objectives and content may take several lessons to achieve, and (b) the objectives for the mathematics may be contained in the scheme of work or the teacher's manuals for published schemes of work. This is not to invite student teachers to be lazy; it simply recognises that duplication may be needless.

EVALUATION, SELF-EVALUATION AND REVIEW

So far this part has been concerned with aims and objectives, the planning of curriculum content and organisation, the need to plan the teaching and learning styles that will be used (discussed in more detail in Part III), together with the planning of resource use and the sequencing of the lesson and schemes of work. The point was made earlier that action planning – at whatever level (overall curriculum strategy, schemes of work, lesson plans) – requires, at some point, a review of the extent to which the plan has been realised in practice, so that the next cycle of action planning can be undertaken.

Moreover, the *levels of planning* discussed earlier indicated that action planning could apply to: (a) an overall curriculum policy (long-term planning); (b) schemes of work (medium-term planning), (c) weekly and daily plans (short-term planning); (d) lesson planning (short-term planning). It was argued that a major component of planning at these levels was the need to set appropriate aims and objectives – objectives for the whole teaching practice, for individual schemes, for a week's work, for a day's work, and for individual lessons. Further, it was suggested that the statements of objectives should apply not only to the children and students but to the student teachers themselves because student teachers undertake teaching practice in order to learn how to teach.

The outcome of these issues is to suggest that *evaluation* must take place with regard to (a)–(d) above. The *form* of evaluation is largely an objectives model[61] which takes its lead from the work of Stake.[62] Stake argues that teaching and curriculum planning begin with a statement of *intentions* (or objectives) with regard to:

1 *antecedents* (the putative initial conditions or state of the class, the student teacher, the students, the curriculum, the resources);

2   *transactions* (the proposed processes that will be experienced in achieving the objectives, with regard to, for example, teaching and learning styles, the structuring, sequencing and organisation of content, the organisation of classroom groups, the nature of the use of resources);

3   *outcomes* (the proposed outcomes with respect to achievement of the objectives, the students' and student teacher's learning and behaviour, the curriculum knowledge, skills and attitudes that have been learnt).

The task of this objectives-based form of evaluation is to chart the extent to which the intentions (objectives and expectations) have been realised in practice, the match between *intentions* and *actuality* in respect of 1–3.

With reference to *antecedents* the student teacher might, for example, have expected the students to have understood simple addition of fractions. Expecting to find this as an initial condition, he or she might start work to build on it, only to discover that in reality several students have no understanding of the addition of fractions. The intended antecedents of another student teacher might have included an expectation that resources for teaching the history of the Victorian age would be plentiful, when in fact they turn out to be very meagre. Another student teacher might have expected to be teaching in a room with enough chairs and tables for every student to be able to sit and see the student teacher, only to find that the room is L-shaped and that, because of the small working areas, there are only enough chairs and tables for three-quarters of the class with the regular class teacher always planning for one group to be out of the room in a 'wet' area that is shared with another class. These examples suggest the pressing need for a full situational analysis of the school and the class before teaching practice begins, including gathering information on children's abilities and prior knowledge.

With reference to *transactions*, the student teacher may have planned collaborative group work, only to find that students cannot handle the apparent freedom and opportunity to talk (often about matters unrelated to the lesson!). Another student teacher may have planned for multimedia resource-based learning, only to find that on the days on which he or she had planned for this to occur some of the computers were booked out for another class, that some children were unsure how to operate equipment, and that others saw the change of student teacher's role from an instructor to a facilitator as a licence to misbehave. Clearly the sessions would have to be rethought.

With reference to *outcomes*, these fall into a variety of fields. The student teacher may wish to know the extent to which the students have acquired the intended knowledge, concepts, skills and attitudes. This is the model of evaluation-as-assessment that underpins the formal assessment of student achievement at the end of each key stage of the national curriculum. The student teacher may have set targets for his or her own learning – the achievement of specified DFEE competences that were introduced in Part I – and wish to reflect on and evaluate his or her achievement of these. Or the student teacher may want to evaluate the extent to which his or her planning for flexible-learning arrangements to improve students' ability to work autonomously (mentioned in Part I) and to speed up their learning progress has been successful.

With regard to *summative* – terminal – assessments (see Part IV) a student teacher might have intended the students to have come to an understanding of the water cycle, only to find at the end of the teaching practice that, though they can identify different *elements* of the water cycle, say evaporation and precipitation, they have been unable to grasp the *cyclical* nature of the water cycle, i.e. they have failed to understand the key concept in question.

In all of these examples the purpose of an objectives model is to evaluate the match between what was proposed and what occurred. This is a very powerful form of evaluation, for it is ruthless. It asks what student teachers and students can do at the end of the teaching practice, week, day or lesson that they could not do at the beginning. Having made explicit what the objectives are for each level and element of planning, this model (we suggested earlier that objectives were to be very specific and concrete) assesses, maybe measures, a level of success or failure in achieving them. The objectives become the criteria for evaluation. As a result of the evaluation a new plan of campaign can be drawn up – the commencement of the next round of action planning.

This model does not look for reasons *why* the objectives were or were not achieved, instead it confines itself to *what* was achieved – the cold, hard edge of success or failure. That is both its strength and weakness. For example, its strength may be to reveal that a clear 30 per cent of the class had understood the multi-faceted notion of social class in a sociology programme; its weakness here is to consign 70 per cent of the class to failure, with the concomitant problems of negative labelling and the lowering of self-esteem (this is one of the major doubts about the efficacy and longer-term benefits of the publication of schools' results on the formal assessments of students' achievements of the national curriculum).[63]

A primary student teacher may have set his or her own objectives to achieve Level 3 of the DFEE levels of competence in subject knowledge; in fact he finds out that he only achieves Level 1. Is this a good or a bad thing? A hard-hearted person would perhaps argue that the student teacher needs to know this and that the evaluation is presenting an objective judgement. It is apposite, in this respect, that the term *objective* can be applied in two different senses – a short-term goal and an unbiased judgement. Another person, seeking to fulfil a more supportive, personalised and developmental role, may regard the cold measure as unhelpful, having little or no diagnostic potential and being demotivating to the student teacher.

The implication of these two examples is to suggest that it is easy to regard the achievement of objectives as 'all or nothing'; either they have been achieved or they have not. This is the error of polarised, bivalent thinking[64] whose roots can be traced back to Aristotle's law of the excluded middle and whose continuing influence and power underpins the information revolution: at the heart of the digital age of computers lies a microprocessing computer chip that is designed *either* to open up a pathway *or* to close down a pathway. We reject this simplistic view in favour of multivalence; the world is grey, we live in the age of 'fuzzy logic' where *degrees* replace *absolutes* in all walks of life. Objectives can be achieved with respect to different elements or areas and with varying degrees of success; this must be reflected in evaluation.

The argument so far points to three major difficulties in using an objectives model. First, Morrison[65] argues that

> [w]hilst the objectives model is very useful in detailing which objectives have been achieved and their level of achievement, it does not address those types of evaluation which seek to explain why the objectives may or may not have been achieved. Hence its simplicity is bought at the price of explanatory potential. It is the model which is useful for describing rather than explaining.

The model is weak on suggesting ways forward for improvement, it has little *formative* potential. Lawton[66] said of this model that it is akin to undertaking intelligence after the war is over.

Secondly, in evaluating the achievement of the objectives the model takes little or no account of matters that were not stated in the objectives. For example, a host of unanticipated but worthwhile matters might have arisen during the course of the teaching practice that the objectives fail to catch. Further, some educationally beneficial activities (for student teachers and students) are not susceptible to formulation in neat objectives; longer-term and deeper qualities that education can develop over time are not easily captured in objectives.

Thirdly, there is a risk in an objectives model that the objectives themselves are not evaluated, their worthwhileness is not considered. This misrepresents the semantic root of evaluation, the notion of *value*. To overcome this problem the student teacher should have considered overall aims of the teaching practice and should have prefaced each scheme of work with a statement of aims. As was mentioned in the earlier discussion of aims, these indicate the main purposes, rationales, principles and values that the school sees itself as serving – the stuff of 'mission statements' that appear in school prospectuses.

The implications of this discussion are that the student teacher, in undertaking evaluations and reviews for the purpose of action planning, will find it useful:

1   to use an objectives model at all levels (relating to schemes of work, weekly, daily and lesson-by-lesson plans);
2   to amplify an objectives-based evaluation with an analytical aspect, a diagnosis of *why* the objectives were or were not achieved;

3   to amplify an objectives-based evaluation with comments on the development of qualities and longer-term, underlying matters that are not measurable;

4   to recognise that achievement of objectives may be partial;

5   to evaluate matters that arose in the teaching practice that were not anticipated;

6   to relate the evaluation of objectives to the development of DFEE competences;

7   to include in evaluation the question of *value*, the *worthwhileness* of activities and plans, particularly in terms of overall aims;

8   to use evaluations *formatively*, as springboards for further action, rather than *summatively*.

We can use these points and the preceding discussion to arrive at a definition of evaluation as 'the provision of information about specified issues upon which judgements are based and from which decisions for action are taken'.[67] Using these principles the evaluations that student teachers conduct will address their success in achieving their overall aims for the teaching practice; their schemes of work; their weekly and daily plans, and their lesson plans. These evaluations will differ in focus, form, methods, evidence – types and sources – and outcomes. This is not the place to look at the whole range of issues in evaluation as some of these go beyond the needs of a student on teaching practice. However, some of them are addressed in the course of the book in the *success criteria* for content and pedagogy, and others feature in Part IV on assessment. This section concerns a student teacher's self-evaluation.

An evaluation of successes or achievements will need to make clear what the *success criteria* are (a feature which, as Part I indicated, is a requisite for effective school-development plans). If a lesson note contains clear, specific, concrete (often behavioural) objectives then these can be used as success criteria; for example, learning the use of the full stop, understanding that ice has a greater volume than its equivalent weight in water. However, as indicated above, it is not always possible, or indeed desirable, to cast objectives or their outcomes in behavioural terms, or to conduct this tightly focused form of evaluation, because events and outcomes are not always precise. This is less true of lesson plans but more true of daily and weekly plans, schemes of work and overall aims of the teaching practice. We address these in turn below.

EVALUATION OF ACHIEVEMENT OF OVERALL AIMS FOR THE TEACHING PRACTICE

The statement of aims and priorities that student teachers write as the outcome of their situational analysis and overall planning are couched in general, non-operational terms (see the earlier discussion of aims and objectives). In this sense also, it is both invidious and impossible to discuss 'achievement' of the aims; because they are infinite (it is impossible to say that a person has achieved a finite state of creativity, imaginativeness, being educated) they will never be achieved finally and completely. They are another example of the multivalent 'fuzzy' logic mentioned above, where simple states of 'either–or' are replaced with grey areas and degrees of success. The overall aims are qualitative, they describe qualities rather than outcomes. It is advisable, then, to evaluate how, how fully and how successfully the aims have been achieved in *qualitative* terms – with informed opinions and judgements based on the professional insights of connoisseurs[68] (in this case experienced teachers, mentors, tutors from institutions of higher education, all of whom are examples of reflective practitioners (see the discussion in Part I of reflective practice)).

This is not to deny the rigour of such an evaluation. Its rigour lies in the student teacher taking each aim in turn and defending – with rational argument and supporting evidence from the teaching practice – his or her achievement of the aim, the way in which it has been addressed and the way in which the priority that was given to it at the beginning has been reflected during the teaching practice. The reliability of the evaluation lies in the arguments and evidence adduced in support not only by the student teacher but by other involved practitioners, for example the class teacher, the mentor, the headteacher, the departmental head, the college or university tutor.

This evaluation will be *summative*, that is, a retrospective, summary review of what has taken place during the practice, couched in terms of the match of intentions and actuality (see the discussion of Stake's 'countenance' model of evaluation above). It will address points 2–7 from the list of considerations outlined on pp. 123–4, and will also focus on the student teacher's own development of reflective practice: the move beyond a technical, recipe-driven view of teaching to a flexible style of teaching that is underpinned by relevant theory (see the discussion of reflective practice in Part I). The evaluation will both *describe* the ways in which the aims have been addressed and *explain* (and justify) why they were addressed in that way.

EVALUATION OF ACHIEVEMENT OF THE SCHEMES OF WORK

The issues involved in evaluating achievement of the aims of schemes of work are the same as those applying to overall aims of the teaching practice and so will not be repeated here. In judging the success of the achievement of objectives an evaluation can focus on objectives that were set out for:

- the *student teacher*, what he or she has learned about: students; preparation; curriculum planning, topic work and subject planning;

organisation, sequencing and structure; assessment; behaviour, relationships, discipline and control; resource preparation and management (e.g.
time, space, materials, staff, children, audio-visual, books, charts,
displays, IT); relationships with colleagues;

- the *students/children*, e.g. interests, motivations; behaviours; abilities,
  progress; achievements, independence and autonomy; self-esteem; interactions; equal opportunities;
- the *organisation of the classroom(s)*, layout, seating arrangements,
  resource access;
- the *curriculum*, framing (e.g. knowledge, concepts, skills, attitudes),
  content, coverage, breadth, balance, relevance, differentiation, progression, continuity, coherence, prioritisation, variety, organisation, structure,
  sequencing, resourcing;
- the *pedagogy*, e.g. structuring activities, use of first- and second-hand
  experiences, drawing on students' contributions, stimulating and motivating students, teaching and learning styles and strategies, resource access
  and use, the use of different types of display, timing and pacing, matching
  and differentiation, class, group and individual work;
- *assessment* and monitoring, opportunities for diagnostic teaching.

The breadth of the review is a function of the breadth of the schemes. Part
of the summative review might consider the appropriateness of the breadth of
the schemes. As with the overall aims discussed above, the review of the
success of the schemes of work will also consider their worthwhileness.
Again, the evaluation will be *summative* and retrospective and qualitative
(using evidence from a variety of sources: personal comments; student
outcomes that have been recorded in the students' ongoing records; weekly,
daily and lesson-by-lesson comments; students' work; students' results on
formal and informal assessments). Additionally, use may be made of 'marks',
grades or other forms of 'hard data'. The evaluation of the scheme of work,
like the evaluation of the overall aims, will describe the main features that
have come out of a review of the schemes with significant adults; though this
may include an analytical or explanatory element it will be minimal here,
being reserved largely for the shorter-term weekly, daily and lesson evaluations.

WEEKLY AND DAILY EVALUATIONS

These evaluations will identify *key points* that the student has learnt over
the previous week or day respectively. They identify *priorities* for the student
teacher in terms of (a) what he or she has learnt about teaching, and (b)
what the implications of this are for subsequent weekly and daily planning.
They are not concerned with *description*, but with *analysis* of and
explanations for the incidence or importance of the major features selected.

For example, they might focus on significant points that the student teacher has learned about: behaviour and discipline, e.g. promotion of positive behaviour patterns, encouraging self-esteem, a range of strategies to avert or minimise bad behaviour, managing the whole class, transitions, use of voice, praise, maintaining high expectations; students; classrooms; curriculum planning and implementation; pedagogy, e.g. successful and unsuccessful strategies, collaborative and group work and seating arrangements; problem-solving and investigational work; resource access, use, organisation and storage; particular types of activity; particular successes and failures and reasons for these.

These evaluations are *formative*, that is, they suggest implications for the immediate future *during* the teaching practice. They concern day-to-day matters and *tactics* for subsequent planning. Weekly evaluations might draw on the student teacher's discussions with his or her mentor, other teachers and involved adults, and they might include personal, subjective comments and self-review. The purpose of these evaluations is to shape what happens next; analyses and reviews of this nature lead into action planning. A weekly review is also an appropriate time for the student to refer to his or her developing abilities in the DFEE competences.

EVALUATION OF SPECIFIC LESSONS

Though these evaluations will be very specific and focused, a student teacher who is developing as a reflective practitioner will need to be selective, to avoid *reportage* and low-level description and to be able to extract from the minutiae of classroom processes the *significant issues* for subsequent practice. A lesson evaluation will ask (and hopefully answer) *why* a specific lesson and elements of that lesson were more or less successful or unsuccessful and what the implications of this analysis are for the immediate future. It will focus on achievement of the concrete objectives that were set out in the lesson plan and the level of success in achieving the elements of the lesson that were included in the lesson plan (see above for the contents of a lesson plan), for example:

- the motivational, managerial and organisational factors during the introductory stages;
- the clarity of communication – questioning, responding, explaining – during the introductory, development and concluding stages of the lesson;
- the success of different stages of the lesson – introduction, development, conclusion;
- the smoothness of the transition from one stage of a lesson to another or from one activity to the next;
- the timing and pacing of different stages of the lesson;

- the quality of the student teacher's feedback that was given to individuals, groups and the whole class;
- the organisation, location, access and uses of resources for the lesson;
- the success in addressing the key teaching points and key questions in the lesson;
- the degree of success of the planned matching and differentiation;
- the worthwhileness and educational significance of the activities planned;
- the development of positive relationships between the student teacher and the students and between the students themselves;
- the promotion of order and good behaviour and the avoidance of bad behaviour;
- the degree of success in achieving the intended learning outcomes for the student teacher;
- the degree of success in achieving the intended learning outcomes for the student teacher/children;
- the degree of success in gaining data for assessment purposes – formal and informal;
- the degree of success in the most efficient and effective use of the student teacher;
- the extent to which the activities drew on subjects and cross-curricular elements of the national curriculum.

These are outline areas only. From our experience of teaching and supervision we would suggest that student teachers will find it useful to consider the following questions in evaluating lessons.

The curriculum

- Aims and objectives.
  Are they clear, worthwhile, useful, appropriate?
- Curriculum content.
  Is it intellectually significant?
  Is it appropriate for the objectives?
  Is it appropriate for the skills to be learned or practised?
  Is it appropriate for the teaching and learning styles used?
  How far does the content address new knowledge?
  How far does the new knowledge relate to existing knowledge?
  How far is the new knowledge appropriate and useful?
  How far does the content provide enrichment and application of existing knowledge?
  How far does the content provide consolidation and practice of existing knowledge?
  How far does the content provide revision of previously learned knowledge?

How far does the content introduce new skills?

How far do the new skills reflect the students' experience and development?

How far does the content develop students' attitudes – what are they?

How interesting is the content?

How far does it allow for understanding?

How can the students use the knowledge?

How far can students share the new knowledge and skills?

How far does the content provide for breadth, balance, depth, relevance, coherence, continuity and progression?

How far does it meet individual needs?

How well matched to the child is the knowledge?

What criteria are being used to address matching?

The teaching and learning

- Task.
  Is the work sequenced at the optimal level?
  Is the work well structured?
  Is there an appropriate balance between choice and direction?
- Time.
  Is the time used most effectively?
  Is the time-scale effective and appropriate?
  Is the time-allowance realistic?
  Is time used flexibly to respond to students' learning styles?
- Space.
  Is space used effectively – to reflect the range and nature of the activities?
  Can students move round the room easily where necessary?
  Can students understand the classroom organisation?
- The student teacher.
  Are praise and blame used appropriately and effectively?
  Is discipline effective?
  Are students well motivated?
  Is the student teacher used to best effect?
  Is there a good rapport between the student teacher and the students?
  Is the student teacher's approach well thought-out?
  Is the student teacher's approach varied and stimulating?
  Does the student teacher's approach respond to the complexity of the content?
  Is the voice used effectively?
  Are the student teacher's gestures and movements used effectively?
  Are instructions clear?
  Is the pacing of the lesson clear, brisk and appropriate?

Is questioning appropriate, varied and effective?

Are the exposition, explanation, discussion, summary effective?

Is the student teacher clear at the beginning, continuation and close of the lesson in the time allotted?

- The students.

Can they see and hear as necessary?

Is allowance made for students' different preferred learning styles?

Is there a suitable use of group, class and individual activities?

Are the students developing socially and emotionally as a consequence of the lesson?

- Resources.

Do the resources reflect the range of the curriculum?

Do the resources reflect the focus of the curriculum (e.g. first-hand and second-hand experience)?

Do the resources reflect the level of the curriculum for each student?

Are they stimulating?

Are they used?

Are they well maintained?

Are they accessible?

Are they appropriate to the task?

Are they of good quality?

Are there sufficient?

Are displays used for learning?

Are displays attractive?

Are displays changed as appropriate?

- Record-keeping.

Are records appropriate, thorough, comprehensive, useful, used?

What is recorded?

Why are different records kept?

How is the progress of each student recorded and monitored?

A more structured and complete set of criteria is provided by Moyles[69] and we advise student teachers to go into her work in detail as it is comprehensive and full, covering: curriculum content; relationships with students; students' progress and achievements; discipline and management; classroom administration, organisation and display; teachers' professional attitudes and personality.

The difficulty in providing lists and suggestions for evaluation is that they can too easily become narrowly prescriptive. On the one hand it could be argued that these lists and suggestions derive from experienced practitioners and that it is a dereliction of their duty if they do not share their experiences. That is not contentious. On the other hand the listing of criteria for evaluation might be seen to go against the grain of the argument advanced throughout this book, *viz.* that the *student teacher*'s action planning is central and that this derives from his or her own agenda, review and target setting.

The reality of the situation is that the two are not mutually exclusive. Be it the setting out of lists from experienced practitioners, academics, or those who composed the DFEE criteria, the point here is that the student teacher is not an island and that he or she may well find it useful and helpful to inform his or her own agenda by investigating and using the ideas and suggestions of others. Indeed, in the case of the DFEE competences this is a requisite. Moreover, the student teacher in school is able to receive a great deal of support and advice from class teachers, subject teachers, department and faculty heads, mentors, college and university tutors. This advice should manifest itself in the student teacher's own development; in turn the student teacher's development should be able to be seen through the lesson, daily and weekly evaluations. In addition to advice from published sources, significant adults and the student teachers themselves a vital source of evaluation data is the students themselves, what they have done in the lesson, what the outcomes are, what written work they have produced, how they have achieved in some form of assessment or test.

The outcome of this discussion should be to guide student teachers to writing useful lesson evaluations. Below is an example of a student teacher's self-evaluation of a lesson and a tutor's evaluation of the same lesson with a class of twenty-eight Year 3 children. Neither evaluation is perfect! For example, the student's evaluation is descriptive, lacking in analysis, rather unselective, and unsuggestive of how it will affect future practice, even though it is clearly authentic. The tutor's evaluation, by contrast, is very long, rather pointed and maybe rather negative.

The student teacher's evaluation of an art and technology lesson

I felt fairly confident about this lesson even though I had not done this sort of thing with children before. I thought the children would like to use all different sorts of materials and beads and to stick them on to paper. James and Donna made a mess of theirs and then went round spoiling others' work; I got cross with them and made them sit in the reading corner out of the way. James, as usual, didn't stay there but got up and carried on wandering round the room. I had to get very cross with him. The children enjoyed looking at the beads and holding them up to the light. I felt very harassed in this lesson as the red group kept arguing about nothing and the group in the corner (Joanne, Billy, etc.) kept shouting for me to go and look at what they were doing. I could have killed Julie when she spilled the box of small beads and everyone came to tell me. At one point I had to stop everyone as too many children were being silly. I think I should have told them about their behaviour and the way to behave in this sort of lesson rather than say how nice some of their pictures were.

This lesson seemed endless. It took them ages to get everything and then they were on the go all the time. I seemed to spend my time stopping things from being spilled and stopping the children from being noisy. I had to get cross with Sharon as she used up three bits of paper. I think I must have told them what to do about a hundred times!

Some of the children made some good pictures and were pleased with them. I let the finished pictures go home.

Points for the future: get everything ready beforehand, show them more clearly what to do, cut down the numbers of children out of their seats, put out fewer materials and spread them round the room rather than having them all in one place with children crowding round each other, stop them much sooner if the lesson is getting noisy.

I enjoyed this lesson (I think) and wouldn't mind doing it again but I need to think about my organisation of the children, materials and classroom.

The tutor's evaluation of an art and technology lesson

Whilst your weekly evaluations are fairly analytical I think your daily and lesson descriptions need a lot more detail and analysis otherwise they simply describe and comment in a way which is not very useful for yourself and future planning. Further, in lesson plans more detail is needed to expose knowledge/concepts/skills/intended learning outcomes more extensively and then to see how these are translated into practice. We need to see evidence in the file of anticipation of organisational problems and how you will deal with these. If you are moving to differentiated work then you will sometimes need to have differentiated objectives.

This is a very ambitious lesson – all doing potentially chaotic activities. Therefore ask yourself: is this the best way to get through the task or would it be better just to have one or two groups on the 'sticky' work? You have set up a situation which requires a lot of movement – are you happy with this? If you *are* happy with this you will need to talk the children through the getting of equipment far more closely, e.g. 'You have two minutes to get what you need; don't start, just get what you need and then sit still.' Then stop them all, talk about the task, then set them away on it. *Or* just have one table at a time getting the equipment. There was a time when only five children were actually sitting down, and only three of them were really doing anything.

The lesson note peters out after the introduction – what will you be doing/teaching during the lesson – we need to know!

You will have to question the wisdom of putting all the resources together, e.g. there was a constant (i.e. for ten minutes) throng round the beads – could this have been re-arranged, or are you making a rule that if there are two or three children there then no-one else is to go there? After five or six minutes stop them all, sit them down, calm them, talk (maybe about teaching points), then set the children away again. This sort of lesson puts you in a high-stress situation – where you are working ten times as much as the children – are you happy with this? When you stopped all the children (after twelve minutes) the effect was positive – you were able to make teaching points – do insist on their attention – tell them to put down scissors, brushes, glue, materials. The dangers of this mass activity is that you end up by having to devote your time to instructions and behavioural points rather than to teaching points – are you happy with this? How else could the lesson have been organised? Was there a fair pay-off in children's work for all your effort? Could you have got a better pay-off by only having one or two groups at a time doing this?

Some of the children are using the materials for patterns, pictures and bas-relief 3D work (using beads for snowmen) – are you happy with this? (You grew aware of this as the lesson went on – it should have been anticipated – proactive rather than reactive teaching.) There are different degrees of accuracy and precision at work here, how will you know how well each child is performing, or are there some children giving less than their best? How can you ensure that the glue keeps off the desk tops? Three desks have sizeable spillages. Are you happy that the children make up their pictures as they go along, rather than trying things out before they start gluing – arranging and re-arranging and then gluing – i.e. are they planning and developing aesthetic criticism or just plonking things on uncritically? Many children were becoming increasingly frustrated because they were 'going wrong', placing before gluing would have averted this.

How can you use this lesson and yourself to develop aesthetic awareness, criticism, awareness of media, materials, form, skills of fine motor control? This is all the stuff of a lesson plan.

It seems on re-reading this that I have been rather negative about this lesson. In fact the children are getting on quite well (after thirty-five minutes) and the results are interesting. You have provided a good variety of materials, the children are quite absorbed in the topic; they are clearly learning about the mechanics of the activity. I am concerned that more could have come out of the activity and that your classroom organisation, organisation of the lesson, questioning of the efficacy of a whole-class activity of this sort would have maximised the high potential of this lesson to really develop the aesthetic aspects of children's development. Do allow a good amount of time to clear up and round off the lesson with comments.

Box 34 A summary of issues in evaluation and self-evaluation

Level	Purposes	Aspects of evaluation and self-evaluation						
		Type	Nature	Data sources	Types of data	Focuses	Reliability
Achievement of overall aims	Review	Summative	Generalised	Significant adults and self	Qualitative, words, informed opinion	Aims	Reference to other adults
Achievement of schemes of work	Review	Summative	General and key points	Significant adults	Qualitative, words, informed opinion	Aims, objectives, student teacher, students, classroom organisation, curriculum, pedagogy, assessment	Reference to other adults and student outcomes
Achievement of weekly and daily plans	Review, analysis of main priorities	Formative	Priorities and key points	Significant adults, self, students' work	Qualitative and quantitative from informed opinion and students' work	Aims, objectives, student teacher, students, classroom organisation, curriculum, pedagogy, assessment	Reference to other adults and student outcomes
Achievement of lesson plans	Review, analyse, explain, shape future practice	Formative	Specific, detailed, concrete	Significant adults, self, students' work	Qualitative and quantitative from informed opinion and students' work	Objectives, student teacher, students, classroom organisation, curriculum, pedagogy, assessment	Reference to other adults and student outcomes

Comment

Though the style and degree of detail are different in the two evaluations, the two parties focus on the same issues: organisation of time, resources, children, layout of the classroom, discipline, degrees of involvement and engagement, rules and routines, anticipating problems and being proactive. The tutor was concerned not only with the 'management' aspects of the lesson but the lesson content itself and the ways in which the activity could address curriculum objectives. The tutor suggested that more detailed attention to the 'nuts and bolts' of the lesson would have been useful, both in the planning and implementation stages. In this former respect the tutor suggested that a more detailed lesson plan might have assisted the student in anticipating problems, rather than waiting for them to happen in the lesson. Clearly the tutor is more analytical than the student teacher and suggests ways of improving matters rather than merely describing the difficulties in the lesson. On the other hand the student teacher's evaluation is honest and formative, suggesting 'points for the future'.

The evaluation of a lesson should be *formative*, it should shape very concretely and specifically the subsequent lessons that the student prepares – maybe to avoid certain types of activity, maybe to emphasise other types of activity, maybe to focus on organisational matters more in the lesson note and the running of the lesson *in situ*. A lesson evaluation should feed directly in the action plan for the next lesson or series of lessons. If it does not do this then its utility is limited. A summary of issues in evaluation and self-evaluation is presented in Box 34.

Part III

Practising teaching

Part III addresses the competences from the DFEE (see Part I) contained within the subsections 2.3 and 2.4 (for secondary student teachers), and 2.5 and 2.6 (for primary student teachers). We have just examined in some detail many of the preparatory aspects of teaching in the classroom – initial acquaintance with one's school, aims and objectives, schemes of work, lesson notes, and observation lessons. We turn now to the practice of teaching itself. We look successively at primary teaching, secondary teaching, language in classrooms, mixed ability teaching, equal opportunities, management and control in the classroom, and finally the classroom environment and situational factors. We have given many additional references in the notes and it is vital that the reader follows up at least some of them in the course of his or her studies.

Chapter 9

Primary teaching

INTRODUCTION

In beginning this part with primary teaching, it is not our intention that the student of primary education confines himself or herself to the next few pages exclusively. There is much of both a specialist and general nature to be had from a perusal of the remaining sections and it is hoped that he or she will at least read through the sections on *equal opportunities* and *management and control in the classroom.* It is also hoped that the primary student will seek out the specialist primary texts referred to for additional guidance.

It would be invidious to commence any outline of primary teaching and learning without an indication of some significant principles that underpin much of primary education. Drawing on a range of texts on ideological, epistemological, psychological and sociological analyses of primary education, Morrison and Ridley[1] suggest that there are several key principles that constitute primary practice:

1 A view of childhood as a state in itself as well as a preparation for adulthood.
2 The use of discovery methods and practical activity.
3 Learning by doing – practical activity.
4 Problem-solving approaches to teaching and learning.
5 Learning in various modes – enactive, iconic, symbolic.
6 Integration and unity of experiences; the integrated curriculum.
7 The value of teaching processes and skills as well as products and bodies of knowledge.
8 The value of content and process as complementary facets of curricular knowledge.
9 A view of educational activities and processes as being intrinsically worthwhile as well as having instrumental and utility value.
10 The value of an enriching social, emotional and physical environment.
11 The need to develop autonomy in children.
12 The provision of a curriculum which demonstrates and allows for

breadth, balance, relevance, continuity and progression, differentiation and consistency.

13　The emphasis given to individual needs, abilities, interests, learning styles and rates as well as a received curriculum.

14　The fostering and satisfaction of curiosity.

15　The value of peer-group support.

16　The value of self-expression.

17　The need for intrinsic as well as extrinsic motivation.

18　The use of the environment to promote learning.

19　The importance of the quality and intensity of a child's experience.

20　The uniqueness of each child.

21　The view of the teacher as a catalyst for all forms of development.

22　An extended view of the 'basics' to comprehend all curriculum areas, not just the three Rs.

23　The need to develop literacy and numeracy through cross-curricular approaches.

We ought to say straight away that this view is not uncontentious. In an important book on primary education theory, Alexander[2] argues for a much more sober examination of integrated curricula, the principle of one teacher to one class for all subjects and the notion of child-centred education. Indeed, in a later work[3] he argues that debates about primary education ought to be stripped of their ideological affiliations and persuasions in order to look more closely at what primary children are actually doing and learning in classrooms and how this can be rendered more efficient and effective.

This view was echoed in the influential document *Curriculum Organisation and Classroom Practice in Primary Schools*[4] in which the three authors (one of whom was Alexander) state that they wish to distance themselves 'as firmly from mindless iconoclasm as from mindless orthodoxy' (p. 10). The authors proscribed the type of education debate that crudely polarised primary education, e.g. as traditional *versus* progressive education or as child-centred *versus* subject-centred curricula, arguing that this misrepresented the complexity of teaching in primary classrooms.

In that spirit they argued that there was a need to look again at the value of topic work, extended group work, the principle of one teacher to one class, different curriculum activities taking place simultaneously in classrooms, in order to judge dispassionately the effectiveness and efficiency of children's learning in school. They advocated a reconsideration of the value of subject teaching, whole-class teaching, undertaking activities in fewer curriculum areas simultaneously, more direct instruction by teachers (e.g. rather than the extended use of worksheets and resource-based learning), and a reduction of the number of teaching and learning strategies that are used in a single session. Indeed, they argued that, though topic approaches could be defended if they demonstrated progression and continuity, 'a national curriculum conceived in terms of distinct subject areas makes it impossible to defend a non-differentiated curriculum'[5] and that 'the introduction of the national curriculum means, however, that a substantial amount of separate subject teaching will be necessary if every aspect of each programme is to be covered effectively'.[6] More recently, Lee and Croll[7] report that streaming and subject teaching are back on the primary agenda, particularly for Key Stage 2 children. In a survey that they carried out in two local authorities they found that over a third of the headteachers involved claimed to see value in streaming and just under a third saw value in subject-specialist teaching, particularly in schools of over 300 children. The debate about subject teaching and topic work has been introduced in Part II. The other issues here will be addressed later in this section. Suffice it here to say that primary teaching is subject to intense educational and political debate.

The children

In this brief review of the children you will be teaching in primary schools, we concentrate on two features: first, the arousal of interest, and second, building up a profile of the class(es) to be taught both collectively and individually.

An important concept to be borne in mind at all levels of teaching and learning is that of *motivation*, and its relevance to the primary classroom in particular needs to be kept well to the fore during teaching-practice periods. Dean[8] has identified a number of factors that can be capitalised upon by the enterprising teacher. There is first the matter of *inner need*. In addition to basic needs for food, drink, warmth and shelter, etc., there are a number of emotional and psychological needs such as love, self-esteem, the desire for recognition and responsibility, etc. All these are underpinned by the fundamental desire to learn. Second, there is the stimulus to interest that comes from *first-hand experience*. Being involved with activities and tasks is itself highly motivating, and such involvement can be enhanced by making use of the senses – sight, sound, touch and smell in particular. Third, motivation can be generated by creating a *stimulating environment*. One of the many positive characteristics of British primary schools has been the imaginative and attractive environments created by class teachers. Decoration, lighting, room arrangement, notice boards and displays have all figured prominently in this connection. Fourth, Dean stresses the importance of *problem-solving* as a means of stimulating children's interests. As she says, 'Problem solving or mastering a skill is an enjoyable human activity ... (and) part of your task as a teacher is to try to offer your children opportunities to work out ideas and tackle problems within their capacity.'[9] The fifth factor is *competition*. Where this is used sensibly it can be an effective incentive to work and to achieve. The important point here is to stress the learning aspect. Self-competition is particularly favoured in this context as the more undesirable features of competition between children are absent. The sixth and final factor, *self-improvement*, is related to self-competition. As Dean comments, 'If you can help a child to identify a set of short-term targets for him to reach, his own natural desire for improvement will support his learning.'[10]

Such motivational factors as these can be all the more effective when you *know your children*. In Part II, we looked at the sort of information to collect during preliminary visits, including the collation of relevant information on the classes you will be teaching. All this seems to be particularly appropriate when you are teaching in primary schools. Dean[11] gives sound advice in this connection and although she has qualified teachers in mind, her suggestions are highly pertinent to student teachers embarking on teaching practice. Thus, she recommends that one should:

1 *Study the children's records and profiles for factual information*: Examine the evidence for general ability, high ability and low ability and especially for marked differences between ability and attainment. Look for information on any physical disabilities like poor eyesight, hearing problems, or difficulties with co-ordination. Make a note of children with learning difficulties and of home factors which may affect a child's behaviour and/or performance.

2 *Talk to the class teacher(s) whose class(es) you will be teaching*: Again, ask for and make a note of factual information on work done. Find out what teaching methods have been used and how effective they are. Information on particular children should be requested, e.g. very high ability, low ability, problem children, children not realising their potential, those who have special skills, etc. In this respect, children with learning difficulties should be identified. A teacher's advice on how to deal with problem cases should always be heeded.

3 *Make the fullest use of your preliminary visits*: Dean suggests you should get the feel of a class or group and note how they respond *as a group*, e.g. to questions, instructions. If possible, talk to some of the children and find out what they have been doing. Examine their work. In particular, Dean recommends that you look for anything unusual, e.g. the child whose work is poor but who has good ideas, children with unusual ideas or viewpoints.

Such detailed scrutiny will enable you to identify broadly three groups of children: *the most able*; *the main body of the class*; *and those with low ability or learning problems*. As Dean notes, 'This is very relevant information for preliminary planning and provides the framework for further investigation of the individuals with problems and those who are exceptionally able.' By keeping a file on each child when you start teaching, your detailed record of work and progress will assist you in lesson planning as well as with your theoretical studies at college.

The teachers

We look here at two aspects of the teacher in the primary school: his or her role and functions, and the knowledge and skills required.

The role and function of the teacher have become increasingly diffuse in recent years and his or her close involvement with society at large means that changes and developments taking place in it directly affect him or her. Two features especially in contemporary Britain make the teacher's role ever more demanding; these are the nature of society itself and developments in technology. As society becomes more complex and its values more pluralistic, so the ensuing changes rebound on the teacher, thus widening the area of his or her responsibilities. And already the role of the teacher has taken on a new dimension with the introduction of computers and microelectronics. In the eyes of the general public, however, the teacher's job is still 'to teach' a broadly agreed body of knowledge and skills and project a set of values that characterise the dominant culture. As Dean[12] says in this regard:

> Society gives teachers the task of mediating the curriculum for each child. Only some parts of the curriculum are clearly defined, but the principle of a remit to teachers still obtains. Any school or teacher attempting something which differs widely from the expectations of the community the school serves will be made aware of this very quickly.

Some of the features of the role and function of the teacher in the primary classroom can be itemised thus:

1 *Manager*: he or she is there to manage the total learning environment. This involves the children as individuals and as a group, the learning programme, the environment and resources.
2 *Observer*: his or her ultimate effectiveness depends on an ability to scrutinise the children closely, their actions, reactions and interactions.
3 *Diagnostician*: as an integral part of observing this involves identifying the strengths and weaknesses of each child and devising programmes accordingly.
4 *Educator*: this involves deciding on aims and objectives, the nature and content of the curriculum and the learning programme.
5 *Organiser*: this entails organising the learning programme once its nature has been specified.
6 *Decision-maker*: choosing appropriate learning materials, deciding on topics and projects, and individual programmes.
7 *Presenter*: this involves the teacher as expositor, narrator, questioner, explainer and instigator of discussions.
8 *Communicator*: implied in the role of presenter, it also involves talking to other members of staff.
9 *Facilitator*: an important aspect of the teacher's work, acting as a mediator between the child or class and the problem in hand.

10 *Motivator*: another important feature of the role entails arousing and sustaining interest.

11 *Counsellor*: in this role the teacher advises on a whole range of problems and issues – educational, personal, social and emotional.

12 *Evaluator*: a crucially professional aspect of the teacher's job, this involves evaluating, assessing and recording children's ability, achievement and progress.

It must seem fairly straightforward drawing up a list of this nature, but the teacher's role and function are not without their difficulties. In Box 35 we list a number of dilemmas identified by Pollard and Tann with which teachers are often presented. They are not easily resolved and often it is a matter of trying to minimise the tension generated by them.

To perform effectively the kinds of roles just listed, the teacher needs to possess an impressive body of knowledge and a considerable range of skills. Dean and Pollard and Tann have identified the more important of these as:

1 *Self-knowledge*: This entails an awareness of your strengths and weaknesses. It is a particularly valuable kind of knowledge to possess when working in the primary school where teachers are expected to teach many things.

2 *Open-mindedness*: This term is used by Pollard and Tann in the sense of 'being willing to reflect upon ourselves and to challenge our assumptions, prejudices and ideologies as well as those of others'.

3 *A personal philosophy*: This can take quite a practical form. As Dean says, 'What you need are thought-out aims and objectives which you can use for assessing your work and for deciding on approach and materials.' Those who have a clear idea of their destination are more likely to arrive there.

4 *Child development*: A good grounding in the theories of child development is essential. These will include theories on intellectual, physical, emotional and social development, as well as on individual differences.

5 *How children learn*: The key concepts and topics here are motivation, theories of learning, the use of rewards and punishments, and the relation between language and experience.

6 *Group behaviour*: As teaching is concerned with handling groups, some awareness of group dynamics is helpful. Dean poses the following questions in this regard: What am I doing to teach children how to work together? Have I got the balance between competition and co-operating about right? Do any of my children cheat in order to win? Is this because there is too much competition? Would rather more competition stimulate some of the most able in the class?

7 *Subject knowledge*: Although a teacher needs to be on top of his or her material, this can sometimes be difficult for the primary teacher who is expected to know a great deal. Indeed, OFSTED[13] found that a teacher's

Box 35

Common dilemmas faced by teachers

Treating each child as a 'whole person'.	Treating each child primarily as a 'pupil'.
Organising the children on an individual basis.	Organising the children as a class.
Giving children a degree of control over their use of time, their activities and their work standards.	Tightening control over children's use of time, their activities and their work standards.
Seeking to motivate the children through intrinsic involvement and enjoyment of activities.	Offering reasons and rewards so that children are extrinsically motivated to tackle tasks.
Developing and negotiating the curriculum from an appreciation of children's interests.	Providing a curriculum which children are deemed to need and which 'society' expects them to receive.
Attempting to integrate various elements of the curriculum.	Dealing systematically with each discrete area of the curriculum.
Aiming for quality in school-work.	Aiming for quantity in school-work.
Focusing on basic skills or on cognitive development.	Focusing on expressive or creative areas of the curriculum.
Trying to build up co-operative and social skills.	Developing self-reliance and self-confidence in individuals.
Inducting the children into a common culture.	Accepting the variety of cultures in a multi-ethnic society.
Allocating teacher time, attention and resources equally among all the children.	Paying attention to the special needs of particular children.
Maintaining consistent rules and understandings about behaviour and school-work.	Being flexible and responsive to particular situations.
Presenting oneself formally to the children.	Relaxing with the children or having a laugh with them.
Working with 'professional' application and care for the children.	Working with consideration of one's personal needs.

Source Pollard and Tann[14]

subject knowledge was very strongly associated with high standards of students' achievements. There may be some areas where his or her expertise is slim and this can sometimes be made worse when an individual child undertakes a topic or project in an unfamiliar area. In such circumstances, where a teacher may feel vulnerable, Dean recommends (1) identifying areas in which he or she feels secure and working with them; (2) using other people's expertise – colleagues', parents', perhaps that of outsiders like the local policeman; and (3) making use of school broadcasting.

The issue of teachers' subject knowledge is topical in the current primary debate and is coupled with the issues of curriculum leadership and teachers' roles in the school. During the 1980s a series of government documents[15] had questioned whether newly qualified and experienced class teachers had sufficient subject knowledge to be able to match work to different abilities, particularly at the upper end of the primary school. HMI had reported since the 1970s that there was a close relationship between a teacher's subject knowledge and the quality of his or her teaching.[16] In the section of their report that is perhaps aptly titled 'The Problem of Curricular Expertise' Alexander et al.[17] argue that 'subject knowledge is a critical factor at every point in the teaching process: in planning, assessing and diagnosing, task setting, questioning, explaining and giving feedback. The key question to be answered is whether the class-teacher system makes impossible demands on the subject knowledge of the generalist primary teacher.' Bennett[18] and Pollard et al.[19] reported that the introduction of the national curriculum had exacerbated teacher stress and that, in part, this was caused by teachers' insufficient subject knowledge.

The outcomes of these debates on subject knowledge can be seen in the increased in-service activities designed to increase teachers' subject knowledge and, more relevant for student teachers, to have specific teachers in the school responsible for curriculum leadership in designated curriculum areas. The student teacher may find it useful to contact the curriculum co-ordinators and curriculum leaders in the teaching-practice school. Morrison[20] argued that subject teaching and curriculum leadership on a subject-specific basis might be very useful because curriculum leaders would possess:

- academic knowledge;
- professional and pedagogic knowledge (experience of how to teach the subject effectively, based on knowledge of how children learn in the subject, how to diagnose children's needs and to plan subsequent curricula and learning pathways for them, how to assess children's performance, how to plan for progression and continuity in the subject);
- awareness of the latest developments and resources in the subject;
- enthusiasm for the subject.

This view was echoed by Alexander et al.[21] when they advocated four broad teaching roles for primary teachers, outlined in Part I:

- 'the *Generalist* who teaches most or all of the curriculum, probably specialising in age-range rather than subject, and does not profess specialist subject knowledge for consultancy'.
- 'the *Generalist/Consultant* who combines a generalist role in part with cross-school co-ordination, advice and support in one or more subjects'.
- 'the *Semi-Specialist* who teaches his/her subject, but who also has a generalist and/or consultancy role'.
- 'the *Specialist* who teaches his/her subject full-time.'

In a follow-up report to Alexander *et al.*,[22] OFSTED found that in over 80 per cent of schools the teachers were generalists, with semi-specialist teaching being undertaken in 15 per cent of schools and the only specialist teaching being undertaken by bought-in part-time teachers. The student teacher will need to find out how curriculum leadership is exercised in the school so that he or she can approach the most appropriate teacher(s) in the school with regard to his or her own planning and implementation of schemes and activities.

Dean and Pollard and Tann identify a number of specific skills an effective teacher requires. These include: observing and interpreting children's behaviour; organisation and control; communication skills; planning skills; problem-solving skills; analytical skills; and evaluative skills. For further detail, consult the authors quoted.

The curriculum

We have seen how the teacher is responsible for 'mediating the curriculum'. Increasingly in recent years curricula in state education have been based upon formally and explicitly stated aims and numerous individuals and official bodies have produced exhaustive compilations of them. The Schools Council *Primary Practice*,[23] for example, has produced a comprehensive set of aims for educational practice in this area. According to these, it is desirable that primary children should be able:

1 to read fluently and accurately, with understanding, feeling and discrimination;
2 to develop a legible style of handwriting and satisfactory standards of spelling, syntax, punctuation and usage;
3 to communicate clearly and confidently in speech and writing, in ways appropriate for various occasions and purposes;
4 to listen attentively and with understanding;
5 to learn how to acquire information from various sources, and to record information and findings in various ways;
6 to apply computational skills with speed and accuracy;
7 to understand the applications of mathematical ideas in various situations in home, classroom, school and local area;

8 to observe living and inanimate things, and to recognise characteristics such as pattern and order;
9 to master basic scientific ideas;
10 to investigate solutions and interpret evidence, to analyse and solve problems;
11 to develop awareness of self and sensitivity to others, acquire a set of moral values and the confidence to make and hold to moral judgements, and develop habits of self-discipline and acceptable behaviour;
12 to know about geographical, historical and social aspects of the local environment and the national heritage, to be aware of other times and places, and to recognise links between local, national and international events;
13 to acquire sufficient control of self or of tools, equipment and instruments to be able to use music, drama and several forms of arts and crafts as means of expression;
14 to develop agility and physical co-ordination, confidence in and through physical activity, and the ability to express feeling through movement.

More recently, Pollard et al.[24] found that teachers stated six main aims:

• obedience to parents, teachers and all reasonable authority;
• moral and social development;
• acquiring respect for their own and others' property;
• becoming fitted for an occupational role in society;
• developing kindness and consideration for others.

This resonated with the educational aims identified by Ashton et al.[25] two decades previously. However, the teachers in Pollard et al. also introduced a new feature – 'achieving as many attainment targets as possible for each child'.[26] The authors argue that there has been a move away from teachers' aims in the early 1990s which has emphasised social, personal and academic concerns: (a) developing children's full potential; (b) being happy and well-balanced; (c) having their interest in learning aroused; (d) developing self-confidence; (e) being kind and considerate. In other words, there has been a shift towards much more societal and instrumental goals.[27] This echoes the aims of education set out in the 1988 Education Act, where the curriculum '(a) promotes the spiritual, moral, cultural, mental and physical development of pupils at the school and of society, and (b) prepares such pupils for the opportunities, responsibilities and experiences of adult life', itself embodying in statute the view expressed in the Consultation Report on the national curriculum which stated that a curriculum should equip students 'with the knowledge, skills and understandings that they need for adult life and employment'.[28]

In the course of initial visits to the school and during teaching practice itself, the student teacher will need to find out as much as he or she can about the way the curriculum is organised in the school as a whole and how his or her particular class fits into the school scheme. The following points may assist the student teacher in this respect:

1   Find out the school's approach to the curriculum. Is the emphasis on direct teaching, for example, or on discovery learning? Or is there a balance between them?
2   What teaching styles are used in the school and do all the teachers adopt the same approach?
3   Do the teachers work together at any point in the week?
4   How are the teaching groups organised?
5   What is done for children with special educational needs and for those with physical handicaps?
6   Do specialist teachers visit the school?
7   What is the school's relationship with the parents? Are they encouraged to visit the school?
8   What are the approaches to individual subjects?

A framework for analysing curriculum tasks is provided by perceiving them in terms of *knowledge*, *concepts*, *skills* and *attitudes*. Pollard and Tann[29] define these terms as follows:

- *Knowledge* The selection of that which is worth knowing and of interest.
- *Concepts* The generalisations and ideas which enable pupils to classify, organise and predict – to understand patterns, relationships and meanings, e.g. continuity/change, cause/consequence, interdependence/adaptation, sequence/duration, nature/purpose, authenticity, power, energy . . .
- *Skills* The capacity or competence to perform a task, e.g. person/social (turn-taking, sharing), physical/practical (fine/gross motor skills), intellectual (observing, identifying, sorting/classifying, hypothesising, reasoning, testing, imagining and evaluating), communication (oracy, literacy, numeracy, graphicacy), etc.
- *Attitudes* The overt expression of values and personal qualities, e.g. curiosity, perseverance, initiative, open-mindedness, trust, honesty, responsibility, respect, confidence, etc.

The authors explain that analytical activities are useful for three reasons: (a) the breadth and balance of curriculum provision can be examined; (b) such activities enable teachers to think accurately about what they are doing; and (c) they provide a framework within which children's learning can be evaluated. For further information on the curriculum in the primary school, consult the DES publication, *The Curriculum from 5 to 16*.[30]

CLASSROOM ORGANISATION

The way one organises one's classroom, especially the primary classroom, exerts a powerful influence on both teaching and learning. Furthermore, the organisation must be seen to relate to the school's/teacher's philosophy, curricular aims, teaching and learning methods and interpersonal relationships. Four features of classroom organisation are especially relevant to the student teacher on teaching practice. They are: *the organisation of the pupils*; *the physical environment*; *the use of space*; and *resources*.

The organisation of the children

There are many ways of organising children, e.g. teaching them as a complete class or dividing the class into a number of groups. There are a number of forms of interaction between teacher and pupils and among pupils themselves which may be found in school learning situations. The particular one operating at any given moment will depend upon the objective of the lesson, the nature of the task in hand and the implied educational philosophy. We now consider six characteristic learning situations which account for the principal patterns of interaction, both formal and informal, which may be found in the context of the school. Our analysis is based upon the work of Oeser.[31]

Situation 1: the teacher-centred lesson

The principle of interaction underlying the teacher-centred situation may be illustrated as in Example 1. Although only five pupils are represented in the diagram, this figure may vary, with perhaps a notional thirty pupils being a more representative number in this kind of situation.

Example 1

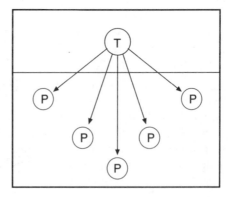

The interaction pattern here is one in which the *teacher speaks and the pupils listen*. As Oeser notes, their relationship to him or her is confined to listening, perceiving and assimilating; and there is no interaction among the pupils themselves.

A social structure of this kind is found in its pure form in a radio or television broadcast. In a school context, it is found in the *talk* or *lecture* where there is a sharp distinction between the teacher and the class (depicted in the diagram by a continuous horizontal line), and in which the teacher's role is authoritarian, exhortatory and directive. This kind of interaction style may also form *part* of a class lesson as, for instance, at the outset when the teacher introduces new learning, or in the course of a lesson when he or she demonstrates a skill, or towards the end of a lesson when he or she sums up what has gone before. Preparation for a formal examination would present occasions when the teacher-centred approach would be an efficient means of teaching and learning.

Situation 2: the lecture-discussion

The second situation may be seen as a variant of the first, being one in which the pattern of interaction is not wholly dominated by the teacher. It is represented diagrammatically in Example 2. Again, the number of pupils may vary, depending upon the circumstances.

Example 2

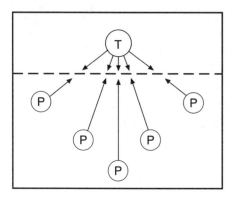

Oeser points out that three of the most important aims of the educator are: to turn the latent leadership of a group in the direction of the educational process; to encourage the individual development of leadership; and to encourage co-operative striving towards common goals while discouraging the exercise of authoritarian leadership. The social structures evolving through situations 2, 3, 4 and 5 provide a framework for the achievement of these aims.

The arrowheads in the diagram indicate more or less continuous verbal interaction between teacher and pupils. Although as leader the teacher asks questions, and receives and gives answers, the initiative need not always be his or hers; and competition may develop among the pupils. The sharp distinction between teacher and taught which was an important feature of the first situation and which was represented in Example 1 by means of a continuous horizontal line is now less obvious – hence the broken horizontal line in Example 2.

This kind of learning situation, the pattern of interaction depicted in Example 1, could develop into the pattern illustrated in Example 2.

Situation 3: active learning

Example 3 depicts a social situation in which the teacher allows discussion and mutual help between pupils.

Example 3

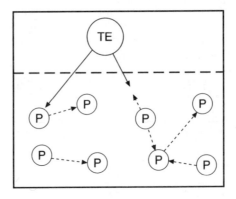

Practical work in a science lesson would be an occasion for this kind of situation. The letters TE in the diagram indicate that the teacher now begins to assume the additional role of expert. As Oeser notes: 'He, of course, retains his other roles as well; but the emphasis in the teaching process now fluctuates between the needs established by the task and the needs of the individual pupils.'[32] For this reason, the situation may be described as *task-* and *pupil-centred* and as one beginning to have a co-operative structure.

Situation 4: active learning; independent planning

Scrutiny of Example 4 shows how this fourth situation evolves logically from the preceding one. The pupils are now active in small groups, and the teacher acts more or less exclusively as an expert-consultant (indicated in the diagram by a wavy line).

As Oeser says: 'Groups map out their work, adapt to each other's pace, discuss their difficulties and agree on solutions. There is independent

Example 4

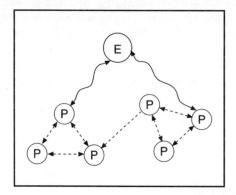

exploration, active learning and a maximal development of a task-directed leadership in each group.'[33] The social climate is co-operative and the situation may be described as *pupil-* and *task-centred*.

Situation 5: task-centred group

A characteristic situation in which a smallish group of individuals is concerned with a particular topic, project or problem, is illustrated in Example 5.

Example 5

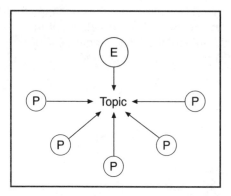

A pattern of this kind may thus be found in a seminar or discussion session. The arrowheads indicate that the group as a whole is concerned with the task – its elucidation, clarification and solution.

The situation is clearly a *task-centred* one in which there is an absence of hierarchical structure. Ideally, the role of the teacher here is simply that of a wise and experienced member of the group (depicted as 'expert' in the diagram). The more coercive roles traditionally associated with the teacher are out of place in this kind of social structure. The attitudes of members of the group to each other will tend to be co-operative and consultative.

Situation 6: independent working; no interaction

This final situation, illustrated in Example 6, arises when pupils are working quite independently and there is no interaction.

Example 6

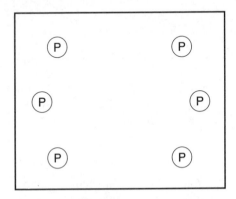

This situation will occur when pupils are working at exercises 'on their own', or in a formal examination session.

In summary, Oeser observes that from situation 1 to 4 there is a progressive change from teacher-centred through task-centred to pupil-centred activities, from passive to active learning and from minimal to maximal participation, with a progressive diminution of the coerciveness of the teacher's roles. In situation 5, the situation is again task-centred, but the teacher's status as such has disappeared.

The six situations outlined above will help the reader not only to understand classroom-based social and learning situations, but also patterns of interaction occurring outside the classroom.

It is of great importance that the student teacher should be aware of the sort of situation he or she wants in a lesson, or at a particular point in it. This will be chiefly determined by his or her lesson objectives, together with the kinds of factors isolated by Oeser which will contribute to defining the overall situation. These include: (1) high–low teacher dominance; (2) large–small number of pupils; (3) high–low academic level of class; (4) active–passive pupil participation; (5) individual–co-operative effort; (6) contentious–non-contentious material; (7) strong–weak needs; (8) task and learning oriented–examination oriented; and (9) directing–helping (counselling).

In writing of the whole-class approach, Pollard and Tann say:

Such opportunities may give the teacher a chance to demonstrate discussion techniques, encourage collaborative learning and stimulate children's thinking by exploring ideas, asking more questions, sharing common problems and encouraging children to join in trying to solve them. However, if classwork is used too extensively, it may pose a severe strain on both the teacher and the listener, for it is very difficult to match the instruction appropriately to each child's different needs without sufficient individual consultation.

Alexander et al.[34] argued that whole-class teaching could 'provide the order, control, purpose and concentration which many critics believe are lacking in modern primary classrooms'. This echoes the research by Galton et al.[35] in the 1980s which showed that whole-class teaching encouraged 'solitary workers' (students working largely on their own although they interact with the teacher and their peers) and 'concentration'; this type of learning style produced the highest degree of time on task in their study (77.1 per cent). Alexander et al. went on to suggest that 'whole class teaching is associated with higher-order questioning, explanations and statements, and these, in turn, correlate with higher levels of pupil performance. Teachers with a substantial commitment to whole class teaching appear, moreover, to be particularly effective in teaching the basic subjects.'[36] Further, this style of teaching accords with their view that 'there are many circumstances in which it is more appropriate to tell than to ask, clearly an advocacy of a more didactic and instructional style of teaching'. This lies uneasily with the notion of differentiation that the same authors advocate and creates potential problems for teachers of children in the early years, where group work has been seen (and shown) to be a positive and valuable teaching strategy.

Group work, too, needs to be planned carefully. Even the most child-centred classroom needs planning; indeed it is a truism to say that the more diverse, complex and 'devolved' on to children is the learning process, the more planned, structured and carefully organised it has to be by the teacher, or else behaviour problems and inefficient learning may result. This echoes the important early study of primary schools by Sharp and Green[37] and the argument from Bernstein[38] that there are 'visible' and 'invisible' pedagogies in schools, neither of which neglects the need for planning. The freer the classroom apparently seems to be, the more carefully it has to be planned and structured.

The several claimed attractions of group work are summarised by Morrison and Ridley,[39] Box 36.

Bennett and Dunne[40] regard group work as an acceptable and manageable compromise between whole-class work and wholly individualised work; the former is seen as unacceptable because it is undifferentiated, the latter is seen as unworkable because there are insufficient resources of time, materials and teaching staff to render this practicable. Indeed, Alexander et al.[42] argue for the need to strike a balance between whole-class and completely

Box 36

Advantages of group work:

helps children to work co-operatively;
enables students to learn from one another;
encourages the involvement of all children;
removes the stigma of failure from children;
enables the teacher to circulate more easily round the class;
enables children to work at their own pace;
enables children to respect others' strengths and weaknesses;
affords children access to scarce equipment;
facilitates collaborative work;
facilitates the integrated day (see below);
encourages joint decision-making;
affords children the opportunity to exercise leadership;
stimulates the development of autonomy, resourcefulness and self-esteem;
focuses on processes as well as products;
promotes high-order thinking;[41]
is particularly effective for problem-solving activities;
promotes mutual integration of children from all ethnic groups;
encourages children to engage the problem of disagreement;
improves discussion and classroom talk.

---

individualised work; they argue that children need experience of class, group and individual work. Pollard *et al.*[43] found that this balance was being struck in about 50 per cent of the classrooms investigated.

Group work is a pedagogical strategy and not simply a seating arrangement. In a much-publicised piece of research, Galton *et al.*[44] found that although primary children sat in groups they in fact worked on their own; there was little collaborative work undertaken for a single, whole-group outcome. One implication of this is that the student teacher must plan tasks, activities and routines which foster and promote interactive learning.[45] This is a significant feature if discipline and good behaviour are to be promoted in classes. Accepting that grouping is a pedagogical device requires the student teacher to be very clear on its purposes and to ensure that the children themselves understand those purposes.

There are limits to the advantages of group work. For example, putting children into groups could replace 'task-enhancing' talk with lower-level 'task-related' talk.[46] Dunne and Bennett[47] found that students of all abilities improved their skills of discussion, suggesting, concluding, testing, inferring and reflecting when working in mixed-ability groups, and that they improved in terms of both co-operation and independence. Bennett and Dunne[48] found that if group work was directed towards a genuinely collaborative activity then task-related activity was very high.

Time will need to be spent on ensuring that children understand the 'rules of the game' in group work (e.g. about talking, moving, allotting tasks) or even on making it clear to children that co-operation is permitted! Cohen[49] argues that students need to know what is involved in co-operation, e.g. listening, explaining, supporting, summarising, sharing ideas. Indeed, Hall[50] demonstrates that children need to become aware of the purposes behind different approaches to learning, particularly when they are being asked to learn through small-group discussion. Without this awareness, he argues, they do not value the various approaches to learning. This is echoed by Harwood,[51] who demonstrated that the presence of the teacher correlated with improved effectiveness of learning in group working where the teacher stimulated the students, elaborated on their ideas, and controlled group dymanics, e.g. avoiding fragmentation of groups, dominance of one student, and scape-goating.

Dunne and Bennett[52] suggest that students need to be told explicitly that they must ask other members of the group for help before coming to the teacher. They also suggest that teachers will have to consider carefully the type of task that groups undertake in order to anticipate the types of demands that will be made on teachers.

There is a significant literature to suggest that students need to be 'trained' in group-work skills. Dunne and Bennett[53] argue that these include: knowledge of acceptable behaviour; listening; questioning; clarifying and challenging skills; posing problems and deciding what to do. Echoing Dunne and Bennett, Harwood argues that teachers need to spend time in the early stages of group work on developing communication skills: listening, asking, explaining, supporting, checking for consensus, providing evidence. Cohen argues that students need to review how successfully they themselves, as a group, are working co-operatively. McAllister[54] extends this point by suggesting that students benefit from analysing their own work and giving feedback to each other in groups. Cohen argues that teachers too need to give feedback to students on how successfully they are working together. McAllister is unequivocal in suggesting that discussion and detailed planning are critical for successful group work, and that these should be stressed very early. Galvin et al.[55] report that, though children work well in groups when the teacher works with them, the level of activity drops to around 50 per cent when the group is working without the teacher.

Further, Mortimore et al.[56] found that whilst group work might be effective if all the groups were working in one or two curriculum areas only (e.g. everyone doing mathematics that is differentiated by task), where three or more curriculum areas were taking place simultaneously children's learning was inefficient. This view was echoed unequivocally by Alexander et al.[57] Too many curriculum areas occurring simultaneously created a level of complexity in organisation and implementation which detracted from efficient learning and efficient use of the teacher – procedural and managerial talk replaced instructional and pedagogical talk. Indeed, Bennett and Dunne suggested that teachers would have to ensure that they made abstract demands as well as action-oriented demands in group work, particularly in the areas of science, technology and mathematics. Pollard et al.[58] reported that teachers who implemented group work involved themselves heavily with low-attaining children: twice as much as they did with high attainers.

There are certain problems with group work. For example, children organised into groups may not see work as their first priority; checking on what a group is doing can sometimes be difficult, especially when it is working independently; and actually organising the groups can be difficult – what principles of organisation does one go by?

Guidance here can be found in Pollard and Tann and Pollard et al., who show how the criteria devised by Kerry and Sands[59] can help to overcome some of the obstacles. The criteria in question are:

1   *Age groups*: These can be useful for some activities, though because of the spread of ability, achievement and interests, etc., they can sometimes be counterproductive when it comes to teaching some subjects.
2   *Attainment groups*: These are useful for well-defined tasks which fit the ability of the children. However, Pollard and Tann consider that they can be divisive if used permanently.
3   *Interest groups*: Grouping children according to interest is always useful and has definite social advantages when there are differences of one sort or another between the children, e.g. race or social class.
4   *Friendship groups*: One of the commonest forms of grouping, these go down well with the children and are a valuable means of social education. However, the teacher must bear in mind the needs of those children who do not mix well.
5   *Convenience groups*: These are used for organisational rather than primarily educational purposes.
6   *Mixed attainment groups* (discussed in more detail later, see p. 202).
7   *Gender groups* (single sex or both sexes).

Pollard et al.[60] found that in 1990 and 1992 80 per cent of teachers grouped children by attainment levels, particularly in mathematics and other curricular areas where differentiation by task was required (e.g. English). Mixed-attainment groups and friendship groups were employed for some of the time, particularly when differentiation by outcome was operating. They reported a decrease in mixed-age groupings – even in rural schools – and a very low incidence of gender-based groups. This study echoed the earlier findings of Bennett and Kell[61] and Kagan.[62] The under-representation of gender-based groups is probably welcome, as Bennett and Dunne[63] found that if a girl was put into a group that comprised mostly boys the amount of participation by girls was reduced and the amount of higher-level talk diminished. Significantly, Pollard *et al.* noted the increase in the amount of grouping by attainment that had occurred since the inception of the national curriculum.

Successful grouping occurs when 'fitness for purpose' is demonstrated. Bennett and Dunne report that group work proceeds optimally when groups comprise no more than four children and where groups are involved in a whole-class activity that includes reporting-back sessions. They define different types of co-operative group work: (a) where children work together on an element of a 'joint' outcome – the 'jigsaw' model; (b) where children work together on a whole task for a whole – joint – outcome; (c) where children work alone for their own individual outcomes but share resources. The latter, of course, is a very limited view of group work. Kagan suggests that having groups of odd numbers is dangerous – a group of three quickly becomes a dyad with an odd one out; a group of five again risks having an odd one out. Further, Dunne and Bennett[64] found that groups of five and six tended to splinter into smaller subgroups.

When organising classes into groups the chief criterion to remember is that of *balance*. As Pollard and Tann say, 'Each group has a different purpose and a specific potential and therefore its own place in the primary classroom.'

Where individual children are chosen to lead groups, as with older children, your expectations have to be explained and the requisite skills developed. Dean has identified five relevant tasks: (1) *Getting ideas from the group* – these then need to be organised and appropriate follow-up action planned. (2) *Allocating tasks* – once ideas have been shaped, tasks can be allocated. Dean recommends *asking* who should do what. (3) *Pacing the work* – monitoring progress involves helping tardy ones to catch up and re-directing early finishers. (4) *Providing encouragement and support* – leaders need to be made aware of this important part of their task. (5) *Fitting it all together* – this involves seeing how the parts fit together and deciding on final presentation. See Dean and Pollard and Tann for further information. In approaching group work a series of questions need to be considered by the student teacher:

1 On what basis will the children be grouped?
2 How permanent is the group?
3 Who will or will not work efficiently with whom if placed in the same group?
4 How long will different groups have to complete the same/different tasks (i.e. what will the student teacher plan for those who finish quickly/ slowly)?
5 Will there be a group leader?
6 Exactly what will each member of the group be required to do – are there enough tasks for each member of the group to be usefully engaged? How will each child know exactly what is expected of her/him?
7 How will the student teacher use himself/herself and intervene most

efficiently, providing instructional and cognitive talk as well as procedural and managerial talk?

8 How will group sessions begin? (i.e. will some children be waiting whilst
the student teacher sets others working; which children can be relied upon
to wait patiently?)

9 How will sessions be rounded off (rather than simply stop for want of
time)?

10 How will reporting back to the whole class be undertaken?

11 What will be done with children who do not wish to work together or who
do not wish to work in any group?

12 What will be done if a child disagrees with a group decision and becomes
uncooperative and uninterested?

McAllister[65] argues that in the early stages of group work students benefit
from being able to work with friends of their own choice. Morrison and
Ridley[66] suggest a seven-stage sequence in introducing and developing group
work:

Stage one   Have only one or two groups working apart from the class at any
one time while the remainder of the class is involved in class or individually
based work.

Stage two   Each group replicates the same activity.

Stage three   Each group works on the same activity or focus in a variety of
ways.

Stage four   Each group works on a variety of aspects of a topic or focus,
one aspect per group.

Stage five   Each group works on a variety of aspects of a topic or focus,
covering many key aspects; children do the planning.

Stage six   Each group works on aspects of a variety of topics or foci.

Whether group work is a resounding success or a demoralising failure is
often a function of planning with management issues in mind. The student
teacher will have to:

- avoid being too ambitious either for himself or herself or for the children;
- only attempt to have more than one curriculum area simultaneously if he
or she and the children can cope with it;
- enable children to practise being in a group (i.e. not expect wonderful
results from novice groups);
- give clear instructions;

- avoid overloading children with instructions all at once, but give instructions at various stages throughout the session;
- be vigilant and attend to the whole class rather than being completely absorbed in one group;
- talk to the class as a whole (e.g. about how well the work is going, how well they are managing to work in the group) as well as talking to groups, i.e. avoid *atomising* the classroom interactions;
- be prepared to stop everyone during the session to calm them down, make a teaching/procedural/managerial/behaviour point.

When it works well, group work can be very productive and satisfying for student teachers and children.[67] Like most moments of bliss, it is 99 per cent hard work and 1 per cent inspiration!

In planning the classroom organisation, then, we argue that the student teacher will need to be guided by the notion of 'fitness for purpose'. For example, Wheldall *et al.*[68] argue that if one wishes students to work co-operatively then a *group* seating arrangement is most appropriate, whilst *independent* work benefits from relative isolation. They argue convincingly that it amounts to cruelty to have students seated in groups and yet expect them to work independently. Further, Hastings and Schwieso[69] suggest that having students seated in rows keeps them on task effectively in individualised work by minimising the opportunities for students to have eye contact with each other and maximising the opportunities for the teacher to have eye contact with the whole class. Group seating arrangements, on the other hand, are suitable for discussions and collaborative activities.

The physical environment

Our brief comments here can be read in conjunction with the relevant parts of *The classroom environment and situational factors* later in this section. The fundamental aim with the classroom environment is to organise it in such a way as to back up whatever your educational purposes are. Most experts in this field advise that you begin by drawing a plan of your classroom, preferably to scale, adding the fixed features like doors and windows first. When you have got a more or less complete picture, you can scrutinise it in the light of your own intentions. The criteria you use could include *aesthetic* ones: do the design, layout, decoration and lighting contribute to a pleasing effect? Is the room pleasurable to be in? Is the room *functional*? Does it do what you will want it to do? Can practical work be undertaken efficiently? Is there sufficient storage? Can different activities take place simultaneously? Are there enough materials and tools? What are the *presentational* aspects like? Are the notice boards and display tables adequate to your needs? Do they achieve what they are supposed to achieve? No room is perfect, so what are the *possibilities* for further improvement? Can greater use be made of the windows, or the ceiling perhaps? Are there enough plants in the room? A particular aspect of the classroom is the extent to which space is used effectively, and it is to this we turn.

The use of space

Kerry and Tollitt[70] describe space as essentially a learning resource and state that for the infant teacher managing space is a vital skill. Much of that management, they explain, is about five principles:

1   providing opportunities for a variety of child-centred but teacher-directed activities (story time);
2   reinforcing children's more formal work through real experience or play (e.g. through display, or in the classroom shop);
3   setting up opportunities for tactile or imaginative play as an aid in itself (sand, water, building blocks);
4   making available the essential resources that pupils need in order to learn; and
5   creating an environment conducive to spontaneous learning.

It can be a useful exercise for the student teacher to work out how much is required for the various activities he or she will be organising. This will be particularly relevant to group work. It would be interesting to see what the differences are in this connection with respect to language skills, mathematics, science, environmental studies, art and craft, the expressive arts, play and religious education.

How best available space can be used can be determined by once again drawing a scale model. Dean suggests that you can go on to make scale cut-outs of the base of each of the pieces of furniture you have. This will allow you to arrange it in different ways. She also advises having different areas for different activities. These can be marked off by the appropriate use of cupboards, screens, shelves or tables. The fundamental divisions are into clean/messy activities and quiet/noisy ones. As Dean explains: 'These need to be separated in time or space. Noisy activities can be confined to a certain time of the day ...' In Box 37 Kerry and Tollitt suggest ideas to start you thinking about 'exploiting space'.

Resources

Our last feature of classroom organisation, resources, is certainly not the least. The availability and use of resources in the primary classroom are of the greatest possible importance for children's learning. Pollard and Tann have suggested four criteria that might be borne in mind when organising and arranging resources. They are of particular value to student teachers when planning lessons and activities. They are:

Box 37

Exploiting space

Floor area	Layout of tables, chairs, etc. will have an effect upon kinds of activities you can employ – think of spaces for individual work, group activity, story time and so on.
Wall space	Can this be exploited for display – of children's work, of stimulus materials, of resource materials around a topic of current concern?
Notice boards	Fixing devices can be more varied here (staple guns, pins). Possible use for more long-term items, e.g. 'word ladders' of basic vocabulary, packs of stimulus cards giving tasks for pupils with 'free' moments.
Black/ whiteboards	Up-dated display of day, date, season, clock-face, 'Word a day' reinforcement.
Storage area	Think out problems of access, cleanliness, layout. If unsightly, how can area be disguised? e.g. doorway 'dressed' as time machine, or attractively curtained.
Horizontal surfaces	Useful for equipment (magnifying glass, Lego, etc.), specimens, 3D artefacts made by children, 3D displays by teacher, plants.
Ceiling beams	In older schools it may be practical to use these as hangers for 'word trees', mobiles, etc.
Bays	Can these be pressed into service as a reading corner, a group-work area, a wet area, a project base?
Windows and views	Artwork can often be displayed effectively when back-lit by window light. Window may look out on to field, with potential for watching wildlife, or on to school yard with bird-feeder.
Wet areas	As well as supporting artwork, cookery, etc. these areas give potential for scientific experiments, volume and quantity work, keeping an aquarium, etc.
Adjacent corridor	Can be decorated to harmonise with any theme developed in the classroom, e.g. some may lend themselves to open-access bookshelves and browsing areas.
Electric points	Enable a range of audio-visual aids to be used in teaching and learning. Pupils can operate tape-recorders or simple slide viewers, so increasing potential for individual or group work, or helping non-readers.

Source Kerry and Tollitt[71]

1   *Appropriateness*: What resources are suitable as an integral part of the learning activities?
2   *Availability*: What is available within the classroom, the school, and the wider environment?
3   *Storage*: How are the resources stored? What is under teacher control and what is freely available to the children? What safety factors need to be remembered?
4   *Maintenance*: What kind of maintenance is required and who is responsible for it?

The reader might, by way of an exercise, select a typical learning activity and then decide on the resources needed using the four criteria identified by Pollard and Tann.

SOME ORGANISATIONAL CONCEPTS IN PRIMARY EDUCATION

We have already introduced in Part II the notion of subject and subject-specialist teaching in the primary school. There is no doubt that this idea has a powerful lobby from many quarters in education and the political field. Further, there is no doubt that its influence is being felt, particularly since the introduction of a subject-framed national curriculum.[72] We will not rehearse the points raised in Part II, but that is not to deny their potency or their significance in primary education today. Indeed, Blyth[73] shows that this form of primary practice has a long tradition which emanated from the elementary tradition of primary education, with an emphasis on the 'basics' and a didactic pedagogical style.

Our intention here is to trace an alternative context of primary education whose history is little shorter than the elementary tradition, *viz.* the notion of child-centred education, for example in the work of Rousseau[74] and Dewey,[75] and enshrined in the famous phrases from the Hadow Report which argued that the curriculum should be thought of in terms of activity and experience rather than knowledge to be learned and facts to be stored.[76] Child-centredness has many hues[77] – from a child-chosen curriculum to the delineation of an active, experiential and concrete form of learning. The notion of child-centred to progressive education has become almost a term of abuse or an accusation against teachers for failing to bring students to the required standards.

However, we argue that a cooler, less fundamentalist, less pejorative and less dismissive reading of child-centred education is tenable. This respects the individuality of the child (in differentiated activities), demonstrates the value of first-hand, experiential learning (implicit in constructivist psychology) which 'begins where the child is', and argues for some form of negotiation with children rather than a steamroller approach with heavy prescription. This will enable teachers to replace the ideological trappings of a romantic ideology with which progressive education has unfortunately been saddled with some enduring and important teaching principles which make for good practice regardless of one's ideological commitments.

A watershed in primary education that emphasised child-centred principles and methods was set out in the Plowden Report.[78] This report proved to be a powerful influence in advocating open schools and open education, concepts which when translated into school practice were to result in a marked shift from the more traditional view of children as learners. In spite of early enthusiasm for the ideas enshrined in this open or progressive philosophy, implementation of the complete package was to prove neither total nor enduring. The open or progressive view of education was characterised by three broad concepts – *freedom*, *activity* and *discovery* – and a concern with *process* as opposed to *content*. It was also noted for its desire to broaden concepts such as *education, learning* and *responsibility*, and it is such concepts and ideas that were to persist and exert an important influence on the organisation of primary-school practice. The emphasis on discovery learning or 'learning to learn', for example, and the highlighting of the needs of the individual child are instances of open education's more lasting influence. Likewise, stress on the value of group work. As Dean says, '[The Plowden Report's] authors saw groups as a natural social unit for primary children, which were part of the process of socialisation.' 'Openness' in terms of attitudes and sharing, and in terms of relationships between teacher and pupil, pupil and pupil, and teacher and teacher also became an increasing feature of the primary world. Some of the concepts emerging from the progressive philosophy admittedly had a certain vagueness that time has not dispelled, and consequently there is not always complete agreement on working definitions. The most we can do here is to take a small selection of the more important concepts and identify some of their characteristics.

The notion of 'open education' was reflected not only in the pedagogical styles adopted (discussed later) but in the physical layout of the school building as a whole and of age-related teaching areas in particular.[79] We are referring here, of course, to the notion of an open-plan or semi-open-plan school, wherein there is joint use of space and materials, concomitant with team teaching and very flexible groupings of children. In a fully open-plan school space is divided up by low furniture, creating bays for study; in a semi-open-plan school teaching spaces are defined by walls with openings into other areas (often shared library, art and technology areas); and flexible open-plan schools have screens and partitions that can be moved to open or close off areas at will.[80]

There are several claimed attractions of open-plan arrangements. These are summarised in Box 38. On the other hand, as with integrated teaching (discussed below), open-plan teaching is not universally popular and not always without its difficulties. These are summarised in Box 39.

Box 38

Advantages of open-plan arrangements:

Open-plan arrangements can:

1   Develop children's autonomy and responsibility (e.g. for working without too close supervision).
2   Maximise space through shared areas.
3   Move away from whole-class instruction to differentiated activities.
4   Support team planning, team teaching and team assessing.
5   Facilitate social learning and peer-group learning.
6   Reduce resource duplication.
7   Encourage co-operative work (by children and teachers).
8   Support flexible group size and membership.
9   Avoid feelings of insecurity and isolation that student teachers (and experienced teachers) may feel in more traditional 'cellular' classrooms.
10 Facilitate consistent and supportive handling of difficult children by more than one teacher.
11 Facilitate the sharing of ideas by students and teachers.

Box 39

Disadvantages of open-plan arrangements:

Open-plan arrangements can:

1   Incur much transition time.
2   Let children 'slip through the net' of being monitored.
3   Fail with uncommitted teachers.
4   Lead to wasteful use of resources.
5   Cause much noise and distraction.
6   Fail to make the most of materials and resources.
7   Lead to over-reliance on worksheets.
8   Cause discipline problems.
9   Cause problems of cover if staff are absent.
10 Cause congestion as children circulate round areas.
11 Provide inadequate display space.
12 Make personality clashes amongst teachers very visible.
13 Require much time for team planning.
14 Cause problems of supervision.

Open-plan teaching makes heavy demands on teachers and planning, echoing the issue raised by Mortimore *et al.*[81] and Alexander *et al.*[82] that having too many groups doing too many different activities in too many curriculum areas is inefficient.

Two key concepts at the heart of educational practice in open and progressive classrooms are the *integrated day* and the *integrated curriculum*, both of which play an important part in primary education today.

The *integrated day* has been described by Dearden[83] as an organisational concept, implying that 'timetables or other formalised ways of changing from one activity to another, are abandoned. Instead, the flow of children's learning activities is broken and changed informally and often individually, with a large element of the children's own choice governing the matters.' In consequence, Dearden adds, a variety of contrasting activities are likely to be in progress simultaneously in the room or area. 'Some children may be reading or writing, others weighing or measuring, some painting, experimenting or modelling, while yet others may be in a group being instructed or questioned by the teacher, or out of the room altogether.'

Dearden considers that at least three things may be said in favour of having an integrated day. First, it allows for more individualised learning in content and pace and this makes for more interest and involvement: 'when curricula and methods are more precisely tailored success is more likely.' Second, because the amount of time a teacher can devote to a particular child is strictly limited, children learn how to learn on their own in those areas of work where this is possible: 'at the primary stage, this principally means acquiring various information-getting skills such as are involved in using reference books, using libraries and writing to relevant people. It also involves acquiring habits of initiative and persistence, so that available opportunities to find out for oneself are not shied away from ...' Third, more individualised learning and developing skills of learning for oneself are closely related to the development of personal autonomy and self-direction.

Advocates of open or progressive education objected to the sharp division among subjects in traditional classrooms. They argued that learning cannot always be neatly wrapped up in separate packages. Many activities involve knowledge of, and skill in, a variety of subjects. Open educators therefore recommended an *integrated curriculum* in which subject boundaries were less distinct. Thus the work of a class could be organised around broad unified themes which encompass a number of subject areas. Skills are studied as they are needed by the activity and are practised in the course of significant tasks. In this connection, Dearden[84] writes:

> Integration logically presupposes differentiation, the differentiated elements being subordinated to some unitary whole. In what might be called 'loose' integration, the subordination of elements is no more than their selection according to relevance to a topic, theme or centre of interest. Thus geography, history, science, music and art may be selectively drawn upon for the contribution they can make to some such theme as canals, the sea,

railways, flight, India or whatever. If the theme is the sea, then there may be maps of oceans, the history of voyages of discovery, experiments on floating in salt and fresh water, the painting of scenes beneath the sea, the playing of 'Fingal's Cave', the singing of sea shanties. *Treasure Island* may be read and the economic uses of the sea may be studied. No doubt the justification for such a 'loose' integration of subjects would be that it naturally follows the course of an interest without any arbitrary inter-ruptions or divisions. And a good deal of such general knowledge is acquired in areas where it is difficult to argue that this rather than that must be known, or that this rather than that must be covered. The strongest argument for loose integration is thus motivational.

Thus the main argument in favour of an integrated curriculum is that pupils are *actively involved* in the learning experience. The teacher is the 'facilitator' who helps to create the conditions for learning, but it is the child who does the learning. Pollard and Tann remind us of two other arguments in favour of the integrated curriculum. First, new subjects have been added to the curriculum which are interdisciplinary and conceptually linked. An example here is environmental studies. The very nature of the subject integrated a number of disciplines. Second, where subject boundaries are reduced, it is possible to reduce the influence of subject content. As the authors explain, 'Having lessened the emphasis on particular subject knowledge, a higher priority can be given to general processes, skills and attitudes.'

Inevitably, in most integrated days there has to be a certain amount of formal time tabling. This usually occurs, as Dearden notes,[85] where the use of common or shared resources, such as in music or television programmes, is involved. Similarly, even though an integrated curriculum may be in operation, a certain amount of differentiation must needs occur. As Dearden explains,[86] 'Physical education for practical reasons, mathematics for reasons of sequence, and language skills because of their arbitrary social conventions all have to be differentiated out, at least for some of the time.'

From the child's perspective, integration in learning is natural during the early years of life. At this stage in her mental development, the child does not see what she learns as classifiable into distinct subject areas or isolated skills. She reads, records, calculates in pursuit of her current interests, and not until the age of 9 or so does she begin to classify what she learns into subject compartments. Integration stems from the child and from the natural ways in which she learns. It is the child who integrates, not the teacher.

Morrison and Ridley[87] identify five stages that the student teacher can follow in introducing the integrated day:[88]

Stage one   Grouping the children and training them in the access, use and return of materials; establishing discipline and control.

Stage two   Using one hour or one block of time to do two specific tasks, the student teacher setting the tasks and the children choosing the order and timing.

Stage three   The student teacher extending the periods of integration and number of tasks, perhaps doing this one group at a time.

Stage four   Reducing the amount of direction by the student teacher, with the children knowing what tasks to do without being told by the teacher; lengthening the period of integration; the student teacher drawing up daily plans for the children.

Stage five   Days of integration moving to a week of integration, perhaps one group at a time, extended use of assignment cards.

One can see from the preceding outline that the integrated day risks being task-focused rather than child- or teacher-focused, i.e. that the amount of child–teacher interaction might become reduced and that the teacher's talk might be managerial and procedural rather than instructional (see the discussion of topic work in Part II). As steps to integration gather momentum so do the possible management problems. The integrated day can lead to the situation where an exhausted teacher is working much harder than the children, where noise levels rise, where lazy children 'slip through the net' (unless scrupulous records are kept and updated on an almost daily basis), where children can move around the room being distracted and distracting others, where assignment cards suffer from the 'death by worksheet' syndrome mentioned later, where some children cannot handle the freedom accorded to them, and where the degree of planning required is greater than the return on the time and effort expended.

We touched earlier upon possibilities for grouping children within a class, sometimes referred to as *intra-class grouping*. We now consider grouping children within the school, or *intra-school grouping*. This can be achieved in terms of *age or ability*. We begin with age. There are three options here: *same-age grouping* (sometimes called horizontal or chronological grouping), *vertical grouping* (or mixed age grouping) and *transitional grouping*.

Same-age grouping (or horizontal or chronological) refers to classes in which children are of the same age-range. This may vary from three months to possibly one year depending on the size of the school. Allen and her colleagues[89] have identified a number of advantages and disadvantages of horizontal grouping. The advantages are that: (1) the narrow age-range may enable teachers to feel more secure and the narrower range of ability may appear to make their task simpler; (2) children and teachers are both able to make a completely new beginning with each new school year; and (3) classes grouped in this manner show greater social cohesion and interaction because they are at similar levels of intellectual, social and emotional development and have similar interests.

Some of the disadvantages are as follows: (1) as the class is new at the start of each year, there is no continuity with the previous year; (2) there is the possibility that children in the younger parallel classes may under-achieve because they are known to be younger and appear less able; (3) a teacher who sees his class as a fairly homogeneous group may be in danger of not noticing the exceptions; and (4) teachers who tend to specialise in one age-group for a number of years will automatically restrict the range of their experience.

Because of the importance of vertical or mixed-age grouping in the primary school, we explore this concept in a little more detail. Vertical grouping may be defined as a method of organising children in such a manner that each class contains children from each age-group in the school. At the present time, vertical grouping is found chiefly in infant schools, and in ones so organised that all classes will be parallel and each class will contain an equal proportion of children of all ages from 4-plus to 7-plus. The children will subsequently remain throughout their infant-school life in the same class under the supervision of the same teacher. Each child will then 'run his own race' in a stable community guided by one teacher. Variations in this pattern abound in the primary sector. In some areas, for example, it is more common to find the reception class or the top infants being taught separately. Such structuring is sometimes termed *partial vertical grouping* or *transitional grouping*. We consider this variant more fully shortly.

Vertical or mixed-age grouping implies a flexible organisation which provides a wide basis for a child's emotional, social and intellectual development. Although a class so structured contains roughly equal proportions of each age, it does not mean that the class is rigidly stratified on this basis. The distinctive strength of this arrangement lies in its fluidity, for individual, group and class work are all possible. Indeed, it is the individual needs and interests of the children, and not their ages, which lie at the basis of group formation and re-formation.

In addition to the flexible organisational structure noted above, vertical grouping possesses a number of additional advantages (some of which it shares with horizontally grouped children being taught on an individual or group basis) which may be listed thus:

1 a more natural and relaxed atmosphere can result from this same flexibility;
2 the organisation minimises problems arising from a child's entering the infant school for the first time – moving into a stable and secure community, the new entrant is able to adjust more quickly and successfully;
3 the organisational flexibility relates more effectively to the children's motivation, to the content of learning, and to the integration of the

curriculum than is the case with more traditional approaches;

4   children are better able to learn from each other as well as from the teacher;

5   the structure allows more effectively for variations in personal growth and development than is the case with more rigid organisational structures, fixed age-groups and set instructional procedures;

6   the organisation increases the likelihood of children interacting with the environment;

7   a wider range of social experience is possible, together with resultant benefits such as a greater sense of belongingness, support and security;

8   should problems arise, a child can be moved to another class without much difficulty;

9   older children develop a sense of responsibility towards the younger ones;

10   the teacher is in a better position to deal with the children individually;

11   communication between teachers benefits, as each teacher is confronted with similar problems of the various age-groups; and

12   teachers using vertical grouping tend to speak favourably of it.

Critics of vertical grouping, however, raise the following objections:

1   the duties of the teacher become excessively onerous;

2   personality clashes between a teacher and child may make it undesirable for a child to spend two or three years in the same class;

3   older children may help younger ones too much, thus hampering their own progress;

4   children on the point of entering the junior school may be given preferential treatment;

5   the noise created by the younger children may disturb the older ones (partial vertical grouping can solve this problem);

6   the structure presents difficulties for activities such as stories and poems, religious education, and those areas such as music and movement and physical education where skill depends on maturation;

7   groups whose teachers are uncommitted or weak will be disadvantaged by a vertically grouped structure; and

8   hostility from parents (though this often arises from misunderstandings).

Mycock[90] has listed *four basic educational principles underlying the practice of vertical grouping*. These may be briefly summarised as follows:

1   being a stable and secure community, the school embodying the principles of vertical grouping provides the continuity and coherence necessary in a child's educational life;

2   a vertically grouped situation caters for a wide age-range in its own right, provides for individual motivation, tempo and maturation, and thus facilitates maximal individual growth;

3   a vertically grouped structure provides for the acceptance of the child as an agent of his own learning. It meets a child's natural urge to explore and discover, and provides a school environment that promotes and develops a child's ability to think by involving him in the selection and rejection of ideas, by developing discrimination and by forming value judgements; and

4   such an organisation provides for the fullest development of the balanced personality. It meets the need for a holistic view of child development which will foster attitudes, qualities and abilities that will enable a child to live a happy, well-adjusted life in a complex and changing social environment.

Although the one essential characteristic of vertical grouping is the age-grouping, some teachers identify two further characteristics. These are: (1) the *integrated* or *unstructured day*. This they perceive as crucial to the successful working of vertical grouping. In so far as it is possible, a school is thus stripped of all artificial divisions. In practice, however, there is a considerable amount of experimentation in this respect. As a general rule, much of the day is left unspecified for both individual and group work, with all the children coming together from time to time for set teaching periods; and (2) a *structured environment*. An unstructured day is only made possible by having a highly organised classroom, and success in vertical grouping rests to a large extent on a highly structured environment. Space and opportunity to spread out are essential; and every classroom should have a good range of basic equipment.

The role of the teacher in a vertically grouped structure, as in other integrated situations, is a complex and subtle one. A selection of his or her functions, though by no means exclusive to vertical grouping, may be itemised as follows:

1   he or she promotes a relaxed and tension-free atmosphere which is conducive to happiness, mutual and self-help;

2   he or she establishes and maintains an appropriate and flexible environment in which children can learn chiefly through their own activities;

3   he or she ensures provision of materials and apparatus;

4   he or she arranges learning situations and opportunities;

5   he or she recognises the needs of each individual child and sees that these are met;

6   he or she is a teacher, guide, source of reference and motivator;

7   he or she establishes standards; and

8   he or she evaluates and records individual effort and progress.

After a prolonged study of a wide variety of primary schools in rural, urban and suburban areas, Allen and her colleagues concluded that the advantages of vertical grouping seemed on balance to outweigh the disadvantages. They felt that the system could be a very positive gain in schools with a large number of immigrant children or in ones situated in deprived areas, in both of which a sense of security among the children was required.

Transitional grouping is a combination of same-age and vertical grouping. Some see it as a compromise between the two. Arrangements for transitional grouping in infant, junior and first schools are extremely flexible. One such arrangement in an infant school would be to have the 5- and 6-year-olds vertically grouped in parallel classes and single-age classes for the 7-year-olds. Allen and her colleagues found in first schools that the fives and sixes were vertically grouped and then proceeded to further vertically grouped classes containing 7- and 8-year-olds.

Transitional grouping has arisen in recognition of the differing intellectual and social needs which distinguish 6- and 7-year-olds. Allen and her colleagues point out that the younger child is largely engaged in the formation of concepts relative to physical and social reality and in learning to separate fact from fantasy and desire. He tends to be adult-oriented and to regard his peer group as rivals.

The 7- or 8-year-old, by contrast, is 'normally engaged in learning to manipulate facts, in acquiring skills and the concepts essential to everyday life. He is learning to be peer-group related and to adopt the appropriate personal and sex role within the group.' Transitional grouping thus caters for these and other differences.

Allen and her associates have further recorded both the advantages of transitional grouping and the disadvantages. Advantages include:

- with transitional grouping, children have the experience of changing to a single-age class within the security of the same school;
- transitional grouping allows children more variety of adult contact;
- separating children at 7 appears to eliminate the need to cater for physical education, story and music at a separate level for certain ages as within the vertically grouped class;
- it helps with the problem of younger children trying to follow too closely the lead of the older children, and losing experience of activities such as fantasy play or the investigation of the properties of materials;
- older children also benefit in that they can expect more opportunity to use materials creatively and more teacher's help with the practice of basic skills;
- some teachers are happier with older children and others are more suited to younger ones; and
- the system appears to be particularly advantageous in a socially deprived school.

Three disadvantages identified by the authors may be listed thus:

- where an individual child has not emotionally or intellectually reached the level of his companions, this is obviously more noticeable on transfer to a 7-year-old class or a vertically grouped 7- to-8-year-old class;

- as with vertically grouped situations, there may well be misunderstandings among parents which need sympathetic explanation by the school; and
- where children have made friends with older or younger children in their vertically grouped class and are now separated, there may be distress which needs to be understood by the school.

Intra-school grouping according to ability offers two possibilities: *the same or similar ability groups* and *mixed-ability groups*. Schools organised on same-ability principles make use of streaming, though it is now comparatively rare to find primary schools employing streaming exclusively. Some of the drawbacks of streaming were revealed in earlier research. Chiefly, teachers working in streamed schools tend to categorise children and make more or less final judgements on them. And research into streamed secondary schools showed that teachers tended to underestimate the less able. They also claimed a flexibility in the extent to which children were moved from one stream to another that was not borne out by the evidence. Another factor which opponents of streaming stress is that pupils in the lower streams tend to develop a negative image of themselves. Dean has pointed out that what is true of streamed classes tends also to be true of streamed groups *within* classes and that teachers ought to be aware of the dangers, especially where the groupings are permanent.

Where streaming is seen as problematic, the answer lies in *mixed-ability grouping*. This refers to classes containing a wide range of ability, and we deal with this topic in relation to older children in a separate chapter. Kerry and Tollitt[91] remind us that at infant level, mixed-ability grouping is rarely made the issue it has become in comprehensive schools. They have identified some of the reasons why teachers in infant schools prefer mixed-ability groups:

1   Grading children by ability is socially divisive.
2   Infant school is too early to make satisfactory judgements about children's academic potential.
3   Children labelled as failures tend to fail.
4   Streaming does not correspond to the way children will live in the community.
5   Children of differing abilities can learn to help or be helped by classmates.

We continue by examining some of the principal teaching and learning styles to be found in primary classrooms. We concentrate on those methods that developed with the emergence of open and progressive classrooms.

TEACHING AND LEARNING STYLES IN PRIMARY CLASSROOMS

One of the most striking features of contemporary primary classrooms is the range and variety of teaching and learning styles operating in them. A teaching style is made up of a cluster of elements:

- the type of discipline;
- the relationships and interactions between teachers and children;
- teacher behaviour;
- the organisation of the class;
- the nature and extent of teacher talk;
- the degree of student choice;
- the nature and use of resources;
- the nature of assessment;
- the organisation of the curriculum;
- the style of learning;
- the atmosphere in the classroom.

A formal style will interpret these very differently from an informal style. For example, a formal style might be characterised by strict, overt discipline, a high degree of social distance between teachers and students, a 'chalk-and-talk' type of lesson with little interaction between one student and another, individual work with no talking, an emphasis on book work, the teacher acting as an expert, the curriculum organised in subjects and students being assessed by standardised tests. An informal style might be characterised by a freer discipline, less social distance between students and teachers, experiential and active learning using a variety of resources, children learning in groups, and assessment being diagnostic.

Early approaches to discussing teaching styles used the concept of a teacher as a 'lion tamer', an 'entertainer', a 'new Romantic',[92] an autocrat, a democrat, and a laissez-faire liberal. Our review of teaching and learning styles includes *individualisation, individual attention, discovery learning, play and talk,* and *topics and projects.* Group teaching we have already touched upon and there is enough guidance on direct, formal teaching in other parts of the book to meet the reader's need.

Individualisation

Individualisation of instruction is based on recognition of the fact that not all children can be expected to learn at the same rate. The approach is used in both traditional and open classrooms, though its relationship to the content of learning is different in each case. In the traditional classroom, individualisation is achieved by varying the pace or duration of learning, by varying the mode of teaching or by modifying the set curriculum in some way. What these variations have in common, however, is the belief that all children must master a specified curriculum determined by the teacher or the system. A consequence of this is the need for frequent evaluation and testing to check the children's progress. In open or progressive classrooms, where individualisation is a key concept, children collaborate in formulating their own curricular goals. As Stephens[93] explains, 'The teacher's responsibility is not to decide in advance exactly what each child will study but rather to provide a climate in which individual children can make choices about the curriculum and explore matters of interest to them.' This does not mean that the child does as he likes, or that the teacher abandons all responsibility in this connection, but that the curriculum is freed from the constraints of the traditional approach and now more appropriately meets the unique needs, interests and abilities of each child. Individualisation is sometimes misinterpreted as meaning that each child works on his own in a physical sense. But this is not the case. It simply means that his individual needs are taken into account. More often than not, these can be most effectively met by grouping – a topic we have already considered.

The key to effective individualised learning lies in the provision of adequate resources and materials, carefully structured and suitable for a child's abilities. Individualisation is but one aspect of the learning process which can benefit enormously from the technological revolution and its application to the classroom. As Dean has noted, 'Micro-technology makes it possible to match a programme to the particular needs of an individual child with a high degree of accuracy and a child working in this way can get immediate feedback on whether the answers he is giving are correct or appropriate.'

Individual attention

Individualisation involves encounters with the teacher, and his or her contribution to the teaching–learning process in the primary classroom can be considered in terms of *individual attention*. The burden of informal encounters between the teacher and child can be very onerous, sometimes totalling as many as a thousand interpersonal contacts a day. For this reason, individual attention can be one of the more problematic concepts in a class environment for it is never far removed from its polar opposite – individual neglect. Two earlier studies conducted in the United States, for example, show that in any given period certain children received most of the attention while others were largely ignored.[94] A British study conducted in the early 1970s[95] revealed that two main groups of children received attention – the active hard workers and the active miscreants. It was concluded that the *average passive* child missed out in this respect, not through any rational policy on the part of the teacher, but because the ongoing classroom pressures limited pupil contact to the two categories identified above. Further, for the neglected child who was also diffident and therefore unlikely to talk even to those other children in his group, the classroom became 'bereft of language, either written or spoken'. Boydell[96] graphically describes the possible consequences of individual neglect.

> Isolation from the teacher, coupled with a fairly high probability that contacts will not be work-oriented when they do occur, is as much a classroom reality for many children as the exhausting never-ending series of individual work conversations are for the teacher. 'It's time to pack up' said by a weary teacher at the end of the afternoon may be all some children have heard her say to them all day!

More recent research[97] in this connection offers more hope, however. Dividing the pupils into three subgroups – high achievers, medium achievers and low achievers – the researchers found that there was, in fact, very little difference in the distribution of teacher–pupil interaction; overall, they found, it was almost identical. They found no evidence that there was any discrimination either in favour of or against any particular group of pupils according to their achievement level.

To return to the problem of individual neglect, this need not bedevil the teacher's efforts if he or she knows what it is he or she has to spot and give attention to. In this connection, Dean gives excellent practical advice. She argues that every class is made up of individuals, but that some will need more attention than others. These children will include: those of low ability; those with specific learning problems; those with emotional or behavioural problems; those with gaps in their schooling; those with language problems, including those of non-English speaking home background; and those with outstanding ability of some kind. For specific advice on how to deal with these kinds of individuals, we refer the reader to Dean's book, pp. 177–89.

Discovery and experiential learning

Discovery and experiential learning are concepts arising from the strategies of topic and project work in progressive environments and are of central importance to the work of the primary classroom. Dean has said of them:

> Discovery learning is one of the most important of the learning approaches because it can be highly motivating and can help children to structure what they are learning. It is also one of the most difficult methods to use well and creating situations in which children can make discoveries which are within their capacity is a fascinating professional task.

Dearden[98] has suggested that by means of discovery learning we may reasonably expect children to learn something new; and to do so through some initiative of their own. He goes on to identify three other points to be borne in mind in any discussion on learning by discovery. First, what is involved primarily is the learning of facts, concepts and principles rather than skills, techniques or sensitivities; and that the subjects most relevant to discovery learning are mathematics, science and environmental studies. Second, discovery learning may be contrasted with the sort of learning usually associated with the traditional classroom, i.e. learning by instruction or demonstration. And third, learning by discovery does not just happen; it comes about as a result of a particular teaching method or strategy. Numerous strategies can be distinguished in this connection; perhaps the commonest one to be found is that of *guided discovery*. By means of this, a teacher supports a child's self-chosen activity with questions, commentary and suggestions.

Another useful typology is that of *open-ended discovery learning* and *planned or structural discovery*. In the case of the former, the situation in which the child is put or which he chooses is such that the teacher does not know the outcome. A topic on some aspect of environmental studies would be an example here. *Planned or structured discovery* occurs when a teacher wants a specific aspect of learning to take place, perhaps with respect to the development or acquisition of scientific or mathematical concepts.

From time to time, discovery learning comes under fire from those holding entrenched traditionalist positions. Such attacks are best countered with the kind of sentiments which Dearden[99] expresses thus:

> Learning by discovery characteristically aims to engender intrinsic interest, both in what is learned and in the process of learning it. It also emphasises the satisfactions of learning independently. But the development of both intrinsic interest and independence in learning are extremely important liberal education aims. If a method in the hands of some teacher is successful in achieving these aims, then it has much to be said for it, at least as one valid method amongst others.

Play and talk

The educational significance of *play* for younger children, say 4- to 7-year-olds, has been a persistent theme in the writings of educational theorists from as early as Plato. The prominent role accorded it by the initiators of the progressive movement in education has now become one of pre-eminence in the theory and practice of infant education. Broadly speaking, *play* serves a twofold purpose in the thinking of specialists. First, it seems to cater for a *fairly wide range of children's needs*. These include psychological, educational, social, emotional and motor. In this sense, play can be an important source of knowledge for the child. Kerry and Tollitt consider that in this connection there is a need for a careful balance between structured and unstructured play in the classroom and playground. The second purpose of play is for it to serve as an *integrative factor*. In this sense, it is a vital means of breaking down traditional divides. Thus play merges with, or becomes indistinguishable from, work; and the boundaries between other traditional dualisms such as doing and knowing, or intellect and emotions, are similarly blurred by the concept. For an overview of the developmental aspects of play in 4-, 5-, 6- and 7-year-olds, consult Kerry and Tollitt, pp. 28–35.

Talk likewise occupies a crucial position in the classroom in any consideration of principal agents of learning. Adelman and Walker express the point thus: 'We consider that the nature of talk is the only readily available manifestation of the extent and process by which mutual understandings of what counts as knowledge in any context are transacted.' It is therefore in the many discussion situations in the classroom that talk as an agent of learning operates most effectively. This means that the problem for the teacher is how to develop and improve children's skills in this respect and indeed his or her own. In the main, discussions take place either between the teacher and class or among small groups with or without the teacher.

Dean advises teachers to think out clearly what it is they hope to get from their discussions and to consider their functions. This involves identifying important questions and having the children's language skills and general experience in mind at the same time. The important points that need to be remembered, in Dean's view, are: *how you receive the children's contributions, scanning the class to spot would-be contributors and those not involved, being able to interpret body language so as to know when children have had enough,* and finally *being able to summarise and structure ideas with a view to taking the discussion further.*

Pollard and Tann have posed further questions which the reader can reflect on, perhaps in the light of his or her own teaching-practice experiences:

1   What is the range of roles participants might play?
2   What do class members learn, including those who do not participate?
3   How do different kinds of tasks, group size and composition affect group processes?
4   How can we use discussion to develop and monitor the participants' discussion skills?

Box 40 contains a framework for monitoring discussion strategies which Pollard and Tann have devised. The reader is recommended to use it in conjunction with at least one discussion session he or she has initiated.

Topic and project work

Tann[100] defines topic work as 'an approach to learning which draws upon children's concerns and which actively involves them in the planning, executing, presenting and evaluating of a negotiated learning experience. In this form of topic work "control" is a shared responsibility.' The use of topics, projects, themes and centres of interest has long been an important feature of primary classrooms, especially in those where child-centred teaching prevails

Box 40

Discussion skills

Aim: To examine discussion skills
A reflective teacher may find it useful to consider the following points:

1   Do the participants take turns or do they frequently talk over or
interrupt?
Do they invite contributions, re-direct contributions for further
comments, give encouragement?
Do they listen to each other? Are they willing to learn from each other
(i.e. respond and react to each other's contributions)?
Or do they indulge in 'parallel' talk (i.e. continue their own line of
thinking)?
Does conflict emerge or is harmony maintained (at all costs)?
are the ideas disputed?
is the speaker attacked?
Is conflict positively handled?
by modifying statements, rather than just reasserting them?
by examining the assumptions, rather than leaving them implicit?
by explaining/accounting for the claim, rather than ignoring the
challenge?
2   Do they elaborate, rather than answer in monosyllables?
by giving details of events, people, feelings?
by providing reasons, explanations, examples?
Do they extend ideas, rather than let ambiguity go unchallenged?
by asking for specific information?
by asking for clarification?
Do they explore suggestions?
by asking for alternatives?
by speculating, imagining and hypothesising?
Do they evaluate?
by pooling ideas and suspending judgement before making choices?

Source Pollard and Tann

(not necessarily the simplistic ideologically puritan version outlined earlier
but the approach that stresses first-hand, experiential learning through a
negotiated order – a view than is not necessarily at odds with the national
curriculum, indeed a view that is deliberately and explicitly stated in the
Curriculum Guidance documents from the former National Curriculum
Council).[101] The reasons for our support of some form of topic work are
numerous – their value in integration and discovery learning, for example,
along with the social benefits that accrue from group work. Of course, the use
of such approaches is not confined to the primary classroom, as an

examination of secondary, further and higher education will disclose. Indeed, projects play a significant role in the coursework of the GCSE. The terms 'topic work' and 'project work' lack precise definitions, but they do possess similarities which have been identified by Rance.[102] Thus, they are practical in nature and attempt to break away from the conventional methods of teaching, placing more emphasis on the child than on the subject; they endeavour to allow the child to construct his or her own methods of approach to knowledge; they give him or her the opportunity to 'learn how to learn'; they break down barriers between school subjects; and they both utilise a child's own interests.

Topic work may be defined as the individual and/or group investigations, recordings and presentations which children undertake when pursuing a topic. As Rance writes:

> It requires the content of normal curricular subjects to be used so that the pupil can develop a simple but logical method of systematically seeking, absorbing, organizing and recording knowledge. This process should be allowed to flourish in a situation which enables the child to make a free choice, within predetermined limits, of the subject he wishes to study and encourages him to create an end-product commensurate with his mental and physical abilities.

Rance further elucidates the terminology used in topic work. Thus, there are two types of topic: the *graded topic* in which the teacher aims at teaching children new methods for obtaining, selecting, recording and presenting knowledge, the emphasis being on method; and the *subject topic*, the chief aim of which is to encourage children to acquire a wide range of information concerning a particular subject. The emphasis here is on content.

An individual topic is carried out by one child; a group topic is undertaken by a group of from four to six children; and a class topic by the whole class. An independent group is a self-sufficient unit contributing to one independent section of the topic; and a linked group collaborates with one or more other groups.

Generally speaking, topics should be freely chosen by the children on the basis of their own interests. They may initially require some suggestions and the teacher can help here with a compiled list of possibilities which can serve as a basis for negotiation. The children, however, should be allowed to make the final choice.

The methods of undertaking a topic vary considerably with its nature and the maturity and experience of the children. The following five-stage plan by Rance, however, would serve as an organisational basis for student teachers embarking on a topic perhaps for the first time:

1   The teacher's preparation of the subject (see also Box 41).
2   Introduction of the subject(s) to the class.

3   The organisation of the subject(s) with the class.
4   The children's research into the subject matter.
5   The end-product.

Box 41

Preparing for topic work

Before the topic begins, teachers should:

1   *Prepare content and teaching methods*
Make flow diagrams or outlines of anticipated directions of study.
Divide the content into the curriculum areas to be covered.
Decide on specific teaching activities or modes for subdivision of the content.
Refer to the school's outline scheme of work.
Read around the subject at their own level.
Make a list of the skills to be taught.
Make notes on classroom-management procedures (e.g. assign pupils to working groups).
Decide on the time-scale of the topic.
Amend flowcharts or plans in consultation with pupils.
Plan lead lessons.

2   *Prepare resources and materials*
Make a search of school and public libraries.
Collect suitable audio-visual software.
Arrange visits and speakers.
Contact museums and other outside organisations.
Prepare worksheets or assignment cards.
Encourage pupils, colleagues or parents to collect materials.
Consult TV and radio programme schedules.
Write letters to supplying agencies.
Visit the local Teachers' Centre.
View in advance any area to be visited later by the class.

3   *Prepare the classroom itself*
Make a display of related charts, reference books, etc.
Prepare a display area.
Prepare resource collections.
Decide on the layout of furniture.
Check that any software or apparatus required is readily available.
Provide suitable folders or storage for pupils' work.
Organise outside or ancillary help.
Explore the potential of school-based facilities (such as rain gauges).

Source Kerry and Tollitt

Rance points out that (a) the form the end-product takes can be discussed during stage 3; and (b) once the five stages have been carried out, it is usual to have a discussion session in which the topic is reviewed and in which improvements for subsequent topics are suggested.

The teacher's functions throughout the sequence of stages are numerous. If the subject centres around a place or building, part of his or her own preparation may be a visit alone. The form his or her introduction takes will depend on the nature of the subject, but it should be done in such a way as to arouse strong initial motivation. He or she may even adopt an imaginative approach, like telling a story or having the children act out some aspect of the theme. Once the topic is underway, the teacher is then available as a consultant and resources person. He or she should be careful not to direct too closely or obviously the actual course of the investigation for, as far as possible, the children themselves should determine how they wish to pursue their research and presentation. From time to time the teacher will need to re-stimulate interest and perhaps suggest new or alternative avenues of approach and exploration to the children as they work on their topics. He or she must constantly be on the alert for waning interest.

The importance of having a *well-defined end-product* agreed at the organisational stage cannot be over-emphasised. No matter how well motivated children are initially, they can easily lose interest as the topic gets underway. If or when this happens, the defined end-product will assist in re-focusing attention and sustaining interest. What form the end-product takes will depend on a number of factors. Common forms of display and presentation include an exhibition, presentation in booklets and folders, displays and murals, tape-recordings, mimes and plays, a talk by one or more members of the group, film-strips or video-recordings, models, collages, a magazine or newspaper, a festival, spoken poetry and prose, or any combination of these.

Readers seeking additional information on the subject of topics are referred to Rance's book, which provides a detailed consideration of the subject. In particular, they are advised to read chapter 10, which examines the special problems of the student teacher when attempting topic work. Other useful sources of information and advice in this respect may be found in the books by Lane and Kemp,[103] Waters,[104] Bradley et al.,[105] and Kerry and Eggleston.[106]

In summary, the reader is reminded that the chief points to bear in mind are: (1) his or her own thorough preparation, and especially the preliminary reading, research and exploration he or she needs to undertake; (2) the organisation of the topic with the class (availability of resources and definition of end-product are important here); (3) making sure that the children enjoy the work; and (4) establishing and maintaining a reasonably high level of motivation and anticipating the points where it can be expected to flag.

For a more detailed checklist for the preparation of topic work, we refer you to Box 41, the items having been devised by Kerry and Tollitt with infants in mind.

It is difficult to establish a clear-cut distinction between topic work and project work. Like the topic, a project can be the work of an individual or a group. Projects, however, do tend to be more substantial than topics, thus requiring longer to accomplish. It is possible, for example, to spend a whole term on a project.

Much of what has been said on topic work will apply to projects. Social studies, environmental studies and science lend themselves particularly well to class projects. Box 42 lists some of the advantages of enquiry-based projects in primary school science.

Box 42

Advantages of enquiry-based projects in primary school science

1   They provide a context which may help children to understand the processes of science by actually doing them.
2   They may encourage children to work together, to share ideas, to challenge one another and to develop a critical awareness.
3   They may change the role of the teacher from being a presenter of knowledge to that of being a resource agent and guide.
4   They may encourage a degree of independence from the teacher and so begin the process of independent learning and judgement.
5   They may encourage children to see science as a tentative discipline and not as an infallible one.

Source Baker[107]

An important factor needing to be confronted in project work is that of structure. In Bonnett's[108] view, the challenge of project work for children lies in the extent to which it enables them to explore themselves in relation to the real world through the thoughtful acknowledgement and pursuit of their concerns. This challenge, Bonnett argues, 'cannot be met by attempts to "order up" projects in advance and standardise their achievements. The structure we should be seeking is one which takes its cue from the children's own relationship with the world, their ways of revealing it to themselves.'

From his study of project work in schools, Bonnett has identified five sources of structure. These may be enshrined in the following principles:

1   *The teacher-centred principle*: This will derive largely from the teacher's own personal associations which in turn result from the teacher's own experiences and world view. As Bonnett says, 'As such it may well

be highly subjective and greatly influenced by his or her own enthusiasm and areas of perceived expertise.'

2   *The knowledge-centred principle*: Where this structuring principle is paramount, the project becomes a vehicle for conveying pre-specified information, concepts and ideas, selected, as the author says, 'on the basis that either they are of value in their own right, and/or learning them forms part of the initiation of the pupil into the wider modes of knowledge and understanding from which they are derived'.

3   *The skills-centred principle*: Where this principle is operative the project is seen as a vehicle for transmitting certain skills which might be grouped under such headings as physical/manipulative, cognitive, social, etc. As Bonnett explains, 'these would be pre-specified relatively independently of a particular knowledge content'.

4   *The problem-centred principle*: Here the structure is determined by the enquiry itself, and content and direction develop according to where that enquiry leads, and, as Bonnett adds, *wherever* it leads.

5   *The child-centred principle*: The structuring principle here is the child's own consciousness – his or her felt needs and concerns and the opportunities provided for choice and responsibility which the genuine exploration of these needs requires.

The criticisms sometimes levelled at projects (that they lack positive educational direction, that they result in mindless copying and futile experiment, and that they at best keep noisy children quiet and at worst lead to boredom and frustration) can be avoided where the practical suggestions offered above are put into practice. For further information on project work in the primary school, we refer you to Haslam.[109]

Chapter 10

Secondary teaching

The topics we have chosen to examine here divide into four groupings: the requisites of a secondary school student teacher, first meeting(s) with one's classes, lesson presentation skills, and teaching styles.

It is not intended that these topics should be read exclusively by intending secondary teachers, as there is a great deal in them of relevance to primary teachers and, indeed, to anyone else concerned with professional instruction.

SOME REQUISITES OF A SECONDARY SCHOOL STUDENT TEACHER

The secondary school teacher is caught up in a web of different (and sometimes conflicting) demands. For example, one can witness significant changes and innovations in secondary-school curricula and teaching, e.g. the increasing certification of vocational courses in GNVQ, B Tec, NVQ, City and Guilds qualifications. Indeed the whole field of certification, assessment and examinations has been the focus of considerable debate in the last decade, covering, for example: (a) the moves to credentialise – award qualifications for – vocational education in an attempt to raise the status of this area of students' development; (b) the moves to harmonise GCSE requirements with the national curriculum requirements at Key Stage 4; (c) the moves to break the academic stranglehold of the post-16 curriculum in the 'gold standard' of A-levels; the debate about the amount and the role of coursework in public examinations; (d) the accreditation of experiences and activities for public examinations, recorded in a record of achievement (ROA) and included in the partner to an ROA – action planning, itself a *leitmotiv* of this book; (e) the moves to ensure that students achieve the National Education and Training Targets.

Further, over the last decade many moves have been made to establish links between the school, the community and local industry. Students typically undertake periods of work placement (e.g. a one-week or two-week block during Key Stage 4; one day per week for a term at age 16) and the outcomes of these are included in a record of achievement. Many schemes for linking schools and industry have been in place since the 1980s, e.g. the Technical and Vocational Education Initiative; the Low Attaining Pupils' Programme; Compacts; the Certificate of Pre-Vocational Education; the Young Ambassadors scheme.

Hence to regard the secondary school teacher as solely a teacher of one or two subjects is to misconceive quite seriously the diversity of the requirements of the teacher. Dowson[1] differentiates between the roles of a teacher as a subject specialist and the wider role of the teacher. With regard to the teacher-as-subject-specialist she argues that the teacher must be able to:

- communicate the special relevance and rewards of the subject;
- support and stretch all students in learning the knowledge, skills and processes of the subject in question;
- achieve the best possible examination results;
- contribute to the running of the department;
- sustain subject expertise and enthusiasm.

In the same volume, Leask[2] argues that subject teachers require subject knowledge, professional judgement and professional knowledge. She argues that it is not enough for the teacher simply to possess academic knowledge; that has to be translated into effective learning by the students. This echoes Morrison,[3] where he writes that subject specialists should possess both *subject* knowledge and *pedagogical* knowledge. Indeed, he goes further than this to suggest that a subject specialist should possess several areas of expertise:

- academic subject knowledge;
- pedagogical knowledge;
- effective interpersonal behaviour;
- enthusiasm and motivating skills;
- understanding of social relations in schools and classrooms;
- skills for developing curricula and schemes of work;
- organisational skills;
- understanding of how students learn;
- awareness of current trends in the content and teaching of the subject;
- management skills – leadership, communication and monitoring;
- skills in assessment, evaluation and record-keeping.

This list is little more than a reiteration of the competences that were outlined in Part I of this book.

In addition to possessing subject-specialist abilities, Dowson argues that the secondary school teacher should be able to (a) integrate cross-curricular dimensions, skills and themes into his or her teaching, (b) become involved in the pastoral aspect of school life, and (c) foster links between the school, the local community and industry.[4] Student teachers, to become full participants in school life, will need to adopt a less synoptic, wider view of their tasks, roles and interpersonal behaviour with staff and students alike. Most secondary school teachers will also be involved in teaching a programme of Personal and Social Education, most will be involved in a tutorial role in the school, most will have pastoral responsibility for a named group of students.

As a 'novice teacher' on school experience, then, the student teacher will have to absorb very rapidly and become part of the several aspects of teaching that are embraced both in subject teaching and the many other aspects of school life: curricular, extra-curricular, cross-curricular, pastoral, disciplinary, interpersonal, managerial. Indeed, Leask[5] argues that the school will have several expectations of the student teacher *qua* trainee professional and guest in the school, covering several areas:

Organisation and teaching approach

You will be expected to:

- be well organised;
- arrive in plenty of time. And that doesn't mean arriving just as the bell goes. It means arriving considerably earlier in order to arrange the classroom; check the availability of books and equipment; test out equipment new to you; talk to staff about the work and the children's progress; and clarify any safety issues;
- plan and prepare thoroughly. Be conscientious in finding out what lesson content and subject knowledge are appropriate to the class you're teaching. In many cases you will be teaching material which is new to you or which you last thought about many years ago. Staff will expect you to ask if you're not sure but to work conscientiously to improve your subject knowledge. They will not be impressed if you frequently show you have not bothered to read around the subject matter of the lesson;
- keep good records: have your file of scheme of work and lesson plans, pupil attendance and homework records up to date. Your evaluations of your lessons are best completed on the same day as the lesson;
- know your subject;
- try out different methods of teaching. Teaching practice is your opportunity to try out different approaches without having to live with the results of failure, but you have a duty to the class teacher not to leave chaos behind you.

Professionalism

You will be expected to:

- act in a professional manner, e.g. with courtesy and tact; and to respect confidentiality of information;

- be open to new learning; seek advice and act on advice;
- be flexible;
- dress appropriately (different schools have different dress codes);
- become familiar with and work within school procedures and policies. These include record-keeping, rewards and sanctions, uniform, relationships between teachers and pupils;
- accept a leadership role. You may find imposing your will on pupils uncomfortable but unless you establish your right to direct the work of the class you will not be able to teach effectively;
- recognise and understand the roles and relationships of staff responsible for your development;
- keep up to date with your subject;
- take active steps to ensure that your pupils learn;
- discuss pupil progress with parents.

Social skills

You will be expected to:

- develop good relationships with pupils and staff;
- keep a sense of humour;
- work well in teams;
- be able to communicate with children as well as adults;
- learn to defuse difficult situations.

The role of the secondary school student teacher, then, is diffuse. We advise the student teacher to find out as much as possible during his or her preliminary visits and initial contact with the school, covering, for example: the school's expectations of him or her; the curricular and pedagogic aspects of the teaching; the students he or she will be teaching; the staff with whom he or she will be working; the administrative and managerial matters in which he or she will be involved.

FIRST MEETING(S) WITH ONE'S CLASSES

We move on to try to establish a few points that will assist student teachers when meeting a class for the first time. We have deliberately pluralised the word *meeting(s)* in parenthesis to stress the fact that although the very first meeting between teacher and class is important, the points implemented on that occasion need to be followed up and consistently reinforced in ensuing lessons. Wragg and Young[6] have pointed out that relatively little research has been undertaken into the first moments of contact between teacher and pupils. Writing of the qualified teacher in this respect, they say: 'The success or failure of a whole year may rest on the impression created, the ethos, rules and relationships established during the first two or three weeks in September.'

In meeting the need for more research in this aspect of teacher–pupil encounters, they observed 313 lessons given by experienced teachers, and B Ed and PGCE students at the beginning of the school year (in the case of the teachers) and on teaching practice. Their subsequent analysis revealed a substantial combined effort by the experienced teachers in September to establish a working climate for the whole of the academic year, and the problems the students had on arriving later when, as the authors put it, 'the territory had been staked out, rules and relationships had been developed and procedures established'.

As regards the experienced teachers, they had a clear idea of how they would conduct themselves before the school year began. Their intentions, expressed in interviews given to the researchers prior to the study, were more or less fulfilled when they were observed at the beginning of the school year. The majority sought to establish a firm presence; they made up their minds about the pupils from their own experience rather than from study of the pupils' records; initial dominance and harshness was leavened by humour; and they used non-verbal means (eye movement, gesture, etc.) to reinforce what they were trying to achieve. They set out to establish rules from the very first and to some of these rules there was a noticeable moral character.

In contrast to the experienced teachers, and as one would perhaps expect, the student teachers were less certain about their rules and what they hoped to do with their pupils. The PGCE students especially tended to identify closely with the pupils and rather hoped that rules could be formulated as the need arose. However, they were well aware of the problems that might arise if they were too informal. They tended to be anxious about interpersonal relationships.

The research also disclosed that both the student teachers and the experienced teachers were able more often than not to establish a high level of pupil involvement with little misbehaviour in the initial lessons. The experienced teachers were considered to be more businesslike, confident, warm and friendly than the students; they made more of a point of learning the students' names; and in the case of the male teachers, humour was employed from quite early in the year.

Encouragingly, the researchers point out that the differences between the two groups did not necessarily persist until the end of the practice. With regard to the PGCE students, for example, most of the initial rawness and hesitation tended to diminish during the term.

From this research and related studies we have set out below a number of factors upon which the reader might reflect with respect to his or her own first and early encounters with classes. The eight points made are not intended to be prescriptive, nor should they be seen as an inventory to be implemented in the first lesson. Evidence of them in initial lessons, however, will undoubtedly contribute to more effective teaching.

(1) Information prior to meeting a class

There is a certain amount of basic information you need to know before taking a class, e.g. which pupils are perennial miscreants, are there any having physical difficulties such as deafness, partial sightedness, approximately what is the range of ability, and are there any striking individual needs? Beyond these points it can sometimes be counterproductive to have too much information and too many preconceived ideas. One needs to maintain a certain amount of spontaneity and freshness.

(2) Thinking in advance

This entails giving due thought before a lesson to such matters as content, timing, presentations, transitions, beginnings and endings, and rules and procedures. Wragg and Young quote a study which confirms the view that prior thought on such matters is a positive help in securing pupil involvement.

(3) Introductions and appearance

Who you are and how you look are matters of great importance to a new class. In another study by Wragg and Young[7] which investigated pupils' appraisals of teaching, it was found that the vast majority expected the teacher to introduce himself or herself with his or her name together with some personal details about interests and hobbies. It can be useful in this connection to write your name on the blackboard during the first meeting. Your general appearance will be a matter of curiosity and it is important that you create a favourable impression in this respect. As regards clothes, for example, either smart formal or smart casual clothes are desirable.

(4) The first lesson, its content and introduction

Particular care needs to be given to the preparation and planning of the very first lesson you will take. It is especially important to find out what has been done with the class before your arrival so that you can break new ground and not find yourself repeating what a class teacher has already done with the group. Such a state of affairs can be undermining, unless it is a revision lesson. The introduction to the lesson should be thought out with great care and imagination so that you can achieve maximum effectiveness. Motivation and interest are key concepts here. See also below for the suggestions given on set induction.

(5) Ethos, image and manner

Whether you are aware of it or not, you will establish an ethos within a short space of time, so it is desirable that you create one that is favourable and to your advantage. Personality and projection are important here. Set out initially to be firm in a friendly way, achieve a degree of dominance, and avoid being soft and weak. Your manner needs to be relaxed without being too laid-back, yet at the same time you need to send out the message that 'you're in charge'. Other qualities you need to display are patience, self-control, fairness and respect for pupils. Project a confident image.

(6) Stereotypes

Related to this last point about image is the need to avoid developing stereotypical patterns of behaviour during early meetings. Wragg[8] gives the example of students who, wanting to establish relaxed relationships with their classes but having difficulties, found themselves yelling for silence all day. Allowing verbal and physical mannerisms to become part of your classroom behaviour should also be avoided. Prefacing all your statements with 'er', or frequently punctuating them with 'OK' are examples of the kind of things that pupils can latch on to. Avoiding such pitfalls requires a degree of self-awareness and self-monitoring that can only come with experience.

(7) Rules and procedures

We deal with the matter of rules in Chapter 14 and it will be helpful to read what we say there in conjunction with this brief review of them in relation to first meetings. Following Hargreaves' advice,[9] it is desirable that the teacher establishes a minimum number of rules during his or her very first encounter with a class. As we say later, these may cover such areas as entering the room, movement about the room, modes of address, when to talk and when not to talk, work and homework, and the distribution of materials and equipment. Try to express them as briefly as possible and then ensure that they are adhered to.

(8) Relationships

A teacher can begin to establish positive relationships with a class both collectively and individually from the very first meeting, in spite of the prohibitive nature of those rules that have to be established on this occasion. Wragg and Young[10] describe a variety of ways in which teachers and student teachers achieve this. Briefly, they are: (a) the judicious use of praise and encouragement; (b) giving attention to individual pupils; (c) being prepared to apologise when a mistake is made; (d) making positive offers to help individual pupils and working alongside them; (e) learning and using the children's names as soon as you can – it doesn't matter if you make a mistake, at least you're seen to be trying; and finally (f) the leaven of humour. As Fontana[11] says, children respond well to a teacher who can share a joke with them, and especially to a teacher who can see the funny side even when the laugh is on him or her. See also our comments on teacher–pupil relationships in Chapter 15.

LESSON PRESENTATION SKILLS

We have just considered the importance of first meetings of teachers and student teachers with their classes. As well as the points we identified as being of importance to the student teacher in particular, there are the specifically professional aspects of presenting material to a group or class. Most traditional lessons, especially at the secondary level, involve the teacher expounding, narrating, lecturing, demonstrating, explaining and directing discussion. As Perrott[12] has said, 'Regardless of the level of the pupils, the necessity of exposing pupils to new facts, concepts and principles; of explaining difficult ideas; of clarifying issues or of exploring relationships more often than not places the teacher in a position where he has to do a great deal of presenting.' She goes on to identify *five skills* that a teacher needs to develop in order to become a successful presenter. These are: (1) set induction; (2) closure; (3) stimulus variation; (4) clarity of explanation; and (5) use of examples. Let us look at each in turn.

(1) Set induction

A 'set' has been defined as 'a temporary, but often recurrent, condition of a person that (a) orients him toward certain environmental stimuli or events rather than towards others, selectively sensitising him for apprehending them; and that (b) facilitates certain activities or responses rather than others'. 'Induction' simply means 'introduction'. So we are talking about saying or doing (or both) specific things prior to a learning situation that will direct the learner's attention to the task in hand. Perrott says that the activities preceding a learning task will have an influence on the outcomes of the task and that some sets are more successful than others in achieving planned outcomes.

She identifies four functions of set induction, thus:

1 Focusing a learner's attention on what is to be learned by gaining their interest.

2 As a means of *transition* from the familiar to the new, from the known to the unknown, from material already covered to new material about to be introduced. At the beginning of a lesson, a transition set is often resorted to, using a question-and-answer session on material covered in the last lesson, thus leading on to the new learning in the current lesson. In addition, as Perrott

says, a transition set may use examples from pupils' general knowledge to move to new material by use of example or analogy.

3 A set induction may be used to provide a *framework* or *structure* for a lesson. Perrott quotes research evidence which indicates that teachers can influence pupils' learning best when they are told in advance, or at the outset, what the teacher expects of them. This kind of set may perhaps be more general and will provide the class with a framework or schema for the lesson. A moment's thought will enable you to realise that there is a close logical connection between a set induction in this sense and the lesson objective, tying us into the objectives model that underpins much of this book.

4 The fourth function of set induction is to give meaning to a new concept or principle. This frequently involves the use of concrete and specific examples and analogies to assist pupils in understanding abstract ideas and concepts.

Perrott summarises the discussion of set induction in Box 43.

Box 43

The use of set induction

In addition to its use at the beginning of a lesson, set induction may also be used during the course of a lesson. Examples of the activities in which it is appropriate are:

1   To begin a new unit of work.
2   To initiate a discussion.
3   To introduce an assignment.
4   To prepare for a field excursion.
5   To prepare for a practical session in the laboratory.
6   To prepare for viewing a film or TV programme.
7   To introduce a guest speaker.

Source Perrott

(2) Closure

If set induction organises a learner's perception in a particular way at the outset of a learning session, *closure*, as Perrott explains, complements set induction by drawing attention to the end of a learning sequence or the end of an entire lesson by focusing attention on what has been learned. Indeed, this is its main function – to help learners remember the main points for a future occasion.

Perrott warns that closure needs to be carefully planned so that it is given due allocation of time. As she says, to be overtaken by the bell is a most ineffective end to a lesson.

She identifies four occasions for using closure during the course of a lesson:

1   to end a discussion by calling on a pupil to summarise the main points covered;
2   to end a laboratory exercise by summarising the stages and findings of the experiment;
3   as a follow up to a film, TV programme, or guest speaker; and
4   to follow up a piece of homework by using praise and encouragement, e.g. 'You tackled a difficult task very creditably, well done!' As Perrott says, this would be an example of social closure in contrast to cognitive closure.

(3) Stimulus variation

The need for this skill – varying the stimulus – arises because sustained uniformity of presentation can lead to boredom and mental inactivity. Again, it is based on research evidence which indicates that changes in perceived environment attract attention and stimulate thought.

Perrott identifies the chief means of varying the stimulus thus:

1 *Teacher movements*: Deliberate and timed shifts about the room can help to revive and/or sustain interest. However, avoid nervous, fussy and irritating movements, like obsessively pacing up and down the same part of the room.

2 *Focusing behaviours*: Communication can be aided by the use of *verbal focusing* (giving emphasis to particular words, statements or directions) and *gestural focusing* (using eye movements, facial expressions, and movement of head, arms and body). As Perrott says, gestures are important as means of communication between teacher and pupil, being used to gain attention and express emotions. *Verbal-gestural focusing*, which is a combination of the two, can also be useful.

3 *Changes in speech patterns*: This involves changing the quality, expressiveness, tone and rate of speech, all of which can increase animation. Planned silences and pauses can also be effective.

4 *Changing interaction*: The need here is to ring the changes on the main types of interaction – teacher and class, teacher and pupil, and pupil and pupil.

5 *Shifting sensory channels*: Information is processed by means of the five senses and research suggests that pupils' ability to take in information can be increased by appealing to sight and sound alternatively. Thus a teacher will follow up a verbal explanation with an accompanying diagram.

(4) Clarity of explanation

Perrott again points out that research findings indicate that *clarity of presentation* is something that can exert considerable influence on effective teaching. She goes on to select a number of factors important in contributing to effectiveness in explanation. They are: (a) *Continuity*: Maintaining a strong connecting thread through a lesson is a matter of great importance. This should be perfectly clear and diversions from it should be kept to a minimum. (b) *Simplicity*: Try to use simple, intelligible and grammatical sentences. As Perrott says, 'A common cause of failure is the inclusion of too much information in one sentence. Keep sentences short, and if relationships are complex consider communicating them by visual means.' As regards vocabulary, use simple words well within the class's own vocabulary. If specialist, subject-specific language is used, make sure the terms employed are carefully defined and understood. (c) *Explicitness*: Perrott explains that one reason for ineffectiveness in presenting new material to a class is the assumption that the children understand more than is in fact the case. Where explanations are concerned, one must be as explicit as possible (see the discussion of *language* below).

(5) Use of examples

The use of examples is a fundamental aspect of teaching and it is hardly necessary to stress its importance, particularly in the presentation of new material. Perrott offers the following guidelines for the effective use of examples.

1   Start with simple examples and work towards more complex ones.
2   Start with examples relevant to pupils' experience and level of knowledge.
3   Relate examples to the principles, idea or generalisation being taught.
4   Check to see whether you have accomplished your objectives by asking the pupils to give you examples which illustrate the point you were trying to make.

TEACHING STYLES

Barnes *et al.*[13] report three significantly different teaching styles that were found on the Technical and Vocational Education Initiative in the 1980s. They were named thus:

- *closed* (a formal, didactic style with little or no negotiation between teachers and students);
- *framed* (where an overall structure for a lesson was given by the teacher but within that there was room for students' own contributions);

- *negotiated* (where teachers and students largely negotiated the content and activities between themselves).

The measure of latitude in the *negotiated* style perhaps has little opportunity to be practised in any widespread way since the inception of the national curriculum. The notion of *framing* reaches back to the work of Bernstein in the 1970s.[14] He argued that *framing* referred to the degree of control that teachers and students possessed over the selection, organisation and pacing of curricular knowledge; weak framing ceded a great deal of control to teachers and students; strong framing offered little opportunity for control. A strongly framed curriculum parallels the *closed* teaching style in Barnes *et al.*, whereas their *negotiated* teaching style parallels Bernstein's notion of weak framing.

One can take from the work of Galton *et al.*[15] in primary education (discussed earlier) an alternative tripartite classification of teaching styles. These are:

- *class enquirers* (characterised by whole-class teaching, together with individuals working on their own, a high level of teacher questioning and a high degree of control exercised by the teacher);
- *individual monitors* (characterised by teachers tending to work with individuals rather than with groups or the class as a whole, and making very stressful demands on the teacher);
- *group instructors* (characterised, as its title suggests, by teachers organising students into groups and working with them in the group situation).

This third style was seen by the researchers as an organisation that minimised the potentially disruptive effect of 'attention seekers' in the class (they would disrupt a group rather than the whole class), whereas the first style – the whole-class approach that is heavily under the control of the teacher – provided a theatre for the attention seeker, with an audience of the remainder of the class.

The student teacher will draw on a range of teaching styles using the criterion of *fitness for purpose*. Some activities will require the student teacher to be very formal and didactic, with little negotiation with the students. In other activities a group or student-driven approach might be more suitable, particularly if there is a wide spread of ability in the class; group work can be seen as a manageable means of organising mixed-ability classes that steers a course between under-differentiated, poorly matched work and work that is so differentiated that it is impossible for the teacher to keep up with each individual's demands. That said, the rise in information technology might herald new possibilities for planning and managing individualised programmes of study for some of the teaching time.

Bearing in mind the comments in Part II about differentiation, we suggest that the student teacher takes the opportunity on teaching practice to try several different styles so that he or she can begin to match up appropriate teaching styles with appropriate learning styles, different curricular areas, different types of activity, different students and different resources.

SOME RELEVANT RESEARCH FINDINGS

Since the 1960s there has been a steady growth in the number of studies of teacher and pupil behaviour in the classroom. Although the complex nature of classroom activity presents significant problems for researchers, the findings yielded by their efforts are of great interest to teachers and particularly student teachers. Flanders,[16] for instance, discovered that teachers who were *not* successful in the classroom tended surprisingly to use many of the same instructional procedures and methods as those who were, except that they used them in more or less rigid fashion. They displayed little variation from one classroom situation to the next and seemed to lack the ability to expand or restrict children's freedom of action through verbal control.

The successful teachers, by contrast, manifested four elements in their teaching: spontaneously, they varied their classroom roles from dominative to supportive ones, and were able to secure both student compliance and initiative as the situation demanded; they could switch at will from one role to another and did not blindly follow a single approach to the exclusion of others; they were able to move easily from their diagnosis of a classroom problem to a follow-up course of action; and they were both critical of their classroom pupils and sensitive to their needs as human beings. Briefly, the study suggests that successful teachers are flexible in their teaching styles and can shift easily and naturally from the direct to the indirect, from being critical observers to sympathetic counsellors, depending on the need.

Flanders subsequently reported that when pupils' ideas are incorporated into the learning activities, they seem to learn more and to develop more positive attitudes to the teacher and the learning situation; and that teachers who are over-critical in class appear consistently to achieve less in most subject areas.

Hamacheck,[17] after a review of available research on teacher classroom behaviour, reports that effective teachers seem to be superior in the following ways: their willingness to be flexible; their capacity to perceive the world from the child's point of view; their ability to 'personalise' their teaching; their willingness to experiment; their skill in asking questions; knowledge of subject matter; their skill in establishing definite examination procedures; their willingness to provide study helps; their capacity to demonstrate an appreciative attitude; and their conversational manner in teaching.

The perceptual differences between good and poor teachers investigated by Combs[18] suggest that good teachers can be distinguished from poor ones with respect to the following perceptions about other people:

The good teacher is more likely to have an internal rather than an external frame of reference. That is, he or she seeks to understand how things seem to others and then uses this as a guide for his or her own behaviour.

The good teacher is more concerned with people and their reactions than with things and events.

The good teacher is more concerned with the subjective-perceptual experience of people than with objective events. He or she is, again, more concerned with how things seem to people than just the so-called or alleged facts.

The good teacher seeks to understand the causes of people's behaviour in terms of their *current* thinking, feeling, beliefs and understandings rather than in terms of forces exerted on them now or in the past.

The good teacher generally trusts other people and perceives them as having the capacity to solve their own problems.

The good teacher sees others as being friendly and enhancing rather than hostile or threatening.

The good teacher tends to see other people as being worthy rather than unworthy. That is, he or she sees all people as possessing a certain dignity and integrity.

The good teacher sees people and their behaviour as essentially developing

Box 44

Good and poor teacher behaviour in the classroom

Barr, using a variety of recording techniques, studied the classroom behaviours of forty-seven social studies teachers who were considered to be superior and forty-seven who were regarded as below average. The following are fragmentary samples of classroom behaviours distinguishing the good from the poor teachers:

Characteristic comments made by poor teachers (but not by good ones):
Are you working hard? ... Aren't you ever going to learn that word? ... Everyone sit up straight, please ... I'm afraid you're confused ... No, that's wrong ... Oh dear, don't you know that? ... Oh, sit down ... Say something ...

Characteristic comments made by good teachers (but not by poor ones):
Aha, that's a new idea ... Are you going to accept that as an answer? ... I should like more proof ... Do you suppose you could supply a better word? ... Can you prove your statement? ... Don't you really think you could? ... I'm not quite clear on that – think a moment ... Let's stick to the question ... Probably my last question wasn't a good one ...

Source Brembeck[19]

from within rather than as a product of external events to be moulded or directed. In other words, she sees people as creative and dynamic rather than passive or inert.

Some characteristics of good and bad teachers are summed up by Brembeck (Box 44).

In a study which investigated pupils' assessments of their teachers, Wragg and Young[20] identified students' opinions using questionnaires and interviews. The school was a sixth-form-entry city comprehensive high school for 12- to 16-year-olds. It had a mixed catchment area drawing partly on a large working-class estate and partly on a middle-class residential area. The school had a good reputation and was a popular choice among parents.

The questionnaire comprised thirty-two five-point scales. The scores ranged from 1 (everyone strongly agrees) to 5 (everyone strongly disagrees). The five items which attracted the strongest agreement were as follows:

Five statements showing strongest agreement

Item		Mean score
1	This teacher would explain things clearly.	1.46
2	This teacher would call you by your first name.	1.61
3	This teacher would help the slower ones catch up in a nice way.	1.65
4	This teacher would help you learn a lot in every lesson.	1.66
5	This teacher would be a good listener.	1.86

As the authors point out, this table confirms findings disclosed in previous studies, chiefly, *that the ability to explain is most highly valued*. It also reveals the importance attached by pupils to good sympathetic personal relationships. In contrast, the five statements attracting greatest disagreement are:

Five statements showing strongest disagreement

Item		Mean score
1	This teacher would hit you.	4.37
2	This teacher would boss you about.	4.28
3	This teacher would sometimes be too busy to talk to you.	3.71
4	This teacher would let you mark your own tests.	3.55
5	This teacher would do something else if that's what the class wants.	3.52

The reader, the authors suggest, can perhaps draw his or her own conclusions from this table about the pupils' views on child-centredness, aggression in teachers, and authoritarian styles. One particularly surprising finding of the study was the lack of difference between sexes and between year groups.

Rogers,[21] approaching the problems of learning from a more existential viewpoint, stresses that the goal of education is the facilitation of learning. His clinical and empirical studies have disclosed three basic qualities in the teacher which help to bring this about. The first is the *realness of the facilitator*. He is much more likely to be effective if he presents his real self to the learner without front or facade. Rogers points out that this is in sharp contrast with the tendency of most teachers to show themselves to their pupils simply as roles. The second quality is *trust and acceptance* and involves respect for the learner's feelings and opinions. It is a caring relationship in a non-possessive sense. The third quality is *empathetic understanding* – the ability to understand the children's reactions from the inside and to be aware of the way the process of learning seems to the child. Children appreciate being understood simply from their point of view without being judged or evaluated. Rogers's studies will repay careful reading by those interested in the kinds of findings experimental and empirical research disclose.

Chapter 11

Mixed-ability teaching

So many books and articles have been written about organising mixed-ability groups in schools and so many definitions of the term 'mixed-ability' are now bandied about that it is quite impossible to discuss the topic of mixed-ability teaching without bearing in mind that the term has different meanings for different people. It can be argued,[1] of course, that all teaching in school is mixed-ability teaching since the moment a teacher has responsibility for teaching more than one child at a time, he or she is faced with the problem of planning worthwhile learning experiences for groups of children which take account of individual differences within the group. This does not get us very far, however, for as student teachers discover in their contacts with schools, there are teachers who appear to ignore or discount the manifest differences among the children they teach.

THE CASE FOR MIXED-ABILITY TEACHING

Mixed-ability teaching is little more than an extension of 'good practice' in terms of organising students to meet individual needs. It is, perhaps, fallacious to assume that whole-class teaching of students with alleged similar abilities was ever more than an administrative or pedagogical convenience for teaching large numbers of students of similar ages – a coping strategy[2] which disguised massive differences of ability within an allegedly 'homogeneous' group. Mixed-ability teaching forces teachers to recognise the problems of having to stretch the brightest students and having to cater for the less able students.[3] The notion of mixed abilities is premised on the view that each student possesses multiple abilities in different curricular and extra-curricular activities. This moves us away from the psychometric paradigm of a single overall ability in students that permeates every activity in which they are involved – such that placement in a stream or band fairly reflects a student's overall ability. Rather, the argument for mixed-ability grouping reflects the view that one student may be excellent in mathematics but have problems in English, another may be outstanding in PE but mediocre in geography. To confine students permanently to a single band or stream is to understate their many abilities.

The evidence is unequivocal in the nature/nurture debate that to prevent the achievement of potential by spurious reference to the *nature* side of the argument – that students are intrinsically or genetically slow or bright overall – is grossly to reduce by distortion the considerable effects of the *nurture* side of the argument.[4] Jackson[5] remarks that excellence and abilities may have genetic limits but we have to go a long way before we reach them. Bailey and Bridges[6] remark that a teacher who writes that a student 'could do better' is reporting little more than a safe and virtually logically necessary truth.

The case for mixed-ability grouping is advanced further by the evidence that a streaming system can easily reproduce a social system, wherein, very crudely speaking, 'bright' streams contain students from the middle and upper classes and 'poor' streams contain students from the working classes. Streams and bands correlate highly with social situation.[7] Indeed, one of the cornerstones of comprehensive schooling is that not only is a social mix desirable within a school, but a social mix is desirable within each class. Students should learn how to work with peers drawn from different social situations, indeed the school has a major function in breaking down patterns of differential status, power and class.

Kelly[8] suggests that the alternatives to mixed-ability teaching – banding and streaming – consign many able students to failure (e.g. through negative labelling and low expectations amongst those students who are not in the upper bands or streams). There is also evidence to suggest that the gaps between streams widen through a student's educational career and beyond to employment. Further, there is a need for organisational strategies to reduce student disaffection and associated teacher stress. The problem of the 'delinquescent subcultures' of disaffected students identified by Hargreaves[9] is exacerbated by streaming that creates 'sink' streams or bands.

Given the influence of teacher expectations on students' performance,[10] the dangers of the self-fulfilling prophecy depressing student performance[11] and the high significance of grouping of students for their subsequent performance and achievement,[12] moves to increase students' self-esteem and raise teachers' expectations (a central feature of school effectiveness) should surely be encouraged. Mixed-ability teaching is one strategy for this. Further, it is not enough simply to provide access for all students to a common curriculum (e.g. the national curriculum): by dint of their home and outside-school circumstances and situations, students will have a differential uptake of this curriculum. This is the 'cultural capital' thesis.[13] It argues that some students have the background cultural and linguistic capital and the necessary dispositions, together with the positive attitudes to school, motivations to learning, parental support, social advantage, ease in dealing with authority figures so that when they meet schooling and school knowledge they can engage it comfortably and take advantage of it. For other students, schools and school knowledge represents an unfamiliar or alien culture and method-ology, they cannot engage it as easily and hence are disadvantaged. For them, schools and the curriculum represent a culture shock.

It can be seen, then, that the argument for mixed-ability teaching *in principle* (and supported by empirical data) is powerful. Empirical research suggests that the evidence is plentiful but conflicting as to the *academic* merits or demerits of mixed-ability teaching. Ross[14] provides pieces of research evidence that are diametrically opposed to each other; Morrison[15] argues that the only general agreement is that there is no agreement on whether mixed-ability teaching is any better or worse than banded or streamed teaching. Newbold[16] suggests that there is little evidence to suggest that high-ability students achieve any less in streamed or mixed-ability classes, and that for low-ability students there was a marked gain in achievements in mixed-ability classes in comparison with streamed classes.

In an important study, Slavin[17] found that there were no significant differences in achievement between secondary school students who were taught in homogeneous and heteregeneous groups. The results were the same for all subjects except for social studies, in which heterogeneous (mixed-ability) groupings seemed to produce better achievement for all students. Slavin argued that his findings contrast with those of other research studies that compare students' achievements in different tracks (streams or bands). These studies, he avers, show that a tracking system operates to the advantage of bright students and to the disadvantage of lower-ability students; they show that tracking has positive effects for high achievers and negative effects for low achievers. His work dispels both the criticisms of mixed-ability teaching and the criticisms of streaming.

Academic standards, then, are not appreciably threatened by mixed-ability teaching (indeed in a global sense they actually rise); one can also identify other advantages of mixed-ability teaching, in particular social, management and personal advantages to students and teachers. These are set out in Box 45.

That said, having mixed-ability teaching groups does not find universal support in schools – particularly in secondary education. It has to be said that the success of mixed-ability teaching is heavily dependent on the commitment to it by teachers. Ball[18] makes the sad comment that, in the school he studied, mixed-ability teaching failed because there was little evidence of teachers moving away from a formal, didactic style of teaching. Indeed, Reid *et al.*[19] comment that success of mixed-ability teaching is contingent upon the school system finding a way of coping with very many factors; see Box 46.

Hence, whilst this form of organisation is desirable for a wealth of reasons – ideological, educational, sociological, etc. – there is clearly a need not only for teacher commitment but also for demanding practical problems to be solved. It is these that we shall address in the remainder of this chapter. Clearly the student teacher will need to ask his or her mentor about these practical issues, the nature of setting arrangements in the school, the composition of the class or set and particular problems within these. Many

Box 45

Advantages of mixed-ability groups

1 There are fewer 'sink' groups in schools.
2 Different teaching styles are opened up, moving away from didactic methods.
3 There is potentially less negative labelling of students.
4 Teachers have contact with a wide range of students.
5 This form of teaching makes for diagnostic teaching.
6 Troublesome students are 'diluted' through the school.
7 A sense of community can be developed in the school (though, it must be said, that this is under threat as schools have an open-access policy, moving them away from being neighbourhood and community schools).
8 There is a wide social mix in classrooms.
9 Students'self-esteem and motivation are promoted.
10 Equality of opportunity and outcome are furthered.
11 Mutual respect, support, understanding and tolerance are developed between students.
12 The classroom reflects the social mix of the world outside school.
13 Teachers develop new teaching skills.
14 Competition is replaced by co-operation.
15 The pastoral aspects of schooling take on increasing significance.
16 The errors of selection are avoided (e.g. where students are incorrectly assigned to bands, streams or tracks).

---

attempts to overcome the practical hurdles in mixed-ability teaching are addressed by having group work in classes (see the discussion of group work earlier). Mixed-ability teaching implies a *certain kind of teaching*, whereas any kind of teaching can, and does, go on in mixed-ability groups.

There is an important difference between *teaching in mixed-ability groups* and *mixed-ability teaching* which we ought to get straight from the outset. Elliott,[20] who makes this important distinction, identifies mixed-ability teaching as occurring when a teacher attempts to regulate his treatment of individual differences by the principle of equality. For example, when teachers adopt a teaching-to-the-whole-class approach in a mixed-ability situation they fail to regulate their teaching by the idea of equality because their teaching style assumes that individual differences do not exist.

In the sections that follow we review some of the more widely practised teaching strategies and learning styles that student teachers are likely to encounter during teaching practice. It is important to stress that in connection with the various teaching strategies we are presenting broad reviews. We do not take account of regional variations with respect to the interpretation (or assumption) of underlying philosophies, organisation and administration of

Box 46

Disadvantages of mixed-ability groups

1 Increased preparation and marking by staff.
2 The need for increased resources and careful use of resources.
3 The demands and stress on teachers.
4 The role uncertainty of teachers.
5 The need for detailed and frequent records of students' progress.
6 Coping with a wide ability range in a class (many secondary schools endeavour to circumvent this problem by setting).
7 Too heavy a reliance on worksheets and published schemes in resource-based learning.
8 For secondary schools, harmonising mixed-ability groups with GCSE examinations that have 'cut-off' grades (i.e. some students in a group being entered for examinations where the highest grade is a C and others in the group being entered for examinations where the highest grade is an A).
9 The avoidance of teacher dependence by students.
10 The attention to teacher input and instruction, i.e. ensuring that teachers are not confined to a class management *modus operandi* and that students are not expected simply to teach themselves.
11 Parental demand for academic excellence (a significant feature where schools compete with each other for students).
12 Balancing individual, group and whole-class teaching.

---

attendant practices, or even nomenclature. Nor, for the same reason, do we draw too fine a distinction between what is done with pupils of different ages.

TEACHING STRATEGIES IN MIXED-ABILITY GROUPS

It is axiomatic that the adoption of mixed-ability grouping requires the teacher to employ methods and means of class management that are compatible with it. Using methods that depend for their success upon a more or less homogeneous range of ability invites difficulty and failure.

Much of the time spent teaching mixed-ability classes will be devoted to individual and small-group work (see the discussions earlier on group work). The advantage of individualised learning in this context is that each student is able to work at a pace best suited to his or her needs and ability. He or she is therefore not stretched beyond his or her capabilities, nor prevented from fully realising his or her potential in a particular direction. One of the most efficient means of achieving individualised learning is through preparing individual programmes for the students concerned. This is especially the case in certain basic subjects like mathematics. The implications of this approach for the student teacher are twofold: (1) a high workload, particularly *before* a lesson; and (2) a considerable amount of record-keeping. Using Oeser's[21] notation we can diagram individualised learning in mixed-ability groups as in Example 7.

Example 7

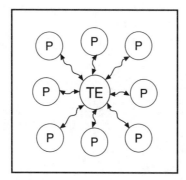

The use of *themes* caters for individual and small-group needs, especially among older children. A theme in this context may be seen as a central idea (e.g. animals, fire, witches and spells) used as a starting point for learning and one which will engage the children's interests. The main advantage of the theme approach is that it offers a framework within which to operate yet at the same time a considerable degree of freedom to both the children and teacher.

The successful outcome of the theme approach depends very much on the right choice of theme at the outset. It should be neither too narrow in scope nor too general; and sub-topics subsumed under the theme must have coherence arising from their logical interrelationships.

The factors that need to be borne in mind when choosing a theme include the ages, interests, aptitudes and abilities of the pupils involved in the enterprise. We suggest, too, that the student teacher finds out in advance which children have learning difficulties, which are poor readers or potentially disruptive. Another fact that must not be overlooked is the competence of the student teacher himself or herself. He or she should be sure of having access to the subject and pedagogical knowledge to undertake this successfully, discussing matters with and seeking advice from the mentor and relevant teachers in the school. Yet another factor concerns the objectives the student teacher has in mind. These must be carefully specified to ensure the successful organisation of the undertaking.

Once a theme has been chosen, the next decision concerns whether all the children will work on the same things and engage in the same activities, or whether they will be allowed to choose their own sub-topic from the theme and devote their attention to that. The decision will be influenced by the teacher's objectives, but most likely he or she will want to make use of one or other of two techniques: the *circus approach* and the *selective approach*. With the former, a pupil will work at each of the sub-topics embraced by the theme in sequence; with the latter, he will select one or two sub-topics and give his attention exclusively to these.

Again, using Oeser's notation, the *circus approach* to a theme in small group work can be diagrammed as in Example 8. The thick arrows show that each small group engages in each of the sub-topics of the theme.

Example 8

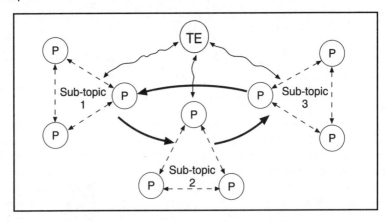

The *selective approach* to a theme in small-group work can be represented as in Example 9.

A theme can be initiated by means of a lead lesson, for this is one of the

Example 9

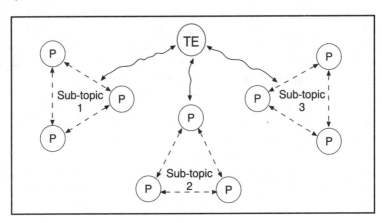

more successful ways of arousing interest. A second means of stimulating interest, if pertinent to the chosen theme, is to visit places in the locality having bearing on the work to be explored – a museum or television studio, for example. To make the most of a visit of this kind, the teacher must plan and prepare carefully so he or she can bring as much as possible to the attention of pupils. A third means of capturing interest would be to surround the children with examples, materials and resources relevant to the theme and suggest what they might possibly do with them. This approach has proved especially useful with primary children.

The organisation of the theme approach can be particularly daunting for student teachers. No matter how much the children's interest has been aroused, it will be to little avail if the organisation is faulty and does not permit the theme's thorough implementation. This can only be achieved by careful preparation and planning.

Once matters are underway, the teacher's main task is to keep a careful watch on the progress of each student. This will mean checking that adequate materials and resources are available, striving to maintain the original motivational level and suggesting ways in which an individual student's efforts may develop. If the work of the class is to be an educational experience, the teacher will find that he or she has to work just as hard as in a more traditional lesson.

One final point arises with subjects which at first glance do not appear to lend themselves to the theme approach. Languages, mathematics and science, for example, generally require a 'linear' approach, that is, knowledge in these areas has to be developed step by step and cannot easily be approached obliquely from a student's own interests. Where this is the case, provision is usually made in the timetable for either formal teaching or individualised work. However, a change of objectives even with subjects of this nature very often discloses potential for a theme approach.

The impact of information technology in schools creates several additions to the examples provided by Oeser. For instance, one can add a new type of teaching arrangement as shown in Example 10. This represents a resource suite in which there are shelves of resources (on the right), computer terminals and PCs, and tables for individual or collaborative work (centre). The teacher is circulating around the class. The essential focus here is on the resources rather than simply the people. Students are interacting with materials principally and with people secondarily. This is by no means a new concept; indeed, this form of organisation rehearses some of the rationale that underpins Example 9, where Oeser writes that a way of capturing students' interest is to surround them with examples, materials and relevant resources and to suggest how they can be used.

Let us summarise some of the points we have been discussing concerning the organisation of group work in mixed-ability classes. Box 47 identifies some of the organisational skills that make for successful teaching in mixed-ability groups.

Example 10

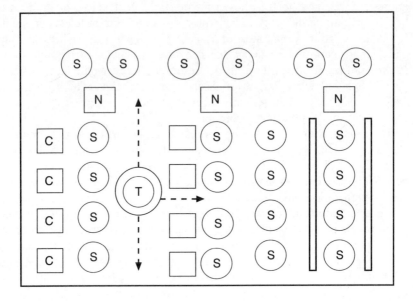

S = Student
T = Teacher
N = Networked computer
C = Stand-alone computer

Box 47

Skills needed for mixed-ability group work

1   *Decide beforehand* how your group will be made up: self-selected, or selected by you, and if so on what criteria?
2   *Decide if your groups will be static* or regrouped for different activities.
3   *Have the lesson carefully prepared* and everything ready beforehand.
4   *Ensure that each group has appropriate subject material* and activities.
5   *Go round from group to group quickly.* Make sure you are still visible by, and still watching, other groups.
6   Do not forget to *look behind you* as you go round.
7   *Be prepared for early finishers* and have things ready for them to do.
8   *Watch for signs* that pupils are unoccupied – unnecessary movement and too much chat, incipient rowdiness.
9   Have a good way of *ending the lesson*.

Source adapted from Kerry and Sands[22]

DIFFERENT ABILITIES WITHIN MIXED-ABILITY CLASSES

The various definitions[23] of mixed-ability organisation in the literature share one thing in common and that is their recognition that mixed-ability classes contain a span of ability ranging from significantly below to significantly above the average.

Arguably, it is at the extremes of the ability range that children have most need of individual attention. For student teachers, it is absolutely vital that they should plan for the range of abilities in preparing their teaching programmes. Kerry and Sands identify some *common problems* which experienced teachers face when dealing with a range of abilities in mixed-ability classes. They are to do with:

- *Dead time* This is the time between a pupil finishing one activity and starting another. Some students complete work quickly because tasks are often too easy for them. Other students can often manage only a sentence or two, and then they feel they have exhausted the topic.
- *Boredom* This may result from spending too much time waiting for the teacher to correct work, approve progress to the next step or take remedial action.
- *Lack of motivation* Children who are often unoccupied and bored can easily lose interest.
- *Disruption* The creative mind continually seeks new diversions. The less able may simply be looking for something more relevant to do! The bored pupil is always a potential trouble-maker.
- *Provision of special work* The previous four problems imply that the teacher must of necessity provide special work for pupils at both ends of the ability spectrum.
- *Increased preparation time by the teacher* Implicitly, providing special work means spending more time in preparing lessons.
- *Linguistic and cognitive levels of worksheets and texts* One perennial problem of mixed-ability classes is that teachers tend to 'teach to the middle'. Part of the 'special provision' for exceptional pupils is to cater for students who need to be stretched intellectually and to cope with others for whom the language of text or instructions may not be clear.
- *Emotional and pastoral problems* Finally, both sets of pupils may (but not necessarily) have problems of a social nature, e.g. concerning peer-group relations. Bright pupils are sometimes rejected as 'teacher's pet', and slower learners are labelled 'thick'. The teacher needs to bear relationship problems in mind when organising classroom work and activities.

Having identified some of the *common problems* that experienced teachers face when dealing with slow learners and bright pupils, let us now examine some of the specific solutions that have been proposed for dealing with these two groups of students.

STUDENTS WITH LEARNING DIFFICULTIES

'How can one use worksheet assignments when half the class can't read?' This must surely be one of the most frequently voiced comments by teachers in any discussion of mixed-ability teaching. Despite the exaggeration in that rhetorical question, a small proportion of children in the classes of most secondary schools which have a truly comprehensive intake will lack basic skills in literacy and numeracy. What is to be done with these pupils? A number of solutions suggest themselves. First, poor readers might be winnowed out at the beginning of their secondary schooling to form a separate group for whom special courses are devised and taught by trained support staff. Second, a programme of part-time extraction might be devised in which children needing special help in literacy and numeracy are withdrawn to receive that tuition. Third, teachers might be encouraged to meet the needs of learners experiencing difficulties entirely within the context of mixed-ability groups.

The appeal of the first solution (that is, the total extraction of pupils needing additional help) lies in the benefits they might enjoy as a result of working in small groups with sympathetic and specialist teachers. The disadvantages of remedial groups, however, may well outweigh the advantages. All too frequently such a degree of separation from fellow pupils generates anti-school attitudes and behaviour problems. The second solution (part-time group extraction for remedial reading) is widely practised in many secondary schools. Davies[24] shows how such a solution can be accomplished:

> Pupils needing remedial attention will be scattered across the whole year group when placed initially in forms under the care of a form tutor. These forms will be permanent units which for three, four or five years will be registered together ... and whose needs will be the concern of the form tutor having responsibility for helping with their problems and keeping their records. These mixed ability units are retained for certain lessons – e.g. Art ... Music, Physical Education. For all other lessons the year group will be settled into more homogeneous groups. In this way children of all abilities might work together for perhaps a quarter of their time at school.

While this pattern of support has much to commend it, contributing as it does both to the educational and the social objectives of mixed-ability teaching, it has been argued that it serves to minimise rather than to remove the problems of teaching students with learning difficulties. Placing children in mixed-ability grouping for only 25 per cent of the school day, Davies suggests, is a guarantee of creating sub-cultures within the student body as a whole, with all the attendant problems that such smaller groupings can generate.

In arguing for the third solution (total retention of students with learning difficulties within mixed-ability groups), both Kelly[25] and Davies are aware of the enormous demands that such a solution imposes upon most teachers. For Kelly, the social and the emotional advantages to be derived make it unwise and undesirable that non-readers should be excluded from mixed-ability work. Kelly's solution is to give these students individual assignments in group projects which capitalise upon what strengths they have, such assignments being based upon as many resources that can be used without reading skills as can be obtained or made. It is doubtful that Kelly's solution arouses much enthusiasm among teachers as a whole. Davies's proposal, based as it is on actual practice, is more realistic:

> At one stage, itinerant remedial help was brought into the mainstream classroom, with a pair of teachers operating in harness, using carefully devised assignments wherein every pupil was guided to tasks with which he or she could cope initially via the use of resources suited to his or her capabilities.

However desirable Davies's solution, it is contingent upon a relatively small number of pupils needing specialised support and the availability of a large number of support staff. In most schools today this is scarcely a viable proposition. By and large, it is the practice of part-time extraction which is chosen as the way of dealing with students with learning difficulties within mixed-ability teaching situations.

BRIGHT PUPILS

What of the fast learner and the gifted child? The following extract from a 14-year-old's essay entitled 'My dream work' illustrates the problem of the gifted child who feels underchallenged in a mixed-ability teaching situation:

> Ever since I can remember I have enjoyed learning. At H.L. (her middle school) I had every encouragement. I was allowed to work at lunchtimes; there were adequate text books which we could bring home, and we were 'set' according to ability and speed of working. That meant that those of us with academic ambitions could help and encourage each other. Those less quick to comprehend had lessons geared to their pace.
>
> Since I have been at R. (secondary comprehensive) I have begun to despair of my dream becoming reality (university degree and a teaching diploma). It is hard to find satisfaction in working from worksheets. Without text books, except for Maths and French, I cannot pursue an idea which interests me, or revise except from my own notes. We have no library at W.E. (her home village) and the public library in L. (nearest town) leaves much to be desired. Why cannot I have text books to bring home? Why was it so outrageous for me to ask to take home an atlas to finish some work? Why must I be taught with pupils who have no desire to learn?

The report by HMI entitled *Gifted Children in Middle and Comprehensive School*[26] highlights the problem of the gifted pupil. *Giftedness* is an ill-defined term. For the vast majority of schools and their teachers, the report concludes, giftedness is neither implicit nor explicit in the day-to-day dialogue of school life. The irony is that whereas gifted children can, and frequently do, work below their potential from lack of challenge or from personal choice, and pass unnoticed, students with learning difficulties can less easily disguise their inability to work at the level and pace of their fellows. This latter observation is supported in the findings of a study[27] of able children in mixed-ability classes in which heads of department were asked to comment on the problems that mixed-ability teaching posed for bright pupils. They identified the following:

1   Teachers spend too much time with students with learning difficulties.
2   Good pupils can get away with not working at an appropriately fast pace.
3   It is hard to cater for the very bright in a mixed situation.
4   Bright pupils fail to cover enough subject content for their needs.
5   Teachers are not doing their best for top pupils – work is aimed at the middle band.
6   The top third of pupils are not stretched.
7   Bright pupils are more difficult to teach than other pupils.

The research concluded that for bright pupils, the following three needs are paramount. First, teachers must help bright children to develop appropriate study skills. *Inter alia*, this will involve producing genuinely graded worksheets and instructing able children in methods of self-testing. Second, teachers need to encourage bright pupils to develop skills of higher-level thinking. This will involve teachers in looking critically at classroom interaction and at their own questioning skills. Third, teachers must come to accept the 'normality' of bright pupils, particularly on the emotional level, even though they may seem 'old for their age'. The desire not to be different on the part of bright pupils sometimes triggers under-achievement. Bright pupils need to be rewarded for scholastic achievement and at the same time to retain their identification with the class group.

RESOURCES

Mixed-ability organisation raises a number of practical problems, not the least of which is the development and utilisation of adequate resources. Unlike traditional whole-class teaching, a mixed-ability regime requires a far greater quantity and variety of learning resources. Most schools that have organised along mixed-ability lines have developed some sort of resource-centre system, either localised within individual subject departments or centralised so as to serve the needs of the whole school. A resource centre involves six essential elements:

1   Production of home-made resources.
2   Selection and acquisition of other resources.
3   Classification and indexing for retrieval.
4   Storage.
5   Use, including guidance and lending, etc.
6   Evaluation and weeding.

The average school resource centre today is likely to contain most or all of the following materials: books, periodicals, video-cassettes, satellite downloading facilities, maps, models, posters, filmstrips, pictures, records, audio-tapes, slides, worksheets, computer programs, CD-ROMs, access to databases and programs outside the school (e.g. using the JANET and Internet resources). The development of computer networking in the school facilitates mixed-ability grouping and working very considerably as students have access to programs that are well matched to their needs and abilities.

WORKCARDS AND WORKSHEETS

Probably the most commonly used resource is the worksheet or workcard. Waters[28] argues that worksheets can free the teacher to move round the class more freely, encourage independent learning, structure learning, enable students to work at their own pace, keep students usefully occupied with work that does not require the teacher, freeing him or her to work with students whose worksheets do require his or her presence, and free the teacher from the role of instructor. One inquiry[29] into the use of worksheets revealed that, at any one time, there were several basic types in operation in the particular school. For example, there was a *single workcard* used by the whole class which, because it lacked structure, failed to satisfy the extremes of ability. Second, there was a *single structured workcard* which started from concrete problems that were within the grasp of the majority of students in the group and proceeded in both depth and breadth to more abstract problems. This type of workcard had the effect of frustrating the least able children, who found little success in this arrangement. A third approach involved *a series of shorter workcards* that were designed to complete the whole programme. The cards were graded in difficulty, the earlier ones presenting concrete problems and providing a series of success points for the less able students. The later ones were designed to extend the more able children and presented them with open-ended, problem-solving tasks. The appeal of this third approach to workcard development is that it allows for a whole range of resource materials to be used as a supplement to the basic programme. Whatever method is adopted, the author (an experienced teacher) identifies certain basic criteria that need consideration. We summarise these in Box 48.

Box 48

Considerations in planning worksheets

1   What exactly is the purpose of the worksheet? Is it to provide information, ask questions, set tasks, record information, promote new learning, revise or apply knowledge, keep students busy, or a combination of these (and others)?

2   Do you actually need a worksheet (e.g. if everyone is to have the worksheet could not its contents simply be written on the chalkboard)?

3   The worksheet must make clear exactly what the students are to do and how they are to record.

4   The language level must be appropriate for the students in terms of vocabulary and readability. Will the children understand the language?

5   How will different worksheets for different students in a single lesson be organised and introduced?

6   Will the worksheet become progressively harder in the knowledge that only the brighter or faster workers will reach the end?

7   The workcard must be attractive and motivating.

8   Will the worksheet be handwritten or word-processed/desktopped? If it is handwritten will it be written in print/'joined up' writing/capitalised/ lower case/in the school's adopted handwriting style? If they are word-processed the letters may be able to be printed in an interesting font or style or in an interesting manner (e.g. a workcard on eggs could have the words written around the perimeter of an egg, a workcard on houses could be shaped like a house). Has the spelling been checked?

9   Will the students know how to answer the questions on the sheet? If they do not, what will be the student teacher's role? How will the students find the answers to the questions?

10   What resources and equipment are required for the tasks on the sheet?

11   What prior knowledge is assumed on the sheet? Whereabouts in the programme of work will it come, e.g. to lead off a programme, to follow it up, to extend and apply knowledge? How will it be introduced? What preliminary activities are necessary?

12   How will students access textbooks for answers – is it necessary to specify to which books etc. the student is to refer?

13   How many activities are there on the sheet? Is that too many/too few?

14   Will there be many activities of the same type on the sheet or activities of a differing type on a single sheet?

15   How attractive is the sheet? Are there too many or too few words?

16   Do some tasks require the student teacher to be on hand for safety reasons, e.g. cutting, heating, handling dangerous equipment?

17   How will the sheet prompt and promote discussion as a whole class or group?

18   Are the questions an appropriate mixture of low and high order, open and closed (see p. 229: *questioning*)?

19   Has a time-scale been specified or anticipated for the completion of the worksheet (i.e. so that the student teacher can plan the most efficient use of his or her own time)?

20   How will the worksheet be linked to displayed material for accessing information?

Box 48 sets out some general *principles* in devising workcards and worksheets together with the very many *practical* issues. These derive from our own analyses of student teachers' workcards and worksheets produced for teaching practice. We list twenty key considerations.

Finally, the oft-quoted description of mixed-ability teaching as 'death by a thousand worksheets' points to the injudicious use some schools make of this key learning resource. The workcard is best seen as one of a number of teaching resources that are appropriate to mixed-ability teaching. An un-relieved diet of workcards is a certain recipe for boredom and indiscipline in any classroom.

IMPLICATIONS FOR STUDENT TEACHERS

By now it is abundantly clear that successful teaching in mixed-ability classrooms involves a wide range of preparation and a variety of professional skills. Is it possible, one might ask, to identify specific factors that make for effective mixed-ability teaching? In proposing a ten-point attack on the challenge of mixed-ability teaching, Wragg has the particular needs of student teachers in mind. Box 49 identifies his proposals which we then present in greater detail.

Box 49

Ten sets of skills for mixed-ability teaching

Preparatory skills
 1 Understanding individual differences among children in the class.
 2 Understanding the importance of issues to do with language in the classroom.
 3 Ability to be a member of a team.
 4 Devising and preparing appropriate curricula.

Teaching strategies
 5 Using whole-class teaching judiciously.
 6 Handling small groups.
 7 Interacting with individual children.
 8 Developing flexibility and adaptability.

Evaluation
 9 Monitoring pupils' progress and keeping records.
 10 Evaluating one's own teaching and undertaking professional self-development.

Source Wragg[30]

Individual differences

Mixed-ability teaching requires a thorough understanding of individual differences. Teachers need to anticipate difficulties by identifying, for example, those who require more time, those who lack self-confidence and those who are impulsive.

Language in the classroom

Unless teachers are aware of the crucial importance of language, much of the teaching in mixed-ability classes will be misguided. The effective preparation of worksheets, charts and wall displays, is contingent upon the use of appropriate language.

Team membership

Considerable interpersonal skills are required in mixed-ability situations where teachers are frequently required to work in teams in the planning and preparation of coursework materials.

Devising and preparing curricula

Because mixed-ability teaching poses more planning problems than other forms of classroom grouping, teachers need to acquire the inventiveness, the sensibility and the determination to devise and prepare appropriate curricula.

Using whole-class teaching

Contrary to popular belief, mixed-ability teaching requires the judicious use of whole-class teaching. Stand-up-and-talk skills are therefore very important. Teachers need to be able to command attention, to explain clearly, to speak audibly and distinctly, and to chair proceedings with large groups.

Handling small groups

Teachers need to develop the ability to handle several groups at once. In mixed-ability teaching such groups often differ in size, constitution and task in hand. Teaching them requires 'with-it-ness', that is, the ability to work with one group while keeping a vigilant eye on others in the classroom.

Interacting with individuals

Interacting with individual students is a vital skill in mixed-ability teaching. Teachers need to be able to secure a high degree of industry from students working on their own. This involves designing appropriate individual assignments and monitoring individual progress.

Developing flexibility and adaptability

Mixed-ability teaching requires numerous decisions to be made during the course of any lesson in which, typically, groups and individuals are engaged in several different activities. Success under such conditions demands flexibility and adaptability on the part of the teacher.

Monitoring student progress

In mixed-ability teaching, regular assessment and recording of students' progress is, if anything, more important than in traditional forms of classroom grouping. Teachers need to learn a wide range of assessment techniques and to develop an awareness of when and why to make evaluative judgements.

Evaluating one's own teaching

As important, perhaps, as evaluating students' work is the student teacher's assessment of his/her own performance. Ultimately, improvement in teaching often only takes place when student teachers decide for themselves to change the ways in which they plan, prepare and initiate learning activities.

Chapter 12

Language in classrooms

Talk occupies a crucial position in the classroom in any consideration of principal agents of learning. Adelman and Walker[1] express the point thus: 'We consider that the nature of talk is the only readily available manifestation of the extent and process by which mutual understandings of what counts as knowledge in any context are transacted.' American and British research[2] showed that talk in classrooms abides by the 'rule of two-thirds' – two-thirds of a lesson is talk; two-thirds of the talk is teacher talk; two thirds of the teacher talk is concerned with discipline and procedural matters rather than the lesson content itself. Whether this reflects a traditional, didactic approach to teaching or a less formal style of teaching, the conventional wisdom of this saying reflects the immense significance of classroom talk, not only for instructional matters but for discipline and control. We consider the question of classroom talk in eight main areas: characteristics of talk in classrooms, exposition, explanation, questioning, discussion, responding, summarising, and language and classroom interaction.

CHARACTERISTICS OF TALK

It is only in the recent past that the value of talk in the classroom has attracted the attention it deserves. This has been manifest in the steady flow of articles and books stressing the need for greater emphasis on spoken work in schools,[3] a need that has come about because, some believe, we have tended to devalue talk in the school and classroom. Whether this is true or not, one cannot deny that a considerable amount of talking does take place in schools; and this is so because our own culture depends to a very large extent on the spoken word as a means of transmitting knowledge. In reviewing the main characteristics of classroom talk, particularly that of older children, Edwards and Furlong[4] consider that not only is there so much of it, but that so much of what is said is both public and highly centralised. What they mean by being 'highly centralised' is that for much of the time in classrooms, there is a *single* verbal encounter in that whatever is being said demands the attention of all.

In pursuing the theme of centralised communication further, Edwards and

Furlong explain that although it plays a very important part in classroom interaction, its role should not be overstated, for considerable amounts of incidental and unofficial talk take place amid official exchanges. The authors further point out that, notwithstanding the occasions when children talk privately to other members of the class, when they offer comments and pose questions when requested to do so, or when they talk 'unofficially', their main communicative role, as far as traditional classrooms are concerned, is *to listen*. This means that the communicative rights of teacher and pupils are very unequal. In effect, the authors point out, teachers usually tell pupils when to talk, what to talk about, when to stop talking and how well they talked. The normal conversation between two equals stands in marked contrast to classroom exchanges because of this very inequality. In the former, no one has overriding claim to speak first, or more than others, or to decide unilaterally on the subject. The difference between an everyday conversation and a classroom exchange is dramatically realised when each kind is recorded and transcribed. In the case of everyday exchanges, statements are often incomplete, they clash with the statements of others and they are interrupted. There are also frequent false starts, hesitations and repetitions. Unless the transcript is edited, it is often difficult to make much sense of. By contrast, exchanges recorded in traditional classrooms are much more orderly and systematic. Indeed, Edwards and Furlong observe that they often look like a play script. As they comment, 'Most utterances are complete, and most speakers seem to know their lines and to recognize their turn to speak. Despite the large number, the talk appears more orderly.' Thus it is that whereas in everyday informal conversations there is always the possibility that several speakers will perversely talk against one another or that one individual will eventually appropriate a disproportionate amount of the talking time, in classroom interaction contributors to a discussion must be carefully controlled. The authors point out that this is much more easily achieved if communication rights are *not* equally shared – 'if one participant can speak whenever he chooses to do so, can normally nominate the next speaker, and can resolve any cases of confusion'.

The authors go on to explain that in so far as pupils are ready to be taught, they are likely to acknowledge that an able teacher has the right to talk first, last and most; to control the content of a lesson; and to organise that content by allocating speaking turns to the pupils. The teacher's right to decide who speaks, when, for how long and to whom, is mirrored in the small number of interactional possibilities in a typical lesson. Edwards and Furlong refer to such arrangements of speakers and listeners as *participant-structures* which they define as communicative networks linking those who are in contact with one another already, or can be if they choose. Enlarging on the nature of them, Edwards and Furlong say:

It is not difficult to link these structures intuitively to certain obvious stages in lessons – for example, to the teacher lecturing, checking on the reception of the lecture, inviting queries, sorting out problems, eliciting discussion, and trusting pupils to work on their own ... What even the simplest list brings out is the limited variety of interactional patterns characteristic of lessons, and how firmly most of them are centred on the teacher. There is usually a formalised allocation of speaking and listening roles. Teachers expect both a 'proper' silence *and* 'proper' willingness to talk, and they manage the interaction so as to produce orderly and relevant pupil participation.

The authors go on to consider how this orderliness is achieved. In the well-ordered classroom, they explain, the teacher's turns at speaking are taken as and when he or she chooses, these being determined by the kinds of pupil he or she addresses and also the subject matter being taught. Thus teachers appear to talk less to younger pupils, to brighter pupils, and when they are teaching English or social studies, for example, as compared with science or modern languages. However interesting these variations are, they are overshadowed by the difficulty most teachers seem to have in limiting themselves to much less than two-thirds of the time available for talking. Because much of the time appropriated by teachers is taken up by giving information and instructions, censuring pupils and evaluating them, Edwards and Furlong consider that most of their talking can be described as *telling*.

In seeing teacher talk in this context as *dominant performance*, Edwards and Furlong suggest that the teacher's message is made all the more effective because of his or her 'front of stage' location. The traditional classroom settings serve as a means of reinforcing the centrally controlled interaction.[5] As they say:

The conventional groupings of desks or tables channel communication to and from the teacher, who is the obvious focus of attention. He can direct his talk to any part of the room, while the natural flow of pupil-talk is either to him or to other pupils through him. It is a setting which makes it difficult for the teacher to avoid talking *at* pupils, or to break up the interaction into more localised encounters. In classrooms which are physically more open, no single focus of attention may be visible at all. Symbolically and practically, there is a switch of emphasis from the teacher to the learner.

But the teacher cannot monopolise the talk totally. There has to be a certain amount of pupil participation; and this presents the teacher with significant managerial problems because of the numbers of children involved. Once a teacher stops talking, Edwards and Furlong ask, how are turns taken? How is the rule of one speaker at a time maintained? Who is to answer a particular question? Normally, it is the teacher's on-the-spot decisions that solve them

– 'Turns are allocated, they are not seized, and pupils have to learn to bid appropriately for the right to speak.'

We have been concerned in this section with some characteristics of talk in classrooms and have seen how most participant-structures focus on the teacher, who either does the talking or nominates others to do it, and the significance of this for controlling the class. Watson[6] outlines six categories of teacher talk that embrace not simply introductory talk but teacher talk at the different points in a lesson. The six categories are:

1   Finding out about students' understanding and knowledge (45 per cent of all teacher talk).
2   Extending students' thinking (25 per cent of all teacher talk).
3   Providing general feedback, e.g. on effort, task difficulty, the need to listen and pay attention, giving rewards (16 per cent of all teacher talk).
4   Modelling reflective teaching (no percentage given).
5   Valuing individuals' contributions (no percentage given).
6   Peers helping, explaining or evaluating (less than 1 per cent).

One can see the dominance of the first three categories (nearly 90 per cent of all teacher talk) and the fact that these, in turn, reflect the teacher's domination of classroom talk. This finding echoes that of Carlsen,[7] who argued that teachers' questioning may reflect and reproduce status differences in classrooms. For further consideration of teacher dominance in this context we refer you to Edwards and Furlong, who go on to examine further aspects of classroom interaction, including the shaping of meaning – the asking of questions, the management of answers, and the constraints imposed by the social nature of the setting.

On a practical level one should note that most students will only be able to be involved in talk for a limited period of time (from seconds to half-hours), both as 'active listeners' and participants in talk. This is a salutary point; many student teachers devote far too long to introductory talk. Be it a one-way exposition, questioning, explaining, discussing or other forms of student participation in talk, it is a brave student teacher who will have too great an amount of introductory talk.

Talk is an oral and aural medium; many students cannot sustain oral and aural concentration for very long without a *visual* focus – be it on pictures, the chalkboard, a video, a piece of work, etc. One can learn from the televisual medium that concentration is highest when students have both an aural and visual focus. Without a visual focus a free-floating discussion can easily float off into irrelevance and concomitant indiscipline.

There is the further issue of *types* of talk. Typically a teacher will engage in *instructional* talk (e.g. cognitive curricular content), *procedural* talk (e.g. pedagogical talk – how students are to work on the content) and *managerial* talk (e.g. how order and acceptable behaviour are promoted and sustained in a lesson). The student teacher will have to consider the emphasis that is placed on each type. Too little *cognitive* talk and the lesson can become undemanding and boring; too much and it can become overwhelming. Too little *procedural* talk and the student will not know how to work on an activity. Too much *procedural* talk and the students' autonomy and metacognitive development are eroded. Too little *managerial* talk and there is a risk of disruption. Too much *managerial* talk risks boredom, demotivating students who, in fact, might be trying hard to be successful and positive with the teacher. The Office for Standards in Education[8] found that poor student achievement was often accompanied by an over-reliance on procedural and managerial talk (i.e. servicing and supervisory talk respectively) and an under-reliance on direct teaching.

EXPOSITION

Numerous authors[9] argue that exposition can have several functions:

- introducing lessons;
- relaying new information;
- getting attention;
- motivating students;
- introducing and using technical language in a controlled way;
- relating to and building upon existing knowledge or understanding (e.g. refreshing students' memories of previous work);
- reinforcement and alternative representation;
- clarifying a sequence of cognitive or practical steps appropriate to learners;
- consolidation;
- defining the nature of an activity;
- setting appropriate expectations.

These functions can serve as criteria for judging the effectiveness of expositions, wherein student teachers clarify the purposes – objectives – of the expositions and then evaluate how successfully these purposes have been achieved, echoing the significance of the objectives model that runs throughout this book. The art of exposition is multifaceted, embracing not only the *content* but also the *effectiveness of 'delivery'* of the exposition. For example, Pollard and Tann[10] set out a useful checklist of questions for evaluating the 'delivery' of the exposition (Box 50).

The exposition stage of classroom talk is a critical factor in judging the effectiveness of a lesson. If it is too long students 'switch off' and bad behaviour can occur. If it is too short students may fail to grasp the significance of what is being said and what is required of them, again resulting in bad behaviour. As was mentioned earlier, talk is an important medium of control and the promotion of good discipline. Many students can only concentrate for one or two minutes (particularly young children); the best

Box 50

Questions to evaluate the 'delivery' of an exposition

Is eye contact sustained, to hold attention and give interim feedback?

Is an interesting, lively tone of voice used?

Is the pace varied for emphasis and interest?

Is the exposition varied by encouraging orderly participation?

Are pauses used to structure each part of the exposition?

Are appropriate examples, objects or pictures used to illustrate the main points?

Are appropriate judgements made regarding the level of cognitive demand, size of conceptual steps, and length of the concentration span required?

Is a written or illustrated record of key points provided as a guide, if listeners need memory aids?

Has the student teacher planned what is going to be said?

Has the student teacher planned the outline structure of the exposition (e.g. by means of 'advance organisers' – signposts to key points that will be met)?

Has the student teacher selected the key points – identified and made explicit the relevance of each and their relationship to each other?

Has the student teacher sequenced the key points appropriately?

Has the student teacher used simple, short sentences, explained specialist vocabulary, provided concrete examples and asked students to generate their own?

Has the student teacher signalled when a new point is made, summarised the key points of the exposition, and sought feedback to check understanding?

Source Pollard and Tann[10]

listeners can only sustain 'active concentration' for a short time – maybe twenty minutes at the very most.

In classroom talk the use of examples can root the topic in the experiences of students and provide an important aid to exposition, explanation, questioning, discussion, responding and summarising (see pp. 225–43). Brown and Wragg[11] argue that it is often useful to convert the topics of an exposition into a series of questions (see below: *questions and questioning*).

EXPLANATION

We have already discussed the work of Perrott[12] concerning effective explanation (see p. 196). Wragg adds that clarity involves a *clear structure*, *clear language*, *clear voice* and *fluency*. The skills involved in explaining and giving explanations have received rather patchy attention from researchers over the years, yet their importance for the teacher in the classroom cannot be overestimated. Indeed, much of his or her time is devoted to explaining in one way or another. Brown and Armstrong[13] have pointed out that at its lowest level the process of explaining involves presenting sets of facts or simple instructions; and that higher levels of explaining go beyond facts to consider relationships between facts and also to consider reasons, motives and causes. Wragg[14] adds to this the view that when concepts (medium- and higher-order levels of explanation) are being expounded the student teacher should make sure that the *label* or *name* of the concept is introduced and its *attributes* are identified (with examples), including necessary and possible attributes. He suggests that explanations can be used to enable students to understand concepts, cause and effect, procedures, purposes and objectives, relationships, processes and consequences.

For Perrott a clear explanation depends upon (a) identifying the elements to be related, e.g. objects, events, processes, generalisations, and (b) identifying the relationships between them, e.g. causal, justifying, interpreting, mechanical. As she says, 'this identification of the components and the relationship between them is something which the teacher has to do first for himself. The teacher's failure to do this is a primary cause of confused presentation.'

She also stresses the need to make an explanation *explicit*, i.e. clearly and openly stated. The danger here is in giving information about the thing in question and leaving the explanation *implicit* in the information supplied. It would appear from research that a student teacher's ability to make his or her explanations *explicit* has a wholly beneficial effect on students' attainment levels. Perrott explains that the majority of sentences which make explicit a relation between two ideas or processes use words or phrases like:

because	as a result of
why	therefore
so that	in order to
by	through

In an empirical study of explaining and explanations, Brown and Armstrong adopted the following working definition: explaining is an attempt to provide understanding of a problem to others. There are three factors for the researchers to bear in mind – the explainer, the problem and the explainees. Thus, 'the explainer has to present or elicit a set of linked statements, each of which is understood by the explainees and which together lead to a solution of the problem for that particular set of explainees'.

At the outset of their study, they used a simple typology which consisted of:

The interpretive: which clarifies, exemplifies or interprets the

	meaning of terms (What is ... ?)
The descriptive:	which describes a process or structure (How is ... ? How does ... ?)
The 'reason giving':	which offers reasons or causes, the occurrence of a phenomenon (Why is ... ?)

This typology provided a basis for the analysis of explanations and for activities concerned with the preparation, design and structuring of explanations. A list of topics illustrating the typology is given in Box 51.

Box 51

Topics for explanatory lessons

Interpretive explanations
   What are phyla?
   What is a biome?
   What is a fossil?
   What is ecological succession?

Descriptive explanations
   Where does the energy of the living world come from?
   How do streams become polluted?
   How do environmental factors influence the number of plants and animals in a particular area?
   How are animals protected against the dangers of dying out?

Reason-giving explanations
   Why are there no polar bears at the South Pole?
   Why is soil considered to be an ecosystem?

Source Brown and Armstrong

In the study, twenty-seven PGCE biology students were required to teach two out of ten specified topics to groups of twelve 11- to 12-year-olds in two ten-minute lessons. Briefly summarising the results, the interpretive lessons revealed the importance of selection of appropriate content. Simple lessons with only one or two new concepts scored more highly than lessons in which the pupils were introduced to a large number of ideas, even though the new ideas were linked together. The lessons involving descriptive explanations disclosed the importance of careful planning and logical structuring as a framework for effective explanations. Finally, the reason-giving lessons underlined the importance of answering the central questions. The better lessons stated the problem and principles relatively early and proceeded to elicit and give examples.

The challenge of effective explaining along with lesson presentation skills and questioning illustrates just what a crucial role language plays in students' education. We cannot overstate the need for student teachers to think through the difficulties that students might encounter in understanding concepts, knowledge, reasons or specific procedural points, and the terminology and vocabulary used in explanations. The student teacher will need to anticipate these difficulties and plan alternative ways of explaining, ensuring that explanations will use concepts, examples, images, metaphors and references that are within the students' understanding and experiences. A general rule is to endeavour to make explanations and examples as *concrete* as possible.

In his important study of explaining, Wragg identified several criteria that student teachers can use to evaluate their explanations. These are summarised in Box 52.

Box 52

Criteria for evaluating explanations

Clear introduction
New terms clarified
Apt word choice
Clear sentence structure
Vagueness avoided
Adequate concrete examples
Within pupils' experience
Voice used to emphasise
Emphasis by gesture
Appropriate pauses
Direct verbal cueing
Repetition used
Many ideas paraphrased
Sound use of media, materials
Pattern of explanation clear
Parts linked to each other
Progressive summary
Pace or level altered
Opportunity for pupils' questions
Grasp of main ideas checked
Pupil commitment sought

Source Wragg

One can see that many features of effective exposition also apply to explanations; indeed notions of clarity, purpose, sequencing, non-verbal support, student involvement, exemplification, timing and pacing are factors that apply to the seven aspects of classroom talk in this chapter: characteristics of classroom talk, exposition, explanation, questioning, discussion, responding, summarising.

QUESTIONS AND QUESTIONING

It is often said that teachers are amongst a small group of adults who ask students questions to which they already know the answer. Anecdotally, a 6-year-old child did not answer a teacher who asked him what 8 + 4 'made', because, as he said, 'the teacher already knew, and I already knew, so I don't know why she asked the question'. This story makes the telling comment that teachers not only need to be sure of the purposes of a question but also need to ensure that the students know what the purposes of the question are. The Leverhulme Primary Project[15] suggested twelve *possible* reasons why questions could be asked (Box 53). One can see in Box 53 that teachers' purposes in planning for the use of questions are very diverse. This is echoed elsewhere in the same study, where teachers' *actual* reasons for asking questions were given (Box 54). One can see in these reasons that the teachers were using questions not only for *cognitive/intellectual* reasons (concerning the subject matter of the lesson) but for *emotional/social* reasons (to cater for different personalities) and for *managerial* reasons (to minimise bad behaviour and to keep students on task).

So far we have discussed the *student teacher's* possible purposes in asking

Box 53

Purposes in asking questions

To arouse interest and curiosity concerning a topic.
To focus attention on a particular issue or concept.
To develop an active approach to learning.
To stimulate pupils to ask questions of themselves and others.
To structure a task in such a way that learning will be maximised.
To diagnose specific difficulties inhibiting pupil learning.
To communicate to the group that involvement in the lesson is expected, and that overt participation by all members of the group is valued.
To provide an opportunity for pupils to assimilate and reflect upon information.
To involve pupils in using an inferred cognitive operation on the assumption that this will assist in developing thinking skills.
To develop reflection and comment by pupils on the responses of other members of the group, both pupils and teachers.
To afford an opportunity for pupils to learn vicariously through discussion.
To express a genuine interest in the ideas and feelings of the pupil.

Source Brown and Edmonson[16]

Box 54

Teachers' reasons for asking questions

Encouraging thought, understanding of ideas, phenomena, procedures and values.	33%
Checking understanding, knowledge and skills.	30%
Gaining attention to task. To enable teacher to move towards teaching point in the hope of eliciting a specific and obscure point, as a warm-up activity for pupils.	28%
Review, revision, recall, reinforcement of recently learnt point, reminder of earlier procedures.	23%
Management, settling down, to stop calling out by pupils, to direct attention to teacher or text, to warn of precautions.	20%
Specifically to teach whole class through pupil answers.	10%
To give everyone a chance to answer.	10%
Ask bright pupils to encourage others.	4%
To draw in shyer pupils.	4%
Probe children's knowledge after critical answers, redirect question to pupils who asked or to other pupils.	3%
To allow expressions of feelings, views and empathy.	3%

Source Brown and Edmonson[17]

questions. Thompson and Feasey[18] argue that, in the context of science teaching, students themselves should be asking questions. Here teachers should encourage students to:

- generate a range of scientific questions;
- ask pertinent questions;
- recognise which questions can be answered;
- appreciate that different kinds of questions can be answered in different ways;
- appreciate that not every question has one correct answer;
- develop a range of strategies to deal with different questions;
- question each other and themselves in a critical manner;
- support answers to questions using data from investigations or other sources;
- question the validity of their own and other data.

Although this list was given in the context of science teaching, it is easy to appreciate that it can be applied in many other curriculum areas. Importantly, Thompson and Feasey suggest several strategies to improve students' abilities to pose and answer questions through teachers' interventions. Interventions, they argue, should: (a) be only occasional, (b) encourage observations; (c) encourage thinking; (d) reflect on what has happened and what might happen next; (e) help students to recognise causal links between events; (f) feed into future planning. Teachers, therefore, should: use many different *types* of question, ask *fewer* direct questions, use questions to *link* what children know to intended learning outcomes, *talk less* and *listen more, use focused questions* for diagnostic purposes, realise that questions have *limitations*, encourage *more questions* from children, use *silence* as thinking time, and support oral questioning with the same *written* question.

The skilful questioning of a class performs a number of important functions. Socially, it helps to establish relationships and integrate groups through face-to-face interaction. Psychologically, it assists in increasing, developing and maintaining a healthy emotional and intellectual climate as well as establishing appropriate levels of motivation.

Educationally, one function of questioning is to elicit information. Thus, it may probe the extent of children's prior learning before a new subject or area of learning is introduced; or it may help to revise earlier learning; or consolidate recent teaching and learning. More than this, however, questions should have teaching value, that is, in asking the question a teacher is helping the pupil 'to focus and clarify, and thus have thoughts and perceptions that he would not have had otherwise'. Indeed the Office for Standards in Education[19] found that *questioning* (closely followed by *exposition*) was the single most important factor in students' achievements of high standards, where questions were used to assess students' knowledge and challenge their thinking.

Framing the question

The value to the student teacher of preparing questions beforehand as part of, or to accompany, a lesson plan cannot be over-emphasised. There are at least three reasons for this need. First, questions should be precisely and unambiguously worded so that they elicit the answer the student teacher intends. The likelihood of misunderstandings and wrong answers is greater with unprepared, impromptu questions. Second, where a connected series of questions is required, it is difficult to organise them sequentially and logically on the spur of the moment. And third, a student teacher is better prepared to deal with the unexpected if he or she possesses a body of well-thought-out questions.

A related issue is the desirability of preparing some questions with particular children in mind. An apt question, for example, worded especially for a timid student or a student with learning difficulties can help develop his/her confidence and sense of achievement.

It is particularly useful when framing questions to distinguish two broad kinds – questions which test knowledge and questions which create knowledge. The former are referred to as lower-order cognitive questions and the latter as higher-order cognitive questions (you may find it easier initially to think of them as 'fact' questions and 'thought' questions respectively, as these are terms of approximate equivalence).

Lower-order cognitive questions embrace chiefly *recall, comprehension* and *application*; higher-order questions, by contrast, involve *analysis, synthesis* and *evaluation*. Low-order questions tend to be *closed* questions (when a known response is sought); higher-order questions tend to be *open* questions (when the type of response is known but the actual response is not, students being free to respond in their own way). With regard to the latter, it is important that students know what *type* of response is being sought so that their responses are relevant and apposite. Brown[20] elucidates the categories of lower- to higher-order questioning thus:

Lower-order cognitive questions

Recall: Does the student recall what he or she has seen or read?
Comprehension: Does the student understand what he or she recalls?
Application: Can the student apply the rules and techniques to solve problems that have single correct answers?

Higher-order cognitive questions

Analysis: Can the student identify motives and causes, make inferences and give examples to support his or her statements?
Synthesis: Can the student make predictions, solve problems or produce interesting juxtapositions of ideas and images?
Evaluation: Can the student judge the quality of ideas, or problem solutions, or works of art? Can he or she give rationally based opinions on issues or controversies?

We give particular examples of these kinds of question in Boxes 55 and 56. For additional information, the reader is referred to Bloom[21] and Brown.[22]

Studies conducted in the United States indicate that many teachers' questions fall into the recall category and that higher-order cognitive questions are rarely used (Gall[23]). Although recall questions are especially useful in testing learning and focusing attention, questioning sessions made up exclusively of them may become boring and place undue emphasis on rote-learning. Ideally, lower-order cognitive questions should be coupled with carefully selected higher-order cognitive ones so that children are led to consider the implications of the facts or circumstances that give rise to them. It must be remembered, however, that there is skill involved in judging the extent to which children are able to respond appropriately to the more difficult and complex higher-order cognitive questions; and such judgement must be based on knowledge of the students' intellectual capabilities. Once a student

Box 55

Categories of teacher questions

Lower-order cognitive questions

Recall:	What were the two kinds of objective identified in Part II?
Comprehension:	What are the differences between an aim and an objective?
Application:	Would you formulate a behavioural objective using the action verb 'list'.

Higher-order cognitive questions

Analysis:	Why did Mr Smith have discipline problems in the lesson you were observing yesterday afternoon?
Synthesis:	What do you think would have happened had Mr Smith adopted a less authoritarian approach?
Evaluation:	Which seems to be the best way to handle his class in that kind of lesson?

---

teacher has this knowledge, he or she should try to get a judicious balance of both types organised in carefully planned sequences. Some questions need to be handled carefully, or, in certain circumstances, avoided altogether. These may be briefly identified as follows.

- Questions inviting a *yes* or *no* answer should not be used excessively, for a student has as much chance of being right as of being wrong if he guesses. *Yes* and *no* answers follow from binary questions of the recall type, and where such answers are unavoidable, another question, such as *how?* or *why?* should follow in order to provide explanatory or supportive evidence for the *yes* or *no*. Occasionally, a *yes* or *no* answer can be of disciplinary assistance when attentions are wandering: 'Do you understand, John?'
- Questions having several equally good answers should be avoided if the teacher has only one answer in mind ('What should a driver have with him?' A map? his licence? a torch? a tool-kit? a first-aid box?). Formulations of this nature invite guessing. Questions having several equally good answers are permissible, however, when a teacher is building up a composite answer, e.g. when introducing a topic or project.
- Composite questions – those involving a number of interrogatives – present difficulties even with brighter children and should be avoided.
- Do not use questions beginning 'Who can tell me ... ?' or 'Does anyone

Box 56

Lower-order and higher-order cognitive questions

The examples below from Brown illustrate how lower-order and higher-order cognitive questions may be formed on the same topic: item (a) questions exemplify lower-order cognitive questions; and item (b) ones, higher-order cognitive questions.

1   (a) What is the largest city in Holland?
     (b) Why is Amsterdam the largest city in Holland? (Analysis)
2   (a) Who is the author of *Catcher in the Rye*?
     (b) Which aspects of *Catcher in the Rye* suggest that the author is a young man? (Analysis)
3   (a) What does the theorem of Pythagoras tell us?
     (b) Why is the theorem of Pythagoras so important in geometry? (Evaluation)
4   (a) Who wrote *Hamlet*?
     (b) Describe the feelings of Hamlet for his mother as portrayed in the play of Shakespeare. (Analysis)
5   (a) What happened in *A Christmas Carol*?
     (b) What kind of relationship did Scrooge have with his employee in *A Christmas Carol*? (Analysis)
6   (a) What is the most common element found in the earth's crust?
     (b) Why is oxygen the most common element found in the earth's crust? (Analysis)
7   (a) What is the most widely spoken indigenous language in Africa?
     (b) Account for the distribution of two of the most widely spoken languages in Africa. (Analysis)
8   (a) Where is Stonehenge?
     (b) Discuss the recent theories of the stone formation at Stonehenge. (Evaluation)
9   (a) How many independent countries have been established in Africa during the past twenty years?
     (b) Why has there been a sudden increase in the number of independent countries in Africa during the past twenty years? (Evaluation)
10 (a) What are the two main levels of questions?
     (b) Which type of questions do you consider the most important? (Evaluation)

Source Brown[24]

know ... ?' as these may lead to various members of the class shouting out answers.

• Questions testing powers of expression should be treated with care. Similarly, those seeking definitions of words or concepts, especially abstract ones, should be handled carefully.

- General questions that are vague and aimless should not be used ('What do you know about the French Revolution?'). Precision and clarity should be sought from the outset.
- Guessing questions are sometimes useful for stimulating a child's imagination and actively involving him in discussion. If used too often, however, they encourage thoughtless responses.
- Leading questions (those framed in such a way as to suggest or imply the desired answer – 'Wordsworth was the author of the first sonnet we read, wasn't he?') and rhetorical questions (those to which the pupil is not expected to reply – 'Do you want me to send you outside?') should be avoided because the former tend to reinforce a student's dependence on the student teacher and undermine independent thought, whereas the latter may provoke unwanted or facetious replies. Questions should be asked only if the student teacher wants a real answer.
- Elliptical questions – those worded so that a child supplies a missing word or missing words – are of value when used to encourage students with learning or behaviour difficulties. Provided they are not used too often, they can give variety to a questioning session.

Box 57 indicates how questions may be related to a typical class.

Asking the question and receiving the answer

Questions should be asked in simple, conversational language and in a friendly and challenging manner, ensuring that the student knows what *kind* of answer is expected (i.e. there is a need to give cues to the students). A useful procedure is as follows: put the question to the class, pause briefly, then name the child you wish to answer. A sequence of this kind encourages everyone to listen and prepare an answer in anticipation of being asked. Respondents should be named at random rather than in a predetermined and systematic way, thus avoiding selective listening. As suggested earlier, it is to the teacher's advantage at this point to have prepared questions with particular children in mind. The more difficult questions for brighter students and easier ones for students experiencing learning difficulties help to sustain different motivational levels and maintain the flow of the lesson. It is especially important in this respect to try to draw out the more shy members of the class. The student teacher should also counter the tendency to overlook students sitting at the back or sides of the classroom when distributing questions. Similarly, student teachers should resist the temptation to ignore those students who happen to be sitting near a supervising tutor or mentor.

Once a question has been put to a student, it should be left with him or her long enough for an answer to emerge. Lack of preparation on the part of the student teacher, or impatience, may lead him or her to follow one question

Box 57

Possible purposes of questioning in relation to the suggested class lesson plan

Stage	*Questioning*
Introduction	to establish human contact
	to assist in establishing set induction devices
	to discover what the class knows
	to revise previous work
	to pose problems which lead to the subject of the lesson
Presentation	to maintain interest and alertness
	to encourage reasoning and logical thinking
	to discover if pupils understand what is going on
Application	to focus and clarify
	to lead the children to make observations and draw inferences for themselves
	to clear up difficulties and misunderstandings and assist individual pupils
Conclusion	to revise the main points of the lesson
	to test the results of the lesson and the extent of the pupils' understanding and assimilation
	to suggest further problems and related issues

---

immediately with others, or to modify the original, qualify it, re-word it or explain it. Such addenda merely confuse students. Indeed, British research indicates that student teachers and beginning teachers often ask more questions than they receive answers. Brown[25] suggests that their failure to obtain answers is often due to lack of pauses and no variation in the delivery of questions. The efficacy of the student teacher sometimes accepting two or three answers before responding should also be noted. A varied pattern of this nature thus encourages volunteering, contributes to group co-operation, and achieves a more realistic social situation which can be further enhanced by allowing other members of the class to respond to a child's answer ('John, was Peter's answer correct?').

The techniques of *prompting* and *probing* are often useful in class questioning sessions. Prompting involves giving hints to help a child. In addition to eliciting appropriate answers, prompts backed up with teacher encouragement help hesitant children reply more confidently. On receiving an answer, it is sometimes necessary to prod a child for additional information and this may be especially the case after a factual question. Probing in this context may take the form of further information, directing the child to think more deeply about his or her answer, inviting a critical interpretation, focusing the response on a related issue or encouraging the child to express himself or herself more clearly. (Two illustrations of prompting and probing are given in Box 58.) As Brown observes, probing questions with older children tap the highest levels of their thinking.

Sometimes a correct answer needs to be repeated to make sure all have

Box 58

Prompting and probing

Prompting

Teacher:	Would you say that nationalism in Africa is now greater or less than it was twenty years ago?
Pupil:	Greater.
Teacher:	Yes. Why is that?
Pupil:	Because there are more nations now.
Teacher:	Yes. Mmm. There's more to it than that. Can anyone else give some reasons?
Class:	(Silence)
Teacher:	Well, basically it's because . . .

This is an example of what frequently happens in the first discussion lessons given by a teacher. The discussion drags and degenerates into an unprepared lecture. This can be avoided by prompting any weak answers given. In the example, the teacher could have said 'Yes. That's right. There are more nations now and there are more nations because African people wanted to be independent of the Europeans. What has happened in the past twenty years which has helped them to become independent?'

Probing

Teacher:	Jessica, you went to Paris this year. What did you think of it?
Jessica:	Mmm. It was nice.
Teacher:	What was nice about it? (Pause)
Jessica:	Well, I liked walking down the avenue which had trees. I liked watching the boats on the river. I liked listening to Frenchmen. The Metro was exciting and, oh, I liked the French bread and butter.

The simple probe 'What was nice about it?' evoked from this 7-year-old girl a series of impressions which revealed her interest in sights, sounds and food.

Source Brown[26]

heard it. It is inadvisable to accept unsolicited answers that have been called out as such habits can lead to problems of control. Wrong answers can be of value in clearing up misunderstandings, obscurities and difficulties providing they are treated tactfully and without disrupting the lesson to any great extent (to respond to a wrong answer, for instance, with 'That's nonsense' or 'What rubbish!' is to ensure that the flow of answers from the class will quickly dry up!). Clearly, a sense of humour is an invaluable asset at this stage in a questioning session.

It is very important for students to receive information on the correctness or otherwise of their answers (see below: *Responding*). This is especially the case for low achievers. Feedback from the teacher is the easiest way to maintain interest and is most effective when given after an individual response. In most instances, the feedback does not need to be long: a word or two will suffice to let a student know that she's on the right lines – 'That's right, Joanne.' Praise and censure should be used with discrimination. Praise is quickly devalued if used too readily; and undue censure can be discouraging. Excessive criticism directed at weaker pupils can do nothing but harm.

One final point remains to be briefly considered: the students' questions to the teacher. As Davies and Shepherd[27] note, nothing shows more clearly that a student teacher and class are on friendly terms than evidence of students sensibly questioning the teacher about difficult points. Desirable as this kind of relationship is, however, it can pose problems for less experienced teachers. They must, for instance, avoid having too many interruptions and being side-tracked from the main theme of their lesson. One way of dealing with difficulties of this kind is to ensure that they anticipated the class's questions with the ones they put to them. Another way is to invite questions from the class at appropriate points in the lesson (towards the end of the *presentation stage*, for example). Some questions may not be directly relevant to the lesson in hand, in which case the student teacher should inform the class that they will be dealt with in future lessons. If you do not know the answer to a question, don't be afraid to admit it, but say you will find out the answers as soon as you can.

When an awkward student proposes a series of difficult or even silly questions which have no direct relationship with the topic under consideration, Davies and Shepherd advise that student teachers are fully justified in setting them aside without prohibiting further questions.

Student teachers anxious to acquire command of this most vital skill of questioning a class should make every effort to build short questioning sessions of from five to ten minutes into their lessons. You can then get some idea of your progress by constructing a simple self-evaluation schedule based on the suggestions outlined earlier and checking your performance, say, once a week as part of your routine lesson criticisms. For further guidance in this respect, we refer readers to Unit VI in Brown, and for additional information on empirical studies in this area, we suggest you consult Turney *et al.*,[28] MacLeod *et al.* (in Chanan and Delamont[29]), and also Brown and Edmonson.[30] In evaluating student teachers' abilities to conduct effective questioning, Brown and Wragg set out some errors that student teachers typically make (Box 59).

Box 59

Common errors in questioning

Asking too many questions at once.
Asking a question and answering yourself.
Asking questions only of the brightest or most likeable students.
Asking a difficult question too early.
Asking irrelevant questions.
Always asking the same types of question.
Asking questions in a threatening way.
Not indicating a change in the type of question.
Not using probing questions.
Not giving pupils time to think.
Not correcting wrong answers.
Ignoring answers.
Failing to see the implications of answers.
Failing to build on answers.

Source Brown and Wragg[31]

As a corollary to this they set out some key factors for effective questioning:

1 *Structuring* (providing signposts for the sequence of questions and the topic, indicating the types of answers expected, using 'advance organisers' to clarify what the children will be doing).
2 *Pitching and putting clearly* (considering: how broad/narrow to make the question, the order of the question – low to high, the vocabulary to be used, the degree of openness or closure of the question).
3 *Directing and distributing* (going around the whole class).
4 *Pausing and pacing* (allowing thinking time, particularly for more complex questions).
5 *Prompting and probing* (considering what to say in a prompt or a probe, rephrasing, reviewing).
6 *Listening and responding* (deciding the most appropriate form of response. See below: *Responding*).
7 *Sequencing* (introducing, opening out, converging, extending, lifting).

These key factors reflect the fact that questioning is both an art and a skill that can be specifically rehearsed for classroom success.

DISCUSSION

It is in the many discussion situations in the classroom that talk as an agent of learning operates most effectively. This means that the problem for the student teacher is how to develop and improve students' skills in this respect, and indeed his or her own. In the main, discussions take place either between the student teacher and class or among small groups with or without the student teacher. There is an important issue of the physical layout of the classroom to be considered here, so that students have the opportunity to hear

Box 60

Discussion skills

A reflective teacher may find it useful to consider the following points:

1   Do the participants take turns or do they frequently talk over or interrupt?
     Do they invite contributions, re-direct contributions for further comments, give encouragement?
     Do they listen to each other? Are they willing to learn from each other (i.e. respond and react to each other's contributions)?
     Or do they indulge in 'parallel' talk (i.e. continue their own line of thinking)?
     Does conflict emerge or is harmony maintained (at all costs)?
     Are the ideas disputed?
     Is the speaker attacked?
     Is conflict positively handled?
     by modifying statements, rather than just reasserting them?
     by examining the assumptions, rather than leaving them implicit?
     by explaining/accounting for the claim, rather than ignoring the challenge?

2   Do they elaborate, rather than answer in monosyllables?
     by giving details of events, people, feelings?
     by providing reasons, explanations, examples?
     Do they extend ideas, rather than let ambiguity go unchallenged?
     by asking for specific information?
     by asking for clarification?
     Do they explore suggestions?
     by asking for alternatives?
     by speculating, imagining and hypothesising?
     Do they evaluate?
     by pooling ideas and suspending judgement before making choices?

Source Pollard and Tann[32]

each other and feel able to contribute in a supportive environment (often facing each other rather than all facing forwards to the teacher). Dean[33] advises student teachers to think out clearly what it is they hope to get from their discussions and to consider their functions. This involves identifying important questions and having the students' language skills and general experience in mind at the same time.

It is important that the student teacher knows where he or she wants the discussion to go and communicates this to the students so that everyone knows what is relevant and what is not. All too often the student teacher accepts as relevant to the discussion anything that the students say. This can quickly degenerate into students calling out anything, making light of the discussion and leading to discipline problems. It can render discussions inconsequential, literally pointless. This returns us to the underlying message of this book – that an objectives model is useful. Student teachers should be clear on the objectives of the discussion – where they want the discussion to go, what they want from the discussion (e.g. the intended pedagogic and knowledge outcomes), and how they will use the discussion to feed into the remainder of the lesson – and they should communicate these intentions clearly so that the students see the relevance of the discussions. Even with the student teacher adopting the role of the 'neutral chairperson'[34] there still needs to be a direction for and outcome of a discussion. The important points that need to be remembered in Dean's view are: how you receive the students' contributions, scanning the class to spot would-be contributors and those not involved, being able to interpret body language so as to know when children have had enough, and finally being able to summarise and structure ideas with a view to taking the discussion further. Discussion involves speaking, listening and taking turns. The student teacher will have to consider how participation and listening skills can be taught and learnt by students.[35] Box 60 contains a framework for monitoring discussion strategies which Pollard and Tann have devised. Readers are recommended to use it in conjunction with at least one discussion session they have initiated.

RESPONDING

In expositions, explanations, questioning and discussions an important skill to be developed is that of responding appropriately to students. Brown and Wragg[36] indicate several types of response that can be made to students' answers and comments. Student teachers can:

- *ignore* the response, moving on to another student, topic or question;
- *acknowledge* the response, building it into the subsequent discussion;
- *repeat* the response verbatim to reinforce the point or to bring it to the attention of those that might not have heard it;
- *repeat part* of the response, to emphasise a particular element of it;

- *paraphrase* the response for clarity and emphasis, and so that it can be built into the ongoing and subsequent discussion;
- *praise* the response (either directly or by implication in extending and building on it for the subsequent part of the discussion);
- *correct* the response (a feature that student teachers are often reluctant to do, thereby sanctioning error and irrelevance);
- *prompt* the students for further information or clarification;
- *probe* the students to develop relevant points.

These features indicate the *type* of response that is possible. There are also some *procedural* matters that echo points made so far, for example: allowing thinking time (particularly for complex responses), affording students the opportunity to correct, clarify and crystallise their responses, once uttered, i.e. not 'jumping onto' a response before a student has had time to finish it; building a student's contribution into the student teacher's own plans for the sequence of the discussion; using a student's contribution to introduce another question to be put to another student. There are also *pedagogic* matters in responding to students' contributions, for example giving feedback to students on the quality, accuracy, range, relevance, amount and significance of their contribution. Students need to know both the positive and the negative aspects of their contributions; to ignore the negative aspects (based, presumably, on the notion of *extinction* in the behaviourist view of learning) might be to leave a student unsure whether everything that he or she has said is relevant or accurate. Pointing out errors or shortcomings need not be done negatively but in a spirit of constructive criticism and in a supportive manner.

SUMMARISING

That there are cognitive and affective aspects of summarising is reflected in the view of Proctor *et al.*[37] that effective summarising can 'reassure, consolidate [and] support' students. Cognitively, the student teacher needs to be able to draw together key points (whether of a discussion, a set of questions, an explanation, a series of instructions or a whole lesson) so that students can differentiate between the highly relevant/important/central points and the less relevant/trivial/marginal/peripheral points. In many cases there should be a match between the contents of a summary and the intended learning outcomes and objectives of a lesson; indeed a student teacher's evaluation of a lesson might reflect on the degree of concordance or discrepancy between the *actual* key points and the *intended* objectives (cognitive, procedural, managerial) of the lesson. This resonates with Stake's[38] view of evaluation as an indication of the degree of congruence between what was intended and what was actually transacted.

Summarising in talk can be undertaken through an admixture of questions, statements and restatements (by the student teacher or the students them-selves), confirmations and highlighting of the most important features of the matters to be summarised. Summaries will link the several sections of a series of questions, discussions or stages of a lesson. They may also establish and clarify links between the current and previous or future lessons, communicat-ing to students the nature of the continuity, progression and relevance of the work. Summarising is a convergent exercise intended to make it clear to students what are the significant features of the work; it is a reductionist exercise which highlights key matters. Bruner[39] argues that the clarification and highlighting of key matters, concepts, issues, etc., facilitates memorising and recall. A summary which recalls contributions from students themselves is a motivational force that engages students emotionally as well as cognitively in a shared enterprise: an exemplification of Vygotsky's[40] argument that higher-order cognitive functions are acquired and transmitted socially – a view shared by practising teachers.[41]

LANGUAGE AND CLASSROOM INTERACTION[42]

The most important reason for observing and studying teacher–pupil dialogue in classrooms is that the dialogue taking place between teachers and pupils *is* the educational process, or the major part of it for most children. No matter how important other factors such as IQ, social background, parental encouragement or children's individual language skills appear to be, they nevertheless remain external influences.[43] Such is the view of Stubbs, who goes on to observe that for all its importance, relatively little research has been undertaken on the *interactional aspects* of the teaching process in classroom settings.

Traditionally, much of the research to do with classrooms has been of a *normative* cast: this is to say that the process of education could best be understood by looking at *input variables* such as intelligence, motivation, social-class background and personality, and comparing them with *output variables* – how well a student has done according to an agreed set of criteria. In other words, what happened between the input and output phases was largely ignored: few seemed to be interested in what was actually taking place *inside* classrooms. Stubbs argues that on common-sense grounds alone, it would seem that an understanding of teaching and learning would have to depend, at least in part, on observation of teachers and learners. Although an impressive body of information on learning theory has been built up this century, it has largely been derived from carefully controlled experimental situations. For this reason, it is extremely difficult to extrapolate the findings to 'real-life' contexts; in other words, we still know very little about *how* children learn in classrooms. Stubbs suggests that the only way to overcome this problem is to observe students in the classroom and, particularly, the way they interact with teachers and fellow students.

In thus pleading for a closer correspondence between what we say about education and detailed empirical investigation of what is actually *said* in the classroom, Stubbs identifies the kind of specific questions to be asked. Given that many messages are conveyed by student teachers to students, just how are they communicated? By *what* 'structure'? What *are* the rules of the verbal game? What specific behaviours? If they are specific, then they can be specified. We might easily continue the list. How are messages received by students? How are they assimilated, comprehended and acted upon? What part does the language of education, or of specialist subjects, play in promoting or hindering communication and learning? And how does a student's background, socially and linguistically, affect the transactions that take place?

Numerous reasons could be advanced, no doubt, to explain why there has been a shortage of naturalistic studies of classroom interaction. We refer to two of them. First, there is the enormous complexity of communicative behaviour, a complexity which can only be unravelled by on-the-spot observation and analysis. Earlier research methods have functioned more as a deterrent than an aid in this respect. The second reason is logically related to the first. Because there have been few naturalistic studies, we lack an appropriate terminology to talk about classroom integration and the teaching process. As Stubbs says in this regard:

> If one talks to teachers about their classroom experiences, one discovers immediately that there is simply no vocabulary of descriptive concepts for talking about teaching. Despite the vast complexity of second-by-second classroom dialogue, the discussion will be conceptually crude and oversimplified. It is time that teachers had an adequate descriptive language for talking about their own professional behaviour.

The descriptive language and body of concepts referred to by Stubbs, together with the theoretical framework to which these will relate, can only come from empirical studies of interactional processes at the centre of action, that is to say, the *classroom itself*. A beginning in such research has been made, and it is fitting to close this section with a brief review of some of the more important studies undertaken in this connection in the past twenty years or so. Most of them are case studies and are thus based on a detailed description of a group of lessons or even a single lesson.

A pioneering study in the field of classroom language is Barnes's 'Language in the Secondary Classroom'.[44] His concern was to record the whole language environment of a first-year class during their first half-term in a comprehensive school with a view to investigating the ways in which a teacher's language might impede rather than facilitate learning because of the terminology or style used. He was thus interested in both spoken and written language, and also in the student as a producer and receiver of language. Being readily accessible and having many good examples of classroom exchanges, the book offers a useful introduction to the topic to student teachers.

In contending that many teachers when talking about their subject use a specialist language of instruction that might be a barrier to students' learning, Barnes identifies three categories: (1) specialist language perceived by the teacher as a potential barrier and therefore carefully 'presented' to them; (2) specialist language not so presented for various reasons; and (3) the language of secondary education which is made up of forms not specific to school subjects, nor likely to be used or heard by pupils in any other situation.

In another study,[45] Barnes assumes that language is a major means of learning and that pupils' uses of language for learning are strongly influenced by the teacher's language which, he argues, prescribes their roles as learners. This assumption thereby involves a shift of emphasis from the more traditional view of language as a *means of teaching*. In operational terms this means that we learn not only by listening passively to the teacher, but by verbalising, by talking, by discussing and arguing. By studying teacher–student interaction, one can begin to see how classroom language offers different possibilities of learning to students. Should students merely be passive listeners? Or should they be allowed to verbalise at some point? Or should active dialogue with the student teacher be encouraged? Just three ways of students' participation in learning, but all under the control of the student teacher's own speech behaviour.

Like Barnes's earlier study, Mishler's work[46] takes extracts of classroom dialogue and subjects them to perceptive analysis. Unlike Barnes, however, Mishler is more concerned with showing how different cognitive strategies as well as different values and norms are carried in the language used, chiefly in the structure of teachers' statements and in the types of exchange developed between them and the children. By contrasting speech recordings of different first-grade teachers with each other, he sets out to extract different features in the language used and to show how these features reflect both different constructions of reality and different ways of learning about it: this is to say that what teachers say and how they say it creates a particular sort of world for the students.

Mishler's main purpose, then, is to show how teachers' cognitive strategies are conveyed in the warp and weft of classroom dialogue. To this end, he is concerned with how attention is focused, with how teachers orient themselves and their pupils to the problem under discussion; the procedures for information search and evaluation; and the structure of alternatives, that is, the number of types of alternative answers to a question and their relationship to each other. Writing of Mishler's work, Stubbs[47] says:

> Mishler's approach is one which could be of direct interest to teachers. By close study of transcribed lessons he shows how quite general teaching strategies are conveyed by the fine grain of a teacher's use of language.

Such a study can therefore begin to throw a little light on how children learn what they do in school. Only by close observation of how teachers and pupils actually talk to each other can one discover how concepts are put across, how some lines of enquiry are opened up and others closed off, how pupils' responses are evaluated, and how their attention is directed to the areas of knowledge which the school regards as valuable.

There is a very frequent pattern of questioning that takes the form of Initiation–Response–Follow-up, for example:

Initiation: How many bones are there in the human body?
Response: Two hundred and six.
Follow-up: Excellent.

This model typifies many classrooms where it is the teacher who is the initiator and who controls the talk. In another study, Stubbs himself described one way in which teachers in relatively traditional lessons control classroom exchanges.[48] A characteristic of much classroom talk is the extent of the teacher's *conversational control* over the topic, over the relevant or correctness of what students say, and over when and how much students may speak. In traditional lessons, students have few conversational rights. Whereas this has often been pointed out in general, the actual verbal strategies used by teachers to control classroom talk have only recently been subjected to systematic study.[49] What Stubbs shows is that a teacher is constantly monitoring the communication system in the classroom by such utterances as 'You see, we're really getting onto the topic now', or 'OK, now listen all of you' or 'Now, we don't want any silly remarks.' The teacher is thus able to check whether students are all on the same wavelength and whether at least some of them follow what is being said. Stubbs refers to such language as *meta-communication*.[50] 'It is', he says, 'communication about communication; messages which refer back to the communication system itself, checking whether it is functioning properly.' In conclusion, he adds:

Such talk is characteristic of teachers' language: utterances which, as it were, stand outside the discourse and comment on it comprise a large percentage of what teachers say to their pupils, and comprise a major way of controlling classroom dialogue. Use of such language is also highly asymmetrical: one would not expect a pupil to say to a teacher: *That's an interesting point.* Such speech acts, in which the teacher monitors and controls the classroom dialogue are, at one level, the very stuff of teaching. They are basic to the activity of teaching, since they are the acts whereby a *teacher controls the flow of information* in the classroom and defines the relevance of what is said.

This chapter, echoing the spirit of the Bullock Report,[51] has argued that talk is not the exclusive or major preserve of teachers. Encouraging students' talk that is relevant, focused, supported, a central feature of a lesson, sensitive to individuals and contexts, is not only a medium of communication but an essential feature of successful teaching. Just as student teachers can develop their own skills in using language in the classroom, so they can facilitate the development of language in their students.

Chapter 13

Equal opportunities

INTRODUCTION

Since the *Sex Discrimination Act* of 1975 and the *Race Relations Act* of 1976 the issue of equal opportunities has taken an increasingly central role in the educational and curricular debate. A series of reports from the 1970s onwards[1] makes it very plain that all students have a right to an 'entitlement' curriculum regardless of sex, race, ethnicity, class, age, ability, special educational needs, sexuality, physical impairment, religion, cultural and linguistic background, or other background aspects in which forms of discrimination might occur.

The Warnock Report of 1978[2] added impetus to this in relation to special educational needs; the Swann Report of 1985[3] and the *Code of Practice* by the Commission for Racial Equality in 1989[4] did the same in respect of ethnicity and race; the government paper *From Policy to Practice* in 1989[5] extended this in its discussion of cultural diversity; the National Curriculum Council's paper *A Curriculum for All* in 1989[6] argued that all students share the right to a broad and balanced curriculum regardless of special educational needs, a view that was echoed in the series of *Curriculum Guidance* documents from the National Curriculum Council between 1989 and 1992;[7] the government paper *Choice and Diversity* in 1992[8] made it clear that every teacher has a duty to provide students everywhere with the same opportunities; the *Handbook for the Inspection of Schools* in 1993[9] made it a requirement that schools should not only have policies for addressing equality of opportunity but that the policy should be seen to be working in practice; the government's *Code of Practice for the Identification and Assessment of Special Needs* in 1994[10] reinforced the need for schools to respond systematically to students with special educational needs.

The three *guidance* documents from OFSTED in 1995[11] made it clear that equality of access and opportunity for all students to learn and to make progress should feature highly on a school's planning and should touch the school's aims, objectives, curriculum and organisation, grouping of students, role models in its teachers, support for learning, and students' achievements.[12]

As was seen in the earlier discussion of the aims of the school (discussed in Part II), the school has a duty to offer high-quality education to all, to promote, foster and fulfil the potential of every student, and to prepare students for adult life after school. Indeed, the Runnymede Trust in 1993[13] argued that these three concerns touch the issues of *quality*, *identity* (individual and cultural), and *society* respectively in addressing *equality assurance* in education.

What is being argued here is that the issue of equal opportunities engages very many important areas of teaching and learning, including: teachers' expectations, students' self-esteem, labelling theory and stereotyping, the formal and hidden curriculum;[14] management, resources (including time, space, materials, teachers, support staff), power and empowerment, inter-actions between all parties in schools, discipline, pedagogy, assessment and a concern for high standards in all students. Newman and Triggs[15] argue that inequality comes about through stereotyping, abuse, bias, omission (i.e. non-representation in the curriculum), discriminatory behaviour and expectations. Clearly these impact on the full gamut of experiences that students have at school and which the student teacher will need to address. Equal opportunities, then, concerns:

- treating students as individuals of equal worth – regardless of gender, race, background, special needs;
- addressing equality of access, uptake and outcome;
- countering stereotypes, discrimination, bias and misperceptions;
- promoting a clearer understanding of equal rights and freedoms;
- celebrating the notion of difference and promoting positive images of a diverse populace;
- identifying how to break down discriminatory practices.

We believe that the case for equal opportunities needs no justification, as it is premised on the notions of justice, democracy, freedom and empowerment, which are the foundations of a just society. The *practical implications* of equal opportunities, however, do need some examination in order to ensure that they are addressed in their many forms. We discuss these in two ways. First, we look at some meanings of equal opportunities. Secondly we examine some implications of these meanings for practice, relating our discussions to gender, ethnicity and special educational needs as examples of how equal opportunities might be addressed in a student teacher's teaching practice.

In addressing equal opportunities it is inadequate simply to ensure that formal equality of opportunity is provided, i.e. that every child is entitled to a broad and balanced curriculum. Rather, teachers and schools should be concerned with *equality of uptake*.[16] As we saw on p. 203, this builds on the 'cultural capital' thesis from Bourdieu.[17] He argues that, though formal equality of opportunity to a curriculum might be offered to all students, there will be a differential uptake because students come from a variety of backgrounds. School knowledge and culture are such that some students find in school an alien culture – and hence are not able to make the most of the education that schools offer – whilst other students find that the school culture accords with their own cultural background (e.g. in terms of acceptance of authority, valuing an academic education, adopting a particular linguistic register) so that they are able to access the curriculum more easily. Equality of opportunity, in this instance, does little to break down equality of access and uptake, indeed it makes for the reproduction of inequality in the wider society (e.g. in terms of employment, power, money, class).

Moreover, equal opportunities should concern not only access and uptake; they should also address *equality of outcome*, i.e. the promotion of freedoms, social justice, choice in lifestyles, life chances, moves towards an egalitarian society. In this respect we are arguing that equal opportunities has a clear political agenda which promotes empowerment in individuals, groups, cultures and society at large, reduces illegitimate differentials of power, and breaks down illegitimate discriminatory practices in society.

Our case, then, is that every student, regardless of differences (and we are all different) should be guaranteed equality of access, uptake, and outcome, and that education should further those practices that break down discrimination, i.e. that every student is of equal *worth* as an individual and as a citizen in society. Education, therefore, is charged with the responsibility to fulfil individual potential and to prepare students for membership of an egalitarian society. We continue our discussions with some general questions that student teachers may find useful to address in approaching equal opportunities. These concern the formal and hidden curricula of schools.

We indicated above that *teachers' expectations* of students exerted a considerable influence on students' learning (discussed in more detail later). Echoing the notion of the self-fulfilling prophecy,[18] the emerging literature on school effectiveness[19] argues that teachers' expectations of students exert a powerful effect on their achievements. Crudely speaking, if teachers have low expectations of a student then the student's performance tends to drop; if teachers have high expectations of students and challenge and 'stretch' them, then their performance rises. In looking at equal opportunities, student teachers ought to be asking themselves about their expectations of students and whether these expectations might be affected by gender, race, class, general abilities, behaviour, linguistic abilities, etc. For example, do all students have their fair share of the student teacher's time and high-quality attention, do all students have equal access to resources, does the student teacher make it clear that she values all of the students equally, does the student teacher hold appropriate expectations regardless of the race, class, sex, special needs, etc., of each student (i.e. to what extent is the student teacher aware of her own stereotyping)?

The student teacher's expectations are often conveyed subtly in classrooms, not simply by what he or she says but how he or she says it and what reinforcers, responses and sanctions he or she uses. For example, a non-response to a student might convey a feeling that the student's contribution is unimportant (see the discussion of language in classrooms earlier). This is reinforced in a powerful critique of classrooms by Fine,[20] in which she shows how students' cultures are confirmed and disconfirmed routinely and differentially in classrooms. The way in which the student teacher acts (and reacts) in incidents of name-calling, bullying, teasing or harassment sends signals to students about the teacher's own values.

Moreover, it is possible for a student teacher to convey a variety of messages through the organisation of the classroom. Do males and females sit together? Do students from diverse racial backgrounds sit together? Are seating arrangements (e.g. males next to females) used as a sanction? Do males undertake certain 'jobs' in the classroom and females undertake others? Which students are not given any jobs to do (or most of the jobs to do)? What kinds of learning activities are provided for males/females, Afro-Caribbean students, Chinese students, students who are physically challenged? How frequently does the student teacher review the grouping arrangements in the class to see whether 'ability' groups contain an acceptable mix of sexes, ethnicity and social classes?[21] How do males and females interact in groups (e.g. can they co-operate, are they abusive to each other, is the work session productive)?[22]

What messages does the student teacher give in his or her control of the teaching space, access to resources, language rights in the classroom (echoing the views set out earlier that the hidden curricula of classrooms reinforce differentials of power, status and rights)? How is non-teaching space used (for example, do boys control the play areas at breaktimes,[23] can students with physical impairments join in breaktime activities)? Does the student teacher use different sanctions for males and females? Does the student teacher speak differently to males, females, Afro-Caribbean students, Asian students, etc. and how is this justified?

The hidden messages that student teachers might convey to students – perhaps unwittingly – can be reinforced by the *resources* that are used. For example, in printed resources how are the 'working classes'[24] portrayed (e.g. coarse, rough, stereotyped by sex roles, sexist, racist)? How is vocabulary used (e.g. 'effeminate', 'fireman', 'headmaster', 'black' as a negative feature and 'white' as a positive feature)? Is the vocabulary gender-neutral? How are male and female roles portrayed[25] (e.g. boys as having practical, exciting adventures out of the house; girls undertaking 'domestic play' in the house; men as active and women as passive; men doing, women watching; men as decision-makers, women as servicing the decision-makers)? Are different ethnic groups portrayed and how are they portrayed (both in words and pictures)? What cultural bias is there in the resources used? Are students with special needs represented in words and pictures? Do role models and resources reinforce or break down discriminatory and stereotypical practices and views respectively?

In *display materials* are all cultures, races, abilities, sexes represented? Do the displays reinforce cultural, sexual, racial stereotypes? Are there any displays that positively discriminate in favour of breaking down stereotypes and dealing with equal opportunities *per se* (e.g. adopting anti-racist stances)? What are people portrayed as doing in displayed materials? What jobs and activities are portrayed?

This simple introduction reinforces our earlier point that the question of equal opportunities needs to be addressed in every aspect of a student's experience in school – in both the formal and the hidden curriculum. The field of equal opportunities is vast and we cannot hope to do full justice to it in the space available here. However, we want to raise some issues that impinge on the student teacher in his or her planning, implementation and evaluation of teaching practice. We concern ourselves with three cognate areas of equal opportunities – sex, ethnicity and special educational needs – but we hope to use these as vehicles for exposing a range of issues that go beyond them. In doing so we shall be attempting to address several components of equal opportunities as they are experienced by teachers and students in schools. There is clearly a difficulty in separating out these three areas as, in practice, for example, sex interacts with and is influenced by race, special needs with race, sex with special needs.[26] Indeed, all three areas are interpenetrated with and mediated by the central issue of differentials of power – structurally, interpersonally and personally. One central purpose of an equal-opportunities policy should be the empowerment of students (and student teachers) to fulfil their own potentials within a just society.

GENDER

Student teachers will encounter a variety of situations where sexist behaviour occurs and where they need to plan to meet the areas in the six 'bullet points' set out above. We identify above three levels at which this might occur – structurally, interpersonally and personally. We shall now deal with each of these in turn.

1 The structural level

At a *structural* level the student teacher will need to plan how to ensure equality of access, uptake and outcome of the curriculum; how the curriculum content and resources not only avoid sex stereotyping but actively promote sexual emancipation; how the curriculum breaks down sex stereotyping in students. Some of this will have been undertaken before the student teacher arrives in school (e.g. the subject options that students choose, the vocational options they follow, the work experience placements they undertake). In practical terms the student teacher may be required to consider the possible sex bias in the curriculum content (perhaps addressing this explicitly with the students in subjects such as the under-representation of women in history ('invisible women')[27] and the ascription of women to domesticity in certain historical periods, geographical areas of the world or religious faiths).

The student teacher will also need to consider, for example, whether equal numbers of women and men are portrayed in resource materials, what they are doing, where they are, what they say, how much control they have over their own lives. Clearly the student teacher needs to review materials before they are used in order to spot any sexist language, so that this issue can be tackled in the classroom. This could be taken further, where the student teacher deliberately selects resources that 'counter-teach', i.e. that raise students' awareness of sexist matters and challenge sexism, for example:

- using books, workcards and media that are written by women;
- using books, workcards and media that portray women in powerful and strong roles;
- using books, workcards and media that portray men in gentler roles;
- using books, workcards and media that present women and men in non-traditional roles;
- using books, workcards and media that raise gender issues.[28]

Delamont[29] and Spender[30] suggest that in several respects schools are more sexist than the 'real' world, segregating the sexes too rigidly (e.g. in cloakrooms, in play areas, on registers, for sports, in uniforms, on records, when lining up), steering boys and girls to different areas (thereby pre-empting future career choices),[31] offering outdated role models, failing to challenge students' own sex-role stereotypes, enforcing exaggeratedly different clothes, demeanours and language.

At a more developed level the student teacher may decide that it is worth attempting a topic on sex stereotyping itself,[32] and the structural causes of sexual inequality in society. The student teacher will have to consider carefully whether this is appropriate, as the handling of such sensitive issues by a relative outsider (the student who arrives at a few weeks' notice and only stays for a few weeks) may require a measure of mutual understanding, mutual confidence, mutual ease, mutual trust and mutual respect that the situation cannot guarantee.

2 The interpersonal level

At an *interpersonal* level the student teacher will need to examine how teaching and learning styles, groupings and interactions can be planned that will address and break down discrimination, prejudice, harassment, verbal and physical abuse, and abuse of power. This level addresses pedagogical and organisational issues. In practical terms this might require the student teacher initially to look at the seating arrangements in the classroom (where students sit and with whom), access to resources, and access to the teacher. Serbin[33] argues that boys receive more attention even if they are not close to the teacher, whereas girls have to stay close to the teacher in order to receive attention. Stanworth[34] demonstrates that boys are likely to receive twice as much attention as girls if the teacher is a woman and ten times as much attention if the teacher is a man – reinforcing the notion of 'invisible women' mentioned above.

In terms of classroom processes the student teacher will need to consider his or her linguistic strategies, e.g. to whom he or she asks questions, the frequency with which males and females are asked questions,[35] what kinds of questions are put to males and females – for example whether males are asked cognitively higher-order questions and females asked cognitively lower-order questions, whether males are asked open questions and females asked closed questions (see the discussion earlier about language in classrooms) – and how the responses are handled.[36] Moreover, the student teacher will need to ensure that he or she is asking equally challenging questions, offering equally challenging activities, and engaging in equally demanding instruction with males and females, i.e. differentiation by input, process and outcome (discussed in Part II). It will also mean giving equal discussion rights and opportunities to males and females (again, see the discussion earlier on language in classrooms).

The student teacher will also need to consider how he or she will respond to sexist incidents in the classroom, for example name-calling, physical abuse, males dominating certain activities or resources (e.g. computers, constructional[37] and building apparatus in primary schools) and females dominating other activities or resources (e.g. the home corner in the infant school).[38] Domination is not simply in terms of *time spent* but also in terms of the *quality* of teaching, learning and activity that occurs.

Moreover, the student teacher will need to consider the balance of activities, for example whether males have more boisterous activities than females, whether males engage in more group activities than females (or *vice versa*), whether females engage in more individual activities than males (or *vice versa*), whether females have more sedentary and quieter activities than males.[39] In connection with this the student teacher will need to look carefully at how he or she plans what he or she will be doing, with whom he or she will be working (also when and for how long), what sanctions and rewards he or she uses and whether these are unacceptably differentiated by sex. This might extend further into the student teacher reviewing the seating and grouping arrangements, the nature of and 'responsibilities' for 'jobs' undertaken by males and females,[40] the motivational strategies that he or she uses for males and females, and the size and constitution of the groups in the classroom. Myers provides a useful checklist that student teachers can use to sensitise themselves to gender issues in the classroom, Box 61.

Box 61

Gender in practice – a checklist

How much time do we spend responding to disruptive behaviour by boys and girls?

How do we evaluate the time we spend with boys and girls in the classroom?

Do we expect girls to be quieter and better behaved?

Do we expect boys to be more imaginative, creative and resourceful?

Do we expect girls to be more sensible and responsible?

Do we expect boys to be stronger and more aggressive?

Do we expect girls to be better at language work and boys to be better at maths and science?

Do we find ourselves commenting more on girls' physical appearance?

Do we ever refer to children by gender groupings, e.g. 'girls line up here'?

Are we conscious of the language we use and do we actively try and avoid sexist terms or references?

Are all classroom jobs done by both boys and girls?

Are boys and girls ever grouped separately for different activities? If so, what questions should we ask to review the practice?

What behaviour do we reward and punish in boys and girls?

How do we encourage other patterns of behaviour, for instance helping girls to participate or boys to listen?

Source Myers[41]

3 The personal level

At a *personal* level the student teacher will need to examine how he or she can promote in students their self-advocacy, appropriate assertiveness and empowerment – setting their own realistic goals, raising their own expectations of themselves, taking control of their own lives, raising their own self-esteem, knowing how to behave appropriately in a group, what is and what is not acceptable to peers, how to respond to inappropriate behaviour, how to handle sexist incidents, comments and behaviour (not necessarily on their own but with the support of others), gaining insights into how they can prepare themselves to be active and authentic citizens. This rather high-sounding agenda implies that the student teacher should attempt to develop in students a self-awareness of their own life situations through an analysis of their own backgrounds and the sociocultural, economic and perhaps political causes of their situations. This is perhaps a high-flown way of saying that the student teacher should attempt to enable each student to reach their full potential, regardless of her or his sex.

The notion of furthering student empowerment – teaching students to value themselves – implies, perhaps, a negotiated approach to teaching and learning, where students take a degree of responsibility for their own learning, echoing Rogers's view that 'I know I cannot teach anyone anything. I can only provide an environment in which he (*sic.*) can learn.'[42] This is a view that is reinforced by Brandes and Ginnis[43] in their view that learning has to be 'owned' by the student and that such ownership is a combination of possession and responsibility. Clearly some students (and indeed some student teachers) may feel uncomfortable with this notion, particularly in the context of a prescribed national curriculum. It may be the case that a step-by-step approach to such a degree of ownership is required, particularly if this has not been the custom and practice in the class(es) that the student teacher inherits. Many students will not relish the idea of ownership as it means a degree of commitment that they may not wish to give.

The student teacher will need to consider carefully how he or she assesses each student, what is assessed (e.g. personality characteristics?), how a student's progress is recorded (particularly in words as words can convey hidden, stereotyped messages about teachers' expectations – discussed in Part IV), how feedback is given to students, what is entered on a record of achievement (e.g. whether females are 'steered' to enter different achievements from boys).

What we are arguing in this section is that the framework of the curriculum, the pedagogical strategies associated with it, and assessment contained within it should be empowering and enabling rather than constraining, a ladder rather than a cage.

ETHNICITY

Immigration to Britain over the past forty years or so has brought about fundamental changes in our society. We are now an ethnically mixed and a culturally varied nation. One consequence of this is that our institutions are having to adapt in order to reflect and to cater for the many mixed communities that now exist throughout the country. Schools in particular are having to change to accommodate the needs of students from many different backgrounds.[44] Whether or not schools are prepared to make sufficient changes and modifications in their organisational policies and practices to meet the needs and aspirations of all their members is a matter of current concern, for as one study shows, many teachers appear to hold what can be described as an *assimilationist* viewpoint with respect to students from minority backgrounds and their needs. (Indeed, it could be argued that many schools cling to the view that there is a white majority when, for example, globally speaking there is a white *minority* rather than a white *majority*).

The term *assimilationist* refers to a point of view that dominated official and educational policy in the early days of immigration in the 1960s. This sought to help immigrants accommodate to the host society by giving them a working knowledge of the English language and of the indigenous culture, and was based on the belief that once English-language proficiency had been acquired, all other problems would diminish. A National Foundation for Educational Research study showed that as far as many teachers are concerned, it is all right to impart information about the religions and homelands of minority groups but beyond this they are divided in their opinions about the extent to which they are prepared to make changes in their curriculum planning and teaching in light of the multicultural composition of contemporary British society.

It is our firm belief that an *assimilationist* viewpoint is both condescending and dismissive of other cultures and lifestyles. All over the world minority groups now actively assert their determination to maintain cultural continuity and to preserve their religious, linguistic and cultural differences. Increasingly, therefore, the host society is turning its attention to the concept of *cultural pluralism*. What exactly does this term imply? Simply that second- and third-generation (43 per cent and 95 per cent of black/Asian people respectively born in Britain[45]) British-born Sikhs, Hindus and Moslems, while sharing many of the same interests and aspirations of white students, are at the same time determined to retain their involvement in the richness of their own minority cultures. Cultural pluralism, then, implies a system that accepts and celebrates the fact that people's lifestyles and customs are different and operates so as to allow equality of opportunity for all to play a full part in society. The partner of cultural pluralism is *cultural diversity*.

The concept of cultural pluralism represents a decisive departure from assimilationist and integrationist viewpoints with their common focus on the perceived *problems* of ethnic-minority pupils and their proposed *remedies* by way of *compensating* for those students' *disabilities*. Nevertheless, cultural pluralism has come in for strong and sustained criticism. One major objection to the cultural-pluralist perspective is its almost exclusive emphasis on *culture*, a vague, ill-defined concept that is open to many interpretations.

Preoccupation with culture, it is said, tends to obscure or to avoid the more fundamental issues to do with *race, power* and *prejudice*,[46] i.e. it fails to address the dynamics of culture. In other words, it fails to address questions[47] in connection with:

1   The economic position of black people in relation to white people.
2   Differences in access to resources and in power to affect events.
3   Discrimination in employment, housing and education.
4   Relations with the police.

A second criticism of the cultural-pluralist position is that it fails to confront what is regarded as the cardinal influence on the life situations of ethnic minority groups in Britain, that is, *racism*. In this respect, racism is not simply prejudiced attitudes held by unenlightened white people; more fundamentally, it refers to the *structural* aspects of racism as manifested both in the education system and in society at large.

The cultural-pluralist response is at best regarded as tokenist, at worst as little better than a form of subtle racism. Rather, an *anti-racist* stance *exposes* inequalities and discrimination in society, for example in employment, in housing, in education, in careers, in 'life chances' and in income, and argues that *positive discrimination* is required to redress the structural inequalities and discrimination in society. In educational terms this argues for the need to raise equality, inequality, discrimination and racism *per se* as issues for students to study in school, directly teaching about these matters, fostering anti-racist attitudes and teaching about anti-discrimination. Negative discrimination can take many forms,[48] for example:

- people illegitimately regarding others as inferior;
- treating persons, on racial grounds (e.g. race, colour, nationality, ethnic origin), less favourably than others;
- restricting opportunities to certain sections of the community or society;
- exclusive or near-exclusive focus on a particular ethnic group (i.e. avoiding the practice of inclusiveness that values everybody's ethnic and cultural background);
- adopting an ethnocentric (often a European or nationalistic) view of society and culture;
- uncritically accepting the views of one culture or group alone;
- holding prejudiced views of others;
- acting prejudicially.

This last feature has taken on an increased importance as we see the resurgence of right-wing groups across Europe and the pressure from the 'cultural restorationists' in the UK[49] to establish curricula and values that hark back to the time when Britain ruled the waves. As with discrimination, so prejudiced behaviour can take many forms, for example:[50]

- *physical assault* that is based on skin colour, ethnicity or culture;
- *verbal assault* that is based on skin colour, ethnicity or culture (e.g. racist jokes, threats, verbal abuse in name-calling, graffiti on books and buildings, attack on personal property, insulting behaviour, the use of racist and offensive language, using language to portray people as inferior – for example 'half-caste');
- *provocative behaviour* (e.g. wearing racist badges and 'T-shirts', insulting the clothes worn by students; circulation of racist literature);
- *attitudinal prejudice* (e.g. regarding other ethnic groups, cultures and societies as inferior);
- *harassment* (of other ethnic groups, cultures and societies);
- *making assumptions* about particular groups in society (e.g. Asian boys work in the family business in the evenings, Moslems bring up their girls

to be passive, domestic and servile, Afro-Caribbean boys are disruptive but good at running);

- *lowering expectations* for certain groups[51] (this affects curricular and pedagogic provision and treatment – e.g. the consigning of a disproportionately high number of students from a particular background to lower sets, achievements and assessment criteria – e.g. using culturally biased tests, undertaking assessments in the students' second language; using assessments to define students as 'linguistically deprived' if they are learning English as a second language (i.e. regarding a student as a problem rather than regarding the learning of a second language as very positive, leading to over-referrals of students from particular racial groups));

- *offending minority groups* in society (e.g. neglect or segregation of the sexes for certain educational activities; insistence on particular uniforms rather than, for example, catering for the Sikh turban, the covering of the legs of Moslems and the wearing of the Jewish skull cap; inappropriate school meals provision; insistence – maybe without consultation with parents – that all students should study multifaith religious education and attend a daily act of worship which, statutorily, must be largely Christian in character).

The debate on multicultural education has shifted considerably during the last few years and is now beginning to reflect greater concern for the role that education can play in countering the pernicious effects of racism both within schools and in society at large. *All* teachers have a vital role to play in the responsible task of preparing *all* students for life in multiracial Britain.

Our task in this section[52] is to discuss an outline for a *multicultural curriculum* which, according to its author, is a natural response to the altered nature of British society and which, from our point of view, exemplifies the practical consequences of a culturally pluralistic position.

A multicultural curriculum

Jeffcoate[53] defines a multicultural curriculum as one in which choice of content reflects the multicultural nature of British society and the world and draws significantly on the experiences of British racial minorities and cultures overseas. He justifies such a curriculum on the following grounds. First, there is what he calls a 'pathological' justification for developing a multicultural curriculum arising out of the pernicious and pervasive racism in British society. Schools, Jeffcoate believes, have a clear duty to make a concerted response to the evil of racism by promoting racial and ethnic self-respect and interracial understanding. Second, a multicultural curriculum can be justified on the notion of minority-group rights. That is to say, ethnic minorities are entitled to expect that their cultures will be positively and prominently represented in the school curriculum. Third, if it is a fundamental task of the school to present an accurate picture of society to its pupils then it follows that other races and cultures are important elements in that picture. Fourth, a multicultural curriculum involves pupils in more interesting, stimulating and challenging experiences than one which is not.

Having set out a justification for a multicultural curriculum, how does one go about selecting learning experiences that might be incorporated within it? As with the issue of gender in the previous section, we argue that decisions for teaching can be made at three levels – the *structural*, the *interpersonal* and the *personal*.

1 The structural level

As in the previous section we suggest that at the *structural* level the student teacher will need to plan: (i) how equality of access, uptake and outcome of the curriculum will be ensured; (ii) how the curriculum content and resources will not only avoid racial and ethnic stereotyping but actively promote emancipation of all groups and cultures in a culturally diverse society; (iii) how the curriculum will break down racial and ethnic stereotyping in students. In practical curriculum terms Jeffcoate sets out five criteria that need to be addressed in curriculum selection and preparation. We summarise these in Box 62.

Box 62

Criteria for selecting learning experiences for a multiracial curriculum

1   A curriculum for the final quarter of the twentieth century needs to be international in its choice of content and in its perspective. An insular curriculum focusing on Britain and British values is unjustifiable and inappropriate.

2   Contemporary British society contains a variety of social and ethnic groups; this variety should be made evident in the visuals, stories and information offered to children.

3   Pupils should have access to accurate information about racial and cultural differences and similarities.

4   People from British minority groups and from other cultures overseas should be presented as individuals with every variety of human quality and attribute.

5   Other cultures and nations have their own validity and should be described in their own terms. Wherever possible they should be allowed to speak for themselves and not be judged exclusively against British or European norms.

Source adapted from Jeffcoate

Drawing on his experiences with the Schools Council, Jeffcoate identifies some limitations in the organisation of materials and methods for multi-cultural classrooms. There is not a lot to be said, he warns, for isolating topics on India, Africa or the Caribbean which are not part of a comprehensive multicultural policy.[54] Indeed, where schools have poor relations such efforts are likely to be counterproductive. A sounder approach is to construct a learning programme around regular themes, drawing on a variety of cultures for source materials with which all pupils can identify. That said, there is still the need for some kind of overt, systematic study since themes of themselves cannot provide pupils with an appreciative understanding of the logic and integrity of a way of life different from their own. Jeffcoate argues that the humanities curriculum should divide its attention evenly between local and international studies, these serving to complement one another in the process whereby children make sense of their world. One can add to this the suggestion[55] that positive role models from members of all ethnic groups should be incorporated into the curriculum, taking examples of the achieve-ments of all ethnic and racial groups (this is an instance of the 'counter-teaching' mentioned above).

Having decided to incorporate minority cultures into their curricula, schools should avoid defining these cultures solely in terms of patterns of life and experience in countries and continents of origin. It may be far more pertinent for children to look at these minority cultures as they are currently evolving and taking shape here in Britain.[56]

Jeffcoate has something to say about development studies, that is to say, those types of investigation of the third world that are particularly popular in secondary schools. Too often, it seems, they infringe the fifth criterion in Box 62, by making European concepts and categories integral to their operations. The multicultural curriculum involves a change in perspective as well as a change in content, an end, in effect, to ethnocentrism which views other cultures in a disparaging, or, at best, condescending way.

In respect of the latter point McFarlane[57] exposes the bias in many non-fiction and textbooks about other countries and cultures. For example, famine may be seen as unavoidable, reliance of the third world on the first world may be accepted as necessary, despite the fact that such reliance replaces self-help, so that a climate and culture of dependency is legitimated. Many textbooks regard the local culture as somehow 'deficient', 'defective', possibly corrupt and not measuring up to the standards of the west. These books communicate hidden messages about inevitable power and wealth differentials; an ethno-centric (and Eurocentric) set of criteria is used to judge other cultures and societies.

Curriculum content, therefore, needs not only to draw on a diversity of cultures but to represent these cultures fairly *in their own terms*, i.e. adopting an anthropological view. An anthropological view defines culture non-judgmentally. For example, Tylor[58] saw culture as 'that complex whole which includes knowledge, belief, art, morals, law, custom, and any other capabilities and habits acquired by [a person] as a member of society'; Linton[59] defined culture as 'the sum total of the knowledge, attitudes and habitual behaviour patterns shared and communicated by the members of a particular society'.

Indeed, it is this view that Lawton[60] used in the 1980s to try to establish a curriculum that was based on cultural analysis. He defined English culture in terms of nine systems: social, economic, communication, rationality, technology, morality, belief, aesthetic and maturation. From his analysis of how these systems were addressed in English society he advanced a case for multicultural, political, economic, vocational and technological education, a multifaith approach to religious education and a respect for minority languages (amongst many other items). Although events overtook him in the national curriculum, nevertheless Lawton's analysis is helpful in raising the agenda of ethnicity.[61]

In Box 62, we listed Jeffcoate's criteria for choosing learning experiences in the multicultural curriculum. In an earlier paper[62] he outlined a *modus operandi* for curriculum planning in the multicultural school based on the traditional objectives model. His expressed intentions were to establish the primacy of objectives in curriculum planning in multicultural education and to explore what factors might govern their selection. We have included the latter in Box 63. Jeffcoate justifies his preference for the objectives model because, as he explains:

> We share the basic assumption of the objectives school that the function of formal education is to bring about desired changes in children. We want them to have acquired certain identifiable knowledge and skills and developed certain identifiable attitudes and behaviours by the time they leave school. We must be prepared to make these knowledge, skills, attitudes and behaviours the starting point and focus for our curriculum planning.

While recognising that the objectives model has certain weaknesses, Jeffcoate is careful to defend his own particular taxonomy. For him, multicultural education is *primarily affective*, being concerned with attitudes and only instrumentally cognitive. But, as he goes on to explain:

> It is a different sort of affectivity from the affectivity of creative work or aesthetic judgement. Even though the overriding objectives, respect for self and others, stipulated in the classification could hardly be called 'correct', they are ones we believe to be necessary for children and for society, and we could go some way to justifying their selection; equally, they are not objectives that could be said to be open to negotiation. Many of the objectives in the classification are knowledge objectives, and I have called these 'instrumental'. In order to come to respect themselves and

others, I am suggesting children must be in possession of certain facts. The first three specific knowledge objectives are, then, a necessary (but not, of course, a sufficient) condition of the overriding objective of respect for others. It is at this point that we find ourselves at odds with the dominant progressive ideology. We do not dissent from the importance they attach to skills but we also attach importance, in a way they would not, to specific items of knowledge which we feel to be predicated by our overall affective targets.

In stressing the need for the acquisition of distinctive knowledge Jeffcoate concedes that he may be adopting a somewhat unfashionable stance. He goes on to discuss factors governing the selection of objectives. In particular, he reviews the way in which they are significantly affected by a school's value system (its philosophy of education) and its definition and analysis of the situation (problems, needs and so on). Each of these three models is sufficiently open-ended and contains sufficient principles to be used as a suitable starting point for the construction of a multicultural curriculum.

Clearly, Jeffcoate's approach is one of *moral persuasion*, concentrating as it does on how respect of self and for others should be the cornerstone of a non-prejudiced society (but *only* from the point of view of the dominant community, notes Gundura).[63] Gundura and others have criticised Jeffcoate's work for its essentially neutral stance. They point to a lack of stress on socio-political aspects of multicultural education[64] and cite a typology for the multicultural curriculum suggested by Williams[65] which includes, *inter alia*, a socio-political perspective which asserts that what passes for knowledge is no more than the dominant ideology of a particular society. Williams calls for a multicultural curriculum which challenges the value consensus in British society and thereby leaves open the possibility of a diverse society consisting of relatively separate but equal groups with equal rights and, importantly, equal powers and representation. Such an approach might focus upon the history and the literature of this country, using historical experiences and literary responses as a key to understanding the effects of colonialism upon our society. Williams further suggests that a multicultural curriculum should teach about race relations and should explore the reasons for migration, government legislation and other controversial issues.

More recently the Runnymede Trust has set out a series of considerations for the planning of the knowledge, skills and attitudes that support the development of personal and cultural identity (see Box 64).

It can be seen that there is as yet little agreement about the aims and objectives of multicultural education or about what ought to constitute a multicultural curriculum. Saunders[66] suggests ways of helping students explore the cultural diversity existing in multicultural classrooms, including *similarity and difference, individual differences, identity, derivation of names, culturally important categories*, and *who is ideal*. The former National

Box 63

A classification of objectives in multiracial education

(A) *Respect for others*:
Cognitive (knowledge)
All pupils should *know*:
the basic facts of race and racial difference;
the customs, values and beliefs of the main cultures represented in Britain and, more particularly, of those forming the local community;
why different groups have immigrated into Britain in the past and how the local community has come to acquire its present ethnic composition.
Cognitive (skills)
All pupils should *be able to*:
detect stereotyping and scapegoating in what they see, hear and read;
evaluate their own cultures objectively.
Affective (attitudes, values and emotional sets)
All pupils should *accept*:
the uniqueness of each individual human being;
the underlying humanity we share;
the principles of equal rights and justice;
and value the achievements of other cultures and nations;
strangeness without feeling threatened;
that Britain is, always has been and always will be a multicultural society;
that no culture is ever static and that constant mutual accommodation will be required of all cultures making up an evolving multicultural society;
that prejudice and discrimination are widespread in Britain and the historical and socio-economic causes which have given rise to them;
the damaging effect of prejudice and discrimination on the rejected groups.

(B) *Respect for self*:
Cognitive (knowledge)
All pupils should *know*:
the history and achievements of their own culture and what is distinctive about it.
Cognitive (skills)
All pupils should *be able to*:
communicate efficiently in English and, if it is not their mother tongue, in their own mother tongue;
learn the other basic skills necessary for success at school.
Affective (attitudes, values and emotional sets)
All pupils should *have developed*:
a positive self-image;
confidence in their sense of their own identity.

Source adapted from Jeffcoate

Box 64 Objectives for personal and cultural identity

Personal and cultural identities: a summary of objectives

Knowledge and understanding
- knowledge of the history and development of one's own cultural traditions, and of the ways in which these both foster and constrain one's own personal identity;
- knowledge of the history of different cultural traditions within Britain, Europe and the wider world;
- knowledge of the physical, social and emotional needs which human beings have in common, including nutrition and shelter, and values relating to freedom, self-respect, belonging, and a sense of meaning and purpose;
- knowledge of the various ways in which different cultures, communities and societies respond to these fundamental needs and moral concerns.

Skills
- ability to contribute to one's own cultural traditions, including the traditions of mainstream public, cultural and political life;
- ability to learn from different cultural experiences, norms and perspectives, and to empathise with people with different traditions;
- ability to analyse and criticise features of cultural traditions, and to identify instances of prejudice, intolerance and discrimination;
- ability to engage in discussion, argument and negotiation with people with traditions other than one's own.

Attitudes
- willingness to sustain the positive aspects of one's own traditions and therefore willingness to be constructively critical when appropriate;
- willingness to learn from different traditions, cultures and identities;
- willingness to challenge instances of prejudice, intolerance and discrimination;
- willingness to accept reasonable and equitable procedures for resolving conflicts.

Source Runnymede Trust[67]

Curriculum Council[68] argued for the need to study the origins and effects of racial prejudice in Britain and other societies. In fact this echoed the view of the Swann Report,[69] which argued that there was a need for all students to understand how racism can operate so that they can influence and be part of positive changes in society in order to reflect more fully the values of a pluralist society. This implies very strongly that multicultural and anti-racist education is not simply the task of teachers in schools that draw on ethnically diverse communities (or indeed, for example, that draw on largely only Asian or Afro-Caribbean or Arabic communities), but is also a task for all-white schools. Britain is a multicultural and multi-ethnic society; we regard it as a dereliction of duty if students in all-white areas are denied access to knowledge of and preparation for membership and practices of these diverse communities. This has implications for the images and texts that are used with all children. Materials should reflect the multicultural and multi-ethnic diversity of the UK and the rest of the world.[70]

Hence we suggest that the student teacher may wish to attempt a topic on racism itself and its structural, interpersonal and personal causes. However, just as we advocated some caution in handling issues of sex stereotyping, we advise each student teacher to consider carefully whether, as a newcomer (and during the comparatively short time that he or she stays in the school), he or she has had sufficient opportunity to establish a degree of mutual trust, respect, understanding and confidence that is often critical in making for success in handling sensitive issues.

In approaching the structure and content of the curriculum in schools, then, we set out a list of 'indicators of good practice' in handling ethnicity and multiculturalism for each curriculum subject. We suggest that the student teacher should ensure that:

- a range of social, cultural, religious, ethnic and political histories, traditions, backgrounds and achievements is represented within and across each subject in the curriculum, drawing on students' own backgrounds and perspectives fully, and is handled sensitively and without causing offence in school;
- students work with culturally diverse and different contents and resources;
- the positive achievements and heritage of people from different ethnic and cultural backgrounds are studied;
- non-western influences on western society and culture are studied;
- judgements of 'better than' or 'worse than' are suspended until greater knowledge and appreciation of other traditions, beliefs, practices, cultures and societies are acquired;
- opportunities are provided for students to develop their own personal and cultural identities;
- opportunities are provided to 'counter-teach' and for students to analyse and break down their own assumptions and to critique the stereotyped assumptions (often negative) of, and racist aspects in others, in curriculum content and in diverse media;
- opportunities are provided for students to examine power, power differentials, legitimate and illegitimate power, the exercise of power, rights, freedoms, responsibilities;
- opportunities are provided for students to explore similarities and

differences between themselves, their own and others' backgrounds, cultures, communities, traditions, beliefs, values and practices;

- students are made aware of global trends and the global contexts of decisions that have implications for their local communities, contexts and everyday lives;
- students study and evaluate other countries, communities, peoples, traditions, economies, politics, religions, cultures in their own terms before making invidious or stereotyped comparisons;
- opportunities are provided for students to study examples of the achievement of emancipation, democracy and empowerment of individuals, groups, communities, societies and the struggles that were involved in reaching emancipation, democracy and empowerment;[71]
- foreign-language teaching and the increasing need for students to speak more than one language are accompanied by an insight into the cultures and societies that speak those languages;
- opportunities are provided for students to see what they have in common with each other as well as how they differ from each other;
- opportunities are provided for students to work in their own first language if this is not English.

2 The interpersonal level

The *interpersonal* level concerns pedagogy. The student teacher will need to be able to draw on the experiences of students from a variety of backgrounds, to have high expectations of all students, developing high standards of achievement in them all. In particular – and this is not exclusive to teaching for ethnic diversity – the student teacher will need to consider how he or she can promote motivation, self-esteem, confidence and tolerance in students (see below: the *personal* level) and how mutual trust and respect can be built up in relationships between students and student teachers.

The development of interpersonal trust, tolerance and respect has implications for the use of workshop approaches, group work and peer-group learning. The student teacher will need to consider, for example, the ethnic and cultural constitution of each group as well as the ethnic and cultural content of the knowledge on which the students are working. Discussion-based activities can explore different aspects of the communities and cultures from which students are drawn and, in so doing, can foster tolerance, mutual respect and co-operation amongst students from diverse backgrounds.

Further, attention to pedagogy will require the student teacher to consider the languages, dialect, accent, oral and written traditions of the students in exploring the communities from which the students are drawn. This might be approached through oral and written media, discussions and drama. The Runnymede Trust[72] suggests that some practical activities can be designed so that students' learning does not depend solely on their abilities in English.

Proficiency in English can be furthered through the use of support teachers and adults who are able to work in community languages as well as English. Indeed, bilingual and trilingual children should have the opportunity to learn *concepts* in their first language as well as in their second or third language. Small-group learning of English can also be an effective strategy.

The issue of pedagogy also requires attention to the learning environment that teachers and students create. For example, it means that classroom displays (a) reflect cultural diversity, (b) break down stereotyping and (c) promote positive role models in relation to cultural identity and ethnicity. At a practical level it will mean that several community languages and scripts might be represented in the displayed materials.

The national curriculum in general, and the cross-curricular themes and dimensions in particular, lay emphasis on the links between schools and the community. In planning for these aspects of the national curriculum a prime opportunity is afforded for the student teacher to involve a diversity of community representatives, both by taking students out into the community and by bringing people from the community into the school. The opportunity for members of the community to discuss with students several aspects of their community is one which is too good to neglect. This is not confined to schools that draw on a diverse catchment area; it applies also to all-white schools; indeed it could be argued that it is more important that all-white schools should become involved in finding out about other communities. Some all-white schools,[73] for example, run exchanges with schools whose students are drawn from culturally and ethnically diverse backgrounds.

As with sexist comments and incidents discussed in the previous section, the student teacher will need to consider how he or she will respond to racist, discriminatory and prejudiced comments and incidents within and outside the classroom (e.g. verbal and physical abuse and bullying, name-calling, antagonistic remarks). As all schools should have a policy on equal opportunities it may be useful for the student teacher to examine these policies and to take other steps in order to find out what strategies the school employs to deal with racist language, assumptions, behaviour and incidents.

3 The personal level

At a *personal* level the student teacher will need to plan how to ensure that *all* students, regardless of ethnicity, develop self-confidence, self-esteem and tolerance. Indeed, the Runnymede Trust[74] suggests that each student should become confident and self-affirming rather than insecure and ashamed of their culture; they should develop an openness to change and a willingness to listen to and learn from others. The student teacher has a significant role to play in this during teaching practice, as he or she will be the planner and provider of opportunities for students to experience success, to have a sense of personal achievement and to value their own communities and traditions.

The student teacher, as the provider of opportunities, experiences and feedback on achievement, shares with other teachers in the school the important responsibility of ensuring that each student fulfils her or his own potentials and ambitions and develops as a responsible member of a democratic society.

Hence the student teacher will need to plan opportunities for students to develop autonomy and personal worth, to resist being stereotyped and stereotyping others, to believe in their own capabilities, to learn how to handle racist comments, incidents and behaviour (not necessarily by themselves but with the support of others), to gain insights into how to work towards countering racism in its several forms, to be able to stand up for themselves, and to appreciate the value of community and cultural solidarity.

Because the issues of ethnicity and multicultural education are contentious, the student teacher will find it essential to discuss his or her planning and experiences with the class teacher or mentor in the school. This ensures not only that the student teacher is operating within the parameters of the school but that he or she has addressed the sensitivities involved in dealing with these delicate issues.

SPECIAL EDUCATIONAL NEEDS

Introduction

We regard as self-evident and incontestable the view that students with special educational needs should receive as broad and balanced an entitlement curriculum as any other students, the same degree of choice and consultation about options as any other students (rather than, for instance, a stripped down narrow diet of 'basics', programmed reading, repetitive teaching styles and simple job training).[75] This is the view that was espoused in the 1981 Education Act[76] and which was echoed in two important documents from the National Curriculum Council in 1989 and 1992[77] with regard to students with special educational needs and severe learning difficulties respectively. Indeed, each document for each national curriculum subject makes it a 'common requirement' that the national curriculum should be taught to as many students as possible in ways appropriate to their abilities.[78] Moreover, the Office for Standards in Education in a series of publications in 1995[79] made explicit its view that schools should ensure that:

- 'provision for special educational needs permeates the school's organisation and curricular structures and the practice in the school;
- all staff work closely with the special educational needs co-ordinator;
- parents know who is their main point of contact (normally the special educational needs co-ordinator) and who is the school's "responsible person";

- resources, including staffing, are managed effectively and efficiently to support special educational needs policies and pupils' identified needs;
- all staff are sufficiently aware of procedures for identifying, assessing and providing for pupils with special educational needs;
- pupils' progress is monitored, especially in relation to annual reviews and individual education plans;
- assessment, recording and reporting satisfy statutory requirements;
- the use of specialist support from outside agencies is well managed within the school'.

This view places on the student teacher the responsibility for finding out (a) how students with special educational needs are identified and assessed; (b) how provision for students' special educational needs is addressed and managed; (c) who is the special educational needs co-ordinator and 'responsible person'; (d) what resources are available to support students with special educational needs (e.g. materials, teaching and ancillary staff, specialist support); (e) which students have a statement of special educational needs; (f) what the students' needs and difficulties are; (g) how recording and reporting is addressed for students with special educational needs; (h) how progress is planned and monitored for students with special educational needs.

Supporting the view that equal opportunities should be provided for all students has certain corollaries for students with special educational needs. For example, it recognises that equality of *access* to a wide curriculum will be a challenging task for many students and teachers.[80] We take up this issue later in this section (see below: the *interpersonal* level and the *personal* level).

Who, then, are the students with special educational needs? The Warnock Report[81] sets the scene here, arguing that any simplistic view of special needs is untenable:

> The idea is deeply ingrained in educational thinking that there are two types of children, the *handicapped* and the *non-handicapped* ... But the complexities of individual need are far greater than this dichotomy implies. ... We wish to see a more positive approach and we have adopted the concept of *special educational need*.

The Warnock Report was a comprehensive review of educational provision in England, Scotland and Wales for students challenged by disabilities of body or mind. One task in this section of the book is to introduce student teachers to some implications of the Warnock Report and the subsequent (and continuing) educational debate about special educational needs, as they impinge upon teachers' work in classrooms in ordinary schools.

One of the most startling statistics to emerge from the Warnock Committee's Report is that at some time during their school career *one in five children* will require some form of special educational provision. Clearly, the Warnock Committee has widened the definition of special education to include students needing relatively mild educational support, and it follows that special provision of this proportion of the school population means *provision in ordinary schools* as well as special schools. Research[82] surveyed by the committee revealed that childhood disabilities giving rise to special educational needs are found in a much larger proportion of the school population than has commonly been assumed. One of the conclusions of the report, therefore, is that the tendency to equate special education with special schooling is inappropriate, given the large number of children with special educational needs in ordinary schools. Indeed, the notion of special educational needs itself should avoid a 'deficiency' or 'pathology' view that confines itself to students with learning difficulties and consider, for example, the special needs and backgrounds of students:

who are able and gifted;
with linguistic diversity;
with ethnic and cultural diversity;
with specific learning needs;
with short-term emotional and behavioural difficulties.[83]

We shall not consider here the very able and gifted, though this is not to minimise the importance of setting them challenging tasks. Indeed, it is probable that many very capable students deliberately under-achieve in order not to stand out as being too different from their peers. The *Code of Practice for the Identification and Assessment of Children with Special Educational Needs* regards any student as having a special educational need if any *special educational provision* is necessary.[84] The authors argue that this will include students with special educational needs in relation to: (a) academic attainment; (b) learning difficulties; (c) specific learning difficulties (e.g. dyslexia); (d) emotional and behavioural difficulties; (e) physical disabilities; (f) sensory impairment (e.g. hearing or visual difficulties); (g) speech and language difficulties; (h) medical conditions.[85] One must be cautious, of course, in labelling students as this can lead to the problem of teachers having low expectations of students that we mentioned earlier. It could be argued, for instance, that *category labels* should be replaced by an engagement with the *quality* of the educational experience that students have, as this recognises the complexity of the issue and the need to act positively.

What does all of this mean for the student teacher? Simply this. A student teacher in a mixed-ability class of thirty in an *ordinary school*, should be aware that as many as six students might require some form of special provision at some time, and about four or five students will need special provision at any given time. Such students (and those currently categorised as educationally sub-normal), the Warnock Report refers to as *children with learning difficulties*, a term it recommends should be employed to embrace students with emotional and behavioural difficulties and those receiving educational support from specialist teachers. While special schools will continue to be the main providers of special education for students with severe or complex physical, sensory or intellectual difficulties, those with behavioural or emotional disorders that are so extreme that they disrupt ordinary school classes, and those with less severe difficulties who even with special help do not perform well in ordinary schools, it follows that the task of recognising early signs of possible special educational need and, where appropriate, coping with them in ordinary classrooms, will increasingly be the responsibility of teachers in ordinary schools.

Is this really feasible, readers may well ask. The answer suggested by the findings of a three-year study[86] is a resounding *yes*. To a far greater extent than is currently practised, the authors conclude, special educational needs can be met in ordinary schools providing, of course, that there are the requisite commitment and resources. Hegarty, Pocklington and Lucas undertook a detailed examination of seventeen integration programmes in fourteen LEAs, the programmes themselves varying enormously in terms of the types of special needs that were catered for and in respect of the ages and the numbers of students involved. The range and the scope of the investigation covered: developmentally delayed, communication disordered, visually impaired, hearing impaired and physically impaired, special educational needs, with needs being met by links between special schools and mainstream schools, special centres, and individual programmes for integration. In the space available to us we focus specifically on the attitudes and reactions of ordinary[87] teachers in the twenty-two schools involved in the research and on the problems of curriculum development in the integration of students with special educational needs into ordinary schools.

Teachers' reactions

Two hundred and forty-seven teachers completed questionnaires revealing their knowledge of students with special needs and their competence in handling and teaching such students. The majority of them responded that they had relatively little or no knowledge when the various integration programmes were begun in their particular schools. At the end of the study, however, teachers were able to report a considerable increase in their understanding of specific difficulties, their greater knowledge being chiefly attributable to two sources: (1) direct experience of the students themselves, and (2) from interaction (largely on an informal basis) with more knowledgeable persons such as specialist teachers, educational psychologists and speech therapists.

Although 'ordinary' teachers felt that they were fairly competent to deal with the students with special needs allocated to their classes, their comments showed that to no small extent their feelings of adequacy reflected the existence of specialist teacher facilities in their schools and the fact that their responsibilities for students with special needs were limited.

What the study clearly revealed was that integrating students with special needs into mainstream schools requires new ways of working on the part of the various professionals involved. There is, the researchers report, a need to collaborate with colleagues, share information, view students' problems in a comprehensive light, disseminate skills and generally move toward inter-disciplinary and collaborative, collegial working. This is very difficult to achieve in light of such obstacles as territoriality and traditions of isolated professionalism among teachers.

The curriculum and integration programmes

What of the curriculum in such programmes of integration? What is actually being offered to students with special needs in ordinary schools? The study revealed considerable diversity in practice. Wade and Moore[88] suggest that the range of special educational provision can be conceived of as a continuum ranging from segregated special schooling to full attendance in a normal class, different forms of provision being seen as different points along the continuum. They argue that one can move from total segregation to *locational*, *social*, *curricular* and *pedagogic* integration, and thence towards *functional* integration where all aspects of the development of students with special needs are both catered for and built into mainstream education: their social, emotional and physical as well as academic and intellectual needs. Hegarty, Pocklington and Lucas propose that the following range be available to pupils with special needs:

1 **Special curriculum**   This is a curriculum that has little or no reference to work being done by age peers. Such curricula, they opine, are unlikely to find a place in integration programmes and are increasingly being called into question as providing a valid approach to special education.

2 **Special curriculum plus**   Special curricula have become less isolated from mainstream curricula as a result of the growing realisation that all children are educable and that it is important to focus on similarities as well as differences. Thus a common curricular pattern, the researchers note, is 'basic skills plus general enrichment', a fair description of the curriculum in many special schools.

3 **Normal curriculum, significant reductions**   Here the emphasis is quite markedly on what students with special needs have in common with their peers. They follow a normal curriculum as far as is possible, with modifications and omissions in order to meet their special needs. This approach is clearly different from one whose starting point is students' special needs, even though such a programme may involve extensive withdrawal and the abandoning of several subjects.

4 Normal curriculum, some modifications   Some students with special needs follow the same curriculum as their peers with some omissions and/or supplementary or alternative activities. Partially sighted students, for example, may be precluded from taking part in certain aspects of art and craft, concentrating instead on sculpture and such activities that are dependent on tactile senses.

5 Normal curriculum, little or no modification   Hegarty and his associates found many students in the same teaching groups as their peers. This was especially the case, they noted, in the case of the physically challenged, but it also applied to others.

There was a broad consensus, the researchers found, among teachers, parents and the students themselves that students with special needs benefit greatly from being placed in integration programmes. There were gains in self-confidence, independence and in the realistic acceptance of an individual's challenging condition. Friendly relationships between students with special needs and their peers did occur but they tended to be limited and often involved outgroups in the school. Negative relationships such as teasing were reported to be comparatively rare. Particularly encouraging was the teachers' thoroughgoing endorsement of the integration programme in their schools.

How does this impact on the work of the student teacher? As with the discussions of sex and ethnicity earlier, we organise our suggestions into three levels, the structural, interpersonal and personal.

1 The structural level

At a *structural* level the student teacher will need to consult with the teachers and the school mentor in order to find out which students have special educational needs (and which students are 'statemented', i.e. have a formal – legal – statement of their needs and proposals for how these are to be met), which are in the process of being statemented,[89] and which students may have special needs though they are not statemented. Further, the student teacher will need to find out what the needs and difficulties of the students in question are and how they are being addressed (i.e. how equality of *access* and *uptake* are addressed). This latter will include where and how support staff are used (and when, e.g. twice a week on a withdrawal basis, three days a week with a support teacher working alongside the class teacher in the class with all of the other students, etc.), details of special resources and equipment available, and particulars of individualised education plans (IEPs).[90]

However, simply focusing on the student with special educational needs in a mainstream class can lead to the stigmatisation (perhaps unwittingly and not deliberately) of that student. Rather, we suggest that the notion of special educational needs is a *societal* rather than an *individual* issue. This implies that the students' peers should have their awareness raised of special educational needs and how to respond to and work with students with such needs. This has to be handled very sensitively, for indelicate handling can cause further stigmatisation rather than help to reduce it. With this caution, however, the student teacher can plan programmes and resources for the whole class or particular teaching groups that address special needs.

At the simplest level, perhaps, a review of texts, pictures and materials can be undertaken to ensure that there is appropriate representation of students with special needs and that that inclusion is presented positively. At another level the student teacher may wish to ensure that a 'special-needs dimension' features in the curriculum content (taking care to avoid the risk of stigmatisation).

At a more developed level the student teacher will need to plan IEPs with the class teacher and/or special needs co-ordinator in which activities 'can be broken down into small and achievable steps for pupils who have marked learning difficulties'.[91] It may well be the case, for instance, that a student may take several years to complete Level 1 of the national curriculum. Further, opportunities for students with special needs to *achieve* visibly a particular task and to *experience success* should be planned; as the *Curriculum Guidance* document from the former National Curriculum Council[92] says: 'pupils learn best when they feel valued and their achievements are recognised'.

2 The interpersonal level

The interpersonal level concerns pedagogy. This, perhaps, lies at the heart of the notions of access and uptake of a curriculum that is formally available to all, regardless of special need. Planning for students' access to the curriculum can be a challenging and daunting task for the student teacher,[93] and clearly he or she must seek advice and support on this. In connection with providing access it is important to note that each national curriculum subject document includes in its *common requirements* the statement that 'appropriate provision should be made for pupils who need to use:

- means of communication other than speech, including computers, technological aids, signing, symbols or lip-reading;
- non-sighted methods of reading, such as braille, or non-visual or non-aural ways of acquiring information;
- technological aids in practical and written work;
- aids or adapted equipment to allow access to practical activities within and beyond school.'[94]

This statement echoes the views of the former National Curriculum Council's *Curriculum Guidance* documents[95] where they argue that there will be occasions where an 'emphasis on oral rather than written work will help some pupils with learning difficulties'[96] and that a range of communication methods should be used that make the best use of students' strengths.[97] There should be access to large-print books and texts where necessary and also to audio-cassettes and adapted word processors to facilitate learning. At another level the student teacher will need to plan for a multi-sensory approach to learning for some students.[98] Further, if the abilities to communicate and to be communicated with are to be addressed then the student teacher will need to provide many opportunities for this to occur. This moves teaching away from formal, didactic and individual styles and towards group work.

Planning to develop communicative competence has significant implications for the use of extended group work, collaborative and co-operative work, in pairs, small groups and larger groups.[99] We suggest that, though many students with special educational needs might find it difficult to develop, meet and practise the social, emotional, linguistic and communicative challenges and demands of being a member of a communicative situation, nevertheless, if that is how students need to develop then student teachers should be planning for such opportunities to occur. The isolated, the marginalised, the stigmatised, the emotionally and behaviourally disturbed students in the classroom are the very ones who need this most, even though they are often the very ones that operate worst in this situation, presenting disruptive and difficult behaviour. The student teacher will have to plan very carefully, of course, the size and constitution of each group in order to minimise difficulties in the students and in order to maximise their social, emotional, cognitive and behavioural development.

The expansion of technological aids in classrooms has a vital part to play in enabling students to learn and to communicate. The use of technology, including concept keyboards and various overlays for computers and word-processing packages can 'facilitate and encourage sensory development, ... increase the range of materials that can be accessed across the curriculum ... [and] encourage pupil interaction'.[100] For example, technology can enable students with severe learning difficulties to generate visual and aural patterns using switches, allow choice and decision-making through 'yes' and 'no' switches, and increase sensory control skills, attending skills and co-operative skills.[101]

At another level the student teacher will need to consider 'environmental factors', for example, whether students are seated so that they can hear and see properly; whether the lighting is adequate for visually impaired students; whether acoustic conditions (and aids) are appropriate for students with hearing impairments; whether the furniture is arranged for easy movement of students with physical impairments.

Most teachers and student teachers will encounter emotionally and behaviourally disturbed and disturbing students. Though we deal with management and control in the next section, we ought to signal here the need for the student teacher to discuss with the class teacher the agreed and most appropriate ways of handling children whose problems cause them to present challenges to the smooth running of the classroom, who disrupt the learning of others and who disrupt their own learning by violent or disturbed behaviour. It is vital that the novice student teacher holds these discussions in order to avoid provoking disturbed behaviour, in order to promote the emotional and behavioural well-being of the student, and in order to know how best to respond to behavioural challenges and emotionally charged behaviour.

Let us not understate the enormity of this task. Students with emotional and behavioural difficulties are very draining on the capabilities of teachers to cope with routine stress, to start each day afresh and to be prepared to try to be positive over and over again with difficult students. It is likely that, in many cases, the student teacher will have to handle a student who presents a combination of emotional, behavioural and learning difficulties. Indeed, some of the behavioural difficulties may stem from frustration caused by learning difficulties and the teacher's poor matching of work, e.g. over-estimating the student's abilities. It is comparatively common to see in a single student a conjunction of learning and behavioural difficulties.

The same situation arises, of course, in connection with students with other special educational needs. For example, a hearing-impaired student may have difficulty in learning and this may produce difficult behaviour (e.g. out of frustration). Often it is necessary to understand and try to address the complexity of the interplay between learning difficulties and physical, emotional, behavioural and sensory difficulties. This implies that planning to meet the needs of the student will have to take place on a variety of fronts – emotional, social, behavioural, cognitive – simultaneously. For the novice student teacher this is a daunting task in which he or she will need to seek and be given guidance and support from teachers not only with experience of handling difficult students but who have knowledge of particular individuals and how best to work with them.

Many schools will have both formal and informal strategies that are agreed for handling specific individuals and their presenting disruptive behaviour in the class, e.g. organisation for learning (maybe the use of group work); the use of practical activity; the cognitive demand, pacing and organisation of tasks; negotiation; confrontation avoidance; withdrawal; involvement of other staff; involvement of parents; the setting of individualised work and agreed contracts for work and behaviour; the use of sanctions, punishments and rewards, etc. The student teacher needs to be apprised of these agreed strategies so that her actions are consistent with them. Further, many teachers (perhaps who are in the process of statementing a student) will require incidents and examples of emotional and behavioural disturbance to be formally recorded so that, if a case conference is held, evidence rather than subjective prejudice and preference will be available to support the discussions. Students with moderate or severe learning difficulties will tax the ingenuity and creativity of student teachers quite heavily, as they will have to devise several ways of addressing, introducing and cementing concepts and areas of knowledge. There will need to be multiple routes to the formation of single and several concepts in students.

As with sexist and racist comments and incidents discussed previously, the student teacher will need to consider how to respond to discriminatory comments and incidents within and outside the classroom (e.g. verbal and physical abuse to students, name-calling, bullying, violent and aggressive language, violent and aggressive non-verbal communication, antagonistic remarks). This should be considered in terms of strategies for handling such incidents generally and with particular individuals.

3 The personal level

Many students with special educational needs have fragile, damaged or low self-esteem and self-concepts. This is one of the most powerful arguments for taking students out of mainstream education and placing them in schools for students with moderate or severe learning difficulties or with emotional and behavioural difficulties, as mainstream education has often not only failed these students but has caused them to fail and to regard themselves as failures. The low expectations that some mainstream teachers may have of students can have seriously depressing and damaging effects on students' self-esteem and motivation to learn. The reduction of threat in some form of special education is invaluable in rebuilding damaged self-concepts.

Many students, for whatever reason, need others to speak and act for them for their greatest benefit, i.e. to act as advocates for their welfare. Though *advocacy* on behalf of students with special needs is important, it is only one side of the coin; the other side is to develop in students their abilities in *self-advocacy*.[102] This is an important issue if students are to be able to have genuine control over their own lives and power to take decisions in their own best interests. Students should be enabled to find, develop and exercise their own autonomy, their 'voice'.[103] It is no accident, perhaps, that a low-ability student is called 'dumb'; it is indicative of their own inabilities and their teachers' inabilities to foster the development of their own 'voice'.

The development of self-advocacy resonates with the points made in discussing sex and ethnicity earlier, that students should be supported in their moves to become as autonomous and fulfilled as possible, and that this process can be facilitated in student-centred, negotiated and flexible learning. This need not be confined to older students; for example the High Scope curriculum accords considerable autonomy, supported decision-making and responsible decision-making in children from the nursery years upwards.[104] Further, Zimiles[105] demonstrates that students brought up in progressive education were able to engage weighty moral issues – punishment, goodness, wrongdoing – more effectively than students whose pedagogical and curricular diet was more formal. At a simple level this might mean that students face up to the consequences of their behaviour and take responsibility for making it more acceptable.

The great difficulty for many student teachers is coping with emotionally and behaviourally disturbed students who are severely disruptive in class. The student teacher wishes, perhaps, that they would cease to advocate themselves in the classroom! There is no simple solution to such behavioural problems; if there were it would have been discovered years ago. There is no simple solution because there is no simple problem. Many disturbed students' behaviour is the outcome of a complex interplay of numerous contributing factors, e.g. home circumstances and relationships, parental problems, parenting difficulties, relationships with peers, physical and mental illness, early childhood experiences, an inability to cope, difficulty in self-restraint or controlling emotions, and school matters (for example, limited academic abilities).

This does not mean that nothing can be done for these students; in fact, just the opposite. It suggests that teachers, if no one else in the students' world, should be able to provide a stable, respectful and supportive environment for these students which affords them some opportunities to develop appropriate self-management skills. It also means that teachers will have to come to know and understand the biography and social and emotional make-up of the students. It involves the teacher understanding and communicating with the parties that are interested in the student, for example parents, welfare workers, etc. Such intimate knowledge takes time to acquire; a student teacher who does not have that time needs, therefore, to try to gain that knowledge rapidly from the class teacher (respecting confidentiality where appropriate) and to use this to try to build up relationships with students.

Many students with special educational needs are the butt of verbal insults, taunts and abuse. Indeed, the notion of having a special educational need is often used as an insult in itself amongst students who are not themselves disadvantaged. Students with special educational needs are surrounded by messages, images and behaviour which indicate that having a special educational need renders them somehow a lesser person or a failure; this can reinforce their low self-esteem. Given this situation it is hardly surprising that for some students with special educational needs the only way of gaining some positive recognition is by aggressive physical and verbal behaviour – that is all that is left open to them. The student teacher needs to discuss with the teacher(s) with whom he or she is working the strategies that are being used to boost self-esteem and to develop in students with special educational needs abilities to handle themselves with self-control, to avoid violence and violent confrontations, to avoid acting abusively themselves, and to preserve their dignity when they are the butt of abuse. This is a difficult lesson for many students to learn; it is a lesson that perhaps needs to be addressed explicitly as part of the curricular experience of all students. Developing a sense of responsibility for actions in students is an important matter, though clearly it is difficult and long-term.

Chapter 14

Management and control in the classroom

INTRODUCTION

This chapter is concerned with management and control in the classroom. It does not pretend to offer a panacea for all the manifold challenges and difficulties that are potentially present in the modern classroom; nor does it attempt to deal with the more problematic aspects of behaviour like bad language, violence and truancy. To do so would be to swing the balance of the pages that follow in the direction of juvenile delinquency and so distort the overall picture of classroom behaviour. In any case, should these and comparable incidents arise in the course of a student teacher's school experience, they should be referred to a senior member of staff as soon as is practically possible. What we do aim to do in this chapter, however, is to offer the reader a framework for securing and maintaining the co-operation of students in classroom activities. To this end, we attempt to bring together a range of stimulating ideas, perspectives and concepts – some theoretical, others the result of recent research – that will provide the student teacher with an operational base for achieving a positive, humane and constructive approach to management and control in the classroom.

A word of caution, however. Important as it is for the reader to consider carefully the points raised in this chapter, particularly if he or she is concerned to achieve good standards of teaching, they cannot really be viewed in isolation. This is to say, they tie up with a whole range of contextual factors, some of which are touched upon elsewhere in the book, such as preparation and planning, suitability of material, teaching methods, teacher–pupil relationships, and so on. If, for example, the work you give to your class tends consistently to be too difficult, or if your relations with the class are permanently abrasive, then no amount of reading or re-reading of this section will help you resolve the difficulties that will inevitably follow. The connections between the factors about to be discussed and the broader issues of pedagogy must be made by the reader.

The point that we wish to emphasise is that management and control is a multifaceted matter, concerning all aspects of life in schools and all aspects of a student's personality and a teacher's craft. Some key elements of good discipline and management are shown in Box 65. This moves away from regarding 'discipline' as an extra to teaching, for example in the view widespread amongst student teachers that discipline comes *after* curricular and pedagogic matters – a view reflected in the practice whereby a student teacher sets students some work and then spends the remainder of the lesson

Box 65

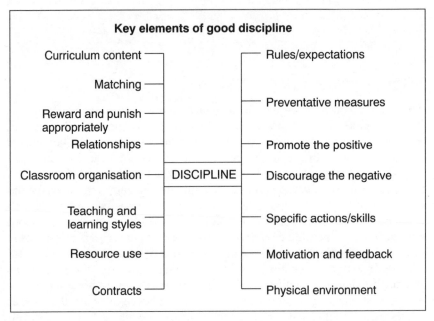

Key elements of good discipline

Curriculum content — Rules/expectations
Matching —
Reward and punish appropriately — Preventative measures
Relationships — Promote the positive
Classroom organisation — DISCIPLINE — Discourage the negative
Teaching and learning styles — Specific actions/skills
Resource use — Motivation and feedback
Contracts — Physical environment

ensuring that students are kept 'on task' and working. The view that we espouse here is that discipline is a 'built-in' element of teaching rather than a 'bolt-on' extra – it touches every aspect of a school. This view finds support from the influential Elton Report[1] on discipline in schools, which suggested that a whole-school policy was vital for effective discipline, ensuring consistency of vision and practice. Further, the Elton Report suggested that this whole-school policy should include:

- systems of incentives, sanction and support;
- shared understanding and mutual support among members of a school staff;
- ways of talking matters over with students;
- curriculum content and teaching styles;
- home/school relationships.

The strength of the Elton Report is a realisation that a behaviour policy is not just about behaviour but touches every aspect of the formal and hidden curriculum of schools and their relationships with the wider community. Good behaviour and good teaching cannot be separated. A student teacher can reasonably expect to be able to look at a school's behaviour and discipline policy as a preparation for teaching practice. A school discipline policy, however, is not guaranteed to reduce misbehaviour. Hart *et al.*[2] demonstrate that there is little relationship between a school's construction and implementation of a discipline policy and the levels of students' misbehaviour or the level of teacher stress caused by misbehaviour. Rather, they aver, it is better to create a supportive atmosphere that helps teachers to cope with the misbehaviour that they have to face.

A range of recent studies[3] all point in the same direction in suggesting that the promotion of good behaviour is founded on several fundamental key principles:

- The need to 'promote the positive' and to build self-esteem in students.
- The need to provide opportunities for students to experience success.
- The centrality of motivation, interest in and enjoyment of all aspects of school life.
- The need to attend to and support the 'whole person'.
- The promotion of empowerment, autonomy and responsibility in students.
- The need for consistency.
- The *inclusive* nature of a policy, involving and addressing all aspects of school life and curricula, all relevant parties (within and outside the school), and all aspects of the student (e.g. psychological and emotional well-being), i.e. a concern for total quality.
- The recognition that pastoral, behavioural and academic needs exist in symbiosis with each other.
- The need to promote a positive ethos and climate in the school and classroom which extends to the physical, emotional, psychological and social as well as to the academic aspects of school.
- The need to consider the 'persona' of the student teacher.
- The need to be proactive, considering preventative measures and measures to de-escalate trouble quickly.
- The need for negotiated and agreed rules, rewards and sanctions.
- The need for communication, e.g. of expectations, boundaries, acceptability, responsibilities, rules, praise, feedback.

It is clear from this summary list that attention is focused on *people*, on *intervention* and on *accentuating the positive*. This accords with the findings of the Elton Report, Mortimore *et al.*,[4] Galvin, Costa and Mercia[5] that punitive schools appeared to promote poor behaviour. The student teacher concerned to demonstrate effective class management and control will need to consider, amongst other things:

1   How to promote positive environments.
2   How to be proactive and fair.
3   How to plan and implement the formal curriculum to support good discipline.
4   How and when to involve other parties.
5   Making plans for management and discipline effective in practice.

With regard to (1) – how to promote positive environments – the student teacher will need to consider:

Promoting the positive

An emphasis on accentuating the positive rather than focusing on the negative.
Encouraging, teaching and rewarding good behaviour and positive relationships.

Motivations, praise and enjoyment

Making school and learning interesting.
Reinforcing the positive, extinguishing the negative.
Providing feedback to students.
Providing opportunities for success.
Providing earned and appropriate verbal and non-verbal praise.
Recognising relative as well as absolute success.
Public recognition of achievement and effort (e.g. in class, assemblies).
Conveying enthusiasm and enjoyment.

Self-esteem and success

Valuing students' contributions and communicating this to them.
Promoting student autonomy, empowerment and 'voice'.
Providing opportunities for success.
Avoiding labelling.
Avoiding humiliation, sarcasm, insult and ridicule.
Asking for students' views/accounts and taking them seriously.
Recognising non-academic achievements.

Ethos and climate

An open, welcoming, stimulating, caring and supportive climate within the classroom environment (however defined).

Equal opportunities

Addressing gender, race, class, abilities, special needs: an equal opportunity to contribute and to learn.

Intervening to reduce stereotyping and stereotyped behaviour.

Responding quickly to incidents and behaviour which violate equal opportunities.

Avoiding stereotyping student teachers' responses to students.

Being alert to racial and sexual harassment and bullying.

Being aware of statemented students and those with special needs.

Valuing all cultures.

Roles and relationships

The promotion of positive role models.

Showing an interest in all aspects of students' lives.

Being friendly and 'human'.

Knowing students as individuals.

Responsibility, self-reliance and respect

Developing autonomy and responsibility in students, e.g. for their work, behaviour, learning.

Providing opportunities for students to exercise autonomy and responsibility.

Being polite and respectful, expecting politeness and respect.

Providing opportunities for self-discipline.

The physical environment

Classroom layout and the use of floor/wall space/furniture, location of and access to resources, students' personal space and personal belongings.

A stimulating, clean and welcoming environment.

Classroom display.

Arrangements for moving round the classroom/teaching spaces, avoiding circulation bottlenecks.

Monitoring entrance/egress of students and monitoring students outside the classroom, e.g. in corridors and play spaces.

Involving students in keeping the physical environment attractive and free from graffiti, litter, etc.

Dealing with those who violate the physical environment.

Being clear on how students should move round the classroom and where they may/may not go.

With regard to (2) – how to be proactive and fair – the student teacher will need to consider:

Expectations and communication

Being overt, clear and precise over expectations.
Teaching appropriate and acceptable behaviour.
Communicating the criteria for acceptable behaviour.
Discouraging anti-social behaviour.
Defusing confrontations and challenging behaviour.
Having high but realistic expectations in a variety of fields and communicating them.
Avoiding the negative self-fulfilling prophecy.
Making criticism constructive.

Being proactive and taking preventative measures

Confrontation avoidance.
Anticipating problems and adjusting demands.
Stopping unacceptable behaviour before it escalates. Spotting incidents in the making.
De-escalating unacceptable and challenging behaviour.
Avoiding 'boxing students into a corner' where staff and students will lose face.
An avoidance of crisis-driven, responsive behaviour wherever possible.
Staying calm and 'taking the heat' out of situations.

Setting and communicating boundaries

Developing routines, e.g. for accessing and returning resources, giving in work, going to the toilet, moving round the classroom, starting sessions, entrance and egress, establishing attention.
Monitoring and intervening in unacceptable behaviour.
Maintaining eye contact.
Being clear and unambiguous, and checking that everyone understands expectations/task.
Avoiding 'bargaining', arguing with students and being pressurised by students.
Being overt on expectations and boundaries and reinforcing these frequently.

Consistency, fairness and whole-school practice

Adhering to the whole-school policy.

Ensuring consistent application of rules, rewards, sanctions, responding to specific presenting behaviours and students.

Being consistent with an individual student and fair in working with all students, i.e. being seen to be consistent.

Sharing individual experiences and supporting individuals.

Consistency of standards of, for example, school uniform, jewellery.

Being consistent in particular ways of working with named students.

Avoiding punishing whole groups if some individuals do not deserve it.

Ensuring appropriate differentiation of application with respect to different students and situations.

Ensuring fairness in administering incentives for good behaviour.

With regard to (3) – how to plan and implement the formal curriculum to support good discipline – the student teacher will need to consider:

Curriculum matters

Matching, differentiation, stimulation, motivation and sustaining interest.

Making demands realistic, meaningful and achievable.

Monitoring and assessing learning and providing feedback to students.

Marking work promptly.

Communicating the purposes of the lesson and the criteria for success/ achieving the purposes.

Provision of extension and reinforcement material.

Planning curricula and activities with discipline considerations in mind.

Examining timetabling to reduce discipline problems, unnecessary movement/disruption/'slack' time.

Avoiding 'slack' time (i.e. time where students can avoid being occupied) and increasing learning/teaching time.

Teaching and learning

Task orientation and a purposeful, brisk rate.

Using group work for social and emotional development.

Using group work to defuse the potential for attention-seeking behaviour to disrupt large numbers of students.

Finding out about and building on students' preferred learning styles.

Finding out and using teaching and learning styles that minimise bad behaviour and accentuate good behaviour.

Providing opportunities for student-centred and student-initiated/self-assessed learning.

Attention to specific classroom teaching skills: beginnings, transitions, conclusions, questioning/explaining/giving instructions/listening and responding/building on students' contributions/checking understanding and working/summarising; vigilance and communicating vigilance, use of voice – volume/speed/pitch/conviction, planning and preparation, timing, accessing and returning resources, being mobile.

Setting and implementing time-limits for work.

Providing variety in curriculum content and teaching styles as well as demand.

Balancing teaching and learning styles.

Preventing troublesome students from dominating the class.

Taking care with worksheets – avoiding 'teaching by proxy' – rather going for the human factor in teaching.

With regard to (4) – how and when to involve other parties – the student teacher will need to consider:

Home, school and community

Peer-group support/pressure.

Two-way communication with home and school.

Communicating not just the negative.

Where relevant, involving parents early in many aspects of education and behaviour, not just as a last resort.

Non-teaching staff

Keeping all adults involved in school informed of relevant policy matters and how they impact on practice and working with students.

Involving non-teaching staff in decision-making.

Providing support for non-teaching staff in their interactions with students.

Lunchtimes and breaks

Supervision by teaching and non-teaching staff.

Making lunchtimes and playtimes interesting and constructive, e.g. with equipment, appropriate supervision, activities.

Arrangements for supervision, behaviour and activities in wet playtimes/ lunchtimes.

Clarity on which students may/may not go into designated areas.

Supervision of students who have been kept in at breaktimes/lunchtimes.

Rules on kinds of activities permitted and forbidden (and reasons for these).

Rules and student involvement

Involving students in devising school and classroom rules.
Developing a limited number of agreed, explicit and memorable rules, e.g. on movement and speed, calling out, listening, going out of the classroom.
Reinforcing rules frequently.
Avoiding idle threats, carrying out threats if made.

With regard to (5) – making plans for management and discipline effective in practice – the student teacher will need to consider:

Rewards, sanctions and protocols

Purposes, scope and rationales of rules and their enforcement.
Appropriate rewards and punishments (to fit the behaviour and the student).
Extrinsic and intrinsic rewards – making rewards tangible and real.
Grading behaviour, rewards and sanctions to fit the incident, e.g. talking out of turn → hindering others → making unnecessary noise → work avoidance → unruly behaviour while waiting → rowdiness and verbal abuse → being cheeky → physical aggression, taking into account possible reasons for the behaviour.
Avoiding over-reacting.
Using a range of individual extrinsic rewards, e.g. individual and public praise, showing work to other students/adults, tokens, points, 'stickers' and badges, certificates, privileges.
Using a range of group/class extrinsic rewards, e.g. points, certificates, plaques, trophies.
Using a range of methods of discouraging unacceptable behaviour, e.g. questioning such behaviour, reprimands, loss of tokens, loss of rights and privileges, punishments, apologising, making amends, e.g. for damage and abusive behaviour, bringing in other staff (e.g. the headteacher), involving parents, temporary separation/isolation, detention, entry in discipline book, restraint, exclusion.
Rewarding/punishing the behaviour, not the student (and making this clear to the students).
Responding quickly.
Avoiding 'blanket' punishments which involve non-offenders.
Agreeing protocols for handling aggressive/weak/inadequate students and parents.
Recording incidents and events.
Arrangements for students who abscond.
Incentives for good behaviour.

Bullying

The school's position on bullying and dealing with it (in all its forms).

Protocols for dealing with incidents of bullying, bullies and victims at the time and follow-up times, recording and reporting incidents, event and follow-up action.

Involving parents openly and having a constructive plan to offer to all parties.

Keeping all involved parties informed.

Rewarding non-aggressive behaviour.

Contracts

Contracts to promote the positive and to negotiate with students.

Reporting on students on a frequent basis where appropriate.

Contracts for returning to the class after a period of exclusion.

Individual programmes of behaviour where appropriate.

The vast set of considerations set out above reflect the complexity of considerations in establishing and maintaining effective management and discipline. No aspect of school and classroom life is untouched by management and discipline matters. The major implication of this for the student teacher is that all his or her planning needs to be addressed with management and discipline in mind, i.e. how it will promote effective discipline and diminish discipline problems. In the following pages the several matters outlined above will be addressed in more detail.

It is useful up to a point to consider a teacher's management and control of his or her pupils in the classroom in terms of the key concepts of *power* and *authority*. Peters,[7] examining these concepts in the sphere of social control, stresses the importance of distinguishing between them. He says of *power* that it 'basically denotes ways in which an individual subjects others to his will by means of physical coercion (e.g. inflicting pain, restriction of movement), or by psychological coercion (e.g. withholding food, water, shelter, or access to means of attaining such necessities), or by the use of less dire forms of sanctions and rewards (e.g. by manipulating access to material resources and rewards, sexual satisfaction, etc.), or by personal influences such as hypnotism or sexual attraction'. On the other hand, *authority* 'involves the appeal to an impersonal normative order or value system which regulates behaviour basically because of acceptance of it on the part of those who comply. It operates because of understanding of and concern for what is intimated within a rule-governed form of life, which those in authority help to create and sustain. Authority, of course, may be and usually is supported by various forms of power.'

The classroom is a particular kind of social context and if the concepts are to be of value to us in our consideration of management and control in the classroom, they need to be interpreted in relation to this context. Take the teacher's power, for instance. Wadd[8] considers that this consists chiefly of four components: (1) charisma – the ability to attract and influence people with one's personality; (2) dominance – the ability to obtain control over a situation; (3) intellectual power – knowledge and mastery of one's subject(s); and (4) resources power – one's ability to organise all aspects of work in the classroom. He argues that the way in which these components function is an important determinant of the extent of the teacher's effectiveness. And further, the influence of each may vary with the particular teaching situation. Thus, resources power may contribute more significantly to the personal power of a teacher practising open education in an open-plan school, whereas a teacher working in a difficult urban school may have to rely on dominance, implying a certain amount of physical or psychological coercion.

The teacher's authority[9] in the classroom will derive not only from his or her traditional role as a teacher, but also from the system of rules operating in the school as a whole and the classroom in particular. We shall shortly consider the importance of establishing a minimum list of rules (or at least revising existing ones) in order to define the classroom situation to the student teacher's advantage and to indicate what is and what is not permitted. The value of arriving at such a list by discussion and consensus lies in the fact that it thus contributes to the 'impersonal normative order' to which both teacher and pupil can refer (or be referred). To enforce this order, however, it must be backed by rewards for those who conform and punishments for those who deviate.

Your control of student behaviour will therefore be through a subtle blending of personal power emanating from your personality and skills, and authority deriving from your status as teacher and from the established system of rules operating in the school and classroom. In the pages that follow, we outline a range of procedures that will assist you in implementing these two crucial concepts in the context of the classroom. We begin by taking a brief look at some of the contrasting views on how the task of classroom management should be approached.

SCHOOLS OF THOUGHT ON CLASSROOM MANAGEMENT

Even the most casual study of teachers in classrooms would lead one to infer that between them they hold a range of viewpoints on the central issue of classroom management. Wragg[10] has identified a number of commonly held views in this respect. In describing them, he warns the reader that the list is not exhaustive and that teachers should not necessarily be assigned to one category exclusively: they may change their view (and behaviour) according to the occasion. Briefly, they are as follows:

1 Authoritarian

According to this view, teachers are held to be in charge: it is their responsibility to establish and maintain order in the school. They make the decisions and give the orders within a well-defined and fairly rigid system of roles. The justification for a teacher assuming this stance resides in his or her greater knowledge and experience. Opponents of this view argue that it can become repressive and that it is not appropriate to an age in which students need to learn independence if society is to become really democratic.

2 Permissive

Usually contrasted with the preceding view, the permissive school emphasises individual freedom and choice. Traditional constraints on behaviour are thus kept to a minimum. The aim is to develop pupil autonomy so that pupils can make their own decisions and be responsible for their own behaviour. The critics of permissiveness contend that it all too often degenerates into a kind of *laissez-faire* situation having little or no real educational significance for those participating.

3 Behaviour modification

This school holds to the view of behaviourist psychology, which stresses the role of rewards and punishments in the control of behaviour. Thus the teacher's job is to encourage desirable behaviour and stamp out undesirable behaviour by administering or withholding suitable reinforcements. It is objected to on the grounds that the treatment is mechanistic and that this implies that the people so treated are regarded as machines and not humans.

4 Interpersonal relationships

The aim of this school of thought is to produce good, positive relationships between the teacher and students and among the students themselves. Emphasis on negotiation and suggestion will result in a healthy classroom climate in which learning will occur automatically. If the trick works, then problems of management will not arise. Critics of this view, however, contend that good personal relationships become an end in themselves and that the real purpose of the classroom enterprise, namely the acquisition of knowledge and skills, takes second place.

5 Scientific

According to this view (which, incidentally, is one held by the present authors – though not exclusively), teaching is an activity which can be studied and analysed. The view can be described as being scientific in the sense of being an objective and systematic analysis and later synthesis of the more important components of teaching and learning. It is also scientific in the sense that it draws on the findings of empirical studies as a means of establishing a body of theory on which practice can be based. Four examples are given here that draw on empirical evidence.[11] Using data from school inspections, the Scottish Council for Research in Education suggested that good lesson organisation and discipline could be developed in a variety of ways, listed in Box 66. This is paralleled by the English Department of Education, which

Box 66

Promoting good discipline in school

(a) Classwork marked regularly and thoroughly.
(b) Materials and equipment readily available.
(c) Teachers anticipate difficulties and react positively to them.
(d) Teachers are seen to be 'fair' by pupils.
(e) Teachers show an interest in their children and work.
(f) Teachers arrive at class punctually.
(g) Pupils come into class in an orderly fashion.
(h) The objectives of the lesson are clear and stated in the early part.
(i) Lessons get off to an interesting and brisk start.
(j) Teachers speak clearly and are audible at all times.
(k) The language is simple, clear and unambiguous.
(l) Brief, snappy questions are used to check children's comprehension.
(m) Teachers avoid slowing down the pace of the lesson.
(n) A constant overview of the class is kept.
(o) Teachers are aware of what individuals are doing.
(p) Interventions are prompt when passions rise.

Source Scottish Council for Research in Education[12]

gives a shorter list of recommendations for good behaviour, set out in Box 67. The many areas of overlap between the two studies ought to inspire student teachers with a degree of confidence in the suggestions provided.

A third example can be given of empirical research containing an important message for discipline. Galton *et al.*[13] showed that the impact of a student who was labelled (perhaps euphemistically!) an 'attention seeker' was greater if a whole-class teaching style were adopted in a lesson (where the attention seeker had a larger theatre) than in a situation where group work was being adopted (where the attention seeker was reduced to gaining the attention of only a group, thereby diluting her or his impact).

Our own experience of supervising students on teaching practice has

Box 67

Factors promoting good discipline

Nurturing of genuine involvement based on understanding of the concepts which underlie those tasks and examples particular to a given lesson.

Materials and preparation to ensure differentiation within tasks for pupils of different abilities.

Sustained hard work on the part of the pupils as well as the teacher.

Specific help for individual pupils without losing sight of the reactions of the whole group.

The encouragement of pupils to contribute ideas.

Careful attention to their contributions, with encouragement to refine their ideas in discussion.

Flexibility in adapting a lesson plan to take account of pupils' contributions and of the mood of the group.

Variation of the pace of a lesson to keep interest and momentum.

Wit and humour, which help pupils to enjoy a lesson and can defuse potential problems, without recourse to sarcasm.

Infectious enthusiasm for the subject, and for pupils and their response to it.

Source Department of Education and Science[14]

enabled us to set out a series of 'tips' under four main headings: talk, classroom management, timing and organisation.

Talk

Vary the voice – its pitch, tone, volume, speed.

Avoid rhetorical questions, e.g. 'Do you know what sitting down means?' – rather give a direct order.

Avoid general exhortations, e.g. 'Come on now' – be specific and concrete.

Do not bargain with students, e.g. 'If you're good we will watch this programme.'

Do not rely on students' good behaviour, e.g. 'You will be good won't you?'

Do not allow students to argue with you.

Do not accept anything that students say if it is ridiculous.

Avoid only speaking with volunteers.

If students were supposed to have listened to an instruction and then ask what to do, tell them off for not listening.

Do not speak too quickly for long, it whips up an excited atmosphere in the classroom.

Do not bombard students with instructions, stage them through the lesson.

Do not talk over students if you are insisting on silence – it gives a mixed message that, in fact, you will tolerate noise whilst asking for silence.

Comment on what students have done and how well they have done it.

Speak firmly and with conviction.

Give explicit instructions that students will understand.

Explain how to commence work.

Be firm without shouting or being unfriendly, maybe use humour to defuse situations.

Do not accept students' shouting out – deal with it.

Convey a realistic sense of urgency in your voice, mean what you say.

Avoid asking a student to tell you what they were supposed to do – it is a rhetorical question.

Avoid going to extremes too rapidly, or from extreme to extreme, e.g. flattery to crossness.

Classroom management

Make very explicit and communicate exactly what the 'ground rules' are – what is acceptable and unacceptable.

Monitor the whole class, even when they are working in groups, stopping regularly if necessary.

Do not become absorbed with individuals or groups at organisationally critical times, e.g. transitions, ending a lesson.

Be in the classroom before the students, organise their entrance and egress.

Avoid being pinned to your desk or being the 'pied piper' with a queue of students behind you – restrict numbers moving round the classroom and in a queue at any one time. Move to the students rather than the students moving to you.

Stop an activity if necessary, sacrificing content to control rather than vice versa.

Insist on acceptable standards of presentation, concentration, behaviour.

Use written work to quieten students if necessary.

When you stop the whole class insist on complete attention.

Anticipate trouble and 'nip it in the bud'.

Avoid being too friendly with the class and then suddenly fierce or vice versa – be consistent.

Be prepared to 'police' a situation at times (even if it is out of your character).

Insist on total concentration at times, even silent working.

Avoid saying something and then not following it through.

Reduce students' fidgeting if they are listening.

Veiled – unspecified – threats, e.g. 'There will be trouble if I have to come over to you again,' may be more useful than specific threats; if a specific threat is given it must be carried out if the infraction continues.

Avoid students pressuring you into repeating something that they should have listened to earlier, it is 'their fault'.

Repeatedly calling out students' names makes a diminishing impact.

Avoid joking in a serious activity.

If a student repeatedly misbehaves avoid treating each incident in isolation, deal with the cumulative effect.

Do not accept everything that the student cares to do.

Be vigilant, developing 'the all-seeing eye'.

Be dynamic.

Allow thinking time in questions, do not always provide answers to students – you may be too helpful for their own good (see earlier: *questioning* and *responding*).

Move round the class.

Initiate good behaviour.

Avoid letting a worksheet replace all of your teaching.

Do not be flustered by several students suddenly requiring help.

Shortly after students have been set to work check that they are, in fact, working.

Do not be fooled by a quiet student or class – it may be a screen for daydreaming.

Make optimum seating arrangements.

Avoid confrontations wherever possible – though some students will not allow you to do this.

Timing

Allow sufficient time to commence and round off sessions.

Set finite time-limits, e.g. 'You have ten minutes to do such-and-such.' Communicate these limits to the students.

Do not spend too long on easy or trivial points, keep a brisk pace.

Try to ensure that work is completed by the dinner break/end of the afternoon (for primary school student teachers).

Allow reasonable time for students to work – set realistic expectations.

Organisation

Be thoroughly prepared.

Be very vigilant at transition points – come out of 'teacher-as-instructor' mode and into 'teacher-as classroom manager' mode.

Anticipate problems and plan how they will be addressed.

Use a visual focus to support an aural focus (e.g. using 'jotters', the chalkboard, flip chart, etc.).

This list of tips may appear unduly antagonistic in tone at first sight. This is not intended; rather the intention here is to signal that the student teacher needs to be proactive, clear and communicative in his or her work and relations with his or her class(es).

What we are arguing is that regarding teaching as a *science* enables us to identify particular teaching skills for effective management that can be developed, for example: beginnings, questioning, explaining, handling transitions, concluding, responding, being vigilant, being prepared, timing and pacing lessons, using eye contact, anticipating what might happen and how difficult situations should and should not be handled. Opponents of this perspective of teaching as a scientific activity argue that teaching is an art and cannot therefore be subjected to such an analysis. For them, teaching – and this includes class management – is intuitive and can depend upon personality.

6 Social systems

The 'social systems' view contends that the school and its inmates constitute a sub-system of the wider social system, influences from which affect the group's behaviour. These include political, social, financial and emotional emanations. The teacher thus needs to understand and be aware of these wider contextual factors in order to work effectively in school, although learning is in essence an individual process. Critics of this view respond by arguing that teachers have little or no control over external factors and must, therefore, function within the framework of the school.

7 Folklore

If the new teacher can assimilate the received wisdom of the profession, the 'tips for teachers' and 'tricks of the trade', then he or she will be suitably equipped to deal with most contingencies. As Wragg[15] explains, critics consider that tips are lacking in any theoretical basis, are random and unrelated to each other, and may suit the person who proffers them but not the recipient. Box 68 contains a number of common tips identified by Wragg in his project. In the same project Wragg outlines several differences between experienced and student teachers. These are shown in Box 69.

We shift our perspective now as we consider the kinds of things students expect of their teachers in the matter of management and control.

STUDENTS' EXPECTATIONS OF TEACHERS

Wragg notes that students are only rarely brought into the act of thinking about classroom processes. (For example, most rules are decided by adults, the content of lessons is frequently chosen by the teacher, and it is assumed

Box 68

Folklore in the classroom

As part of the Teacher Education Project, Wragg collected from student teachers tips or 'tricks of the trade' that they had found most useful. The twenty-five most common are given below in descending order of frequency. Go through the list and consider their value.

1   Start by being firm with pupils: you can relax later.
2   Get silence before you start speaking to the class.
3   Control the pupils' entry to the classroom.
4   Know and use the pupils' names.
5   Prepare lessons thoroughly and structure them firmly.
6   Arrive at the classroom before the pupils.
7   Prepare furniture and apparatus before the pupils arrive.
8   Know how to use apparatus, and be familiar with experiments before you use them in class.
9   Be mobile: walk around the class.
10 Start the lesson with a 'bang' and sustain interest and curiosity.
11 Give clear instructions.
12 Learn voice control.
13 Have additional material prepared to cope with e.g. bright and slow pupils' needs.
14 Look at the class when speaking, and learn how to scan.
15 Make written work appropriate (e.g. to the age, ability, cultural background of pupils).
16 Develop an effective question technique.
17 Develop the art of timing your lessons to fit the available period.
18 Vary your teaching techniques.
19 Anticipate discipline problems and act quickly.
20 Be firm and consistent in giving punishments.
21 Avoid confrontation.
22 Clarify and insist on *your* standards.
23 Show yourself as a helper or facilitator to the pupils.
24 Do not patronise pupils, treat them as responsible beings.
25 Use humour constructively.

Source Wragg

that students must know how to learn on their own or in groups.) Wragg then refers to examples of proposals that have been put forward for involving students more in this matter of classroom processes. Glasser,[16] for instance, has suggested that students should be involved in discussion about rules and procedures during lessons. He suggests that class time should be used for the teacher to explain about classroom rules and that discussion should take place about these during which they could be adjusted, new rules could be

Box 69 Differences between experienced and student teachers

Experienced teachers

were usually very clear about their classroom rules;
did not hesitate to describe what they thought was 'right' and 'proper';
were conscious of the massive effort needed to establish relationships
with a new class;
used their eyes a great deal to scan the class or look at individuals;
were quick to deal publicly with infraction of their rules;
were more 'formal' than usual;
were especially brisk and businesslike;
established their presence in the corridor before the class even entered
the room;
introduced themselves formally.

Student teachers

were not so clear about classroom rules, either their own or those of other
teachers in the school;
did not use terms such as 'right' and 'proper' when talking about rules;
were unaware of the massive collective effort the school and individual
teachers had put into starting off the school year;
made less use of eye contact and were very conscious of themselves
being looked at;
often neglected early infringements of classroom rules which then
escalated into larger problems;
concentrated in their preparation on lesson *content* rather than rules and
relationships.

Source Wragg

negotiated and problems discussed. Gordon, meanwhile, contends that to
solve a problem one must decide who 'owns it'. Is it the teacher, the students
or is it shared? He recommends a six-step approach: (1) define the problem;
(2) generate possible solutions; (3) evaluate these solutions; (4) decide which
solutions seem best; (5) decide how to implement the chosen solutions; and
(6) assess the effectiveness of the solutions chosen. Both Glasser's and
Gordon's approaches demand greater responsibility on the part of the pupils
than is normally the case.

Another approach to involving students is to find out from them what they
consider are the characteristics of good teachers, for it is generally known that
good teachers are capable of maintaining good discipline. Nash,[17] for
example, found that 12-year-old pupils in a Scottish secondary school
regarded favourably teachers who kept order, were strict and punished
students; who actually taught them and kept them busy with work; who gave
explanations, were helpful and could be understood; who were interesting,

unusual and different; who were fair, consistent and had no favourites; and who were friendly, kind, talked gently and joked. A composite picture of the effective teacher is to be found in Box 70.

Box 70 Characteristics of good teachers

The good teacher

Since as early as the 1960s researchers have endeavoured to ascertain students' definitions of the 'good' teacher. After studying the findings of the more important studies in this connection, Saunders constructed a composite picture which suggests that the good teacher:

is purposeful and in control of herself/himself;
knows what s/he wants to teach and checks that the students are learning;
takes positive action when s/he discovers they are not making adequate progress;
is sensitive to the reactions of the students and responds by changing role smoothly and appropriately;
tries to understand the point of view of the learner;
shows respect for others;
is concerned for all the students.

Source Saunders[18]

A more dynamic view of how students see effective teachers is to be found in Gannaway's study.[19] On the basis of interviews and observation, he constructed a dynamic model by proposing that teachers are progressively typified by pupils in a given sequence. The teachers are, in effect, subjected to a systematic series of tests by students, the first of which is *Can the teacher keep order?* The next test is *Can he have a laugh?* And the final test to which the teacher is subjected is *Does he understand pupils?* Gannaway suggests that provided the answer to each of these is *yes*, and provided the teacher can put over something of interest in the lesson, then he or she 'has it made'. The implications of these questions are of particular interest. The first test, for instance, *Can the teacher keep order?*, implies that the students expect him to do just that, to keep order. Of equal importance is the second challenge, *Can he have a laugh?* What is implied here is that in expecting the teacher to keep order, students do not expect him or her to be *too* strict, to impose a regime so harsh that the pupils will eventually rebel (we touch on this as a possible cause of misbehaviour in the next section). What is called for is a 'nice strictness' in preference to a 'nasty strictness'.[20]

The final test, *Does he understand students?*, is in some ways the most interesting of the three for it implies an understanding of the class, *as a class*, *as a group*, in contrast to understanding *individual* students, or a group of students on an individual basis. The difference is significant, for it means that understanding a group is of a different order to understanding the individual: a different standpoint is required and different knowledge and skills. Before we identify some of the causes of misbehaviour in the classroom, we look at a psychologist's account of some of the factors affecting classroom behaviour.

SOME FACTORS AFFECTING BEHAVIOUR IN CLASSROOMS

As part of his concern to understand the reasons behind students' behaviour, Fontana[21] has identified some of the differences among students which influence how they behave. Briefly, these include the following.

1 Age-related differences in behaviour

The effective teacher is aware of the need to adjust the way that motives are imputed to students' behaviour as they grow older. There are also other reasons why age should be regarded as an important factor in dealing with problems of class control. Briefly listing these, they are: the nature of students' demands and expectations of the teacher change as they grow older; the nature of students' relationships with each other changes as they grow older; students grow bigger and stronger as they get older; generally students are more critical of adult behaviour the older they become; older students are often readier to blame adults for their own failures and shortcomings; and students' concentration span and their ability to do theoretical work increases as they develop intellectually.

2 Ability-related differences in behaviour

Differences in behaviour stemming from variations in ability which Fontana considers important may be briefly stated as follows: motivation for schoolwork will differ markedly from high ability to low ability; different ability levels in students make different demands upon the teacher in terms of personal qualities such as patience and sympathy; the criteria for success and failure differ from one ability level to the next; and the facilities and equipment available for students at different ability levels may differ markedly.

3 Sex-related differences in behaviour

Fontana considers that the abilities and potential that boys and girls have in common are more important from an educational point of view than any differences. Those differences that do exist are often the result of expectations. Boys are expected to be rowdy and girls more emotional. And in practice each group tends to meet such expectations.

In the primary classroom there may be clear social and academic differences. Girls are more helpful and co-operative, whereas boys show greater interest in sports and practical activities. Boys are more drawn to mathematics, while girls are attracted to reading and writing. Ideally, however, the good teacher will endeavour to minimise differences and provide the sort of learning environment that offers both boys and girls the same kind of opportunities.

The same impartiality should be evident in matters of class control. The good teacher, for example, will give praise to categories of behaviour that are the same for both boys and girls and will thus avoid the kind of situation where boys are praised for good classwork and girls for good social behaviour.

4 Socio-economic related differences in behaviour

Fontana argues that with the spread of comprehensive schools differences in the socio-economic character of schools are not as great as they used to be, though they still exist. He identifies the following differences between upper-socio-economic-status (SES) pupils and lower-SES pupils. In terms of their relevance to class control, they are: students from lower-SES backgrounds tend to be lower in self-esteem, perhaps because of their underprivileged environment, than those from upper-SES backgrounds; the values and standards taught in schools tend to accord more with those taught in upper-SES homes than with those taught in lower-SES homes; students from lower-SES homes are more likely to find themselves in low-ability groups than students from upper-SES homes; and upper-SES students are more likely than lower-SES students to practise and understand the importance of deferral of satisfaction.

5 Culturally related differences in behaviour

By culture, Fontana refers not only to sub-cultural variations arising from socio-economic factors, but to variables associated with a child's ethnic group. As he explains, cultural variables may overlap with socio-economic ones, but at the same time they introduce a number of factors potentially important with regard to class control. The more important of these can be summarised thus: religious and moral codes of behaviour may be more strict in certain cultural groups; religious observances and rituals may influence the school behaviours of some students; rivalry and hostility may develop between different cultural groups; students from non-white ethnic groups may experience language problems in the classroom; and the degree to which students from different cultural groups are taught emotional and social restraint may vary.

We shall have more to say about behavioural problems with some ethnic-minority students at the end of this section.

WHAT MAKES PUPILS MISBEHAVE?

To answer this question comprehensively would require the wisdom of Solomon and more. Fortunately, our intentions in posing it are more modest. Briefly, they are to identify broad types of disruptive behaviour so that the beginning teacher can know what to look for, have some idea of the cause(s), and decide what action (which may sometimes mean inaction) is called for on his or her part.

Saunders[22] has identified four main patterns of disruptive behaviour arising from social causes. These are:

1 Antipathy to school

For some students, school is seen as having no place or purpose in their lives. It is an irrelevance for them and consequently they dismiss both school and teachers. This is by no means an uncommon cause of difficulties in the contemporary classroom. Indeed, as unemployment queues lengthen and jobs become more elusive, one could expect such antipathy to spread. The teacher's task in such circumstances is to know how to make schoolwork more relevant and meaningful. Related to this factor of antipathy is what has been termed *conflicts of interest*. This embraces differences in needs, values and goals between the student and the system as embodied in the teacher, and usually results in a show of nonconformity by the students in question.[23] Resolving conflicts of this kind involves *negotiation*: the pupil and teacher working out a mutually acceptable settlement. A model for negotiation is set out in Box 71.

2 Social dominance

Saunders regards this as an extension of the antipathetic syndrome. He writes:

> Some physically and socially mature pupils seem to have a need for frequent reinforcement in the form of attention from their peers. This is often achieved at school by challenging the authority of the teacher. If the challenge is not met it can be taken up by other pupils and the lesson ruined, and as a result the assertion of the teacher's authority becomes more difficult in future lessons.

Box 71

Negotiating a settlement of a conflict of interest

Step 1: confronting the opposition
A direct expression of one's viewpoint and one's feelings is vital from the outset. Equally important is an invitation to the opposition to be as forthright themselves. Expressing feelings is often difficult but it must be undertaken and should be directed at the issues involved, *not* at the persons who are in conflict.

Step 2: jointly defining the conflict
Resolving a conflict necessitates defining it in a way that is acceptable to both sides. Therefore, focus on behaviour, not on individual characteristics; centre discussion on issues, not on personalities. Try to define the conflict as a problem to be solved, not as a battle to be won at all costs. Coercing students into doing what the teacher requires is a short-term strategy with poor long-term pay-offs. The smaller and more precise the conflict, the easier it will be to resolve.

Step 3: communicating co-operative intentions
A candid expression of one's intention to co-operate results in: (a) agreements being reached more quickly; (b) a reduction in an opponent's suspicion and defensiveness; (e) a greater comprehension by each protagonist of the other's point of view; and (d) more positive perceptions by both parties to the dispute of each other as understanding and accepting persons.

Step 4: negotiating and perspective-taking
Successful negotiation requires sufficient detachment from one's original position to be capable of looking at an issue from alternative perspectives. Perspective-taking involves demonstrating to an opponent that one is capable of accurately perceiving his position and his feelings. This can be achieved by temporarily arguing an opponent's position.

A central aspect of successful negotiations, therefore, is taking the perspective of one's opponents and influencing them to do the same.

Source Johnson[24]

How one counters this sort of machismo posturing is a perennial problem for teachers in present-day classrooms.

3 Social isolation

Some students have strong acceptance needs and a strong yearning to be wanted by their peers. However, they tend to be on the periphery of the group instead of being fully integrated into it. To achieve a sort of affiliation, therefore, they adopt the group's behaviour, often in extreme form.

4 Inconsequential behaviour

Saunders here refers to those students who seem unable or unwilling to anticipate the consequences of their actions. Such a student, Saunders examples, 'behaves impulsively instead of reflecting on the courses of action which are open to him and of the possible consequences of each; or he may be unable to inhibit the urge to meet a challenge'. Anticipating an action requires a degree of reflection that, judging from the frequency of this kind of problem in the classroom, many students are incapable of achieving.

To these patterns of disruptive behaviour we can add the following causes of misbehaviour set out by Gnagey.[25] One or other of them will have been experienced already by the student teacher. Thus:

5 Ignorance of the rules

Ignorance of the rules of classroom behaviour is a common cause of misbehaviour. This is particularly the case during a teacher's early contacts with a class. As we shall see in the next section, it takes a while to implement a rule, for it has to be learned over a period of time by interpreting it in relation to specific concrete situations. In this respect, Gnagey distinguishes between *verbal* and *actual* rules, that is, rules that are acted upon and those that are not. As he says, 'Even if a pupil is presented with a neatly organized set of by-laws, he never really knows which statutes are operational and which are just on paper. As every seasoned teacher knows, classes have a very practical way of solving this problem. They simply proceed to try the teacher out, to see what they can get away with.'

6 Conflicting rules

Difficulties can sometimes arise for the teacher when a student is presented with two sets of conflicting rules – those of the classroom and those of his home. What is permissible in one situation is frowned upon in the other. Invariably it is the home that is the more permissive environment. Alternatively, the clash may occur between classroom norms and those of the peer-group culture outside school. Where the clash is a marked one, the teacher would be best advised to seek a negotiated settlement with the student in question if lasting peace is to be achieved.

7 Displacement

As we have just seen, inappropriate behaviour may occur in the classroom because it is perfectly acceptable in another context, like the home or neighbourhood. A similar situation may occur with respect to *feelings*; inappropriate feelings are often displaced onto people and objects in the school. Thus, a student's hatred for his father may be transferred to his male form teacher. In an age where there is increased social dislocation through divorce, separation and one-parent families, displacement as a cause of disruptive behaviour may be more widespread than ever before. In a study by Thurston, Feldhusen and Benning, quoted in Gnagey, several factors appeared again and again in the home situations of students who regularly misbehaved at school. These we have listed in Box 72.

Box 72

Home situations of badly behaved children

In a study conducted in the United States, the following factors appear regularly in the home situations of children who constantly behaved badly in the classroom:

1 Discipline by the father is either lax, overtly strict or erratic.
2 Supervision by the mother is at best only fair, or it is downright inadequate.
3 Parents are either indifferent or even hostile toward the child.
4 Family members are scattered in diverse activities and operate only somewhat as a unit or perhaps not at all.
5 Parents find it difficult to talk things over regarding the child.
6 The husband–wife relationship lacks closeness and equality or partnership.
7 The parents find many things to disapprove of in their child.
8 The mothers are not happy with the communities in which they live.
9 The parents resort to angry physical punishments when the child does wrong. Temper control is a difficult problem for them at this time.
10 The parents believe they have little influence on the development of their child.
11 The parents believe that other children exert bad influences on their child.
12 The parents' leisure-time activities lack much of a constructive element.
13 The parents, particularly the father, report no church membership. Even if they are members, their attendance tends to be sporadic.

Source Thurston, Feldhusen and Benning[26]

8 Anxiety

A great deal of misbehaviour in the classroom is caused by anxious reactions to features in the educational environment – examinations, having to speak in class, being judged publicly, etc. Earlier research by Gnagey[27] disclosed that disruptive students tended to be more afraid than their well-behaved classmates.

9 Leadership styles as causes of misbehaviour

Finally, Gnagey identifies a number of leadership styles on the part of teachers that can incite disciplinary problems rather than solve them. These include the *despot* and the *nonentity*. The despot, as he explains, embraces a *custodial* view of student control and his or her main concern is with keeping order. He or she tends to view students in negative and stereotypical terms. Student response to a lasting tyrannical style of this kind is invariably anger, which can manifest itself in a variety of ways, often indirectly as with vandalism or bullying or, in more extreme cases, arson. In a word, *displacement* is operating.

The nonentity, as the name suggests, is totally ineffectual. His or her generally over-permissive, non-interventionist approach, combined with an unwillingness to utilise such fundamental psychological principles as motivation and rewards, is likely to generate feelings of restlessness on the part of pupils and a tendency to be easily distracted.

It may be of some interest to student teachers at this point to know what British teachers think about causes of misbehaviour. In a study by Dierenfield[28] (quoted in Watkins and Wagner[29]) teachers in a sample of English comprehensive schools were asked to rate ten provided causes of disruptive behaviour. The proportion who rated each item as 'an important cause' was as follows:

Unsettled home environment	49.6%
Peer pressure	35.6%
Lack of interest in subject	30.7%
General disinterest in school	30.5%
Pupil psychological or emotional instability	29.4%
Inability to do classwork	21.9%
Revolt against adult authority	20.8%
Lack of self-esteem	13.7%
Dislike of teacher	12.7%
Use of drugs	4.9%

School processes can clearly be seen as a source of problems resulting in disruptive behaviour. The questionnaire also revealed that heads and deputy heads endorsed extra-school factors, i.e. home, peers and instability, as significant causes more than teachers.

When it came to the kinds of response teachers should make to such causes, the ten most frequently rated were:

Positive teacher personality	89.7%
Effective teaching methods	87.6%
Establishing and maintaining behaviour standards early on	86.3%
Firm support of teacher discipline measures by head	70.8%
Consistent application of behaviour standards to all pupils	69.3%
Support of school by parents	68.7%
Treating causes of behaviour problems	66.6%
Influence of head	56.0%
Pastoral-care programme	40.3%
Strict disciplinary measures by teacher	39.9%

The teacher and school aspects feature strongly here. Measures such as exclusion, special classes, streaming and the school social worker received less support, though they were still seen as useful possibilities. Head teachers and their deputies gave above-average support to those factors involving parents and the pastoral-care programme.

One way of preventing behaviour problems arising in the first place is to have adequate rules as means of controlling student behaviour. It is to a consideration of this topic that we now address ourselves.

RULES AND ROUTINES IN THE CLASSROOM

Hargreaves[30] reminds us that rules specify acceptable forms of classroom conduct and that they are either laid down by the teacher or arrived at by agreement between him or her and the students. Rules play an important part in helping to define the classroom situation in terms of the teacher's dominance; and if this is not established early on, then the students will define the situation to their advantage and very much to the teacher's discomfort.

Gnagey[31] likewise notes that the teacher defines the behaviour and misbehaviour by the number and kinds of rules he makes and enforces in his room. Indeed, reminders of 'expected' behaviour as defined by rules of this kind make up one of the most frequently used techniques for controlling individuals and groups.[32] Although each teacher makes a somewhat different list, most rules are based *on moral, personal, legal, safety* and *educational* considerations.

Educational settings have traditionally featured too many rules, especially punitive ones,[33] and it is important that such a list be kept to a minimum for at least three reasons: (1) the number of disciplinary actions a teacher takes is kept to a minimum also; (2) rules contribute to stultifying the atmosphere of school and classroom; and (3) there is some evidence from research[34] that rules by themselves exert little influence on classroom behaviour; in other words, they need to be seen in relation to other factors in the classroom situation. The criteria for helping to achieve such a minimum list are *relevance*, *meaningfulness* and *positiveness*. Thus:

Relevance

Making one's list relevant requires that a teacher has a clear idea of the objectives of a particular lesson or course of lessons. It follows that the list may be flexible and may vary from lesson to lesson, though not to an extent that would confuse students or give them an opportunity to justify misbehaviour.

Meaningfulness

Rules that are seen to derive logically from the nature of the task are more acceptable to students than ones that are imposed arbitrarily by the teacher and are not easily seen to relate to the task or context. What seems to be required here is a degree of negotiation between the teacher and his pupils. Wragg[35] found a striking difference between experienced teachers and student teachers in this matter of 'meaningful' rules. Whereas the experienced teachers stressed the moral rules about 'right', 'proper' and 'sensible' behaviour, the student teachers never mentioned such rules (see Box 73).

Positiveness

Where possible, rules should be expressed positively, since a positive statement offers a goal to work towards rather than something to avoid. Thus, 'work quietly' is preferable to 'do not talk'. A list of *don'ts* can have an inhibiting effect on classroom behaviour.

Hargreaves[36] suggests that the teacher should attempt to lay down his or her minimum list during the very first encounter with a class. Rules may cover such areas as entering the room, movement about the room, modes of address, when to talk and when not to talk, work and homework attitudes, and the distribution and use of materials and equipment. He also recommends that these rules should be fairly comprehensive, though not so general as to offer little guidance in specific situations; and that during subsequent meetings with the class the teacher should ensure that the rules are understood, learned and conformed to.

Defining the situation in terms acceptable to the teacher will take some weeks because, as Hargreaves explains:

Box 73

Rules in school

When, as part of the Teacher Education Project, *experienced* teachers were interviewed about their classroom rules, most were clear about them and were quick to enforce them. *Student* teachers, on the other hand, were much more vague and spoke of rules being established 'as the need arose'. Experienced teachers worked very hard in their first few lessons to put over their rules, student teachers often found students having to 'test the limits' to see what the rules were. Rules in school come from several sources. In addition to society's laws and conventions which apply during school hours, there are three further sources:

1   *Local authority*: such as county-wide rules about behaviour in the laboratory or gymnasium which may be written in official circulars.
2   *School*: for example, over uniform or running in the corridor, which may be contained in printed school rules or announced at assembly, having been agreed among the staff or decreed by the senior people in the school.
3   *Teacher*: such as 'no eating in class', 'must raise hand when answering', which will vary from teacher to teacher, as may the interpretation and enforcement of school and local authority rules. In the Teacher Education Project studies it was found that most rules were made by the teacher rather than discussed with pupils. Experienced teachers stressed the moral rules about 'right', 'proper' and 'sensible' behaviour, student teachers never mentioned such rules.

Rules are established in different ways. Some are announced amid considerable ceremony at an assembly or in a first lesson, often given out in printed form to emphasise their 'official' standing. Other rules or norms, especially at classroom level, are established by case law; for example, when someone calls out and the teacher asks him to raise his hand in future.

Source Wragg

The rules must be often created and always clarified in relation to concrete incidents where the rules are applicable; because the pupils need time to learn the rules and how they apply in given situations; and because the teacher must be able to demonstrate his power to enforce the rules and gain conformity to them. The definition of the situation is, in short, a progressive and cumulative process. It is built up day by day, incident by incident, into a consistent whole.

As well as establishing rules, the student teacher should make explicit to the students during his or her early contact with them just what they can take for granted, e.g. can they use the pencil sharpener without asking permission? Clarification of this kind serves a dual purpose – it keeps formal rules to a minimum and cuts out undue fussiness.

Other procedures (if not already established), though not strictly codifiable as rules, should likewise be made explicit early on, certainly during the first few contacts, e.g. do you require all the students' written work to be headed with the date? If so, make it clear to them when the first occasion for written work occurs and specify how you want it presented. A new line? On the left-hand side? Underlined? No abbreviations . . . or whatever.

In addition to rules formally laid down by the teacher or school, there are often supplementary rules of a more informal nature. Writing of such, Denscombe[37] says

> In one sense these informal rules are much more localised than general school rules. They operate in particular classrooms, at particular times and with particular people: they are 'context specific'. So, for example, rules about the amount of noise which is permissible will depend on the kind of lesson being taught, on the teacher in charge, on the kinds of pupils, on the phase of the lesson, and on the day/week/term. Even then, these rules can be altered, suspended or renegotiated depending on the circumstances.

Indeed, as the author later points out, rules are not always imposed on students but are often the result of negotiation and re-negotiation – 'the end product of a subtle bargaining procedure between teacher and students in which disagreement and resistance need to be overcome'.

In summary, good classroom management involves establishing clear rules where rules are needed, avoiding unnecessary ones, eliminating punitive ones, reviewing them periodically, and changing or dropping them when appropriate. Additionally, greater flexibility may be introduced by having recourse to more informal arrangements, frequently arrived at by negotiations and bargaining.

The partner to rules is routines (discussed in Part II). There is a certain security in routines which can promote good behaviour. So, for example, the student teacher would be well advised to assimilate the existing routines of the class(es) and, if there are none, generate some of his or her own and communicate these to the students, covering, for example:

- entering and leaving the classroom
- accessing, giving out, sharing and putting away materials
- having work marked
- leaving seats and moving around the classroom
- attracting and maintaining the attention of the class
- changing activities
- catching up on incomplete work
- occupying students who complete work quickly

- going to the toilet
- using resources from other rooms
- preparing for registration/assemblies/dismissal

We continue by identifying some of the well-tried techniques used by experienced teachers for dealing with unacceptable behaviour in the class-room.

SUGGESTIONS FOR HANDLING MINOR MISBEHAVIOUR PROBLEMS

The techniques reviewed below may be of some assistance to student teachers when dealing with minor misbehaviour problems of a passing kind such as inattention, distraction or mischievousness. When faced with infringements of this nature, the aim of the teacher should be to cut short the incipient misbehaviour before it develops and spreads, without interrupting the flow of the lesson or distracting other students unnecessarily.

Constant monitoring of the class

Good and Brophy[38] have emphasised the need for monitoring or scanning as an important factor in successful classroom management. By this they mean keeping the class and its individual members constantly under observation. Kounin,[39] likewise, stresses the value of this technique, noting that teachers possessing it show *with-it-ness*, that is, an awareness of what is happening in class. And Peters[40] says, 'The good teacher is always, as it were, "out there" in the classroom, not wrapped up in his own involuted musings. He is aware of everything that is going on and the students sense vividly his perception of them as well as his grasp of his subject matter.' A teacher with this kind of awareness can respond immediately to a minor problem before it has time to develop into something more disruptive.

Brown[41] summarises the main signals to look for when monitoring a class in this way. Briefly, these are:

1 *Posture*: Are the students turned towards or away from the object of the lesson?
2 *Head orientation*: Are the students looking at or away from the object of the lesson?
3 *Face*: Do the students look sleepy or awake? Do they look withdrawn or involved? Do they look interested or uninterested?
4 *Activities*: Are the students working on something related to the lesson, or are they attending to something else? Where they are talking to their fellow pupils are their discussions task-oriented or not?
5 *Responses*: Are the students making appropriate or inappropriate responses to your questions?

The vital need, then, is for the student teacher constantly to scan his or her group in an active, alert and expectant manner. Not only is he or she thus in a position to check or deter incipient disturbances, he or she also shows the class an awareness of what is going on. There are some classroom situations where the student teacher is restricted in this respect – when writing on the chalkboard, sitting at the desk or at a piano, or when dealing with an individual student or small group. On such occasions, he or she must not only be extra vigilant, but must be seen to be so.

On a more positive note, lively and interested students, as Brown notes, usually sit with their heads slightly forward and their eyes wide open; a few eagerly wait for a chance to speak.

Ignoring minor misbehaviour

Good and Brophy[42] consider that it is not necessary for a teacher to intervene in a direct way every time he or she notices a minor control problem. Indeed, research evidence[43] suggests that the combination of ignoring inappropriate

Box 74

Noise in the classroom

Denscombe's case studies of three schools disclosed the following broad categories of noise:

Allowable noise: This came from such lessons as PE, drama and music where it was recognised that the normal rules could not reasonably operate and where, within bounds, more noise could be tolerated without impugning the competence of the teacher in charge.

Unavoidable noise: Although the blaring of a tape-recorder or the rasping noise of classroom furniture being scraped across a floor may be a nuisance that interferes with an adjacent lesson, such noise does not immediately signify poor control.

Acceptable occasional noise: From time to time a teacher may have a lively class and a lively lesson where the presence of noise would be interpreted as a sign of action and enthusiasm rather than apathy or poor control.

Unacceptable noise: Here, pupil-initiated noise, created by pupils and/or their teacher's responses, is taken to be an indication of a lack of control in the classroom. The cacophony of talking students interspersed with the raised voice of a teacher invariably carries the connotation of a control problem. However, noise appears to be excusable when emanating from groups that all teachers find difficult to control.

Source adapted from Denscombe[44]

behaviour and showing approval for desirable behaviour can sometimes be a more effective way of achieving better classroom behaviour. Further, the disruptive effect of the teacher's intervention, as Good and Brophy point out, can sometimes create a greater problem than the one the teacher is attempting to solve.

Having made the above recommendation, however, we need to file a caveat in the case of the student teacher experiencing his or her first teaching practice. The overlooking of a minor discipline problem by a *student* teacher, especially where the class knows the person teaching them is a student, could easily be misconstrued as either weakness or lack of awareness. Students may even seize the opportunity to test the teacher out in his or her newness – 'We've got away with it once, let's go one better!' As the outcomes of a student teacher's first few encounters with the students are vital to him or her in defining the situation and establishing the power structure he or she wants, it is advisable that all early challenges to authority be checked and that he or she explores the more subtle technique of 'turning a blind eye' *later* in the practice, when he or she has the measure of the group.

This is perhaps a suitable juncture for the reader to give some consideration to what is often the bane of a student teacher's life: noise. In Box 74 we summarise some of the findings of case studies of three schools by Denscombe. Review the points made in relation to yourself and your own subject specialism(s).

DEALING WITH REPEATED MINOR MISBEHAVIOUR

There are several techniques available to student teachers for intervening in cases of *repeated* minor misbehaviour when it threatens to disrupt a lesson or spread to other students in the class. These should be used in preference to more dramatic procedures whenever the student teacher wishes to check, for example, persistent inattentiveness or restlessness without distracting others. The more obviously useful of these techniques include the following:

Eye contact

One of the most effective ways of checking a minor infraction is simply to look at the offender and establish eye contact with him or her. A cold, glassy stare has an eloquence of its own. An accompanying nod or gesture will assist in re-focusing the student's attention on the task in hand.

Touch and gesture

A particularly useful technique in small group situations is the use of touch and gesture. A misbehaving student near at hand can easily be checked by touching his head or shoulder lightly (obviously taking care to avoid any behaviour that could be construed as assault), or by gesturing. The non-verbal nature of this approach ensures that others are not distracted, that is, Kounin's notion of *smoothness* is preserved.

Physical closeness

Minor misbehaviour can also be eliminated or inhibited by moving towards the offender. This is especially useful with older students. If they know what they should be doing, the mere act of moving in their direction will assist in re-directing their attention to their work.

Inviting a response

Another effective means of summoning a student's wandering attention is to ask him or her a question. The utility of questioning for control purposes is often overlooked. It would seem reasonable to relate a question used for this end to the content of the lesson at the time of the incident, that is, to make it 'task-centred', not 'teacher-centred'. Thus, 'What would you have done in such a situation, John?' is preferable to 'What did I just say, John?'

Other non-verbal gestures

In addition to the ones noted above, there are other non-verbal means of expressing disapproval or checking an infraction. Common examples would include frowning, raising the eyebrows, wagging or 'clicking' a finger or shaking the head negatively.

The advantages of these and similar techniques are that they enable to teacher to eliminate minor problems without disrupting the activity or calling attention to the misdeed. Eye contact, touch and gesture, physical propinquity and other non-verbal gestures are the simplest, since no verbalisation is involved.

DEALING WITH PERSISTENT DISRUPTIVE BEHAVIOUR

The techniques described so far will assist the student teacher in solving relatively minor problems of control and management. For more serious disruptions, we make the following additional suggestions.

Direct intervention

Good and Brophy note that the direct intervention required for more serious misbehaviour may take two forms. First, a student teacher can command an end to the behaviour and follow this up by indicating what alternative behaviour would be appropriate. In such a situation, intervention should be short, direct and to the point: *name the student, identify the misbehaviour* and *indicate what should be done instead.* When a student knows he or she is misbehaving, a brief directive should be sufficient; 'Janet, finish the exercise I gave you.'

The second direct intervention technique which Good and Brophy suggest is simply to remind the students of relevant rules and expected behaviour. As suggested earlier, clear-cut rules defining acceptable classroom behaviour should be formulated early on in the practice (or revised if you take over the class teacher's existing rules), possibly after explanation and discussion with the students if they are old enough. Where this has been done, all the student teacher has to do is to remind the class or student of them as soon as a problem manifests itself.

Another useful guide in this context is suggested by the work of O'Leary, Kaufman, Kass and Drabman,[45] who studied the effects of loud and soft reprimands on the behaviour of disruptive students. Briefly, two students in each of five classes were selected for a four-month study because of their high rates of disruptive behaviour. In the first phase of the study, almost all reprimands were found to be of a loud nature and could be heard by many other students in the class. During the second phase, however, the teachers were asked to use mainly soft reprimands which were audible only to the students being reprimanded. With the institution of soft reprimands, the frequency of disruptive behaviour declined in most of the students. This sequence was repeated, with the same results.

Here is a finding, then, which could play an important part in class management yet which is at variance with the more traditional approach that recommends addressing the culprit in a loud voice.

Interview techniques

In his discussion of management techniques in the classroom, Saunders[46] outlines two forms of interview that may be used for achieving workable arrangements with those students presenting lasting behaviour problems for the teacher. The *investigative interview* is a useful strategy where the more serious forms of misbehaviour are present and may be used where one or more students are involved. Saunders recommends that the interview should concern only the student or students involved in the incident for, as he explains, this reduces the possibility of 'acting up' and bias resulting from group pressures. Ideally, the student or students should be given time to 'cool off'. Where more than one is involved, each should be allowed to give his version of what took place, the student teacher only interrupting to clarify questions of fact and to distinguish fact from opinion. Discrepancies in the story line should be resolved and a final account established that is acceptable to all. Saunders is of the opinion that defence mechanisms or strategies are often used by students when giving explanations in order to protect them from anxiety regarding the consequences of their behaviour. Those commonly used are *denial, projection* and *rationalisation*. Where possible these should be identified and brought out into the open. The interview will eventually lead to appropriate action which may take the form of striking a deal with the students, punishment or referral to a higher authority. Box 75 summarises the main points.

Box 75

Investigative interviews

Investigative interviews may be summarised as follows:

> try not to become emotionally involved;
> if possible exclude anyone not involved in the incident;
> each student should be required to give his/her own version of what happened;
> the teacher should clarify the facts and differentiate them from opinion;
> try to recognise the use of defence mechanisms;
> if possible, explain their use to the student;
> take further appropriate action;
> remember your actions may serve as models for other students.

Source adapted from Saunders

The second form of interview discussed by Saunders is the *reality interview*. This depends for its effectiveness on good personal relations between the student teacher and student and on the knowledge that neither will be intimidated by each other. Given these conditions, the student teacher should get the pupil to admit the misbehaviour. This achieved, the discussion should move on to an evaluation of the behaviour in question. Cause and effect links should be established. Finally, Saunders considers that the student should be encouraged to discuss a more effective course of action for the future, with the teacher impressing on him or her that he or she is responsible for his or her own behaviour and will subsequently be accountable for it. The main steps in this process are summarised in Box 76.

Conflict-resolving strategies and techniques

Saunders further discusses the strategies and techniques that student teachers sometimes resort to in order to resolve conflict situations. These he considers in three broad categories: avoidance strategies, diffusion strategies and confrontation strategies.

First, *avoidance strategies*. These include high tolerance, feigned illness and engaging in banter. If a student teacher can build up high tolerance, he

Box 76

Reality interviews

The principal guidelines to reality interviewing are:

discuss in private;
with no hint of intimidation from either side;
start from an existing relationship, if possible;
establish the need for frankness;
evaluate the misdeed;
link cause and effect;
establish other causes of action and their consequences;
discuss the most effective action for the future.

Source Saunders

or she will be in a position to ignore conflict until a breakdown point is reached. Retreating from a conflict situation under the guise of illness is another technique sometimes employed. And engaging in banter with pupils is yet another means of side-stepping conflict. As Saunders says, 'Avoidance strategies may have some survival value, but they are maladaptive in so far as the individual teacher does not receive any measure of professional satisfaction and the conflict is not resolved.'

Second, *diffusion strategies*. These include delaying action, tangential responses, evasion and appeals to generalisability. Delaying action, as it suggests, involves putting off a decision to avoid precipitating a crisis. A tangential response is one that deals with peripheral issues, thus leaving the main source of conflict unresolved. Evasion is resorted to when a student teacher is called on to justify his or her position and side-steps the issue. And an appeal to generalisability is resorted to when a student teacher concedes that a demand is reasonable when it is made by one person, but not if others make a similar request. Like avoidance strategies, diffusion strategies are generally unsatisfactory.

Finally, *confrontation strategies*. These include the use of power and negotiation strategies. A student teacher resorts to power strategies when he or she uses the divide-and-rule approach; when he or she resorts to pseudo-power by threatening sanctions which cannot be implemented; by manipulating rewards; and by resorting to school tradition – 'This isn't the way we do it here.' Negotiation strategies are invoked when there is the possibility of a rational solution to the difficulty. Saunders identifies three approaches in this respect: compromise, affiliative appeal and pseudo-compromise.

Watkins and Wagner[47] suggest a number of principles which would serve to de-escalate a developing confrontation. These have much in common with Saunders's strategies, as a comparison between the two approaches will show:

1   Avoid public arenas in which people may crystallise their position in front of an audience.
2   Ask, 'Is what has led to this really so important as to justify this escalation?'
3   Avoid threats of any sort, especially those which could be perceived as physical.
4   Look for an alternative in which *both* can 'win'.
5   Encourage the student to say more about his or her perception of what is going on.
6   Explain your own view of things clearly, and in a way which is not simplified.

With practice, Watkins and Wagner suggest that 'these principles can be applied in such a way that student teachers' common reactions about feelings of "condoning" or "climbing down" are not precipitated, and teachers can agree that desired behaviour from pupils is not brought about by confrontation'.

In summary, then, whereas the conflict-avoidance strategies may have a certain survival value to all teachers at some stage in their careers, as permanent features of one's professional behavioural repertoire they need to be regarded with suspicion because they offer neither long-term solutions nor personal satisfaction.

We next consider how a reprimand from a teacher can influence the response of the rest of the class.

THE RIPPLE EFFECT

Research by Kounin,[48] who video-taped many hours of teaching in his study of indiscipline in the classroom, has revealed that a reprimand from a teacher to a student misbehaving in his or her class may influence the rest of the group although they are not actually party to the misdemeanour. Kounin labelled this *the ripple effect*; it may have either positive or negative influences from the student teacher's point of view. When, for instance, a student being reprimanded is of high standing in the sociometric structure of the group, the ripple effect from an encounter with the student teacher is usually strong. If the student teacher succeeds in checking the misbehaviour, the effect on the rest of the class from the student teacher's perspective is positive in that they will tend to accept the reprimand as fair and think of the student teacher as an effective disciplinarian. In practical terms, it means that they will either improve their behaviour or be less likely to behave unsatisfactorily. If, however, the high prestige student rebels at the student teacher's efforts to control him or her, this feeling may spread to classmates, who may then consider the teacher's handling of the situation unsatisfactory and consequently perceive him or her as weak and ineffectual. The practical consequences could be an escalation of the problem, with the rest of the class expressing resentment or generally creating an atmosphere not conducive to meaningful work.

Since it is therefore important to produce a positive ripple effect, that is, an improvement or inhibition of the behaviour of other pupils, certain characteristics of control need to be borne in mind. Gnagey[49] identified a number of such factors including *clarity, firmness, task-centred techniques, high-prestige pupils* and *roughness*. Each will be considered briefly.

Clarity

What Gnagey describes as a clear control technique, one embodying *clarity*, is one that specifies the defiant, the deviancy and the preferred alternative behaviour. Thus, 'John, stop talking and finish your essay' is preferable to 'Cut out the talking at the back there', for it is a clear command and can be expected to have two beneficial effects on the rest of the class: they will be less likely to talk themselves and less likely to be disrupted in their own work than would probably be the case with a command lacking clarity.

Firmness

Firm control techniques prevent disruption more effectively than tentative ones. Gnagey recommends that they can best be implemented by moving towards the offender, issuing the command in an 'I-mean-it' tone, and following through by seeing the command is obeyed before continuing with the lesson. Kounin and Gump[50] found that students responded to rules that were actually enforced ('followed through') but ignored those lacking conviction and enforcement ('follow-through').

Task-centred techniques

A *task-centred approach* produces a more desirable ripple effect than one that is teacher-centred. By this is meant the need to stress the task in hand, or the effects of deviancy on the task, rather than the student teacher or the student teacher's relationship with the pupil. Thus, 'John, stop whispering and watch the demonstration, or else you won't understand when you have to do it yourself later' is better than, 'Pay attention and listen to me.'

High-prestige students

Gnagey recommends that *high-prestige students* be identified and studied. He writes, 'As their responses to your influence have such a strong ripple effect on others, it will pay to find out which control techniques cause them to respond submissively with the least amount of belligerence.' In this connection, the reader is referred to the account of sociometric techniques in Oeser.[51]

Roughness

Gnagey explains that *roughness* refers to the use of threatening or violent control techniques on the part of the teacher which in turn are likely to produce negative ripples – anger, resentment, feelings of injustice or displacement – as well as being illegal. Kounin, Gump and Ryan[52] found that such techniques produced a considerable amount of disruptive behaviour among students who were not originally misbehaving themselves. A further consequence was that they also held the student teacher in lower esteem because of his or her manner.

In summary, the beginning teacher should seek positive ripples through clarity, firmness, task-centred techniques, capitalising on high-prestige students and the avoidance of roughness. We continue by taking the important skill of giving orders and instructions a little further.

ISSUING ORDERS AND INSTRUCTIONS

Although some teachers are more effective at it than others, giving instructions to an individual, group or class is a skill that can be learned and improved with practice. Like other techniques, issuing instructions, orders and commands can be broken down into their basic components such as content, phrasing, manner of delivery and context.

The prevailing conditions play a part in the overall effectiveness of instructions; the class must be *still and silent*, ideally before an instruction is given. Say, 'Stop whatever you are doing, please; no more talking, stop writing.' Then give your instruction.

The manner of delivery is also important. You have to avoid being too stern and imperious on the one hand, yet too diffident and unconvincing on the other. The one approach can induce fear (which is not desirable); the other, an ineffectualness on the teacher's part. A firm but pleasant manner is required. Marland's[53] advice in this connection is eminently practical: 'It is worth practising instructions on your own. Then listen to yourself as you give them in school and observe the response. *Develop a firm warmth, or a warm firmness.*'

Generally speaking, instructions tend to be more effective and to be accepted more gracefully when phrased in a positive, rather than a negative, manner. Accordingly, 'Be early for the practical lesson on Monday' in preference to 'Don't be late for Monday's lesson.' Or, 'Leave the room as tidy as you found it' rather than 'Don't leave the room in such a mess this week.'

Marland warns against framing an instruction in the form of a question. For example, the organisational and management problems encouraged by,

'Anyone need paper?' will be minimised by expressing the point thus, 'Put your hands up if you're without paper.'

You should not give a second instruction until the first one has been obeyed. Take time to glance round the room and check that everyone has understood and carried out your order.

Finally, the following points may be useful to the reader in his or her consideration of the use of commands as a technique of control.

- Task-oriented commands are often preferable to status-oriented ones. As Peters[54] observes, 'If commands are task-oriented rather than status-oriented they are a thoroughly rational device for controlling and directing situations where unambiguous directions or prohibitions are obviously necessary.'

- Generally speaking, the reason for a command should not be given, as this introduces an element of doubt or suggests that it may not or need not be obeyed. In any case, if the system of rules operating in the classroom has been explained to the group at an earlier stage, there should be no need for elaboration.

- A command should not be coupled with a statement of grievance, as this may arouse hostility towards, or induce disrespect for, the person issuing the command. For example, avoid this sort of utterance: 'Stop moving the chairs to the back of the room. I'm tired of telling you. You do it every time you come into the room.' Similarly, a command couched in the language of a whine 'operates powerfully to bring about its own frustration'.[55]

- Once you have got to know your class, requests – a more polite form of command – may be all that you need to structure the situation.

- The voice issuing the command should be strong, decisive and warm.

- The student teacher's own expectations play a part, too. Students will tend to conform not so much to what he or she says in words but to what he or she actually *expects*. He or she must therefore expect more or less instant obedience to her commands as a matter of course.

- The verbal context of the message is also important. It is vital that it stands out in relief from what the teacher has said immediately preceding its issue and, especially, from what he or she says subsequently. A directive can easily lose much of its force by becoming indistinguishable from its context in terms of timbre, tone, dynamics, manner and speed of delivery. Timing, the judicious use of pauses and silence, social dynamics, facial expressions and a touch of drama will all assist in achieving greater salience.

- A student teacher may further enhance the effectiveness of his or her commands by having the class come to associate them with certain additional non-verbal features such as clapping the hands, snapping the fingers, staring, gesturing or moving to a focal point in the room.

REWARDS AND PUNISHMENTS

Rewards

Older books on the psychology of education make great play with the concepts of *extrinsic* and *intrinsic* rewards as aids to motivation and to a lesser extent classroom management and control. Their validity and usefulness in these respects still hold good. Extrinsic rewards such as marks, grades, stars, prizes and public commendation are stock examples and are there for the student teacher to exploit. Intrinsic rewards like the warm feeling from a job well done, or satisfying one's innate curiosity, or the kick one gets from solving a problem or achieving a standard one has set oneself, belong to an individual's subjective world and so are beyond the student teacher's direct control. But he or she can influence them *indirectly* through the use of extrinsic rewards. The connection between the two is often overlooked, for the skilful manipulation of extrinsic rewards over a period of time can lead to the more desirable intrinsic kind. Contrasting perspectives on rewards in the classroom by pupils and teachers respectively are indicated in Box 77.

Box 77

Pupil and teacher perspectives on rewards

In a study on the relative effectiveness of various incentives and deterrents as judged by pupils and teachers, it was found that:

1   *Pupils preferred:*
        favourable home report
        to do well in a test
        to be given a prize
        to receive good marks for written work
2   *whereas the staff thought the most effective rewards were:*
        to be praised in the presence of others
        good marks for written work
        elected to leadership by fellow pupils
        teacher expressing quiet appreciation

Source adapted from Burns[56]

Merrett and Jones[57] classified three 'grades' of extrinsic rewards. Lower-order rewards include: praise, points, credits and tokens. Medium-order rewards include: certificates, badges, being allowed privileges, comments put on reports, a letter home.[58] Higher-order rewards include prizes and very public credit. Capel[59] indicates that students can be very motivated by achievement, enjoyment of a task, satisfaction (the feeling that one is improving) and success (e.g. in an examination). She outlines four types of reward:

- *social rewards* (social contact and pleasant interaction with other people);
- *token rewards* (house points, certificates);
- *material rewards* (tangible, usable items);
- *activity rewards* (opportunities for enjoyable activities).

Perhaps the most immediately accessible means of reward for the student teacher is the *use of praise*, and its value in the classroom should not be overlooked. It has been demonstrated by Madsen, Becker and Thomas[60] that showing approval for appropriate behaviour is probably the key to effective classroom management. Much of this kind of approval will take the form of *verbal praise* so it is important for the teacher to understand both the constructive and damaging effects of its classroom use. Waller's[61] comments are apposite here:

> The whole matter of control by praise is puzzling and a bit paradoxical. Where it is wisely carried on, it may result in the most happy relations between students and teachers. Where it is unwisely applied it is absurdly ineffective and ultimately very damaging to the child. Praise must always be merited, and it must always be discreet, else all standards disappear. Cheap praise both offends and disappoints, and it breaks down the distinction between good and bad performances. Praise must always be measured; it must not resort to superlatives, for superlatives give the comfortable but deadening sense of a goal attained. Such praise as is used must open the way to development and not close it. Praise must always be sincere, for otherwise it is very difficult to make it sincere, and if it does not seem sincere it fails to hearten. Praise as a means of control must be adapted to particular students. It is a device to be used frequently but only on a fitting occasion rather than an unvaried policy.

Everyone enjoys praise and you should try to direct it at both the individual and the class as a whole, as well as to a range of classroom behaviours – work, good behaviour, helpfulness, a quick answer. Nor should personal praise be overlooked. It is not always necessary to select the *best* work and behaviour, as one is not seeking absolute performance. Nor should you invariably praise only those who 'shine' naturally, as the idea is to get over to the child that praise is accessible to all and can be earned by them with striving. In some instances, especially where slower students are involved, it is more desirable to praise *effort* rather than the finished product.

There are two main ways of praising an individual student: either publicly or in private. Public praise in front of the rest of the class (or at morning assembly, in some circumstances) can be effective and appreciated providing it is not overdone or too effusive. The quiet private word of praise with a student is an approach which student teachers tend to overlook. In a large survey of over 1,700 8–11-year-olds Merrett and Man Tang[62] reported that younger children found praise more acceptable if it was given quietly (and reprimands more acceptable if given publicly!). This mirrored an earlier study in secondary school students.[63]

The persistent trouble-maker should be praised with care. Of him (or her), Marland[64] writes:

> If, as is often the case, he is seeking group status by his ostentatious behaviour, he will resent the public praise as an attack on his reputation, and as likely as not he will find some technique of expression or gesture that not only nullifies the praise but, worse than that, actually associates your praise with his scorn – thus devaluing it for others ... This does not, however, normally mean that he does not want the praise, merely that he doesn't want it openly. For such a pupil, the private word of praise is essential, and frequently effective.

There is a whole range of non-verbal signals that can be used to indicate approval; these can be used to reinforce verbal praise or else independently. For example, a smile, an affirmative nod of the head, a pat on the back or a hand on the shoulder all indicate acceptance of student behaviour. Similarly, the use and display of students' ideas, like writing comments on the board, holding up a student's work for the class to see or displaying it on a display board, can also be regarded as non-verbal expressions of approval. And merely showing interest in student behaviour and presence by establishing and maintaining eye contact is yet another rewarding (from the student's point of view) use of non-verbal signals.[65]

Some American research findings[66] are worth mentioning in this context. Teachers use praise sparingly in standard classrooms. Further, teachers give more praise to high-achieving pupils; pupils to whom they feel more attached, or less indifferent; pupils whom they say they favour; and pupils for whom they have expectations of high future occupational status. The researches also indicate that boys receive more praise than girls and that praise varies with the social class status of the school's location. However, Bourne[67] argues that praise is not enough. She suggests that students need cognitive feedback as well as praise if their motivation (linked to successful achievements) is to be raised. She demonstrates that teachers give more feedback to high achievers so that they know how to improve, but give only praise to low achievers, without indicating to them how they could improve their work.

Merrett and Jones[68] indicate a significant discrepancy in teachers' behaviour, of rewarding students' academic achievements more than their achievements in terms of behaviour. In primary schools they noted that 50 per cent of teachers' comments on students' academic achievements were positive and 16 per cent were negative; only 6 per cent of teachers' comments on behaviour were positive, whilst 28 per cent were negative. In secondary schools the researchers noted that 45 per cent of teachers' comments on students' academic achievements were positive and 15 per cent were negative; only 10 per cent of teachers' comments on behaviour were positive and 30 per cent were negative. Not only does this show that more rewards were given for academic attainments than for behaviour, but teachers were much more negative about behaviour than they were about academic matters. A curious anomaly is shown here, for, if a positive approach seems to be successful in the academic area, it is surprising that the same teachers did not use this approach for promoting good behaviour. This echoes our opening comments on class management – that it is essential to work on the positive rather than focus on the negative. In academic terms a teacher's first reaction to students making a mistake is usually to teach them; it is paradoxical that when students make a mistake in their behaviour a teacher's first reaction is to criticise or punish them.

Punishments

We saw earlier how a teacher's control may be seen as stemming chiefly from a combination of personal power and authority. Discipline in a classroom is achieved by the successful exercising of this control to ensure conformity to the established rules. It is when there is a serious breach of the rules, a breakdown of discipline, that the need for punishment may arise. The Elton Report[69] was careful to endorse the view that 'the punishment should fit the crime', i.e. that student teachers should avoid over-reacting and under-reacting; misbehaviour was 'graded' from the trivial to the serious in the sequence that follows:

talking out of turn
preventing others from working
making unnecessary noise (not just talking but, e.g., by scraping chairs)
leaving a seat or room without permission
calculated idleness or avoidance of work
general rowdiness
verbal abuse to other students
physical aggression to other students
lateness or unauthorised absence
persistence in infringement of class and school rules
cheekiness to teachers
physical destructiveness
verbal abuse of teachers
physical aggression to teachers

The Elton Report indicated that there was a high incidence of low-level stress from low-level disruptions, a feature indicated by Wheldall and Merrett[70] and reinforced in comparative studies such as a piece of research by Johnson *et al.*[71] in South Australia that was deliberately designed to replicate Elton's methodology and instrumentation, and a study of first and middle schools in St. Helena in which, for example, the researchers reported that talking out of turn was the most commonly occurring problem[72] (43 per cent of all cases reported). Charlton and David[73] comment that the incidence of low-level behaviour infractions and irritants is responsive to relatively simple methods (outlined below).

In response to 'graded' degrees of seriousness the Elton Report indicated that several strategies were used that, themselves, were graded in order of 'seriousness', from least to most serious in the sequence that follows:

reasoning with a student within the classroom
reasoning with a student outside the classroom
setting extra work
deliberately ignoring minor infractions
keeping students in during and after school
discussing with the whole class why things are going wrong
temporarily withdrawing a student from the class
referring a student to another teacher
removing privileges
sending a student to a senior figure in the school
involving parents
suspension from the school

In their important study, Merrett and Jones classified three gradations of sanctions: *Low-order sanctions* included: telling off (publicly and privately); detention; lines or tables; comments on reports; confiscation of property; short exclusion from the lesson. *Middle-order sanctions* included: those that involved another member of the management staff; placing a student 'on report'; sending a letter home; denying the student certain activities; meeting with parents. *Higher-order sanctions* included: exclusion; suspension; expulsion and other actions that involved an outside authority.

Johnson *et al.* set out a list of the most to the least effective strategies for handling unacceptable behaviour in the primary school. These are shown in Box 78. The further one goes down the list the less effective is the strategy. This list is similar to the Elton Report's suggestions for secondary school students, with the exception that detentions are seen as being more effective. The Elton Report comments that for both primary and secondary school students it is important not to ignore minor infractions which might easily escalate into major problems.

Peters[74] points out that punishment is a much more specific notion than discipline and that at least three criteria must be met if we are to call something a case of punishment. These are (1) intentional infliction of pain or unpleasantness (2) by someone in authority (3) on a person as a consequence of a breach of rules on his part. Although some actions in the

Box 78

Strategies for handling unacceptable behaviour

Discuss the problem with the student in the class.
Have the student leave the class.
Reason with the student outside the class.
Remove privileges.
Seek parental involvement.
Have a conference with the student and the parent(s).
Set extra work.
Ignore minor disruptions.
Detention.
Refer the student to another teacher.
Send the student to the head teacher.
Remove the student from the school.

Source Johnson *et al.*[75]

school situation are loosely referred to as cases of 'punishment' without meeting all these criteria, e.g. asking a student to do a piece of work again, they do nevertheless provide us with a useful frame of reference for our brief consideration of this important subject.

For some considerable time, the use of punishment as a means of assisting in the upbringing and education of students was discouraged not only on ethical grounds but also because of the possible harmful side effects. More recently, however, interest in the subject has revived and research undertaken latterly does seem to indicate that punishment may very well have a valuable part to play in the development and control of students.

Of course, a teacher who comes to rely heavily on punishment cannot hope to succeed except in a narrow and temporary sense. Whatever he or she achieves will be at the cost of undue negative emotional reactions such as anxiety and frustration and a permanent impairing of relationships. Nevertheless, a teacher should not hesitate to resort to punishment when the occasion demands, for, when properly used, it is a legitimate and helpful means of dealing with certain disciplinary problems.

We now consider the forms which punishment in the classroom might take, the occasions for punishment and ways of administering it.

Forms of punishment

Before deciding the forms of punishment you intend to use during your teaching practice, should the need for them arise, there are two points worth bearing in mind. First, you are not starting from square one: most schools will have an established system of punishment as part of their tradition and no doubt the forms it takes will be related to the rules that are operative in the school. You should thus find out what alternatives exist within the tradition so that you can use them when necessary. Do not use corporal punishment – you could be prosecuted for assault. Second, it is better whenever possible to anticipate and thereby avoid incidents likely to culminate in the need for punishment. As Peters says, 'Under normal conditions enthusiasm for the enterprise, combined with imaginative techniques of presentation and efficient class management will avert the need for punishment. Boredom is one of the most potent causes of disorder.'

Keeping a class in after school can be an effective deterrent and a particularly useful one for the student teacher, although this form of punishment does present the kind of dilemma to which Peters draws attention: 'There is also the problem of what to do with them when they are so detained. It becomes a farcical situation, and one that is very difficult to manage, if nothing constructive is done. Yet the conditions are scarcely ideal for doing much of educational value.' A further disadvantage with keeping students after school lies in the fact that some schools insist on giving students at least twenty-four hours' notice of the detention. Although sound practical reasons usually account for such a ruling, it can weaken the connection between the offence and the punishment.

A useful form of punishment for the individual offender is that of isolation. Its efficacy was noted by Waller when he referred to it as 'a long lever that makes for conformity'. It is important for the student teacher to remember that it is not necessary to send a student out of the room to achieve isolation. Setting him apart from the rest of the class *within* the classroom can be just as effective and may be achieved by having him stand in a corner, or, better still, sit at a desk away from the others. This kind of psychological banishment can be especially effective providing it does not last too long. Offenders who have been particularly disruptive may be isolated with their work, but again the isolation should not last too long. Thompson[76] advises that no matter how naughty a child has been he should be given innumerable 'fresh starts', for students have a strong corporate feeling so that isolation counts as a severe punishment.

Negative utilitarian controls are frequently used by teachers. These may take the form of *behaviour restrictions* and *limitations of privilege* and may thus include missing part of a favourite lesson, a desired recreational activity or playtime, or not being allowed to sit near the back of the class. You will quickly discover additional means of controlling misbehaviour along similar lines. Forms of punishment are outlined in Box 79.

Some kinds of punishments are better avoided, and may be itemised as follows:

1   school work should not be used as a punishment. A child kept in from

Box 79

Forms of punishment

Reasonable punishment can take many forms, but some account must be taken of the forms customarily used in your school with the age range in question. Some common practices are:

- keeping a student behind for a few minutes' discussion after the rest of the class have left, so that he or she is last in the queue for lunch, or it causes his or her friends to wait;
- formal detention with some task to do that is not directly connected with the lesson so that his or her antipathy for the lesson is not increased by the punishment;
- detention to finish work deliberately not completed in lesson time;
- withdrawal of privileges, such as the use of a tuck-shop at break, or access to a common room or classroom other than when essential;
- isolation or exclusion with work, either in a corner of the classroom or in another part of the school;
- if property is damaged the student may be required to repair the article, if such action is appropriate; or to do a socially useful task such as tidying the classroom or picking up paper in the playground;
- as a response to unacceptable language the pupil might be required to write out the offending words several times.

Source Saunders[77]

play or games, for instance, should not be given additional school work such as writing or mathematics. These should be associated with enjoyment.

2   Avoid collective punishments, such as keeping a whole class in when only one or two individuals are culpable.[78] Such action will provoke unnecessary resentment from the innocent members.

3   Forms of mental punishment such as severe personal criticism, ridicule, sarcasm and so on are not recommended.

4   Coercive sanctions, those involving a physical component such as caning, strapping, striking or shaking, should not be used; these forms of punishment are illegal.

5   Only send a child to the head teacher as a last resort, or when you are confronted with a particularly serious case of misbehaviour. Such an action can be seen as weakening the teacher's authority (though, in some schools it is seen very positively as the teacher simply not putting up with bad behaviour at any price). However, do not hesitate to seek advice privately from other members of staff when you need help.

6   Avoid banishing a student from the classroom if possible. Where you feel isolation is warranted, try to let it be within the classroom.

The 'when' and the 'how' of punishment

Good and Brophy[79] in their analysis of punishment make a number of interesting points concerning *when* to resort to punishment. Generally speaking, punishment is appropriate only in dealing with *repeated* misbehaviour, not for single, isolated incidents, no matter how serious. It is a measure to be taken when a student persists in the same kinds of misbehaviour in spite of continued expressions of concern and disapproval from the student teacher. Resorting to punishment is not a step to be taken lightly since it signifies that neither the student teacher nor the student can handle the situation. One other point: punishment should not be administered if it is apparent that the student is trying to improve. He or she should be given the benefit of the doubt and, where possible, rewarded for attempts at improvement.

In considering the nature of punishment and the forms it may take in the classroom, we can easily lose sight of the way in which it should be administered. A moment's reflection tells us that we should at least be *systematic* and consistent in its application. So once again the efficacy of having agreed on a few basic classroom rules is brought home to us, for in providing an impartial frame of reference for student teacher and students alike, not only do they ensure we will achieve the consistency we seek, they also guarantee that the recipients, in recognising the logic and fairness of the punishment, will be less likely to respond emotionally.

Another factor in the punishing situation concerns the nature and extent of the talk the teacher engages in. Wright[80] explains that this can serve a number of functions, one of which is to help the student 'to construe his actions in a certain way, to structure them cognitively and relate them to general rules'. In thus justifying the punishment to the student, the student teacher's explanatory talk will clarify the nature of the offence, will provide reasons for judging it wrong, will explain its effects on others and will relate it to future occasions. A consistent *modus operandi* of this nature will give the student the necessary criteria for making his or her own judgements.

A third factor concerns the temporal relationship between the offence and the punishment. Wright points out that punishments placing restrictions on a student will be most effective if they are related to the offence, if they follow closely after it, and if removal of the restrictions is conditional upon improvement of behaviour. Punishment logically related to the offence is more easily perceived as fair. A sanction should therefore be immediate and inevitable so that the cause and effect relationship is apparent. If it is prolonged to the point where the relationship becomes tenuous, the offender may become resentful.

BEHAVIOUR MODIFICATION AND ASSERTIVE DISCIPLINE

Psychologists have long been aware that most behaviour is affected by its consequences. These consequences may be seen as rewarding or reinforcing if, as a result, the behaviour persists or increases, and punishing if the behaviour ceases or decreases. In some circumstances behaviour may be extinguished if there is no consequence.

Behaviour modification

The principles set out above lie at the heart of the approach to dealing with undesirable or maladaptive classroom behaviour known as *behaviour modification*, the techniques of which are used to change specific patterns of inappropriate behaviour, e.g. hyperactivity in the classroom, excessive movement about the room, talking too much or disobedience. This method of handling behaviour problems is preferred by those who find the use of punishment in the classroom distasteful and who seek a non-punitive, positive approach as an alternative.

The behaviour-modification approach in its most basic form consists of three components: (1) specification of the undesirable behaviour to be extinguished or minimised and the preferred desirable behaviour that is to replace it; (2) identification first of the rewards and reinforcements sustaining the unwanted behaviour so that they may be avoided, and second of the rewards and reinforcements that will increase the frequency of the preferred alternative behaviour; and (3) the consistent and systematic avoidance and application of these respective rewards and reinforcements over a period of time, together with a systematic record of changes in behaviour. A reinforcer in this context is defined by its ability to accelerate, or increase, the rate at which a behaviour will occur, or, more simply, its effect on the learner.

There are a number of types of reinforcer that may be used in this context. The most natural and effective for teachers are *social reinforcers*. Student-teacher attention, student-teacher praise, student-teacher approval and disapproval are powerful factors affecting students' behaviour, and they can be systematically varied to produce the sort of behaviour desired by the student teacher. When employing these techniques, however, the student teacher must be sure to reinforce the desirable behaviour as well as ignore the undesirable if she is to achieve her objective of creating the most favourable conditions for learning.

A particular instance of the application of behaviour-modification techniques may concern some form of consistent anti-social behaviour on the part of a student in class. This kind of behaviour may be sustained by reinforcements in the form of student-teacher attention or by the approval or perhaps disapproval of the rest of the class. If this is the case, the behaviour-modification approach would recommend ignoring the attention-seeking behaviour (e.g. a student constantly moving out of his or her seat) and making sure that the sought-after alternative behaviour (e.g. the student remaining in his or her place) is rewarded or reinforced with appropriate action (attention, praise or some kind of non-verbal approval like smiling) on the part of the student teacher.

Such techniques may also be useful in the following situations providing they are employed systematically, consistently and over a period of time: failure to pay attention, day-dreaming, failure to show interest in work, not meeting work requirements, being uncommunicative and withdrawn, breaking class rules, overreacting to stressful conditions, insensitivity to other people, anti-social behaviours, hyperactivity, attention-seeking, disobedience and disrespect.

The results of experimental studies in behaviour modification are encouraging. A study by Thomas, Becker and Armstrong,[81] for example, demonstrates the possibilities of the approach. They showed that approving teacher responses served a positive reinforcing function in maintaining appropriate classroom behaviours. Disruptive behaviours increased each time approving teaching behaviour (praise, smiles, contacts, etc.) was withdrawn. When the teacher's disapproving behaviours (verbal reprimands, physical restraints, etc.) were tripled, there was much greater disruption, i.e. an increase in noise and movement about the room. The findings, therefore, emphasise the important role of the teacher in producing, maintaining and eliminating both desirable and disruptive classroom behaviour. Summaries of findings of similar studies in which the techniques of behaviour modification have been successfully supplied to a range of maladaptive behaviours may be found in Hewett.[82]

Of course, from the student teacher's point of view, teaching practice is not the most ideal context for putting the techniques of behaviour modification to the test because of its length – a few weeks at most. Nevertheless, he or she may be in a position to select some consistently manifested behaviour problem and attempt to remedy it along the lines suggested above. He or she could then at least be satisfied that the principles are sufficiently sound to warrant further investigation at a later date.

In this regard we refer to a project by Lawrence, Steed and Young,[83] the implications of which have immediate relevance for student teachers on teaching practice in that while on the surface the approach appears to be basic common-sense, it does encapsulate positive behaviour-modification techniques. The project concerned a group of teachers working with a problematic class in a difficult school. The techniques the teachers used were controlled systematic rewards (praise, attention and encouragement) for appropriate behaviour, and ignoring unwanted behaviour, except when it was dangerous. 'Encouragement' with respect to this particular project included:

1   Praise of all kinds, for the student's work and behaviour.
2   Attention to the student.
3   Interest in the student.
4   Help to the student.
5   Increasing the student's self-respect or self-esteem.

The class in question was a third-year boys' class, with thirty-two on the roll, in the middle stream of three. All recorded IQs were low average. There were no parental occupations in social class I or II and the class was racially mixed. Six had appeared at least once before a juvenile court.

Some of the principles emerging from the study, and which hold good for both sexes, are as follows:

1   'Encouragement' is a very powerful means of improving both a student's behaviour and the work he or she does.
2   The *more* encouragement for appropriate behaviour and work he or she receives, the *better* he or she will behave and work.
3   A teacher may *think* he or she is encouraging a student a great deal but in practice may not be, e.g. what he or she considers encouraging may not appear so to the student, or the encouragement may not be expressed in a way clear to the student, or it may not be enough to influence him or her.
4   Misbehaviour can often be cancelled out if, when it is observed, the teacher ignores the student but simultaneously praises another who is behaving correctly. The teacher then returns to encourage the first student *as soon as* he or she is behaving appropriately (e.g. by saying 'That's more like it!' or 'I'm pleased to see you're behaving like an adult now').
5   Another way of handling inappropriate behaviour is simply to ignore it, but to praise as soon as appropriate behaviour occurs.

Practical implications following from the project can be summarised:

•   Moving quickly around the class saying 'that's right' or 'good' is a way of settling the class down and getting it to work speedily.
•   Small groups can be similarly encouraged.
•   Encouraging a student can include having a word with him before or after a lesson.
•   Students at this age like to be treated as adults.
•   All work discussed in a lesson, including homework, can be used for encouragement purposes.
•   'Spell out' your praise even at the risk of overdoing it.
•   Use the student's own words when praising, or make your meaning quite clear.
•   Displaying a student's work is a visible sign of praise.
•   A person-to-person chat at an adult level is often appreciated, especially on a topic of adult interest.

For further information on this subject we suggest you read Gropper and Kress[84] and Sloane.[85] The latter is particularly useful in that within the framework of behaviour modification it presents practical, positive procedures for solving and preventing problems of management and control. The concrete suggestions throughout the text will help the reader to develop a systematic approach to all areas of classroom management. A similarly useful text is Clarizio's,[86] which offers a wealth of practical suggestions on rewards, extinction and punishment. Two introductory guides which outline the main principles of behaviour modification in the classroom are those by Givner and Graubard[87] and McAuley and McAuley.[88] Finally, a text dealing with the planning and implementation of behaviour-modification programmes for severely handicapped students is Morris's.[89]

Assertive Discipline

A comparatively recent approach to behaviour management which has affinities with behaviour modification is Canter and Canter's[90] *Assertive Discipline*. Although this was introduced in the 1970s, it has crossed the Atlantic to the UK with some force in the 1990s. Assertive discipline is premised on five key principles:

1   Clear expectations for the required behaviour are set out by the teacher.
2   Specific, concrete and verbal praise and rewards are given for the behaviour.
3   There is a graded sequence of negative consequences of undesirable behaviour.
4   The teacher is assertive in insisting on the application of the rewards and sanctions.
5   Power resides with the teacher, while informed choice of whether to follow a path that leads to rewards or sanctions resides with the student.

In this approach a student who is misbehaving is told to stop and told explicitly what will happen if he or she does not stop. The student can choose to comply with the teacher's orders (i.e. to stop) or not to comply (i.e. to demonstrate the undesirable behaviour again and, thereby, to incur the negative sanctions). If the unacceptable behaviour persists, then stronger sanctions are imposed. Nicholls and Houghton[91] report that, overall, using the methods saw significant increase in teacher approval, decrease in teacher disapproval, increase in students' 'on-task' behaviour and decrease in disruptive behaviour.

On the other hand very severe questions have been raised against this approach. In a hard-hitting paper, Robinson and Maines[92] argue that the approach is not only under-researched but that it embodies many of the negative features of behaviourism, for example: students are passive receivers to be trained in predetermined behaviours; it demonstrates a crude instrumentalism and technicism; it replaces understanding with knee-jerk reactions; it reduces education to trivial matters of the observable. Robinson and Maines argue forcefully that Assertive Discipline (a) confuses consequences with punishments, (b) is demeaning, humiliating and insulting to students, (c) neglects the circumstances that lead to the behaviour (resulting in a student's sense of injustice), (d) disregards the need of difficult students for a flexible approach based on encouragement rather than a rigid approach that deploys punishment, (e) involves public humiliation of an offender which is itself 'an offence against confidentiality', and (f) denies basic agency and freedoms because students and teachers have unequal rights to be listened to and powers to create a negotiated environment. This litany of concerns is not empty argument. Martin[93] argues that the approach can easily fail because it needs whole-staff commitment and training but the issues and methods are so contentious that such a consensus is almost impossible to secure.

Hence, though this approach aspires to being a 'movement', with Canter speaking at venues across the globe, the student teacher will need to consider carefully its merits and demerits. If he or she is in a school where Assertive Discipline is practised, careful observation of its efficacy and its problems will be worthwhile.

ANTICIPATING MANAGEMENT AND CONTROL PROBLEMS IN THE CLASSROOM

There are certain aspects and structural features of one's lesson that need handling with particular care and foresight because they can be the cause of quite serious problems of management and control. The beginning of a lesson, for example, requires special thought because it sets the tone for the rest of the lesson. Similarly, transitions from one activity to another are potentially disruptive. As we have already considered these features of the lesson, it is sufficient for us at this point to suggest that you revise the appropriate sections.

Another important point for student teachers to bear in mind concerns their first meeting with a new class. As Wragg has observed, the very first lesson with a class can go a long way towards establishing the kind of climate that will prevail for the rest of the practice or term. In the Teacher Education Project, he and his colleagues observed a hundred lessons given by thirteen experienced teachers at the beginning of the school year, and two hundred given by student teachers at the beginning of teaching practice. The differences between the two groups are listed in Box 69, and we refer readers back to this.

The importance of the first meeting with a class is also stressed by Robertson,[94] who argues that teachers who want to establish their authority should behave as if they were already in authority. As he says:

A teacher, by virtue of his higher status, has certain rights to behave in ways denied his pupils, and in exercising those rights he reinforces his authority. This does not mean that he should be repressive or authoritarian, but rather that his behaviour should be consistent with his status.

Among factors highlighted by Robertson as being of crucial importance in conveying this status, especially during initial meetings, are:

1 Firmness and confidence

When a student teacher feels confident and assured, the students are consequently more responsive and this in turn reinforces his or her own confidence. If, on the other hand, the student teacher is lacking in confidence, the reverse can occur and he or she may go to pieces.

2 Bodily behaviour

Non-verbal behaviour is important and two factors apply here: *immediacy* between a teacher and class which is achieved by a sensitive awareness of such factors as posture, positioning, bodily orientation, eye contact, gesture and touching (these, Robertson explains, focus or intensify communication between people); and *relaxation*, by which Robertson means an asymmetrical positioning of the limbs, openness of arm position, a sideways lean and tilt of the head or, if seated, a more reclined position. A higher-status person assumes a more relaxed posture than a lower-status one.

BEHAVIOURAL PROBLEMS WITH SOME ETHNIC-MINORITY STUDENTS

That there are differences in the incidence, form and extent of behavioural problems among students differentiated in terms of their ethnicity is indisputable. Moreover, a review of the research literature on multicultural classrooms over the past twenty years or so suggests that references to 'behavioural problems with *some* ethnic minority students' are almost invariably concerned with students of Afro-Caribbean origin.

Whilst an adequate explanation of the complex interrelationships of structural, interpersonal and personal factors that account for misbehaviour in specific ethnic minority groups has yet to be made, the research literature points to some issues which are of crucial importance to beginning (and, indeed, experienced) teachers alike. We deal with two vital areas.

Earlier in the chapter we made reference to the work of Fontana and Saunders, both of whom sought to relate socio-economic and cultural differences to the incidence of classroom misbehaviour. Saunders's concern, for example, was with *antipathy to school*, displayed by those students for whom school seemed irrelevant in terms of their future life chances. Such antipathy brings to mind the language teacher in Carrington's study of Hillsview Comprehensive School[95] reporting a conversation with one of her older black students: 'Miss, – you're wasting your time, – School doesn't matter. I shan't get a job. – I don't want to know.'

Fontana's focus, *inter alia*, was directed towards socio-economic factors that relate to poor attitudes and student underachievement. A recent appraisal[96] of Department of Social Security data, exploring the relationship between poverty and inequality and using indices such as population density, overcrowding, non-white children, levels of benefit payments and infant mortality, concluded that 'inequality in our society is clearly growing.... In terms of real income, the poor have got relatively poorer and the rich have got relatively richer between 1979 and 1991/2.' To *structural factors* which point to associations between, on the one hand, poor attitudes, poor behaviour and poor achievement in school and on the other, worsening socio-economic circumstances must be added *interpersonal factors* that impinge directly on teacher–student relationships in schools.

Carrington's case study of Hillsview Comprehensive pulls no punches in its dissection of the channelling processes initiated by teachers that directed students of Afro-Caribbean origin away from academic pursuits and towards sporting activities, 'twentieth century gladiators for white Britain' as Carrington observes. Teachers were ingenuously open about their differential treatment of black students: 'I'm reluctant to push black kids too hard.... I frequently indulge them ...' 'Inevitably, I'm more lenient towards blacks.... I try to avoid confrontation.' Some Hillsview teachers, moreover, operated with well-documented pejorative stereotypes of Afro-Caribbean students whose behaviour, academic abilities and parent cultures they viewed in a negative manner. There were several occasions in interview when teachers referred to the students as 'lacking in ability', 'unable to concentrate', 'indolent', 'insolent', 'aggressive' and 'disrespectful of authority'.

Green's study[97] is more disturbing still. After 3,000 observations of teacher–student interactions were recorded *in each classroom*, Green then invited the seventy participating teachers to complete an attitude inventory in which a twenty-five-item prejudice scale had been 'buried'. Only after identifying twelve highly intolerant teachers did Green return to examine the interaction data. He found that *highly intolerant teachers*:

- gave significantly *less time to accepting the feelings* of the children of Afro-Caribbean origin;
- gave *only minimal praise* to children of Afro-Caribbean origin;
- gave significantly *less attention to the ideas* of children of Afro-Caribbean origin;
- gave significantly *more authoritative directions* to children of Afro-Caribbean origin;

- gave significantly *less time* to children of Afro-Caribbean origin *to initiate contributions to class discussions.*

The Carrington and Green studies reveal teacher behaviour that is highly injurious to the personalities, the self-esteem and the life chances of the students involved. Whereas, perhaps, the Hillsview data reflect an 'unintentional racism'[98] on the part of some members of staff, the evidence from Green's study is unequivocal in its mapping of systematic racist behaviour on the part of certain teachers. Whatever its origin, such unjust behaviour towards any student is totally unacceptable in today's classrooms. It is worthwhile, at this point, to reiterate some 'ethical absolutes' which have already appeared in our earlier discussions of equal opportunities and classroom management and control. It is a requirement of student teachers to:

- support and stretch *all* students in the learning process;
- remove the stigma of failure from students;
- treat students as individuals of equal worth regardless of gender, race or background;
- celebrate the notion of difference and promote positive images of a diverse populace;
- counter stereotypes, discrimination, bias and misperceptions;
- identify how to break down discriminatory practices.

Finally, lest readers think that what has been reiterated above is unnecessarily hortative, a recent study[99] involving intending teachers on university and college of higher education courses found that whilst the majority of student teachers recognised and wholeheartedly disowned overt, racist behaviour on the part of the practising teacher in the video presentations that they witnessed, there was a minority of intending teachers who singularly failed to recognise many offensive and discriminatory actions in the lifelike portrayals of management and control problems in ethnically mixed secondary school classrooms.

CLASS MANAGEMENT ON TEACHING PRACTICE

We close this chapter on management and control with reference to a study by Wragg and Dooley[100] into student teachers' class management. The research was undertaken in two parts. The first part, a pilot study, involved fifty-six case studies of student teachers thought to be good or poor at handling classes. The subsequent main enquiry involved 204 lessons given by thirty-four PGCE students at six Nottingham comprehensive schools, three in the city and three in other parts of the county.[101]

With regard to the pilot study, the tentative conclusions indicated that effective managers were well prepared, anticipated difficulties, and reacted quickly to disruption rather than allowing it to escalate. Good management

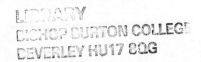

Box 80 Common forms of misbehaviour

Most common forms of misbehaviour observed	
Misbehaviour	*Percentage*
excessively noisy talk	38
non-verbal behaviour not appropriate to tasks	24
irrelevant talk	23
inappropriate use of materials/equipment	20
illicit eating/drinking	12
movement at the wrong time	11
fidgeting	9
provoking laughter (derision, not shared humour)	6
teacher interrupted (excluding normal exchanges)	5
physical aggression	2
damage to materials/equipment	1.5
disobeying teacher	1.5
cheating	1.5
pupil insulted	1.5
teacher insulted	1

Source Wragg and Dooley

was often executed with briskness and verbal deftness. It was also noted that successful student teachers usually arrived at the classroom before the students, personally admitted them into the room, established a presence, and were seen to be in charge in an unobtrusive way. Conversely, unsuccessful managers tried to start their lessons before attention had been secured, and were unable to deal effectively with concomitant distractions like late arrivals.

With regard to the main study, analysis of the 204 lessons taught by the thirty-four PGCE students revealed that most acts of deviance occurring in their lessons were of a minor nature, as the authors say, 'typically the buzz of chatter punctuated by requests or commands to desist'. Few of the student teachers observed had serious discipline problems, and hardly any examples of serious disruption occurred, although many lessons became mildly chaotic and suffered from sustained minor deviance. Deviance most often occurred with 13- and 14-year-old students and then during transitions or changes of activity, particularly when movement was involved.

Box 80 lists the most common forms of misbehaviour observed. In each

Box 81

Student teachers' reactions to misbehaviour

Reaction	*Percentage*
order to cease	61
reprimand	25
statement of rule	24
proximity (moving towards pupils)	20
involving pupils in their work	16
threat	10
facial expression	8
dramatic pause	7
gesture	5
pupil moved	3
humour	2
touch	1
ridicule	1
punishment	1

Source Wragg and Dooley

case they are percentages of all 1,020 segments in which the particular piece of misbehaviour occurred. Student teachers' reactions to misbehaviour are recorded in Box 81. They are expressed as percentages of the 543 lesson segments in which a response to deviancy was noted.

Chapter 15

The classroom environment and situational factors

INTRODUCTION

So far in this part we have looked at some of the more specifically pedagogical aspects of the teacher's work and how they affect the pupil: primary and secondary approaches to teaching, mixed-ability teaching, equal opportunities and management and control, for example. In this section we examine some of the features that make up the classroom environment and some situational factors that impinge on effective teaching and learning. As regards situational factors in school learning, there are literally countless factors operating singly or interactively which impinge directly or indirectly on the student teacher's and students' efforts throughout a lesson. Indeed, the *lack* of effort on the part of student teacher or student could be seen as one such factor, and obviously a very important one. Even if, through some miracle, it were possible to identify all these factors, it would be quite impossible to discuss them all in a book of this nature. What we have done, therefore, is to select those that we feel the reader ought especially to be aware of. We begin with a review of the *physical environment*, and go on to consider successively the *emotional environment, teacher–pupil relationships, the use of modelling* and then *teachers' attitudes and expectations*.

THE PHYSICAL ENVIRONMENT

The physical environment is the framework for learning and as it can contribute to either promoting or impeding learning, it must be under the student teacher's control as far as possible. Indeed, the physical environment suitably ordered makes up part of the student teacher's *resources power* and thus contributes to his or her *personal power*.[1] We therefore recommend that the student teacher devotes meticulous care to the planning and organisation of his or her teaching environment, for his or her authority and power as a classroom performer derive in part from such preparation.

What does the ordering and controlling of one's physical environment entail? For both the traditional classroom and open-plan areas, a multiplicity of factors are involved, but chiefly it entails arranging, organising or utilising satisfactorily such matters as seating and layout, teaching aids, equipment for practical lessons, audio-visual apparatus, activity corners and areas, notice boards, blackboards and display tables. Thoroughly organising one's needs in this respect helps to establish an environment conducive to learning.

The importance of the classroom environment has been stressed by Marland,[2] who writes, 'It would be fair to say that the physical impression of the classroom can be an ally or an enemy in teaching, and part of the art of the classroom is to *use* the room itself. Its arrangement can contribute to the control, the learning, the relationships and the pleasure of working together.'

A student teacher on teaching practice is not often in a position to make significant changes to a room. He or she is only in the school for a comparatively short period of time and even then may not have a regular base from which to operate, having to move from room to room (particularly in a secondary school). For the qualified teacher in a permanent post, however, it is highly desirable that he or she gives evidence of 'ownership' of a room. This may take the form of changes in decoration, how facilities for display are used, lighting and classroom layout. Teachers' problems can sometimes be traced to such factors, as Watkins and Wagner[3] observe: 'On occasions of giving assistance to teachers experiencing difficulty it is not unusual to see them conveying the message that they have little control or ownership of the situation's physical features, let alone other aspects.' As they advise: 'considerations of display, colour, and even lighting can lead to easy changes which affect pupil behaviour.'

The competent student teacher, then, must have the classroom environment – just as much as the students and the content of lessons – well under control, or as much under control as is practically possible in the circumstances. Moving to different rooms for different lessons will, of course, minimise this, though one must do the best one can in the circumstances. We now consider three factors which are particularly relevant in this connection.

Preparation – equipment

It is especially important for the student teacher in an unfamiliar school to find out what equipment is available and where it is located. Many schools have the following: a radio, television, video recorder, record player, tape recorder, computers of manifold types, cassette tape recorder, microphone, loud-speakers, movie projector, camcorder, strip projector and an episcope. The student teacher should also find out where in the school these may be used. Particular items, like a cassette tape recorder, may be in great demand, so the student teacher should plan well ahead and book equipment he or she needs in good time.

Specialist teachers should get to know what is available in their subjects. Thus, a geographer may want to know what the school has in the way of atlases, wall maps and facilities for duplicating; the mathematics teacher may want to use calculators and computers; the music teacher will be interested in the content of the school's music library, the range of musical instruments and texts; and the PE specialist will need to find out what equipment, apparatus and facilities are available. Science teachers will want to know what equipment there is for experiments and practical lessons. It is particularly important where class practicals are involved to check that there is sufficient equipment and that it will be available when required. In schools where the laboratory technician is normally responsible for preparing equipment for teacher and pupil use, it is usually necessary to give him or her two or three days' notice of whatever will be required.

Primary teachers will want to know what basic materials are available for their use, and the range of additional material for various activities. West[4] has compiled lists of equipment and material the primary teacher can expect to draw upon. For money transactions in maths, for example, he lists plastic money, paper money, real money, used stamps, PO counterfoils, used bus tickets, price lists from local shops, bill heads for shipping, charts of wrappers of priced goods and charts of coin values. Further information may be found from the same source, pages 43–7.

Notice boards

Notice boards and display boards are to be found in most classrooms and at various strategic points around the school. Apart from their basic function in communicating important information – timetables, class lists, fire regulations, etc. – they may also be used to display aids for learning, students' work and exhibitions arranged by the students or teachers – pictures, clippings, posters, etc.

A student teacher on arriving at his or her school can quickly discover the notice boards and assess the standards of presentation and maintenance. If inexperienced in such matters, he or she can find ideas and inspiration for the upkeep of the boards for which he or she will be responsible by studying those in the school that have been well kept. Two important criteria are *freshness* and *relevance*.

We offer a few suggestions by way of a beginning:

1   Ask your class teacher to allocate you an area of display space for your exclusive use during the practice.
2   Divide it up so that a smallish part may be reserved for the students' personal interests and their own contributions. The larger part of the display space can be used for material relating to your own teaching – information, charts, diagrams for a project, for example. You can reserve another small part for a representative sample of the students' work. This last section should be changed frequently.

3   Take particular care with the labelling of the various exhibits. Bold, eye-catching lettering is desirable.
4   Information is not simply stuck on the board to be forgotten. Refer to and use whatever is displayed in the course of your lessons. Marland[5] suggests that the final minutes of a lesson can be given over to questions and answers in connection with work or information thus presented. Alternatively, a class can be sent in groups to do a worksheet based on a display.
5   Encourage the class to share in the maintenance of the display and notice boards.

You should remember that visitors to a classroom – and especially those of particular significance to you, like supervising tutors, school mentors and external examiners – sometimes form their earliest and often lasting impressions of the student teacher from the appearance of displays. And of course the same holds for those display tables for which the student teacher is responsible. Bear in mind that notice boards and other means of display reflect something of the philosophy of education that prevails in the classroom.

Seating

It is the view of experienced teachers that careful attention to seating arrangements contributes as effectively as any other aspect of classroom management and control to overall success with a class. Although we fully realise that in most cases the student teacher must accept and use the classroom seating as he or she finds it, nevertheless we feel it important to establish one or two points of particular relevance.

First, the teacher's desk or table. In the past this was often positioned on a raised platform in the front centre position. As there is no longer the same need for it to occupy such a dominating location, teachers have experimented with different placings and many consider that for most purposes a front side position is probably the best (or even that it might not be necessary to have a 'teacher's desk'). A desk placed at a front side position meets the criteria suggested by Marland: (1) all the students can see the student teacher when he or she is at the desk; and (2) the desk is clearly visible from the door. He further notes that he prefers to have this desk in a position which is easy for the student teacher to get at and round, which is adjacent to the best focal position for board work and questions, and which allows him or her to observe the class when helping an individual pupil.

The second point of relevance concerns the students' desks or tables. As Watkins and Wagner note:[6]

The layout of furniture and the arrangement of seating carries a number of potential messages about expectations of work patterns, who is to be attended to, who work partners are, to indicate what sort of learner the pupil is expected to be ... The messages conveyed concern the activity level which is expected of pupils, the amount of interaction which is expected between them, the types of tasks they will tackle and, by implication, who is to be responsible for the learning.

Arrangements will largely be determined by the age and needs of the students. Formal rows will give 14-year-olds elbow room and privacy for individual work; four tables arranged as a rectangle will permit four to six 8-year-olds to work together. While recognising that there is rarely an ideal layout, Marland suggests that an optimum one is worth striving for, yet at the same time preserving a reasonable amount of circulatory space. One feature to be avoided in this connection is what Watkins and Wagner term traffic 'hot spots' which can generate unwelcome behaviour.

Readers should remember not to attempt to teach or address a class of students arranged in groups without first ensuring that where necessary chairs have been turned to face the student teacher. One often sees students uncomfortably screwing their necks round to attend to the student teacher while their chairs continue to face away from him or her.

Should students be allowed to sit where they like? Or should their seating be determined by the student teacher? Although having a secondary or middle school classroom in mind, Marland strongly recommends that the initial seating of a class be done by the student teacher and to a plan devised by him or her. He further suggests arranging a class alphabetically, a procedure which is simple, defensible, and which has practical advantages, one of which is apparent where mixed classes are involved.

Two additional points with regard to the importance of seating will be mentioned. The first concerns what to do with spare seats in a situation where there are more places than students. Marland advises:

> I strongly recommend that you exploit the spare seats as buffers to improve the psychological separation of pupils or groups ... It might be wise with one class to keep the back row, the trouble-maker's instinctive chair-swinging row, empty. In another class you may distribute the empty chairs here and there, merely to thin the seating out. You may use your knowledge of the pupils in another class to decide that Gary or Elaine is best left sitting in isolation.

The second point arises from mixed-ability classes, in which the arranging of seating is even more important than in classes of like ability. Mixed-ability grouping involves individual work, group work and sometimes class teaching. Whatever the need, planned seating can assist in achieving the appropriate learning situation and educational outcomes. As Marland says:

> The greater fluidity of mixed ability teaching implies the need for the control that comes from controlled seating. The seating plan, then, is a

method of assisting the psychological insulation of crowded pupils, and can sometimes be subtly manipulated to separate certain individuals or leave others entirely on their own.

We hope that in the light of all this readers will be a little more sensitive to the importance of seating arrangements and give it high priority in their consideration of the classroom environment.

THE EMOTIONAL ENVIRONMENT

Important as the physical characteristics of the classroom are, the learning environment is more than just the sum of them. It also embraces such features as the student teacher's voice, his or her attitudes and expectations, belief system, humour, techniques of control, favoured leadership styles and the use of praise. These contribute to what may be described as the *emotional environment*. This may be even more important than the physical environment, for not even the most desirable ordering and use of the physical environment can compensate for an impoverished emotional one.

We will now look briefly at some of these factors determining or contributing to a classroom's emotional tone.

Voice

The student teacher's voice is of considerable importance in establishing emotional tone in a classroom. If it is relaxed, natural and mainly conversational in manner, it will assist in creating a relaxed, tension-free atmosphere favourable to interaction and learning. Further, the students' voices will in turn tend to reflect similar qualities. Conversely, the emotional tone will be adversely affected by an anxious, high-pitched voice which will tend to generate a correspondingly tense atmosphere.

It is mainly the non-verbal aspects of speech – timbre, pitch, manner and speed of delivery, smoothness and flow – which contribute for good or ill to the classroom atmosphere.

Attitudes and expectations

The part played by a student teacher's attitudes and expectations in the educational outcomes of a lesson is examined later in this section. It is important to note that they also assist in establishing the 'feeling tone' (caring atmosphere) of a classroom. A student teacher who habitually maintains a cheerful, optimistic frame of mind, who expects the best from his or her pupils, and who is able to appraise the students' abilities and efforts realistically will be well rewarded, not least in the kind of atmosphere produced.

Teachers' beliefs, classroom atmosphere and students' behaviour

A further important determinant of a classroom's emotional tone concerns the teacher's professional orientation. A study by Harvey, Prather, White and Hoffmeister[7] replicating earlier studies found that teachers' belief systems determine the general tone or atmosphere of the classroom, and that this in turn affects the children in significant ways. Thus, teachers manifesting greater *abstractness* (i.e. those who were more resourceful, less dictatorial and less punitive) were associated with more educationally preferable behaviour in the children. By contrast, teachers having more *concrete* belief systems (i.e. less resourceful, more dictatorial and more punitive) affected children's performance less favourably.

Briefly then, the results show that the belief systems of teachers do affect their overt classroom behaviour and that this in turn is significantly related to the children's behaviour.

Humour

Another indispensable feature contributing to a favourable classroom atmosphere is humour. In the well-structured, purposeful organisation of an effective classroom, there will be many opportunities for humour. Its manifold functions are more or less self-evident: it relaxes tension, helps establish natural relationships, facilitates learning and is of great value as a means of restoring sanity to a classroom after a disciplinary incident. Peters[8] remarks: 'Humour is a great catalyst in a classroom; for if people can laugh together they step out of the self-reference cast by age, sex and position.' Marland's advice on humour bears the stamp of experience:

> A joke goes a long way. Try to be light-hearted whenever you feel up to it. Try to chivvy recalcitrant pupils jokingly rather than by being indignant ... Be willing to make jokes at your own expense, and to laugh at your own foibles. Teachers' jokes don't have to be very good to be nevertheless highly acceptable.

He goes on to warn young teachers with high ideals and considerable theoretical understanding from taking themselves, their responsibilities and their students too seriously. Their 'humourless indignation' and 'sad intensity' may alienate their charges.

Leadership styles and teaching methods

The emotional ambience is very considerably affected by the kind of leadership style a teacher provides and the methods of teaching he or she adopts. One of the earliest attempts to observe and control objectively the climate variable in group life was White and Lippitt's.[9] Working with boys' clubs, they demonstrated the influence of leadership style on group life, its social-emotional climate, and productivity, findings which have strong implications for teachers and education. Two of White and Lippitt's major conclusions were: (1) that different styles of leadership behaviour produce differing social climates and differing group and individual behaviours; and (2) that group members in a democratic social climate were more friendly to each other, showed more group-mindedness, were more work-minded, showed greater initiative and had a higher level of frustration tolerance than members in groups governed by either autocratic or *laissez-faire* leadership styles.

More recent classroom research in America indicates that teachers who have an *indirect* influence on children (i.e. those who accept the 'feeling tone' of the students in a non-threatening manner; who praise and encourage students' efforts; who accept and use students' ideas; and who ask questions) create a more favourable emotional tone than those having a *direct* influence (i.e. those who tend to lecture students; who act in an authoritarian manner; who give directions; and who are unduly critical).

Although *indirect* influences contribute to the 'warmth' of a classroom, research shows that most teachers adopt *direct*, traditional approaches, and that classrooms are neither 'warm' nor 'cold', but primarily neutral in tone.

Self-esteem

Self-esteem is generally seen as an important correlate of educational and scholastic achievement. It is also an important contributory factor to the emotional tone of the classroom and it is from this perspective that we briefly consider the concept here.

Self-esteem has been defined by Lawrence[10] as the individual's evaluation of the discrepancy between his self-image and his ideal self. He describes it as an affective process and as such is a measure of the extent to which the individual cares about the discrepancy. Since high self-esteem is going to improve the emotional ambience of a classroom, it is in the student teacher's best interests to enhance and develop this factor in individual students mainly through fostering suitable interpersonal relationships and providing opportunities for success. In a series of projects which took place over a number of years, Lawrence found evidence that teachers can enhance self-esteem both through their day-to-day contacts with the students and through their teaching methods. He identified a number of factors that need to be borne in mind by the teacher consciously setting out to enhance self-esteem in his or her students. We summarise them thus:

1 *Teacher self-esteem*: A teacher with high self-esteem is likely to engender high self-esteem in his or her students.

2 *Desirable personal characteristics*: Originally stressed by Carl Rogers, these are:
Acceptance: This means being non-judgemental with respect to the student and accepting his or her personality as it is.
Genuineness: This means being a 'real person' and not hiding behind a professional mask. Being spontaneous rather than defensive.
Empathy: This means being able to appreciate what it feels like to be another person and involves the challenging task of 'listening to feelings'.

3 *Communication*: This takes two forms:
Verbal: Verbal messages can enhance or reduce self-esteem in a student. To achieve the desired enhancement of self-esteem, the student teacher will need to use words and phrases that are encouraging, praising, valuing, and generally relaxing.
Non-verbal: Non-verbal behaviour is particularly powerful in this context, students being extremely sensitive to such signals. Body posture, body orientation, eye contact, pauses in speech, tone, speed of delivery, gesture, can all be used to indicate the extent to which a person likes or dislikes, feels involved or uninvolved, feels superior or inferior to another.

4 *Preferred teaching style*: Self-esteem can be enhanced more effectively when a teacher uses a teaching style of his or her choice.

5 *Everyday contacts*: A self-evident truth is well supported by research. Of all the factors considered, a student teacher's everyday contacts with students have most effect on self-esteem. Desirably, personal contacts should be made each day – a smile, a word of praise or encouragement can sometimes be sufficient.

The following comments on teacher–student relationships will also be highly pertinent to self-esteem.

TEACHER–STUDENT RELATIONSHIPS

Good relationships between teachers and students are vitally important in the give and take of classroom life: where they exist there is less likelihood of difficulties arising. 'Teacher–pupil relations' is a fairly general term and, as Evans points out,[11] covers such topics as the influence of teachers on the immediate behaviour of their students and on their intellectual and social development, the contribution which teachers make to the mental health and adjustment of students, the students' likes and dislikes with regard to their teacher, and the effects on the teachers of daily contact with their students.

At the heart of effective teacher–pupil relations lies *respect for persons*. Dawney[12] considers that this involves 'treating children as individuals, recognizing and valuing their singular characteristics'. She goes on:

For a child to develop and function as a person, he needs to be treated as someone who is important in his own right and not just as a member of a category. He needs help in developing the kind of self-concept that allows him to regard himself as of value. To treat children as persons in their own right involves regarding them as responsible for their own actions and therefore having some control over what they do.

She warns us, however, against showing an uninformed and uncritical respect towards students. This would be inappropriate, as she explains:

It would be misguided for a teacher to let his respect for a child's point of view prevent him from showing his pupils what moral and intellectual standards imply. Constructive criticism of a pupil helps him to develop the sort of self-image and self-esteem that enable him to develop as an autonomous being, and thus has an important part to play in the judgements we make of him and to him.

Many factors contributing to effective teacher–student relationships, e.g. the personality of the students, are clearly beyond the control of the teacher and have therefore to be taken as 'given' when interactions occur. None the less, as Kutnick[13] observes, effective relationships do not just 'happen'. Teachers must plan for particular relationships and not leave their occurrence to the 'hidden curriculum of everyday life in the classroom'. One factor that it does lie within the student teacher's power to manipulate is what has been termed 'non-verbal immediacy behaviours'.[14] These signal that the initiator, namely the student teacher, is approachable and available for communication. In that they thus communicate interpersonal closeness and warmth, they can contribute positively to relationships. Indeed, research on immediacy constructs suggests that they can be a positive force in the classroom, particularly in bringing about better teacher–pupil relationships.

The article by Andersen and Andersen reviews a whole range of non-verbal immediacy behaviours in the context of the classroom. They include the following:

Proxemics or the use of interpersonal space and distance. There are two aspects here: physical distance and bodily orientation.

In the case of physical distance, many student teachers fail to establish interpersonal closeness with a class because they remain physically remote in the sense that they stand at the front of the classroom or sit at a desk. Confident, effective student teachers use the entire room and move among students.

As regards orientation of the speaker, more 'immediacy' is communicated when the student teacher *faces* the class. As the authors say:

Many teachers do not fully face their class when teaching. They hide behind desks, podiums and tables, and often continuously write on the blackboard, with their backs to the class. Not only does this reduce the immediacy between teachers and their classes, it also removes any visual communication between them.

Kinetics or communication by body movement. Four aspects are relevant here – smiling, head nods, bodily relaxation and gestural behaviour – though a very full analysis of this is provided by Neill and Caswell.[15]

One of the most effective immediacy cues is smiling. Research shows that smiling produces substantial positive therapeutic effects in relationships, including an increase in interpersonal acceptance. As Andersen and Andersen say, 'Teachers who frequently smile are communicating immediacy in one of the easiest and most powerful ways. Pupils at all levels are sensitive to smiles as a sign of positive affect and warmth.'

Head nods are another effective means of indicating immediacy, especially when used by a listener in response to a speaker. When used by a teacher to his or her class they provide reinforcement and indicate that the teacher is listening to and understanding what they say.

Bodily relaxation communicates immediacy by indicating freedom from stress and anxiety. It has been found that more 'immediate' teachers are more relaxed, whereas tense and anxious teachers communicate negative attitudes to their students who perceive them as cold and inaccessible.

Gestures, particularly hand and arm movements, communicate interest, warmth and involvement. In these respects they contribute positively to both interpersonal transactions and teaching.

Oculesics is the study of messages sent by the eyes. Eye contact is an invitation to communicate and a powerful immediacy cue.[16] As we saw earlier, student teachers who use eye contact can more easily monitor the behaviour of their classes. They can also communicate more warmth and involvement to their students. The authors advise that student teachers should position themselves so that they can and do establish eye contact with every student in the class, warning that immediacy cannot be successfully established by a student teacher in the absence of eye contact.

In thus making themselves more accessible by incorporating these skills into their classroom behaviour, student teachers are in a position to strengthen the relations they have with their students. Other practical ways of building up relationships are suggested in Box 82.

Another important factor in helping to establish good relationships and another that also lies within the teacher's control is that of teaching and learning styles. In this respect, the importance of *co-operative learning* must be stressed. According to Kutnick,[17] 'It has been shown to promote more effective mixed ability teaching, inter-racial friendships, sensitivity between pupils, helping, the integration of handicapped children, and more.' As he later explains, putting students into groups enables them to learn very effectively with collective reinforcement – more effectively than in individualistic and competitive reward situations. He considers that co-operative

Box 82

Teacher–student relationships

Relationships can be established in many different ways. Teachers who
have harmonious relationships with their classes often establish and cement
these in a number of contexts by occasionally or regularly doing, among
other things, some of the following:
Out of class

crossing the yard or walking down corridors talking to students;
chatting casually to groups or individuals during breaks or lunch hours;
looking out for quieter or more difficult students to talk to away from the
classroom;
showing interest in extra-curricular activities such as clubs, sports, plays,
music, etc.
meeting parents at parents' evening or other school events;
knowing the school's catchment area and understanding the way of life of
the people who work and live in it;
taking an interest, in a discreet way, in the social problems encountered
by students;
being familiar with and understanding the leisure and recreational
pursuits of the age group.

In class

talking to students in a friendly way as they enter the room;
monitoring students' work on an *individual* basis;
learning and using students' names;
sharing jokes and sharing good humour;
creating a sense of collective pride in the work which students do.

Source Wragg[18]

learning should become a dominant learning style because of the social and
emotional developments that ensue. Some of the benefits of co-operative
learning are listed in Box 83. These findings and recommendations will be of
particular relevance to primary teachers, for whom the opportunities for
organising co-operative learning are probably greater.

MODELLING

Good and Brophy[19] have noted that many things may be learned in
classrooms without deliberate instruction by the teacher or deliberate practice
by the learner; and that such observations are supported by a growing body
of experimental evidence. The learner only needs to see a particular behaviour
demonstrated by another person before imitating it himself, sometimes
consciously, sometimes not. The person who demonstrates the behaviour is

Box 83

Some benefits of co-operative learning

1   Inter-racial school friendships were shown to develop in heterogeneously structured groups. These friendships were generally reciprocated, and minority-group academic performance correspondingly improved.
2   Co-operative learning helped to overcome interactional barriers in groups including mixed-ability and physically handicapped children.
3   Children's self-esteem was enhanced in a majority of studies.
4   Children generally increased their within-classroom friendships, with corresponding increases in their feelings of altruism and social perspective-taking.

Source adapted from Kutnick[20]

called *the model* and the form of learning, *modelling*.

Modelling can be a most useful device for the student teacher. Many skills, for example, can be learned more easily through observation and imitation than by trying to understand and respond to only verbal explanation and instruction. This is especially true for younger children, whose abilities to follow detailed verbal instructions are limited. The process of modelling may thus be seen as a means of enabling a child to re-assemble components of behaviour he or she already possesses into new and alternative combinations.

The pervasiveness of modelling

Most teachers recognise the value of prepared demonstrations as teaching tools, especially in practical subjects. However, they are usually less aware of the more general modelling effects that may occur incidentally in the classroom, and are therefore less likely to take advantage of them through deliberate, planned modelling behaviour. There is thus a need for teachers to know that modelling effects can occur at any time.

In this connection, it is important to remember that if students detect discrepancies between what the student teacher says and what he or she actually does, they will ignore what is said and be affected much more by what is done. Further, if they see discrepancies between what he or she says he or she expects and what he or she allows, they will tend to be influenced by what is allowed. This aspect of modelling has important consequences for discipline, especially for the student teacher, who, having once established a particular standard of behaviour, should insist that it is maintained.

What is learned from models

Good and Brophy suggest that exposure to a model can result in either or both of two responses by the learner: *imitation* and *incidental learning*. Imitation, perhaps the more obviously useful for the student teacher, is the simpler: the learner observes the model's behaviour and then imitates it, making it his or her own. For example, a class will tend to respond to tactful and sympathetic treatment in the same vein; likewise, sarcasm or ridicule on the part of the student teacher invariably produces a negative response from a class.

Incidental learning is a more subtle form of modelling than imitation. The learner observes the model's behaviour in specific situations and on the basis of these observations makes inferences about the model's beliefs, attitudes, values and personality. These inferences may subsequently affect a student's own behaviour.

Factors affecting what is learned from observing a model

The amount and kind of learning that results from observing others depends on a number of factors, one of the more important of which is *the situation*. Modelling effects are far more likely to occur in *new* situations where the expected behaviour of both the student teacher and learner is unclear. When such ambiguous situations occur in the classroom, the potential for modelling will be considerable, especially at the beginning of a new academic year or, in the case of the student teacher, at the start of a teaching practice. As a result of such early contacts with their student teacher, then, students will make inferences about him or her and decide whether they like him or her; they will form views of what kind of person he or she is and how they ought to respond to him or her. Further, the student teacher's early behaviour will contribute to establishing the emotional and intellectual climate of the classroom. It is thus vital for the student teacher to model appropriate behaviour from his or her first day in the school. Opportunities to teach through modelling will be greater at this time because many things will still be fluid and ambiguous. Later, when both student teacher and class settle into predictable routines, it will be more difficult to bring about changes.

A second factor affecting what is learned from modelling is *the personality of the teacher*. A warm and enthusiastic teacher whom the students like will be imitated by them. There is the possibility that some of the students will adopt, or be influenced by, his or her attitudes and beliefs; and they may imitate his or her behaviour. However, students will be less likely to imitate a student teacher whom they dislike or do not respect, particularly in the sense of adopting or conforming to his or her ideals.

Teaching through modelling

To illustrate the value of modelling as a teaching device, two areas of behaviour will be briefly described which exemplify the two kinds of response identified above, namely, imitation and incidental learning.

Imitation will be illustrated by the use of demonstrations in the classroom. These must be the most obvious means of using modelling as a teaching aid before a group. Many skills can be taught best by demonstration, especially with younger children. Some skills can be demonstrated with little or no verbalisation. However, demonstrations tend to be more effective when accompanied by some verbalisation. Demonstrations usually provide examples of more general principles that a teacher wants his or her students to learn. Thus, to maximise transfer value, a demonstration should not only show a student the physical movements involved in performing a task, it should also include explanations of the thinking that lies behind the movements.

Research shows that people tend to leave out important pieces of information when explaining or demonstrating something, assuming that the listener sees the situation in the same way they do. The expert instructor, however, breaks down a task into step-by-step operations, assuming little or no knowledge on the part of the learner. Each component or part of the task is identified and placed in context. The learner can thus master one step at a time.

Thinking aloud at each step in this way is crucial when the task is primarily cognitive and the physical movements involved are relatively less important or negligible. A task such as making an incision will require verbal commentary if the pupil is to understand fully. Where the processes are not verbalised, they will possibly be hidden from the learner.

Teachers not only educate through modelling, they also socialise students by influencing attitudes and values. In other words, they contribute to incidental learning. For example, good teachers model respect for others by treating students politely and pleasantly, and by avoiding behaviour that would cause them to suffer indignities. Many well-intentioned attempts to help students learn appropriate forms of social behaviour in this way are undermined by teachers not modelling the behaviours they would wish to promote. In this connection, Rutter and his colleagues[21] make the following observations:

> Standards of behaviour in school are also set by the behaviour of the staff. There is an extensive research literature which shows that children have a strong tendency to copy the behaviour of other people – especially people in positions of authority whom they like and respect. Moreover, not only do they copy specific behaviours, but they also tend to identify in a more general way with the people whom they follow, and come to adopt what they perceive to be their values and attitudes. This means that pupils are likely to be influenced – either for good or ill – by the models of behaviour

provided by teachers both in the classroom and elsewhere. These will not be restricted to the ways in which teachers treat the children, but may also include the ways staff interact with one another, and how they view the school.

We suggest that the reader considers ways in which he or she can consciously use modelling processes in his or her own work. For example, at a cognitive level, helping students to develop skills in logical thinking and problem-solving; at an attitudinal level, encouraging them to develop an interest in learning for its own sake; at a social level, fostering a favourable group climate; and in a general way, adopting a humane and rational approach to life.

STUDENT TEACHERS' ATTITUDES AND EXPECTATIONS AND THE INFLUENCE THEY EXERT ON CLASSROOM BEHAVIOUR

It is apparent from a commonsense viewpoint that the attitudes and expectations a student teacher holds with respect to the students he or she teaches considerably affect his or her behaviour towards them; and that this in turn influences *their* responses in a variety of ways. There is now a significant body of evidence illustrating the more negative aspects of these observations which is of particular interest to the student teacher.

Studies conducted in the United States, for instance, indicate that students of differing achievement levels were treated differently by their teachers; and that there were important differences in both the *frequency* and *quality* of the contacts between them.[22] Some of the consequences were that high achievers received more opportunity to respond than low achievers. They also tended to ask more questions. Further, teachers waited significantly longer for the more capable students to respond before giving an answer or calling on another student.

The findings disclosed, too, that teachers praised high achievers more than low achievers, the latter being more likely to be criticised for a wrong answer. Teachers also tended to 'give up' more readily with students who did not know, or who answered incorrectly, and this suggests that they expect and demand higher performance from high achievers. Related evidence from these same studies indicates that physically separating poor performers from the rest of the class by regrouping them increases the likelihood of their being treated differently and inappropriately.

There have been a number of studies which reveal that in some situations differential teacher behaviour and expectations affect students' behaviour and achievement. Findings by Douglas[23] and Mackler,[24] for example, show that teachers' expectations about a student's achievement can be affected by factors having little or nothing to do with his or her ability; and that these expectations can determine the student's level of achievement by confining his or her learning opportunities to those available in a particular class. A student who is placed needlessly in a low grade is unlikely to realise his or her potential because teachers do not expect much of him or her and his or her achievement motivation will be affected accordingly.

Good and Brophy suggest a model to demonstrate how teachers' expectations can function as self-fulfilling prophecies; we illustrate this in Box 84. It indicates that the teacher's expectations are not automatically self-fulfilling. To become so, they must be translated into consistent behaviour patterns.

Box 84

Teachers' expectations as self-fulfilling prophecies

1   The teacher expects specific behaviour and achievement from particular children.
2   Because of his different expectations, he behaves differently towards the different children.
3   The teacher's treatment tells each child what behaviours and achievements the teacher expects from him and this in turn affects his self-concept, achievement motivation and level of aspiration.
4   If the teacher's treatment is consistent over time, and if the child does not actively resist or change in some way, it will tend to shape his achievements and behaviour.
5   With time, the child's achievements and behaviour will conform more and more closely to what was originally expected of him.

Source Good and Brophy[25]

The importance of these and similar findings for the student teacher is self-evident, for his or her success in the classroom is dependent in part on the adoption of suitable attitudes and expectations even though, as a student teacher, he or she may only be in school for relatively short periods of time. Because students are individuals, it is natural for student teachers to form different attitudes and expectations concerning them, and as long as these are accurate and appropriate, they will be helpful in planning ways to meet the students' needs. However, they must be constantly reviewed and evaluated to ensure that they are modified in response to changes in the student's behaviour. Unless a student teacher is prepared to monitor his or her view of a student in this way, he or she may get caught in a 'vicious circle of failure'.

As Good and Brophy observe, attitudes and expectations may be a teacher's allies if properly maintained and used. However, as Lawrence[26] has pointed out, although a teacher may influence a student to behave in ways which the teacher expects, this will only occur when the relationship between them is a close one. The expectation factor therefore does not operate in all circumstances. Nevertheless, teachers need to be aware of what is possible in this respect and act accordingly.

In conclusion, one further point of interest may be added which again stresses the reciprocity of the relationship and it is this: a student will tend to fulfil the positive expectations *of a teacher whom he respects*. It is therefore incumbent upon the student teacher to strive to earn respect from the outset.

Part IV

Assessment, record-keeping and records of achievement

Chapter 16

Assessment

Part IV addresses the DFEE competences (see Part I) that are contained within subsections 2.5 (for secondary student teachers) and 2.4 (for primary student teachers). Assessment itself is not a new phenomenon, though the considerable attention it has received in the last decade certainly is. This part sets out a range of issues and practices in assessment and indicates how student teachers might approach it on their teaching practice. It will be argued that, though assessment opportunities should be found in everyday teaching, a degree of rigour should be shown in planning, conducting, recording and reporting assessments. It is useful, first, to know 'where assessment is coming from', to find out why and how it has come to gain the centre ground in education and educational policy-making. This can be seen by examining the international and national contexts. Then a series of key issues for planning assessments is outlined, including the purposes of assessment, the types of assessment, reliability and validity in assessments, methods of gathering assessment data, providing opportunities for assessment to take place and when to assess. Part IV closes with some guidelines for planning, recording and reporting assessments in the context of a formal report and a record of achievement.

INTERNATIONAL CONTEXT OF ASSESSMENT

The attention that has been given to assessment since the 1988 Education Act has been considerable.[1] This is not an issue simply for the UK; launching a new journal about assessment in 1994 the editor opened with the words 'assessment is on the agenda'[2] and then proceeded to document the increasing attention that has been given to assessment world-wide. This is reinforced by Morrison,[3] who charts a list of concerns about the attention that is being given to assessment internationally. On the one hand assessment is being used for educational improvement, increased school effectiveness and curriculum reform, and on the other hand it is being used for political control of teachers, students and curricula,[4] centralised policy-making,[5] narrow accountability,[6] credentialism,[7] educational selection,[8] and the determination of life chances in competitive markets.[9]

Furthermore, assessment is becoming redefined internationally as test-ing,[10] diagnostic and formative assessment are being overtaken by summative examinations. One can detect increasing national control of assessment, an increasing uniformity of styles and practices of assessment, an increasing importance of assessment, an increasing amount of assessment activity, an increasing scope of assessment, and a uniformity of purposes of assessment. Harlen et al.[11] argue that when 'the stakes are high', e.g. when assessment is used for certification, selection, job opportunities, further and higher educa-tion, and accountability, as in the publication of 'league tables' of results of schools' examination successes, or when assessment features highly on a political agenda, then assessment takes the form of public examinations.

At the extreme of uniformity is the *sole* use of national examinations (for example in China[12]) and the *extensive* use of national examinations, for example in the USA,[13] the UK and New Zealand – where the minister of education publishes national achievement standards.[14] At the extreme of devolution is the practice in Austria,[15] where transition to secondary school is contingent upon successful grades which primary school teachers award subjectively, with no moderation across the country. The extent of decentrali-sation and centralisation of assessment is phase-specific; typically the older the student is the more formal and centralised is the assessment system, culminating in the national examinations at the end of a student's secondary school career.

The issue of control, however, is capable of different interpretations. In China control of the contents of examinations, their marking and consequent determination of results is undertaken at a national level. A similar practice exists in the USA, where tests are developed, disseminated and marked by commercial companies.[16] In some countries this degree of control is attenuated in two ways, either by providing a national framework within which teachers' assessments are undertaken, or by combining national and teacher assessments.

Several attempts have been made to combine national examinations with teachers' assessments of students (e.g. Sweden, the United Kingdom, Germany, New Zealand). In the United Kingdom students are compulsorily examined at four points in their school careers – at ages 7, 11, 14 and 16 – with the examination being a composite of national tests and teachers' assessments. In this context procedures for moderation are vital[17] if parity across teachers, schools and regions is to be established. A balance between a uniform, objective national system or framework and a local assessment is an attempt to embrace the notion of parity of standards on the one hand and a person-centred approach to assessment which recognises teachers' pro-fessionalism and the rights and individuality of students on the other.

An international perspective on assessment reveals that the higher the significance which is accorded to assessment, the greater is the use of machine-scorable, closed-format styles of nationally prescribed examinations. The uniform rise in interest in assessment internationally has been met with limited diversity of response. At one extreme is the burgeoning rise of the closed multiple-choice, cloze-procedure style and 'tick-box' forms of assessment which focus on low-level recall of factual knowledge, where content is elevated over skills and where assessment is largely undertaken by written examination. At the other extreme is the open-ended profile of achievements which teachers and students keep and which draws on a variety of assessment evidence – written or otherwise – and which is used to record the whole gamut of achievements of a student (e.g. academic, social, extra-curricular).

The purchase in the UK[18] of optical mark readers which are capable of scanning and processing up to 10,000 forms per hour and the development of machine-scorable examinations in China[19] and the USA[20] which are cheap to administer are indices of the increasing reliance on the 'tick-box', multiple-choice style of assessment. Marks are aggregated to give an overall score, grade or level in a subject (e.g. in the assessment of a child's achievement of the national curriculum in the UK), a process which degrades data and thereby reduces validity[21] (discussed later).

The negative aspects of this style of assessment are legion: the diminishing of education to training students to perform certain prescribed behaviours,[22] the emphasis on outcomes rather than processes, the passive nature of learning, the elevation of trivial, observable, measurable, short-term behaviours over serious, high-order, unmeasurable, creative, person-oriented, open-ended, lifelong aspects of education. The move towards criterion-referenced assessments, whilst it addresses validity in requiring specific, detailed 'evidence' to inform teachers' assessments (rather than their intuitions or hunches), does not herald a move away from behaviourism, rather it provides teachers with more to measure, more to assess.

At the opposite pole of behaviourism is the open-ended profile of students' achievements which is evidenced in records of achievement (ROAs) in the United Kingdom.[23] Here assessments include the 'non-cognitive' qualities of students,[24] grades awarded in formal examination, and a whole prcfile of a student's achievements and awards – curricular and extra-curricular, personal, social, community-based and academic. The National Record of Achievement,[25] for example, sets out the following categories: qualifications and credits, employment history, school achievements (subject by subject), other achievements and experiences (e.g. sporting, clubs, community work, voluntary work). Whilst these have the attraction of being a personalised portfolio which motivates their owners,[26] they carry the risk of building in the prejudices and biases of teachers, of including illegitimate, value-laden and generalised statements[27] and of being insufficiently discriminating in their coverage of the significant and the trivial. Furthermore, completing this open-ended record is time-consuming.

Where education has a high political profile the first casualties in assessment are validity and reliability.[28] For example, the UK has witnessed criterion-referenced assessment data being used not as they were intended – for diagnostic and formative purposes – but normatively to compare school with school in a published 'league table' of results, a practice which is replicated in the USA.[29] Furthermore, the style of assessment has to take account of issues of equal opportunities.[30] For example, in the UK the Department of Education and Science[31] indicated that boys performed better in multiple-choice examinations than girls, and that girls performed better in written work than boys. Goulding[32] indicated that continuous assessment of coursework enabled a truer picture of girls' achievements in mathematics to be presented than that yielded by results on a written examination.

This latter example goes to the very heart of assessment – the questions of the validity and ethics of assessment – as information acquired for one set of purposes, for example motivation, diagnosis and action planning, in fact might be used for another set of purposes, for example selection, competition, employment and unemployment. The provision of an extended profile of achievements and personal qualities might simply provide employers and higher education with more evidence to use *against* a student rather than *for* the student as was intended.

Essentially what is being striven for is a balance between using insufficient and thereby invalid evidence formatively and using so much assessment that it becomes 'interrogation without end'[33] and a means of providing material to hold teachers accountable for aspects of students' development over which they exercise little or no control. The international context of assessment shows its potential dangers, the need to clarify its educational purposes, and the need to take steps to address reliability and validity in formative and diagnostic assessment, i.e. to select the most appropriate types and methods of assessment (discussed later).

UK CONTEXT OF ASSESSMENT

In the United Kingdom one can trace four major contexts of assessment. *First*, assessment results (e.g. the results of students' test scores) are being used to serve the issue of *accountability*. The statutory publication of schools' results in league tables is seen as a way of ensuring that schools are accountable to the 'consumers' of education, principally parents. In this context assessment is but one of a battery of managerialist measures that have been introduced to serve accountability, e.g. teacher appraisal, the Pay and Conditions Act of 1986, and the proposal to introduce performance-related pay.

Secondly, rehearsing the comments made in Part II about the moves to link education and the economy more securely, assessment of academic and vocational aspects of education, coupled with an 'entitlement' curriculum, is seen as a way of 'credentialising' – giving recognised qualifications for – vocational courses in schools and preparation generally for the world of work.

Thirdly, there is a vast political dimension to assessment. Since the 1960s teachers – in particular 'progressive' teachers – have been castigated for falling standards in schools and the diminished economic performance of the country. The series of publications entitled the Black Papers in Education,[34] essentially inflammatory collections of newspaper cuttings held together with short polemical essays, fanned the flames of criticism of teachers. Since then there have been several examples of the increasing attention to assessment: the setting up of the Assessment of Performance Unit and the publication of several reports about standards and curricula (e.g. the Bullock Report on English,[35] the Cockcroft Report on mathematics,[36] the Turner Report on reading,[37] the publications of the IEA (International Association for the Evaluation of Achievement) comparative studies of educational achievements in the developed and developing world[38]). Further, the government's decision not to act on the recommendations of the Higginson Report,[39] which argued for the reform of A-level examinations, reflects a concern that there should be a 'gold standard' of academic qualification for the intellectual elite.

The political context of assessment is further revealed in the increasing control of assessment and examination boards,[40] a feature that was noted in the outline above of international trends in assessment. The 1988 Education Act brought about a centrally controlled curriculum and assessment that was launched with a plethora of documents from the then DFE – a clear indication of the link between the bureaucratisation of education, increased attention to managerialism in education, and the thirst for centralised control that was revealed, among other ways, in the reduction of the power of local education authorities.[41]

Fourthly, there is a clear intention to improve education through reform – hence the title of the Education Reform Act of 1988. This followed the consultation wherein it was asserted that the national curriculum, backed by clear assessment arrangements, would improve standards.[42] The government's desire to incorporate new and developing assessment practices into its plans for education is revealed in:

- its adoption of the principles of profiling and records of achievement[43] and its eventual issue of the National Record of Achievement;[44]
- the use of criterion-referenced assessments in standard assessment tasks (SATs), the GCSE examination and records of achievement;
- the move away from psychometrics and towards a more extended and detailed approach to assessment;[45]
- the extension of moderation activities to include teachers' assessments in a formal programme of assessment of students.

Assessment was a single device or mechanism which could meet all four requirements of the UK context set out above: accountability, credentialism, political agendas and educational reform and improvement. Little wonder it should have received so much attention.

Students were to be assessed at ages 7, 11, 14 and 16 in order to determine where their achievements placed them on a ten-level standard. At age 7 the 'average child' should have reached or nearly reached Level 2; at age 11 the 'average' child should be working in Level 4; at age 14 the 'average' student should have cleared Level 5; at age 16 the 'average' student should have cleared Level 6.[46] Notionally, then, each level would take the 'average' student two years to complete. That this exemplifies a norm-referenced approach using 'average' students (discussed later) betrays the spirit of the original intention for assessments which was that they were to be criterion-referenced. The two types of assessment exist in a relationship of tension with each other, as discussed later.

The original proposals for national assessment suggested that it should be:

1   formative (diagnostic)
2   criterion-referenced
3   moderated
4   related to progression.

However, these quickly ran into difficulties. With regard to (1), formative, diagnostic assessments – where specific information could be gathered to diagnose a student's strengths and weaknesses so that effective planning for future teaching and development could take place – were seen to place an enormous burden on teachers in terms of extensive record-keeping and time to actually undertake the diagnoses.[47] This resulted in many teachers having to set 'holding' tasks for students in the class who were not being assessed, thereby reducing the speed of their learning and risking a lowering of their standards.[48]

With regard to (2), criterion-referenced assessments – where the achievements of a student are assessed relative to predetermined specific criteria[49] – were subverted, in effect, by using the results normatively to compare students and schools (through the publication of 'league tables'). Criterion-referenced assessments generated vast lists of criteria redolent of the long lists of behavioural objectives in the 1960s and 1970s, and became unmanageable.[50] Further, the reliability of the results could be questioned – how could students' achievement of a criterion be assured; what if they achieved the criterion on the day of the assessment and subsequently were unable to achieve it?

Moreover, the intention of criterion-referencing was to provide specific and focused information; however, the data from the assessments were aggregated to give an overall score for each student on each subject – the specificity and utility were lost.[51] This can be illustrated by an example in English. Let us say that I receive a Level 3 for spelling and a Level 5 for reading; if I aggregate the scores to give me an average level I will be awarded a Level 4. But what does this Level 4 really mean; what does it indicate? It is a meaningless number that tells me nothing about my specific achievements in the contributing criteria; I am unable to use the result for subsequent planning – the formative potential of criterion referencing has been lost.

With regard to (3), moderation turned out to be a very costly exercise because of the inclusion of teachers' assessments of students. Ensuring parity of standards of teachers' assessments initially required teachers to be taken out of school for training and agreement trials, though agreement trials now take place in schools.[52]

With regard to (4), progression was to be judged in terms of the national curriculum levels, which, as was argued in parts I and II, misrepresented the nature of students' learning and falsely assumed that each of the ten levels of the national curriculum was objectively more difficult than the previous one. The difficulties of delineating objective levels of difficulty were made clear in the criticisms of the Rasch model of objective difficulty for use by the Assessment of Performance Unit.[53]

One can see, then, that the four original pillars of national curriculum testing and assessment were problematic. One can speculate that the DFE wanted cheap, summative, comparative testing, whereas the original proposals for assessment were expensive, formative and focused on specific diagnostic assessments.

Lest we be accused of adopting a solely negative stance to assessment arrangements, we ought to record the positive advances claimed for increased assessment activity in schools. For example, assessments were to be based on *evidence* rather than intuition or hunch,[54] they would foster *diagnostic teaching* and increased diagnosis of *students* which in turn would promote greater levels of *match* in the work set (see the discussion of differentiation in Part II[55]), and the backwash effect of having to assess and report on students' achievements of all aspects of the curriculum would result in the *full* national curriculum being taught.[56] Indeed, evidence from the initial introduction of formal assessment indicated that young children positively enjoyed the increased individual attention[57] they received from the teacher during periods of assessment.

The international and national contexts of assessment reveal it to be a politically and educationally highly charged activity. This suggests to us that the several elements of assessment need to be addressed in detail and fully understood. This will be undertaken below and will lead into a discussion of how student teachers can plan, implement, record and report assessments and the results of assessments.

THE PURPOSES OF ASSESSMENT

Nevo[58] sets out a range of purposes of assessment that fairly capture the flavour of discussions concerning them. He suggests that assessments serve a series of *primary functions* wherein they are used for:

- *certification*, qualifying students for their lives beyond school by awarding passes, fails, grades and marks;
- *diagnosis*, identifying a student's particular strengths, weaknesses, difficulties and needs in order that an appropriate curriculum can be planned;
- *improvement of learning and teaching*, providing feedback to students and teachers respectively so that action can be planned, moving away from marks and grades and towards comments, discussions, and suggestions for how students and teachers can improve – a formative intention. It also enables greater precision in matching to be addressed.

One can add to Nevo's suggestions the following primary purposes of assessment:

- *to select* for future education, setting and banding, options, level of examination entry or level at which to enter students for formal assessments (the former applying to GCSE examinations and the latter applying to SATs);
- *to provide evidence of achievement* both of the national curriculum and beyond;
- *to see the extent* to which intended learning outcomes have become *actual* learning outcomes;
- *to chart rates of progress* in learning;
- *to compare students*, for example with others in the class, set, year, school or indeed with national levels of performance;
- *to report* what students can do and what they have achieved.[59]

Nevo goes on to suggest that assessments can serve a series of *secondary functions* wherein they are used for:

- *accountability* of teachers and students to interested parties – to report on standards;
- *motivating students and teachers*,[60] though this is dependent upon the type of assessments adopted – tests tending to be demotivating while formative assessment and feedback tend to be more motivating. Further, because SATs and GCSEs require teachers to decide the entry levels of students this may be a demotivation, for example if a student resents being entered for a differentiated GCSE examination where the highest possible grade he or she could obtain is a grade C.[61]
- *discipline*, though Nevo does not advocate this policy of lowering or raising grades gained from assessments dependent on students' behaviour or misbehaviour.

One can add to Nevo's secondary suggestions the control of the curriculum, for the 'backwash effect' on the curriculum is strong in 'high stakes' – external – assessment.[62] It is important to be clear on one's purposes in assessment, for, as will be argued later, the choice of method of assessment, follow-up to assessment, types of data sought, types of assessment are all governed by the notion of *fitness for purpose*.[63] We suggest that several of the purposes set out above are in a relation of tension to each other.[64] For example, using assessments for the purposes of selection and certification may be intensely demotivating for many students and may prevent them from improving; the award of a grade or mark has very limited formative potential, even though it would be politically attractive; internally conducted assessment has greater educational validity than externally conducted assessment. Using a diagnostic form of assessment is very different in purpose, detail, contents and implementation from assessment by an end-of-course GCSE examination. Using assessment results as performance indicators can detract from a policy of providing formative feedback to improve learning. The notion of fitness for purpose returns us to a central principle of this book, *viz.* the need to clarify and address the objectives of the exercise. We support the view that student teachers should be concerned with diagnostic and formative assessments which are geared to improvements in teaching and learning, as these are more educationally worthwhile and practicable over the period of a teaching practice. The purposes of assessment here are educative rather than political or managerial.

TYPES OF ASSESSMENT

One major type of assessment is *criterion-referenced* assessment, brought into the educational arena by Glaser[65] in 1963. Here the specific criteria for success are set out in advance and students are assessed on the extent to which they have achieved them, without any reference being made to the achievements of other students (which is norm-referencing). There are minimum competency cut-off levels, below which students are deemed not to have achieved the criteria, and above which different grades or levels can be awarded for the achievement of criteria – for example, a grade A, B, C, etc. for a criterion-referenced piece of coursework at GCSE level.

A common example of a simple criterion-referenced examination is a driving test. Here a dichotomous view of criterion-referencing is adopted wherein the driver either can or cannot perform the elements of the test – reversing round a corner without mounting the pavement, performing an emergency stop without ejecting the examiner through the windscreen, overtaking without killing passers-by. The example of a driving test is useful for it indicates a problem in criterion-referenced assessment, *viz.* whether a student needs to pass each and every element (to meet every single criterion) or whether high success in one element can compensate for failure in another. Strictly speaking in an overall criterion-referenced system the former should apply,[66] which is draconian since a student could fail a whole course by dint of failing one small element, a common feature of the driving test. This is a problem that has been recognised in modular courses, particularly where one or more compulsory modules have to be passed.[67] This also raises another problem in the educational sphere, *viz.* that the dichotomous view of pass/fail – *either* able *or* unable to perform a task – is unhelpful to teaching and assessment. Abilities are not of the 'either/or' type: that is the error of bivalent western thinking that was discussed in Part II. Rather in an educational context a multivalent, 'fuzzy logic'[68] should apply which recognises that a task can be performed with differential degrees of success in its different elements or as a whole.

Another example of criterion-referenced assessment is the music perform-ance examinations of the Associated Board of the Royal Colleges of Music. Let us say that I am taking one of their piano examinations which requires me to play the scale of C sharp minor in double thirds for four octaves. If I play it successfully I pass that element of the examination; if I play it very well I receive a higher mark in that element of the examination; if I play it to the standard of a concert pianist I receive an even higher mark. Then I fail my performance of a Bach fugue, missing notes, failing to bring out the fugue's subject in the stretto sections and playing the wrong notes, thereby failing this element of the examination. However, the music examination differs from the driving test in that my marks in the former are *aggregated* so that one strong element can compensate for one weak element,[69] so that overall I may pass the music examination even though I am carrying a failed element.

The example of the piano examination is useful also, for it indicates that a measure of subtlety can be used in handling marks. These stand in contrast to the national curriculum assessments where *levels*, not marks, are being used; this is problematic because marks are more reliable than levels, retaining a degree of detail which is automatically lost when marks are combined to give a level. The problem is exacerbated further in the national curriculum because the levels that were crude aggregates of marks are themselves aggregated to give an overall level in a subject. We are only one stage away from aggregating all of the subjects to give a single level index of a student! There are several advantages in using *marks* rather than *levels* for assessment purposes:[70]

- it enables partial completion of a task to be recognised, wherein students can gain marks in proportion to how much of the task they have completed successfully;
- it affords the student the opportunity to compensate for doing badly in some elements of a task by doing well in others;
- it enables credit to be given for successful completion of parts of a task, reflecting considerations of the length of the task, the time required to complete it, and the perceived difficulty of the task;
- it enables weightings to be given to different elements of the task.

The question of aggregation is troublesome for criterion-referenced tests.[71]

If one were being true to the specificity of criterion-referencing one would argue against aggregation at all, since collapsing details in an overall aggregate loses the very specificity and diagnostic/formative potential upon which criterion-referencing is premised. However, if one fails one criterion out of a large number of criteria in an assessment then one fails the overall assessment.

The problem of aggregation in criterion-referencing is compounded because criterion-referencing suggests the compilation of long lists of criteria for each element of an assessment, echoing the dangers of behavioural objectives.[72] The parallel with behavioural objectives is not empty, for, just as with behavioural objectives, the danger of criterion-referencing is that one only plans for and assesses the observable, performatory and often superficial, trivial aspects of education and proceeds to record them in pages of tick boxes. Attempts to minimise these problems and to make criterion-referenced tasks manageable can easily result in generalised and inaccurate data that are meaningless.

The task, then, for users of criterion-referenced assessments is to select limited *sample* criteria that fairly represent a wider field, balancing specificity and generality whilst adhering to notions of: (1) *item discriminability* – 'the potential of the item in question to be answered correctly by those students who have a lot of the particular quality that the item is designed to measure and to be answered incorrectly by those students who have less of the particular quality that the same item is designed to measure';[73] (2) *item difficulty* – where the item is not so difficult that nobody answers correctly and not so easy that everyone answers it correctly.

A second main type of assessment is *norm-referenced* assessment. A norm-referenced assessment measures a student's achievements as compared to other students, for example a commercially produced intelligence test or national test of reading ability that has been standardised so that, for instance, we can understand that a score of 100 is of a notional 'average' student and that a score of 120 describes a student who is notionally above 'average'. The concept of 'average' only makes sense when it is derived from or used for a comparison of students. A norm-referenced assessment enables the teacher to put students in a rank order of achievement.[74] That is both its greatest strength and its greatest weakness. Whilst it enables comparisons of students to be made it can risk negative labelling and the operation of the self-fulfilling prophecy.[75]

A third type of assessment is *diagnostic assessment*, which is often used in the preparation of a statement for a student with special educational needs, describing exactly what the problems and needs are so that a programme of remediation can be focused and appropriate.[76] Not that this applies only to children with difficulties; indeed, given the discussion in Part II of teachers' apparent inabilities to match work to high achievers, there is a clear need for careful diagnosis of every student to take place in order than a better level of matching can be achieved.

Diagnostic assessment shares with *formative assessment* the intention of being able to suggest and shape the contents and processes of future plans. Formative assessment provides feedback to teachers and students on their current performances, achievements, strengths and weaknesses in such a form that it is clear what the student or the teacher can do next either to improve, enhance or extend learning and achievement. In this sense formative assessment is constructive and useful;[77] it sets an agenda for improvement. It takes place *during* a programme so that it can shape the forthcoming areas of the programme. Formative assessment can be frequent and informal, thereby really assisting teachers and students in the day-to-day business of improvement.

Diagnostic and formative assessments, then, are integral to the everyday learning that takes place in schools. In common with the discussions of evaluation in Part II, diagnostic and formative assessments require the exercise of *judgement* about exactly what a student needs to do next and why, thereby respecting the professional judgement of teachers. Formative assessment and the feedback gained from it by students and teachers can also be a motivator, as it outlines successes and shows how weaknesses or failures can be remedied – it is designed to be positive, supportive and helpful. It recognises a student's positive achievements and builds on these.[78] It is optimistic in indicating that there is a way forward.

Formative assessment contrasts with *summative* assessment both in timing and purpose. Summative assessment is terminal; it comes at the end of a programme and assesses, for example, students' achievements in the programme and overall knowledge acquisition and practice. It is the stuff of the GCSE formal examination, the end of term test, the A-level, the final examinations for a degree programme. A summative assessment might be to provide data on what the student has achieved at the point of time at the end of a course; it might also be more of a retrospective review of what has taken place during the course and what has been learned from it. Summative assessment is often concerned with certification, the awarding of marks and grades and public recognition of achievement.

Summative, diagnostic and formative assessments have an important part to play in action planning – a key *leitmotiv* of this book. A summative assessment provides data on achievements; a diagnostic assessment analyses and unpicks the reasons behind the achievements and the elements or fields of these achievements. Together they constitute the *review* stage of action planning wherein judgements are made about the levels of achievement of the *success criteria*. From there a formative assessment identifies new objectives and ways forward – not only *target setting* but indicating *ways of achieving the targets*. In action planning the summative and diagnostic outcomes can be discussed with the teacher, and the contents of the formative aspect can be arrived at through a process of discussion, consultation and negotiation between the student and the teacher. The teacher acts as a facilitator rather than as a director, drawing upon his or her own epistemic authority to make positive suggestions to the student. In this respect action planning is akin to, and forms part of, a record of achievement (discussed later).

The discussion of action planning takes us into the final type of assessment to be considered here: *ipsative assessment*.[79] Ipsative assessment (derived from the Latin 'ipse' – meaning 'herself' or 'himself') refers to a process in which students identify their own starting points or, in the language of action planning and school development planning, *initial conditions*. This is undertaken *in the student's own terms* (hence the appeal to the Latin root). From this analysis the student sets targets for future learning and achievements, often in conjunction with the setting of a time-frame. When the student arrives at the end of the nominated time-frame he or she reviews his or her progress within that time and the levels of achievement of self-set targets. This accords with Dean's[80] view that students should be given the opportunity to reflect on their own learning. Ipsative assessment starts and finishes with the student setting the agenda; it may not relate to formal assessment in form, content, process or timing, but it is valuable in that the student has a degree of ownership of the assessment process. It is much less threatening to many students than external and formal assessments. Furthermore, it can focus on aspects of development that do not necessarily feature in formal assessments, for example social, moral and emotional development.

Ipsative assessment feeds directly into the process of keeping a record of achievement – the contents of which are the students' own property – and is a useful parallel to, or complement to, the more academic, curriculum-oriented view of action planning. As with action planning that uses feedback from assessment formatively, ipsative assessment need not be undertaken by the student in splendid isolation, rather it can be undertaken with a teacher as facilitator and negotiator.

We commented earlier that the purposes of assessment not only are distinct but stand in tension with one another: the more assessment serves one purpose the less it can serve another. This is true for some types of assessment. For example, the more we move towards summative, grade-related examinations the more we move away from formative and diagnostic assessments that require detailed – often qualitative – comments; the more we move towards standardised tests the more we move away from ipsative assessments; the more we move towards norm-referenced assessments that often yield a single score or grade the more we move away from criterion-referenced assessments that will yield specific details about a range of elements; the more we use external, objective instruments the less opportunity we have to use internal, teacher-devised instruments (often simply as a function of the time available).[81] We suggest that student teachers should be concerned with diagnostic and formative assessments, providing useful feedback to students, i.e. feedback to improve learning, and that these can be part of ipsative assessment and action planning. Further, by involving students in ipsative assessment and by providing feedback upon which they can act to improve, positive interpersonal relationships are developed between students and student teachers which themselves support enhanced learning through engagement and motivation.

RELIABILITY AND VALIDITY IN ASSESSMENTS

As educators we need reliable data on students' achievements so that we can have confidence both in how we judge students and in what we subsequently plan for them. Further, we need to be assured that the assessments actually assess what they are intended to assess or else subsequent planning begins from the wrong place.

Reliability is an index of consistency,[82] for example of marking practices/ conventions and of standards – quality assurance and quality control respectively.[83] An assessment would have little reliability if it yielded different results in the hands of another assessor or different results for similar students. Reliability, then, requires comparability of practices to be addressed.[84] This can be undertaken prior to assessments by agreement trials, so that a range of assessors can agree on the specific marks and grades to be awarded for particular samples of work, examination scripts, coursework and marks scored in elements of an overall assessment, though in practice it often only becomes an issue in the post-assessment standardisation and agreement of marks and awards. Reliability affects the *degree of confidence* that one can place in assessment data and their interpretation (discussed later).

Reliability is an important issue given the significant role of teachers in formal assessments and examinations, and the need for external markers of examination scripts to be fair to all candidates, neither too harsh nor too generous in comparison with other external examiners. When external examiners commit breaches of reliability it often makes the national press; this echoes the comment made earlier that when 'the stakes are high' attention focuses on reliability in graded examinations.[85]

Not only must reliability be addressed but it must be seen to be addressed; marking must be seen to be fair. This issue was highlighted in a collection of papers from the British Educational Research Association's (BERA) Policy Task Group on Assessment, where the notion of 'transparency' was included in discussions of reliability.[86] It comes as no surprise, therefore, that the significance of reliability and transparency should lead to objective, standardised, national, externally marked tests and that this should accord with the views of a government which replaced the four criteria for assessment, specified earlier as being *formative, criterion-referenced, moderated* and *related to progression*, in favour of summative, norm-referenced, externally moderated pencil-and-paper tests. As was indicated earlier, assessment plays its part in a political agenda.

In an educational context most standardised tests include 'technical' details in their test manuals; these report the levels of reliability of the test. In test construction, reliability is a statistical concept which refers to numerical indices of *stability* (the test–re-test form of reliability), high correlations with results obtained in *equivalent forms* of a test, and high correlations between different items of a single test (*internal consistency*).[87] For reasons that will become clear later when comparing validity and reliability, we shall not dwell on the formulae for calculating reliability coefficients; rather we shall remain with the concept of consistency *qua* concept.

In endeavouring to attend to reliability, the School Curriculum and Assessment Authority suggested that reliability in teachers' assessment at key stages 1, 2 and 3 could be improved by, amongst other things:

- joint planning between teachers in the same year or department, across years or across key stages;
- using the programme(s) of study to agree objectives for teaching, learning and assessment;
- developing common activities focused on agreed objectives;
- discussing and marking work to develop shared expectations of performance;
- comparing the performance of pupils from different classes on common activities;
- referring to SCAA's *Exemplification of Standards*[88] booklets;
- referring to national tests and tasks;
- agreeing standards of samples of work from a range of contexts relating to particular level descriptions or end of key stage assessments;
- developing a common understanding of judgements about the work of individual pupils;
- identifying inconsistencies in pupils' performance;
- referring to examples of work whose standards have already been agreed and which are held in a school portfolio of work for facilitating moderation and consistency of grading;
- attending meetings outside the school for confirming judgements about standards, i.e. using external referents for moderation purposes.

It can be seen merely from the size of this (incomplete) list that reliability features highly when assessment is undertaken externally and by teachers. It enters the assessment arena at the point of agreeing marks, i.e. after the product – the examination script or the coursework for assessment, for example – has been made. The analogy with an industrial process is deliberate, for it is only after the product has been made that quality control comes into operation, selecting out the damaged goods. Indeed the BERA group mentioned above talks in terms of reliability as *post hoc* quality control.

There are several threats to reliability in assessments. For example:[89]

1   Students can execute a mathematics operation in the mathematics class but they cannot perform the same operation in, for example, a physics class; students will disregard English grammar in a science class but observe it in an English class. This raises the issue of the number of contexts in which the behaviour must be demonstrated before a criterion is deemed to have been achieved.[90] The question of transferability of knowledge and skills is also raised in this connection.

2   Motivation and interest in the task has a considerable effect on performance. Clearly, students need to be motivated if they are going to make a serious attempt at any test, whether motivation is *intrinsic* (doing something for its own sake) or *extrinsic* (doing something for an external reason, e.g. obtaining a certificate or employment or entry into higher education). The results of a test completed in a desultory fashion by resentful pupils are hardly likely to supply the student teacher with reliable information about the students' capabilities.[91] Research suggests that motivation to participate in test-taking sessions is strongest when students have been helped to see its purpose, and where the examiner maintains a warm, purposeful attitude toward them during the testing session (Hudson[92]).

3   The relationship (positive to negative) between the assessor and the assessee exerts an influence on the assessment. There is sufficient research evidence to show that test-takers and test-givers mutually influence one another during examinations, oral assessments and the like.[93] During the test situation, students respond to such characteristics as the evaluator's sex, age and personality. Although the student teacher can do little about his or her sex and age, it is important (and may indeed at times be comforting) to realise that these latent identities do exert potent influence. It could well be, for example, that the problems experienced by a female student teacher conducting a test with older secondary school boys have little if anything to do with the quality of the test material or the amount of prior preparation she has put into the testing programme.

4   The language of the assessment and the assessor exerts an influence on the assessee, for example if the assessment is carried out in the assessee's second language.[94]

5   The conditions – physical, emotional, social – exert an influence on the assessment, particularly if they are unfamiliar. The advice generally given in connection with the location of a test or examination is that the test-room should be well-lit, quiet and adequately ventilated. To this we would add that, wherever possible, students should take tests in familiar settings, preferably in their own form rooms under normal school conditions. Research suggests that distractions in the form of extraneous noise, walking about the room by the examiner, and intrusions into the room, all have significant impact upon the scores of the test-takers,

particularly when they are younger pupils (Lewis[95]). An important factor in reducing students' anxiety and tension during an examination is the extent to which they are quite clear about what exactly they are required to do. Simple instructions, clearly and calmly given by the examiner, can significantly lower the general level of tension in the test-room. Student teachers who intend to conduct testing sessions may find it beneficial to rehearse the instructions they wish to give to pupils *before* the actual testing session. Ideally, test instructions should be simple, direct and as brief as possible.

6 The readability level of the task can exert an influence on the assessment, e.g. a difficulty in reading may distract from the purpose of an assessment which is to test the use of a mathematical algorithm.

7 The Hawthorne Effect, wherein, in this context, simply informing a student that this is an assessment situation will be enough to disturb his or her performance – for the better or the worse (either case not being a fair reflection of his or her usual abilities).[96]

8 The Halo Effect, wherein a student who is judged to do well or badly in one assessment is given undeserved favourable or unfavourable assessment respectively in other areas.[97]

9 The size and complexity of numbers or operations in an assessment (e.g. in mathematics) which may distract the assessee who actually understands the operations and concepts.

10 The number and type of operations and stages in a task. A student may know how to perform each element, but when they are presented in combination the size of the task can be overwhelming.

11 Distractions (including superfluous information).

12 A considerable and growing body of research in the general area of *teacher expectancies* suggests that students respond to the *teacher-assessor* in terms of their perceptions of what he or she expects of them (Nash[98]). It follows, then, that the calm, well-organised student teacher embarking purposefully upon some aspect of evaluation probably induces different attitudes (and *responses*) among his or her class of children than an anxious, ill-organised colleague.

13 The time of the day, week, month will exert an influence on performance. Some students are fresher in the morning and more capable of concentration.[99]

What we are saying is that specific contextual factors can exert a significant influence on learning and that this has to be recognised in conducting assessments,[100] rendering an assessment as unthreatening and natural as possible.

With specific reference to the national curriculum standard assessment tasks (SATs) it has been argued that some tasks which meet the criteria for a higher level may in fact be easier than other tasks[101] for lower levels, depending on the previous experiences of the students. In other words, as was mentioned before, there are no objective levels of difficulty. The construction of difficulty is in the mind of the individual. Further, there is a problem connected with levels of maturation and age of the students. For example, a task for a Level 5 student may be suitable for an 11-year-old but may be given to a 16-year-old; students of different ages (and not necessarily different abilities) make qualitatively different responses to the same task.[102] This is unremarkable; student teachers who found their GCSE examinations difficult could probably pass them with ease now that they are older.

Validity in assessment is defined as ensuring that the assessment in fact assesses what it purports to assess. This is a problem when defining and operationalising abstract constructs like intelligence, creativity, imaginativeness, anxiety. Validity[103] refers to appropriateness, meaningfulness, usefulness, specificity, diagnostic potential, inferential utility and adequacy (i.e. *consequential validity* wherein the inferences that can be made from the assessment are sound). One can see that validity is concerned with detail – with criterion-referencing perhaps – and with the ability of an assessment to explain a student's performance in ways that feed into future planning. This external interpretation of validity resonates with the discussion of the diagnostic and formative potential of assessments. The utility value of valid data for teachers is considerable because the data are idiographic (individualistic), diagnostic and suggestive of the contents of further teaching and learning needs.

So here we have a dilemma. We commented earlier on the tensions between competing purposes of assessment and competing types of assessment. We argued that one has to select which purposes and types of assessment will be used, because a single assessment cannot serve all purposes and types of assessment, they being incompatible with each other. So it is with reliability and validity. The more we steer towards reliability, consistency, uniformity, standardisation and their outcomes in nominal grades, the more we move away from the valid data upon which teachers can take action. Conversely, the more we move towards teacher- and student-defined, personalised valid data the less generalisable, standardisable, comparable and consistent are the results (though no less transparent provided that the criteria are made public). The notion of representativeness of a wide population in reliability becomes redefined as representing and capturing the specific needs, abilities and achievement of each individual student.[104] We advocate addressing the latter rather than the former set of issues.

Moreover, Lambert[105] argues that not only are reliability and validity in a state of tension with each other but that a third factor – manageability – may reduce reliability and validity.

The remarks made earlier about classrooms being non-linear exemplars of chaos theory are relevant again here, for classrooms are individualistic, teachers and teaching practice are individualistic, students respond to being treated as individuals. This means that attempts to move towards reliability as standardisation are fundamentally misconceived because they misrepresent the dynamics and individuality of the teaching process. This echoes Nevo's[106] comment that while consistency is a crucial feature for the trivial it is misleading for the insightful. We are reminded of Wittgenstein's[107] words: 'when all possible scientific questions have been answered, the problems of life remain completely untouched.' In this respect assessment is an inherently inexact science.[108] Indeed, it is an art rather than a science. Now, perhaps, the reason becomes clearer why (as we said earlier) additional time will not be spent on the statistical intricacies of reliability formulae! We have moved from defining *quality control* as attention to a finished product, to *quality assurance*, as indicating that quality has to be built in from the design stage to the processes; it is intrinsic and integral, not extra and terminal.[109] As Pirsig[110] writes in *Zen and the Art of Motorcycle Maintenance*:

> Quality isn't something you lay on top of subjects and objects like tinsel on a Christmas tree. Real quality must be the source of the subjects and objects, the cone from which the tree must start. . . . You want to know how to paint a perfect painting? It's easy. Make yourself perfect and then just paint naturally.

The trick, of course, is to be able to generate both reliable and valid data, to avoid devaluing that which is not assessed, and to ensure that the gathering of reliable and valid data is, in fact, practicable and manageable.[111] The argument so far has indicated the problematic nature of assessment issues. These are summarised in Box 85.

We suggest that student teachers should be primarily concerned to address validity because this has strong individualistic, diagnostic and formative potential. This is not to say that reliability should be neglected; indeed, student teachers will find it useful to compare their own assessments of work with those contained in the school portfolio of moderated work that are exemplars of different levels and attainment targets. We suggest that student teachers should be concerned with *quality assurance*, i.e. carefully planned and differentiated work that is well matched to students' needs. Intended learning outcomes for students are communicated to them and discussed with them – generating their involvement and 'ownership' – as mentioned in Part II. Diagnostic assessment feeds into diagnostic teaching. This renders validity, particularly 'consequential validity', a significant issue. Assessment takes place in the course of everyday teaching. Where assessment is more 'formal', i.e. less embedded in everyday teaching, care should be taken to reduce stress as much as possible and to address as far as practicable the thirteen features of reliability outlined above.

Assessment is an inherently inexact activity; this suggests to us that a counsel of perfection should give way to a counsel of utility, practicability, validity and strong formative potential. That said, it would be a useful

Box 85 Reliability and validity as quality control and quality assurance

Quality control	Quality assurance
Reliability (consistency, comparability, fairness, transparency, objectivity, standardisation to external norms)	Validity (meaningfulness, specificity, utility, criterion-referenced, diagnostic potential, providing ongoing feedback)
External use (audit moderation; teachers' attendance at moderation meetings, school and department-wide moderation)	Internal use (school portfolio; individual and full students' records)
Externally set standards (teachers as technicians)	Internally set standards (teachers as professional experts)
Summative Level descriptions	Formative Programmes of study
Product-focused	Process-focused
Undertaken after assessments have been completed (i.e. adjustment to standard scores)	Undertaken before assessments are completed (i.e. to plan for the provision of useful feedback to students to enable them to improve)
Norm-referenced (measuring)	Criterion-referenced (diagnosing)
Formal	Formal and informal

experience for student teachers to take the opportunity to conduct a standardised test or assessment.

METHODS OF GATHERING ASSESSMENT DATA

The student teacher has several ways of gathering assessment data. These can be divided into two main types: *written sources of assessment data* and *non-written sources of assessment data*.[112] Mitchell and Koshy[113] also suggest that formative assessment by teachers can address what a student does, says and writes. Written sources include tests and written examinations (including essays), samples of students' work, records and self-completed, self-referenced assessments. Non-written sources include observation (visual, oral), practical activities with concrete outcomes, questioning, interviews and conferencing, presentations and exhibitions, video and audio recordings, and photographs. We shall deal with these in turn.

Written sources of data collection

Tests

The major means of gathering assessment data over the years have been tests and examinations. Published tests are commercially produced and they take various forms: *diagnostic* tests (e.g. the Metropolitan Diagnostic Tests), *aptitude* tests (which predict a person's aptitude in a named area, e.g. the Comprehensive Test of Adaptive Behaviour, the McCarthy Screening Test, the Assessment for Training and Employment Test), *achievement* tests, *norm-referenced* tests (e.g. the Boehm Test of Basic Concepts), *criterion-referenced* tests (e.g. the GCSE examinations of coursework), *reading* tests (e.g. the Edinburgh Reading Test), *verbal reasoning* tests (e.g. the Wechsler Adult Intelligence Scale and tests published by the National Foundation for Educational Research), tests of *critical thinking* (e.g. the Watson–Glaser Critical Thinking Appraisal), tests of *social adjustment* (e.g. the British Social Adjustment Test and the Kohn Social Competence Scale), *baseline assessment* tests (e.g. the Basic Achievement Skills Individual Screener). Several commercial companies hold tests that have restricted release or availability, requiring the teacher or school to register with a particular company. For example, in the United Kingdom the Psychological Corporation Ltd not only holds the rights to a world-wide battery of tests but has different levels of clearance for different users. Having different levels of clearance attempts to ensure, for example, that students are not 'prepared' for the test by coaching on the various items.[114]

Published tests have several attractions: they are objective and standardised (as a result of piloting and refinement), they declare their levels of reliability and validity through the inclusion of statistical data, they come complete with instructions for administration and processing, they are often straightforward and quick to administer and mark, and an accompanying manual gives guidance for the interpretation of results.

On the other hand, simply *because* they have been standardised on a wide population and are generalisable, by definition they are not tailored to an individual institution, a local context or specific needs. Hence if published tests are to be used they must serve the desired purposes of the assessment – the notion of fitness for purpose that was mentioned earlier is crucial in selecting from a battery of tests in the public domain.[115]

A test that is devised by the teacher for a specific purpose, while it does not have the level of standardisation of a commercially produced test, nevertheless will be tailored to that teacher's particular needs. Morrison[116] provides some guidelines for the construction of a test by a teacher:

- the *purposes* of the test must be explicit (i.e. to provide data for a particular type of assessment);
- the *type* of test must be appropriate (e.g. diagnostic, achievement, aptitude, criterion-referenced, norm-referenced);
- the *objectives* of the test need to be stated in operational terms;
- the *content* of the test must be suitable;
- the *construction* of the test must address *item analysis* (e.g. ensuring that each item in the test serves one or more specified objectives), *item discriminability* and *item difficulty* (see the discussion of these topics on page 373);
- the *format, readability and layout* of the test must be appropriate and clear for students;
- the *validity and reliability* of the test must be appropriate (see the discussion above of these two areas);
- the *marking criteria and marking conventions* for the test must be explicit, including the weightings of various elements.

Lewis[117] sets out a *freedom of response continuum* in discussing the relative 'openness' or 'closedness' of various types of test. These are represented in Box 86.

Box 86 A freedom of response continuum

'Open' essays

Essays

'Factual' and 'directed' essays

Short answer questions

Divergent thinking items

Completion items

Multiple-choice items

Source Lewis

Many objective tests are composed of a number of items – for example, missing words, incomplete sentences or incomplete, unlabelled diagrams, true/false statements, open-ended questions where students are given guide-lines for how much to write (e.g. a sentence, a paragraph, 300 words, etc.), closed questions, multiple-choice questions, matching pairs of statements and responses. They can test recall, knowledge, comprehension, application, analysis, synthesis, and evaluation, i.e. different orders of thinking. These take their rationale from the work of Bloom *et al.*[118] in 1956 on hierarchies of cognitive abilities – from low-order thinking (comprehension, application) to higher-order thinking (evaluation). Clearly the student teacher will need to know the order of the thinking being tested in the test.

Essays

A more open-ended type of written test is an essay. It is the freedom of response which is possible in the essay form of examination that is held to be its most important asset. Unlike the objective test, the essay allows the candidate to organise his or her thoughts and to communicate them in his or her own style; in short, it gives him or her freedom to be creative and imaginative in the communication of ideas. There are disadvantages, however, in the essay as a gatherer of information. Essays are difficult to assess reliably. With only one or two assessors a considerable degree of unreliability can creep into the assessment of essays, i.e. 'inter-rater' reliability may be limited. Even with analytical marking schemes (see below) the degree of agreement between markers may be low. Since only a limited number of essay titles can be answered in one examination, only a limited part of a syllabus of work can be addressed by the candidate. The student who has the misfortune to choose the 'wrong' essay title may produce work that does not fairly represent his or her true abilities. Chase[119] has suggested some ways of overcoming these weaknesses. First, all students may be asked to write on the same essay title(s), the principle being that individuals can only be compared to the extent that they have 'jumped the same hurdles'. Second, marking should be *analytic* rather than *impressionistic*. Analytic marking is based upon *prior decisions* about what exactly is being assessed in the essay – the content? the style? the grammar? the punctuation? the handwriting? (i.e. criterion-referencing should apply). On the question of the low agreement between essay markers, Lewis suggests the following ways of reducing the subjective element:

- by marking for substantive content rather than style;
- by fixing a maximum penalty for mistakes in grammar, syntax and spelling;
- by multiple marking followed by a further close scrutiny of those essays placed near the pass–fail line.

For public examinations this problem can also be addressed by agreement trials and moderation. Again the notion of fitness for purpose must be the criterion to judge the openness of the essay and its marking frame.

Samples of work

Throughout the years of schooling samples of work can be used to provide assessment data, be they pieces of coursework specifically undertaken for assessment purposes (for example, the coursework elements for GCSE examinations) or pieces of work undertaken as part of everyday learning. As with the devising and use of tests, the use of the coursework or other written work must be appropriate to the purposes and objectives of the assessment and, like most samples, be representative of the wider range of work that a student has done. Samples of work are one of the most widely used means of assessment because they are ongoing and are rooted in the reality of classroom life.

Ensuring that the samples of work fit the objectives and purposes of the assessment means that the criteria for setting the work in the first place must fit those purposes and that the assessment or marking of the work must make explicit the criteria to be used and disclose these to the students. In the interests of good teaching and natural justice there is little justification for withholding from students the purposes of the written work and the criteria that will be used to assess it. It is unacceptable to have students 'play a game' whose rules they have not been told. Students will be more likely to feel involved in the process of assessment if it is made clear to them what it will be and what criteria will be used[120] (see the discussion earlier about reliability, motivation, the relations between the assessor and assessee and the assessee's 'nerves' during the assessment). This breaks with the traditional type of assessments where contents and criteria were kept secret.

Both the School Curriculum and Assessment Authority[121] and OFSTED[122] suggest that schools should have a marking policy that is consistent and consistently used through the school. This policy might include, for example, the proportions of marks to be given for coverage of content, depth of own research, grammar, spelling, presentation, effort, achievement, together with weightings for these several elements.

For marking GCSE coursework the criteria for assessment are explicit and are given by the examining body; they constitute the 'analytical' marking schemes described above. For other pieces of work and for pre-GCSE students the criteria may be those set out in the national curriculum documentation. With reference to the national curriculum, though the School Curriculum and Assessment Authority[123] has suggested that level descriptions and end of key stage statements should be used for assessment purposes, in practice some of these are too generalised to provide *operational* criteria; the student teacher might be better advised to refer to the programmes of study and the attainment targets in the national curriculum for more concrete criteria – or to operationalise the level descriptions and end of key stage statements in more detail.

To be able to assess a sample of work in terms of its demonstration of the achievement of a particular aspect or subject of the national curriculum the School Curriculum and Assessment Authority has suggested that each school and department keeps a *portfolio* of samples of work which, by a process of internal moderation,[124] external moderation and agreement trials, have been judged to demonstrate a particular level of achievement in every subject of the national curriculum. When a teacher wishes to assess a sample of work he or she can refer to these samples in the school portfolio in order to match his or her own assessment standards with the agreed standards for the samples of work contained in it. The DFEE indicated that the school portfolio should contain (a) work to cover the levels of each core subject of the national curriculum, (b) two or three examples for each level in each subject, and (c) examples of work that are at the top of each level.

Records

Student teachers on teaching practice will be required to keep records of students' progress. The issues of record-keeping will be addressed later in this part. For the present we note that the day-to-day, week-to-week and term-by-term records should provide clear evidence for student teachers' and teachers' assessments of students, in a subject-specific form as well as in terms of a student's wider development (including, for example, social and emotional factors).

Teachers are required to report on a student's progress in every national curriculum area each year; to be able to do this entails keeping records throughout the year so that a student's achievement can be documented, difficulties noted and particularly strong features recorded. These records are *informal*, though not necessarily private documents. For a *formal* assessment record the teacher can review the data and match them to the level descriptions and attainment targets of the national curriculum in order to document the student's level of achievement. The corollary of this is that the student teacher will be well advised to ensure that the ongoing record-keeping system that he or she adopts is framed in terms of the national curriculum as well as including other elements. By dating each entry a student's *rate of progress* will be indicated, showing where there have been periods of rapid progress and limited progress, periods of consolidation and periods where very little seems to have happened. Student teachers would be well advised to practise writing short, punchy accounts, often in note form.[125]

Self-referenced assessments

A final type of written sources of assessment data is self-assessment undertaken by students. It was suggested in the comments earlier about ipsative assessments that a student could set his or her own targets (often in discussion with the teacher) and refer back to these at a given point in time in order to assess how successfully he or she has met those targets. As was mentioned earlier, the targets might be focused on academic knowledge and the national curriculum subjects or they might also include other aspects of development such as confidence and motivation, what has been found easy or difficult (and why), what has been achieved in social behaviour, how the student has managed to stay calm in difficult situations, and so on.

One must recognise that to give many students a blank sheet of paper and ask them to complete a self-assessment in their own terms is sheer folly; they

Box 87 Written sources of assessment data

Method	Strengths	Weaknesses
Tests	Targeted, specific, written, flexible, many types, marks can give credit and compensation for partial answers	Unnatural, threatening, outcome focused, the Hawthorne Effect, simplistic, often only one 'correct' answer
Essays	Open-ended, enable individuality to be demonstrated, much formative potential	Prone to unreliability, poor coverage of a whole course, risks of not showing a student's overall abilities, problems of comparability between different essay titles
Samples of work	Rooted in everyday teaching and learning, much formative potential, criterion-specific, public criteria, much formative potential, ongoing	Need to ensure validity, much hinges on single items, problems for poor writers, neglects processes
Records	Specific, detailed, focused, much formative potential, charts rates of progress, honest, ongoing, cumulative	Time-consuming, risk of subjectivity
Self-referenced assessments	Authentic, focused, honest, highlight priorities, high student ownership	Irrelevant for national curriculum assessment, problems for poor writers, problem of institutional response only

Source Morrison[126]

will have little or no understanding of what to do, limited ability to decide the focuses of the comments, and limited ability to write the comments. In these circumstances a 'scaffolding' or framework for analysis can be helpful – either provided entirely by the student teacher or arrived at through a process of discussion and negotiation with the student.

A summary of methods of data collection from written sources is provided in Box 87. We suggest that each student teacher should select the most appropriate form(s) for his or her requirements – to address the notion of *fitness for purpose* – and that caution may have to be exercised in interpreting written data, particularly from students for whom writing is difficult, demotivating or threatening. That said, many lessons which require a written outcome can also become, thereby, opportunities for assessment.

Non-written sources of data collection

Non-written sources of assessment data may be particularly appropriate for students whose written abilities are limited.[127] They enable credit to be given for work other than written work. There are several sources of non-written data, including questioning, observations, interviews and conferences, presentations, video and audio recording, and photographs.

Questions

Perhaps the most commonly used way of gathering informal assessment data is by asking the students questions, because that is what teachers do for much of their time anyway. This form of data gathering is true to everyday classroom life.[128] Effective questioning is quite a skill, as was demonstrated in Part III. Asking the 'right' questions in order to elicit required information is an art that the student teacher would do well to rehearse beforehand, rather than trying to organise his or her questioning on the spur of the moment (see Part II on planning the specific questions that will be asked). Further, the student teacher may wish to rehearse different ways of putting questions in order to help the respondent. Kerry[129] suggests seven factors to consider in questioning:

- structure;
- pitching (the level and the words chosen) and putting;
- distributing (the spread and focus) and directing;
- pausing and pace (allowing thinking time);
- prompting (for clarification) and probing (for follow-up);
- listening and responding (for follow-up);
- sequencing (logical, psychological, chronological).

Questions can be open-ended, which is particularly useful for asking higher-order, evaluative questions and 'why-type' questions.[130] Open-ended questions offer the respondent the opportunity to answer in an individualistic way, though, for assessment purposes, some prompts and probes from the student teacher may be useful. Open-ended questions for assessment purposes enable a series of prespecified focuses to be addressed but answered by the students in their own terms. Closed, highly structured, often lower- and middle-order questions (engaging the levels of recall, comprehension, application, analysis from Bloom's taxonomy) are useful for eliciting very specific information, for example a student's grasp of a mathematical proof, or knowledge of a chemical process, or an explanation of how the rain cycle operates. Kerry echoes this where he suggests that there are four main types of questioning: for *recalling information*, for *reasoning* (asking why), for *speculating* (the subjunctive 'what if ...' question[131]) and for *personal response*.

The student teacher will have to plan the type, sequence, level, wording, number, focus and purposes of questions if they are to yield reliable and valid data. There is also the issue of the timing of different types of question; for example, at the start of a session the questions might refer back to previous teaching and then move to more speculative, open-ended questions, whereas questioning at the end of a session might be for summarising and review, using more closed questions. The focus of the questions can be derived from the purposes and focuses of the assessment, which, in turn, are informed by the contents of the national curriculum. What is required, then, is for the student teacher to *operationalise* the relevant contents of the national curriculum so that appropriate, concrete, specific questions can be asked of the students. Such operationalisation should not be difficult as it should have formed part of the process of planning schemes of work and weekly, daily and lesson plans (see Part II).

We end this section on a cautionary note. Many students may be extremely threatened if a teacher poses a battery of questions, particularly if the respondent does not know the answer.[132] Many student teachers will have insufficient knowledge of particular students to be able to ask questions appropriately, discreetly and unthreateningly. Indeed, some students may consider the posing of a range of questions by a relative outsider an invasion of their privacy. All of these constitute significant threats to reliability.

Observation

For the most part observation is a very useful tool for collecting assessment data because it need not interrupt or upset the daily life of classrooms – thereby being strong on validity and reliability. Observation can play a highly significant part in assessment. Some activities can only be assessed by observation *in situ*, for example in PE the student teacher will need to watch the performance of a handstand or a forward roll as it happens. Notes on the performance can be made at the same time or written up shortly afterwards.

The former School Examination and Assessment Council (SEAC) suggested that, in planning observations, attention should be given to the *methods and recording, the focus* and the *role of the teacher*.[133]

With regard to methods and recording one suggestion from SEAC was that observation could be *systematic*, i.e. at regular intervals of time in an activity, at certain points in or stages of the activity, or by working down the list of students to be observed. Another suggestion was that observation could be targeted at specific *critical incidents* (where the teacher is present when an unanticipated event occurs that yields assessment data). In truth, these two types of observation lie at two poles of a continuum in observation.

At one pole is *structured* observation[134] where the observer knows in advance what he or she will be looking for and enters data on a previously worked out pro forma. One such pro forma is for *event sampling*. Here a tally mark is entered whenever the looked-for behaviour occurs over a given time period, for example, whenever the student reads on his or her own, writes without assistance, addresses safety factors in the laboratory. For example:

1   The student fetches safety glasses /////
2   The student checks that his or her shirt or blouse cuffs are tucked into an overall //
3   The student keeps the Bunsen burner flame yellow when not in use ////
4   The student wears gloves when handling acids ///////

In this example the event (4) occurs most frequently and event (2) least frequently. Event sampling enables the observer to note the incidence and frequency of the looked-for behaviour; the result may indicate to the student teacher whether a student has learnt something and can apply it confidently and securely.

There are other forms of structured observation, *viz. instantaneous sampling* and *interval recording*. Both require data to be entered on to an observation grid of looked-for behaviours, using some form of coding symbols for speed of entry. We consider it unlikely that at this stage the student teacher would have sufficient time available to conduct this type of observation, so we shall not dwell on it here.

In structured observation the focus of the observation can be decided by reviewing the level descriptions, the attainment targets in question or the programmes of study of the national curriculum. It is likely that this has already been undertaken at the planning stage (see Part II); in this case the student can refer to the lesson plans where 'assessment data' and 'intended learning outcomes' were specified. These can then be operationalised into specific items to feature in the observation. We would argue against too structured an observation unless it is for in-depth assessment as it is very time-consuming, unnatural (unlike an everyday teaching situation) and potentially very threatening to students.

An *unstructured* observation (of critical incidents) records incidents that take place spontaneously. Here data are usually entered in the form of words and descriptions; these are reviewed later in light of the criteria used for assessment – perhaps derived from the national curriculum level descriptions or attainment targets, lesson plans, or objectives of the scheme of work. We would argue against a completely unstructured observation as it may be time-wasting. Nevertheless *a responsive observation* – where a student teacher notes down an unanticipated event, reaction, or outcome – may be useful for assessment purposes.

Between structured and unstructured observation comes *semi-structured* observation, where the teacher has a range of points about which to gather data (e.g. the students' ability to plan, undertake and evaluate a piece of design technology), but the nature of the entry about the features or behaviour looked for is open-ended, enabling a tailored response to be written. The observer has to know what is being looked for in the observation.[135] For example, the student teacher might be interested in assessing a student's abilities to conduct an experiment, e.g. finding out which kind of paper towel absorbs most liquid. He or she might divide the assessment activity into eight areas:

1   Pinpointing exactly what the problem is in the experiment.
2   Identifying key variables.
3   Isolating and controlling the variables in order to conduct a fair test.
4   Operationalising the experiment.
5   Conducting the experiment.
6   Recording the results.
7   Interpreting the results.
8   Evaluating the experiment (e.g. how it could have been improved).

Each of these eight points is listed and comments are written about the student's performance in each. The comments might also include numbers (marks for the student's achievement in different aspects of the activity).

We advocate very strongly a semi-structured observation as it sets an agenda of areas and items to be observed but is sufficiently open-ended to allow an individual, 'customised' response in the form of words. This respects the student teacher's growing professional insight and judgement.

With regard to the *role of the teacher* in gathering observational data, the SEAC advice was that attention needed to be given to whether the teacher was to be a participant or non-participant observer, though SEAC was unforth-coming on what this might mean and how it might be addressed. We can surmise that teachers are intended to be aware that if they intervene too greatly in the activity they may reduce the reliability of the data they acquire.

With regard to the *focus of the observation* SEAC indicated that this should consider individual and group activities. Indeed, one of their early comments indicated that the assessment activity should resemble normal classroom practice as far as possible so that the problem of the Hawthorne Effect and the other threats to reliability set out earlier could be reduced. In reality this implies that collaborative group projects should feature in an assessment. Whilst this is a very positive factor it does create some problems for the assessor:

- how to minimise students copying from one another;
- how to identify an individual's contribution, particularly if it did not result in a visible outcome;
- the composition, size, dynamics of, and personalities in, the group that might exert a significant influence on an individual's contribution, for example if there is a dominant student;
- how tasks are shared out in the group;
- the degree of co-operation, sharing and collaboration;
- the make-up of abilities in the group (e.g. mixed abilities, poor abilities, high abilities, a homogeneity of abilities, a polarisation of abilities);
- what kind and level of involvement each individual has in the task;
- what is the focus of the group talk (e.g. task-related or unrelated to the task – resulting in students being off-task).

SEAC suggested that some of these problems could be minimised if: (a) the teacher clarifies what each student will be doing in the group (perhaps after the group itself has discussed this); (b) every student has the opportunity to make a contribution; (c) it is possible to identify how each individual has enabled the task to move forward; (d) the teacher builds into the task the opportunity for individual discussions between himself or herself and each student.

Interviews and conferencing

This 'live' form of data collection involves recording data as the interview takes place or shortly afterwards. Interviews and conferencing can take place on a one-to-one basis, with groups of students, and with the student(s), parent(s) and teacher(s) present. In the case of the latter the interview might be recorded; this is useful but very time consuming. Interviews, like observations, vary from the structured to the unstructured. *Highly structured* interviews will have the contents, wording and sequence of questions worked out in advance.[136] *Semi-structured* interviews will have a list of topics and questions planned but the sequence and wording will follow the flow of the interview. Questions here are open-ended as well as closed, enabling respondents/participants to address matters in their own terms and in their own words. The assessor might have a list of *prompts* and *probes* ready to use if students are unforthcoming or if they are able to be pressed into further comments respectively. Honesty, candour, depth and authenticity of response are the hallmarks of validity in a semi-structured interview.

An *unstructured* interview cannot, by definition, set its own agenda. It is more like an everyday conversation, open-ended and uncontrived. Though this may yield assessment data there is a risk that it may not yield anything – just as many everyday conversations are comparatively inconsequential. We would not advocate this form of interview as it is time-consuming and sometimes fruitless.

Interviewing and conferencing have commanded significant attention in the last ten years. Given impetus by the former Inner London Education Authority[137] in its *Primary Language Record* – of which conferences with parents, teachers and children were the foundation stones – this was later developed much more fully and extended to all age groups and areas of school life with the rise of records of achievement and action planning. Both of these have conferencing at their heart, whether it be to engage in a process of review or to decide future targets, success criteria and ways of achieving the targets. The importance of interviewing and conferencing in this book's advocacy of action planning cannot be overstated. Interviews and conferencing can be motivating for students and student teachers; many students respond positively to the individual attention they receive in a conference and this form of action planning has student involvement and engagement in learning as a high priority. Using interviews and conferencing for teaching and learning purposes and for assessment purposes gives this form of data collection an authenticity which is derived from its rootedness in the everyday life of classrooms.

Presentations

Data can be acquired from students making short presentations to their peers or to the student teacher. A presentation might be in the form of a play, reporting what they have done in a particular lesson, leading a debate, reporting how they conducted a traffic census, introducing work that they have done as a group, reporting on a collaborative project, etc., presenting their exhibits of art or design technology work. An oral rather than a written medium enables students to use their own ideas in their own words. As a 'live' event it can involve students more in their own learning and engage them in the activity in question, raising their motivation and interest. This is particularly true for students who find writing difficult or unpleasurable.

On the other hand, this activity can be very threatening for inarticulate, reticent or shy students who might become a target for public embarrassment and humiliation, condemning themselves from their own mouths. Alternatively, it might give centre stage to a student who loves the limelight and public acclaim and who has an ego to match. Presentations are very personality-specific; while this virtually guarantees authenticity it may reduce their degree of validity.

Video and audio recordings, and photographs

These sources of assessment data capture the unfolding complexity of classrooms and are particularly suitable for acquiring data from students whose written abilities are limited. For this reason they are frequently used with students with special educational needs. Though they can capture 'live' events they can only do so if the equipment is trained on the appropriate parties. For example, a video recorder can be selective in its focus and may need to be moved from place to place (which can cause a major disturbance). The student teacher ought also to be warned about the cost of these forms of acquiring assessment data. With regard to photography there is the cost of the film and processing; with regard to audio and video cassettes there is the cost not only in terms of equipment but in terms of time spent setting it up and analysing the results – an hour's video time might take three hours of analysis, an hour's audio cassette time might take five hours of analysis. These latter two forms of acquiring assessment data are perhaps unrealistic for general and widespread use though they may be very useful indeed for in-depth, focused assessment of specific students or aspects of work.

Role play

This activity may enable students who are inhibited in one context to demonstrate looked-for abilities in another. For example, a student who is reluctant to contribute much to a class discussion may turn out to be highly articulate in a spontaneous piece of drama. Knowing that many behaviours are context-dependent (see the discussions of reliability earlier), this is a useful way of trying to gather assessment data through additional channels. On the other hand, of course, some students may not take to role-play activities; they may be overshadowed by more assertive members of a drama group and thus unable to show enough freedom in decision-making for the student teacher to gather useful assessment data.

A summary of methods of collecting assessment data from non-written sources is presented in Box 88. Lambert[138] also includes *graphic evidence* (e.g. pictures, diagrams, charts and graphs, computer printouts) and *products* (e.g. artefacts, models and 3D constructions). These may be particularly useful for catching assessment data from students whose written and oral skills are undeveloped.

The selection of which non-written form of data collection to use should be influenced by the criterion of fitness for purpose. Less tightly structured, non-written methods are often truer to everyday life. Unstructured methods risk being too time-wasting. As with written sources of data, we advocate semi-structured methods of data collection as these have a set agenda but are sufficiently open-ended to permit a response that is tailored to individuals. In planning how to gather assessment data the student teacher needs first to be

Box 88 Non-written sources of assessment data

Method	Strengths	Weaknesses
Questions	Focused, formative, specific, true to everyday life in school	Threat, needs skills to put the questions, problems if students are inarticulate, perceived invasion of privacy
Observation	Strong on reality, takes in context, high validity, reliability	Distracting for teachers, time-consuming
Interviews/ conferencing	Built on known relationships, can be detailed, deep and focused, enables freedom of response, links with action planning and records of achievement	Time-consuming to administer and analyse, students may be inhibited
Presentations	Enables students to present outcomes in their own terms, useful for poor writers, captures factors that written forms miss, can be true to everyday classroom processes, motivating	Threat, public humiliation or 'showing-off', difficult to isolate an individual's contribution, difficult to build out the influence of others, students may be inhibited
Video/audio recording and photographs	Live, captures complexity, records the non-written, suits poor writers	Selective, time-consuming to set up and analyse, expensive materials
Role play	May enable a student to show different abilities	Students may be shy, a dominant student might bias another student's 'performance'

Source Morrison[139]

clear on the purposes of the assessment; this will determine the level of formality of the assessment. The purposes and degree of formality will indicate whether written or graphic types of data are appropriate, how structured and closed or semi-structured and open the data-collection methods are to be, and how reliability and validity will be addressed.

PROVIDING OPPORTUNITIES FOR ASSESSMENT

In addition to the obvious point that students perform differently at different times of the day and the week, a more detailed analysis reveals that *opportunities* have to be provided for students to demonstrate their abilities, achievements and understandings.[140] There are plenty of occasions in classrooms when assessment data can be collected: in *writing times* – factual, stories, poems, handwriting, spelling; in *speaking and listening* times – asking and answering questions, participating in discussions; following instructions, compiling charts and spreadsheets; when students are *reading* all manner of literature and documents; undertaking practical activities, using equipment, solving problems, investigating, working with computers.

Moreover, not only do occasions within the field of *curriculum content* provide opportunities for assessment, but there is a range of *pedagogical* opportunities that can be used to collect assessment data: working individually, in pairs, in a small group; in the home corner, in the science laboratory, in the resources centre, in the music room, in a flexible-learning suite. Clearly if this is to be developed it requires teachers, departments and faculties to be prepared to share information about students other than in their own curriculum area. For example, since the publication of the Bullock Report mentioned earlier the point has been made that language is a cross-curricular responsibility of every teacher, yet how many secondary teachers are there who do not teach English but who have been expected to contribute to a discussion of a student's performance in English; probably rather fewer than the Bullock Report recommended!

In devising assessments, then, opportunities for assessment to occur not only have to be planned but have to be seized as part of the normal everyday teaching process, rendering assessment as close as possible to a 'natural' teaching situation. Put simply, not only is it desirable *in principle* that assessment should be integral to learning but, *in practice* a school day, week, term or year does not have sufficient slack time to allow assessments to be *extra* to teaching; they are *built-in* not *bolt-on* elements of teaching. Lambert[141] suggests that a lesson plan, for example, should include references to *assessment opportunities, assessment methods* and *evidence of attainment* (see also the lesson plans set out in Part II).

DESIGNING AN ASSESSMENT TASK

So far this chapter has set out a range of issues in planning assessments. We turn now to seeing how these issues can be addressed in planning specific assessments. For clarity these are set out in an annotated sequential list.[142] The planning issues addressed locate assessment not only in general contexts but with specific reference to the national curriculum.

- Identify the target group.

Considerations: will it be one or more groups from a whole class; a whole class; students from across more than one class; one or more age groups; one or more ability groups; how will reliability be addressed if too many students are involved?

- Decide the number of students who can be working on the activity and who can be assessed by the activity.

Considerations: will there be some students who are working on the task but who will not be assessed; what criteria will be used to decide on the numbers of students being assessed, e.g. ability, practicability, relationships, resources; how will children with special needs be part of the activity?

- Decide the purpose of the assessment.

Considerations: will it be to grade, to diagnose, to provide feedback to students, to decide future class placement (i.e. for selection), to measure achievement, to chart rates of progress, to compare students; who will be the audiences of the data collected, i.e. what are the objectives of the assessment and what learning outcomes will the assessment serve (applying the objectives model adopted throughout this book)?

- Decide the type of assessment.

Considerations: what are the most suitable types of assessment for the purposes, e.g. criterion-referenced, norm-referenced, diagnostic, formative, summative, ipsative?

- Decide the assessment opportunities in a 'normal' teaching and learning activity.

Considerations: how can you derive assessment data from everyday activities rather than having to set a task specifically for assessment purposes; what assessment data and criteria are possible in a given lesson and its outcomes?

- Decide what kind of task will most fittingly serve the purposes of the assessment.

Considerations: exactly what will the assessment activity be assessing; how will validity be addressed; what will the focus of the activity be?

- Decide whether the activity is an individual or group activity and how you will assess an individual's performance in a group activity (if applicable).

Considerations: what makes the activity specifically a group activity; is the difficulty with assessing an individual's contribution to a group activity insurmountable or worth the effort; how will group interactions feature in acting on the data? Do not attempt to work with more than four groups if the students are unfamiliar with working in groups.[143]

- Decide the attainment target(s) to be assessed.

Considerations: will you focus on one attainment target or more than one; what ways are there to conduct assessments in the attainment target(s)?

- Decide the range of levels in which the activity will enable you to place students as a result of the assessment.

Considerations: for standard assessment tasks (SATs) the teacher has to decide the most appropriate entry level as different SATs apply to different entry levels – will you have different activities for different entry levels or different elements of an activity for different entry levels; have you looked at the criteria for achievement at the lowest and highest levels; how will you accurately be able to distinguish levels of achievement in the activity?

- Decide how to render the activity as close as possible to everyday classroom practice.

Considerations: how important is it that students know that they are being assessed;[144] how will a student's awareness that he or she is being assessed affect his or her performance; is it possible to undertake the assessments without the timetable being disrupted; which children will be anxious; what can be done to allay anxieties?[145]

- Decide the timing and time-scale of the activity.

Considerations: examine the normal teaching timetable and activities to identify assessment opportunities in everyday teaching. How will you judge how much time is required; why might you be putting time constraints at all on a criterion-referenced assessment; what time of the day or the week is most suitable for the students; how will you make allowances for fast and slow workers?

- Decide what assessment evidence you need to collect.

Considerations: will you focus on processes or outcomes; how will you decide what valid and reliable evidence is required?

- Decide the most appropriate ways of gathering the assessment evidence.

Considerations: decide which parts of the assessment data can only be gathered *in situ* (e.g. a PE performance or musical performance) and which data can be reviewed out of school (e.g. by looking at samples of written work or notes made during an activity); decide whether, and which, written or non-written forms of data are most appropriate to address the purposes and focuses of the assessment (or whether a combination of written and non-written forms might be more suitable).

- Analyse the type of task required.

Considerations: is the task an application of material already learnt, application of new material, a practice task, the synthesis of existing knowledge, the synthesis of existing and new knowledge (or a combination of these, and, if so, which parts of the task address different types of task and why are you making differential task demands); how do you know what demands the task will place on students; how precisely[146] do you know what the demands on students will be?

- Analyse the task requirements.

Considerations: look at the task requirements[147] to see if all elements of the task are equally difficult. Why are you including elements of the task which are easier or more difficult than others; what is it that makes some elements of the task more difficult than others; are the tasks sufficiently concrete and within the experience of the students; does the number of elements in the task prevent students from demonstrating that, in fact, they might understand each element but be overwhelmed when they are put together?

- Decide options in the task.

Considerations: will some students select an easier option than others (e.g. a way of working) and what will happen if students select an easy way of working when they are capable of much more; how will the task-selection process affect an individual student's recorded attainment; will the students appreciate the relevance of the task to their own lives?

- Clarify the criteria for marking (where applicable).

Considerations: how many relevant tasks does the student have to complete successfully before being credited with having reached a particular level of achievement? Consider marking conventions, criteria and weightings.

- Decide how the activity will be introduced (the *presentation* mode); what the students will actually be doing in the activity (the *operation* mode); what form the outcome will take (the *response* mode).[148]

Considerations: how well matched are these modes to the students; how will you know whether, for example, a language difficulty is preventing a student from demonstrating his or her scientific or mathematical abilities; how will you support students whose first language is not English?[149] Decide the method of delivery in: (a) the *presentation mode* (e.g. oral, written, pictorial, video, IT, practical); (b) the *operation mode* (e.g. mental, written, practical, oral); (c) the *response mode* (e.g. a multiple-choice test, essay, short piece of writing, picture, oral, practical, display, presentation, role play, computer data).

- Decide how to reduce threats to reliability and validity.

Considerations: how will extraneous influences on performance be reduced; when will you address reliability issues, e.g. in devising the task (quality assurance) or in marking the outcome (quality control); attempt an assessment that is 'good enough' rather than striving for perfection – be realistic.[150] When will you halt the activity if students are struggling; how will you take account of teacher intervention or interventions by other students; how will the situation be made less threatening; how positive are the relationships between the assessor and the assessee; how have you addressed readability; how consistent is the proposed assessment task with the usual ways of working in the class; what other contextual variables do you need to consider that might influence the reliability of the assessment and the data that it yields?

- Decide exactly which national curriculum criteria you will be using in judging the assessment evidence.

Considerations: some level descriptions may be imprecise, in which case the attainment targets and programmes of study may be more helpful; reference to the school portfolio of agreed standards may be helpful here.

- Decide the information/records/evidence/data that will be brought to a moderation meeting.

Considerations: how will the issue of sampling be addressed, i.e. how will you decide what is a representative sample of each student's work and several students' work?

- Decide how the results will be used as part of an ongoing recording system.

Considerations: ensure that your decisions fall in line with the school policy; decide on whether and how to aggregate marks (if applicable); how often will you update your formal records?

- Decide how to report the results and to whom.

Considerations: what will be reported to students, parents, other teachers, and other interested parties; what will go into each student's portfolio?

This long list of points and considerations is perhaps daunting, yet, for the sake of reliability and validity, these are important issues that cannot be overlooked. As the opening comments in this chapter suggest, reliability and validity all too easily become the casualties of ill-prepared, over-politicised or 'high-stakes' assessments. There is no doubt that assessment in the United Kingdom is a 'high-stakes' activity, both politically and educationally, particularly since teacher assessment in the national curriculum has assumed an almost equal footing at key stages 1, 2 and 3 with externally set and externally marked SATs.

That said, a much shorter list of considerations for teacher assessment was provided by SEAC, which built on the acronym of INFORM.[151] An updated version of the SEAC acronym can be seen below:

1   Identify the elements of the national curriculum (attainment targets, level descriptions, programmes of study) that the lesson will address.
2   Note opportunities for the student to demonstrate attainment.
3   Focus on the performance, looking for evidence of achievement.
4   Offer the student the opportunity to discuss what was achieved.
5   Record what was identified as important and noteworthy.
6   Modify lesson plans for the student if necessary.

What is very clear in this six-stage process is that the teacher assessment envisaged is formative, criterion-referenced, related to progression, evidential, perhaps even related to action planning at stage 6, and, because the teacher has to relate her standard of marking to agreed criteria and standards, moderated. Hence, though formal teacher assessment and SATs might take us into simplistic summative assessments with limited formative potential, in the day-to-day assessments of students a more educationally beneficial set of practices might still operate. What is very clear is that the SEAC recommendations place assessment and forward planning as partners in promoting learning.[152]

Drawing together the several strands of the arguments and issues raised in this chapter, we suggest fourteen principles to guide the student teacher who is preparing to assess students during teaching practice:

1   The purposes are to be diagnostic and formative, providing feedback and being educative.
2   The assessments should be criterion-referenced and the criteria should be public.
3   The assessments should lead to diagnostic teaching.
4   The assessments should be built on evidence rather than on intuition.
5   Assessment data should be derived from everyday classroom activities.
6   Assessment opportunities should be sought in everyday classroom activities.
7   Semi-structured approaches to gathering data are recommended, generating words rather than numbers (measures).

8   Assessments should be linked to the student teacher's and the student's action planning.

9   Involve the students in the assessment process.

10   Communicate the assessment criteria to students where appropriate.

11   Demonstrate validity and reliability in the assessments, addressing particularly 'consequential validity'.

12   Demonstrate *fitness for purpose* in deciding the method(s) of gathering assessment data and setting assessment tasks.

13   Address quality assurance and quality control.

14   Select assessment methods that accord strongly with everyday teaching and learning processes.

A WORKED EXAMPLE OF AN ASSESSMENT ACTIVITY

Target child   The target child is a Year 2 (7-year-old) girl whom we shall call Saira.

Activity/assessment opportunity   We decide to assess her in a group situation with two other children; they will be playing a group game called 'The Snake Game'. In this game different coloured snakes have different numbers on them, some with numbers less than 10, others with numbers of 10 or greater. The number is the same for a snake of the same colour: 2 for a green snake, 3 for a yellow snake, 5 for a red snake, 10 for a brown snake, 12 for an orange snake, 15 for a white snake. The children can choose any snake if they answer correctly a question that is printed on each card in a set of cards. The cards can ask them: (a) to add single digits; (b) to add numbers greater than 10; (c) to subtract single digits from numbers between 10 and 100; (d) to subtract numbers over 10 from numbers between 11 and 100; (e) to count up the next 3 of a sequence, e.g. 2–4–6–8–10; 3–6–9–12–15; 5–10–15–20–25; (f) to count down the next 3 of a sequence, e.g. 30–25–20–15–10; 24–20–16–12–8; 30–27–24–21–18. Each child must write down the answer to each question, though they don't need to 'show the working' if they don't wish to. The winner is the child who is first to reach 100.

The purpose of the assessment   The assessment is diagnostic and formative and has several purposes:

(a) to see how well the child can read, write and order whole numbers up to 100 and to identify areas of strength and weakness in this;

(b) to see how secure the child's understanding is of place value up to 100, and to identify areas of strength and weakness in this;

(c) to see how well the child can add numbers below 10, greater than 10 (whose totals do not exceed 100), both mentally and on paper, and to identify areas of strength and weakness in this;

(d) to see how well the child can subtract numbers below 10 from totals of 100 or less, both mentally and on paper, and to identify areas of strength and weakness in this;

(e) to see how well the child can use repeated addition and subtraction in a number pattern.

The attainment target(s) and level of the national curriculum to be covered   Mathematics, attainment target 2 (number and algebra), Level 2 (though the level might turn out to be Level 1).

The timing and time-scale of the activity   A fifteen-minute activity in the mid-morning of a Wednesday.

Presentation mode, operation mode, response mode   The teacher will show the children what to do and give them practice in the mechanics of the game; the children will play the game, writing down algorithms and 'sums' where necessary; the response will be written.

The assessment evidence to be collected   Listening to the child's conversation and confidence in the activity (observation); her ability to work out 'sums' mentally (questioning); the contents of her written work (written); responses to the teacher's questions (questioning).

The (a) easy, (b) moderately difficult and (c) difficult aspects of the activity   (a) the addition (single figures) and subtraction (single figures – no decomposition); (b) addition and subtraction (double figures – no decomposition); (c) handling large numbers and subtraction with decomposition respectively.

The type of task   The application of already learnt material.

Threats to reliability and validity   The desire to win, the effect of losing or being incorrect or having difficulty, the effects of the other two children in the group, struggling to understand the rules of the game.

Addressing threats to reliability and validity   By discussion with the child; by ensuring that the child knows exactly what to do (with a demonstration by the child and the teacher before the assessment begins); by giving the child the opportunity to practise the 'mechanics' of how to play the game (i.e. so that the rules of the game do not obstruct the processes of using algorithms).

What to do if the child has difficulties   The teacher will prompt the child and indicate this in the assessment, suggesting that further work/practice is required.

The exact criteria to be used to judge the child's performance   See p. 403 – the purpose of the assessment.

The data/records to be brought to a moderation meeting   The teacher's written comments, a photocopy of the child's written work.

The record of the results   The work and the results will be held in the child's own portfolio and the teacher's record book.

Reporting the results   A summary report, together with the teacher's own record for discussion with the parents.

The report of the results   Saira was eager to play the game and was able to keep the other players enthusiastic, even though they were not winning very much. Saira usually chose 'high-value' snakes (bearing numbers greater than 10). She was able to count up and down in 2s, 3s, and 5s mentally but needed to write down the additions of numbers over 10 when her running total exceeded 30. Her written calculations were always correct in addition, and in subtraction where single digits were being subtracted. She sometimes used counters for this latter activity. Her subtraction of numbers over 10 from larger numbers (over 20) was correct if there was no decomposition but incorrect if decomposition was involved, e.g. $60 - 12 =$ and $53 - 15 =$. When I asked her how she 'worked out' the sums in her head she was clear on place value; when I asked her 'extension' questions about adding on in patterns of 2, 3 and 5 she was clear and correct, although when she was subtracting these mentally she was clear on what to do but sometimes incorrect in actually manipulating the numbers.

Assessment analysis   Saira has a good grasp of place value to 100, mental addition to 30 and simple subtraction without decomposition. She shows understanding of, and confidence in, using the correct algorithms for these processes. She can recognise and use number patterns of 2, 3, and 5. In national curriculum terms she is operating at Level 2 of the mathematics attainment target 2.

Recommendations   Saira is ready to apply the algorithms to larger numbers in addition (up to 100) in written and mental work, and to be introduced to decomposition in subtraction – using single figures only at this stage with much practical concept reinforcement before too much written (procedural) work.

It can be seen from this fairly lengthy example that the activity bears a strong similarity to the everyday activity of a 7-year-old in school and that the assessment has been planned with reference to, or derived from, the level descriptions and programmes of study of the national curriculum. Clearly, in the day-to-day work of the teacher the level of background detail reported here would not need to be formally recorded (e.g. the details of the game, perhaps the purpose of the assessment) – the details are written here for the purpose of explication and example. They indicate, in fact, that the teacher has taken account of the several factors involved in planning the assessment; the difference between this and the normal activity of the teacher is the degree of formality involved – the teacher might be advised to go through the series of planning considerations in her mind rather than on paper.

Chapter 17

Record-keeping

INTRODUCTION

During teaching practice the student teacher has a clear obligation to continue the day-to-day running of classes in line with the organisation and methods employed by the regular class teachers. In certain forms of classroom and school organisation, for example, where continuous assessment is practised, where vertical grouping and related schemes operate, adequate record-keeping is essential to the success of the educational programmes. Similarly, in systems practising 'individualised learning' the need for individual records is crucial. Further, with the rise of assessment and the increased attention given to the reporting of achievement there is a marked increase in the amount of record-keeping that is taking place in the school. It is the student teacher's responsibility to participate fully in the record-keeping system that is used in the school to which he or she is attached. What follows is an outline of the use of records and some suggestions for student teachers who find themselves faced with the task of designing record systems for their own use.

Record-keeping is often considered an irksome chore by many teachers. Since the 1988 Education Act the amount of record-keeping that teachers have to do has increased tremendously. In many cases the official records that schools used to keep of names, address, date of birth, previous schooling, contact telephone numbers, etc. are stored on computers; these are not the present subject of discussion. Rather, our concern is with the records that the teacher keeps in connection with the ongoing work in class and the progress of students at school. In many cases there is a 'house style' of record-keeping in schools, though this is usually for the more formal reporting to parents, the next school, the next teacher, the curriculum co-ordinator and the head-teacher. On the other hand many teachers keep personal records on their students, often for their own use rather than to be shown to others. Many considerations determine the records kept by teachers, for example:

- the purposes and uses of the record;
- the use of records for reporting;

- the formality of the record;
- the contents and level of detail of the record;
- the audience(s) of the record;
- the style (format) of the record;
- the timing of the record entry.

Different parties will be interested in different matters, for example a class teacher may wish to have a more detailed day-to-day record than, say, parents. A new school may seek a combination of a general record on a student's overall achievements together with specific details of particular strengths and weaknesses. A head of year or age phase or a teacher concerned with the pastoral aspects of schooling may wish to have information about students who are experiencing or have experienced personal, emotional, social or behavioural difficulties and how these have been met successfully by previous teachers. The different purposes that records serve require different contents and formats. For example, it may be that parents wish to have a jargon-free and easy-to-read summary of their child's progress whereas a receiving teacher may wish to have a more detailed and diagnostic record within each national curriculum subject. Records for a student teacher's personal use may contain notes and symbols that are unintelligible to others.

Some records may document curriculum content covered (e.g. by lists, schemes of work, web diagrams, flow charts, half-termly, weekly or daily plans that can also double up as records); others may be records of marks gained on students' written work. There may be individual students' records, group records, a whole class record. Some records may be numerical (e.g. marks scored); others may be verbal (a teacher's comments on progress, etc.); others may be samples of a student's own work; others may be photographic. Some records may be open-ended; others may be closed 'tick boxes'. As with assessment, the guiding principle for record-keeping must be 'fitness for purpose'. The implication of this is that student teachers initially must be clear about the purposes of their records, so that the contents, style and format, and level of detail serve the purposes clearly.

THE PURPOSES OF RECORD-KEEPING

Throughout this book we have advocated the objectives model as being useful for planning. The same holds true here: it is essential for the student teacher to be very clear on the purposes – the objectives – of the record-keeping. In one study,[1] typical reasons given by teachers for keeping records were:

- to chart pupil progress and achievement;
- to communicate information to other teachers;
- to ensure continuity of education through the school;
- to ensure continuity of education on transfer to other schools;
- to guide a replacement or a supply teacher;

- for diagnostic purposes – to spot problems, identify underachievement and pupils needing extra help;
- to provide teachers with information on the success (or failure) of teaching methods and materials;
- as a statement of 'what has happened' – to inform interested parties (parents, educational psychologists, headteacher);
- to give headteachers a general picture of achievement within the school.

A teacher may wish to augment these points by using records:

- to document effort;
- to record experiences to which the students have been exposed;
- to record a student's physical, emotional, social, intellectual development;
- to compare students;
- to chart rates of progress;
- to inform subsequent curriculum planning.

USE OF THE RECORD FOR REPORTING PURPOSES

A distinction has to be drawn between a record and a report. Typically a report is a selection from or a summary of details contained in teachers' records. The formal requirements of reporting to parents, for instance, is that by 31 July each year[2] parents should have received a written report on the student's attendance, achievement and performance in each subject of the national curriculum, including the results of public examinations where relevant and some comments on non-national curriculum subjects, together with reports of the student's level of attainment on the 10-level scale of each national curriculum subject at the end of each key stage. The report should include a commentary and explanation by the teacher of what the achievements and attainments mean.

Though such reporting can draw on teachers' detailed notes and records, one can argue that this level of reporting is not specific enough for a teacher's detailed diagnostic records. Indeed, reporting to parents is often of a summative nature whereas the records that teachers keep are both summative and formative.

THE FORMALITY OF THE RECORD

A record for a teacher's 'private consumption' might take the form of short notes on a particular student's progress in various areas of the national curriculum, complemented by scores on tests and details of a student's achievement in the formal assessments of the national curriculum (e.g. his or her level of achievement of the several attainment targets in the national curriculum). The teacher may review and select from his or her private records data that are to become part of a more formal record for 'public consumption', e.g. for the next teacher, for a student's parents or guardians. A teacher may wish to record some particular personal details, e.g. about a student's behaviour during breaks or lunchtimes, that he or she may not wish to make public unless matters reach a critical point (though the Data Protection Act[3] makes it a requirement that students should be able to see all records that are held on them). The Education Reform Act of 1988 made it a legal requirement that reports should be given to parents and guardians on their child's performance in the national curriculum at a minimum of once each year. A formal record may be more generalised than an informal record, the former being largely summative and the latter being largely formative. A formal report might include statements from the national curriculum attainment targets or level descriptions that teachers complete with a mark against each statement. A statement of special educational needs is a legal document which specifies action to be taken to meet the special needs of a student; the framing, terminology and detail of the record require careful consideration. Some formal records are anodyne or only contain positive achievements; others are very much more detailed and diagnostic.

Many student teachers will not be required to contribute to or complete a formal record as this is usually undertaken by teachers. However, many student teachers will be teaching one class or more for a substantial period of time, typically up to nearly a term for a final teaching practice. This means that student teachers will probably have to provide teachers with specific data for use in the formal record. Further, given that student teachers will eventually become qualified themselves, it is important that they have the opportunity to look at, discuss and provide data for the formal records that schools keep.

CONTENTS OF THE RECORD

The contents of some records are prescribed by law, regarding a student's coverage of and achievements in the national curriculum. However, the national curriculum is only one element of a student's experiences at school. There are other equally important matters that may feature in a record, such as social, emotional and moral development; a student's overall standard of behaviour; confidence; effort; motivation; interests and enthusiasms; friends and friendship patterns. A diagnostic record will necessarily be more detailed that a summative record of achievements and progress because it is usually criterion-referenced in order that action may be taken on specific matters. The contents of a record will reflect the focus of interest, the level of detail required, the level of formality and sense of audience, and the framing of the record, for example whether it will be strictly in the terminology of the national curriculum, whether it will comment on knowledge, concepts, skills and attitudes, subject-specific and cross-curricular matters, personal and social development, medical factors (e.g. speech, co-ordination, overall health).

Student teachers will find it useful to examine records as a way of finding out rapidly about curricula for, and assessments of, students in the classes that they will be teaching. These records might be in the form of an individual student's record (in which case permission has to be obtained to look at the record) or a record of work undertaken and curricula experienced by a whole class or particular groups.

THE AUDIENCES OF THE RECORD

Different audiences find different types of information useful. Barrs and Johnson[4] identify eight different audiences of records and indicate how the functions of records differ according to their audience(s), for example: the teacher himself/herself; other teachers who have contact with the student; receiving teachers; other teachers in the school; the headteacher; parents; local authority assessment moderators; wider audiences. This is not to deny interested parties access to different information; rather it reflects different interests at work. There are many different 'stakeholders' in education who may require different types of information and who may use data for different purposes. In some respects this is akin to assessment, which was seen in Chapter 16 to serve political agendas of control and managerialist agendas of accountability of schools to their consumers. Records can be used for accountability (e.g. in the documenting and reporting of students' achievements in external tests) and for more educational purposes (e.g. planning and implementing a well-matched curriculum).

It is significant that Barrs and Johnson include only adults in the audiences of records, neglecting the students themselves. This reflects the bureaucratic and managerialist tenor of much record-keeping. However, we commented earlier that one important purpose of assessment was to be able to give feedback to students so that they would become involved in their own learning. So it is with records; they provide information which can form the basis of, or contribute to, discussions between students and student teachers as one stage in the action-planning cycle that has featured throughout this book.

STYLE AND FORMAT OF THE RECORD

There are several ways of entering data on a record that resonate with the ways of entering assessment results, for example by using numbers, words, samples of work, photographic evidence. As with the recording of assessments these ways can vary from the closed 'tick-box' approach to the open-ended record that enables the student teacher to write comments about a given matter (e.g. speaking and listening skills) that are tailored to a specific student. Recording might take the form of:

1 Marks or grades recorded on coursework or non-standardised tests, ensuring that the criteria for mark ranges or grades are discrete, clear, hierarchical (i.e. progressively difficult), defined in concrete terms, and recognising that the extremes of the lowest and highest levels may only apply to a small number of students.

2 Personal observations (from structured or semi-structured observation), for example:

Joanne

Mathematics: A fast worker who prefers to work alone. She can represent and access complex data on a histogram, bar chart and line graph, using appropriate scales. She is able to access data on a pie chart and can use the computer to enter data for a pie chart; she understands the notion of proportions in a pie chart and is beginning to be able to construct simple pie charts that show this understanding.

Shaun

English (writing): Is able to express himself well on a wide variety of matters using appropriate vocabulary and registers. He enjoys writing non-fiction accounts, where his grasp of grammatical structure and clarity of style indicate his ability to explain complex phenomena straightforwardly. Shaun is able to write imaginatively and creatively in a range of fiction areas though he particularly enjoys science fiction.

3 Self-recording charts that students complete as they progress through a scheme of work, for example the self-recording charts that accompany many commercially produced mathematics and language schemes of work. This form of self-recording is usually very straightforward, comprising details of the pages that have been read in a reading book, the mathematics exercises that have been completed, with maybe some very simple extensions, e.g. what was found easy/difficult/interesting, rather than a fuller type of self-assessment.

4 Results of standardised tests and assessments (e.g. of achievements of the national curriculum) for each student, for example Box 89.

5 Ticks against statements with room for a student teacher's own comments (perhaps using the terms of the national curriculum statements of attainment and/or level descriptions, though these may be too generalised for student teachers who are only in the school for a limited period of time, in which case they may have to use more specific terminology than used in the national curriculum), for example Box 90 (for each child).

The four statements in the box are taken from the national curriculum for mathematics at Key Stage 4. It can be seen immediately that space (and time) can be saved if statements are not written verbatim from the national curriculum documents but a shorthand version is used.

6 Coded entries and comments against particular statements, for example:

Box 89 Recording results of formal assessments

ENGLISH	Level 1	Level 2	Level 3	Level 4	Level 5
	TA SAT	TA SAT	TA SAT	TA SAT	TA SAT
AT1 Speaking and listening					
AT2 Reading					
AT3 Writing					

Box 90 Recording specific details of students' progress

Can vary the flow of electricity in a simple circuit and observe the effects.	**Comments**
(a) Can use sampling methods, considering their reliability.	
(b) Has extended skills in handling data into constructing and interpreting histograms.	
(c) Can describe the dispersion of a set of data; can find and interpret the standard deviation of a set of data.	
(d) Understands when and how to estimate conditional probabilities.	

Measuring temperature using a thermometer.
A tick – introduced, continue to reinforce
A tick crossed through with another line – needs further help

Either of the above together with a circle around the tick – ready to advance

This example identifies the starting point at which a student has been introduced to a curriculum feature. It is cumulative in practice in that improvement is recorded by adding to a given symbol (putting a line through an existing tick) rather than requiring the student teacher to erase the first or second symbol in order to replace it with another. While the example shows how a closed record-keeping system can be used, in practice the difficulty in this type of recording is that it runs away with itself; the student teacher ends up spending as much time on the recording as the planning. Whilst this approach may be useful in providing an in-depth approach to record-keeping, in practice it often becomes unworkably detailed (e.g. in a primary school it could generate 30 students × 10 subjects × 30 statements = 9,000 statements to be reviewed). The secret here is to operationalise the statements without generating a level of detail that is overwhelming; this is exactly the same problem as that mentioned earlier in connection with criterion-referenced assessment.

This type of 'coded' response is particularly useful where the student teacher wishes to have a whole-class or group record rather than an individual student's record (see Box 91). On this class record the student teacher can

Box 91 A whole-class or group record

Student's name	Activity 1	Activity 2	Activity 3	Activity 4
Martin Armstrong				
Janice Asher				
Ahmet Al-Sabah				
Ruth Brown				
Soo-Lee Chang				
Joanna Davison				

specify exactly what items 1, 2, 3 and 4 are. In each cell the student teacher can enter comments and/or a code:

| = Has had experience of
+ = Needs further reinforcement
* = Ready to move on

A second example of this approach will list the names of the students targeted and then indicate the activity that is the focus of the record, for example Box 92. There is also a space for individual comments to be written if required.

Box 92 A class or group record of an activity

Student's name	Cutting sticky squares into halves and quarters	Naming the fractions formed – quarter, half, three-quarters	Finding equivalencies – quarter, half, three-quarters
Michaela Bayes			
Angela Downs			
Peter Forrest			
James Kelly			

A third example might break down an activity into significant elements, with space provided for a student teacher's comments, for example Box 93.

A fourth example of codes and comments is of a record of activities undertaken over a period of time, maybe each week, for example Box 94. Here space is required for the student teacher to specify in more detail in the appropriate cells exactly what each student has done (unless it is possible to have included this in the column descriptor) together with relevant comments and codes to reflect effort, achievement and a diagnosis of the success of the outcome.

What we have, then, is a combination of a closed record-keeping system and an open-ended system, numbers/codes and words respectively, i.e. a double entry. Having a system that enables data about many students to be entered on a single record facilitates comparisons between students. Some

Box 93 Recording several aspects of an activity

Student's name	Designing a crane	Making the crane	Testing the crane	Evaluating the results	Improving the design
Sahira Anwaz					
Zoe Bond					
James Clinton					
Sean Davison					
Jane Flynn					

Box 94 Recording activities over a period of time

Student's name	Language task	Science investigation	Art activity	History project
Yasmin Bakhtar				
Paula Bates				
John Clements				
Alan Dodds				
Susan Evans				

record-keeping systems might be structured to provide room for a double entry wherein a code is used to indicate achievement and another code for effort, for example:

A =   all points clearly understood
B =   reinforce a little
C =   reinforce a great deal

1 =   has made a very good effort
2 =   has made an acceptable effort
3 =   has made little or no effort

7 Multiple-choice statements (where each statement must be discrete and it must be made clear whether more than one statement in a group of statements can be selected).

8 Open-ended areas for comment (where an element of, say, language is indicated, e.g. a student's response to a piece of literature) and space provided for comments to be written, or where national curriculum statements are given, for example in mathematics:

Mathematics (understanding and using measures): Develop an understanding of the difference between discrete and continuous measures; read and interpret scales, including decimal scales, and understand the degree of accuracy that is possible, or appropriate, for a given purpose.

Alan has a sound grasp of the difference between discrete and continuous measures and has acquired this understanding through representing and interpreting different types of data using a variety of scales, including decimal scales. He is able to choose appropriate scales for different types of data and different purposes.

Another example of an open-ended record-keeping system is presented in Box 95. This type of record is useful providing it is focused and selective (i.e. identifying priorities) and recognises that a particular activity may serve more than one curriculum area, for example language, mathematics, IT and history.

A compromise between too closed and too open a record can be seen where an agenda and major focuses are established but the student teacher is able to tailor comments to individuals. For example:

Speaking and listening (identifying major strengths and needs in relation to personal accounts, providing information and explanation, participation in class discussions, collaboration within a small group, awareness of register and vocabulary).

Reading (identifying major strengths and needs in relation to the range of the reading diet, fluency and reading strategies used, understanding and recall, responding to literature, study skills, enjoyment).

Box 95 An open-ended record-keeping system

Student's name	Activity/task	Knowledge, concepts, skills, attitudes	Comment on effort and achievement (what was learnt)	Action needed
Deborah Roe				
Alex Sanders				
Mary Slater				
Paula Squires				

Writing (identifying major strengths and needs in relation to awareness of audience, conveying meaning clearly and appropriately, use of vocabulary and syntax, drafting, using different forms of writing, spelling, use of word-processing facilities).

In this example the rubric suggests areas of focus for the student teacher, but there is no necessity for slavish adherence to these if they are inappropriate. A much-publicised example of this type of record is the Primary Language Record from the former ILEA.[5]

There is a well-documented problem concerning open-ended statements and comments that teachers write, *viz.* that the statement reflects more the biases, preferences and subjectivity of the record writer (the teacher) than the student. Law[6] draws attention to six problematical types of statement in connection with this:

1   Undefined statements – which use jargon that is inappropriate for the target audience or that conceals the writer's true intentions, for example: 'has difficulty interpreting interpersonal behaviour and modifying own response when necessary' (i.e. is a major disruptive influence in the class or I don't like this student); 'can use phonic skills, particularly digraphs, in monosyllabic word attack' (i.e. can read simple single-syllable words).
2   Mixed statements – which say more than one thing at a time. The writer is attempting a nuanced statement but a reader does not know which part

of the statement to emphasise, for example: 'can take initiative but prefers guidance'; 'is absent regularly but apparently with good reason'; 'is an intelligent and amusing talker'.

3   Non-operational statements – which, although apparently based on observed behaviours and events, use language which renders it difficult to imagine the behaviour that gave rise to the comment, for example: 'is very polite and creates a good impression' (i.e. shows off to visitors or is genuinely polite to all teachers in all lessons and all situations); 'has distinct leadership potential' (i.e. the ringleader of disruptive behaviour or is able to organise other students very positively and supportively); 'has a very strong personality' (i.e. is awkward and a bully or reacted very well when finding the work difficult).

4   Generalised statements – where a statement about one facet of a student is made in such a way as to render it applicable to all facets of the student (when the teacher does not see all facets of a student), for example: 'is reluctant to try new ideas' (i.e. did not enjoy the new history topic or preferred to work on his or her own); 'does not like to be in the limelight' (i.e. did not want to take part in the school pantomime or was very modest about ten grade-A passes at GCSE); 'needs constant encouragement to relate to others' (was very difficult in my music lessons or was very shy in my class drama lessons).

5   Interpretive statements – which point to underlying states and conditions rather than to specific behaviour, where the knowledge of the underlying states and conditions can only flow from an intimate knowledge of the student (which the teacher rarely has), for example: 'is capable of sustained friendships' (i.e. always chooses to work with the same two other students); 'has exceptional self-confidence' (i.e. did not bother to consider other approaches to solving a problem); 'is very resilient' (i.e. always undertook corrections without complaint).

6   Value-laden statements – where the student is judged according to the personal preferences of the teacher, for example: 'is lazy and unhelpful' (i.e. I didn't like the way that he or she responded to failure); 'has a friendly, helpful attitude' (i.e. I always give him or her the jobs to do in the classroom); 'makes constructive contributions to classsroom discussions and activities' (i.e. I always ask him or her to speak first in a class discussion).

All of these examples show (a) how easy it can be for a record to be interpreted in a way not intended by the writer, and (b) how easy it is for the writer's personality and preferences to colour the comments in a record. In one sense this is an intractable problem as long as people use words, for a writer's vocabulary may be similar to a reader's but they may identify different connotations in the same words. A record writer, then, may find it salutary to consider whether: (a) he or she likes students who resemble him or her in temperament and personality; (b) he or she dislikes students who resemble him or her in temperament and personality; (c) students whom he or she likes have characteristics that he or she likes; (d) students whom he or she dislikes have characteristics that he or she dislikes. We are not suggesting that teachers deliberately misrepresent their students; rather we are arguing that biases can all too easily slip in unnoticed by the record-keeper – be they positive or negative they can easily misrepresent the student.

It is important, then, for word-based statements to be framed as objectively and evidentially as possible, so that solutions to the six problems outlined above can be met by ensuring that statements are:

(a) defined – so that everybody who reads them will understand them in the same way;
(b) singular – they say one thing at a time;
(c) operational – they describe what the student has been doing to give rise to the comment;
(d) specific – they indicate the circumstances in which the characteristic has been demonstrated;
(e) guess-free – they say only what can be correctly known about the student;
(f) value-neutral – they do not voice the writer's preferences for one student over another.

This is an art that needs to be practised by student teachers looking critically at comments that are written about a student in a record. It also applies very particularly to a record of achievement (discussed later) where even greater opportunities exist for open-ended, subjective, prejudiced remarks to be made.

9 Comments taken from lesson, daily and weekly evaluations and plans. It is often the case that student teachers refer to particular students or groups in a class when they are writing evaluations on lessons, a day's activities or a weekly review. These evaluations can provide important data for record-keeping.

10 Photographs.

11 Flow charts, web diagrams, descriptions of curricula studied (where a planning document doubles as a recording document).

12 There is also a completely open-ended type of record that begins life as a sheet of paper bearing only a student's name, and the student teacher enters notes made about unanticipated behaviours, learning, comments by a student. This is a salutary exercise, for the student teacher can review these sheets after a few weeks and think why more notes have been made on one student than on another (e.g. is the student teacher concentrating more of his or her attention on one student rather than another, and if so, why?).

A standardised format enables data to be entered fairly rapidly and enables the student teacher to compare one student with another. Moreover, a standardised format may enable some useful parity to be achieved between teachers and age phases, enabling continuity to be addressed – vertically across several teachers of a specified age group and laterally across several teachers as a student moves up through a school. On the other hand tick-boxes and closed forms of recording may fail to catch some important individual features about a student. In this case it may be more advisable to have a semi-structured approach to record-keeping, wherein an area for comment is specified (maybe with reference to attainment targets of the national curriculum) and space is provided for a student teacher's individual comments, carefully referenced to specific individuals and activities. There is a danger in more open forms of recording that the record may become platitudinous and generalised, saying more about the student teacher's likes and dislikes than the student's (discussed later). Open-ended forms of recording must confine themselves to evidential matters, noting the context and activity that gave rise to the record entry.

There is a tension, therefore, between the need for standardisation and the need to be able to catch each student's individuality on a record. Further, there is another tension between the overall desirability of parsimony in a record – for rapidity and ease of completion – and the need for a record to be sufficiently detailed and comprehensive to provide useful data (i.e. data upon which action can be taken). There is a third tension between the ability of the record to enable the student teacher to enter data in his or her own preferred manner and the need to avoid so personalised a style or format that personal prejudices can appear.

TIMING OF THE RECORD ENTRY

The notion of 'fitness for purpose' that was mentioned earlier also applies to the timing of record entries. It might be most fitting to complete a summative record each half-term whereas it might be more fitting to review detailed records on a daily or weekly basis. All data entered on a record should be dated in order that the student teacher can chart rates of progress. Timing of data entry varies according to the purpose (formative/summative) of the record, the level of detail required (the less the detail, the less frequent the record) and the focus (the more specific the focus the more frequent the entry, though more open entries are not necessarily less frequent). Moreover, we have assumed so far that the timing of the data entry will be regular – once a day, once a week, once a term, etc. This need not be the case. For example, an entry in a record could be made whenever a particular event occurs, which may be once in a day or once in a week. This echoes the comments on 'event sampling' earlier, where the occurrence of the event is recorded (and dated) rather than the number of occasions on which it occurs in a given period of time. This raises the important concept of the 'critical-incident' approach[7] where the significance of an event can be recognised (e.g. when a child first writes her name correctly) rather than its frequency. This type of data entry enables unanticipated events, comments and behaviour to be noted.

The picture of record-keeping that we have painted so far has portrayed it as being a relatively complex activity which has increased in tandem with the bureaucratisation and management of education. We recognise that this may be off-putting for student teachers. Nevertheless, throughout the discussion here we have provided examples of different record-keeping systems that student teachers may wish to adopt during their teaching practice. We suggest that student teachers do not confine themselves simply to recording students' achievements of the national curriculum but keep notes on all aspects of a student's development, strengths, needs, interests, and social and emotional make-up.

Part I included reference to the particular competences in record-keeping framed by the DFEE. These competences required student teachers to be able to record systematically, use these results for subsequent planning and teaching, and record a student's progress in terms of the national curriculum. A student teacher undertaking a short teaching practice might not be in the school or class for a sufficient length of time to be able to complete the most perfunctory records. However, many student teachers are placed in a school for up to a term's duration; in light of this as a minimum requirement we suggest that a student teacher's records for a term's teaching practice should include:

(a) A record of work and activities undertaken in each curriculum area taught. This might be in the form of a web or flow diagram, a sequence of lessons, a scheme of work, an ongoing record of activities undertaken.
(b) A formative and diagnostic record of every student's progress in the national curriculum areas taught, highlighting particular successes and difficulties encountered.
(c) A summative record of every student's achievements and efforts for every national curriculum subject taught (for primary school student teachers this will probably be with reference to a single class of children; for secondary school student teachers this will probably be with reference to a single main subject together with personal and social education).
(d) A 'blank sheet' type of record for each student (though this is perhaps more practicable in primary than in secondary school classes in the time available) which records unanticipated events, observations, comments, etc. that move beyond the narrow intellectual or academic record and towards a more holistic record on a student's whole personality, personal, emotional and social development, particular strengths and needs, particular achievements and interests.

Unfortunately, for many teachers record-keeping seems to be a bureaucratic chore. However, we suggest that this need not be the case. Records that are linked to assessment which, in turn, is linked to planning, can provide important documentation for addressing progression and continuity. Above all they must be useful; a cosmetic record that has no formative or summative potential is a sheer waste of time. Students on teaching practice may find that they are requested to deposit a copy of their records with the school for the school's own record-keeping purposes.

Chapter 18

Records of achievement

BACKGROUND

So great has been the impact of records of achievement (ROAs) that commentators often talk of the records of achievement 'movement' which began in the late 1970s and early 1980s. This notion captures the zeal with which ROAs were discussed, the strength of feeling – both positive and negative – that ROAs engendered, and the recognition that ROAs can be a major lever of change throughout a school.

In terms of management implications, the decision to implement ROAs can lead to the appointment of an ROA/assessment co-ordinator, particularly in secondary schools. There is also a time dimension: time must be allocated for the co-ordinator to undertake the role, and the implementation of ROAs requires time to be found during lessons for the necessary review and action-planning processes and for the discussions involved in negotiating and setting objectives for the future – academic or otherwise. This requires a relationship between teacher and student wherein social distance is reduced. The teacher moves from being solely a judge, provider of information, expert, director, instructor, controller and sometimes a dictator to being a witness, provider of opportunity, partner, consultant, counsellor, enabler and negotiator. This constitutes a major cultural and pedagogical shift in roles and role relations which opens up the pastoral side of education. Considerable courage is required for staff to accept that they may be deskilled and that they need reskilling in different pedagogical practices.

Hoyle[1] comments that curriculum innovation requires a major change in the internal organisation of the school and that changing the internal organisation of the school is itself a major innovation. Implementing ROAs and new pedagogical practices has major resource implications (including resources of time, money, space, materials and people) not only within the school but in the field of in-service education (INSET) to support the change (e.g. to develop counselling skills in teachers).

Traditional assessment cast the teacher as the assessor who set summative examinations, marked them in private and wrote a report about the student's success or failure in private, to be delivered to the student's parents or guardian. The student was largely kept out of the assessment and report construction. By contrast an ROA – also called a profile – is the outcome of a joint discussion and joint assessment between the teacher and the student in which all of the statements are positive (it is a record of achievement, not failure), there is a strong formative potential in the comments made, where the student and teacher together plan targets (see the comments earlier on ipsative assessment). Indeed, the National Record of Achievement[2] argues that the process of recording achievements and planning future developments helps people to take greater control of their education and training and to take pride in their achievements. Student involvement and ownership is high, indeed it is the case that the ROA is the student's property,[3] to be shown to, or withheld from, certain audiences at the discretion of the student. An ROA is intended to have high student involvement and ownership, with concomitant motivational significance for the student.

An ROA is not a report, nor is it a reference. It is more akin to a *curriculum vitae* (CV) in which achievements are noted; indeed, many ROAs contain a CV. Many teachers feel uncomfortable in omitting negative comments from an ROA, arguing that it is a dereliction of their duty not to make clear the weaknesses as well as the strengths of a student. However, a teacher has opportunities to comment on weaknesses as well as strengths in a report or a reference – written or oral. A report is a separate document or event altogether. Given that many parents (and teachers) are disturbed by the ROA, believing that it distorts the student's abilities by not commenting on the negative aspects or areas of weakness, there is an important message to be communicated to parents (and teachers) about the nature of the ROA and its relationship to formal reports and references, to say what an ROA is not and what a report or reference is.

THE PURPOSES OF A RECORD OF ACHIEVEMENT

Although the DES found considerable variety in the nature of the records and the processes involved in compiling them, nevertheless some common features were found, *viz.*, 'they set out to record achievements of young people, or assessment of their personal qualities, which go beyond examination results'.[4] One can see from this definition that the significant features of an ROA are that it:

- is an ongoing and cumulative record of a student's achievements in school and out of school, including curricular and extra-curricular activities;
- is the outcome of a discussion between the teacher and the student;
- is based on identifiable evidence from a wide data source;
- records success and positive achievements;

- is designed to involve and motivate students, raising their self-awareness, self-esteem and confidence, and thereby enhance learning;
- makes clear to students and other interested parties the criteria that are being used to make comments and judgements;
- is the student's own property.

This accords with the four aims of an ROA set out by the DES:[5]

1   Recognition of achievement (not solely in terms of public examinations but in other ways).
2   Motivation and personal development (increasing students' awareness of strengths, weaknesses and opportunities).
3   Enhancement of the curriculum and organisation for the student (considering how well the curriculum, teaching and organisation enable students to develop general, practical and social skills).
4   A document or record when leaving school (for employers and institutions of further and higher education).

It was envisaged that an ROA would enhance employment prospects for students and, indeed, that employers might be involved in contributing to the ROA. As the secretary of state for education remarked when introducing the National Record of Achievement (NRA):[6]

> The economic well-being of the country relies on having the right people with the right skills in the right jobs. We will only achieve that if we can secure the commitment of employers and employees to effective education. The Government is committed to the concept of life-long learning. As a further step to support that process we are introducing the National Record of Achievement (NRA). Records of achievement have significant value in motivating learners, whether at school, in further or higher education, training or employment and the NRA is one of the cornerstones of the ROA process. The NRA is designed to present a simple record, in summary form, of an individual's achievements throughout education, training and working life. It encourages people to take an active part in their own training and development, and gives employers a convenient and comprehensible record of what somebody can do. The relevant parts of the NRA might additionally help schools to report to parents on the achievements of pupils aged 16–18.

One can see from this lengthy catch-all quotation that the secretary of state's view of the NRA is that it can be used in employment, that keeping an ROA is summative though the ongoing processes are formative, that it can be used in a variety of contexts and shown to a variety of audiences, that it can contribute to the educative process and raise motivation by involving students, that it uses a wide data source, and that it is criterion-referenced. This view was enhanced by the Department of Employment in 1991[7] when they explicitly stated that the 'National Record of Achievement is just one of the ways the Departments of Employment and Education and Science are working together to help you create that better skilled, better qualified workforce'.

These elements are both the greatest strengths and greatest weaknesses of an ROA. Hargreaves[8] adopts a much less sanguine view of ROAs, arguing that the involvement of potential employers and their use in seeking employment might result in the ROA being used against a student – for selection rather than motivation – as one student's ROA may be less impressive than another's. The results could be demotivating for students. Further, Hargreaves argues that, in fact, an ROA is a sop for disaffected students who will not meet the gold standard of academic qualifications, that: (a) they will see through the ROA in the course of time, as the academic agenda for education is comparatively unchanged and unchangeable by students – it is still a 'given' rather than a negotiable curriculum; and (b) the academically gifted will not require an ROA to gain access to higher education and better employment prospects.

The key tension that Hargreaves exposes is between using an ROA either for motivation or for selection; the more one serves the former the less one serves the latter and vice versa. This tension is not resolved in the government's view of an ROA, indeed it is exacerbated in that there is a requirement that a student's achievements in the national curriculum should be recorded in the ROA.[9] Hargreaves is arguing that the ROA can be seen as a government response to a motivational crisis in education, the economy and society and that, by stressing motivation, the government is able to appeal to very different sectors – employers, students, parents and educators. Hargreaves's argument is useful in that it sets out the potential chasm between the rhetoric and the reality of ROAs. This is discussed in more detail later in this chapter; for the present, we confine ourselves to setting out the main features and contents of an ROA and the principal benefits to be derived from them.

If this tension (principle *versus* practice) is combined with the realisation that ROAs are very time-consuming to complete (both for students and teachers) one has to question whether the claims that are made for ROAs in principle can be sustained in practice. Practical difficulties include negotiating the contents and finding time for completion of the records.

CONTENTS OF A RECORD OF ACHIEVEMENT

An important feature of an ROA is its intention to embrace more than the national curriculum or the successful learning of an academic curriculum. Hence its contents can include:

- subject-specific achievements, attainments and targets (for students who will not be leaving school at the time of entering data on the ROA), for example in terms of knowledge, concepts, skills and attitudes (within and outside the national curriculum, both award-bearing and non-award-bearing) together with samples of work where relevant;

- cross-curricular achievements, attainments and targets (for students who will not be leaving school at the time of entering data on the ROA), for example in terms of knowledge, concepts, skills and attitudes;
- personal and social skills and achievements;
- other experiences and achievements (including events, awards, interests and activities undertaken);
- a personal statement written by the student.

In most cases the contents (and often the format) of the ROA are similar, comprising:

1 An introductory sheet to the ROA that indicates its overall purpose, contents and contributors.

2 A sheet with factual information, for example: the student's name, address and date of birth; the school(s) attended (with dates); courses followed (e.g. in secondary school for GCSE, B Tec, GNVQ and A-level); attendance figures; punctuality; a place for the student and class teacher/ headteacher to sign.

3 A sheet for curricular achievements (in the national curriculum, public examinations – where relevant – and other areas), with appropriate marks, grades, awards and a commentary.

4 A sheet for general achievements, experiences[10] and interests (e.g. sports, extra-curricular activities at school and out of school, work experience). These may include:
core skills (communication, Information Technology, personal skills, numeracy, problem-solving);
personal and social qualities (e.g. self-reliance, coping with pressure, perseverance, determination, supporting others, working collaboratively, including samples of certificates or special commendations that have been gained in school);
other qualifications (e.g. in music examinations of the Associated Board of the Royal Colleges of Music, First Aid certificates of the St. John Ambulance Brigade, the Duke of Edinburgh's award).

5 Employment history (part time and full time), including community participation.

6 A sheet for an action plan that might include agreed statements between the student, teacher and parent(s) covering, for example:
Where am I now? (review)
Where am I going? (goals)
What are my next steps? (targets)
How will I get there? (arrangements).

7   A sheet for a personal statement, in which the student might comment on himself or herself in different contexts (e.g. at school, at home, in the community),[11] interests and activities that he or she has particularly enjoyed (at school and out of school), particular abilities and achievements, looking forward to the coming months (e.g. moving to the secondary school, college, employment, higher education).

8   Samples of work (if desired, i.e. a portfolio of work that might be selected to reflect the spread of experiences, work of particular interest to the student, examples of high-quality work, favourite pieces of work, important pieces of work) together with the student's commentary on the samples.

9   Statements by the class teacher/headteacher and parent(s).

An ROA contains both a review and an action plan. This sets it at the heart of this book's support for action planning. The review, action plan and personal statement specify behaviours rather than qualities, i.e. concrete matters rather than non-concrete matters, enabling specific targets to be set and reviewed. Typically the entries in the ROA will be made by students themselves, though in many cases entries are also made by teachers, parents and other 'significant adults'. Entries will be numerical – maybe marks, grades or levels of achievement – and verbal, including commentaries on particular achievements.

It is sometimes the case that item banks of statements by teachers are held on computer and are called up and combined to make the commentary and teachers' comments. That this is problematical can be seen at parents' evenings – often at secondary school level – when parents, initially believing that the comments made about their child are unique, speak to other parents only to find that in many cases the comments are the same or nearly the same for other children. On occasions the parents' feeling of betrayal spills over into anger! On the other hand, given the size of the task facing a teacher who may teach 200 students a week, it is scarcely surprising that he or she may use computer software to ease this enormous task.

FINDING TIME TO COMPLETE A RECORD OF ACHIEVEMENT

In recognition of the significant time-implications of keeping ROAs the Schools Examinations and Assessment Council[12] suggested several ways in which time might be found to write them:

1   'Directed time' after school (i.e. that time that the headteacher can fix at his or her discretion to be used for a named activity).

2   For primary teachers, bringing in secondary teachers who have non-contact time after their students have completed their public examinations.

3   For secondary teachers, using colleagues who have non-contact time after

their students have completed their public examinations.

4   Building in non-contact time on the timetable and budgeting.

5   Releasing staff when a nominated member of staff (e.g. the headteacher) takes a whole-school or year-group assembly.

6   Team-teaching/team covering.

7   Splitting classes with work set, where students undertake the work in another teacher's class.

8   For primary teachers, providing 'busy boxes' of educationally worthwhile activities that can be undertaken whilst the teacher completes an ROA.

9   Bringing in other adults (including parents) to assist in classes.

Quite how realistic these suggestions are is highly questionable. Teachers find their non-contact time is taken up with preparation and marking; primary (and some secondary) children simply cannot be left to 'get on' with activities that are largely unsupervised (regardless of the legal implications); schools do not have enough money to provide 'supply cover' to release teachers; splitting a class often requires more time in preparation and follow-up than the lesson itself; team-teaching implies that the whole team is with the students.

What is certain is that, because of the centrality of negotiation in an ROA, time must be found to complete elements of the ROA with the students during teaching time rather than away from them in the teacher's directed time. As was mentioned earlier, this has pedagogical implications; for example, lessons will require careful planning to free the teacher to work with one student at a time on his or her ROA – setting work to occupy the other students productively.

WRITING COMMENTS ON A RECORD OF ACHIEVEMENT

Comments should spring from discussions between the teacher and the student. That is to say, the student's comments should figure in the ROA. This is a very difficult task for inarticulate students, slow or poor writers (particularly young children) or for some students whose first language is not English. The problem is compounded for students who seem to have made only minimal progress over a period of time – what do they have to report? The question arises of whether the ROA is as motivating as the claims made for it. It could well be the case (and often is) that teachers discuss progress with the student but the teacher writes the statements, the student's contribution being confined to the personal statement. The comments in an ROA should reflect positive achievements, however minimal these might be.

It was mentioned in connection with assessment that the nature of the referent should be made clear,[13] for example whether an assessment has been criterion-referenced, norm-referenced, self-referenced (ipsative-referenced).

The same is true for ROAs. For example, in the following comments on an ROA the referent is often unclear:

'Paul makes every effort to concentrate on his handwriting' (is this ipsative-referencing or norm-referencing, i.e. are Paul's efforts good for Paul or good in comparison to the rest of the class?).

'Susan has made a little progress this year in her geography map-reading' (is this ipsative-referencing (in comparison to her progress last year), norm-referencing (in comparison with other students), or criterion-referencing (in her achievement of the national curriculum)?).

'This term Jamila has been more successful in keeping up with the history work' (is this ipsative-referencing (Jamila has been better this term in comparison with a previous term), norm-referencing (when compared to others in the class), or criterion-referencing (in meeting the specific demands of the history topic)?).

'Michael has found the physics topic quite demanding this term but overall he has improved' (is this ipsative-referencing (in comparison with the physics that was studied in the previous term), norm-referencing (in comparison with his peers), or criterion-referencing (in terms of meeting the specific academic demands of the physics topic)?).

'Ahmed adopts a mature approach to the mathematics' (is this ipsative-referencing (where Ahmed has settled down to study more than in the previous term), norm-referencing (saying that Ahmed is more studious than his peers), criterion-referencing (that Ahmed meets the criteria for a student working at Level 9 in the national curriculum)?).

As with assessment, the data entered on an ROA must be evidential, concrete and specific so that the reader knows exactly what the referent is and the context and activity that gave rise to the comment.

Many students may find very threatening the whole business of sitting with a teacher to discuss their progress and achievements. This requires considerable thought by the teacher and, in many cases, in-service preparation for counselling skills: listening, responding, summarising, conferencing, asking unthreatening questions, being very aware of non-verbal indications of stress in the student – the tight body position, the anxious swing of the leg, the avoidance of eye contact, the protective folding of the arms. For some students having a teacher sitting next to them – rather than opposite them across a table – might reduce stress, for others it might increase stress, particularly if the teacher is male and the student is female. In many cases the teacher will need to practise questioning, initiating, summarising skills so they are not threatening. Moreover, it is useful for the teacher to review who set the agenda, who did the most talking, who took the lead in a session designed to be a partnership in reviewing progress and action planning, whose comments actually appear on the ROA, whether the discussion that led to the comments was more like a dissemination of the teacher's judgements, a consultation about a given agenda, or a genuine focused discussion on mutually agreed matters.

Clearly the completion of an ROA exercises the mind of the experienced teacher; the student teacher who takes part in the completion of an ROA will need to plan very carefully how the session will run. This will include what he or she will say, how he or she will find the words to express positive achievements, how he or she will phrase questions and comments, what he or she will avoid (i.e. threatening, closed questions, ascription of blame), how to move from discussion to entering data on the ROA.

EQUAL OPPORTUNITIES AND RECORDS OF ACHIEVEMENT

It has already been mentioned that students whose written or oral skills are limited may find the completion of an ROA unnecessarily challenging – even if they are completing only the personal statement. One has to ask whether the ROA favours the more articulate students, the faster writers, the higher-ability students, the student whose first language is English, the well-off student who simply can afford to do more exciting out-of-school activities than others and those students with a high measure of those indicators of cultural capital that many schools seem to value. For example, disco dancing may be less valued by schools or post-school readers of the ROA than it is by the student. The teacher, wittingly or unwittingly, might vet the ROA, discouraging entries that may appear less important in the eyes of some readers and encouraging entries that might be more appealing to employers or higher-education interviewers. The teacher may suggest excisions or inclusions in the interests of students, but this does throw into high relief the issue of who controls, and contributes to, the ROA and how authentic the ROA will be. The National Record of Achievement is explicit on this matter, stating that the individual student holds and compiles the ROA.

Further, there is an argument to suggest that the ROA is seen by many students as a 'second best' in comparison with success in external examinations – many students may believe that possessing three A-level successes is much more valuable than having one A-level pass and a good ROA. We see here the problem alluded to earlier, *viz.* that the ROA may be used for selection rather than motivation.

Another feature in the issue of equal opportunities is that many girls tend to take the completion of the ROA more seriously than many boys. Whilst this may or may not be a 'good thing' is irrelevant; if the ROA has differential value to a large sector of the school population then its utility needs to be questioned. One also has to question whether the completion of an ROA favours different personality types, *viz.* the more extrovert and social student who does not mind revealing his or her personality and matters of significance to him or her. Students of a more private, retiring nature may wish to withhold information, fearing or disliking exposure of the personal to a public audience or maintaining a tactful silence on some issues.[14] Some students may regard the ROA as yet another assessment measure, in which case the less that the student says the less he or she is susceptible to the results of assessment and comments in the ROA. There is a fine line between the rights of an individual to silence and privacy and the rights of the public to know about the student in order, for example, to be able to plan future curricula, to offer employment or a place in higher education.

Summarising the outline of ROAs so far raises more questions than it answers, for example:

- How do ROAs vary by age, gender, ethnic origin (of the student and the teacher)?
- How do ROAs vary in relation to the values, attitudes, personality, abilities, socio-economic status, of the teacher and the student?
- How do ROAs vary in relation to teaching and learning styles and interpersonal relationships between students and teachers?
- How do ROAs vary in relation to their perceived utility by, commitment of, and recognition of the significance of ROAs by students and teachers?
- To what extent do ROAs vary with the teacher's and student's abilities to participate in, lead and conduct discussions (in the teacher's case their tutoring and counselling skills; in the student's case abilities and willingness to participate in discussions)?
- To what extent does the success of ROAs vary with the time spent on them by teachers and students?
- To what extent do ROAs vary according to the degree of 'vetting' (conscious or subliminal) of the contents by teachers?

What we are arguing is that many variables exert an influence on the success of ROAs, and that the teacher and student teacher have to be mindful of all of these when participating in the ROA process. This is not to be negative about ROAs, indeed their value has been shown to be great;[15] rather it is to show that the compiling and keeping of an ROA engages complex and sensitive matters.

For student teachers on teaching practice the implementation of ROAs can be threatening as they require a degree of confidence, knowledge about a student, reduction of the social distance between student teacher and student, that either the student teacher does not possess or is reluctant to exercise when, in many cases, their concern is to establish and maintain order in the classroom. In these cases it may be advisable for the student teacher to participate in a comparatively limited though none the less significant way with ROAs, perhaps being involved with only a small number of students, or providing data for a three-way discussion between the student teacher, the class teacher and the student.

Given the sensitivity of some aspects of the completion of an ROA, student teachers should regard their involvement in the ROA as an important part of their preparation for newly qualified teacher status but as one to be handled with care and guidance from more experienced teachers and mentors. This can take the form of:

- sitting-in on discussions between the teacher and students;
- contributing to discussions between teacher and student;
- holding a discussion/conference with a small number of students;
- practising writing sample comments for an ROA – to be shown to and discussed with the class teacher or mentor;
- looking at examples of ROAs in the teaching-practice school, including the contents and types of comments that are entered (and by whom);
- observing how time is created to enable the contents of ROAs to be discussed with students during lesson times;
- finding out how the teacher has had to alter his or her teaching styles and how the students have had to alter their learning styles in order to enable ROAs and the action plans contained in them to become significant features of the lessons and curricula;
- discussing with teachers and students the relative strengths, weaknesses, positive and negative outcomes of ROAs;
- contributing in some part to the written record in the ROA.

Whichever of these forms of involvement are undertaken by student teachers we advocate that they attempt to ascertain the strengths, weaknesses and problematic areas of keeping an ROA, along with students' perceptions of the ROA and the process of compiling it. Given that it embraces a central pillar of this book – the need for action planning – we advise student teachers to ask teachers and students exactly how the ROA fits into their action planning, what they think the ROA contributes to the process of action planning, and how successful a device it is.

Postscript

We began in Part I by presenting some perspectives on teaching and learning, and by relating teaching practice to the wider framework and contexts of teacher education. The second part of the book was devoted to preparing and planning for teaching practice. We looked at the purpose of the preliminary visit and the kinds of information that may be obtained. Aims and objectives were examined in some detail and after discussing planning schemes of work, we concluded with an extended review of the lesson note. We were concerned to address significant features of planning throughout, for example progression, continuity, differentiation and matching. We attempted to locate these discussions within the context of current educational debate (e.g. of specialist teaching in the primary school, of topic approaches and subject-specific teaching). Part III was concerned with the practice of teaching and embraced teaching strategies, the classroom environment, situational factors and classroom organisation, mixed-ability teaching, language in classrooms, control and discipline, and equal opportunities. The final part looked at assessment, record-keeping and records of achievement.

We have introduced a wide range of concepts and drawn upon a considerable amount of research evidence in the hope that you will be all the more able to understand and come to grips with the exciting challenges offered to you by teaching practice.

It only remains for us to wish you every success and satisfaction in the venture.

Notes

1 THE POLITICISATION OF EDUCATION

1 Department of Education and Science (1988) *Education Reform Act*. London: HMSO.
2 Department of Education and Science (1992) *Choice and Diversity: A New Framework for Schools*. London: HMSO.
3 Morrison, K. R. B. (1994) Centralism and the education market: why emulate the United Kingdom? *European Journal of Education*, 29 (4), pp. 415–24.
4 Department of Education and Science (1987) *The National Curriculum 5–16: a Consultation Document*. London: HMSO.
5 Brighouse, T. and Tomlinson, J. (1991) *Successful Schools*, Education and Training Paper No. 4. London: Institute for Public Policy Research. See also J. Tomlinson (1993) *The Control of Education*. London: Cassell.
6 Apple, M. (1993) The politics of official knowledge: does a national curriculum make sense? *Teachers College Record*, 95 (2), pp. 222–41.
7 Tomlinson, *The Control of Education*.
8 Penney, D. and Evans J. (1995) Changing structures; changing rules: the development of the 'internal market', *School Organisation*, 15 (1), pp. 13–21. See also S. Ball (1990) *Politics and Policy Making in Education*. London: Routledge; Bowe, R., Ball, S. and Gold, A. (1992) *Reforming Education and Changing Schools*. London: Routledge.
9 Simon, B. (1988) *Bending the Rules: the Baker Reforms of Education*. London: Lawrence and Wishart; Tomlinson, *The Control of Education*.
10 Hargreaves, D. and Hopkins, D. (1991) *The Empowered School*. London: Cassell.
11 Reynolds, D. (1995) The effective school, *Evaluation and Research in Education*, 9 (2), pp. 57–73.
12 Dalin, P. (1993) *Changing the School Culture*. London: Cassell.
13 Department for Education (1992) *The Parents' Charter*. London: HMSO.
14 Alexander, R., Rose, J. and Woodhead, C. (1992) *Curriculum Organisation and Classroom Practice in Primary Schools*. London: HMSO.
15 Halsey, A. H. (1981) Education can compensate, in W. Swann (ed.) *The Practice of Special Education*. Oxford: Basil Blackwell.
16 National Commission on Education (1995) *Learning to Succeed: the Way Forward*. London: National Commission on Education. See also Shephard's vouchers dismissed as a con, *Times Educational Supplement*, 14 July 1995, p. 4.
17 Young, S. (1995) Reformers angered by lack of action, *Times Educational Supplement*, 3 March 1995, p. 3; Young, S. (1995) Inaction speaks louder than words, *Times Educational Supplement*, 16 June 1995, p. 6.

18   Quicke, J. (1988) The 'New Right' and education, *British Journal of Educational Studies*, 26 (91), pp. 5–20. See also Morrison, Centralism and the education market: why emulate the United Kingdom?

19   Lawlor, S. (1988) *Away with LEAs: ILEA Abolition as a Pilot*. London: Centre for Policy Studies.

20   Adam Smith Institute (1984) *Education Policy (The Omega Report)*. London: Adam Smith Institute.

21   Kirkman, S. (1995) Reconnect the life support system, *Times Educational Supplement*, 28 July 1995, p. 8.

22   Jackson, M. (1982) Teach the moral virtues of profit – Sir Keith, *Times Educational Supplement*, 26 March 1982, p. 8.

23   National Curriculum Council (1990) *Education for Economic and Industrial Understanding*. York: National Curriculum Council.

24   National Curriculum Council (1990) *Careers Education and Guidance*. York: National Curriculum Council.

25   Morrison, K. R. B. (1994) *Implementing Cross-Curricular Themes*. London: David Fulton.

26   This was part of the remit of the Dearing Committee's review of the national curriculum and post-16 education in 1994 and 1995. See also National Commission on Education, *Learning to Succeed: the Way Forward*. It is noteworthy, also, that in 1995 the Department for Education was merged with the Department of Employment, creating the Department of Education and Employment.

27   See note 26 and Nash, I. (1995) Traffic builds up on vocational route, *Times Educational Supplement*, 7 May 1995, p. 9; Department for Education (1993) *Final Report on the National Curriculum and its Assessment, The Government's Response*. London: HMSO; Twining, J. (1992) *Vocational Education and Training in the United Kingdom*. Berlin: CEDEFOP.

28   Hall, S., Critcher, C., Jefferson, T., Clarke, C. and Roberts, B. (eds) (1978) *Policing the Crisis*. London: Macmillan.

29   The delineation of different types of crisis derives from Habermas, J. (1976) *Legitimation Crisis* (trans. T. McCarthy). London: Heinemann. See also Hargreaves, A. (1989) *Curriculum and Assessment Reform*. Oxford: Basil Blackwell and the Open University Press.

30   School Curriculum and Assessment Authority (1995) *Planning the Curriculum at Key Stages 1 and 2*. London: School Curriculum and Assessment Authority.

31   Ball, *Politics and Policy Making in Education*; Bowe, Ball and Gold, *Reforming Education and Changing Schools*.

32   Morrison, K. R. B. (1995) *Habermas and the School Curriculum: an Evaluation and Case Study*. Unpublished Ph.D. thesis, School of Education, University of Durham.

33   Adam Smith Institute, *Education Policy*.

34   Galton, M. and Simon, B. (1980) *Inside the Primary Classroom*. London: Routledge & Kegan Paul.

35   Alexander, Rose and Woodhead, *Curriculum Organisation and Classroom Practice in Primary Schools*.

36   Alexander, R. (1992) *Policy and Practice in Primary Education*. London: Routledge.

37   Mortimore, P., Sammons, P., Stoll, L., Lewis, D. and Ecob, R. (1988) *School Matters*. Salisbury: Open Books.

38   Galton and Simon, *Inside the Primary Classroom*.

39   Office for Standards in Education (1993) *Curriculum Organisation and Classroom Practice in Primary Schools, a Follow-up Report*. London: Office for Standards in Education.

40   Department of Education and Science (1978) *Primary Education in England; a*

Survey by HM Inspectors of Schools. London: HMSO.

41   Alexander, Rose and Woodhead, *Curriculum Organisation and Classroom Practice in Primary Schools.*

42   See note 40 and Department of Education and Science (1983) *9–13 Middle Schools; an Illustrative Survey.* London: HMSO; Department of Education and Science (1985) *Better Schools.* London: HMSO.

43   Morrison, K. (1986) Primary school subject specialists as agents of school-based curriculum change, *School Organisation*, 6 (2), pp. 175–83.

44   Bennett, N., Desforges, C., Cockburn, A. and Wilkinson, B. (1984) *The Quality of Pupil Learning Experiences.* London: Lawrence Erlbaum.

45   Davis, A. (1993) Matching and assessment, *Journal of Curriculum Studies*, 25 (3), pp. 267–79.

46   Department of Education and Science, *Primary Education in England; a Survey by HM Inspectors of Schools*; Borg, W. (1966) *Ability Grouping in the Public Schools: a Field Survey.* Dembar Educational Research Services; Newbold, D. (1977) *Ability Grouping – the Banbury Enquiry.* Slough: NFER; Reid, M. (1981) *Mixed Ability Teaching: Problems and Possibilities.* Slough: NFER; Smith, I. (1981) Curriculum placement in comprehensive schools, *British Educational Research Journal*, 7 (2), pp. 111–24; Slavin, R. (1987) Ability grouping and student achievement in elementary schools: a best-evidence synthesis, *Review of Educational Research*, 57 (3), pp. 293–336; Slavin, R. (1987) Ability grouping in elementary schools: do we really know nothing until we know everything? *Review of Educational Research*, 57 (3), pp. 347–50.

47   See notes 14, 39, 46 and Kelly, A. V. (1978) *Mixed Ability Grouping: Theory and Practice.* London: Harper & Row.

48   For example, Vygotsky, L. (1978) *Mind in Society: the Development of Higher Psychological Processes* (ed. M. Cole). Cambridge, Mass.: Harvard University Press; Hargreaves, D. (1982) *The Challenge for the Comprehensive School.* London: Routledge & Kegan Paul.

49   Bennett, N. and Carré, C. (1993) *Learning to Teach.* London: Routledge.

50   Galton and Simon, *Inside the Primary Classroom.*

51   Alexander, *Policy and Practice in Primary Education.*

52   Morrison, K. R. B. (1995) *Structuralism, Postmodernity and the Discourses of Control in Education*, mimeo, School of Education, University of Durham.

53   Whetton, C., Ruddock, G. and Hopkins, S. (1991) *The Pilot Study of Standard Assessment Tasks for Key Stage 1: A Report.* London: School Examinations and Assessment Council. See also Wilian, D. (1993) Validity, dependability and reliability in National Curriculum assessment, *The Curriculum Journal*, 4 (3), pp. 335–50.

54   Sockett, H., Bailey, C., Bridges, D., Elliott, J., Gibson, R., Scrimshaw, P. and White, J. (1980) *Accountability in the English Educational System.* Sevenoaks: Hodder & Stoughton.

55   Department of Education and Science (1988) *National Curriculum, Task Group on Assessment and Testing: A Report.* London: HMSO. For an outline of how the principles in this report have been abandoned see Hackett, G. (1995) Tests 'unreliable' claims ex-adviser, *Times Educational Supplement*, 14 July 1995, p. 9.

56   Goulding, M. (1992) Let's hear it for the girls, *Times Educational Supplement*, 21 February 1992, p. 38; Department of Education and Science, *National Curriculum, Task Group on Assessment and Testing: A Report.*

57   Department for Education, *Final Report on the National Curriculum and its Assessment, The Government's Response.* The document begins with an indication that the government accepts in full the main recommendations of the Dearing Committee (which recommended the moratorium).

2 INFORMATION TECHNOLOGY AND CHANGES IN TEACHING AND LEARNING

1   Toffler, A. (1971) *Future Shock*. London: Pan Books Ltd.
2   Illich, I. (1972) *Deschooling Society*. Harmondsworth: Penguin; Hargreaves, D. (1982) *The Challenge for the Comprehensive School*. London: Routledge & Kegan Paul; Entwistle, H. (1980) Work, leisure and life styles, in B. Simon and W. Taylor (eds) *Education in the Eighties*. London: Batsford; Stonier, T. (1982) Changes in Western society, in C. Richards (ed.) *New Directions in Primary Education*. Lewes: Falmer.
3   Department of Employment (1993) *Flexible Learning: A Framework for Education and Training in the Skills Decade*. Sheffield: Department of Employment; Eraut, M. (1991) *Flexible Learning in Schools*. Institute of Continuing and Professional Education: University of Sussex.
4   Morrison, K. R. B. (1994) Uniformity and diversity in assessment: an international perspective and agenda, *Compare*, 24 (1), pp. 5–15.
5   Entwistle, H. (1980) Work, leisure and life styles, in B. Simon and W. Taylor (eds) *Education in the Eighties*. London: Batsford.
6   Handy, C. (1989) *The Age of Unreason*. London: Business Books Ltd.

3 ACTION PLANNING IN TEACHING AND LEARNING

1   Morrison, K. R. B. (1994) *Implementing Cross-Curricular Themes*. London: David Fulton.
2   Moon, B. (1988) *Modular Curriculum*, London: Paul Chapman Publishing.
3   Morrison, K. R. B. and Ridley, K. (1988) *Curriculum Planning and the Primary School*. London: Paul Chapman Publishing.
4   Hohmann, M., Bunet, B. and Weikart, D. W. (1979) *Young Children in Action*. Michigan: The High Scope Press.
5   Department for Education (1992) *Initial Teacher Training (Secondary) (Circular 9/92)*. London: Department for Education; Department for Education (1993) *The Initial Training of Primary School Teachers: New Criteria for Courses (Circular 14/93)*. London: Department for Education.
6   Morrison, *Implementing Cross-Curricular Themes*; Department of Employment (1993) *Flexible Learning: A Framework for Education and Training in the Skills Decade*. Sheffield: Department of Employment; Eraut, M. (1991) *Flexible Learning in Schools*. Institute of Continuing and Professional Education: University of Sussex.
7   Hargreaves, D. and Hopkins, D. (1991) *The Empowered School*. London: Cassell.

4 THE IMPACT OF SCHOOL-BASED INITIAL TEACHER EDUCATION

1   Department for Education (1992) *Initial Teacher Training (Secondary) (Circular 9/92)*. London: Department for Education; Department for Education (1993) *The Initial Training of Primary School Teachers: New Criteria for Courses (Circular 14/93)*. London: Department for Education.
2   Furlong, V. J., Hirst, P. H., Pocklington, K. and Miles, S. (1988) *Initial Teacher Training and the Role of the School*. Milton Keynes: Open University Press; Wilkin, M. and Sankey, D. (eds) (1994) *Collaboration and Transition in Initial Teacher Training*. London: Kogan Page.
3   Wilkin, M. (ed.) (1992) *Mentoring in Schools*, London: Kogan Page.

4   Department for Education, *Initial Teacher Training (Secondary)* and *The Initial Training of Primary School Teachers.*

5   Ibid.

6   Ibid.

7   McCulloch, M. (1994) Teacher competences and their assessment, in M. McCulloch and B. Fidler (eds) *Improving Initial Teacher Training?* Harlow: Longman.

8   Eisner, E. (1985) *The Art of Educational Evaluation.* Lewes: Falmer.

9   Department of Education and Science (1989) *Initial Teacher Training: Approval of Courses (Circular 24/98).* London: Department for Education.

10   Mager, R. F. (1962) *Preparing Instructional Objectives.* Belmont, Calif.: Fearon Publishers; Wiles, J. and Bondi, J. C. (1984) *Curriculum Development; a Guide to Practice.* Columbus, Ohio: Charles E. Merrill Publishing; Morrison, K. R. B. and Ridley, K. (1988) *Curriculum Planning and the Primary School.* London: Paul Chapman Publishing.

11   Whitty, G. and Willmott, E. (1991) Competence-based teacher education: approaches and issues, *Cambridge Journal of Education*, 21 (3), pp. 309–18.

12   Morrison and Ridley, *Curriculum Planning and the Primary School.*

13   Mountford, B. (1993) Mentoring and initial teacher education, in P. Smith and J. West-Burnham (eds) *Mentoring in the Effective School.* Harlow: Longman.

14   Tomlinson, P. (1995) *Understanding Mentoring.* Buckingham: Open University Press. See also note 13.

15   Nolder, R., Smith, S. and Melrose, J. (1994) Working together: roles and relationships in the mentoring process, in B. Jaworski and A. Watson (eds) *Mentoring in Mathematics Teaching.* London: Falmer.

16   Tomlinson, *Understanding Mentoring.* See also note 13 and McPartland, M. (1995) On being a geography mentor, *Teaching Geography*, January 1995, pp. 35–7, and Stephenson, J. (1995) Significant others – the primary student teacher's view of practice in schools. *Educational Studies*, 21 (3), pp. 323–33.

17   Jackson, P. (1968) *Life in Classrooms.* New York: Holt, Rinehart & Winston.

18   Holt, J. (1969) *How Children Fail.* Harmondsworth: Penguin.

5 AN OVERVIEW OF THE NATIONAL CURRICULUM OF ENGLAND AND WALES

1   Department of Education and Science (1988) *Education Reform Act.* London: HMSO.

2   Department of Education and Science (1985) *The Curriculum from 5–16*, Curriculum Matters 2. London: HMSO.

3   Morrison, K. R. B. and Ridley, K. (1988) *Curriculum Planning and the Primary School*. London: Paul Chapman Publishing; Kelly, A. (1986) *Knowledge and Curriculum Planning.* London: Harper & Row.

4   These skills are direct derivatives of those outlined by HMI in 1985, see note 2.

5   Morrison, K. R. B. (1994) *Implementing Cross-Curricular Themes.* London: David Fulton.

6   National Curriculum Council (1990) *The Whole Curriculum.* York: National Curriculum Council.

7   Morrison, *Implementing Cross-Curricular Themes.*

8   National Curriculum Council (1990) *Education for Economic and Industrial Understanding.* York: National Curriculum Council; National Curriculum Council (1990) *Health Education.* York: National Curriculum Council; National Curriculum Council (1990) *Careers Education and Guidance.* York: National Curriculum Council; National Curriculum Council (1990) *Environmental Education.* York: National Curriculum Council; National Curriculum Council (1990) *Education for*

Citizenship. York: National Curriculum Council.
9   Hartnett, A. and Naish, M. (1976) *Theory and Practice of Education*. London: Heinemann.

INTRODUCTION TO PART II

1   Jeffcoate, R. (1976) Curriculum planning in multiracial education. *Educational Research*, 18 (3), pp. 192–200.
2   Shipman, M. D. (1972) Contrasting views of a curriculum project. *Journal of Curriculum Studies*, November.
3   Morrison, K. R. B. and Ridley, K. (1988) *Curriculum Planning and the Primary School*. London: Paul Chapman Publishing.
4   Jeffcoate, Curriculum planning in multiracial education.
5   Taba, H. (1962) *Curriculum Development: Theory and Practice*. New York: Harcourt, Brace & World.
6   Stake, R. E. (1976) The countenance of educational evaluation, cited in D. Jenkins, Six alternative models of curriculum evaluation, Unit 20, E203, *Curriculum Design and Development*. Milton Keynes: Open University Press.

6 THE PRELIMINARY VISIT

1   Hagger, H., Burn, K. and McIntyre, D. (1993) *The School Mentor Handbook*. London: Kogan Page.
2   Hargreaves, D. H., Hestor, S. K. and Mellor, F. J. (1975) *Deviance in Classrooms*. London: Routledge & Kegan Paul.
3   Davis, I. K. (1976) *Objectives in Curriculum Design*. New York: McGraw Hill.
4   Haysom, J. and Sutton, C. (1974) *Theory into Practice*. Maidenhead: McGraw-Hill.
5   Jackson, P. W. (1968) *Life in Classrooms*. Eastbourne: Holt, Rinehart & Winston.
6   This point is echoed in the writings of Holt, for example: Holt, J. (1969) *How Children Fail*. Harmondsworth: Penguin.

7 AIMS AND OBJECTIVES

1   Davis, I. K. (1976) *Objectives in Curriculum Design*. New York: McGraw Hill.
2   Wheeler, D. K. (1967) *Curriculum Process*. London: University of London Press.
3   Ashton, P., Kneen, P. and Davies, F. (1975) *Aims into Practice in the Primary School*. London: University of London Press.
4   Wheeler, *Curriculum Process*.
5   Hirst, P. H. (1974) *Knowledge and the Curriculum*. London: Routledge & Kegan Paul.
6   Rowntree, D. (1974) *Educational Technology in Curriculum Development*. New York: Harper & Row.
7   Gerlach, V. S. and Ely, D. P. (1971) *Teaching and Media: A Systematic Approach*. Englewood Cliffs, NJ: Prentice-Hall.
8   Wiles, J. and Bondi, J. C. (1984) *Curriculum Development: A Guide to Practice* (2nd edn). Columbus, Ohio: Charles E. Merrill Publishing.
9   Note: the original painting is in the Tate Gallery, London. A colour reproduction may be found in Bullock, A. (ed.) (1971) *The Twentieth Century*, plate 80, p. 228. London: Thames & Hudson.
10   Note: photographs of the house may be found in Scully Jr., V. (1960) *Frank Lloyd Wright*. London: Mayflower. A colour photograph can be seen in Raeburn, M. (1973) *An Outline of World Architecture*, p. 116. London: Octopus Books.

11   Tyler, R. W. (1973) *Basic Principles of Curriculum and Instruction*. Chicago: University of Chicago Press.
12   Ibid.
13   Shulman, L. S. and Keislar, E. R. (eds) (1966) *Learning by Discovery*. Chicago: Rand McNally.
14   Saylor, J. G. and Alexander, W. M. (1974) *Planning Curriculum for Schools*. New York: Holt, Rinehart & Winston.
15   Peters, R. S. (1966) *Ethics and Education*. London: Routledge & Kegan Paul.
16   MacDonald-Ross, M. (1973) Behavioural objectives – a critical review. *Instructional Science*, 2, pp. 1–51.
17   Kibler, R. J., Cegala, D. J., Barker, L. L. and Miles, D. T. (1974) *Objectives for Instruction and Evaluation*. Boston: Allyn and Bacon. See also Davis, *Objectives in Curriculum Design*; Morrison, K. R. B. and Ridley, K. (1988) *Curriculum Planning and the Primary School*. London: Paul Chapman Publishing.
18   Dean, J. (1983) *Organising Learning in the Primary School Classroom*. Beckenham: Croom Helm.

8 BEGINNING CURRICULUM PLANNING

1   Mortimore, P., Sammons, P. and Ecob, R. (1988) *School Matters: The Junior Years*. Salisbury: Open Books; Levine, D. and Lezotte, L. (1990) *Unusually Effective Schools: A Review and Analysis of Research and Practice*. Madison: NCESRD Publications; Brighouse, T. and Tomlinson, J. (1991) *Successful Schools*. Education and Training Paper No. 4. London: Institute of Public Policy Research. Alexander, R., Rose, J. and Woodhead, C. (1992) *Curriculum Organisation and Classroom Practice in Primary Schools*. London: Department of Education and Science; Reynolds, D. and Cuttance, P. (1992) *School Effectiveness: Research, Policy and Practice*. London: Cassell; Reynolds, D., Creemers, B. P. M., Stringfield, S., Teddlie, C., Schaffer, E. and Nesselrodt, P. (1994) *Advances in School Effectiveness Research: Policy and Practice*. London: Cassell; Office for Standards in Education (1994) *Primary Matters: A Discussion of Teaching and Learning in Primary Schools*. London: Office for Standards in Education; Reynolds, D. (1995) The effective school. *Evaluation and Research in Education*, 9 (2), pp. 57–73; Sammons, P., Hillman, J. and Mortimore, P. (1995) *Key Characteristics of Effective Schools: a Review of School Effectiveness Research*. London: OFSTED.
2   Office for Standards in Education (OFSTED) (1994) *Handbook for the Inspection of Schools*. London: OFSTED.
3   A useful summary of the principles for planning can be seen in Galvin, P., Mercia, S. and Costa, P. (1990) *Building a Better Behaved School*. Harlow: Longman.
4   School Curriculum and Assessment Authority (1995) *Planning the Curriculum at Key Stages 1 and 2*. London: School Curriculum and Assessment Authority, p. 9.
5   Ibid., p. 11.
6   Ibid., p. 15.
7   Ibid., p. 21.
8   Ibid., p. 21.
9   Ibid., p. 21. The School Curriculum and Assessment Authority provides examples in the same booklet in order to assist teachers' planning.
10   Morrison, K. R. B. (1994) *Implementing Cross-curricular Themes*. London: David Fulton.
11   Department of Education and Science (1985) *The Curriculum from 5 to 16* (Curriculum Matters 2). London: HMSO.
12   Ibid., paras. 106–33.

13   Department of Education and Science (1983) *Curriculum 11–16. Towards a Statement of Entitlement, Curricular Reappraisal in Action*. London: HMSO.

14   Department of Education and Science, *The Curriculum from 5 to 16*, paras. 32–89.

15   Ibid., para. 58.

16   Morrison, K. R. B. and Ridley, K. (1988) *Curriculum Planning and the Primary School*. London: Paul Chapman. Morrison and Ridley also discuss the *Core Curriculum for Australian Schools*. Canberra: Curriculum Development Centre.

17   Department of Education and Science, *The Curriculum from 5 to 16*, paras. 112–15.

18   Department of Education and Science (1981) *Curriculum 11–16: A Review of Progress*. London: HMSO, para. 2.9.6.

19   Morrison and Ridley, *Curriculum Planning and the Primary School*, pp. 130–3.

20   Alexander, Rose and Woodhead, *Curriculum Organisation and Classroom Practice in Primary Schools*, para. 76.

21   Department of Education and Science, *The Curriculum from 5–16*, paras. 116–20.

22   School Curriculum and Assessment Authority, *Planning the Curriculum at Key Stages 1 and 2*, p. 21.

23   Vygotsky, L. S. (1978) *Mind in Society: The Development of Higher Psychological Processes*. Cambridge, Mass.: Harvard University Press.

24   Schools Council (1981) *The Practical Curriculum* (working paper 70). London: Methuen.

25   School Curriculum and Assessment Authority, *Planning the Curriculum at Key Stages 1 and 2*, p. 11.

26   Morrison and Ridley, *Curriculum Planning and the Primary School*, pp. 137–9.

27   Galvin, P., Mercia, S. and Costa, P. (1990) *Building a Better Behaved School*. Harlow: Longman.

28   Vygotsky, *Mind in Society*.

29   Department of Education and Science, *The Curriculum from 5 to 16*, paras. 124–33.

30   School Curriculum and Assessment Authority, *Planning the Curriculum at Key Stages 1 and 2*, p. 39.

31   Hirst, P. (1967) The logical and psychological aspects of teaching a subject, in R. S. Peters (ed.) *The Concept of Education*. London: Routledge & Kegan Paul.

32   Lacey, C. and Lawton, D. (eds) *Issues in Evaluation and Accountability*. London: Methuen.

33   See Morrison and Ridley, *Curriculum Planning and the Primary School*, pp. 136–7.

34   Desforges, C. (1987) *Understanding the Mathematics Teacher*. Lewes: Falmer.

35   For example: Department of Education and Science (1978) *Primary Education in England: A Survey by HMI*. London: HMSO; Department of Education and Science (1982) *Education 5–9*. London: HMSO; Department of Education and Science (1991) *Testing 7 Year Olds in 1991: Results of the National Curriculum Tests in England*. London: HMSO.

36   Bennett, S. N., Desforges, C., Cockburn., A. and Wilkinson, B. (1984) *The Quality of Pupil Learning Experiences*. London: Lawrence Erlbaum Associates.

37   The student teacher, of course, will have to rely on discussions with individual teachers. See, for example, Hagger, H., Burn, K. and McIntyre, D. (1993) *The School Mentor Handbook*. London: Kogan Page.

38   Davis, A. J. (1993) Matching and assessment. *Journal of Curriculum Studies*, 25 (3), pp. 267–79.

39   Morrison and Ridley, *Curriculum Planning and the Primary School*, chapter 5.

40   Withers, R. and Eke, R. (1995) Reclaiming matching from the critics of primary education. *Educational Review*, 37 (1), pp. 59–73.

41   Alexander, Rose and Woodhead, *Curriculum Organisation and Classroom Practice in Primary Schools*, para. 97.

42   Morrison and Ridley argue for a much more complex view of differentiation, to
     include many variables in differentiating by process. See Morrison and Ridley,
     Curriculum Planning and the Primary School, pp. 134–6.
43   Central Advisory Council for Education (1967) *Children and Their Primary Schools*
     (Plowden Report). London: HMSO.
44   For example: Blenkin, G. and Kelly, A. V. (1981) *The Primary Curriculum*. London:
     Harper & Row; Walkerdine, V. (1983) It's only natural: rethinking child-centred
     pedagogy, in A. M. Wolpe and J. Donald (eds) *Is There Anyone Here from Education?*
     London: Pluto Press; Alexander, R. (1984) *Primary Teaching*. Eastbourne: Holt,
     Rinehart & Winston; Morrison and Ridley, *Curriculum Planning and the Primary
     School*.
45   Pollard, A. and Tann, S. (1993) *Reflective Teaching in the Primary School* (2nd edn).
     London: Cassell.
46   Alexander, *Primary Teaching*.
47   Walkerdine, It's only natural: rethinking child-centred pedagogy.
48   Entwistle, H. (1971) *Child-Centred Education*. London: Methuen.
49   Eggleston, J. and Kerry, T. (1985) Integrated studies, in S. N. Bennett and C. Desforges
     (eds) *Recent Advances in Classroom Research. British Journal of Educational
     Psychology Monographs Series No. 2*. Edinburgh: Scottish Academic Press.
50   Alexander, Rose and Woodhead, *Curriculum Organisation and Classroom Practice
     in Primary Schools*, para. 64.
51   Morrison, K. R. B. (1986) Primary school subject specialists as agents of school-
     based curriculum change. *School Organisation*, 6 (2), pp. 175–83.
52   For example: Department of Education and Science, *Primary Education in England:
     A Survey by HMI*; Department of Education and Science (1983) *9–13 Middle Schools*.
     London: HMSO.
53   Office for Standards in Education (1993) *Curriculum Organisation and Classroom
     Practice in Primary Schools: A Follow-up Report*. London: OFSTED; Office for
     Standards in Education (1994) *Primary Matters: A Discussion of Teaching and
     Learning in Primary Schools*. London: OFSTED.
54   Alexander, Rose and Woodhead, *Curriculum Organisation and Classroom Practice
     in Primary Schools*, para. 64.
55   Pollard, A., Broadfoot, P., Croll, P., Osborn, M. and Abbott, D. (1994) *Changing
     English Primary Schools?* London: Cassell.
56   Morrison, *Implementing Cross-Curricular Themes*.
57   A straightforward introduction to this field can be seen in Gleick, J. (1988) *Chaos*.
     London: Abacus.
58   Stenhouse, L. (1975) *An Introduction to Curriculum Research and Development*.
     London: Heinemann.
59   Bernstein, B. (1977) Class and pedagogies – visible and invisible, in B. Bernstein
     Class, Codes and Control, Volume Three. London: Routledge & Kegan Paul.
60   Sharp, R. and Green, A. (1975) *Education and Social Control*. London: Routledge &
     Kegan Paul.
61   This is expounded in Morrison, K. R. B. (1993) *Planning and Accomplishing School-
     Centred Evaluation*. Norfolk: Peter Francis Publishers.
62   Stake, R. E. (1976) The countenance of educational evaluation, cited in D. Jenkins,
     Six alternative models of curriculum evaluation, Unit 20, E203, *Curriculum Design
     and Development*. Milton Keynes: Open University Press.
63   For a statement of the need for young children to learn their own capabilities from
     a very early age see Letwin, O. (1987) Testing issues. *Times Educational Supplement*,
     18 September 1987.
64   For an interesting overview of the strengths and weaknesses of bivalent and

multivalent thinking see Kosko, B. (1994) *Fuzzy Thinking*. London: Flamingo.

65 Morrison, *Planning and Accomplishing School-Centred Evaluation*, p. 41.
66 Lawton, D. (1973) *Social Change, Educational Theory and Curriculum Planning*. London: University of London Press.
67 Morrison, *Planning and Accomplishing School-Centred Evaluation*, p. 2.
68 For an overview of 'connoisseurship' in educational evaluation see Eisner, E. (1985) *The Art of Educational Evaluation*. Lewes: Falmer.
69 Moyles, J. (1988) *Self-Evaluation: A Teacher's Guide*. Slough: National Foundation for Educational Research.

9 PRIMARY TEACHING

1   Morrison, K. R. B. and Ridley, K. (1988) *Curriculum Planning and the Primary School*. London: Paul Chapman Publishing, p. 22.
2   Alexander, R. J. (1984) *Primary Teaching*. Eastbourne: Holt, Rinehart & Winston.
3   Alexander, R. J. (1992) *Policy and Practice in Primary Education*. London: Routledge.
4   Alexander, R. J., Rose, J. and Woodhead, C. (1992) *Curriculum Organisation and Classroom Practice in Primary Schools*. London: Routledge, para. 23.
5   Ibid., para. 66.
6   Ibid., para. 71.
7   Lee, J. and Croll, P. (1995) Streaming and subject specialism at key stage 2: a survey in two local authorities. *Educational Studies* 21 (2), pp. 155–65.
8   Dean, J. (1983) *Organising Learning in the Primary School Classroom*. London: Croom Helm (rep. Routledge 1988).
9   Pollard, A. and Tann, S. (1988) *Reflective Teaching in the Primary School*. London: Cassell.
10 Dean, *Organising Learning in the Primary School Classroom*.
11 Ibid.
12 Ibid.
13 Office for Standards in Education (1994) *Primary Matters: A Discussion of Teaching and Learning in Primary Schools*. London: Office for Standards in Education, paras. 13–19.
14 Pollard and Tann, *Reflective Teaching in the Primary School*.
15 For example: Department of Education and Science (1982) *The New Teacher in School*. London: HMSO; Department of Education and Science (1985) *Better Schools*. Cmnd. 9469. London: HMSO; Department of Education and Science (1988) *The New Teacher in School*. London: HMSO.
16 Department of Education and Science (1978) *Primary Education in England: a Survey by HMI*. London: HMSO; Department of Education and Science (1982) *The New Teacher in School*; Department of Education and Science (1988) *The New Teacher in School*.
17 Alexander, Rose and Woodhead, *Curriculum Organisation and Classroom Practice in Primary Schools*, para. 77. See also Pollard, A. and Tann, S. (1993) *Reflective Teaching in the Primary School* (2nd edn). London: Cassell, p. 149.
18 Bennett, S. N., Wragg, E. C., Carré, C. G. and Carter, D. S. G. (1992) A longitudinal study of primary teachers' perceived competence in, and concerns about, national curriculum implementation. *Research Papers in Education* 7 (1), pp. 53–78.
19 Pollard, A., Broadfoot, P., Croll, P., Osborn, M. and Abbott, D. (1994) *Changing English Primary Schools?* London: Cassell.
20 Morrison, K. R. B. (1986) Primary school subject specialists as agents of school-based curriculum change. *School Organisation* 6 (2), pp. 175–83.

21   Alexander, Rose and Woodhead, *Curriculum Organisation and Classroom Practice in Primary Schools*, para. 146.

22   Office for Standards in Education (OFSTED) (1993) *Curriculum Organisation and Classroom Practice in Primary School: a Follow-up Report*. London: OFSTED, para. 10.

23   Schools Council (1983) *Primary Practice*, working paper 75. London: Schools Council, 16–17.

24   Pollard, Broadfoot, Croll, Osborn and Abbott, *Changing English Primary Schools?* pp. 106–12.

25   Ashton, P., Kneen, P., Davies, F. and Holley, B. J. (1975) *The Aims of Primary Education: a Study of Teachers' Opinions*. London: Macmillan.

26   Pollard, Broadfoot, Croll, Osborn and Abbott, *Changing English Primary Schools?* p. 109.

27   Ibid., pp. 110–12.

28   Department of Education and Science (1987) *The National Curriculum 5–16: a Consultation Document*. London: HMSO, para. 7.

29   Pollard and Tann, *Reflective Teaching in the Primary School*.

30   Department of Education and Science (1985) *The Curriculum from 5 to 16*, (Curriculum Matters 2). London: HMSO.

31   Oeser, O. A. (1966) *Teacher, Pupil and Task*. London: Tavistock Publications.

32   Ibid., p. 54.

33   Ibid., p. 55.

34   Alexander, Rose and Woodhead, *Curriculum Organisation and Classroom Practice in Primary Schools*, para. 89.

35   For example: Galton, M., Simon, B. and Croll, P. (1980) *Inside the Primary Classroom*. London: Routledge & Kegan Paul; Galton, M. and Simon, B. (eds) (1980) *Progress and Performance in the Primary Classroom*. London: Routledge. This view is echoed by Dunne and Bennett, see Dunne, E. and Bennett, N. (1991) *Talking and Learning in Groups*. Basingstoke: Macmillan.

36   Alexander, Rose and Woodhead, *Curriculum Organisation and Classroom Practice in Primary Schools*, para. 90.

37   Sharp, R. and Green, A. (1975) *Education and Social Control*. London: Routledge & Kegan Paul.

38   Bernstein, B. (1977) Class and pedagogies – visible and invisible, in B. Bernstein *Class, Codes and Control*. London: Routledge & Kegan Paul.

39   Morrison and Ridley, *Curriculum Planning and the Primary School*, pp. 85–9.

40   Bennett, S. N. and Dunne, E. (1992) *Managing Classroom/Learning Groups*. Hemel Hempstead: Simon & Shuster.

41   Vygotsky, L. S. (1978) *Mind in Society: The Development of Higher Psychological Processes*. Cambridge, Mass.: Harvard University Press. Cooper and McIntyre suggest that teachers themselves accord significance to the social dimension of classrooms in promoting effective teaching and learning. See Cooper, P. and McIntyre, D. (1996) The importance of power sharing in classroom learning, in M. Hughes (ed.) *Teaching and Learning in Changing Times*. Oxford: Blackwell.

42   Alexander, Rose and Woodhead, *Curriculum Organisation and Classroom Practice in Primary Schools*, para. 99.

43   Pollard, Broadfoot, Croll, Osborn and Abbott, *Changing English Primary Schools?*, p. 166.

44   Galton, Simon and Croll, *Inside the Primary Classroom*.

45   Pollard, Broadfoot, Croll, Osborn and Abbott, *Changing English Primary Schools?*

46   Galvin, P., Mercia, S. and Costa, P. (1990) *Building a Better Behaved School*. Harlow: Longman.

47   Dunne and Bennett, *Talking and Learning in Groups*, p. 4.
48   Bennett and Dunne, *Managing Classroom Groups*.
49   Cohen, E. (1994) Restructuring the classroom – conditions for productive small groups. *Review of Educational Research*, 64 (1), pp. 11–35.
50   Hall, K. (1995) Learning modes: an investigation of perceptions in five Kent classrooms. *Educational Research*, 3 (1), pp. 21–32.
51   Harwood, D. (1995) The pedagogy of the World Studies 8–13 Project: the influence of the presence/absence of the teacher upon primary children's collaborative group work. *British Educational Research Journal*, 21 (5), pp. 587–611.
52   Dunne and Bennett, *Talking and Learning in Groups*, p. 31.
53   Ibid., pp. 32–3.
54   McAllister, W. (1995) Are pupils equipped for group work without training or instruction? *British Educational Research Journal*, 21 (3), p. 403.
55   Galvin, Mercia and Costa, *Building a Better Behaved School*, provide a useful summary of relevant issues and research on this matter.
56   Mortimore, P., Sammons, P. and Ecob, R. (1988) *School Matters: The Junior Years*. Salisbury: Open Books.
57   Alexander, Rose and Woodhead, *Curriculum Organisation and Classroom Practice in Primary Schools*, para. 97.
58   Pollard, Broadfoot, Croll, Osborn and Abbott, *Changing English Primary Schools?*, p. 161.
59   Kerry, T. and Sands, M. K. (1982) *Handling Classroom Groups*. London: Macmillan.
60   Pollard, Broadfoot, Croll, Osborn and Abbott, *Changing English Primary Schools?*, p. 160.
61   Bennett, S. N. and Kell, J. A. (1989) *A Good Start? Four Year Olds in Infant Schools*. Oxford: Blackwell.
62   Kagan, S. (1988) *Cooperative Learning: Resources for Teachers*. University of California: Riverside Books.
63   Bennett and Dunne, *Managing Classroom Groups*, p. 27.
64   Dunne and Bennett, *Talking and Learning in Groups*, p. 27.
65   McAllister, Are pupils equipped for group work without training or instruction?, p. 404.
66   Morrison and Ridley, *Curriculum Planning and the Primary School*, p. 88.
67   A useful overview of issues in this field can be found in Slavin, R. (1983) *Cooperative Learning*. New York: Longman; and Slavin, R. *et al.* (1985) *Learning to Cooperate: Cooperating to Learn*. New York: Plenum Books.
68   Wheldall, K. *et al.* (1981), Rows versus tables: an example of behavioural ecology in two classes of eleven-year-old children. *Educational Psychology*, 1 (2), pp. 171–84.
69   Hastings, N. and Schwieso, J. (1995) Tasks and tables: the effects of seating arrangements on task engagement in primary classrooms. *Educational Research* 37 (3), pp. 279–91.
70   Kerry, T. and Tollitt, J. (1987) *Teaching Infants*. Oxford: Basil Blackwell.
71   Ibid.
72   Pollard, Broadfoot, Croll, Osborn and Abbott, *Changing English Primary Schools?*, chapter 7.
73   Blyth, W. A. L. (1965) *English Primary Education, Volume One*. London: Routledge & Kegan Paul.
74   Rousseau, J. J. (1911) *Emile*. London: Everyman.
75   Dewey, J. (1916) *Democracy and Education*. New York: Macmillan; Dewey, J. (1938) *Experience and Education*. New York: Collier.
76   Board of Education (1931) *Report of the Consultative Committee of the Board of Education on the Primary School*. London: Board of Education, p. 93.

77   Entwistle, H. (1970) *Child-Centred Education*. London: Methuen; Morrison, K. R. B. (1985) Tensions in subject specialist teaching in primary schools. *Curriculum*, 6 (2), pp. 24–9.
78   Central Advisory Council for Education (1967) *Children and Their Primary Schools* (the Plowden Report). London: HMSO.
79   Morrison and Ridley, *Curriculum Planning and the Primary School*, p. 91.
80   Bennett, S. N., Andrea, J., Hegarty, P. and Wade, B. (1980) *Open Plan Schools: Teaching, Curriculum, Design*. Slough: National Foundation for Educational Research.
81   Mortimore, Sammons and Ecob, *School Matters: The Junior Years*.
82   Alexander, Rose and Woodhead, *Curriculum Organisation and Classroom Practice in Primary Schools*, para. 97.
83   Dearden, R. F. (1971) What is the integrated day? In Walton, J. (ed.) *The Integrated Day in Theory and Practice*. London: Ward Lock Educational.
84   Dearden, R. F. (1976) *Problems in Primary Education*. London: Routledge & Kegan Paul.
85   Dearden, What is the integrated day?
86   Dearden, *Problems in Primary Education*.
87   Morrison and Ridley, *Curriculum Planning and the Primary School*, pp. 89–91.
88   See Taylor, J. (1983) *Organizing and Integrating the First School Day*. London: Allen & Unwin.
89   Allen, I., Dover, K., Gaff, M., Gray, E., Griffiths, C., Ryall, N. and Toone, E. (1975) *Working an Integrated Day*. London: Ward Lock Educational.
90   Mycock, M. A. (1970) Vertical grouping in the primary school. In Rogers, V. R. (ed.) *Teaching in the British Primary School*. London: Macmillan.
91   Kerry and Tollitt, *Teaching Infants*.
92   Hargreaves, D. H. (1973) *Interpersonal Relations and Education*. London: Routledge & Kegan Paul.
93   Stephens, L. S. (1974) *The Teacher's Guide to Open Education*. New York: Holt, Rinehart & Winston.
94   Withal, R. (1956) An objective measurement of a teacher's classroom interactions. *Journal of Educational Psychology*, 47. See also Resnick, L. B. (1972) Teacher behaviour in the informal classroom. *Journal of Curriculum Studies*, 4 (2), pp. 99–109.
95   Garner, J. and Byng, M. (1973) Inequalities of teacher–pupil contact. *British Journal of Educational Psychology*, 43, pp. 234–43.
96   Boydell, D. (1975) Individual attention: the child's eye view. *Education 3–13*, 3 (April), pp. 9–13.
97   Adelman, C. and Walker, R. (1974) Open space – open classrooms. *Education 3–13*, 2 (October), pp. 103–7.
98   Dearden, *Problems in Primary Education*.
99   Ibid.
100   Tann, C. S. (1988) The rationale for topic work. In C. S. Tann (ed.) *Developing Topic Work in the Primary School*. Lewes: Falmer, p. 4.
101   For example: National Curriculum Council (1989) *A Framework for the Primary Curriculum*. York: National Curriculum Council; National Curriculum Council (1990) *The Whole Curriculum*. York: National Curriculum Council.
102   Rance, P. (1968) *Teaching by Topics*. London: Ward Lock Educational.
103   Lane, S. M. and Kemp, M. (1973) *An Approach to Topic Work in the Primary School*. London: Blackie.
104   Waters, D. (1982) *Primary School Projects*. London: Heinemann Educational.
105   Bradley, H., Eggleston, J., Kerry, T. and Cooper, D. (1985) *Developing Pupils'*

Thinking Through Topic Work: a Starter Course. London: Longman.

106 Kerry, T. and Eggleston, J. (1988) *Topic Work in the Primary School*. London: Routledge.

107 Baker, R. (1987) Developing educational relevance in primary school science. CASTME *Journal*, 7 (1), pp. 28–39.

108 Bonnett, M. (1986) Child-centredness and the problem of structure in project work. *Cambridge Journal of Education*, 16 (1), pp. 3–6.

109 Haslam, K. R. (1971) *Learning in the Primary School*. London: George Allen & Unwin.

10 SECONDARY TEACHING

1 Dowson, J. (1995) The school curriculum, in S. Capel, M. Leask and T. Turner, *Learning to Teach in the Secondary School*. London: Routledge.

2 Leask, M. (1995) What do teachers do?, in S. Capel, M. Leask and T. Turner, *Learning to Teach in the Secondary School*. London: Routledge.

3 Morrison, K. R. B. (1986) Primary school subject specialists as agents of school-based curriculum change. *School Organisation*, 6 (2), pp. 175–83.

4 Dowson, J. (1995) The National Curriculum, in S. Capel, M. Leask and T. Turner, *Learning to Teach in the Secondary School*. London: Routledge, p. 338.

5 Leask, What do teachers do?

6 Wragg, E. C. and Young, E. K. (1984) Teachers' first encounters with their classes, in E. C. Wragg (ed.) *Classroom Teaching Skills*. London: Croom Helm.

7 Wragg, E. C. and Young, E. K. (1984) Pupil appraisal of teaching, in E. C. Wragg (ed.) *Classroom Teaching Skills*. London: Croom Helm.

8 Wragg, E. C. (1984) Training skilful teachers: some implications for practice, in E. C. Wragg (ed.) *Classroom Teaching Skills*. London: Croom Helm.

9 Hargreaves, D. H. (1973) *Interpersonal Relations and Education*. London: Routledge & Kegan Paul.

10 Wragg and Young, Teachers' first encounters with their classes.

11 Fontana, D. (1985) *Classroom Control: Understanding and Guiding Classroom Behaviour*. London: British Psychological Society and Methuen. See particularly in this respect pp. 138–42.

12 Perrott, E. (1982) *Effective Teaching: A Practical Guide to Improving your Teaching*. London: Longman.

13 Barnes, B. (1987) *Learning Styles in TVEI: Evaluation Report No. 3*. Leeds University for the MSC.

14 Bernstein, B. (1971) On the classification and framing of educational objectives, in M. F. D. Young (ed.) *Knowledge and Control*. Basingstoke: Collier-Macmillan.

15 Galton, M. and Simon, B. (1980) *Inside the Primary Classroom*. London: Routledge & Kegan Paul.

16 Flanders, N. A. (1970) *Analysing Teacher Behaviour*. Reading, Mass.: Addison Wesley.

17 Hamacheck, D. E. (1968) *Human Dynamics in Psychology and Education*. Boston: Allyn & Bacon.

18 Combs, A. (1965) *The Professional Education of Teachers*. Boston: Allyn & Bacon.

19 Brembeck, C. S. (1971) *Social Foundations of Education*. New York: J. Wiley & Sons.

20 Wragg and Young, Pupil appraisal of teaching.

21 Rogers, C. R. (1969) *Freedom to Learn*. Columbus, Ohio: Charles E. Merrill. See also the same author's (1984) *A Way of Being*. Boston: Houghton Mifflin.

11 MIXED-ABILITY TEACHING

1 Ridley, K. (1982) Mixed ability teaching in the primary school. In M. Sands and T. Kerry (eds) *Mixed Ability Teaching*. London: Croom Helm.

2 Pollard, A. (1982) A model of coping strategies. *British Journal of Sociology of Education*, 3 (1), pp. 19–37.

3 Inner London Education Authority (1976) *Mixed Ability Grouping*. London: Inner London Education Authority, p. 15.

4 Walkerdine, V. (1983) It's only natural: rethinking child-centred pedagogy. In A. M. Wolpe and J. Donald (eds) *Is There Anyone Here from Education?* London: Pluto Press. See also R. J. Alexander (1984) *Primary Teaching*. Eastbourne: Holt, Rinehart & Winston.

5 Jackson, B. (1964) *Streaming: an Education System in Miniature*. London: Routledge & Kegan Paul.

6 Bailey, C. and Bridges, D. (1983) *Mixed Ability Grouping: a Philosophical Perspective*. London: Allen & Unwin.

7 Bourdieu, P. (1977) Cultural reproduction and educational reproduction. In J. Karabel and A. H. Halsey (eds) *Power and Ideology in Education*, London: Oxford University Press; Woods, P. (1979) *The Divided School*. London: Routledge & Kegan Paul; Halsey, A. H., Heath, A., and Ridge, J. (1980) *Origins and Destinations*. London: Oxford University Press; Ball, S. (1981) *Beachside Comprehensive*. London: Cambridge University Press; Hargreaves, D. H. (1982) *The Challenge for the Comprehensive School*. London: Routledge & Kegan Paul.

8 Kelly, A. V. (1978) *Mixed Ability Grouping: Theory and Practice*. London: Harper & Row.

9 Hargreaves, D. H. (1978) The two curricula and the community. *Westminster Studies in Education*, 1 (1), pp. 31–41.

10 Rosenthal, J. and Jacobson, L. (1968) *Pygmalion in the Classroom: Teacher Expectation and Pupils' Intellectual Development*. New York: Holt, Rinehart & Winston; Woods, P. (1980) *Teacher Strategies: Explorations in the Sociology of the School*, London: Croom Helm.

11 Hurn, C. J. (1978) *The Limits and Possibilities of Schooling*. New York: Allyn & Bacon; Esland, G. (1971) Teaching and learning as the organization of knowledge. In M. F. D. Young (ed.) *Knowledge and Control*. Basingstoke: Collier-Macmillan; Keddie, N. (1971) Classroom knowledge, in Young (ed.) *Knowledge and Control*; Woods, *The Divided School*; Peak, B. and Morrison, K. R. B. (1988) Investigating banding origins and destinations in a comprehensive school. *School Organisation*, 8 (3), pp. 339–49.

12 Chapman, R. (1979) Schools do make a difference. *British Educational Research Journal*, 5 (1), pp. 115–24; Smith, I. (1981) Curriculum placement in comprehensive schools. *British Educational Research Journal*, 7 (2), pp. 111–24; Reynolds, D. (1995) The effective school. *Evaluation and Research in Education*, 9 (2), pp. 57–73.

13 Bourdieu, P. (1976) The school as a conservative force. In R. Dale, G. Esland, M. MacDonald (1976) *Schooling and Capitalism*. London: Routledge & Kegan Paul.

14 Ross, J. (1972) *A Critical Appraisal of Comprehensive Education*. Slough: National Foundation for Educational Research.

15 Morrison, C. (1976) *Ability Grouping and Mixed Ability Grouping in Secondary Schools*. Edinburgh: Scottish Council for Educational Research. This view is supported by Passow, A. (1966) *The Effects of Ability Grouping*. Teachers College, Columbia University, New York: Teachers College Press; Borg, W. (1966) *Ability Grouping in the Public Schools: a Field Survey*. New York: Dembar Educational Research Services; Postlethwaite, K. and Denton, C. (1978) *Streams for the Future*. Banbury: Pubansco; Hargreaves, *The Challenge for the Comprehensive School*.

16 Newbold, D. (1977) *Ability Grouping – The Banbury Enquiry.* Slough: National Foundation for Educational Research.
17 Slavin, R. (1990) Achievement effects of ability grouping in secondary schools: a best evidence synthesis. *Review of Educational Research,* 60 (3), pp. 471–99.
18 Ball, *Beachside Comprehensive.*
19 Reid, M., Clunies-Ross, L., Goacher, B. and Vile, C. (1981) *Mixed Ability Teaching: Problems and Possibilities.* Slough: National Foundation for Educational Research.
20 Bailey, M. Mixed teaching and the defence of subjects, cited in Elliott, J. (1976) The problems and dilemmas of mixed ability teaching and the issues of teacher accountability. *Cambridge Journal of Education,* 6 (2), pp. 3–14.
21 Oeser, O. (1966) *Teacher, Pupil and Task.* London: Tavistock Publications.
22 Kerry, T. and Sands, M. (1982) *Mixed Ability Teaching in the Early Years of the Secondary School.* London: Macmillan.
23 Reid, Clunies-Ross, Goacher and Vile, *Mixed Ability Teaching: Problems and Possibilities.*
24 Davies, R. P. (1975) *Mixed Ability Grouping.* London: Temple Smith.
25 Kelly, *Mixed Ability Grouping: Theory and Practice.*
26 Department of Education and Science (1977) *Gifted Children in Middle and Comprehensive Schools.* London: HMSO.
27 Kerry, T. (1978) Bright pupils in mixed ability classes. *British Educational Research Journal,* 4 (2), pp. 103–11.
28 Waters, D. (1982) *Primary School Projects.* London: Heinemann.
29 Wyatt, H. (1976) Mixed ability teaching in practice. *Forum,* 18 (2), pp. 45–9.
30 Wragg, E. C. (1978) Training teachers for mixed ability classes: a ten-point attack. *Forum,* 20 (2), pp. 39–42.

12 LANGUAGE IN CLASSROOMS

1 Adelman, C. and Walker, R. (1974) Open space – open classrooms. *Education 3–13,* 2 (October), pp. 103–7.
2 For example: Flanders, N. A. (1970) *Analysing Teacher Behaviour.* Reading, Mass.: Addison Wesley; Edwards, A. D. and Furlong, V. J. (1978) *The Language of Teaching.* London: Heinemann.
3 See, for example: Jones, A. and Mulford, J. (eds) (1971) *Children Using Language.* London: Oxford University Press; Rosen, C. and Rosen, H. (1973) *The Language of Primary School Children.* Harmondsworth: Penguin.
4 Edwards and Furlong, *The Language of Teaching.*
5 Stebbins, R. (1973) Physical context influences on behaviour; the case of classroom disorderliness. *Environment and Behaviour,* 5, pp. 291–314.
6 Watson, L. (1995) Talk and pupil thought. *Educational Psychology,* 15 (1), pp. 57–68.
7 Carlsen W. (1991) Questioning in classrooms. *Review of Educational Research,* 61 (2), pp. 157–78.
8 Office for Standards in Education (1994) *Primary Matters: A Discussion of Teaching and Learning in Primary Schools.* London: Office for Standards in Education.
9 For example: Wragg, E. C. (1993) *Explaining.* London: Routledge; Pollard, A. and Tann, S. (1993) *Reflective Teaching in the Primary School* (2nd edn). London: Cassell. Proctor, A., Entwistle, M., Judge, B. and McKenzie-Murdoch, S. (1995) *Learning to Teach in the Primary Classroom.* London: Routledge, pp. 78–80.
10 Pollard and Tann, *Reflective Teaching in the Primary School.*
11 Brown, G. and Wragg, E. C. (1993) *Questioning.* London: Routledge.
12 Perrott, E. (1982) *Effective Teaching.* London: Longman.

13   Brown, G. and Armstrong, S. (1984) Explaining and explanations, in E. C. Wragg (ed.) *Classroom Teaching Skills*. London: Croom Helm.
14   Wragg, *Explaining*.
15   See Brown and Wragg, *Questioning*.
16   Brown, G. and Edmonson, R. (1984) Asking questions, in Wragg (ed.) *Classroom Teaching Skills*.
17   Ibid.
18   Thompson, L. and Feasey, R. (1992) *Questioning in Science*. Mimeo: School of Education, University of Durham.
19   Office for Standards in Education, *Primary Matters*, para. 11.
20   Brown, G. (1975) *Microteaching*. London: Methuen.
21   Bloom, B. (ed.) *Taxonomy of Educational Objectives Handbook 1: Cognitive Domain*. London: Longman.
22   Brown, *Microteaching*.
23   Gall, M. D. (1970) The use of questioning. *Review of Educational Research*, 40, pp. 707–21.
24   Brown, *Microteaching*.
25   Brown, *Microteaching*.
26   Ibid.
27   Davies, W. T. and Shepherd, T. B. (1949) *Teaching: Begin Here*. London: Epworth Press.
28   Turney, C., Clift, J. C., Dunkin, M. J. and Trail, R. D. (1973) *Microteaching: Research, Theory and Practice*. Sydney: Sydney University Press.
29   Chanan, G. and Delamont, S. (1975) *Frontiers of Classroom Research*. Windsor: National Foundation for Educational Research.
30   Brown and Edmonson, Asking questions, in Wragg (ed.) *Classroom Teaching Skills*.
31   Brown and Wragg, *Questioning*.
32   Pollard and Tann, *Reflective Teaching in the Primary School*.
33   Dean, J. (1983) *Organising Learning in the Primary School Classroom*. Beckenham: Croom Helm.
34   Turner, T. (1995) Moral development and values, in S. Capel, M. Leask and T. Turner, *Learning to Teach in the Secondary School*. London: Routledge.
35   Capel, Leask and Turner, *Learning to Teach in the Secondary School*.
36   Brown and Wragg, *Questioning*.
37   Proctor, Entwistle, Judge and McKenzie-Murdoch, *Learning to Teach in the Primary Classroom*, p. 79.
38   Stake, R. (1976) The countenance of educational evaluation, cited in D. Jenkins, Six alternative models of curriculum evaluation, Unit 20, E203, *Curriculum Design and Development*. Milton Keynes: Open University Press.
39   Bruner, J. S. (1966) *Towards a Theory of Instruction*. Cambridge, Mass.: Harvard University Press.
40   Vygotsky, L. (1978) *Mind and Society: The Development of Higher Psychological Processes*. Cambridge, Mass.: Harvard University Press.
41   Cooper, P. and McIntyre, D. (1996) The importance of power sharing in classroom learning, in M. Hughes (ed.) *Teaching and Learning in Changing Times*. Oxford: Blackwell. Gipps adds to this the view that adult–child interactions, if they are to promote learning, should be sustained and challenging rather than short, fragmented or routine, see Gipps, C. (1994) What we know about effective primary teaching, in J. Bourne (ed.) *Thinking Through Primary Practice*. Buckingham: Open University Press.
42   This section draws on material contained in Cohen, L. and Manion, L. (1981) *Perspectives in Classrooms and Schools*. Eastbourne: Holt, Rinehart & Winston, chapters 6 and 8.

43 Stubbs, M. (1983) *Language, Schools and Classrooms* (2nd edn). London: Methuen.
44 Barnes, D. (1971) Language in the secondary classroom, in D. Barnes, J. Britton and H. Rosen, *Language, the Learner and the School*. Harmondsworth: Penguin.
45 Barnes, D. (1971) Language and learning in the classroom. *Journal of Curriculum Studies*, 3 (1), pp. 27–38.
46 Mishler, E. G. (1972) Implications of teaching strategies for language and cognition: observations in first-grade classrooms, in C. B. Cazden, V. P. John and D. Hymes, *Functions of Language in the Classroom*. Teachers College, Columbia University, New York: Teachers College Press.
47 Stubbs, M. (1976) Keeping in touch: some functions of teacher-talk, in M. Stubbs and S. Delamont (eds) *Explorations in Classroom Observation*. London: Wiley.
48 Stubbs, *Language, Schools and Classrooms*.
49 See, for example: Edwards, D. and Mercer, N. M. (1987) *Common Knowledge: The Development of Understanding in the Classroom*. London: Routledge; Edwards, D. (1991) Discourse and the development of understanding in the classroom, in O. Boyd-Barratt and E. Scanlon (eds) *Computers and Learning*. Wokingham: Addison-Wesley, pp. 186–204; Edwards, D. (1993) Concepts, memory and the organisation of pedagogic discourse: a case study. *International Journal of Educational Research*, 19 (3), pp. 205–25.
50 Stubbs, *Language, Schools and Classrooms*.
51 Department of Education and Science (1975) *A Language for Life* (the Bullock Report). London: HMSO.

13 EQUAL OPPORTUNITIES

1 For example, the *Sex Discrimination Act* (1975). London: HMSO; the *Race Relations Act*, (1976). London: HMSO; Department of Education and Science (1978) *Special Educational Needs* (the Warnock Report). London: HMSO; Department of Education and Science (1985) *Better Schools*. London: HMSO; Department of Education and Science (1986) *The Curriculum from 5 to 16*. London: HMSO; Department of Education and Science (1985) *Education for All* (the Swann Report). London: HMSO; Department of Education and Science (1989) *From Policy to Practice*. London: HMSO; Department for Education (1992) *Choice and Diversity: a New Framework for Schools*. London: DFE.
2 Department of Education and Science, *Special Educational Needs* (the Warnock Report).
3 Department of Education and Science (1985) *Education for All* (the Swann Report).
4 Commission for Racial Equality (1989) *Code of Practice for the Elimination of Racial Discrimination in Education*. London: Commission for Racial Equality.
5 Department of Education and Science, *From Policy to Practice*.
6 National Curriculum Council (NCC) (1989) *A Curriculum for All*. York: National Curriculum Council.
7 National Curriculum Council (1989) *A Framework for the Primary Curriculum*. York: National Curriculum Council; National Curriculum Council, *A Curriculum for All*; National Curriculum Council (1989) *The Whole Curriculum*. York: National Curriculum Council; National Curriculum Council (1990) *Education for Economic and Industrial Understanding*. York: National Curriculum Council; National Curriculum Council (1990) *Health Education*. York: National Curriculum Council; National Curriculum Council (1990) *Careers Education and Guidance*. York: National Curriculum Council; National Curriculum Council (1990) *Environmental Education*. York: National Curriculum Council; National Curriculum Council (1990) *Education for Citizenship*. York: National Curriculum Council; National Curriculum Council

(1992) *The National Curriculum and Pupils with Severe Learning Difficulties*. York: National Curriculum Council.

8   Department for Education, *Choice and Diversity*.

9   Office for Standards in Education (OFSTED) (1993) *Handbook for the Inspection of Schools*. London: OFSTED.

10   Department for Education (1994) *Code of Practice for the Identification and Assessment of Special Educational Needs*. London: DFE.

11   Office for Standards in Education (OFSTED) (1995) *Guidance on the Inspection of Nursery and Primary Schools*. London: OFSTED, p. 77; OFSTED (1995) *Guidance on the Inspection of Secondary Schools*. London: OFSTED, p. 82; OFSTED (1995) *Guidance on the Inspection of Special Schools*. London: OFSTED, p. 80.

12   Ibid., pp. 106, 112 and 112 respectively.

13   The Runnymede Trust (1993) *Equality Assurance in Schools*. London: The Runnymede Trust with Trentham Books.

14   Equal Opportunities Commission (1984) *Do You Provide Equal Educational Opportunities?* Manchester: Equal Opportunities Commission, p. 7.

15   Newman, E. and Triggs, P. (eds) (1991) *Equal Opportunities in the Primary School*. Bristol: Bristol Polytechnic, pp. 28–9.

16   Department of Education and Science (1989) *From Policy to Practice*. London: HMSO.

17   Bourdieu, P. (1976) The school as a conservative force. In R. Dale, G. Esland and M. MacDonald (eds) *Schooling and Capitalism*. London: Routledge & Kegan Paul in association with the Open University Press.

18   Rosenthal, R. and Jacobson, L. (1968) *Pygmalion in the Classroom: Teacher Expectation and Pupils' Intellectual Ability*. New York: Holt, Rinehart & Winston. See also C. J. Hurn (1978) *The Limits and Possibilities of Schooling*. New York: Allyn & Bacon Inc. Rosenthal's and Jacobson's findings are not uncontentious, however. Wineburg (1987) indicates that their research contained several flaws, has not been able to be replicated, and owes its high profile to its concordance with a political crest of a wave – the time was ripe for such research findings when they appeared. See Wineburg, S. S. (1987) The self-fulfilment of the self-fulfilling prophecy. *Educational Researcher* 16 (9), pp. 28–37.

19   For example, Mortimore, P., Sammons, P., Stoll, L., Lewis, D. and Ecob, R. (1988) *School Matters: the Junior Years*. Shepton Mallett: Open Books; Reynolds, D. and Cuttance, P. (1992) *School Effectiveness: Research, Policy and Practice*. London: Cassell; Alexander, R., Rose, D. and Woodhead, C. (1992) *Curriculum Organisation and Classroom Practice in Primary Schools*. London: Department for Education.

20   Fine, M. (1987) Silencing in public schools. *Language Arts*, 64 (2), pp. 157–74.

21   Gibb, M., Paulin, G. and Hibbs, M. (1991) Equal opportunities, Unit 7, in G. Tilley and D. King (eds) *Cross-Curricular Issues: an INSET Manual for Secondary Schools*. Harlow: Longman, p. 718.

22   Myers, K. (1987) *Genderwatch*. London: School Curriculum Development Committee, p. 25.

23   Boulton, M. (1992) Participants in playground activities at middle school. *Educational Research*, 34 (3), pp. 167–82.

24   McFarlane, C. (1986) *Hidden Messages?* Birmingham: Development Education Centre, p. 7.

25   Lobban, G. (1975) Sex roles in reading schemes. *Forum for the Discussion of New Trends in Education*, 16 (2), pp. 57–60.

26   Meighan, R. (1981) *A Sociology of Educating*. Eastbourne: Holt, Rinehart & Winston.

27   Deem, R. (1978) *Women and Schooling*. London: Routledge & Kegan Paul.

28   Myers, *Genderwatch*, pp. 158–9.
29   Delamont, S. (1980) *Sex Roles and the School*. London: Methuen.
30   Spender, D. (1980) *Man Made Language*. London: Routledge & Kegan Paul.
31   Byrne, E. (1978) *Women and Education*. London: Tavistock.
32   McFarlane, *Hidden Messages*.
33   Serbin, L. (1978) Teachers, peers and play preferences, in B. Spring (ed.) *Perspectives on Non-Sexist Early Childhood Education*. Columbia University, New York: Teachers College Press.
34   Stanworth, M. (1981) *Gender and Schooling: a Study of Sexual Divisions in the Classroom*. London: Women's Research and Resources Centre Publications.
35   Myers, *Genderwatch*, p. 26.
36   Ibid., pp. 126–7.
37   Equal Opportunities Commission (1984) *Do You Provide Equal Educational Opportunities?* Manchester: Equal Opportunities Commission, p. 7.
38   Myers, *Genderwatch*, p. 70.
39   Ibid., p. 90.
40   Ibid., p. 96.
41   Myers, *Genderwatch*, p. 26.
42   Rogers, C. (1965) *Client Centred Therapy*. Boston: Houghton Mifflin Co., p. 389.
43   Brandes, D. and Ginnis, P. (1986) *A Guide to Student-Centred Learning*. Oxford: Basil Blackwell, p. 26.
44   Department of Education and Science, *Education for All* (the Swann Report).
45   Gaine, C. (1991) What do we call people?, in E. Newman and P. Triggs (eds) *Equal Opportunities in the Primary School*. Bristol: Bristol Polytechnic.
46   This is the substance of Whitty's criticisms of Lawton's attempts to derive a curriculum from an analysis of culture, see Whitty, G. (1985) *Sociology and School Knowledge*. London: Methuen.
47   Inner London Education Authority (1983) *Race, Sex and Class 3. A Policy for Equality*. London: ILEA.
48   *The Race Relations Act* (1976). London: HMSO. See also the Commission for Racial Equality, *Code of Practice for the Elimination of Racial Discrimination in Education*.
49   Ball, S. (1994) *Education Reform: a Critical and Post-structural Approach*. Buckingham: Open University Press.
50   Allcott, T., Smith, P., Burgoyne, N., Gibb, M. and Paulin, G. (1991) The multicultural dimension, in Tilley and King (eds) *Cross-Curricular Issues: an INSET Manual for Secondary Schools*.
51   Office for Standards in Education, *Guidance on the Inspection of Nursery and Primary Schools*, *Guidance on the Inspection of Special Schools* and *Guidance on the Inspection of Secondary Schools*.
52   We draw on material in L. Cohen and L. Manion (1982) *Multicultural Classrooms: Perspectives for Teachers*. London: Croom Helm, chapter 8.
53   Jeffcoate, R. (1979) A multicultural curriculum: beyond the orthodoxy. *Trends in Education* 4, pp. 8–12. See also G. Gerzina (1996) *Black Britain: Life Before Emancipation*. London: John Murray.
54   See also C. McFarlane (1986) *Hidden Messages? – Activities for Exploring Bias*. Birmingham: Development Education Centre.
55   Inner London Education Authority, *Race, Sex and Class 3*; Allcott, Smith, Burgoyne, Gibb and Paulin, The multicultural dimension.
56   Lawton, D. (1983) *Curriculum Studies and Educational Planning*. Sevenoaks: Hodder & Stoughton; Lawton, D. (1989) *Education, Culture and the National Curriculum*. Sevenoaks: Hodder & Stoughton.

57 McFarlane, C. (1986) *Hidden Messages?*, pp. 38–9.

58 Tylor, E. B. (1871) *Primitive Culture*. London: Murray.

59 Linton, R. (ed.) (1940) *Acculturation*. New York: Appleton-Century-Crofts.

60 The Runnymede Trust, *Equality Assurance in Schools*. Such work develops ideas from Lawton, D. (1973) *Social Change, Educational Theory and Curriculum Planning*. London: Hodder & Stoughton.

61 Lawton's work is not without its critics. For a summary of the criticisms of his work see Whitty, G. (1985) *Sociology and School Knowledge*. London: Methuen.

62 Jeffcoate, R. (1976) Curriculum planning in multiracial education. *Educational Research* 18 (3), pp. 192–200.

63 Gundura, J. (1982) Approaches to multicultural education, in Tierney, J. (ed.) *Race, Migration and Schooling*, Eastbourne: Holt, Rinehart & Winston.

64 Whether this particular criticism is justified in light of the contents of Box 63 we leave readers to judge.

65 Williams, J. (1979) *The Social Science Teacher*, 8 (4), cited in Gundura, Approaches to multicultural education.

66 Saunders, M. (1981) *Multicultural Teaching: A Guide for the Classroom*. Maidenhead: McGraw-Hill.

67 The Runnymede Trust, *Equality Assurance in Schools*.

68 National Curriculum Council (1991) *Circular 11: Linguistic Diversity and the National Curriculum*. York: National Curriculum Council.

69 The Swann Report drew upon the comments of many witnesses and a range of relevant literature.

70 Brown, C., Barnfield, J. and Stone, M. (1990) *Spanner in the Works: Education for Racial Equality and Social Justice in Primary Schools*. London: Trentham Books.

71 In response to the possible criticism that we are putting forward our own case for democracy we are reminded of Winston Churchill's view that 'democracy is the worst form of government devised by man [*in original*] apart from all the rest'.

72 The book from the Runnymede Trust, *Equality Assurance in Schools*, is an accessible source which indicates matters of direct importance to student teachers.

73 This counters the comments that are frequently heard in all-white schools, *viz.* 'We don't have a multi-cultural problem here'!

74 The Runnymede Trust, *Equality Assurance in Schools*, p. 13.

75 Morrison, K. R. B. (1992) Review of B. Wade and M. Moore 'Patterns of Educational Integration'. *British Journal of Educational Studies* 40 (3), pp. 304–6.

76 *The Education Act 1981*. London: HMSO.

77 National Curriculum Council, *A Curriculum for All* and *The National Curriculum and Pupils with Severe Learning Difficulties*.

78 For example, Department for Education (1995) *Mathematics in the National Curriculum*. London: HMSO.

79 Office for Standards in Education, *Guidance on the Inspection of Secondary Schools*, p. 113, and *Guidance on the Inspection of Nursery and Primary Schools*, p. 107.

80 National Curriculum Council, *The National Curriculum and Pupils with Severe Learning Difficulties*, p. 3.

81 Department of Education and Science, *Special Educational Needs* (the Warnock Report).

82 Pringle, M. L. K., Rutter, M. and Davie, E. (1966) *11,000 Seven Year Olds*. Harlow: Longman; Fogelman, K. (1976) *Britain's Sixteen Year Olds*. London: National Children's Bureau; Rutter, M., Tizard, J. and Whitemore, K. (1970) *Education, Health and Behaviour*. Harlow: Longman.

83 Centre for the Study of Comprehensive Schools (1994) *Managing Special Educational Needs*. School of Education, University of Leicester, Centre for the Study of

Comprehensive Schools and the National Association of Head Teachers, p. 2.

84 Department for Education (1994) *Code of Practice for the Identification and Assessment of Children with Special Educational Needs*. London: HMSO, para. 2.1.

85 Ibid., section 3.

86 Hegarty, S., Pocklington, K. and Lucas, D. (1981) *Educating Pupils with Special Needs in the Ordinary School*. Windsor: NFER-Nelson. For a comprehensive account of the problems of categorisation, selection, assessment and provision for children with special educational needs see A. Cohen and L. Cohen (eds) (1986) *Special Educational Needs in the Ordinary School: A Sourcebook for Teachers*. London: Harper & Row.

87 'Ordinary' teacher refers simply to any teacher who does not have a special role in relation to students with special educational needs.

88 Wade, B. and Moore, M. (1992) *Patterns of Educational Integration*. Wallingford: Triangle Books Ltd.

89 The Department for Education (1994) *Code of Practice for the Identification and Assessment of Children with Special Educational Needs* sets out a clearly defined five-stage model for assessment and statementing of students.

90 See, for example, OFSTED (1995) *Guidance on the Inspection of Secondary Schools*, p. 57; and the Department for Education *Code of Practice*.

91 National Curriculum Council, *A Curriculum for All*, p. 6.

92 Ibid., p. 15.

93 National Curriculum Council, *The National Curriculum and Pupils with Severe Learning Difficulties*, p. 6.

94 For example, Department for Education, *Mathematics in the National Curriculum*, p. 1.

95 National Curriculum Council, *A Curriculum for All* and *The National Curriculum and Pupils with Severe Learning Difficulties*.

96 National Curriculum Council, *A Curriculum for All*, p. 6.

97 Ibid., p. 8.

98 Ibid., p. 19.

99 North American research by Davidson and Slavin has shown that very considerable benefit can be derived from co-operative group work in enhancing students' performance. See Davidson, N. (1990) Co-operative learning research in mathematics. Paper given at the *IACSE 5th International Convention on Co-operative Learning*. Baltimore, MD; Slavin, R. (1990) *Co-operative Learning: Theory, Research and Practice*. Englewood Cliffs, NJ: Prentice Hall.

100 National Curriculum Council, *The National Curriculum and Pupils with Severe Learning Difficulties*, p. 5.

101 Ibid., pp. 48–9.

102 Garner, P. and Sandow, S. (eds) (1995) *Advocacy, Self-Advocacy and Special Needs*. London: David Fulton Publishers.

103 Fine, M. (1987) Silencing in public schools. *Language Arts*, 64 (2), pp. 157–74.

104 Hohmann, M., Bunet, B. and Weikart, D. W. (1979) *Young Children in Action*. Michigan: High Scope Press.

105 Zimiles, H. (1987) Progressive education: on the limits of evaluation and the development of empowerment. *Teachers College Record*, 89 (2), pp. 201–17.

14 MANAGEMENT AND CONTROL IN THE CLASSROOM

1 Department of Education and Science (1989) *Discipline in Schools* (The Elton Report). London: HMSO.

2 Hart, P., Wearing, A. and Conn, M. (1995) Conventional wisdom is a poor predictor

of the relationship between student misbehaviour and teacher stress. *British Journal of Educational Psychology*, 65 (1), pp. 27–48.

3   Docking, J. (1987) *Control and Discipline in Schools*, London: Harper & Row; Department of Education and Science, *Discipline in Schools* (The Elton Report); Docking, J. (1990) *Managing Behaviour in the Primary School*. London: David Fulton; Galvin, P., Mercia, S. and Costa, P. (1990) *Building a Better Behaved School*. Harlow: Longman; McGuiness, J. (1989) *A Whole School Approach to Pastoral Care*. London: Kogan Page; Thompson, D. and Arora, T. (1991) Why do students bully? An evaluation of the long-term effectiveness of a whole-school policy to minimize bullying. *Pastoral Care in Education*, 9 (4), pp. 8–12; Topping, K. (1992) School-based behaviour management work with families. *Pastoral Care in Education*, 10 (1), pp. 7–17; Canter, L. and Canter, M. (1992) *Assertive Discipline*. London: Lee Canter Associates; Munn, P., Johnstone, M. and Chalmers V. (1992) *Effective Discipline in Primary Schools and Classrooms*. London: Paul Chapman Publishing; Boulton, M. (1993) Aggressive fighting in British middle school students. *Educational Studies*, 19 (1), pp. 19–40; McGuiness, J. (1993) *Teachers, Pupils and Behaviour – a Managerial Approach*. London: Cassell; Office for Standards in Education (1993) *Achieving Good Behaviour in Schools*. London: Office for Standards in Education; Miller, A. (1995) Teachers' attributions of causality, control and responsibility and its successful management. *Educational Psychology*, 15 (4), pp. 457–71.

4   Mortimore, P., Sammons, P., Stoll, L., Lewis, D. and Ecob, R. (1988) *School Matters: the Junior Years*. Salisbury: Open Books.

5   Galvin, Mercia and Costa, *Building a Better Behaved School*.

6   Morrison, K. R. B. (1996) Developing a whole-school behaviour policy in primary schools. *Pastoral Care in Education*; Office for Standards in Education, *Achieving Good Behaviour in Schools*; Department for Education (1994) *Pupil Behaviour and Discipline* (Circular 8/94). London: HMSO; Department for Education (1994) *The Education of Children with Emotional and Behavioural Difficulties*. London: HMSO. These works are also relevant to points (4) and (5).

7   Peters, R. S. (1966) *Ethics and Education*. London: George Allen & Unwin.

8   Wadd, K. (1973) Classroom power, in B. Turner (ed.) *Discipline in Schools*. London: Ward Lock Educational.

9   The past few years have witnessed a considerable erosion of the teacher's authority. Some of the reasons for this change are rooted in the dramatic changes in society's beliefs and values that have taken place since the 1960s. For a brilliant account of these processes of change and the effects they have had on features of contemporary life such as the arts, popular culture and education, see B. Martion (1981) *A Sociology of Contemporary Cultural Change*. Oxford: Basil Blackwell.

10   Wragg, E. C. (1981) *Class Management and Control: A Teaching Skills Workbook*. DES Teacher Education Project, Focus Books; Series Editor, Trevor Kerry. London: Macmillan.

11   Morrison, Developing a whole-school behaviour policy in primary schools; Office for Standards in Education, *Achieving Good Behaviour in Schools*; Department for Education, *Pupil Behaviour and Discipline* and *The Education of Children with Emotional and Behavioural Difficulties*.

12   Johnstone, M. and Munn, P. (1987) *Discipline in School*. Edinburgh: Scottish Council for Research in Education.

13   Galton, M., Simon, B. and Croll, P. (eds) (1980) *Progress and Performance in the Primary Classroom*. London: Routledge & Kegan Paul.

14   Department of Education and Science (1989) *Education Observed 5: Good Behaviour and Discipline in Schools* (1989 edn). London: HMSO.

15   Wragg, *Class Management and Control*.

16   Glasser, W. (1969) *Schools without Failure*. New York: Harper & Row.
17   Nash, R. (1976) *Teacher Expectations and Pupil Learning*. London: Routledge & Kegan Paul.
18   Saunders, M. (1979) *Class Control and Behaviour Problems: A Guide for Teachers*. Maidenhead: McGraw-Hill.
19   Gannaway, H. (1976) Making sense of school, in M. Stubbs and S. Delamont (eds) *Explorations in Classroom Observation*. London: John Wiley.
20   Meighan, R. (1981) *A Sociology of Educating*. Eastbourne: Holt, Rinehart & Winston.
21   Fontana, D. (1985) *Classroom Control: Understanding and Guiding Classroom Behaviour*. London: British Psychological Society.
22   Saunders, *Class Control and Behaviour Problems*.
23   For a fascinating study of a small group of working-class boys who reject the norms and values put forward by their teachers, see P. Willis (1977) *Learning to Labour*. Farnborough: Saxon House.
24   Johnson, D. W. (1978) Conflict management in the school and classroom, in D. Bar-Tal and L. Saxe (eds) *Social Psychology of Education: Theory and Research*. New York: John Wiley & Sons.
25   Gnagey, W. J. (1981) *Motivating Classroom Discipline*. New York: Macmillan. London: Collier-Macmillan.
26   Thurston, J. E., Feldhusen, J. F. and Benning, J. J. (1973) A longitudinal study of delinquency and other aspects of students' behaviour. *International Journal of Criminology and Penology*, 1, November, pp. 341–51.
27   Gnagey, W. J. (1980) Locus of control, motives and crime prevention attitudes of classroom facilitators and inhibitors. Paper read at AERA, Boston.
28   Dierenfield, R. B. (1982) *Classroom Disruption in English Comprehensive Schools*. Minnesota: Macalester College Education Department.
29   Watkins, C. and Wagner, P. (1987) *School Discipline: A Whole-School Approach*. Oxford: Basil Blackwell.
30   Hargreaves, D. H. (1972) *Interpersonal Relations in Education*. London: Routledge & Kegan Paul.
31   Gnagey, W. J. (1968) *The Psychology of Classroom Discipline*. New York: Macmillan. London: Collier-Macmillan.
32   Goodlad, J. I., Klein, M. F. and associates (1974) *Looking behind the Classroom Door*. Worthington, Ohio: Charles A. Jones.
33   McIntyre, R. W. (1974) Guidelines for using behaviour modification in education, in R. Ulrich, T. Stachnik and J. Mabry (eds) *Control of Human Behaviour*, Volume III. Glenview, Illinois: Scott, Foresman.
34   Madsen, C. H. (Jnr.), Becker, W. C. and Thomas, D. R. (1968) Rules, praise and ignoring: elements of elementary classroom control. *Journal of Applied Behaviour Analysis*, 1, pp. 139–50.
35   Wragg, *Class Management and Control*.
36   Hargreaves, *Interpersonal Relations in Education*.
37   Denscombe, M. (1985) *Classroom Control: A Sociological Perspective*. London: George Allen & Unwin.
38   Good, T. L. and Brophy, J. E. (1973) *Looking in Classrooms*. New York: Harper & Row.
39   Kounin, J. S. (1970) *Discipline and Group Management in Classrooms*. New York: Holt, Rinehart & Winston.
40   Peters, *Ethics and Education*.
41   Brown, G. A. (1975) *Microteaching*. London: Methuen.
42   Good and Brophy, *Looking in Classrooms*.

43 Madsen, Becker and Thomas, Rules, praise and ignoring.
44 Denscombe, *Classroom Control.*
45 O'Leary, K. D., Kaufman, K. F., Kass, R. E. and Drabman, R. S. (1970) The effects of loud and soft reprimands on the behaviour of disruptive students. *Exceptional Students*, 37 (October), pp. 45–55.
46 Saunders, *Class Control and Behaviour Problems.*
47 Watkins and Wagner, *School Discipline.*
48 Kounin, *Discipline and Group Management in Classrooms.*
49 Gnagey, *The Psychology of Classroom Discipline.*
50 Kounin, J. S. and Gump, P. V. (1958) The ripple effect in discipline. *Elementary School Journal*, 35, pp. 158–62.
51 Oeser, O. A. (1966) *Teacher, Pupil and Task.* London: Tavistock Publications.
52 Kounin, J. S., Gump, P. V. and Ryan, J. J. (1961) Explorations in classroom management. *Journal of Teacher Education*, 12, pp. 235–47.
53 Marland, M. (1975) *The Craft of the Classroom.* London: Heinemann Educational.
54 Peters, *Ethics and Education.*
55 Waller, W. (1932) *The Sociology of Teaching.* New York: John Wiley.
56 Burns, R. B. (1978) The relative effectiveness of various incentives and deterrents as judged by pupils and teachers. *Educational Studies*, 4 (3), pp. 229–43.
57 Merrett, F. and Jones, L. (1994) Rules, sanctions and rewards in primary schools. *Educational Studies*, 20 (3), pp. 345–56.
58 Merrett, F. and Man Tang, W. (1994) The attitudes of British primary school pupils to praise, rewards, punishments and reprimands. *British Journal of Educational Psychology*, 64, pp. 91–103.
59 Capel, S. (1995) Motivating pupils, in S. Capel, M. Leask and T. Turner, *Learning to Teach in the Secondary School.* London: Routledge, p. 95.
60 Madsen, Becker and Thomas, Rules, praise and ignoring.
61 Waller, *The Sociology of Teaching.*
62 Merrett and Man Tang, The attitudes of British primary school pupils to praise, rewards, punishments and reprimands.
63 Houghton, S., Merrett, F. and Wheldall, K. (1988) The attitudes of British secondary school pupils to praise, rewards, punishments and reprimands: a further study. *New Zealand Journal of Educational Studies*, 23, pp. 201–14.
64 Marland, *The Craft of the Classroom.*
65 Note: for a review of the main features of non-verbal behaviour and their relevance in the classroom, see L. Cohen and L. Manion (1981) *Perspectives on Classrooms and Schools.* Eastbourne: Holt, Rinehart & Winston.
66 Dunkin, M. J. and Biddle, B. J. (1974) *The Study of Teaching.* New York: Holt, Rinehart & Winston.
67 Bourne, J. (1994) *Thinking Through Primary Practice.* Buckingham: Open University Press.
68 Merrett and Jones, Rules, sanctions and rewards in primary schools.
69 Department of Education and Science, *Discipline in Schools* (The Elton Report).
70 Wheldall, K. and Merrett, F. (1988) Which classroom behaviours do primary teachers say they find most troublesome? *Educational Review*, 40 (1), pp. 14–27.
71 Johnson, B., Oswald, M. and Adey, K. (1993) Discipline in South Australian primary schools. *Educational Studies*, 19 (3), pp. 289–305.
72 Jones, K., Charlton, T. and Wilkin, J. (1995) Classroom behaviours which first and middle school teachers in St. Helena find troublesome. *Educational Studies*, 21 (2), pp. 139–53.
73 Charlton, T. and David, K. (1993) *Managing Misbehaviour in Schools.* London: Routledge.

74   Peters, *Ethics and Education.*
75   Johnson, Oswald and Adey, Discipline in South Australian primary schools.
76   Thompson, B. (1973) *Learning to Teach.* London: Sidgwick & Jackson.
77   Saunders, *Class Control and Behaviour Problems.*
78   Department for Education, *Pupil Behaviour and Discipline*, para. 39.
79   Good and Brophy, *Looking in Classrooms.*
80   Wright, D. (1973) The punishment of students, in B. Turner (ed.) *Discipline in Schools.*
81   Thomas, D. R., Becker, W. C. and Armstrong, M. (1968) Production and elimination of disruptive classroom behaviour by systematically varying the teacher's behaviour. *Journal of Applied Behaviour Analysis*, 1, pp. 35–45.
82   Hewett, F. M. (1972) Educational programmes for students with behaviour disorders, in H. C. Quay and J. S. Querry (eds) *Psychopathological Disorders of Childhood.* New York: John Wiley.
83   Lawrence, J., Steed, D. and Young, P. (1984) *Disruptive Students – Disruptive Schools?* London: Croom Helm.
84   Gropper, G. L. and Kress, G. C. (1970) *Managing Problem Behaviour in the Classroom.* New York: New Century, Educational Division/Meredith Corporation.
85   Sloane, H. N. (1976) *Classroom Management: Remediation and Prevention.* New York: John Wiley.
86   Clarizio, H. F. (1976) *Toward Positive Classroom Discipline.* New York: John Wiley.
87   Givner, A. and Graubard, P. S. (1974) *A Handbook of Behaviour Modification for the Classroom.* New York: Holt, Rinehart & Winston.
88   McAuley, R. and McAuley, P. (1977) *Child Behaviour Problems.* London: Macmillan.
89   Morris, R. J. (1976) *Behaviour Modification with Students.* Cambridge, Mass.: Winthrop.
90   Canter, L. and Canter, M. (1992) *Assertive Discipline.* London: Lee Canter Associates.
91   Nicholls, D. and Houghton, S. (1995) The effect of Canter's Assertive Discipline program on teacher and student behaviour. *British Journal of Educational Psychology*, 65 (2), pp. 197–210.
92   Robinson, G. and Maines, N. (1994) Who manages pupil behaviour? Assertive Discipline – a blunt instrument for a fine task. *Pastoral Care in Education*, 12 (3), pp. 30–5.
93   Martin, S. (1994) A preliminary evaluation of the adoption and implementation of Assertive Discipline at Robinson high school. *School Organisation*, 14 (3), pp. 321–9.
94   Robertson, J. (1981) *Effective Classroom Control.* Sevenoaks: Hodder & Stoughton.
95   Carrington, B. (1986) Sport as a side-track: an analysis of West Indian involvement in extra-curricular sport, in L. Cohen and A. Cohen (eds) *Multicultural Education: A Sourcebook for Teachers.* London: Harper & Row.
96   Reid, I. (1994) Inequality, Society and Education. Inaugural lecture, Loughborough University Department of Education. See also Department of Social Security (1994) *Households Below Average Income: A Statistical Analaysis 1979–1991/1992.* London: HMSO.
97   Green, P. A. (1982) Teachers' influence on the self concept of ethnic minority pupils. Unpublished Ph.D. thesis. University of Durham.
98   The Rampton Committee (1981) *West Indian Children in Our Schools.* Interim Report. London: HMSO.
99   Cohen, L. (1993) *Racism Awareness Materials in Initial Teacher Training.* (Report to the Leverhulme Trust: 15–19, New Fetter Lane, London.) See also P. Naylor (1995)

Pupil perceptions of teacher racism. Unpublished Ph.D. thesis. Loughborough University of Technology.

100   Wragg, E. C. and Dooley, P. A. (1984) Class management during teaching practice, in E. C. Wragg (ed.) *Classroom Teaching Skills*. London: Croom Helm.

101   Wragg, *Classroom Teaching Skills*.

15 THE CLASSROOM ENVIRONMENT AND SITUATIONAL FACTORS

1   Wadd, K. (1973) Classroom power, in B. Turner (ed.) *Discipline in Schools*. London: Ward Lock Educational.

2   Marland, M. (1975) *The Craft of the Classroom*. London: Heinemann Educational.

3   Watkins, C. and Wagner, P. (1987) *School Discipline: A Whole-School Approach*. Oxford: Basil Blackwell.

4   West, R. H. (1967) *Organization in the Classroom*. Oxford: Basil Blackwell.

5   Marland, *The Craft of the Classroom*.

6   Watkins and Wagner, *School Discipline*.

7   Harvey, O. J., Prather, M., White, B. J. and Hoffmeister, J. K. (1968) Teachers' beliefs, classroom atmosphere and student behaviour. *American Educational Research Journal*, 5 (2), pp. 151–66.

8   Peters, R. S. (1966) *Ethics and Education*. London: George Allen & Unwin.

9   White, R. K. and Lippitt, R. (1960) *Autocracy and Democracy: An Experimental Inquiry*. New York: Harper & Row.

10   Lawrence, D. (1987) *Enhancing Self-Esteem in the Classroom*. London: Paul Chapman Publishing Ltd.

11   Evans, K. M. (1958) The teacher–pupil relationship. *Educational Research*, 2, pp. 3–8.

12   Dawney, M. (1977) *Interpersonal Judgements in Education*. London: Harper & Row.

13   Kutnick, P. J. (1988) *Relationships in the Primary School Classroom*. London: Paul Chapman Publishing Ltd.

14   Andersen, P. and Andersen, J. (1982) Nonverbal immediacy in instruction, in L. L. Barker (ed.) *Communication in the Classroom*. Englewood Cliffs, NJ: Prentice-Hall.

15   Neill, S. and Caswell, C. (1993) *Body Language for Competent Teachers*. London: Routledge.

16   Wragg, E. C. (1981) *Class Management and Control: A Teaching Skills Workbook*. DES Teacher Education Project, Focus Books. Series Editor: Trevor Kerry. London: Macmillan.

17   Kutnick, *Relationships in the Primary School Classroom*.

18   Wragg, E. C. (1981) *Class Management and Control: A Teaching Skills Workbook*.

19   Good, T. L. and Brophy, J. E. (1973) *Looking in Classrooms*. New York: Harper & Row.

20   Kutnick, *Relationships in the Primary School Classroom*.

21   Rutter, M., Maughan, B., Mortimore, P. and Ouston, J. (1979) *Fifteen Thousand Hours*. London: Open Books.

22   For example: Good, T. L. (1970) Which pupils do teachers call on? *Elementary School Journal*, 70, pp. 190–8; Jones, V. (1971) The influence of teacher–student introversion, achievement and similarity on teacher–student dyadic classroom interactions. Doctoral dissertation, University of Texas at Austin; Brophy, J. E. and Good, T. L. (1970) Teachers' communications of differential expectations for children's classroom performance; some behavioural data. *Journal of Educational Psychology*, 61, pp. 365–74.

23   Douglas, J. (1964) *The Home and the School: A Study of Ability and Attainment in*

the Primary School. London: McGibbon & Kee.

24 Mackler, B. (1969) Grouping in the ghetto. *Education and Urban Society*, 2, pp. 80–95.

25 Good, T. L. and Brophy, J. E. (1974) The influence of teachers' attitudes and expectations on classroom behaviour, in R. H. Coop and K. White (eds) *Psychological Concepts in the Classroom*. New York: Harper & Row.

26 Lawrence, *Enhancing Self-Esteem in the Classroom*.

16 ASSESSMENT

1 Pollard *et al.* show that between 1990 and 1992 nearly all the teachers surveyed reported massive increases in the amount of time that they spent on assessment. See Pollard, A., Broadfoot, P., Croll, P., Osborn, M. and Abbott, D. (1994) *Changing English Primary Schools?* London: Cassell.

2 Broadfoot, P. (1994) Editorial to *Assessment*, 1 (1), pp. 1–7.

3 Morrison, K. R. B. (1994) Uniformity and diversity in assessment: an international perspective and agenda. *Compare*, 24 (1), pp. 5–15.

4 McLean, L. (1988) Possibilities and limitations in cross-national comparisons of educational achievement, in P. Broadfoot, R. Murphy and H. Torrance (eds) *Changing Educational Assessment*. London: Routledge; Harnisch, D. L. and Mabry, L. (1993) Issues in the development and evaluation of alternative assessments. *Journal of Curriculum Studies*, 25 (2), pp. 179–87.

5 Ibid.

6 Gipps, C. (1988) National assessment: a comparison of English and American trends, in Broadfoot *et al.*, *Changing Educational Assessment*; Noah, H. J. and Eckstein, M. A. (1988) Trade-offs in examination policies: an international comparative perspective, in Broadfoot *et al.*, *Changing Educational Assessment*.

7 Singh, J. S., Marimuthu, T. and Mukherjee, H. (1988) Learning motivation and work: a Malaysian perspective, in Broadfoot *et al.*, *Changing Educational Assessment*.

8 Halsey, A. (1992) An international comparison of access to higher education, in D. Phillips (ed.) *Lessons of Cross-national Comparison in Education*. Wallingford: Triangle Books.

9 Okano, K. (1993) *School to Work Transition in Japan*. Clevedon: Multilingual Matters Ltd.

10 Harnisch and Mabry, Issues in the development and evaluation of alternative assessments.

11 Harlen, W. (1994) Issues and approaches to quality assurance and quality control in assessment, in W. Harlen (ed.) *Enhancing Quality in Assessment*. London: Paul Chapman Publishing.

12 Singer, R. (1990) Profiling: the role of technology, in C. Bell and D. Harris (eds) *World Yearbook of Education Assessment and Evaluation*. London: Kogan Page.

13 Harnisch and Mabry, Issues in the development and evaluation of alternative assessments.

14 Lee, H. (1992) Examining the New Zealand school system, in G. McCullough (ed.) *The School Curriculum in New Zealand*. New Zealand: The Dunmore Press.

15 Gruber, K. H. (1992) Unlearnt European lessons: why Austria abandoned the comprehensive school experiments and restored the Gymnasium, in Phillips (ed.) *Lessons of Cross-national Comparison in Education*.

16 Harnisch and Mabry, Issues in the development and evaluation of alternative assessments.

17 Pennycuick, D. (1991) Moderation of continuous assessment systems in developing countries, *Compare*, 21 (2), pp. 145–52.

18 Singer, Profiling.
19 Singer, R. (1990b) Optical mark reading technology in Chinese educational development, in Bell and Harris (eds) *World Yearbook of Education Assessment and Evaluation.*
20 Harnisch and Mabry, Issues in the development and evaluation of alternative assessments.
21 Cresswell, M. J. and Houston, J. G. (1991) Assessment of the National Curriculum – some fundamental considerations. *Educational Review*, 43 (1), pp. 63–78.
22 Nixon, N. J. (1990) Assessment issues in relation to experience-based learning on placements within courses, in Bell and Harris (eds) *World Yearbook of Education Assessment and Evaluation*, p. 90.
23 Department of Education and Science (1984) *Records of Achievement: A Statement of Policy.* London: HMSO.
24 Law, B. (1984) *Uses and Abuses of Profiling.* London: Harper & Row.
25 Department of Education and Science (1991) *National Record of Achievement.* London: HMSO.
26 Hargreaves, A. (1989) *Curriculum and Assessment Reform*, London: Basil Blackwell and The Open University Press.
27 Law, *Uses and Abuses of Profiling.*
28 Morrison, Uniformity and diversity in assessment.
29 Harnisch and Mabry, Issues in the development and evaluation of alternative assessments.
30 Gipps, C. (1990) *Assessment: A Teacher's Guide to the Issues.* London: Hodder & Stoughton, chapter five.
31 Task Group on Assessment and Testing (TGAT) (1987) *National Curriculum Assessment and Testing: a Report.* London: HMSO.
32 Goulding, M. (1992) Let's hear it for the girls. *Times Educational Supplement*, 21 February 1992, p. 38.
33 Hargreaves, *Curriculum and Assessment Reform.*
34 For example: Cox, C. B. and Dyson, A. E. (1971) *The Black Papers on Education.* London: Davis-Poynter Ltd.; Boyson, R. and Cox, C. B. (1975) *The Black Paper 1975: The Fight for Education.* London: Dent; Cox, C. B. and Dyson, A. E. (eds) (1977) *Black Paper Two: The Crisis in Education.* London: The Critical Quarterly Society.
35 Department of Education and Science (1975) *A Language for Life* (the Bullock Report). London: HMSO.
36 Department of Education and Science (1982) *Mathematics Counts* (the Cockcroft Report). London: HMSO.
37 Turner, M. (1990) *Sponsored Reading Failure: an Object Lesson.* IPSET Education Unit.
38 See for example the papers in Broadfoot, Murphy and Torrance (eds) *Changing Educational Assessment.*
39 Department of Education and Science (1988) *Advancing A Levels* (the Higginson Report). London: HMSO.
40 Burke, P. K. (1990) The role of examination groups in the curriculum, in T. Brown and K. R. B. Morrison (eds) *The Curriculum Handbook.* Harlow: Longman.
41 Tomlinson, J. (1993) *The Control of Education.* London: Cassell.
42 Department of Education and Science (1987) *The National Curriculum 5–16: a Consultative Document.* London: HMSO.
43 Department of Education and Science, *Records of Achievement.*
44 Department of Education and Science, *National Record of Achievement.*
45 Gipps, C. (1994) *Beyond Testing.* London: Falmer.
46 Task Group on Assessment and Testing, *National Curriculum Assessment and Testing.*

47   Pollard, Broadfoot, Croll, Osborn and Abbott, *Changing English Primary Schools?*

48   Morrison, K. R. B. (1990) An ideological masquerade. *Forum*, 31 (1), pp. 7–8.

49   Nevo, D. (1995) *School-Based Evaluation: a Dialogue for School Improvement.* Kidlington, Oxford: Pergamon.

50   For a review of this see L. Stenhouse (1975) *An Introduction to Curriculum Research and Development.* London: Heinemann.

51   Gipps, *Beyond Testing.*

52   For example, School Curriculum and Assessment Authority (1995) *Consistency in Teacher Assessment.* London: School Curriculum and Assessment Authority.

53   Lacey, C. and Lawton, D. (eds) (1981) *Issues in Evaluation and Accountability.* London: Methuen.

54   McCallum, B., McAlister, S., Brown, M. and Gipps, C. (1993) Teacher assessment at Key Stage One. *Research Papers in Education*, 8 (3), pp. 305–27.

55   Tizard, B., Blatchford, P., Burke, J., Farquar, C. and Plewis, I. (1988) *Young Children at School in the Inner City.* London: Lawrence Erlbaum Associates; Hart, K., Johnson, D. C., Brown, M., Dickson, L. and Clarkson, R. (1989) *Children's Mathematical Frameworks: 8–13.* Windsor: NFER-Nelson.

56   Makins, V. (1995) License to convert a waiting room. *Times Educational Supplement*, 23 June 1995, p. 6.

57   See, for example: Bennett, S. N., Desforges, C., Cockburn, A. and Wilkinson, B. (1984) *The Quality of Pupil Learning Experiences.* London: Lawrence Erlbaum Associates.

58   Nevo, *School-Based Evaluation.*

59   Lambert, D. (1995) Assessing and recording pupils' work, in. S. Capel, M. Leask and T. Turner, *Learning to Teach in the Secondary School.* London: Routledge, chapter 6.

60   Stiggins, J. C. and Conklin, N. F. (1992) *In Teachers' Hands: Investigating the Practice of Classroom Assessment.* New York: SUNY Press.

61   Gipps, *Assessment*, pp. 87–94.

62   Ibid., pp. 12–13.

63   Morrison, Uniformity and diversity in assessment.

64   Harlen, W. (1994) Introduction to *Enhancing Quality in Assessment.*

65   Glaser, R. (1963) Instructional technology and the measurement of learning outcomes: some questions. *American Psychologist*, 18, pp. 519–21.

66   Gipps, *Beyond Testing.*

67   Morrison, K. R. B. (1993) Building progression into modular higher degrees in education. *British Journal of In-Service Education*, 19 (3), pp. 5–11.

68   Kosko, B. (1994) *Fuzzy Thinking.* London: Flamingo.

69   Cresswell and Houston, Assessment of the national curriculum – some fundamental considerations.

70   Ibid.

71   Gipps, *Beyond Testing.*

72   For a discussion of this see Morrison, K. R. B. and Ridley, K. (1988) *Curriculum Planning and the Primary School.* London: Paul Chapman Publishing.

73   Morrison, K. R. B. (1993) *Planning and Accomplishing School-Centred Evaluation.* Norfolk: Peter Francis Publishing, p. 103.

74   School Examination and Assessment Council (1990) *A Guide to Teacher Assessment Pack C: A Source Book of Teacher Assessment.* London: Heinemann for the School Examination and Assessment Council, p. 84.

75   For an introduction to the notion of the self-fulfilling prophecy see C. Hurn (1977) *The Limits and Possibilities of Schooling.* New York: Allyn & Bacon.

76   Nevo, *School-based Evaluation*, p. 55.

77 Horton, T. (1990) *Assessment Debates*. London: Hodder & Stoughton, p. 31.
78 Department of Education and Science, *National Record of Achievement*.
79 Proctor, A., Entwistle, M. Judge, B. and McKenzie-Murdoch, S. (1995) *Learning to Teach in the Primary Classroom*. London: Routledge.
80 Dean, J. (1983) *Organising Learning in the Primary School*. London: Croom Helm.
81 Harlen, Issues and approaches to quality assurance and quality control in assessment.
82 School Curriculum and Assessment Authority, *Consistency in Teacher Assessment*.
83 Harnisch and Mabry, Issues in the development and evaluation of alternative assessments.
84 School Curriculum and Assessment Authority, *Consistency in Teacher Assessment*.
85 Clear examples of this can be seen in Watts, A. (1995) Double entendre. *Times Educational Supplement*, 9 June 1995, p. 3; Hofkins, D. (1995) Cheating 'rife' in national tests. *Times Educational Supplement*, 16 June 1995, p. 1; Maxwell, E. (1995) Anger intensifies over English tests marking. *Times Educational Supplement*, 30 June 1995; Hofkins, D. (1995) English scripts sent back for remarking. *Times Educational Supplement*, 7 July 1995, p. 2; Budge, D. (1995) Complaints pour in over national test results. *Times Educational Supplement*, 28 July 1995, p. 1.
86 Harlen (ed.) *Enhancing Quality in Assessment*.
87 Morrison, *Planning and Accomplishing School-Centred Evaluation*.
88 The School Curriculum and Assessment Authority (1995) has produced these for each of the core subjects of the national curriculum at each key stage.
89 See Nuttall, D. (1987) The validity of assessments. *European Journal of Psychology of Education*, 11 (2), pp. 109–18. See also Cresswell and Houston, Assessment of the national curriculum – some fundamental considerations.
90 Desforges, C. (1989) *Testing and Assessment*. London: Cassell.
91 Gipps, *Beyond Testing*, pp. 87–94.
92 Hudson, B. (1973) *Assessment Techniques: An Introduction*. London: Methuen.
93 See, for example: Rosenthal, R. and Jacobson, L. (1968) *Pygmalion in the Classroom: Teacher Expectation and Pupils' Intellectual Ability*. New York: Holt, Rinehart & Winston; Good, T. L. and Brophy, J. E. (1974) The influence of teachers' attitudes and expectations on classroom behaviour, in R. H. Coop and K. White (eds) *Psychological Concepts in the Classroom*. New York: Harper & Row; Mortimore, P., Sammons, P., Stoll, L., Lewis, D. and Ecob, R. (1988) *School Matters: The Junior Years*. Salisbury: Open Books.
94 School Examination and Assessment Council, *A Guide to Teacher Assessment Pack C*, pp. 14–15.
95 Lewis, D. G. (1974) *Assessment in Education*. London: University of London Press.
96 The Hawthorne Effect is discussed clearly in J. A. Hughes (1976) *Sociological Analysis: Methods of Discovery*. Sunbury-on-Thames: Nelson, pp. 94–7.
97 See School Examination and Assessment Council, *A Guide to Teacher Assessment Pack C*, p. 83.
98 Nash, R. (1976) *Teacher Expectations and Pupil Learning*. London: Routledge & Kegan Paul.
99 Times Educational Supplement (1995) Testing times for the timetable in Modedon Junior School. *Times Educational Supplement*, 16 June 1995, p. 6.
100 Mitchell, C. and Koshy, V. (1993) *Effective Teacher Assessment*. London: Hodder & Stoughton, p. 29.
101 Whetton, C., Ruddock, G. and Hopkins, S. (1991) *The Pilot Study of Standard Assessment Tasks for Key Stage 1: A Report*. London: School Examination and Assessment Council.
102 Cresswell and Houston, Assessment of the national curriculum – some fundamental considerations.

103   Gipps, *Beyond Testing*, chapter 4.
104   For a fuller discussion of this see Gipps, *Beyond Testing* and Nevo, *School-based Evaluation*.
105   Lambert, D. (1995) Assessment and improving the quality of pupils' work, in Capel, Leask and Turner, *Learning to Teach in the Secondary School*.
106   Nevo, *School-based Evaluation*, p. 100.
107   Wittgenstein, L. (1974) *Tractatus Logico-Philosophicus*. London: Routledge & Kegan Paul, p. 73.
108   Sutton, R. (1993) *A Framework for Assessment* (2nd edn). Slough: NFER-Nelson, p. 48.
109   Harlen, Issues and approaches to quality assurance and quality control in assessment.
110   Pirsig, R. M. (1976) *Zen and the Art of Motorcycle Maintenance*. London: Corgi, pp. 286 and 318.
111   Morrison, An ideological masquerade.
112   Morrison, K. R. B. (1994) *Implementing Cross-curricular Themes*. London: David Fulton, pp. 112–13.
113   Mitchell and Koshy, *Effective Teacher Assessment*, p. 38.
114   For details of tests mentioned in this paragraph, see the publications catalogue of The Psychological Corporation. London: Psychological Corporation.
115   Morrison, *Planning and Accomplishing School-centred Evaluation*.
116   Ibid.
117   Lewis, *Assessment in Education*.
118   Bloom, B. (ed.) (1956) *Taxonomy of Educational Objectives Handbook 1: Cognitive Domain*. London: Longman.
119   Chase, C. I. (1974) *Measurement for Educational Evaluation*. Reading, Mass.: Addison-Wesley.
120   School Examination and Assessment Council, *A Guide to Teacher Assessment Pack C*, p. 20.
121   School Curriculum and Assessment Authority, *Consistency in Teacher Assessment*.
122   Office for Standards in Education (OFSTED) (1995) *Guidance for the Inspection of Secondary Schools*. London: OFSTED.
123   This instruction is contained in the first section of each of the national curriculum subject documents (1994).
124   Department for Education (DFE) (1994) *Circular 21/94*. London: DFE.
125   Mitchell and Koshy, *Effective Teacher Assessment*, p. 66.
126   Morrison, *Implementing Cross-curricular Themes*.
127   Ibid.
128   Kyriacou, C. (1994) *Essential Teaching Skills*. London: Simon & Schuster, p. 37.
129   Kerry, T. (1982) *Effective Questioning: a Teaching Skills Workbook*. London: Macmillan.
130   Bloom, *Taxonomy of Educational Objectives Handbook 1*.
131   McLaren argues that there are too few subjunctive moments in classrooms, see P. McLaren (1993) *Schooling as a Ritual Performance* (2nd edn). London: Routledge, p. 142.
132   Simons, H. (1982) Conversation piece: the practice of interviewing in case study research, in R. McCormick (ed.) *Calling Education to Account*. London: Heinemann, chapter 3.6. See also R. McCormick and M. James (1988) *Curriculum Evaluation in Schools* (2nd edn). London: Routledge, chapter 8.
133   School Examination and Assessment Council, *A Guide to Teacher Assessment Pack C*, p. 37.
134   Morrison, *Planning and Accomplishing School-centred Evaluation*, chapter 3.
135   Gipps, *Beyond Testing*, p. 60.

136   Morrison, *Planning and Accomplishing School-centred Evaluation*, chapter 3.
137   Inner London Education Authority (1988) *The Primary Language Record*. London: Inner London Education Authority.
138   Lambert, D. (1995) An overview of assessment: principles and practice, in Capel, Leask and Turner, *Learning to Teach in the Secondary School*, p. 275.
139   Morrison, *Implementing Cross-curricular Themes*.
140   School Examination and Assessment Council, *A Guide to Teacher Assessment Pack C*, p. 20.
141   Lambert, Assessment and improving the quality of pupils' work.
142   See also Morrison, K. R. B. (1990) The assessment of skills, in P. Neal and J. Palmer, *Environmental Education in the Primary School*. Oxford: Basil Blackwell, pp. 92–7.
143   School Examination and Assessment Council, *A Guide to Teacher Assessment Pack C*, p. 11.
144   Pollard *et al.* indicated that 7-year-olds in 1992 showed less awareness of being assessed than 7-year-olds in 1991. See Pollard *et al.*, *Changing English Primary Schools*, p. 224.
145   School Examination and Assessment Council, *A Guide to Teacher Assessment Pack C*, p. 16.
146   Davis, A. J. (1993) Matching and assessment. *Journal of Curriculum Studies*, 25 (3), pp. 267–79.
147   See Cresswell and Houston, Assessment of the national curriculum – some fundamental considerations; Nuttall, The validity of assessments.
148   Task Group on Assessment and Testing, *National Curriculum Assessment and Testing*.
149   School Examination and Assessment Council, *A Guide to Teacher Assessment Pack C*, p. 14.
150   Mitchell and Koshy, *Effective Teacher Assessment*, p. 39.
151   School Examination and Assessment Council, *A Guide to Teacher Assessment Pack C*, p. 20.
152   Ibid., p. 6.

17 RECORD-KEEPING

1   Clift, P., Weiner, G. and Wilson, E. (1981) *Record-keeping in Primary Schools*. Schools Council Research Studies. London: Methuen.
2   See, for example: Department for Education (1992) *Reporting Pupils' Achievement to Parents* (Circular 5/92). London: HMSO; Department for Education and Employment (1995) *Reports on Pupils' Achievements in 1994/95* (Circular 1/95). These requirements are updated by the DFEE each year, though the stipulated date seems not to be consistent.
3   *The Data Protection Act* (1984). London: HMSO.
4   Barrs, M. and Johnson, G. (1993) *Record-keeping in the Primary School*. London: Hodder & Stoughton.
5   Inner London Education Authority (1988) *The Primary Language Record*. London: Inner London Education Authority.
6   Law, B. (1984) *Uses and Abuses of Profiling*. London: Harper & Row.
7   School Examination and Assessment Council (1990) *A Guide to Teacher Assessment: A Source Book of Teacher Assessment (Book C)*. London: Heinemann for the School Examination and Assessment Council, p. 38.

18 RECORDS OF ACHIEVEMENT

1   Hoyle, E. (1975) The creativity of the school in Britain, in A. Harris, M. Lawn and W. Prescott (eds) *Curriculum Innovation*. London: Croom Helm in association with the Open University Press, p. 332.

2   Department of Education and Science (1991) *The National Record of Achievement*. London: HMSO.

3   Department of Education and Science (1984) *Records of Achievement: A Statement of Policy*. London: HMSO, para. 40.

4   Ibid., para. 5.

5   Ibid., para. 11.

6   Department of Education and Science and the Employment Department (undated) *National Record of Achievement* (accompanying paper to the National Record of Achievement (1991), signatories, M. Howard and K. Clark), paras. 1–3.

7   Employment Department (1991) *National Record of Achievement: A Business Guide*. Sheffield: Employment Department, p. 2.

8   Hargreaves, A. (1989) *Curriculum and Assessment Reform*. Oxford: Basil Blackwell with the Open University Press.

9   Department of Education and Science (1991) *The National Record of Achievement*. London: HMSO, page ref. NRA/C/1191.

10 Ibid., page ref. NRA/OA/1191.

11 Ibid., page ref. NRA/PS/1191.

12 School Examination and Assessment Council (SEAC) (1990) *Records of Achievement in the Primary School*. London: SEAC.

13 Johnson, G., Hill, B. and Tunstall, P. (1992) *Primary Records of Achievement: A Teachers' Guide to Reviewing, Recording and Reporting*. London: Hodder & Stoughton.

14 Munby, S. (1989) *Assessing and Recording Achievement*. Oxford: Blackwell.

15 University of Bristol (1988) *Pilot Records of Achievement in Schools Evaluation: Final Report* (PRAISE Report). Bristol: University of Bristol; Department of Education and Science (1989) *Report of the Records of Achievement National Steering Committee* (RANSC Report). London: HMSO.

Bibliography

Adam Smith Institute (1984) *Education Policy (The Omega Report)*. London: Adam Smith Institute.

Adelman, C. and Walker, R. (1974) Open space – open classrooms. *Education 3–13*, 2 (October), pp. 103–7.

Alexander, R. (1984) *Primary Teaching*. Eastbourne: Holt, Rinehart & Winston.

Alexander, R. (1992) *Policy and Practice in Primary Education*. London: Routledge.

Alexander, R., Rose, J. and Woodhead, C. (1992) *Curriculum Organisation and Classroom Practice in Primary Schools*. London: HMSO.

Allcott, T., Smith, P., Burgoyne, N., Gibb, M. and Paulin, G. (1991) The multicultural dimension. In G. Tilley and D. King, *Cross-Curricular Issues: an INSET Manual for Secondary Schools*. Harlow: Longman.

Allen, I., Dover, K., Gaff, M., Gray, E., Griffiths, C., Ryall, N. and Toone, E. (1975) *Working an Integrated Day*. London: Ward Lock Educational.

Andersen, P. and Andersen, J. (1982) Nonverbal immediacy in instruction. In L. L. Barker (ed.) *Communication in the Classroom*. Englewood Cliffs, NJ: Prentice-Hall.

Apple, M. (1993) The politics of official knowledge: does a national curriculum make sense? *Teachers College Record*, 95 (2), pp. 222–41.

Ashton, P., Kneen, P. and Davies, F. (1975) *Aims into Practice in the Primary School*. London: University of London Press.

Ashton, P., Kneen, P., Davies, F. and Holley, B. J. (1975) *The Aims of Primary Education: a Study of Teachers' Opinions*. London: Macmillan.

Bailey, C. and Bridges, D. (1983) *Mixed Ability Grouping: a Philosophical Perspective*. London: Allen & Unwin.

Bailey, M. Mixed teaching and the defence of subjects, cited in J. Elliott (1976) The problems and dilemmas of mixed ability teaching and the issues of teacher accountability. *Cambridge Journal of Education*, 6 (2), pp. 3–14.

Baker, R. (1987) Developing educational relevance in primary school science. *CASTME Journal*, 7 (1), pp. 28–39.

Ball, S. (1981) *Beachside Comprehensive*. London: Cambridge University Press.

Ball, S. (1990) *Politics and Policy Making in Education*. London: Routledge.

Ball, S. (1994) *Education Reform: a Critical and Post-structural Approach*. Buckingham: Open University Press.

Barnes, B. (1987) *Learning Styles in TVEI: Evaluation Report No. 3*. Leeds University for the MSC.

Barnes, D. (1971) Language in the secondary classroom. In D. Barnes, J. Britton and H. Rosen, *Language, the Learner and the School*. Harmondsworth: Penguin.

Barnes, D. (1971) Language and learning in the classroom. *Journal of Curriculum Studies*, 3 (1), pp. 27–38.

Barrs, M. and Johnson, G. (1993) *Record-keeping in the Primary School*. London: Hodder & Stoughton.

Bennett, N. and Carré, C. (1993) *Learning to Teach*. London: Routledge.

Bennett, N. and Dunne, E. (1992) *Managing Classroom Groups*. Hemel Hempstead: Simon & Schuster.

Bennett, N., Desforges, C., Cockburn, A. and Wilkinson, B. (1984) *The Quality of Pupil Learning Experiences*. London: Lawrence Erlbaum.

Bennett, N., Wragg, E. C., Carré, C. G. and Carter, D. S. G. (1992) A longitudinal study of primary teachers' perceived competence in, and concerns about, national curriculum implementation. *Research Papers in Education* 7 (1), pp. 53–78.

Bennett, S. N. and Kell, J. A. (1989) *A Good Start? Four Year Olds in Infant Schools*. Oxford: Blackwell.

Bennett, S. N., Andrea, J., Hegarty, P. and Wade, B. (1980) *Open Plan Schools: Teaching, Curriculum, Design*. Slough: National Foundation for Educational Research.

Bernstein, B. (1971) On the classification and framing of educational objectives. In M. F. D. Young (ed.) *Knowledge and Control*. Basingstoke: Collier-Macmillan.

Bernstein, B. (1977) Class and pedagogies – visible and invisible. In B. Bernstein, *Class, Codes and Control, Volume Three*. London: Routledge & Kegan Paul.

Blenkin, G. and Kelly, A. V. (1981) *The Primary Curriculum*. London: Harper & Row.

Bloom, B. (ed.) *Taxonomy of Educational Objectives Handbook 1: Cognitive Domain*. London: Longman.

Blyth, W. A. L. (1965) *English Primary Education, Volume One*. London: Routledge & Kegan Paul.

Board of Education (1931) *Report of the Consultative Committee of the Board of Education on the Primary School*. London: Board of Education.

Bonnett, M. (1986) Child-centredness and the problem of structure in project work. *Cambridge Journal of Education*, 16 (1), pp. 3–6.

Borg, W. (1966) *Ability Grouping in the Public Schools: a Field Survey*. New York: Dembar Educational Research Services.

Boulton, M. (1992) Participants in playground activities at middle school. *Educational Research*, 34 (3), pp. 167–82.

Boulton, M. (1993) Aggressive fighting in British middle school students. *Educational Studies*, 19 (1), pp. 19–40.

Bourdieu, P. (1976) The school as a conservative force. In R. Dale, G. Esland and M. MacDonald (1976) *Schooling and Capitalism*. London: Routledge & Kegan Paul.

Bourdieu, P. (1977) Cultural reproduction and educational reproduction. In J. Karabel and A. H. Halsey (eds) *Power and Ideology in Education*. London: Oxford University Press.

Bourne, J. (1994) A question of quality. In J. Bourne (ed.) *Thinking Through Primary Practice*. Buckingham: Open University Press.

Bourne, J. (1994) A question of ability. In J. Bourne (ed.) *Thinking Through Primary Practice*. Buckingham: Open University Press.

Bowe, R., Ball, S. and Gold, A. (1992) *Reforming Education and Changing Schools*. London: Routledge.

Boydell, D. (1975) Individual attention: the child's eye view. *Education 3–13*, 3 (April), pp. 9–13.

Boyson, R. and Cox, C. B. (1975) *The Black Paper 1975: The Fight for Education*. London: Dent.

Bradley, H., Eggleston, J., Kerry, T. and Cooper, D. (1985) *Developing Pupils' Thinking Through Topic Work: a Starter Course*. London: Longman.

Brandes, D. and Ginnis, P. (1986) *A Guide to Student-Centred Learning*. Oxford: Basil Blackwell, p. 26.

Brembeck, C. S. (1971) *Social Foundations of Education*. New York: J. Wiley & Sons.

Brighouse, T. and Tomlinson, J. (1991) *Successful Schools*, Education and Training Paper No. 4. London: Institute for Public Policy Research.

Broadfoot, P. (1994) Editorial to *Assessment*, 1 (1), pp. 1–7.

Brophy, J. E. and Good, T. L. (1970) Teachers' communications of differential expectations for children's classroom performance; some behavioural data. *Journal of Educational Psychology*, 61, pp. 365–74.

Brown, C., Barnfield, J. and Stone, M. (1990) *Spanner in the Works: Education for Racial Equality and Social Justice in Primary Schools*. London: Trentham Books.

Brown, G. (1975) *Microteaching*. London: Methuen.

Brown, G. and Armstrong, S. (1984) Explaining and explanations. In E. C. Wragg (ed.) *Classroom Teaching Skills*. London: Croom Helm.

Brown, G. A. and Edmonson, R. (1984) Asking questions. In E. C. Wragg (ed.) *Classroom Teaching Skills*. London: Croom Helm.

Brown, G. and Wragg, E. C. (1993) *Questioning*. London: Routledge.

Bruner, J. S. (1966) *Towards a Theory of Instruction*. Cambridge, Mass.: Harvard University Press.

Budge, D. (1995) Complaints pour in over national test results. *Times Educational Supplement*, 28 July 1995, p. 1.

Bullock, A. (ed.) (1971) *The Twentieth Century*. London: Thames & Hudson.

Burke, P. K. (1990) The role of examination groups in the curriculum. In T. Brown and K. R. B. Morrison (eds) *The Curriculum Handbook*. Harlow: Longman.

Burns, R. B. (1978) The relative effectiveness of various incentives and deterrents as judged by pupils and teachers. *Educational Studies*, 4 (3), pp. 229–43.

Byrne, E. (1978) *Women and Education*. London: Tavistock.

Canter, L. and Canter, M. (1992) *Assertive Discipline*. London: Lee Canter Associates.

Capel, S. (1995) Motivating pupils. In S. Capel, M. Leask and T. Turner, *Learning to Teach in the Secondary School*. London: Routledge.

Capel, S., Leask, M. and Turner, T. (1995) *Learning to Teach in the Secondary School*. London: Routledge.

Carlsen W. (1991) Questioning in classrooms. *Review of Educational Research*, 61 (2), pp. 157–78.

Carrington, B. (1986) Sport as a side-track: an analysis of West Indian involvement in extra-curricular sport. In L. Cohen and A. Cohen (eds) *Multicultural Education: A Sourcebook for Teachers*. London: Harper & Row.

Central Advisory Council for Education (1967) *Children and Their Primary Schools* (Plowden Report). London: HMSO.

Centre for the Study of Comprehensive Schools (1994) *Managing Special Educational Needs*. School of Education, University of Leicester, Centre for the Study of Comprehensive Schools and the National Association of Head Teachers.

Chanan, G. and Delamont, S. (1975) *Frontiers of Classroom Research*. Windsor: National Foundation for Educational Research.

Chapman, R. (1979) Schools do make a difference. *British Educational Research Journal*, 5 (1), pp. 115–24.

Charlton, T. and David, K. (1993) *Managing Misbehaviour in Schools*. London: Routledge.

Chase, C. I. (1974) *Measurement for Educational Evaluation*. Reading, Mass.: Addison-Wesley.

Clarizio, H. F. (1976) *Toward Positive Classroom Discipline*. New York: John Wiley.

Clift, P., Weiner, G. and Wilson, E. (1981) *Record-keeping in Primary Schools*. Schools Council Research Studies. London: Methuen.

Cohen, A. and Cohen, L. (eds) (1986) *Special Educational Needs in the Ordinary School:*

A Sourcebook for Teachers. London: Harper & Row.

Cohen, E. (1994) Restructuring the classroom – conditions for productive small groups. *Review of Educational Research*, 64 (1), pp. 1–35.

Cohen, L. (1993) *Racism Awareness Materials in Initial Teacher Training*. Report to the Leverhulme Trust, 15–19, New Fetter Lane, London.

Cohen, L. and Cohen, A. (eds) (1986) *Multicultural Education: A Sourcebook for Teachers*. London: Harper & Row.

Cohen, L. and Manion, L. (1981) *Perspectives in Classrooms and Schools*. Eastbourne: Holt, Rinehart & Winston.

Cohen, L. and Manion, L. (1982) *Multicultural Classrooms: Perspectives for Teachers*. London: Croom Helm.

Combs, A. (1965) *The Professional Education of Teachers*. Boston: Allyn & Bacon.

Commission for Racial Equality (1989) *Code of Practice for the Elimination of Racial Discrimination in Education*. London: Commission for Racial Equality.

Cooper, P. and McIntyre, D. (1996) The importance of power sharing in classroom learning. In M. Hughes (ed.) *Teaching and Learning in Changing Times*. Oxford: Blackwell.

Cox, C. B. and Dyson, A. E. (1971) *The Black Papers on Education*. London: Davis-Poynter Ltd.

Cox, C. B. and Dyson, A. E. (eds) (1977) *Black Paper Two: The Crisis in Education*. London: The Critical Quarterly Society.

Cresswell, M. J. and Houston, J. G. (1991) Assessment of the national curriculum – some fundamental considerations. *Educational Review*, 43 (1), pp. 63–78.

Curriculum Development Centre (1980) *Core Curriculum for Australian Schools*. Canberra: Curriculum Development Centre.

Dalin, P. (1993) *Changing the School Culture*. London: Cassell.

Data Protection Act (1984). London: HMSO.

Davidson, N. (1990) Co-operative learning research in mathematics. Paper given at the *IACSE 5th International Convention on Co-operative Learning*. Baltimore, MD.

Davies, I. K. (1976) *Objectives in Curriculum Design*. Maidenhead: McGraw Hill.

Davies, R. P. (1975) *Mixed Ability Grouping*. London: Temple Smith.

Davies, W. T. and Shepherd, T. B. (1949) *Teaching: Begin Here*. London: Epworth Press.

Davis, A. (1993) Matching and assessment. *Journal of Curriculum Studies*, 25 (3), pp. 267–79.

Dawney, M. (1977) *Interpersonal Judgements in Education*. London: Harper & Row.

Dean, J. (1983) *Organising Learning in the Primary School Classroom*. Beckenham: Croom Helm, reprinted by Routledge (1988).

Dearden, R. F. (1971) What is the integrated day? In J. Walton (ed.) *The Integrated Day in Theory and Practice*. London: Ward Lock Educational.

Dearden, R. F. (1976) *Problems in Primary Education*. London: Routledge & Kegan Paul.

Deem, R. (1978) *Women and Schooling*. London: Routledge & Kegan Paul.

Delamont, S. (1980) *Sex Roles and the School*. London: Methuen.

Denscombe, M. (1985) *Classroom Control: A Sociological Perspective*. London: George Allen & Unwin.

Department for Education (1992) *Initial Teacher Training (Secondary) (Circular 9/92)*. London: Department for Education.

Department for Education (1992) *The Parents' Charter*. London: HMSO.

Department for Education (1992) *Reporting Pupils' Achievement to Parents (Circular 5/92)*. London: HMSO.

Department for Education (1993) *Final Report on the National Curriculum and its Assessment: The Government's Response*. London: HMSO.

Department for Education (1993) *The Initial Training of Primary School Teachers: New*

Criteria for Courses (Circular 14/93). London: Department for Education.

Department for Education (1994) *Code of Practice for the Identification and Assessment of Special Educational Needs*. London: Department for Education.

Department for Education (1994) *Pupil Behaviour and Discipline (Circular 8/94)*. London: HMSO.

Department for Education (1994) *The Education of Children with Emotional and Behavioural Difficulties (Circular 9/94)*. London: HMSO.

Department for Education (DFE) (1994) *Circular 21/94*. London: DFE.

Department for Education (1995) *Mathematics in the National Curriculum*. London: HMSO.

Department for Education and Employment (1995) *Reports on Pupils' Achievements in 1994/95 (Circular 1/95)*.

Department of Education and Science (1975) *A Language for Life* (the Bullock Report). London: HMSO.

Department of Education and Science (1977) *Gifted Children in Middle and Comprehensive Schools*. London: HMSO.

Department of Education and Science (1978) *Special Educational Needs* (the Warnock Report). London: HMSO.

Department of Education and Science (1978) *Primary Education in England: a Survey by HM Inspectors of Schools*. London: HMSO.

Department of Education and Science (1981) *The Education Act 1981*. London: HMSO.

Department of Education and Science (1982) *Education 5–9*. London: HMSO.

Department of Education and Science (1982) *The New Teacher in School*. London: HMSO.

Department of Education and Science (1982) *Mathematics Counts* (the Cockcroft Report). London: HMSO.

Department of Education and Science (1983) *9–13 Middle Schools: an Illustrative Survey*. London: HMSO.

Department of Education and Science (1983) *Curriculum 11–16. Towards a Statement of Entitlement, Curricular Reappraisal in Action*. London: HMSO.

Department of Education and Science (1984) *Records of Achievement: A Statement of Policy*. London: HMSO.

Department of Education and Science (1985) *The Curriculum from 5 to 16*, Curriculum Matters 2. London: HMSO.

Department of Education and Science (1985) *Better Schools*. Cmnd 9469. London: HMSO.

Department of Education and Science (1985) *Education for All* (the Swann Report). London: HMSO.

Department of Education and Science (1987) *The National Curriculum 5–16: a Consultation Document*. London: HMSO.

Department of Education and Science (1988) *Education Reform Act*. London: HMSO.

Department of Education and Science (1988) *The New Teacher in School*. London: HMSO.

Department of Education and Science (1988) *National Curriculum, Task Group on Assessment and Testing: A Report*. London: HMSO.

Department of Education and Science (1988) *Advancing A Levels* (the Higginson Report). London: HMSO.

Department of Education and Science (1989) *Report of the Records of Achievement National Steering Committee* (RANSC Report). London: HMSO.

Department of Education and Science (1989) *From Policy to Practice*. London: HMSO.

Department of Education and Science (1989) *Initial Teacher Training: Approval of Courses (Circular 24/89)*. London: HMSO.

Department of Education and Science (1989) *Discipline in Schools* (the Elton Report). London: HMSO.

Department of Education and Science (1989) *Education Observed 5: Good Behaviour and Discipline in Schools* (1989 edn). London: HMSO.

Department of Education and Science (1991) *National Record of Achievement*. London: HMSO.

Department of Education and Science and the Employment Department (1991) *National Record of Achievement* (accompanying paper to the National Record of Achievement, signatories, M. Howard and K. Clark).

Department of Education and Science (1991) *Testing 7 Year Olds in 1991: Results of the National Curriculum Tests in England*. London: HMSO.

Department of Education and Science (1992) *Choice and Diversity: A New Framework for Schools*. London: HMSO.

Department of Employment (1993) *Flexible Learning: A Framework for Education and Training in the Skills Decade*. Sheffield: Department of Employment.

Department of Social Security (1994) *Households Below Average Income: A Statistical Analysis 1979–1991/1992*. London: HMSO.

Desforges, C. (1987) *Understanding the Mathematics Teacher*. Lewes: Falmer.

Desforges, C. (1989) *Testing and Assessment*. London: Cassell.

Dewey, J. (1916) *Democracy and Education*. New York: Macmillan.

Dewey, J. (1938) *Experience and Education*. New York: Collier.

Dierenfield, R. B. (1982) *Classroom Disruption in English Comprehensive Schools*. Minnesota: Macalester College Education Department.

Docking, J. (1987) *Control and Discipline in Schools*. London: Harper & Row.

Docking, J. (1990) *Managing Behaviour in the Primary School*. London: David Fulton.

Douglas, J. (1964) *The Home and the School: A Study of Ability and Attainment in the Primary School*. London: McGibbon & Kee.

Dowson, J. (1995) The National Curriculum. In S. Capel, M. Leask and T. Turner, *Learning to Teach in the Secondary School*. London: Routledge.

Dowson, J. (1995) The school curriculum. In S. Capel, M. Leask and T. Turner, *Learning to Teach in the Secondary School*. London: Routledge.

Dunkin, M. J. and Biddle, B. J. (1974) *The Study of Teaching*. New York: Holt, Rinehart & Winston.

Dunne, E. and Bennett, N. (1990) *Talking and Learning in Groups*. Basingstoke: Macmillan.

Edwards, A. D. and Furlong, V. J. (1978) *The Language of Teaching*. London: Heinemann.

Edwards, D. (1991) Discourse and the development of understanding in the classroom. In O. Boyd and E. Scanlon (eds) *Computers and Learning*. Wokingham: Addison-Wesley Publishers, pp. 186–204.

Edwards, D. (1993) Concepts, memory and the organisation of pedagogic discourse: a case study. *International Journal of Educational Research*, 19 (3), pp. 205–25.

Edwards, D. and Mercer, N. M. (1987) *Common Knowledge: The Development of Understanding in the Classroom*. London: Routledge & Kegan Paul.

Eggleston, J. and Kerry, T. (1985) Integrated studies. In S. N. Bennett and C. Desforges (eds) *Recent Advances in Classroom Research. British Journal of Educational Psychology Monographs Series No. 2*. Edinburgh: Scottish Academic Press.

Eisner, E. (1985) *The Art of Educational Evaluation*. Lewes: Falmer.

Employment Department (1991) *National Record of Achievement: A Business Guide*. Sheffield: Employment Department.

Entwistle, H. (1970) *Child-Centred Education*. London: Methuen.

Entwistle, H. (1980) Work, leisure and life styles. In B. Simon and W. Taylor (eds) *Education in the Eighties*. London: Batsford.

Equal Opportunities Commission (1984) *Do You Provide Equal Educational Opportunities?* Manchester: Equal Opportunities Commission.

Eraut, M. (1991) *Flexible Learning in Schools*. Institute of Continuing and Professional Education: University of Sussex.

Esland, G. (1971) Teaching and learning as the organization of knowledge. In M. F. D. Young (ed.) *Knowledge and Control*. Basingstoke: Collier-Macmillan.

Evans, K. M. (1958) The teacher–pupil relationship. *Educational Research*, 2, pp. 3–8.

Fine, M. (1987) Silencing in public schools. *Language Arts*, 64 (2), pp. 157–74.

Flanders, N. A. (1970) *Analysing Teacher Behaviour*. Reading, Mass.: Addison-Wesley.

Fogelman, K. (1976) *Britain's Sixteen Year Olds*. London: National Children's Bureau.

Fontana, D. (1985) *Classroom Control: Understanding and Guiding Classroom Behaviour*. London: British Psychological Society and Methuen.

Furlong, V. J., Hirst, P. H., Pocklington, K. and Miles, S. (1988) *Initial Teacher Training and the Role of the School*. Milton Keynes: Open University Press.

Gaine, C. (1991) What do we call people? In E. Newman and P. Triggs (eds) *Equal Opportunities in the Primary School*. Bristol: Bristol Polytechnic.

Gall, M. D. (1970) The use of questioning. *Review of Educational Research*, 40, pp. 707–21.

Galton, M. and Simon, B. (1980) *Inside the Primary Classroom*. London: Routledge & Kegan Paul.

Galton, M., Simon, B. and Croll, P. (eds) (1980) *Progress and Performance in the Primary Classroom*. London: Routledge.

Galvin, P., Mercia, S. and Costa, P. (1990) *Building a Better Behaved School*. Harlow: Longman.

Gannaway, H. (1976) Making sense of school. In M. Stubbs and S. Delamont (eds) *Explorations in Classroom Observation*. London: John Wiley.

Garner, J. and Byng, M. (1973) Inequalities of teacher–pupil contact. *British Journal of Educational Psychology*, 43, pp. 234–43.

Garner, P. and Sandow, S. (eds) (1995) *Advocacy, Self-Advocacy and Special Needs*. London: David Fulton Publishers.

Gerlach, V. S. and Ely, D. P. (1971) *Teaching and Media: A Systematic Approach*. Englewood Cliffs, NJ: Prentice-Hall.

Gerzina, G. (1996) *Black Britain: Life Before Emancipation*. London: John Murray.

Gibb, M., Paulin, G. and Hibbs, M. (1991) Equal opportunities, Unit 7. In G. Tilley and D. King (eds) *Cross-Curricular Issues: an INSET Manual for Secondary Schools*. Harlow: Longman.

Gipps, C. (1988) National assessment: a comparison of English and American trends. In P. Broadfoot, R. Murphy and H. Torrance (eds) *Changing Educational Assessment*. London: Routledge.

Gipps, C. (1990) *Assessment: A Teacher's Guide to the Issues*. London: Hodder & Stoughton.

Gipps, C. (1994) *Beyond Testing*. London: Falmer.

Gipps, C. (1994) What we know about effective primary teaching. In J. Bourne (ed.) *Thinking Through Primary Practice*. Buckingham: Open University Press.

Givner, A. and Graubard, P. S. (1974) *A Handbook of Behaviour Modification for the Classroom*. New York: Holt, Rinehart & Winston.

Glaser, R. (1963) Instructional technology and the measurement of learning outcomes: some questions. *American Psychologist*, 18, pp. 519–21.

Glasser, W. (1969) *Schools without Failure*. New York: Harper & Row.

Gleick, J. (1988) *Chaos*. London: Abacus.

Gnagey, W. J. (1968) *The Psychology of Classroom Discipline*. New York: Macmillan. London: Collier-Macmillan.

Gnagey, W. J. (1980) Locus of control, motives and crime prevention attitudes of classroom facilitators and inhibitors. Paper read at AERA, Boston.

Gnagey, W. J. (1981) *Motivating Classroom Discipline*. New York: Macmillan. London: Collier-Macmillan.

Good, T. L. (1970) Which pupils do teachers call on? *Elementary School Journal*, 70, pp. 190–8.

Good, T. L. and Brophy, J. E. (1973) *Looking in Classrooms*. New York: Harper & Row.

Good, T. L. and Brophy, J. E. (1974) The influence of teachers' attitudes and expectations on classroom behaviour. In R. H. Coop and K. White (eds) *Psychological Concepts in the Classroom*. New York: Harper & Row.

Goodlad, J. I., Klein, M. F. and associates (1974) *Looking behind the Classroom Door*. Worthington, Ohio: Charles A. Jones.

Goulding, M. (1992) Let's hear it for the girls. *Times Educational Supplement*, 21 February 1992, p. 38.

Graves, N. and Graves, T. D. (1985) Creating a cooperative learning environment. In R. Slavin, S. Sharan, S. Kagan, R. Lazarowitz, C. Webb and R. Schmuck (eds) *Learning to Cooperate, Cooperating to Learn*. New York: Plenum Books.

Green, P. A. (1982) Teachers' influence on the self concept of ethnic minority pupils. Unpublished PhD thesis. University of Durham.

Gropper, G. L. and Kress, G. C. (1970) *Managing Problem Behaviour in the Classroom*. New York: New Century, Educational Division/Meredith Corporation.

Gruber, K. H. (1992) Unlearnt European lessons: why Austria abandoned the comprehensive school experiments and restored the Gymnasium. In D. Phillips (ed.) *Lessons of Cross-national Comparison in Education*. Wallingford: Triangle Books.

Gundura, J. (1982) Approaches to multicultural education. In J. Tierney (ed.) *Race, Migration and Schooling*. Eastbourne: Holt, Rinehart & Winston.

Habermas, J. (1976) *Legitimation Crisis* (trans. T. McCarthy). London: Heinemann.

Hackett, G. (1995) Tests 'unreliable' claims ex-adviser. *Times Educational Supplement*, 14 July 1995, p. 9.

Hagger, H., Burn, K. and McIntyre, D. (1993) *The School Mentor Handbook*. London: Kogan Page.

Hall, K. (1995) Learning modes: an investigation of perceptions in five Kent classrooms. *Educational Research*, 3 (1), pp. 21–32.

Hall, S., Critcher, C., Jefferson, T., Clarke, C. and Roberts, B. (eds) (1978) *Policing the Crisis*. London: Macmillan.

Halsey, A. H. (1981) Education can compensate. In W. Swann (ed.) *The Practice of Special Education*. Oxford: Basil Blackwell.

Halsey, A. H. (1992) An international comparison of access to higher education. In D. Phillips (ed.) *Lessons of Cross-national Comparison in Education*. Wallingford: Triangle Books.

Halsey, A. H., Heath, A. and Ridge, J. (1980) *Origins and Destinations*. London: Oxford University Press.

Hamacheck, D. E. (1968) *Human Dynamics in Psychology and Education*. Boston: Allyn & Bacon.

Handy, C. (1989) *The Age of Unreason*. London: Business Books Ltd.

Hargreaves, A. (1989) *Curriculum and Assessment Reform*. Oxford: Basil Blackwell and the Open University Press.

Hargreaves, D. H. (1973) *Interpersonal Relations and Education*. London: Routledge & Kegan Paul.

Hargreaves, D. H. (1978) The two curricula and the community. *Westminster Studies in Education*, 1 (1), pp. 31–41.

Hargreaves, D. H. (1982) *The Challenge for the Comprehensive School*. London: Routledge & Kegan Paul.

Hargreaves, D. H. and Hopkins, D. (1991) *The Empowered School*. London: Cassell.

Hargreaves, D. H., Hestor, S. K. and Mellor, F. J. (1975) *Deviance in Classrooms*. London: Routledge & Kegan Paul.

Harlen, W. (1994) Introduction to W. Harlen (ed.) *Enhancing Quality in Assessment*. London: Paul Chapman Publishing.

Harlen, W. (1994) Issues and approaches to quality assurance and quality control in assessment. In W. Harlen (ed.) *Enhancing Quality in Assessment*. London: Paul Chapman Publishing.

Harlen, W. (ed.) (1994) *Enhancing Quality in Assessment*. London: Paul Chapman Publishing.

Harnisch, D. L. and Mabry, L. (1993) Issues in the development and evaluation of alternative assessments. *Journal of Curriculum Studies*, 25 (2), pp. 179–87.

Hart, K., Johnson, D. C., Brown, M., Dickson, L. and Clarkson, R. (1989) *Children's Mathematical Frameworks: 8–13*. Windsor: NFER-Nelson.

Hart, P., Wearing, A. and Conn, M. (1995) Conventional wisdom is a poor predictor of the relationship between student misbehaviour and teacher stress. *British Journal of Educational Psychology*, 65 (1), pp. 27–48.

Hartnett, A. and Naish, M. (1976) *Theory and Practice of Education*. London: Heinemann.

Harvey, O. J., Prather, M., White, B. J. and Hoffmeister, J. K. (1968) Teachers' beliefs, classroom atmosphere and student behaviour. *American Educational Research Journal*, 5 (2), pp. 151–66.

Harwood, D. (1995) The pedagogy of the World Studies 8–13 Project: the influence of the presence/absence of the teacher upon primary children's collaborative group work. *British Educational Research Journal*, 21 (5), pp. 587–611.

Haslam, K. R. (1971) *Learning in the Primary School*. London: George Allen & Unwin.

Hastings, N. and Schwieso, J. (1995) Tasks and tables: the effects of seating arrangements on task engagement in primary classrooms. *Educational Research*, 37 (3), pp. 279–91.

Haysom, J. and Sutton, C. (1974) *Theory into Practice*. Maidenhead: McGraw-Hill.

Hegarty, S., Pocklington, K. and Lucas, D. (1981) *Educating Pupils with Special Needs in the Ordinary School*. Windsor: NFER-Nelson.

Hewett, F. M. (1972) Educational programmes for students with behaviour disorders. In H. C. Quay and J. S. Querry (eds) *Psychopathological Disorders of Childhood*. New York: John Wiley.

Hirst, P. (1967) The logical and psychological aspects of teaching a subject. In R. S. Peters (ed.) *The Concept of Education*. London: Routledge & Kegan Paul.

Hirst, P. H. (1974) *Knowledge and the Curriculum*. London: Routledge & Kegan Paul.

Hofkins, D. (1995) Cheating 'rife' in national tests. *Times Educational Supplement*, 16 June 1995, p. 1.

Hofkins, D. (1995) English scripts sent back for remarking. *Times Educational Supplement*, 7 July 1995, p. 2.

Hohmann, M., Bunet, B. and Weikart, D. W. (1979) *Young Children in Action*. Michigan: The High Scope Press.

Holt, J. (1969) *How Children Fail*. Harmondsworth: Penguin.

Horton, T. (1990) *Assessment Debates*. London: Hodder & Stoughton.

Houghton, S., Merrett, F. and Wheldall, K. (1988) The attitudes of British secondary school pupils to praise, rewards, punishments and reprimands: a further study. *New Zealand Journal of Educational Studies*, 23, pp. 201–14.

Hoyle, E. (1975) The creativity of the school in Britain. In A. Harris, M. Lawn and W.

Prescott (eds) *Curriculum Innovation*. London: Croom Helm in association with the Open University Press.

Hudson, B. (1973) *Assessment Techniques: An Introduction*. London: Methuen.

Hughes, J. A. (1976) *Sociological Analysis: Methods of Discovery*. Sunbury-on-Thames: Nelson, pp. 94–7.

Hurn, C. J. (1978) *The Limits and Possibilities of Schooling*. New York: Allyn & Bacon.

Illich, I. (1972) *Deschooling Society*. Harmondsworth: Penguin.

Inner London Education Authority (1976) *Mixed Ability Grouping*. London: Inner London Education Authority.

Inner London Education Authority (1983) *Race, Sex and Class 3. A Policy for Equality*. London: Inner London Education Authority.

Inner London Education Authority (1988) *The Primary Language Record*. London: Inner London Education Authority.

Jackson, B. (1964) *Streaming: an Education System in Miniature*. London: Routledge & Kegan Paul.

Jackson, M. (1982) Teach the moral virtues of profit – Sir Keith. *Times Educational Supplement*, 26 March 1982, p. 8.

Jackson, P. (1968) *Life in Classrooms*. New York: Holt, Rinehart & Winston.

Jeffcoate, R. (1976) Curriculum planning in multiracial education. *Educational Research*, 18 (3), pp. 192–200.

Jeffcoate, R. (1979) A multicultural curriculum: beyond the orthodoxy. *Trends in Education*, 4, pp. 8–12.

Johnson, B., Oswald, M. and Adey, K. (1993) Discipline in South Australian primary schools. *Educational Studies*, 19 (3), pp. 289–305.

Johnson, D. W. (1978) Conflict management in the school and classroom. In D. Bar-Tal and L. Saxe (eds) *Social Psychology of Education: Theory and Research*. New York: John Wiley & Sons.

Johnson, G., Hill, B. and Tunstall, P. (1992) *Primary Records of Achievement: A Teachers' Guide to Reviewing, Recording and Reporting*. London: Hodder & Stoughton.

Johnstone, M. and Munn, P. (1987) *Discipline in School*. Edinburgh: Scottish Council for Research in Education.

Jones, A. and Mulford, J. (eds) (1971) *Children Using Language*. London: Oxford University Press.

Jones, K., Charlton, T. and Wilkin, J. (1995) Classroom behaviours which first and middle school teachers in St. Helena find troublesome. *Educational Studies*, 21 (2), pp. 139–53.

Jones, V. (1971) The influence of teacher–student introversion, achievement and similarity on teacher–student dyadic classroom interactions. Doctoral dissertation, University of Texas at Austin.

Kagan, S. (1985) Dimensions of cooperative classroom structures. In R. Slavin, S. Sharan, S. Kagan, R. Lazarowitz, C. Webb and R. Schmuck (eds) *Learning to Cooperate, Cooperating to Learn*. New York: Plenum Books.

Kagan, S. (1988) *Cooperative Learning: Resources for Teachers*. University of California: Riverside Books.

Keddie, N. (1971) Classroom knowledge. In M. F. D. Young (ed.) *Knowledge and Control*. Basingstoke: Collier-Macmillan.

Kelly, A. V. (1978) *Mixed Ability Grouping: Theory and Practice*. London: Harper & Row.

Kelly, A. (1986) *Knowledge and Curriculum Planning*. London: Harper & Row.

Kerry, T. (1978) Bright pupils in mixed ability classes. *British Educational Research Journal*, 4 (2), pp. 103–11.

Kerry, T. (1982) *Effective Questioning: a Teaching Skills Workbook*. London: Macmillan.

Kerry, T. and Eggleston, J. (1988) *Topic Work in the Primary School*. London: Routledge.

Kerry, T. and Sands, M. K. (1982) *Handling Classroom Groups*. London: Macmillan.

Kerry, T. and Sands, M. (1982) *Mixed Ability Teaching in the Early Years of the Secondary School*. London: Macmillan.

Kerry, T. and Tollitt, J. (1987) *Teaching Infants*. Oxford: Basil Blackwell.

Kibler, R. J., Cegala, D. J., Barker, L. L. and Miles, D. T. (1974) *Objectives for Instruction and Evaluation*. Boston: Allyn & Bacon.

Kirkman, S. (1995) Reconnect the life support system. *Times Educational Supplement*, 28 July 1995, p. 8.

Kosko, B. (1994) *Fuzzy Thinking*. London: Flamingo.

Kounin, J. S. (1970) *Discipline and Group Management in Classrooms*. New York: Holt, Rinehart & Winston.

Kounin, J. S. and Gump, P. V. (1958) The ripple effect in discipline. *Elementary School Journal*, 35, pp. 158–62.

Kounin, J. S., Gump, P. V. and Ryan, J. J. (1961) Explorations in classroom management. *Journal of Teacher Education*, 12, pp. 235–47.

Kutnick, P. J. (1988) *Relationships in the Primary School Classroom*. London: Paul Chapman Publishing Ltd.

Kyriacou, C. (1994) *Essential Teaching Skills*. London: Simon & Schuster.

Lacey, C. and Lawton, D. (eds) *Issues in Evaluation and Accountability*. London: Methuen.

Lambert, D. (1995) Assessing and recording pupils' work. In S. Capel, M. Leask and T. Turner, *Learning to Teach in the Secondary School*. London: Routledge.

Lane, S. M. and Kemp, M. (1973) *An Approach to Topic Work in the Primary School*. London: Blackie.

Law, B. (1984) *Uses and Abuses of Profiling*. London: Harper & Row.

Lawlor, S. (1988) *Away with LEAs: ILEA Abolition as a Pilot*. London: Centre for Policy Studies.

Lawrence, D. (1987) *Enhancing Self-Esteem in the Classroom*. London: Paul Chapman Publishing Ltd.

Lawrence, J., Steed, D. and Young, P. (1984) *Disruptive Students – Disruptive Schools?* London: Croom Helm.

Lawton, D. (1973) *Social Change, Educational Theory and Curriculum Planning*. London: University of London Press.

Lawton, D. (1983) *Curriculum Studies and Educational Planning*. Sevenoaks: Hodder & Stoughton.

Lawton, D. (1989) *Education, Culture and the National Curriculum*. Sevenoaks: Hodder & Stoughton.

Leask, M. (1995) What do teachers do? In S. Capel, M. Leask and T. Turner, *Learning to Teach in the Secondary School*. London: Routledge.

Lee, H. (1992) Examining the New Zealand school system. In G. McCullough (ed.) *The School Curriculum in New Zealand*. New Zealand: The Dunmore Press.

Lee, J. and Croll, P. (1995) Streaming and subject specialism at key stage 2: a survey in two local authorities. *Educational Studies*, 21 (2), pp. 155–65.

Letwin, O. (1987) Testing issues. *Times Educational Supplement*, 18 September 1987.

Levine, D. and Lezotte, L. (1990) *Unusually Effective Schools: A Review and Analysis of Research and Practice*. Madison: NCESRD Publications.

Lewis, D. G. (1974) *Assessment in Education*. London: University of London Press.

Linton, R. (ed.) (1940) *Acculturation*. New York: Appleton-Century-Crofts.

Lobban, G. (1975) Sex roles in reading schemes. *Forum for the Discussion of New Trends in Education*, 16 (2), pp. 57–60.

McAllister, W. (1995) Are pupils equipped for group work without training or instruction?

British Educational Research Journal, 21 (3), pp. 395–404.

McAuley, R. and McAuley, P. (1977) *Child Behaviour Problems*. London: Macmillan.

McCallum, B., McAlister, S., Brown, M. and Gipps, C. (1993) Teacher assessment at Key Stage One. *Research Papers in Education*, 8 (3), pp. 305–27.

McCormick, R. and James, M. (1988) *Curriculum Evaluation in Schools* (2nd edn). London: Routledge.

McCulloch, M. (1994) Teacher competences and their assessment. In M. McCulloch and B. Fidler (eds) *Improving Initial Teacher Training?* Harlow: Longman.

MacDonald-Ross, M. (1973) Behavioural objectives – a critical review. *Instructional Science*, 2, pp. 1–51.

McFarlane, C. (1986) *Hidden Messages? – Activities for Exploring Bias*. Birmingham: Development Education Centre.

McFarlane, C. and Sinclair, S. (1986) *A Sense of School*. Birmingham: Development Education Centre, p. 29.

McGuiness, J. (1989) *A Whole School Approach to Pastoral Care*. London: Kogan Page.

McGuiness, J. (1993) *Teachers, Pupils and Behaviour – a Managerial Approach*. London: Cassell.

McIntyre, R. W. (1974) Guidelines for using behaviour modification in education. In R. Ulrich, T. Stachnik and J. Mabry (eds) *Control of Human Behaviour*, Volume III. Glenview, Illinois: Scott, Foresman.

McLaren, P. (1993) *Schooling as a Ritual Performance* (2nd edn). London: Routledge.

McLean, L. (1988) Possibilities and limitations in cross-national comparisons of educational achievement. In P. Broadfoot, R. Murphy and H. Torrance (eds) *Changing Educational Assessment*. London: Routledge.

McPartland, M. (1995) On being a geography mentor. *Teaching Geography*, January 1995, pp. 35–7.

Mackler, B. (1969) Grouping in the ghetto. *Education and Urban Society*, 2, pp. 80–95.

Madsen, C. H. (Jnr.), Becker, W. C. and Thomas, D. R. (1968) Rules, praise and ignoring: elements of elementary classroom control. *Journal of Applied Behaviour Analysis*, 1, pp. 139–50.

Mager, R. F. (1962) *Preparing Instructional Objectives*. Belmont, Calif.: Fearon Publishers.

Makins, V. (1995) License to convert a waiting room. *Times Educational Supplement*, 23 June 1995, p. 6.

Marland, M. (1975) *The Craft of the Classroom*. London: Heinemann Educational.

Martin, S. (1994) A preliminary evaluation of the adoption and implementation of Assertive Discipline at Robinson high school. *School Organisation*, 14 (3), pp. 321–9.

Martion, B. (1981) *A Sociology of Contemporary Cultural Change*. Oxford: Basil Blackwell.

Maxwell, E. (1995) Anger intensifies over English tests marking. *Times Educational Supplement*, 30 June 1995.

Meighan, R. (1981) *A Sociology of Educating*. Eastbourne: Holt, Rinehart & Winston.

Merrett, F. and Jones, L. (1994) Rules, sanctions and rewards in primary schools. *Educational Studies*, 20 (3), pp. 345–56.

Merrett, F. and Man Tang, W. (1994) The attitudes of British primary school pupils to praise, rewards, punishments and reprimands. *British Journal of Educational Psychology*, 64, pp. 91–103.

Miller, A. (1995) Teachers' attributions of causality, control and responsibility and its successful management. *Educational Psychology* 15 (4), pp. 457–71.

Mishler, E. G. (1972) Implications of teaching strategies for language and cognition: observations in first-grade classrooms. In C. B. Cazden, V. P. John, and D. Hymes, *Functions of Language in the Classroom*. Teachers College, Columbia University, New York: Teachers College Press.

Mitchell, C. and Koshy, V. (1993) *Effective Teacher Assessment*. London: Hodder & Stoughton.

Moon, B. (1988) *Modular Curriculum*. London: Paul Chapman Publishing.

Morris, R. J. (1976) *Behaviour Modification with Students*. Cambridge, Mass.: Winthrop.

Morrison, C. (1976) *Ability Grouping and Mixed Ability Grouping in Secondary Schools*. Edinburgh: Scottish Council for Educational Research.

Morrison, K. R. B. (1985) Tensions in subject specialist teaching in primary schools. *Curriculum*, 6 (2), pp. 24–9.

Morrison, K. (1986) Primary school subject specialists as agents of school-based curriculum change. *School Organisation*, 6 (2), pp. 175–83.

Morrison, K. R. B. (1990) An ideological masquerade. *Forum*, 31 (1), pp. 7–8.

Morrison, K. R. B. (1990) The assessment of skills. In P. Neal and J. Palmer, *Environmental Education in the Primary School*. Oxford: Basil Blackwell.

Morrison, K. R. B. (1992) Review of B. Wade and M. Moore, 'Patterns of Educational Integration'. *British Journal of Educational Studies*, 40 (3), pp. 304–6.

Morrison, K. R. B. (1993) Building progression into modular higher degrees in education. *British Journal of In-Service Education*, 19 (3), pp. 5–11.

Morrison, K. R. B. (1993) *Planning and Accomplishing School-Centred Evaluation*. Norfolk: Peter Francis Publishers.

Morrison, K. R. B. (1994) Uniformity and diversity in assessment: an international perspective and agenda. *Compare*, 24 (1), pp. 5–15.

Morrison, K. R. B. (1994) Centralism and the education market: why emulate the United Kingdom? *European Journal of Education*, 29 (4), pp. 415–24.

Morrison, K. R. B. (1994) *Implementing Cross-Curricular Themes*. London: David Fulton.

Morrison, K. R. B. (1995) *Habermas and the School Curriculum: an Evaluation and Case Study*. Unpublished PhD thesis, School of Education, University of Durham.

Morrison, K. R. B. (1995) *Structuralism, Postmodernity and the Discourses of Control in Education*, mimeo, School of Education, University of Durham.

Morrison, K. R. B. (1996) Developing a whole-school behaviour policy in primary schools. *Pastoral Care in Education* 14(1), pp. 22–30.

Morrison, K. R. B. and Ridley, K. (1988) *Curriculum Planning and the Primary School*. London: Paul Chapman Publishing.

Mortimore, P., Sammons, P., Stoll, L., Lewis, D. and Ecob, R. (1988) *School Matters*. Shepton Mallett: Open Books.

Mountford, B. (1993) Mentoring and initial teacher education. In P. Smith and J. West-Burnham (eds) *Mentoring in the Effective School*. Harlow: Longman.

Moyles, J. (1988) *Self-Evaluation: A Teacher's Guide*. Slough: National Foundation for Educational Research.

Munby, S. (1989) *Assessing and Recording Achievement*. Oxford: Blackwell.

Munn P., Johnstone M. and Chalmers, V. (1992) *Effective Discipline in Primary Schools and Classrooms*. London: Paul Chapman Publishing.

Mycock, M. A. (1970) Vertical grouping in the primary school. In V. R. Rogers (ed.) *Teaching in the British Primary School*. London: Macmillan.

Myers, K. (1987) *Genderwatch*. London: School Curriculum Development Committee.

Nash, I. (1995) Traffic builds up on vocational route. *Times Educational Supplement*, 7 May 1995, p. 9.

Nash, R. (1976) *Teacher Expectations and Pupil Learning*. London: Routledge & Kegan Paul.

National Commission on Education (1995) *Learning to Succeed: the Way Forward*. London: National Commission on Education.

National Curriculum Council (1989) *A Curriculum for All*. York: National Curriculum Council.

National Curriculum Council (1989) *A Framework for the Primary Curriculum.* York: National Curriculum Council.

National Curriculum Council (1990) *The Whole Curriculum.* York: National Curriculum Council.

National Curriculum Council (1990) *Education for Economic and Industrial Understanding.* York: National Curriculum Council.

National Curriculum Council (1990) *Careers Education and Guidance.* York: National Curriculum Council.

National Curriculum Council (1990) *Health Education.* York: National Curriculum Council.

National Curriculum Council (1990) *Environmental Education.* York: National Curriculum Council.

National Curriculum Council (1990) *Education for Citizenship.* York: National Curriculum Council.

National Curriculum Council (1991) *Circular 11: Linguistic Diversity and the National Curriculum.* York: National Curriculum Council.

National Curriculum Council (1992) *The National Curriculum and Pupils with Severe Learning Difficulties.* York: National Curriculum Council.

Naylor, P. (1995) Pupil perceptions of teacher racism. Unpublished PhD thesis, Loughborough University of Technology.

Neill, S. and Caswell, C. (1993) *Body Language for Competent Teachers.* London: Routledge.

Nevo, D. (1995) *School-Based Evaluation: a Dialogue for School Improvement.* Kidlington, Oxford: Pergamon.

Newbold, D. (1977) *Ability Grouping – The Banbury Enquiry.* Slough: National Foundation for Educational Research.

Newman, E. and Triggs, P. (eds) (1991) *Equal Opportunities in the Primary School.* Bristol: Bristol Polytechnic, pp. 28–9.

Nicholls, D. and Houghton, S. (1995) The effect of Canter's Assertive Discipline program on teacher and student behaviour. *British Journal of Educational Psychology,* 65 (2), pp. 197–210.

Nixon, N. J. (1990) Assessment issues in relation to experience-based learning on placements within courses. In C. Bell and D. Harris (eds) *World Yearbook of Education Assessment and Evaluation.* London: Kogan Page.

Noah, H. J. and Eckstein, M. A. (1988) Trade-offs in examination policies: an international comparative perspective. In P. Broadfoot, R. Murphy and H. Torrance (eds) *Changing Educational Assessment.* London: Routledge.

Nolder, R., Smith, S. and Melrose, J. (1994) Working together: roles and relationships in the mentoring process. In B. Jaworski and A. Watson (eds) *Mentoring in Mathematics Teaching.* London: Falmer.

Nuttall, D. (1987) The validity of assessments. *European Journal of Psychology of Education,* 11 (2), pp. 109–18.

Oeser, O. A. (1966) *Teacher, Pupil and Task.* London: Tavistock Publications.

Office for Standards in Education (1993) *Curriculum Organisation and Classroom Practice in Primary Schools, a Follow-up Report.* London: Office for Standards in Education.

Office for Standards in Education (1993) *Achieving Good Behaviour in Schools.* London: Office for Standards in Education.

Office for Standards in Education (1993) *Handbook for the Inspection of Schools.* London: Office for Standards in Education.

Office for Standards in Education (1994) *Primary Matters: a Discussion on Teaching and Learning in Primary Schools.* London: Office for Standards in Education.

Office for Standards in Education (1994) *Handbook for the Inspection of Schools*. London: Office for Standards in Education.

Office for Standards in Education (1995) *Guidance on the Inspection of Nursery and Primary Schools*. London: Office for Standards in Education.

Office for Standards in Education (1995) *Guidance on the Inspection of Secondary Schools*. London: Office for Standards in Education.

Office for Standards in Education (1995) *Guidance on the Inspection of Special Schools*. London: Office for Standards in Education.

Okano, K. (1993) *School to Work Transition in Japan*. Clevedon: Multilingual Matters Ltd.

O'Leary, K. D., Kaufman, K. F., Kass, R. E. and Drabman, R. S. (1970) The effects of loud and soft reprimands on the behaviour of disruptive students. *Exceptional Students*, 37 (October), pp. 145–55.

Passow, A. (1966) *The Effects of Ability Grouping*. Teachers College, Columbia University, New York: Teachers College Press.

Peak, B. and Morrison, K. R. B. (1988) Investigating banding origins and destinations in a comprehensive school. *School Organisation*, 8 (3), pp. 339–49.

Penney, D. and Evans, J. (1995) Changing structures; changing rules: the development of the 'internal market'. *School Organisation*, 15 (1), pp. 13–21.

Pennycuick, D. (1991) Moderation of continuous assessment systems in developing countries. *Compare*, 21 (2), pp. 145–52.

Perrott, E. (1982) *Effective Teaching: A Practical Guide to Improving your Teaching*. London: Longman.

Peters, R. S. (1966) *Ethics and Education*. London: George Allen & Unwin.

Pirsig, R. M. (1976) *Zen and the Art of Motorcycle Maintenance*. London: Corgi.

Pollard, A. (1982) A model of coping strategies. *British Journal of Sociology of Education*, 3 (1), pp. 19–37.

Pollard, A. and Tann, S. (1993) *Reflective Teaching in the Primary School* (2nd edn). London: Cassell.

Pollard, A., Broadfoot, P., Croll, P., Osborn, M. and Abbott, D. (1994) *Changing English Primary Schools?* London: Cassell.

Postlethwaite, K. and Denton, C. (1978) *Streams for the Future*. Banbury: Pubansco.

Pringle, M. L. K., Rutter, M. and Davie, E. (1966) *11,000 Seven Year Olds*. Harlow: Longman.

Proctor, A., Entwistle, M., Judge, B. and McKenzie-Murdoch, S. (1995) *Learning to Teach in the Primary Classroom*. London: Routledge.

Quicke, J. (1988) The 'New Right' and education. *British Journal of Educational Studies*, 26 (91), pp. 5–20.

Race Relations Act (1976). London: HMSO.

Raeburn, M. (1973) *An Outline of World Architecture*. London: Octopus Books.

Rampton Committee Report (1981) *West Indian Children in Our Schools*. Interim Report. London: HMSO.

Rance, P. (1968) *Teaching by Topics*. London: Ward Lock Educational.

Reid, I. (1994) *Inequality, Society and Education*. Inaugural lecture, Loughborough University Department of Education. See also Department of Social Security (1994) *Households Below Average Income: A Statistical Analysis 1979–1991/2*.

Reid, M., Clunies-Ross, L., Goacher, B. and Vile, C. (1981) *Mixed Ability Teaching: Problems and Possibilities*. Slough: National Foundation for Educational Research.

Resnick, L. B. (1972) Teacher behaviour in the informal classroom. *Journal of Curriculum Studies*, 4 (2), pp. 99–109.

Reynolds, D. (1995) The effective school. *Evaluation and Research in Education*, 9 (2), pp. 57–73.

Reynolds, D. and Cuttance, P. (1992) *School Effectiveness: Research, Policy and Practice.* London: Cassell.

Reynolds, D., Creemers, B. P. M., Stringfield, S., Teddlie, C., Schaffer, E. and Nesselrodt, P. (1994) *Advances in School Effectiveness Research: Policy and Practice.* London: Cassell.

Ridley, K. (1982) Mixed ability teaching in the primary school. In M. Sands and T. Kerry (eds) *Mixed Ability Teaching.* London: Croom Helm.

Robertson, J. (1981) *Effective Classroom Control.* Sevenoaks: Hodder & Stoughton.

Robinson, G. and Maines, N. (1994) Who manages pupil behaviour? Assertive Discipline – a blunt instrument for a fine task. *Pastoral Care in Education,* 12 (3), pp. 30–5.

Rogers, C. R. (1965) *Client Centred Therapy.* Boston: Houghton Mifflin Co.

Rogers, C. R. (1969) *Freedom to Learn.* Columbus, Ohio: Charles E. Merrill.

Rogers, C. R. (1984) *A Way of Being.* Boston: Houghton Mifflin.

Rosen, C. and Rosen, H. (1973) *The Language of Primary School Children.* Harmondsworth: Penguin.

Rosenthal, J. and Jacobson, L. (1968) *Pygmalion in the Classroom: Teacher Expectation and Pupils' Intellectual Development.* New York: Holt, Rinehart & Winston.

Ross, J. (1972) *A Critical Appraisal of Comprehensive Education.* Slough: National Foundation for Educational Research.

Rousseau, J. J. (1911) *Emile.* London: Everyman.

Rowntree, D. (1974) *Educational Technology in Curriculum Development.* New York: Harper & Row.

Runnymede Trust (1993) *Equality Assurance in Schools.* London: the Runnymede Trust with Trentham Books.

Rutter, M., Tizard, J. and Whitemore, K. (1970) *Education, Health and Behaviour.* Harlow: Longman.

Rutter, M., Maughan, B., Mortimore, P. and Ouston, J. (1979) *Fifteen Thousand Hours.* London: Open Books.

Sammons, P., Hillman, J. and Mortimore, P. (1995) *Key Characteristics of Effective Schools: a Review of School Effectiveness Research.* London: Office for Standards in Education.

Saunders, M. (1979) *Class Control and Behaviour Problems: A Guide for Teachers.* Maidenhead: McGraw-Hill.

Saunders, M. (1981) *Multicultural Teaching: A Guide for the Classroom.* Maidenhead: McGraw-Hill.

Saylor, J. G. and Alexander, W. M. (1974) *Planning Curriculum for Schools.* New York: Holt, Rinehart & Winston.

School Curriculum and Assessment Authority (1995) *Planning the Curriculum at Key Stages 1 and 2.* London: School Curriculum and Assessment Authority.

School Curriculum and Assessment Authority (1995) *Consistency in Teacher Assessment.* London: School Curriculum and Assessment Authority.

Schools Council (1981) *The Practical Curriculum* (working paper 70). London: Methuen.

Schools Council (1983) *Primary Practice,* working paper 75. London: Schools Council, pp. 16–17.

School Examination and Assessment Council (1990) *Records of Achievement in the Primary School.* London: School Examination and Assessment Council.

School Examination and Assessment Council (1990) *A Guide to Teacher Assessment Pack C: A Source Book of Teacher Assessment.* London: Heinemann for the School Examination and Assessment Council.

Scully Jr., V. (1960) *Frank Lloyd Wright.* London: Mayflower.

Serbin, L. (1978) Teachers, peers and play preferences. In B. Spring (ed.) *Perspectives on Non-Sexist Early Childhood Education.* Columbia University: Teachers College Press.

Sex Discrimination Act (1975). London: HMSO.

Sharp, R. and Green, A. (1975) *Education and Social Control.* London: Routledge & Kegan Paul.

Shipman, M. D. (1972) Contrasting views of a curriculum project. *Journal of Curriculum Studies,* November.

Shulman, L. S. and Keislar, E. R. (eds) (1966) *Learning by Discovery.* Chicago: Rand McNally.

Simon, B. (1988) *Bending the Rules: the Baker Reforms of Education.* London: Lawrence & Wishart.

Simons, H. (1982) Conversation piece: the practice of interviewing in case study research. In R. McCormick (ed.) *Calling Education to Account.* London: Heinemann.

Singer, R. (1990a) Profiling: the role of technology. In C. Bell and D. Harris (eds) *World Yearbook of Education Assessment and Evaluation.* London: Kogan Page.

Singer, R. (1990b) Optical mark reading technology in Chinese educational development. In C. Bell and D. Harris (eds) *World Yearbook of Education Assessment and Evaluation.* London: Kogan Page.

Singh, J. S., Marimuthu, T. and Mukherjee, H. (1988) Learning motivation and work: a Malaysian perspective. In P. Broadfoot, R. Murphy and H. Torrance (eds) *Changing Educational Assessment.* London: Routledge.

Slavin, R. (1987) Ability grouping and student achievement in elementary schools: a best-evidence synthesis. *Review of Educational Research,* 57 (3), pp. 293–336.

Slavin, R. (1987) Ability grouping in elementary schools: do we really know nothing until we know everything? *Review of Educational Research,* 57 (3), pp. 347–50.

Slavin, R. (1990) Achievement effects of ability grouping in secondary schools: a best-evidence synthesis. *Review of Educational Research,* 60 (3), pp. 471–99.

Slavin, R. (1990) *Co-operative Learning: Theory, Research and Practice.* Englewood Cliffs, NJ: Prentice Hall.

Slavin, R., Sharan, S., Kagan, S., Lazarowitz, R., Webb, C. and Schmuck, R. (eds) (1985) *Learning to Cooperate, Cooperating to Learn.* New York: Plenum Books.

Sloane, H. N. (1976) *Classroom Management: Remediation and Prevention.* New York: John Wiley.

Smith, I. (1981) Curriculum placement in comprehensive schools. *British Educational Research Journal,* 7 (2), pp. 111–24.

Sockett, H., Bailey, C., Bridges, D., Elliott, J., Gibson, R., Scrimshaw, P. and White, J. (1980) *Accountability in the English Educational System.* Sevenoaks: Hodder & Stoughton.

Spender, D. (1980) *Man Made Language.* London: Routledge & Kegan Paul.

Stake, R. E. (1976) The countenance of educational evaluation, cited in D. Jenkins, Six alternative models of curriculum evaluation, Unit 20, E203, *Curriculum Design and Development.* Milton Keynes: Open University Press.

Stanworth, M. (1981) *Gender and Schooling: a Study of Sexual Divisions in the Classroom.* London: Women's Research and Resources Centre Publications.

Stebbins, R. (1973) Physical context influences on behaviour; the case of classroom disorderliness. *Environment and Behaviour,* 5, pp. 291–314.

Stenhouse, L. (1975) *An Introduction to Curriculum Research and Development.* London: Heinemann.

Stephens, L. S. (1974) *The Teacher's Guide to Open Education.* New York: Holt, Rinehart & Winston.

Stephenson, J. (1995) Significant others – the primary student teacher's view of practice in schools. *Educational Studies,* 21 (3), pp. 323–33.

Stiggins, J. C. and Conklin, N. F. (1992) *In Teachers' Hands: Investigating the Practice of Classroom Assessment.* New York: SUNY Press.

Stonier, T. (1982) Changes in Western society. In C. Richards (ed.) *New Directions in Primary Education*. Lewes: Falmer.

Stubbs, M. (1976) Keeping in touch: some functions of teacher-talk. In M. Stubbs and S. Delamont (eds) *Explorations in Classroom Observation*. London: Wiley.

Stubbs, M. (1983) *Language, Schools and Classrooms* (2nd edn). London: Methuen.

Sutton, R. (1993) *A Framework for Assessment* (2nd edn). Slough: NFER-Nelson.

Taba, H. (1962) *Curriculum Development: Theory and Practice*. New York: Harcourt, Brace & World.

Tann C. S. (1988) The rationale for topic work. In C. S. Tann (ed.) *Developing Topic Work in the Primary School*. Lewes: Falmer.

Taylor, J. (1983) *Organizing and Integrating the First School Day*. London: Allen & Unwin.

Thomas, D. R., Becker, W. C. and Armstrong, M. (1968) Production and elimination of disruptive classroom behaviour by systematically varying the teacher's behaviour. *Journal of Applied Behaviour Analysis*, 1, pp. 35–45.

Thompson, B. (1973) *Learning to Teach*. London: Sidgwick & Jackson.

Thompson, D. and Arora, T. (1991) Why do students bully? An evaluation of the long-term effectiveness of a whole-school policy to minimize bullying. *Pastoral Care in Education*, 9 (4), pp. 8–12.

Thompson, L. and Feasey, R. (1992) *Questioning in Science*. Mimeo: School of Education, University of Durham.

Thurston, J. E., Feldhusen, J. F. and Benning, J. J. (1973) A longitudinal study of delinquency and other aspects of students' behaviour. *International Journal of Criminology and Penology*, 1 (November), pp. 341–51.

Times Educational Supplement (1995) Testing times for the timetable in Modedon Junior School. *Times Educational Supplement*, 16 June 1995, p. 6.

Tizard, B., Blatchford, P., Burke, J., Farquar, C. and Plewis, I. (1988) *Young Children at School in the Inner City*. London: Lawrence Erlbaum Associates.

Toffler, A. (1971) *Future Shock*. London: Pan Books Ltd.

Tomlinson, J. (1993) *The Control of Education*. London: Cassell.

Tomlinson, P. (1995) *Understanding Mentoring*. Buckingham: Open University Press.

Topping, K. (1992) School-based behaviour management work with families. *Pastoral Care in Education*, 10 (1), pp. 7–17.

Turner, M. (1990) *Sponsored Reading Failure: an Object Lesson*. IPSET Education Unit.

Turner, T. (1995) Moral development and values. In S. Capel, M. Leask and T. Turner, *Learning to Teach in the Secondary School*. London: Routledge.

Turney, C., Clift, J. C., Dunkin, M. J. and Trail, R. D. (1973) *Microteaching: Research, Theory and Practice*. Sydney: Sydney University Press.

Twining, J. (1992) *Vocational Education and Training in the United Kingdom*. Berlin: CEDEFOP.

Tyler, R. W. (1973) *Basic Principles of Curriculum and Instruction*. Chicago: University of Chicago Press.

Tylor, E. B. (1871) *Primitive Culture*. London: Murray.

University of Bristol (1988) *Pilot Records of Achievement in Schools Evaluation: Final Report* (PRAISE Report). Bristol: University of Bristol.

Vygotsky, L. (1978) *Mind in Society: the Development of Higher Psychological Processes* (ed. M. Cole). Cambridge, Mass.: Harvard University Press.

Wadd, K. (1973) Classroom power. In B. Turner (ed.) *Discipline in Schools*. London: Ward Lock Educational.

Wade, B. and Moore, M. (1992) *Patterns of Educational Integration*. Wallingford: Triangle Books Ltd.

Walkerdine, V. (1983) It's only natural: rethinking child-centred pedagogy. In A. M. Wolpe and J. Donald (eds) *Is There Anyone Here from Education?* London: Pluto Press.

Waller, W. (1932) *The Sociology of Teaching*. New York: John Wiley.

Waters, D. (1982) *Primary School Projects*. London: Heinemann.

Watkins, C. and Wagner, P. (1987) *School Discipline: A Whole-School Approach*. Oxford: Basil Blackwell.

Watson, L. (1995) Talk and pupil thought. *Educational Psychology*, 15 (1), pp. 57–68.

Watts, A. (1995) Double entendre. *Times Educational Supplement*, 9 June 1995, p. III.

West, R. H. (1967) *Organization in the Classroom*. Oxford: Basil Blackwell.

Wheeler, D. K. (1967) *Curriculum Process*. London: University of London Press.

Wheldall, K. and Merrett, F. (1988) Which classroom behaviours do primary teachers say they find most troublesome? *Educational Review*, 40 (1), pp. 14–27.

Wheldall, K., Morris, M., Vaughan P. and Ng, Y. Y. (1981) Rows versus tables: an example of behavioural ecology in two classes of eleven year old children. *Educational Psychology*, 1 (2), pp. 171–84.

Whetton, C., Ruddock, G. and Hopkins, S. (1991) *The Pilot Study of Standard Assessment Tasks for Key Stage 1: A Report*. London: School Examinations and Assessment Council.

White, R. K. and Lippitt, R. (1960) *Autocracy and Democracy: An Experimental Inquiry*. New York: Harper & Row.

Whitty, G. (1985) *Sociology and School Knowledge*. London: Methuen.

Whitty, G. and Willmott, E. (1991) Competence-based teacher education: approaches and issues. *Cambridge Journal of Education*, 21 (3), pp. 309–18.

Wiles, J. and Bondi, J. C. (1984) *Curriculum Development: a Guide to Practice* (2nd edn). Columbus, Ohio: Charles E. Merrill Publishing.

Wilian, D. (1993) Validity, dependability and reliability in National Curriculum assessment. *The Curriculum Journal*, 4 (3), pp. 335–50.

Wilkin, M. (ed.) (1992) *Mentoring in Schools*. London: Kogan Page.

Wilkin, M. and Sankey, D. (eds) (1994) *Collaboration and Transition in Initial Teacher Training*. London: Kogan Page.

Williams, J. (1979) *The Social Science Teacher*, 8 (4), cited in J. Gundura (1982) Approaches to multicultural education. In J. Tierney (ed.) *Race, Migration and Schooling*. Eastbourne: Holt, Rinehart & Winston.

Willis, P. (1977) *Learning to Labour*. Farnborough: Saxon House.

Wineburg, S. S. (1987) The self-fulfilment of the self-fulfilling prophecy. *Educational Researcher*, 16 (9), pp. 28–37.

Withal, R. (1956) An objective measurement of a teacher's classroom interactions. *Journal of Educational Psychology*, 47.

Withers, R. and Eke, R. (1995) Reclaiming matching from the critics of primary education. *Educational Review*, 37 (1), pp. 59–73.

Wittgenstein, L. (1974) *Tractatus Logico-Philosophicus*. London: Routledge & Kegan Paul.

Woods, P. (1979) *The Divided School*. London: Routledge & Kegan Paul.

Woods, P. (1980) *Teacher Strategies: Explorations in the Sociology of the School*. London: Croom Helm.

Wragg, E. C. (1978) Training teachers for mixed ability classes: a ten-point attack. *Forum*, 20 (2), pp. 39–42.

Wragg, E. C. (1981) *Class Management and Control: A Teaching Skills Workbook*. DES Teacher Education Project, Focus Books; Series Editor, Trevor Kerry. London: Macmillan.

Wragg, E. C. (1984) (ed.) *Classroom Teaching Skills*. London: Croom Helm.

Wragg, E. C. (1984) Training skilful teachers: some implications for practice. In E. C. Wragg (ed.) *Classroom Teaching Skills*. London: Croom Helm.

Wragg, E. C. (1993) *Explaining*. London: Routledge.

Wragg, E. C. and Dooley, P. A. (1984) Class management during teaching practice. In E. C. Wragg (ed.) *Classroom Teaching Skills*. London: Croom Helm.

Wragg, E. C. and Young, E. K. (1984) Pupil appraisal of teaching. In E. C. Wragg (ed.) *Classroom Teaching Skills*. London: Croom Helm.

Wragg, E. C. and Young, E. K. (1984) Teachers' first encounters with their classes. In E. C. Wragg (ed.) *Classroom Teaching Skills*. London: Croom Helm.

Wright, D. (1973) The punishment of students. In B. Turner (ed.) *Discipline in Schools*. London: Ward Lock Educational.

Wyatt, H. (1976) Mixed ability teaching in practice. *Forum*, 18 (2), pp. 45–9.

Young, S. (1995) Reformers angered by lack of action. *Times Educational Supplement*, 3 June 1995, p. 3.

Young, S. (1995) Inaction speaks louder than words. *Times Educational Supplement*, 16 June 1995, p. 6.

Zimiles, H. (1987) Progressive education: on the limits of evaluation and the development of empowerment. *Teachers College Record*, 89 (2), pp. 201–17.

Index